W9-DIF-998

WITHDRAWN

OUTLINES.

I LOV'D SHAKESPEARE AND DO HONOUR HIS MEMORY, ON THIS SIDE IDOLATRY, AS MUCH AS ANY. HE WAS, INDEED, HONEST, AND OF AN OPEN AND FREE NATURE; HAD AN EXCELLENT FANCY, BRAVE NOTIONS AND GENTLE EXPRESSIONS.

BEN JONSON.

OUTLINES

OF THE

LIFE OF SHAKESPEARE.

BY

J. O. HALLIWELL-PHILLIPPS, F.R.S.,

F.S.A., Hon. M.R.S.L., Hon. M.R.I.A.

THE SIXTH EDITION.

When to the sessions of sweet silent thought
I summon up remembrance of things past,
I sigh the lack of many a thing I sought.
—*The Thirtieth Sonnet.*

VOLUME THE SECOND.

LONDON :—LONGMANS, GREEN, AND CO.

M.DCCC.LXXXVI.

PREFACE.

The biographical lines upon which the present work is constructed have already been sufficiently exhibited, but in commencing a new volume, one in which so many of the leading documentary evidences are introduced, a few words in explanation of the system that has been adopted in the typographical reproduction of those materials may not be unacceptable.

In the consideration of this subject it is not only important to bear in mind that it is beyond the power of type to convey an exact notion of the ancient hands but also that, if it is employed in their imitation, the student often incurs a greater risk of error by forming his judgment on a view of the letterpress than if he were to accept the readings of an experienced paleographer who had consulted the originals. These are drawbacks that outweigh any possible benefits that could be derived from the use of typographical copies of the early symbols. There are, it is true, several contracted forms, especially in the Latin, that admit of more than one interpretation, but it is very rarely found that the uncertainty attending an extension creates an obscurity in the writer's meaning ; and in the latter event the only satisfactory course, that which is here taken, is to present the reader with a facsimile, the elucidation of every serious difficulty of the kind being thus placed under the student's own control.

With the exception of the contractions there are few peculiarities in the Latin documents that invite special remark. There are only a few unimportant anomalies in the orthography, the main diversities consisting in the use of unclassical forms of the language and of what are termed, in an old legal vocabulary, "words significant and known to the sages of the law, but not allowed by grammarians nor having any countenance of Latin"

The whole of the English documents that are here given belong to a period after that in which the mere form of a spelling had an occasional grammatic significance, and before there was an approach to an orthographical standard. Every one in the poet's time spelt according to his fancy, usually with a tendency to a literal redundancy, so that there was scarcely a word that did not appear in a variety of fashions, every section of the language being exposed to the universal irregularity. So widely diffused was this anarchy in the realms of penmanship that it would have been exceedingly difficult to have lighted upon an individual who would have cared for the preservation of uniformity even in the record of his own family surname, and it may, indeed, be explicitly asserted that there was not a single other kind of word of any description which had then taken an established form by rule or precedent,—not one which can now be thought to possess the slightest biographical or historical value in the mere constitution of its letters. Neither is there any such value in the forms of the characters or in the desultory punctuation. Under these circumstances it was thought to be altogether unnecessary to furnish a precise repetition of the old cacography and its surroundings, but some of its main features have been retained for the sake of the natural inclusion of the obscure archaisms which every now and then baffle the resources of modernization.

It may be added generally, and in conclusion, that the system followed in the preparation of the documentary copies has been regulated by a desire to exhibit them in the most legible form that is consistent with an accurate enunciation of the included facts;—facts only, for it should be borne in mind that no advantage would be gained by subjecting a work of this description to the influence of minutiæ that do not affect their determination, such, for example, as those which are solely of importance in verbal criticism or in discussions of a philological character.

HOLLINGBURY COPSE, BRIGHTON.
May, 1886.

SYMBOLS AND RULES.

The following directions have been observed in the reproduction of the documentary evidences and in the quotations from early printed books.

1. The symbol ⑤ is to be affixed to a word in a case in which the original is followed in what appears to be an erroneous reading.

2. The same character is to be subjoined if an antecedent omission is suspected.

3. The division between lines of poetry which are not given separately is to be indicated by the parallel marks =.

4. A person's mark-signature, when not given in facsimile, is to be denoted by a simple cross, +, irrespective of the form in which it appears in the original manuscript.

5. Use the letters V.L. for *verbatim et literatim.*

6. A discretionary power is to be exercised in trivial cases in which there is no possibility of ascertaining the intentions of the original scribe. It is often, for example, a matter of uncertainty whether the final stroke of a word was intended for a letter or a flourish, whether o^r was put for *our* or for *or*, or even sometimes if a vertical mark was or was not the symbol of a contraction. Amongst other matters of this kind may be noticed the frequent impossibility of deciding between the relative appearances of the *u* and the *w*.

7. Individual errors which are obviously merely clerical ones may be corrected, but the original words are to be retained when there happens to be a cluster of inaccuracies.

8. The duplication of the letter *f* at the commencement of a word, being merely an old form of the capital, is not to be retained.

9. There is seldom a necessity for the reproduction of either italics or the long *s*, but, with those exceptions, whenever a quotation is accompanied by the letters V.L., the original text is to be followed with minute accuracy.

10. An absolute modernization is to be effected in all other cases, the old spelling, however, being retained excepting where there are obsolete uses of the letters *i*, *u* and *v*.

ESTATE RECORDS.

This section is formed of records, bearing date from 1579 to 1618, which relate to properties in which it is known that Shakespeare had, at any time of his life, either contingent or absolute interests. It has not been thought necessary to give the later estate documents at length, those passages in them which are of the slightest value being quoted either in the illustrative notes or in the essays.

I. The Note of a Fine levied when an Estate at Aston Cantlowe was mortgaged by Shakespeare's Parents, Easter Term, 21 Eliz., 1579.

Inter Edmundum Lambert, querentem, et Johannem Shakespere et Mariam, uxorem ejus, deforciantes, de duobus mesuagiis, duobus gardinis, quinquaginta acris terre, duabus acris prati, quatuor acris pasture, et communia pasture pro omnimodis averiis, cum pertinenciis, in Awston Cawntlett ; unde placitum convencionis summonitum fuit inter eos, etc., scilicet, quod predicti Johannes et Maria recognoverunt predicta tenementa et communiam pasture, cum pertinenciis, esse jus ipsius Edmundi, ut illa que idem Edmundus habet de dono predictorum Johannis et Marie ; et illa remiserunt et quietumclamaverunt de ipsis Johanne et Maria, et heredibus suis, predicto Edmundo, et heredibus suis, imperpetuum. Et, preterea, iidem Johannes et Maria concesserunt, pro se et heredibus ipsius Marie, quod ipsi warantizabunt predicto Edmundo, et heredibus suis, predicta tenementa et communiam pasture, cum pertinenciis, contra predictos Johannem et Mariam, et heredes ipsius Marie, imperpetuum ; et pro hac recognicione, remissione, quietaclamancia, warantia, fine, etc., idem Edmundus dedit predictis Johanni et Marie quadraginta libras sterlingorum.

II. A Bill of Complaint brought by the Poet's Father against John Lambert in the Court of Queen's Bench, 1589, respecting an estate at Wilmecote near Stratford-on-Avon. From the Coram Rege Rolls, Term. Mich. 31-32 Eliz. This document contains the only positive notices of the great dramatist between the years 1585 and 1592 which have yet been discovered.

WARR :—Memorandum quod alias, scilicet, termino Sancti Michaelis ultimo preterito, coram domina regina apud Westmonasterium venit Johannes Shackspere, per Johannem Harborne, attornatum suum, et protulit hic in curiam dicte domine regine tunc ibidem quandam billam suam versus Johannem Lambert, filium et heredem Edmundi Lamberte nuper de Barton Henmershe in comitatu predicto yoman, in custodia marescalli &c., de placito transgressionis super casum ; et sunt plegii de prosequendo, scilicet, Johannes Doo et Ricardus Roo, que quidem billa sequitur in hec verba,—WARR:, Johannes Shackespere queritur de Johanne Lamberte, filio et herede Edmundi Lamberte nuper de Barton Henmershe in comitatu predicto yoman, in custodia marescalli Marescallie domine regine, coram ipsa regina existente, pro eo, videlicet, quod cum idem Edmundus in vita sua, scilicet, decimo quarto die Novembris anno regni domine Elizabethe nunc regine Anglie vicesimo, per quandam indenturam gerentem datam die et anno predictis, emisset sibi et heredibus suis de prefato Johanne Shackespere et Maria uxore ejus unum mesuagium sive tenementum, unam virgatam terre et quatuor acras terre arrabilis cum pertinentiis in Wilmecote in dicto comitatu Warwici, habendum et tenendum mesuagium sive tenementum predictum,

et alia premissa cum pertinentiis, prefato Edmundo, heredibus et assignatis suis, imperpetuum ; proviso semper quod si dictus Johannes Shackespere, heredes, executores,
administratores vel assignati sui, solverent seu solvi causarent prefato Edmundo
quadraginta libras legalis monete Anglie in die festi sancti Michaelis Archangeli,
quod tunc esset in anno Domini millesimo quingentesimo et octogesimo, quod tunc
deinceps indentura predicta, et omnia in eadem contenta, vacua forent ; virtute cujus
idem Edmundus in tenementa predicta, cum pertinentiis, intravit, et fuit inde seisitus
in dominico suo ut de feodo, et, sic inde seisitus existens, postea, scilicet, primo die
Marcii anno regni dicte domine regine nunc vicesimo nono, apud Barton Henmershe
predictam obiit, post cujus mortem mesuagium predictum et cetera premissa, cum
pertinentiis, discendebant prefato Johanni Lamberte, ut filio et heredi dicti Edmundi ;
dictusque Johannes Lamberte, dubitans statum et interesse sua de et in tenementis
predictis, cum pertinentiis, esse vacua, et noticiam habens quod predictus Johannes
Shackespere eum implacitare vellet et intendisset pro premissis, in consideracione quod
predictus Johannes Shackespere adtunc imposterum non implacitaret dictum Johannem
Lamberte pro mesuagio predicto et ceteris premissis, cum pertinentiis ; et quod dictus
Johannes Shackespere et Maria uxor ejus, simulcum Willielmo Shackespere filio suo,
cum inde requisiti essent, assurarent mesuagium predictum et cetera premissa, cum
pertinentiis, prefato Johanni Lamberte, et deliberarent omnia scripta et evidencias
premissa predicta concernentia ; predictus Johannes Lamberte, vicesimo sexto die
Septembris anno regni dicte domine regine vicesimo nono, apud Stratforde-super-Avon
in comitatu predicto, in consideracione inde super se assumpsit et prefato Johanni
Shackespere, adtunc et ibidem fideliter promisit, quod ipse, idem Johannes Lambert,
viginti libras legalis monete Anglie prefato Johanni Shackespere modo et forma
sequentibus, videlicet, in et super decimum-octavum diem Novembris tunc proximo
sequentem viginti solidos, et in et super vicesimum tercium diem ejusdem mensis tres
libras, et in et super quartum diem Decembris tunc proximo sequentem sexdecim
libras, predictarum viginti librarum residuum, apud domum mancionalem cujusdam
Anthonii Ingram generosi, scituatam et existentem in Walford Parva in comitatu
predicto, bene et fideliter solvere et contentare vellet ; et predictus Johannes Shackespere in facto dicit quod ipse hucusque non implacitavit dictum Johannem Lambert
pro premissis, nec aliqua inde parcella, et insuper quod ipse, idem Johannes
Shackespere et Maria uxor ejus, simulcum Willielmo Shackespere filio suo, semper
hactenus parati fuerunt tam ad assurandum premissa predicta quam ad deliberandum
eidem Johanni Lamberte omnia scripta et evidencias eadem premissa concernentia ;
predictus tamen Johannes Lamberte, promissionem et assumpcionem suas predictas
minime curans, set machinans et fraudulenter intendens ipsum Johannem Shackspere
de predictis viginti libris callide et subdole decipere et defraudare, easdem viginti
libras prefato Johanni Shackespere, juxta promissionem et assumpcionem, suas
hucusque non solvit, nec aliqualiter pro eisdem contentavit licet ad hoc per eundem
Johannem Shackespere postea, scilicet, primo die Septembris anno regni dicte
domine regine nunc tricesimo, apud Barton Henmershe predictam ın comitatu
predicto, sepius requisitus fuit, per quod idem Johannes Shackspere totum lucrum,
commodum et proficuum, que ipse, cum predictis viginti libris emendo et barganizando,
habere et lucrari potuisset totaliter perdidit et amisit, ad dampnum ipsius Johannis
Shackspeare triginta librarum, ac inde producit sectam.—Et modo ad hunc diem,
scilicet, diem Jovis proximum post octabas sancti Michaelis isto eodem termino, usque
quem diem predictus Johannes Lamberte habuit licenciam ad billam interloquendam
et tunc ad respondendam, etc., coram domina regina apud Westmonasterium, veniunt
tam predictus Johannes Shackspere, per attornatum suum predictum, quam predictus
Johannes Lamberte, per Johannem Boldero, attornatum suum, et idem Johannes
Lamberte defendit vim et ınjuriam quando, etc., et dicit quod ipse non assumpsit
super se modo et forma prout predictus Johannes Shackespere superius versus eum

narravit, et de hoc ponit se super patriam ; et predictus Johannes Shackespere similiter, etc. Ideo veniat inde jurata coram domina regina apud Westmonasterium die Veneris proximo post octabas Sancti Hillarii, et qui etc., ad recognoscendum etc., quia tam etc. Idem dies datus est partibus predictis ibidem etc.

III. A Deed of Conveyance, from John Shakespeare to George Badger, of a slip of land belonging to the Birth-Place estate, January, 1596-7.

Omnibus Christi fidelibus ad quos hoc presens scriptum pervenerit, Johannes Shakespere de Stratford-super-Avon in comitatu Warrewicensi, yoman, salutem in Domino sempiternam. Noveritis me, prefatum Johannem, pro et in consideracione summe quinquaginta solidorum bone et legalis monete Anglie mihi per quendam Georgium Badger de Stretford predicta, draper, premanibus solutorum, unde fateor me fideliter esse solutum et satisfactum, dictumque Georgium Badger heredes, executores et administratores suos, inde quietos esse et exoneratos imperpetuum, per presentes barganizavi et vendidi, necnon dedi et concessi, et hac presenti carta mea confirmavi, prefato Georgio Badger, heredibus et assignatis suis, totum illud toftum et parcellam terre mee cum pertinenciis jacentem et existentem in Stretford-super-Avon predicta, in quodam vico ibidem vocato Henlye Strete, inter liberum tenementum mei, predicti Johannis Shakespere, ex parte orientali, et liberum tenementum predicti Georgii Badger ex parte occidentali, continentem in latitudine per estimacionem dimidium unius virgate apud uterque fines, et jacet in longitudine a predicto vico vocato Henlye Strete ex parte australi usque regiam viam ibidem vocatam Gyll-Pyttes ex parte boreali, continens per estimacionem in longitudine viginti et octo virgatas vel circa, et modo est in tenura sive occupacione mei, predicti Johannis Shakespere, habendum et tenendum predictum toftum et parcellam terre, cum pertinenciis, prefato Georgio Badger, heredibus et assignatis suis, ad solum et proprium opus et usum ejusdem Georgii, heredum et assignatorum suorum, imperpetuum, tenenda de capitalibus dominis feodi illius per servicium inde prius debitum et de jure consuetum. Et ego vero, predictus Johannes Shakespere, et heredes mei, totum predictum toftum et parcellam terre cum pertinenciis prefato Georgio Badger, heredibus et assignatis suis, ad opus et usum supradictis contra omnes gentes warrantizabimus et imperpetuum defendemus per presentes. Sciatis insuper me, prefatum Johannem Shakespere, plenam et pacificam possessionem et seisinam de et in predicto tofto et parcella terre, cum pertinenciis, prefato Georgio Badger, secundum vim, formam, tenorem et effectum hujus presentis carte mee inde ei confecte, in propria persona mea tradisse® et deliberasse. In cujus rei testimonium huic presenti scripto meo sigillum meum apposui. Datum vicesimo-sexto die Januarij, anno regni domine nostre Elizabethe, Dei gracia Anglie Francie et Hibernie regine, fidei defensoris, etc., tricesimo nono, 1596.

Sigillatum et deliberatum, ac pacifica possessio et seisina de tofto et parcella terre infrascriptis, deliberata fuit per infranominatum Johannem Shakespere infrascripto Georgio Badger, die et anno infrascriptis, secundum formam, tenorem et effectum hujus presentis carte, in presencia, viz., Richard Lane, Henry Walker, per me Willielmum Courte, scriptorem, Thomas Loche, Thomas Beseley.

IV. Papers in a Chancery Suit respecting an Estate at Wilmecote, Michaelmas Term, 1598. The father and mother of Shakespeare were the plaintiffs, and John Lambert, son of the poet's maternal uncle, the defendant.

24 Nov., 1597. To the righte honorable Sir Thomas Egerton, knighte, lorde keper of the greate seale of Englande.—In most humble wise complayninge, sheweth unto your good lordshippe your dailye oratours, John Shakespere of Stratford-upon-Avon, in the county of Warwicke, and Mary his wief, that, whereas your saide oratours were lawfully seised in their demesne as of fee, as in the righte of the saide Mary, of and in one mesuage and one yarde lande with thappurtenaunces, lyinge and beinge in Wylnecote, in the saide county; and they beinge thereof so seised, for and in con-sideracion of the somme of fowerty poundes to them by one Edmounde Lamberte of Barton-on-the-Heath in the saide countie paide, your sayde oratours were contente that he, the saide Edmounde Lamberte, shoulde have and enjoye the same premisses untill suche tyme as your sayde oratours did repaie unto him the saide somme of fowertie poundes; by reasone whereof the saide Edmounde did enter into the premisses and did occupie the same for the space of three or fower yeares, and thissues and profyttes thereof did receyve and take; after which your saide oratours did tender unto the saide Edmounde the sayde somme of fowerty poundes, and desired that they mighte have agayne the sayde premisses according to theire agreement; which money he the sayde Edmounde then refused to receyve, sayinge that he woulde not receyve the same, nor suffer your sayde oratours to have the saide premisses agayne, unlesse they woulde paye unto him certayne other money which they did owe unto him for other matters; all which notwithstandinge, nowe so yt ys; and yt maye please your good lordshippe that, shortelie after the tendringe of the sayde fowertie poundes to the saide Edmounde, and the desyre of your sayde oratours to have theire lande agayne from him, he the saide Edmounde att Barton aforesayde dyed, after whose deathe one John Lamberte, as sonne and heire of the saide Edmounde, entred into the saide premisses and occupied the same; after which entrie of the sayde John your said oratours came to him and tendred the saide money unto him, and likewise requested him that he woulde suffer them to have and enjoye the sayde premisses according to theire righte and tytle therein and the promise of his saide father to your saide oratours made, which he, the saide John, denyed in all thinges, and did withstande them for entringe into the premisses, and as yet doeth so contynewe still; and by reasone that certaine deedes and other evydences concer-ninge the premisses, and that of righte belonge to your saide oratours, are coumme to the handes and possession of the sayde John, he wrongfullie still keepeth and detayneth the possession of the saide premisses from your saide oratours, and will in noe wise permytt and suffer them to have and enjoye the sayde premisses accordinge to theire righte in and to the same; and he, the saide John Lamberte, hathe of late made sondrie secreate estates of the premisses to dyvers persones to your said oratours unknowen, whereby your saide oratours cannot tell againste whome to bringe theire accions att the comen lawe for the recovery of the premisses; in tender consideracion whereof, and for so muche as your saide oratours knowe not the certaine dates nor contentes of the saide wrytinges, nor whether the same be contayned in bagge, boxe or cheste, sealed, locked or noe, and therefore have no remeadie to recover the same evydences and wrytinges by the due course of the comen lawes of this realme; and for that also, by reasone of the saide secreate estates so made by the saide John Lamberte as aforesaide, and want of your saide oratours havinge of the evidences and wrytinges as aforesaide, your sayde oratours cannot tell what accions or against whome, or in what manner, to bringe theire accion for the recoverie of the premisses att the comen lawe; and for that also the sayde John Lamberte ys of greate wealthe and abilitie, and well frended and alied amongest gentlemen and freeholders of the countrey in the saide countie of Warwicke, where he dwelleth, and your saide oratours are of small

wealthe and verey fewe frendes and alyance in the saide countie, maye yt therefore please your good lordshippe to graunt unto your saide oratours the Queenes Majesties moste gracyous writte of subpena, to be directed to the saide John Lamberte, comandinge him thereby att a certaine daie, and under a certaine payne therein to be lymytted, personally to appeare before your good lordshippe in Her Majesties highnes courte of Chauncerie, then and there to answere the premisses ; and further to stande to and abyde suche order and direction therein as to your good lordshippe shall seeme best to stande with righte, equytie and good conscyence, and your sayde oratours shall daylie praye to God for the prosperous healthe of your good lordshippe with increase of honour longe to contynewe.

Juratus coram me, Thomam Legge, 24 Novembris, 1597.—The answeare of John Lamberte, defendante, to the byll of complainte of John Shakspeere and Mary his wief, complainantes.—The said defendante, savinge to himselfe both nowe, and att all tymes hereafter, all advantage of excepcion to the uncertentie and insufficiencie of the said complainantes byll, and also savinge to this defendante such advantage as by the order of this honorable courte he shal be adjudged to have, for that the like byll, in effecte conteyninge the selfe-same matter, hath byne heretofore exhibited into this honorable courte againste this defendante, wherunto this defendante hath made a full and directe answeare, wherin the said complainante hath not proceeded to hearinge ; for a seconde full and directe answeare unto the said complainantes byll sayeth that true yt is, as this defendante verylie thinkethe, that the said complainantes were, or one of them was, lawfully seized in theire or one of theire demeasne, as of fee, of and in one messuage and one yearde and fower acres of lande with thappurtenaunces, lyeinge and beinge in Wilmecott, in the parishe of Aston Cawntloe, in the countie of Warwicke, and that they or one of them soe beinge thereof seized, the said complainante, John Shakspeere, by indenture beringe date uppon or about the fowertenth daye of November, in the twenteth yeare of the raigne of our Sovereigne Lady the Queenes Majestie that now ys, for and in consideracion of the summe of fortie powndes of lawfull Englishe monney unto the said complainante paide by Edmunde Lamberte, this defendantes father in the said byll named, did geve, graunte, bargaine and sell the said messuage, and one yearde and fower acres of lande with thappurtenaunces, unto the said Edmunde Lamberte, and his heires and assignes, to have and to holde the said messuage, one yearde and fower acres of lande, with thappurtenaunces, unto the saide Edmunde Lamberte, his heires and assignes, for ever ; in which indenture there is a condicionall provisoe conteyned that, if the said complainante did paye unto the said Edmunde Lamberte the summe of fortie powndes uppon the feast daie of St. Michell tharchangell which shoulde be in the yeare of our Lorde God one thousande fyve hundred and eightie, att the dwellinge howse of the said Edmund Lamberte, in Barton-on-the-Heath in the said countie of Warwicke, that then the said graunte, bargaine, and sale, and all the covenauntes, grauntes and agreementes therin conteyned, shulde cease and be voyde, as by the said indenture, wherunto this defendante for his better certentie doth referre himselfe, maye appeare ; and afterwardes, the saide complainante John Shakspeere, by his Deede Pole and Liverie theruppon made, did infeoffe the said Edmunde Lamberte of the saide premisses, to have and to holde unto him the said Edmunde Lamberte and his heires for ever ; after all which, in the terme of Ester, in the one and twenteth yeare of the Queenes Majesties raigne that nowe ys, the said complainantes in due forme of lawe did levye a fyne of the said messuage and yearde lande, and other the premisses, before the Queenes Majesties justices of the comon plees att Westminster, unto the saide Edmunde Lamberte, and his heires, sur conuzance de droyt, as that which the said Edmunde had of the gifte of the said John Shakspeere, as by the said pole deede, and the chirographe of the said fine, wherunto this defendante for his better certentie referreth himselfe, yt doth and maye appeare ; and this defendante further sayeth that the said complainante did not tender or paye the said summe of fortie powndes unto the said Edmunde Lamberte, this defendantes father, uppon the saide feaste daye, which was in the yeare of our Lorde God one thowsande fyve hundred and eightie, according to the said provisoe in the said indenture expressed. By reason whereof this defendantes said father was lawfully and absolutly seized of the said premisses in his demeasne as of fee, and, aboute eleven yeares laste paste thereof, dyed seized ; by and after whose decease the said messuage and premisses with thappurtenaunces descended and came, as of righte the same oughte to descende and come, unto this defendante, as sonne and nexte heire of the said Edmunde ; by vertue whereof this defendante was and yet is of the said messuage, yearde lande and premisses, lawfully seized in his demeasne as of fee, which this defendante hopeth he oughte both by lawe and equitie to enjoye, accordinge to his lawfull righte and tytle therin ; and this defendante further sayeth that the said messuage, yearde lande and other the said premisses, or the moste parte thereof, have ever, sythence the purches therof by this defendantes father, byne in lease by the demise of the said complainante ; and the lease therof beinge nowe somewhat nere expyred, wherby a greater value is to be yearly raised therby, they, the said complainantes, doe now trowble and moleste this defendante by unjuste sutes in lawe, thinkinge therby, as yt shoulde seme, to wringe from him this defendante some further recompence for the said premisses then they have alreddy received ; without that, that yt was agreed that the said Edmunde Lamberte shoulde have and enjoye the said premisses in anie other manner and forme, to the knowledge of this defendante, then this defendante hath in his said answeare heretofore expressed ; and without that, that anie deedes or evidences concernynge the premisses that of righte belonge to the said complainantes are come to the handes and possession of this defendante, as in the said byll is untruly supposed ; and without that, that anie other matter, cause or thinge, in the said complainantes byll conteined, materiall or effectuall in the lawe, to be answeared unto, towchinge or concernynge him, this defendante, and hereinbefore not answeared unto, confessed and avoyded, traversed or denied, is true, to this defendantes knowledge or remembrance, in suche manner and forme as in the said byll the same is sett downe and declared. All which matters this defendante is reddy to averre and prove, as this honorable courte shall awarde, and prayethe to be dismissed therhence with his reasonable costes and charges in this wrongfull sute by him unjustly susteyned.

The replicacion of John Shakespere and Mary his wiefe, plentiffes, to the answere of John Lamberte, defendant.—The said complaynantes, for replicacion to the answere of the said defendant, saie that theire bill of complaynt ys certayne and sufficient in the lawe to be answered ; which said bill, and matters therein contayned, these complainants will avowe, verefie, and justifie to be true and sufficient in the lawe to be answered unto, in such sorte, manner and forme as the same be sett forthe and declared in the said bill : and further they saie that thanswere of the said defenndant is untrue and insufficient in lawe to be replied unto, for many apparent causes in the same appearinge, thadvantage whereof these complainantes praie may be to theym nowe and at all tymes saved, then and not ells ; for further replicacion to the said answere they saie that, according to the condicion or proviso mencioned in the said indenture of bargaine and sale of the premisses mencioned in the said bill of complaynt, he this complaynant, John Shakspere, did come to the dwellinge-house of the said Edmunde Lambert, in Barton-uppon-the-Heathe, uppon the feaste daie of St. Michaell tharcheangell, which was in the yeare of our Lorde God one thousand fyve hundred and eightie, and then and there tendered to paie unto him the said Edmunde Lambert the said fortie poundes, which he was to paie for the redempcion of the said premisses ; which somme the said Edmunde did refuse to receyve, sayinge that he owed him other money, and unles that he, the said John, would paie him altogether, as well the said fortie poundes as the other money, which he owed him over and above, he would not receave the said fortie poundes, and imediatlie after he, the said Edmunde, dyed, and by reason thereof, he, the said defendant, entered into the said premisses, and wrongfullie kepeth and detayneth the said premisses from him the said complaynant ; without that, any other matter or thinge, materiall or effectuall, for these complaynantes to replie unto, and not herein sufficientlie confessed and avoyded, denyed and traversed, ys true ; all which matters and thinges thes complaynantes are redie to averr and prove, as this honourable court will awarde, and pray as before in theire said bill they have praied.—*In dorso*, Ter. Michael. annis 40 et 41.

V. *The original Conveyance of over a hundred acres of land from William and John Combe to Shakespeare, May, 1602.*

This Indenture made the firste daie of Maye, in the fowre and fortieth yeare of the raigne of our Soveraigne Ladie Elizabeth, by the grace of God, of England, Fraunce and Ireland, Queene, Defendresse of the Faithe, &c., betweene William Combe of Warrwicke, in the countie of Warrwick, esquier, and John Combe of Olde Stretford, in the countie aforesaide, gentleman, on the one partie, and William Shakespere of Stretford-uppon-Avon, in the countie aforesaide, gentleman, on thother partye ; Witnesseth that the saide William Combe and John Combe, for and in consideracion of the somme of three hundred and twentie poundes of currant Englishe money to them in hande, at and before the ensealinge and deliverie of theis presentes, well and trulie satisfied, contented and paide ; wherof and wherwith they acknowledge themselves fullie satisfied, contented and paide, and therof, and of everie parte and parcell therof, doe clearlie, exonerate, acquite and discharge the saide William Shakespere, his heires, executors, administrators and assignes for ever by theis presentes, have aliened, bargayned, solde, geven, graunted and confirmed, and, by theis presentes, doe fullye, clearlie and absolutelie alien, bargayne, sell, give, graunte and confirme unto the saide William Shakespere, all and singuler those errable landes, with thappurtenaunces, conteyninge by estymacion fowre yarde lande of errable lande, scytuate, lyinge and beinge within the parrishe, feildes or towne of Olde Stretford aforesaide, in the saide countie of Warrwick, conteyninge by estimacion one hundred and seaven acres, be they more or lesse ; and also all the common of pasture for sheepe, horse, kyne or other cattle, in the feildes of Olde Stretford aforesaide, to the saide fowre yarde lande belonginge or in any wise apperteyninge ; and also all hades, leys, tyinges, proffittes, advantages and commodities whatsoever, with their and everie of their appurtenaunces to the saide bargayned premisses belonginge or apperteyninge, or hertofore reputed, taken, knowne or occupied as parte, parcell or member of the same, and the revercion and revercions of all and singuler the same bargayned premisses, and of everie parte and parcell therof, nowe or late in the severall tenures or occupacions of Thomas Hiccoxe and Lewes Hiccoxe, or of either of them, or of their assignes, or any of them ; together also with all charters, deedes, writinges, escriptes, and mynumentes whatsoever, touchinge or concerninge the same premisses onlie, or only any parte or parcell therof ; and also the true copies of all other deedes, evidences, charters, writinges, escriptes and mynumentes, which doe touche and concerne the saide premisses before bargayned and solde, or any parte or parcell therof, which the saide William Combe or John Combe nowe have in their custodie, or herafter may have, or which they may lawfullye gett, or come by, without suite in lawe ; to have and to holde the saide fowre yarde of errable lande, conteyninge by estymacion one hundred and seaven acres, be they more or lesse, and all and singuler other the premisses before by theis presentes aliened and solde, or mencioned or entended to be aliened and solde, and everie parte and parcell therof ; and all deedes, charters, writinges, escriptes and mynumentes, before by theis presentes bargayned and solde unto the saide William Shakespere, his heires and assignes for ever, to the onlie proper use and behoofe of the saide William Shakespere, his heires and assignes for ever. And the saide William

Combe and John Combe, for them, their heires, executors and administrators, doe covenant, promise, and graunte to and with the saide William Shakespere, his heires, executors and assignes, by theis presentes, that they, the saide William and John Combe, are seazde, or one of them is seazde, of a good, sure, perfect and absolute estate, in fee simple, of the same premisses before by theis presentes bargayned and solde, or ment or mencioned to be bargayned and solde, without any further condicion or lymyttacion of use or estate, uses or estates ; and that he, the saide John Combe, his heires and assignes, shall and will, from tyme to tyme, and at all tymes herafter, well and sufficientlie save and keepe harmles and indempnified as well the saide fowre yardes of errable lande, conteyninge one hundred and seaven acres, and all other the premisses, with their appurtenaunces, before bargayned and solde, or mencioned or entended to be bargayned and solde, and everie parte and parcell therof, as also the saide William Shakespere, and his heires and assignes, and everie of them, of and from all former bargaynes, sales, leases, joyntures, dowers, wills, statutes, recognizances, writinges obligatorie, fynes, feoffamentes, entayles, judgmentes, execucions, charges, titles, forfeytures and encombrances whatsoever, at any tyme before the ensealinge herof, had, made, knowledged, done or suffred by the saide John Combe, or by the saide William Combe, or either of them, or by any other person or persons whatsoever, any thinge lawfullye clayminge or havinge, from, by or under them, or either of them, the rentes and services herafter to be due, in respect of the premisses before mencioned or entended to be bargayned and solde, to the cheife lorde or lordes of the fee or fees onlie excepted and foreprized. And the saide William Combe and John Combe, for them, their heires, executors, administrators and assignes, doe covenant, promise and graunte to and with the saide William Shakespere, his heires and assignes, by theis presentes, that they, the saide William and John Combe, or one of them, hathe right, full power and lawfull aucthoritie for any acte or actes done by them, the saide William and John Combe, or by the sufferance or procurement of them, the saide William and John Combe, to geve, graunte, bargayne, sell, convey and assure the saide fowre yardes of errable lande, conteyninge one hundred and seaven acres, and all other the premisses before by theis presentes bargayned and solde, or ment or mencioned to be bargayned and solde, and everie parte and parcell therof, to the saide William Shakespere, his heires and assignes, in suche manner and forme as in and by theis presentes is lymytted, expressed, and declared ; and that they, the saide William and John Combe, and their heires, and also all and everie other person and persons, and their heires, nowe or herafter havinge or clayminge any lawfull estate righte, title or interest, of, in or to the saide errable lande, and all other the premisses before by theis presentes bargayned and solde, with their and everie of their appurtenaunces, —other then the cheife lorde or lordes of the fee or fees of the premisses, for their rentes and services only,—at all tymes herafter, duringe the space of fyve yeares next ensewinge the date herof, shall doe, cause, knowledge and suffer to be done and knowledged, all and every suche further lawfull and reasonable acte and actes, thinge and thinges, devise and devises, conveyances and assurances whatsoever, for the further, more better and perfect assurance, suretie, sure makinge and conveyinge of all the saide premisses before bargayned and solde, or mencioned to be bargayned and solde, with their appurtenaunces, and everie parte and parcell therof, to the saide William Shakespere, his heires and assignes, for ever, accordinge to the true entent and meaninge of theis presentes, as by the saide William Shakespere, his heires and assignes, or his or their learned counsell in the lawe, shal be reasonablye devized or advized, and required, be yt bye fyne or fynes with proclamacion, recoverye with voucher or vouchers over, deede or deedes enrolled, enrollment of theis presentes, feoffament, releaze, confirmacion or otherwise ; with warrantie against the saide William Combe and John Combe, their heires and assignes, and all other persons clayminge by, from or under them, or any of them, or without warrantie, at the costes and charges in the lawe of the saide William Shakespere, his heires, executors, administrators or assignes, so as, for the makinge of any suche estate or assurance, the saide William and John Combe be not compeld to travell above sixe myles. And the saide William Combe and John Combe, for them, their heires, executors, administrators and assignes, doe covenant, promise and graunte to and with the saide William Shakespere, his heires, executors, administrators and assignes, by theis presentes, that the saide William Shakespere, his heires and assignes, shall or may, from tyme to tyme, from henceforth for ever, peaceably and quietlye have, holde, occupie, possesse and enjoye the saide fowre yardes of errable lande, and all other the bargayned premisses, with their appurtenaunces, and everie parte and parcell therof, without any manner of lett, trouble or eviccion of them, the saide William Combe and John Combe, their heires or assignes ; and without the lawfull lett, trouble or eviccion of any other person or persons whatsoever, lawfullie havinge or clayminge any thinge in, of or out of the saide premisses, or any parte therof, by, from or under them, the saide William Combe and John Combe, or either of them, or the heires or assignes of them, or either of them, or their or any of their estate, title or interest. In wytnes wherof the parties to theis presentes have enterchangeably sette their handes and seales, the daie and yeare first above written, 1602.—*W. Combe.—Jo. Combe.*—Sealed and delivered to Gilbert Shakespere, to the use of the within-named William Shakespere, in the presence of Anthony Nasshe, William Sheldon, Humfrey Maynwaringe, Rychard Mason, Jhon Nashe.

VI. An Extract from the Court-rolls of the Manor of Rowington, being the Surrender from Walter Getley to Shakespeare of premises in Chapel Lane, Stratford-on-Avon, 1602.

Rowington.—Visus franci plegii cum curia baronis prenobilis domine Anne, Comitisse Warwici, ibidem tentus vicesimo octavo die Septembris, anno regni dominę nostre Elizabethe, Dei gracia Anglie, Francie et Hibernie regine, fidei defensoris, etc., quadragesimo quarto, coram Henrico Michell, generoso, deputato scenescallo Johannis Huggeford, armigeri, capitalis scenescalli ibidem.—Ad hanc curiam venit Walterus Getley, per Thomam Tibbottes, juniorem, attornatum suum, unum customariorum tenencium manerii predicti, predicto Thoma Tibbottes jurato pro veritate inde, et sursum reddidit in manus domine manerii predicti unum cotagium, cum pertinenciis, scituatum, jacens et existens in Stratford-super-Avon, in quodam vico ibidem vocato Walkers Streete alias Dead Lane, ad opus et usum Willielmi Shackespere et heredum suorum imperpetuum, secundum consuetudinem manerii predicti ; et sic remanet in manibus domine manerii predicti, quousque predictus Willielmus Shakespere venerit ad capiendum premissa predicta. In cujus rei testimonium predictus Henricus Michell huic presenti copie sigillum suum apposuit die et anno supradictis.—*Per me, Henricum Michell.*

VII. The conveyance to Shakespeare in 1605 of the moiety of a lease, granted in 1544, of the tithes of Stratford-on-Avon, Old Stratford, Welcombe and Bishopton.

This indenture made the foure and twentythe daye of Julye in the yeares of the raigne of our soveraigne Lorde James, by the grace of God of Englande, Scotlande, Fraunce and Irelande, kinge, Defender of the Fayeth, &tc., that is to saye, of Englande, Fraunce and Irelande the thirde, and of Scotlande the eighte and thirtythe, Betweene Raphe Hubande of Ippesley in the countye of Warr., esquier, on thone parte, and William Shakespear of Stratforde-upon-Avon in the sayed countye of Warr., gent., on thother parte ; Whereas Anthonye Barker, clarke, late Warden of the Colledge or Collegiate Churche of Stratforde-upon-Avon aforesayed, in the sayed countye of Warr., and Gyles Coventrie, subwarden there, and the whole chapiter of the same late colledge, by their deade indented, sealed with their chapter seale, dated the seaventh daye of September in the sixe and thirtyth yeare of the raigne of the late kinge of

B 2

famous memorie, Kinge Henrye the eighte, demysed, graunted and to farme lett, amongste diverse other thinges, unto one William Barker of Sonnynge in the countye of Bark., gent., all and all manner of tythes of corne, grayne, blade and heye, yearelye and from tyme to tyme comynge, encreasinge, reneweinge, arrysinge, groweinge, yssueinge or happeninge, or to bee had, receyved, perceyved or taken out, upon, of or in the townes, villages, hamlettes, groundes and fyeldes of Stratforde-upon-Avon, Olde Stratforde, Welcombe and Bushopton, in the sayed countye of Warr., and alsoe all and all manner of tythes of wooll, lambe and other small and pryvie tythes, oblacions, obvencions, alterages, mynumentes and offeringes whatsoever, yearelye and from tyme to tyme cominge, encreasinge, reneweinge or happeninge, or to bee had, receyved, perceyved or taken within the parishe of Stratforde-upon-Avon aforesayed, in the sayed countye of Warr., by the name or names of all and singuler their mannors, landes, tene-mentes, meadowes, pastures, feedinges, woodes, underwoodes, rentes, revercions, services, courtes, leetes, releeves, wardes, marriages, harriottes, perquisites of courtes, liberties, jurisdiccions, and all other hereditamentes, with all and singuler other rightes, com-modities, and their appurtenaunces, togeather with all manner of parsonages, gleebe landes, tythes, alterages, oblacions, obvencions, mynumentes, offeringes, and all other issues, proffittes, emolumentes and advantages in the countye of Warr. or Worcester, or elcewhere whatsoever they bee, unto the sayed then colledge apperteyninge,—the mancionhouse and the scite of the sayed colledge, with their appurtenaunces, within the precinctes of the walls of the sayed colledge, unto the sayed warden and subwarden onelye excepted,—To have and to holde all the sayed mannors, landes, tenementes, and all other the premisses, with all and singuler their appurtenaunces, excepte before excepted, unto the sayed colledge belonginge or in anie wyse apperteyninge, unto the sayed William Barker, his executors and assignes, from the feast of St. Michaell tharchangell then laste paste before the date of the sayed indenture, unto thend and terme of fourescore and twelve yeares then nexte ensueinge, yeldinge and payeinge therefore yearelye unto the sayed warden and subwarden and their successors att the sayed colledge, cxxij.*li.* xviij.*s.* ix.*d.* of lawfull money of Englande, as more playnely appeareth by the sayed indenture ; and whereas alsoe the revercion of all and singuler the sayed premisses, amonge other thinges, by vertue of the Acte of Parliament, made in the fyrst yeare of the raigne of the late soveraigne lorde Kinge Edwarde the sixte, for the dissolucion of chauntries, colledges, and free chappels, or by somme other meanes, came to the handes and possession of the sayed late Kinge Edwarde ; and whereas the sayed late Kinge Edwarde the sixte beinge seised, as in right of his crowne of Englande, of and in the revercion of all and singuler the premisses, by his lettres patentes, bearinge date the eight and twentyth daye of June in the seaventh yeare of his raigne, for the consideracion therein expressed, did gyve and graunte unto the baylief and burgesses of Stratforde aforesayed, and to their successors, amonge other thinges, all and all manner of the sayed tythes of corne, graine and heye, comynge, encreasinge or arrysinge, in the villages and fyeldes of Olde Stratforde, Welcombe and Bushopton aforesayed, in the sayed countye of Warr., then or late in the tenure of John Barker, and to the late Colledge of Stratforde-upon-Avon in the sayed countye of Warr. of late belonginge and apperteyninge, and parcell of the possessions thereof beinge ; and alsoe all and all manner of the sayed tythes of wooll, lambe, and other smalle and pryvie tythes, oblacions and alterages, whatsoever, within the parishe of Stratford-upon-Avon aforesayed, and to the sayed late Colledge of Stratforde-upon-Avon belonginge or apperteyninge, and then or late in the tenure of William Barker or of his assignes, and the revercion and revercions whatsoever of all and singler the sayed tythes, and everye parte and parcell thereof, and the rentes, revenues, and other yearelye proffittes whatsoever reserved upon anye demise or graunte of the sayed tythes, or anie parte or parcell thereof : and whereas alsoe the interest of the sayed premisses in the sayed originall lease mencioned. and the interest of certein copieholdes in Shotterie in the parishe of Stratford aforesayed, beinge by good and lawfull conveyans and assurance in the lawe before that tyme conveyed and assured to John Barker of Hurste in the sayed countye of Berk., hee, the sayed John Barker, by his indenture bearinge date the foure and twentyth daye of June in the twoe and twentythe yeare of the raigne of the late Queene Elizabeth, for the consideracions therein specifyed did gyve, graunte, assigne and sett over unto Sir John Hubande, knighte, brother of the sayed Raphe Hubande, all and singuler the sayed laste mencioned premisses, and all his estate, right, title and interest that hee then had to come, of, in and to all and singuler the sayed premisses, and of all other mannors, messuages, landes, tenementes, gleebe landes, tythes, oblacions, commodities and proffittes in the sayed originall lease mencioned, for and duringe all the yeares and terme then to come unexpired in the sayed originall lease, exceptinge as in and by the sayed laste mencioned indenture is excepted,—as by the same indenture more att large maye appeare ; to have and to holde all and singuler the sayed recyted premisses, excepte before excepted, to the sayed Sir John Hubande, his executors and assignes, for and duringe the yeares then to come of and in the same, yeldinge and payeinge therefore yearelye, after the feast of St. Michaell tharchangell nexte ensueinge the date of the sayed laste mencioned indenture, for and duringe all the yeares mencioned in the sayed first mencioned indenture then to come and not expired, unto the sayed John Barker, his executors, administrators and assignes, one annuall or yearelye rente of twentye seaven poundes thirteene shillinges foure pence by the yeare, to be yssueinge and goeinge out of all the mannors, landes, tenementes, tythes and hereditamentes, in the sayed indenture specyfied, to bee payed yearlye to the sayed John Barker, his executors, administrators and assignes, by the sayed Sir John Hubande, his executors, administrators and assignes, att the feastes of the Anunciacion of our Ladye and St. Michaell tharchangell, or within fortye dayes after the sayed feastes, in the porche of the Parishe Churche of Stratford aforesayed, by even porcions, and further payeinge, doeinge and performinge all suche other rentes, dutyes and servyces, as att anie tyme from thencefourth, and from tyme to tyme, for and duringe the terme aforesayed, should become due to anie personne or personns for the same premisses, or anie parte thereof, and thereof to discharge the sayed John Barker, his executors and administrators ; and yf yt shoulde happen the sayed twentye-seaven poundes thirteene shillinges foure pence to bee behinde and unpayed, in parte or in all, by the space of fortye dayes nexte after anie of the sayed feastes or daies of paye-ment, in which, as is aforesayed, it ought to bee payed, beinge lawfullie asked, that then yt shoulde bee lawfull to and for the sayed John Barker, his executors, adminis-trators and assignes, into all and singuler the premisses, with their appurtenaunces, and everye parte and parcell thereof, to re-enter, and the same to have againe, as in his or their former righte, and that then and from thenceforthe the sayed recyted indenture of assignement, and everye article, covenaunte, clause, provisoe and agree-ment therein conteyned, on the parte and behalf of the sayed John Barker, his executors, administrators and assignes, to bee performed, should ceasse and bee utterlie voyde and of none effect ; with diverse other covenauntes, grauntes, articles and agreementes in the sayed indenture of assignemente specified to bee observed and performed by the sayed Sir John Hubande, his executors and assignes, as in and by the sayed recyted indenture it doth and maye appeare. And whereas the sayed Sir John Hubande did, by his deade obligatorie, bynd himself and his heires to the sayed John Barker in a greate some of money for the performance of all and singuler the cove-nauntes, grauntes, articles and agreementes, which, on the parte of the sayed Sir John Huband, were to bee observed and performed, conteyned and specyfied as well in the sayed recyted indenture of assignement, as alsoe in one other indenture, bearinge the date of the sayed recyted indenture of assignemente, made betweene the sayed John Barker on thone partie and the sayed Sir John Hubande on thother partie, as by the sayed deade obligatorie more att large it doth and maye appeare. And whereas alsoe the sayed Sir John Hubande, by his laste will and testament in writinge, did gyve and bequeath unto his executors, amongst other thinges, the moytie or one half of all and singuler the sayed tythes, as well greate as smalle, before mencioned, to bee graunted to the sayed baylyffe and burgesses of Stratford, for and duringe soe longe tyme, and untill, of the yssues and proffittes thereof, soe much as with other thinges in his sayed will to that purposse willed, lymitted or appointed, shoulde bee sufficient to discharge, beare, and paye, his funeralls debtes and legacies ; and alsoe, by his sayed laste will and testament, did gyve and bequeath the other moytie, or one half of the sayed tythes, unto the sayed Raphe Hubande and his assignes, duringe all the yeares to come in the sayed first mencioned indenture and not expired, payeinge the one half of the rentes and other charges dewe or goeinge out of or for the same, that is to saye the one half of tenne poundes by yeare to bee payed to the sayed John Barker over and above the rentes thereof reserved upon the sayed originall lease for the same, as by the sayed will and testament more playnelye appeareth ;— This indenture nowe witnesseth that the sayed Raphe Hubande, for and in consideracion of the somme of foure hundred and fourtye poundes of lawfull Englishe money to him by the sayed William Shakespear, before thensealinge and deliverye of thees presentes, well and truelye contented and payed, whereof and of everye parte and parcell whereof hee, the sayed Raphe Hubande, dothe by thees presentes acknowledge the receipt, and thereof and of everye parte and parcell thereof dothe clerelye acquite, exonerate and discharge the sayed William Shakespear, his executors and administrators, for ever by thees presentes,—hathe demised, graunted, assigned and sett over, and by thees presentes dothe demise, graunte, assigne and sett over unto the sayed William Shakespear, his executors and assignes, the moytie or one half of all and singuler the sayed tythes of corne, grayne, blade and heye, yearelye, and from tyme to tyme cominge, encreasinge, reneweinge, arrysinge, groweinge, issueinge or happenynge, or to bee had, receyved, perceyved or taken out, of, upon or in the townes, villages, hamlettes, groundes and fyeldes of Stratforde, Olde Stratforde, Welcombe and Bushopton aforesayed in the sayed countye of Warr., and alsoe the moytie or one half of all and singuler the sayed tythes of wooll, lambe, and other smalle and pryvie tythes, herbage, oblacions, obvencions, alterages, mynumentes and offeringes whatsoever, yearelye, and from tyme to tyme, cominge, encreasinge, reneweinge or happeninge, or to bee had, receyved, perceyved or taken, within the parishe of Stratforde-upon-Avon aforesayed : and alsoe the moytie or one half of all and all manner of tythes, as well greate as smalle whatsoever, which were by the laste will and testament of the sayed Sir John Hubande gyven and bequeathed to the sayed Raphe Hubande, arrysing, encreasinge, reneweinge or groweinge within the sayed parishe of Stratford-upon-Avon, and whereof the sayed Raphe Hubande hath att anie tyme heretofore been, or of right ought to have been, possessed, or whereunto hee nowe hath, or att anie tyme hereafter should have, anie estate, right or interest, in possession or revercion ; and all thestate, right, tytle, interest, terme, claime and demaunde whatsoever, of the sayed Raphe Hubande, of, in and to all and singuler the premisses hereby lastelye mencioned to bee graunted and assigned, and everie or anie parte or parcell thereof, and the revercion and revercions of all and singuler the sayed premisses, and all and singuler rentes and yearely proffyttes reserved upon anie demise, graunte or assignement thereof, or of anie parte or partes thereof heretofore made,—the pryvie tythes of Luddington and suche parte of the tythe-heye, and pryvie tythes of Bushopton, as of right doe belonge to the vicar, curate or minister there, for the tyme beinge, always excepted and foreprised,—To have and to holde all and everye the sayed moyties or one halfe of all and singuler the sayed tythes, before in and by thees presentes lastelye mencioned to bee graunted and assigned, and everye parte and parcell of them, and everye of them, and all thestate, righte, tytle and intereste of the sayed Raphe Huband of, in and to the same, and all other thafore demised premisses, and everye parte and parcell thereof, except before excepted, unto the sayed William Shakespear, his executors and assignes, from the daye of the date hereof, for and duringe the residewe of the sayed terme of fourescore and twelve yeares in the sayed first recyted indenture mencioned, and for suche and soe longe terme and tyme, and in as large, ample and benefyciall manner as the sayed Raphe Hubande shoulde or oughte enjoye the same, yeldinge and payeinge therefore yearely duringe the residewe of the sayed terme of fourescore and twelve yeares which bee yet to come and unexpired, the rentes hereafter mencioned, in manner and forme followeinge, that is to saye, unto the baylyffe and burgesses of Stratford aforesaied, and their successors, the yearelye rent of seaventeene poundes att the feastes of St. Michaell tharchangell and the anunciacion of blessed Marye the Virgin by equall porcions, and unto the sayed John Barker, his executors, administrators or assignes, the annuall or yearelye rente of fyve poundes att the feaste dayes and place lymitted, appointed and mencioned in the sayed recyted indenture of assignement made by the sayed John Barker, or within fortye dayes after the sayed feaste dayes by even porcions, as parcell of the sayed annuall rent of twentye seaven poundes thirteene shillinges foure pence in the sayed assignement mencioned ; and the sayed Raphe Hubande dothe by thees presentes, for him, his heires, executors and administrators, covenaunte and graunte to and with the sayed William Shakespear, his executors, administrators and assignes, that hee, the sayed Raphe Hubande, att the tyme of thensealinge and delyverye of thees presentes, hath, and att the tyme of the first execucion, or intencion of anie execucion, of anie estate by force of thees presentes shall have, full power, and lawfull and sufficient aucthoritie certeinlie, suerlye and absolutelie, to graunte, demise, assigne and sett over all and everye the sayed moyties, or one halfe of all and singuler the sayed tythes, and other the premisses before in thees presentes lastelye mencioned to bee assigned and sett over, and everye parte and parcell thereof, unto the sayed William Shakespear, his executors and assignes, accordinge to the true meaninge of thees presentes ; and alsoe that the sayed William Shakespear, his executors, administrators or assignes, shall and maye from tyme to tyme, and att all tymes duringe the residewe of the sayed terme of foure score and twelve yeares yet to come and unexpired, for the yearelye severall rentes above by thees presentes reserved, peaceablie, lawfullye and quietlie have, holde, occupie, possesse and enjoye all and everye the sayed moyties, or one halfe of all and singuler the sayed tythes of corne, graine, blade, heye, woolle, lambe, and other smalle and pryvie tythes, herbage, oblacions, obvencions, offeringes, and other the premisses before by thees presentes graunted and assigned, and everye parte and parcell thereof, excepte before excepted, without anie lett, trouble, entrie, distresse, claime, deniall, interrupcion or molestacion whatsoever of the sayed Raphe Hubande, his executors, administrators or assignes, or of anie other personne or personns havinge or clayminge to have, or which, att anie tyme or tymes hereafter, shall or maye have, or claime to have, anie thinge of, in or to the afore graunted premisses or anie parte thereof, by, from or under the sayed Raphe Huband, his executors, administrators or assignes, or anie of them, or by, from, or under the sayed Sir John Hubande, or by their or anie of their meanes, consent, forfeiture, act or procurement, and without anie lawfull lett, trouble, distresse, claime, denyall, entrie or demaunde whatsoever, other then for the sayed yearely rent of twentye seaven poundes thirteene shillinges fourepence by the sayed recyted assignement reserved of the sayed John Barker, his executors, administrators or assignes, or anie of them, or of anie personne or personns clayeming by, from or under them, or anie of them,— thestate and interest of the Lorde Carewe of, in and to the tythes of Bridgtowne and Ryen Clyfforde, and the interest of Sir Edwarde Grevill, knight, of and in the moytie of the tythe-heye, woolle, lambe, and other smalle and pryvie tythes, oblacions, obvencions, offeringes and proffittes before by thees presentes graunted and assigned unto the sayed William Shakespear, which is to endure untill the feast of St. Michaell tharchangell next ensueinge the date hereof, and noe longer, onelye excepted and foreprised ;—and the sayed Raphe Hubande doth by thees presentes, for him his heires, executors and administrators, covenaunte and graunte to and with the sayed William Shakespear, his executors, administrators and assignes, that all and everye the sayed moyties of the sayed tythes before mencioned to be graunted to the sayed William Shakespear, and other the premisses, except before excepted, nowe are, and soe from tyme to tyme, and att all tymes hereafter duringe the residewe of the saied terme of fourescore and twelve yeares yet to come and unexpired, according to the true meaninge hereof shal be, remaine, and contynewe unto the sayed William, his executors or assignes, free and clere, and freelye and clerelye acquyted, exonerated and discharged, or well and sufficientlie saved and kept harmelesse, of and from all and all manner of bargaines, sales, guiftes, assignementes, leases, recognizances, statutes mercheant and of the staple, outlaries, judgementes, execucions, titles, troubles, charges, encumbraunces and demaundes whatsoever, heretofore had, made, done, comitted, omitted or suffered, or hereafter to bee had, made, done, comitted, omitted or suffered, by the sayed Raphe Hubande, Sir John Hubande and John Barker, or anie of them, their or anie of their executors, administrators or assignes, or anie of them, or by anie personne or personns whatsoever clayminge by, from or under them or anie of them, or by their or anie of their meanes, act, title, graunte, forfeiture, consent or procurement, except before excepted ; and alsoe that hee, the sayed Raphe Hubande, his executors, adminis- trators and assignes, shall and will, from tyme to tyme and att all tymes duringe the space of three yeares next ensueing, upon reasonable requeste, and att the costes and charges in the lawe of the sayed William Shakespear, his executors or assignes, doe performe and execute, and cause, permitt and suffer to bee done, performed and executed, all and everye suche further and reasonable acte and actes, thinge and thinges, devyse and devyses in the lawe whatsoever, bee yt or they by anie meane, course, acte, devise or assurans in the lawe whatsoever, as by the sayed William Shakespear, his executors or assignes, or his or their learned councell, shal be reason- ablie devised, advised or required for the confirmacion of thees presentes, or for the further or more better or firmer assurans, suertye, suer makinge and conveyeinge of all and singler the premisses before by thees presentes demised and assigned, or ment or intended to bee demised and assigned, and everye parte and parcell thereof, unto the sayed William Shakespear, his executors and assignes, for and duringe all the residewe of the sayed terme of fourescore and twelve yeares which bee yet to come and unexpired, according to the tenor and true meaninge of thees presentes, soe as the sayed Raphe Hubande, his executors or assignes, bee not hereby compelled to travell from Ippesley aforesayed for the doeinge thereof ; and the sayed William Shakespear doth by thees presentes, for him, his heires, executors and administrators, covenaunte and graunte to and with the sayed Raphe Hubande, his executors, administrators and assignes, that hee, the sayed William Shakespeare, his executors, administrators or assignes, shall and will, duringe the residewe of the sayed terme of fourescore and twelve yeares which bee yet to comme and unexpired, yearelie content and paye the severall rentes above mencioned, vidlt., seaventene poundes to the baylief and burgesses of Stratford aforesayed, and fyve poundes to the sayed John Barker, his executors or assignes, att the dayes and places aforesayed in which it ought to bee payed accordinge to the purporte and true meaninge of thees presentes, and thereof shall and will discharge the saied Raphe Hubande, his executors, adminis- trators and assignes. In witnes whereof the partyes abovesayed to thees presentes interchangeablie have sett their seales the daie and yeare fyrst above written.—*Raffe Huband.*—Sealde and delivered in the presence of William Huband, Anthony Nasshe, Fra : Collyns.

Bond for the Performance of Covenants.—Noverint universi per presentes me, Radulphum Huband, de Ippesley in comitatu Warwici, armigerum, teneri et firmiter obligari Willielmo Shakespear, de Stratforde-super-Avon in dicto comitatu Warwici, generoso, in octingentis libris bone et legalis monete Anglie solvendis eidem Willielmo, aut suo certo attornato, executoribus vel assignatis suis, ad quam quidem solucionem bene et fideliter faciendam obligo me, heredes, executores et administratores meos, firmiter per presentes sigillo meo sigillatas. Datum vicesimo quarto die Julii, annis regni domini nostri Jacobi, Dei gracia Anglie, Scocie, Francie et Hibernie regis, fidei defensoris, etc., scilicet, Anglie, Francie et Hibernie tercio, et Scocie tricesimo octavo.— The condicion of this obligacion is suche, that if thabove bounden Raphe Hubande, his heires, executors, administrators and assignes, and everye of them, shall and doe, from tyme to tyme and att all tymes, well and truelye observe, performe, fulfill and keepe all and everye covenaunte, graunte, article, clause, sentence and thinge mencioned, expressed and declared, in a certein writinge indented, bearinge date with thees presentes, made betweene the sayed Raphe Hubande on thone parte and the abovenamed William Shakespear on thother parte, and which, on the parte and behalf of the saied Raphe, his heires, executors, administrators and assignes, or anie of them, are to bee observed, performed, fulfilled or kept, according to the purporte and true meaninge of the saied writinge, that then this present obligacion to bee voyde and of none effect, or els to stand and abide in full force, power and vertue.— *Raffe Huband.*—Sealed and delivered in the presens of William Huband, Anthony Nasshe and Fra. Collyns.

VIII. The Note of a Fine levied in Trinity Term, 8 Jac. I., 1610, on the Estate purchased by Shakespeare from the Combes.

Inter Willielmum Shakespere, generosum, querentem, et Willielmum Combe, armigerum, et Johannem Combe, generosum, deforciantes, de centum et septem acris terre et viginti acris pasture, cum pertinenciis, in Old Stratforde et Stratforde-super-Avon ; unde placitum convencionis summonitum fuit inter eos, etc., scilicet, quod predicti Willielmus Combe et Johannes recognoverunt predicta tenementa, cum pertinenciis, esse jus ipsius Willielmi Shakespere, ut illa que idem Willielmus habet de dono predictorum Willielmi Combe et Johannis, et illa remiserunt et quietum-clamaverunt de ipsis Willielmo Combe et Johanne, et heredibus suis, predicto Willielmo Shakespere et heredibus suis imperpetuum ; et, preterea, idem Willielmus Combe concessit, pro se et heredibus suis, quod ipsi warantizabunt predicto Willielmo Shakespere, et heredibus suis, predicta tenementa, cum pertinenciis, contra predictum Willielmum Combe, et heredes suos, in perpetuum. Et ulterius idem Johannes concessit, pro se et heredibus suis, quod ipsi warantizabunt predicto Willielmo Shakespere, et heredibus suis, predicta tenementa, cum pertinenciis, contra predictum Johannem, et heredes suos, imperpetuum. Et pro hac, etc., idem Willielmus Shakespere dedit predictis Willielmo Combe et Johanni centum libras sterlingorum.

IX. A Draft of a Bill of Complaint respecting the tithes, Shakespeare being one of the plaintiffs, 1612. In this manuscript there are several interlineations and corrections in the handwriting of Thomas Greene. The following is a copy of the document in its corrected state, none of the variations and notes that are found in the original draft being of the slightest interest in connexion with the history of the poet's ownership of the moiety. The original is preserved at Stratford-on-Avon.

Richard Lane et alii querentes, et Dominus Carewe et alii defendentes, in Cancellaria billa.—To the Right Honorable Thomas Lord Ellesmere, Lord Chauncellour of England. In humble wise complayninge, shewen unto your honorable good Lordshipp, your dayly oratours Richard Lane, of Awston in the county of Warwicke, esquire, Thomas Greene, of Stratford-uppon-Avon in the said county of Warwicke, esquire, and William Shackspeare, of Stratford-uppon-Avon aforesaid in the said county of Warwicke, gentleman, that whereas Anthonie Barker, clarke, late warden of the late dissolved Colledge of Stratford-uppon-Avon aforesaid in the said county of Warwicke, and Gyles Coventrey, late subwarden of the same colledge, and the chapter of the said colledge, were heretofore seised in their demesne as of fee in the right of the said colledge, of and in divers messuages, landes, tenementes and glebe landes, scituate, lyeinge and beinge within the parishe of Stratford-uppon-Avon aforesaid, and of and in the tythes of corne, grayne and haye, and of and in all and all manner of tythes of wooll, lambe, and all other small and pryvye tythes and oblacions and alterages whatsoever, cominge, groweinge, aryseinge, reneweinge or happeninge within the whole parishe of Stratford-uppon-Avon aforesaid ; and beinge soe thereof seised, by their indenture beareinge date in or aboute the seaventh day of September, in the six and thirtyth yeare of the raigne of our late soveraigne lord of famous memory, Kinge Henry the Eight, sealed with their chapter seale, they did demise, graunte and to ferme lett, amongst divers mannors and other messuages, landes, tepementes and hereditamentes, unto one William Barker, gentleman, nowe deceassed, the aforesaid messuages, landes, tenementes and glebe landes, scituate, lyeinge and beinge within the said parishe of Stratford-uppon-Avon aforesaid, and the aforesaid tythes of corne, grayne and hay, and all and all manner other the said tythes of wooll, lambe, and smale and pryvie tythes, oblacions and alterages whatsoever ; To have and to hould from the feast of Ste. Michaell tharchangell then last past, for and duringe the terme of fourescore and twelve yeares thence next and imediately followeinge and fully to be compleate and ended ; by vertue of which demise the said William Barker entred into the said demised premisses, and was thereof possessed for all the said terme of yeares, and beinge soe thereof possessed of such estate, terme and interest, the said estate, terme and interest of the said William Barker, by some sufficient meanes in the law afterwards, came unto one John Barker, gent., by vertue whereof the said John Barker entred into the same premisses soe demised to the said William Barker, and was thereof possessed for and duringe the residue of the sayd terme of yeares then to come and not expired ; and beinge soe thereof possessed, he, the said John Barker, in or aboute the xxij.th yeare of the raigne of our late soveraigne lady Queene Elizabeth, by sufficiente assureance and conveyance in the lawe, did assigne assure and convey over unto Sir John Huband, knight, synce deceassed, the said messuages, landes, tenementes and glebe landes, scituate, lyeinge and beinge within the said parishe of Stratford-uppon-Avon, and all and singuler the tythes before specified, and all his estate, right, tytle, interest and terme of yeares of and in the same ; to have and to hould for and duringe all the residue of the said terme of lxxxxij. yeares then to come and not expired, reserveinge uppon and by the said assureance and conveyance the annuell or yearely rente of xxvij.*li.* xiij.*s.* iiij.*d.* of lawfull money of England at the feastes of Ste. Michaell tharchangell and thanunciacion of our blessed lady Ste. Mary the Virgin, by even and equall porcions ; in and by which said assureance and conveyance, as one Henry Barker, gent., executor of the last will and testamente of the said John Barker, or administrator of his goodes and chattles, or otherwise assignee of the said rente from the said John Barker, hath divers and sundry tymes given forth ; and which, yf the said rente of xxvij.*li.* xiij.*s.* iiij.*d.* or anie parte thereof shall happe at anie tyme to be unpaid, the tenauntes of the said premisses, as he sayeth, shall find, there was, by some sufficiente meanes, good and sufficiente provision causion and securyty hadd and made, that yf the said annuell or yearely rente, or anie parte thereof, should be behind and unpaid, in parte or in all, after eyther of the said feaste dayes wherein the same ought to be paid by the space of forty dayes, beinge lawfully demaunded at the porch of the parishe church of Stratford aforesaid, that then yt should and might be lawfull to and for the said William Barker, his executors, administrators and assignes, into all and singuler the said messuages, landes, tenementes, glebe lands and tythes, and other the premisses soe assured and assigned unto the said Sir

John Huband, to enter, and the same to have againe, reposseede⑧, and enjoy as in his or their former estate ; by vertue of which said assignemente, assureance and conveyance soe made to the said Sir John Huband, he, the said Sir John Huband, entred into all and singuler the same premisses soe assigned unto him, and was thereof possessed for and duringe all the residue of the said terme of lxxxxij. yeares then to come and not expired, under the condicion aforesaid, and subjecte to the forfeyture of all the said terme to him assured and conveyed, yf defaulte of payemente of the aforesaid rente xxvij.*li.* xiij.*s.* iiij.*d.* happened to be mad contrary to the true entente and meaninge of the said provision and security in and uppon the same assureance soe hadd and made ; and whereas sythence the said assureance and conveyance soe made to the said Sir John Huband, all the said assigned premisses are of divers and sundry parcells, and by divers and sundry severall sufficiente meane assignementes and under estates deryved under the said assureance and conveyance soe made unto the said Sir John Huband, for very greate summes of money and valuable consideracions, come unto and nowe remayne in your said oratours, and other the persons hereafter in theis presentes named, and they have severall estates of and in the same parcells, as followeth ; that is to saie, your oratour Richard Lane, an estate or interest for and duringe all the residue of the said terme of and in the tythes of corne and grayne of and in the barony of Clopton and the village of Shottery, being of and within the parishe of Stratford-uppon-Avon, of the yearely value of lxxx.*li.*, and of and in divers messuages, landes, tenementes and other hereditamentes in Shottery aforesaid and Drayton, within the said parishe of Stratford-uppon-Avon, of the yearely value of xxx.*li.* by the yeare ; and your oratour Thomas Greene, an estate or interest for and duringe all the residue of the said terme of and in one messuage with thappurtenaunces in Old Stratford, of the yearely value of three powndes ; and your oratour William Shackspeare hath an estate and interest of and in the moyty or one half of all tythes of corne and grayne aryseinge within the townes villages and fieldes of Old Stratford, Byshopton and Welcombe, being of and in the said parishe of Stratford, and of and in the moity or half of all tythes of wooll and lambe, and of all small and pryvy tythes, oblaciones, and alterages arisynge or increasyng in or within the wholl parishe of Stratford-upon-Avon aforesayd, for and duringe all the residue of the said terme, beinge of the yearely value of threescore powndes ; and the right honorable Sir George Carewe, knight, Lord Carewe of Clopton, hath an estate and interest, for the terme of nyneteene yeares or thereaboutes yet to come, of and in the tythes of corne grayne and hay aryseinge in the village and fieldes of Bridgtowne, in the said parishe of Stratford, of the value of xx.*li.* ; and your oratour, the said Richard Lane, an estate of and in the same in reversion thereof, for and duringe all the residue of the said terme of lxxxxij. yeares then to come and not expired ; and Sir Edward Grevill, knight, the reversion of one messuage in Stratford aforesaid, after the estate of one John Lupton therein determined, for and duringe all the residue of the said terme of lxxxxij. yeares, beinge of the yearely value of forty shillinges or thereaboutes ; and Sir Edward Conway, knight, hath an estate and interest for and duringe the residue of the said terme of and in the tythes of corne, grayne and haye of Loddington, another village of and within the said parishe of Stratford-uppon-Avon, of the yearely value of xxx.*li.* ; and Mary Combe, widowe, and William Combe, gent., and John Combe, gent., or some or one of them, an estate for the terme of six yeares or thereaboutes yet to come of and in the other moyty or half of the tythes of corne and grayne aryseinge within the townes, villages and fieldes of Old Stratford aforesaid, and Bishopton and Welcome in the said parishe of Stratford, and of and in the moyty or half of all tythes of wooll and lambe, and of all smale and pryvy tythes, oblacions and alterages ariseinge or encreasinge in or within the wholl parishe of Stratford-uppon-Avon aforesaid, of the yearely value of lx.*li.*. and of and in the tythes of corne, grayne and hay of Rien Clyfford, within the parishe of Stratford aforesaid, of the yearely value of x.*li.* ; and the said Thomas

Greene, an estate of and in the reversion of the same moyty of all the same tythes of corne and grayne, and wooll and lambe, and smale and privie tythes, oblacions and alterages, for and during all the residue of the said terme of fourescore and twelve yeares which after the feast day of thanunciacion of our blessed lady Ste. Mary the Virgin which shal be in the yeare of our Lord God 1613, shal be to come and unexpired ; and John Nashe, gent., an estate of and in the tythes of corne, grayne and haie aryseinge within the village and fieldes of Drayton within the parishe of Stratford aforesaid, of the yearely value of xx. markes, for and duringe all the residue of the said terme of lxxxxij. yeares ; and John Lane, gent., an estate, for and duringe all the residue of the said terme, of and in one hereditamente in Stratford aforesaid, heretofore called Byddles Barne, lately made and converted into divers and sundry tenementes or dwellinge-howses, and divers other messuages or tenementes, of the yearely value of viij.*li.* or thereaboutes ; and Anthonie Nashe, an estate of and in one messuage or tenemente in Bridgstreete in Stratford aforesaid, of the yearely value of foure powndes, for and duringe all the residue of the said terme of yeares yet to come ; the said William Combe and Mary Combe, widowe, mother of the said William, or one of them, an estate of and in divers cottages and gardens in Old Stratford, and of and in fyve leyes of pasture in Ryen-Clyfford in the said parishe of Stratford aforesaid, and of and in certayne landes or leyes in their or one of their closse or enclosure called Ste. Hill in the same parishe, of the yearely value of fyve powndes or thereaboutes, for and duringe all the residue of the said terme of lxxxxij. yeares yet to come and unexpired ; Daniell Baker, gent., an estate and® in the tythes of Shottery meadowe and Broad Meadowe within the said parishe, of the yearely value of xx.*li.*, for and duringe all the residue of the sayd terme of lxxxxij. yeares yet to come and unexpired ; John Smyth, gent., an estate of and in divers messuages, tenementes, barnes, and gardens in Stratford-uppon-Avon aforesaid, of the yearely value of viij.*li.* by the yeare, for and duringe all the residue of the said terme of lxxxxij. yeares yet to come and unexpired ; Frauncys Smyth the younger, gent., an estate of and in two barnes and divers messuages and tenementes with thappurtenaunces in the parishe of Stratford aforesaid, of the yearely value of xij.*li.*, for and duringe all the residue of the said terme of lxxxxij. yeares yet to come and unexpired ; William Walford, draper, an estate of and in two messuages or tenementes lyeinge and beinge in the Chappell Streete in Stratford-uppon-Avon aforesaid, of the yearely value of xl.*s.*, for and duringe all the residue of the said terme of lxxxxij. yeares yet to come and unexpired ; William Courte, gent., an estate of and in two messuages or tenementes in the Chappell streete in Stratford-uppon-Avon aforesaid, of the yearely value of iij.*li.*, for and duringe all the residue of the said terme of lxxxxij. yeares yet to come and unexpired ; John Browne, gent., an estate of and in one messuage in Bridge streete aforesaid, in Stratford-uppon-Avon aforesaid, of the yearely value of iiij.*li.*, for and duringe all the residue of the said terme of lxxxxij. yeares yet to come and unexpired ; Christopher Smyth of Willmecott, an estate of and in one messuage with the appurtenaunces in Henley Streete in Stratford-uppon-Avon aforesaid, of the yearely value of iiij.*li.*, for and duringe all the residue of the said terme of lxxxxij. yeares yet to come and unexpired ; Thomas Jakeman, an estate of and in one yard land in Shottery aforesayd in the parishe of Stratford aforesaid, of the yearely value of x.*li.*, for and duringe all the residue of the said terme of lxxxxij. yeares yet to come and unexpired ; and Richard Kempson of Bynton, one yard land and a half in Bynton, of the yerely value of eight powndes, for and duryng all the residue of the sayd terme of lxxxxij. yeres yet to come and unexpired ; Stephen Burman, an estate of and in one yard land and a half in Shottery aforesaid in the parishe of Stratford aforesaid, of the yearely value of xv.*li.*, for and duringe all the residue of the said terme of lxxxxij. yeares yet to come and not expired ; Thomas Burman, an estate of and in half a yard land in Shottery in the parishe of Stratford aforesaid, of the yearely value of v.*li.*, for and duringe all the residue of the said terme of lxxxxij. yeares yet to come and not expired ; and William Burman and the said Thomas Burman, executors of the last will and testament of one Stephen Burman, late deceassed, an estate of and in one tenemente in Church Streete in Stratford aforesaid, of the yearely value of iij.*li*., for and duringe all the residue of the said terme of lxxxxij. yet⑧ to come and not expired ; Thomas Horneby, an estate of and in the messuage wherein he nowe dwelleth in Stratford-uppon-Avon aforesaid, of the yearely value of iij.*li*. x.*s*., for and duringe all the residue of the said terme of lxxxxij. yeares yet to come and not expired ; Thomas Hamond, John Fifield, William Smarte, Thomas Aynge, Thomas Holmes, Edward Ingram, Richard Ingram, Thomas Bucke, Thomas Gryffin, Edward Wylkes, . . Brunte widowe, Thomas Vicars, Roberte Gryffin, Phillipp Rogers, . . Peare widowe, . . Younge, widowe, and . . Byddle, have every of them severall estates for all the residue of the said terme of lxxxxij. yeares, some of them of and in severall messuages with thappurtenaunces, and others of them of and in severall shoppes, barnes and severall gardens, every of the said severall messuages and partes of the premisses, wherein they severally have such estates, beinge of the severall yearely values of three powndes by the yeare or thereaboutes ; and by reason of the said severall estates and interestes soe respectyvely beinge in the said Lord Carewe, Sir Edward Grevill, Sir Edward Conway, and in your said orators, and in the sayd Mary Combe, William Combe, John Combe, John Lane, Anthonie Nashe, Thomas Barber, Daniell Baker, John Smyth, Frauncys Smyth, John Nashe, William Walford, William Courte, John Browne, Christopher Smyth, Thomas Jakeman, Stephen Burman, William Burman, Thomas Burman, John Lupton, Thomas Horneby, Thomas Hamond, John Fifield, William Smarte, Thomas Aynge, Thomas Holmes, Edward Ingram, Richard Ingram, Thomas Bucke, Thomas Gryffin, Edward Wylkes, . . Brunte, Thomas Vicars, Roberte Gryffin, Phillipp Rogers, . . Fletcher, . . Peare, . . Younge, and . . Byddle, every of them, and every of their executors and assignes, ought in all right, equity, reason and good conscience, for and duringe the severall respectyve contynuances of their severall respectyve interestes, estates and termes in the premisses, and accordinge to the severall values of the said severall premisses soe enjoyed by them, and the rentes they doe yearely receyve for the same, to pay unto the executors, administrators or assignes of the said John Barker a ratable and proporcionable parte and porcion of the said annuell or yearely rente of xxvij.*li*. xiij.*s*. iiij.*d*. by and uppon the said assureance and conveyance soe as aforesaid by the said John Barker made unto the said Sir John Huband reserved and payeable ; but soe yt is, yf yt may please your honorable good lordshippe, that the said Lord Carewe, Sir Edward Grevill, Sir Edward Conway, Mary Combe, William Combe, or anie other the said other partyes, at anie tyme synce the said assureances and conveyances soe made and derived from or under the said interest of the said Sir John Huband, for that uppon or by the deedes of their severall under estates or assignementes unto them made, they, or those under whom they clayme, excepte the said Mary Combe, Thomas Greene, William Combe, John Combe, and William Shackspeare, whoe only are to pay for tythes of their said severall moytyes before specified v.*li*., and noe more, yearely duringe their said respectyve interestes, were not directed nor appoynted, nor anie covenauntes by them or anie of them, or anie other under whom they or anie of them doe clayme, excepte touchinge the said severall yearely fyve powndes soe to be paid for the said moytyes, were made, whereby yt might appeare howe much of the same rente of xxvij.*li*. xiij.*s*. iiij.*d*. ought to be paid for every of the said severall premisses, excepte concernyng the sayd moityes, could never yet be drawen to agree howe to paye the residue of the said rente, or be brought to pay anie precise parte or porcion at all towardes the same ; but divers of them, beinge of greate ability, doe divers tymes forebeare and deny to pay anie parte at all towardes the same, except the persons before excepted only as touchinge the said severall fyve powndes for their said severall moytyes, alledginge and saieinge, Lett them that are affrayd to forfeyte or loose their estates looke to yt, and amongst them see the said rente be truely and duelye paid, for they doubte but they shall doe well enoughe with the executors or assignes of the said Jo. Barker; further excusinge their not payeinge anie rente at all for the residue of the premisses other then the said moytyes, by sayeinge that, yf they could fynd anie thinge in anie of their deedes of assignmentes or conveyances chargeinge them precisely with any part thereof, or in anie wise declareinge howe much they are to pay, they would willingly, as is fitt, pay such rate and porcion as they were soe bownd unto, but because they find noe such matter to charge them, excepte the said parties excepted, which by the deedes of their estates are directed for the said severall moytyes to pay the said severall yearely rentes of v.*li.* apeece, therefore they will not paye anie thinge at all towardes the said residue of the said rente of xxvij.*li.* xiij.*s.* iiij.*d.*, untyll, by some legall course or proceedinge in some courte of equity, yt shal be declared what parte or porcion in reason and equity every severall owner of the said severall premisses ought to pay towardes the same, and be judicially ordered thereunto, which lett them that thinke that a good course endevour to bringe to passe, when they shall see good, or wordes to such lyke effecte; soe as your oratours, their said respectyve estates and interestes of and in their said severall premisses aforesaid, and the estates of divers of the said partyes, which would gladly pay a reasonable parte towardes the said rente, but doe nowe refuse to joyne with your said oratours in this their said suite, for feare of some other of the said parties which doe soe refuse to contrybute, doe remayne and stand subjecte to be forfeyted by the negligence or willfullnes of divers or anie other of the said partyes, which manie tymes will pay nothinge, whenas your oratours Richard Lane and William Shackspeare, and some fewe others of the said parties, are wholly, and against all equity and good conscience, usually dryven to pay the same for preservacion of their estates of and in the partes of the premisses belonginge unto them; and albeyt your said oratours have taken greate paynes and travayle in entreatinge and endevoringe to bringe the said parties of their owne accordes, and without suite of lawe, to agree every one to a reasonable contribucion toward the same residue of the said rente of xxvij.*li.* xiij.*s.* iiij.*d.*, accordinge to the value of such of the premisses as they enjoy, and onely for their respectyve tymes and termes therein, yet have they refused and denied, and styll doe refuse and deny, to be perswaded or drawen thereunto, and some of them beinge encoraged, as yt should seme, by some frendly and kind promise of the said Henry Barker, assignee of the said John Barker, that they should find favour, thoughe their said estates should be all forfeyted, have given yt forth that they should be glade and cared not a whitt yf the estates of some or all the said premisses should be forfeyted, for they should doe well enoughe with the sayd Henry Barker. In tender consideracion whereof, and for soe much as yt is against all equitye and reason that the estates of some that are willinge to paie a reasonable parte toward the said residue of the said rente of xxvij.*li.* xiij.*s.* iiij.*d.*, haveinge respecte to the smalnes of the values of the thinges they doe possesse, should depend uppon the carlesnes and frowardnes or other practices of others, which will not paie a reasonable parte or anie thinge at all toward the same; and for that yt is most agreeable to all reason, equity and good conscience, that every person, his executors and assignes, should be ratably charged with a yearely porcion toward the said residue of the sayd rente, accordinge to the yearely benefitt he enjoyeth or receaveth; and for that your oratours have noe meanes, by the order or course of the common lawes of this realme, to enforce or compell anie of the said partyes to yeald anie certayne contrybucion toward the same, and soe are and styll shal bee remediles therein unles they may be in that behalf relieved by your Lordshippes gracious clemency and relyef to others in such lyke cases extended; May yt therefore please your good lordshippe, the premisses considered, and yt beinge alsoe considered that very manie poore peoples estates are subjecte to be overthrowen by breach of the condicion aforesaid, and thereby doe depend uppon the negligences, wills or practices of others, and shall contynue daylye in doubte to be turned out of doores, with their wives and families, thorough the practice or wilfullnes of such others, to write your honorable lettres unto the said Lord Carewe, thereby requiringe him to appeare in the Highe Courte of Chauncery to answere to the premisses, and to graunte unto your said oratours his Majesties most gracious writtes of subpena to be directed unto the said Sir Edward Grevill, Sir Edward Conway, and other the said parties before named, and to the said Henry Barker, whoe claymeth under the right and tytle of the said John Barker, and usually receyveth the said rente in his owne name, and usually maketh acquittaunces upon the receipt thereof, under his owne hand and in his owne name, as in his owne right, and usually maketh acquittances of divers partes thereof, thereby comaundinge them and every of them at a certayne day, and under a certayne payne therein to be lymitted, to be and personally appeare before your good lordshippe in his highnes most honorable Courte of Chauncery, fully, perfectly and directly to awnswere to all and every the premisses, and to sett forth the severall yearely values of the severall premisses soe by them enjoyed, and to shewe good cause whie a comission should not be awarded forth of the said most honorable courte for the examininge of wittnesses to the severall values aforesaid, and for the assessinge, taxinge and ratinge thereof, that thereuppon yt may appeare howe much every of the said parties, and their executors, administrators and assignes, for and duringe their said severall respectyve estates and interestes, ought in reason proporcionably to pay for the same towardes the said residue of the said yearely rente of xxvij.*li.* xiij.*s.* iiij.*d.*, that the same may be ordered and established by decree of your most honorable good Lordshippe accordingly ; and the said Henry Barker to awnswere to the premisses, and to sett forth what estate or interest he claymeth in the said rente of xxvij.*li.* xiij.*s.* iiij.*d.*, and alsoe to shewe good cause whie he should not be ordered to accept the rentes ratablye to be assessed as aforesaid, and to enter onely into the tenement and estate onely of such persons which shall refuse or neglecte to pay such parte of the said rente, as by your most honorable order there shal be sett downe and rated uppon them severally to paie, and further to stand to and abide such further and other order and direccions touchinge the premisses as to your good Lordshipp shall seeme to stand with right equity and good conscience. And your Lordshippes said oratours shall dayly pray unto thalmightie for your Lordshippes health, with dayly encrease in all honour and happines.—*Endorsed*, Lane, Greene et Shakspeare contra W. Combe et alios respondentes.

X. The Deed of Bargain and Sale of the Blackfriars Estate from Henry Walker to Shakespeare and Trustees, 10th March, 1612-3. This indenture was the one that was enrolled by the vendor in the Court of Chancery, and that which was afterwards held by the purchaser. From the original preserved at Hollingbury Copse.

This Indenture made the tenthe day of March, in the yeare of our Lord God, according to the computacion of the Church of England, one thowsand six hundred and twelve, and in the yeares of the reigne of our sovereigne Lord James, by the grace of God king of England, Scotland, Fraunce and Ireland, defender of the faithe, &c., that is to saie, of England, Fraunce and Ireland the tenth, and of Scotland the six and fortith, Betweene Henry Walker, citizein and minstrell of London, of th'one partie, and William Shakespeare of Stratford-upon-Avon in the countie of Warwick, gentle-man, William Johnson, citizein and vintener of London, John Jackson and John Hemmyng of London, gentlemen, of th'other partie ; Witnesseth that the said Henry Walker, for and in consideracion of the somme of one hundred and fortie poundes of lawfull money of England to him in hande, before th'ensealing hereof, by the said William Shakespeare well and trulie paid, whereof and wherewith hee, the said Henry

Walker, doth acknowledge himselfe fullie satisfied and contented, and thereof, and of every part and parcell thereof, doth cleerlie acquite and discharge the said William Shakespeare, his heires, executours, administratours and assignes, and every of them by theis presentes, hath bargayned and soulde, and by theis presentes doth fullie cleerlie, and absolutlie bargayne and sell unto the said William Shakespeare, William Johnson, John Jackson, and John Hemmyng, their heires, and assignes for ever, All that dwelling-house or tenement, with th'appurtenaunces, situate and being within the precinct, circuit and compasse of the late Black Fryers, London, sometymes in the tenure of James Gardyner, esquiour, and since that in the tenure of John Fortescue, gent., and now or late being in the tenure or occupacion of one William Ireland, or of his assignee or assignes, abutting upon a streete leading downe to Pudle Wharffe on the east part, right against the Kinges Majesties Wardrobe ; part of which said tenement is erected over a great gate leading to a capitall mesuage which sometyme was in the tenure of William Blackwell, esquiour, deceased, and since that in the tenure or occupacion of the right Honourable Henry, now Earle of Northumberland ; and also all that plott of ground on the west side of the same tenement, which was lately inclosed with boordes on two sides thereof by Anne Bacon, widow, soe farre and in such sorte as the same was inclosed by the said Anne Bacon, and not otherwise, and being on the third side inclosed with an olde bricke wall ; which said plott of ground was sometyme parcell and taken out of a great peece of voyde ground lately used for a garden ; and also the soyle whereupon the said tenement standeth ; and also the said brick wall and boordes which doe inclose the said plott of ground ; with free entrie, accesse, ingresse, egresse and regresse, in, by and through the said greate gate and yarde thereunto the usuall dore of the said tenement ; and also all and singuler cellours, sollers, romes, lightes, easiamentes, profittes, commodities and hereditamentes whatsoever to the said dwelling-house or tenement belonging or in any wise apperteyning ; and the reversion and reversions whatsoever of all and singuler the premisses, and of every parcell thereof ; and also all rentes and yearlie profittes whatsoever reserved and from hensforth to growe due and paiable upon whatsoever lease, dimise or graunt, leases, dimises or grauntes, made of the premisses or of any parcell thereof ; and also all th'estate, right, title, interest, propertie, use, possession, clayme and demaund whatsoever, which hee, the said Henry Walker, now hath, or of right may, might, should, or ought to have, of, in or to the premisses or any parcell thereof ; and also all and every the deedes, evidences, charters, escriptes, minimentes and writinges whatsoever, which hee, the said Henry Walker, now hath, or any other person or persons to his use have or hath, or which hee may lawfullie come by without suite in the lawe, which touch or concerne the premisses onlie, or onlie any part or parcell thereof, togeither with the true copies of all such deedes, evidences and writinges as concerne the premisses, amounges other thinges, to bee written and taken out at the onlie costes and charges of the said William Shakespeare, his heires or assignes ; which said dwelling-house or tenement, and other the premisses above by theis presentes mencioned to bee bargayned and soulde, the said Henry Walker late purchased and hadd to him, his heires and assignes, for ever, of Mathie Bacon, of Graies Inne in the countie of Midd., gentleman, by indenture bearing date the fifteenth day of October, in the yeare of our Lord God one thowsand six hundred and fower, and in the yeares of the reigne of our said sovereigne lord king James, of his realmes of England, Fraunce and Ireland, the seconde, and of Scotland the eight and thirtith ; to have and to holde the said dwelling-house or tenement, shopps, cellors, sollers, plott of ground and all and singuler other the premisses above by theis presentes mencioned to bee bargayned and soulde, and every part and parcell thereof, with th'appurtenaunces, unto the said William Shakespeare, William Johnson, John Jackson and John Hemmyng, their heires and assignes, for ever, to th'onlie and proper use and behoofe of the said William Shakespeare, William Johnson, John Jackson and John Hemmyng, their heires and assignes for ever. And the said Henry Walker, for himselfe, his heires, executours, administratours, and assignes, and for every of them, doth covenaunte, promisse and graunt to and with the said William Shakespeare, his heires and assignes, by theis presentes, in forme following, that is to saie, that hee, the said Henry Walker, his heires, executours, administratours or assignes, shall and will cleerlie acquite, exonerate and discharge, or otherwise from tyme to tyme and at all tymes hereafter well and sufficientlie save and keepe harmles, the said William Shakespeare, his heires and assignes and every of them, of, for and concernyng the bargayne and sale of the premisses, and the said bargayned premisses, and every part and parcell thereof, with th'appurtenaunces, of and from all and al manner of former bargaynes, sales, guiftes, grauntes, leases, statutes, recognizaunces, joyntures, dowers, intailes, lymittacion and lymittacions of use and uses, extentes, judgmentes, execucions, annuities, and of and from all and every other charges, titles and incumbraunces whatsoever, wittinglie and wilfullie had, made, committed, suffered or donne by him, the said Henry Walker, or any other under his aucthoritie or right, before th'ensealing and deliverie of theis presentes, except the rentes and services to the cheefe lord or lordes of the fee or fees of the premisses from hensforth for or in respecte of his or their seigniorie or seigniories onlie to bee due and donne. And further the said Henry Walker, for himselfe, his heires, executours and administratours, and for every of them, doth covenaunte, promisse and graunt to and with the saide William Shakespeare, his heires and assignes, by theis presentes in forme following, that is to saie, that for and notwith-standing any acte or thing donne by him, the said Henry Walker, to the contrary, hee, the said William Shakespeare, his heires and assignes, shall or lawfullie may peace-ablie and quietlie have, holde, occupie and enjoye the said dwelling-house or tenement, cellours, sollers, and all and singuler other the premisses above by theis presentes mencioned to bee bargayned and soulde, and every part and parcell thereof, with th'appurtenaunces, and the rentes, yssues and profittes thereof, and of every part and parcell thereof, to his and their owne use receave, perceave, take and enjoye from hensforth for ever without the lett, troble, eviccion or interrupcion of the said Henry Walker, his heires, executours or administratours, or any of them, or of or by any other person or persons which have, or maye before the date hereof pretend to have, any lawfull estate, right, title, use or interest, in or to the premisses or any parcell thereof, by, from or under him, the said Henry Walker. And also that hee, the said Henry Walker and his heires, and all and every other person and persons and their heires, which have, or that shall lawfullie and rightfullie have or clayme to have, any lawfull and right-full estate, righte, title or interest, in or to the premisses or any parcell thereof, by, from or under the said Henry Walker, shall and will, from tyme to tyme and at all tymes from hensforth, for and during the space of three yeares now next ensuing, at or upon the reasonable request and costes and charges in the lawe of the said William Shakespeare, his heires and assignes, doe make, knowledge and suffer to bee donne, made and know-ledged, all and every such further lawfull and reasonable acte and actes, thing and thinges, devise and devises in the lawe whatsoever, for the conveying of the premisses, bee it by deed or deedes inrolled or not inrolled, inrolment of theis presentes, fyne, feoffa-ment, recoverye, release, confirmacion or otherwise, with warrantie of the said Henry Walker and his heires against him the said Henry Walker and his heires onlie, or otherwise, without warrantie, or by all, any or as many of the wayes, meanes and devises aforesaid, as by the said William Shakespeare, his heires or assignes, or his or their councell learned in the lawe shal bee reasonablie devised or advised, for the further, better and more perfect assurance, suertie, suermaking and conveying of all and singuler the premisses, and every parcell thereof, with th'appurtenaunces, unto the said William Shakespeare, his heires and assignes, for ever, to th'use and in forme aforesaid ; and further that all and every fyne and fynes to bee levyed, recoveryes to bee suffered, estates and assurances at any tyme or tymes hereafter to bee had, made, executed or passed by or betweene the said parties of the premisses, or of any parcell thereof, shal bee, and shal bee esteemed, adjudged, deemed and taken to bee, to th'onlie and proper use and behoofe of the said William Shakespeare, his heires and assignes, for ever, and to none other use, intent or purpose. In witnesse whereof the said parties to theis indentures interchaungablie have sett their seales. Yeoven the day and yeares first above written.—*Henry Walker.*—Sealed and delivered in the presence of Will. Atkinson ; Robert Andrewes, scr. ; Edw. Ouery ; Henry Lawrence, servant to the same Scr.

XI. The opening Paragraphs and the Termination of the Counterpart of the preceding Indenture of the 10th of March, 1612–3, the former being the deed which was held by the vendor. With the exceptions of the signatures and the attestation, and an erasure of a few lines referring to a lease of the premises which had been granted by Walker in December, 1604, the whole of the counterpart is verbally identical with the deed that is given at length in the last article. From the original in the Library of the City of London.

1. This indenture made the tenthe day of Marche, in the yeare of our Lord God, according to the computacion of the Church of England, one thowsand six hundred and twelve, and in the yeares of the reigne of our sovereigne Lord James, by the grace of God King of England, Scotland, Fraunce and Ireland, defender of the faith, &c., that is to saie, of England, Fraunce and Ireland the tenth and of Scotland the six and fortith, betweene Henry Walker, citizein and minstrell of London of th'one partie, and William Shakespeare, of Stratford-upon-Avon in the countie of Warwick, gentleman, William Johnson, citizein and vintener of London, John Jackson and John Hemmyng, of London, gentlemen, of th'other partie.

2. And further, that all and every fyne and fynes to bee levyed, recoveryes to bee suffered, estates and assurances at any tyme or tymes hereafter to bee had, made, executed or passed by or betweene the said parties of the premisses, or of any parcell thereof, shal bee, and shal bee esteemed, adjudged, deemed and taken to bee, to th'onlie and proper use and behoofe of the said William Shakespeare, his heires and assignes, for ever, and to none other use, intent or purpose. In witnesse whereof the said parties to theis indentures interchaungablie have sett their seales. Yeoven the day and yeares first above written.—*William Shakspere.—Wm. Johnson.—Jo. Jackson.*—Sealed and delivered by the said William Shakespeare, William Johnson, and John Jackson, in the presence of Will : Atkinson ; Ed. Ouery ; Robert Andrewes, scr. ; Henry Lawrence, servant to the same scr.

XII. The deed from Shakespeare and Trustees to Henry Walker, by which the Blackfriars Estate was mortgaged to the latter, 11th March, 1612–3. From the original in the Library of the British Museum.

This Indenture made the eleventh day of March, in the yeares of the reigne of our Sovereigne Lord James, by the grace of God, king of England, Scotland, Fraunce and Ireland, defender of the Faith, &c., that is to saie, of England, Fraunce and Ireland the tenth, and of Scotland the six and fortith ; betweene William Shakespeare, of Stratford-upon-Avon in the countie of Warwick, gentleman, William Johnson, citizein and vintener of London, John Jackson and John Hemmyng, of London, gentlemen, of th'one partie, and Henry Walker, citizein and minstrell of London, of th'other partie : Witnesseth that the said William Shakespeare, William Johnson, John Jackson and John Hemmyng, have dimised, graunted and to ferme letten, and by theis presentes doe dimise, graunt and to ferme lett unto the said Henry Walker all that dwelling-house or tenement, with th'appurtenaunces, situate and being within the precinct, circuit and compasse of the late Black Fryers, London, sometymes in the tenure of James Gardyner, esquiour, and since that in the tenure of John Fortescue, gent., and now or late being in the tenure or occupacion of one William Ireland, or of his assignee or assignes, abutting upon a streete leading downe to Puddle Wharffe on the east part, right against the Kinges Majesties Wardrobe; part of which said tenement is erected over a greate gate leading to a capitall mesuage which some-tyme was in the tenure of William Blackwell, esquiour, deceased, and since that in the tenure or occupacion of the right honourable Henry, now Earle of Northumberland; and also all that plott of ground, on the west side of the same tenement, which was lately inclosed with boordes on two sides thereof by Anne Bacon, widow, soe farre and in such sorte as the same was inclosed by the said Anne Bacon, and not otherwise, and being on the third side inclosed with an olde brick wall; which said plott of ground was sometyme parcell and taken out of a great voyde peece of ground lately used for a garden; and also the soyle whereuppon the said tenement standeth, and also the said brick wall and boordes which doe inclose the said plott of ground, with free entrie, accesse, ingresse, egresse and regresse, in, by and through the said great gate and yarde there, unto the usuall dore of the said tenement; and also all and singuler cellours, sollers, romes, lightes, easiamentes, profittes, commodities and appurtenaunces whatsoever to the said dwelling-house or tenement belonging, or in any wise apper-teyning; to have and to holde the said dwelling-house or tenement, cellers, sollers, romes, plott of ground, and all and singuler other the premisses above by theis presentes mencioned to bee dimised, and every part and parcell thereof, with th'appurtenaunces, unto the said Henrye Walker, his executours, administratours and assignes, from the feast of th'annunciacion of the blessed Virgin Marye next comming after the date hereof, unto th'ende and terme of one hundred yeares from thence next ensuing, and fullie to bee compleat and ended, without ympeachment of or for any manner of waste; yeelding and paying therefore yearlie during the said terme unto the said William Shakespeare, William Johnson, John Jackson and John Hemmyng, their heires and assignes, a peppercorne at the feast of Easter yearlie, yf the same bee law-fullie demaunded, and noe more; provided alwayes that if the said William Shake-speare, his heires, executours, administratours or assignes, or any of them, doe well and trulie paie or cause to bee paid to the said Henry Walker, his executours, administratours or assignes, the some of threescore poundes of lawfull money of England in and upon the nyne and twentith day of September next comming after the date hereof, at or in the nowe dwelling-house of the said Henry Walker, situate and being in the parish of Saint Martyn neere Ludgate, of London, at one entier payment without delaie, that then and from thensforth this presente lease, dimise and graunt, and all and every matter and thing herein conteyned, other then this provisoe, shall cease, determyne, and bee utterlie voyde, frustrate, and of none effect, as though the same had never beene had ne made, theis presentes, or any thing therein conteyned to the contrary thereof, in any wise notwithstanding. And the said William Shake-speare, for himselfe, his heires, executours and administratours, and for every of them, doth covenaunt, promise and graunt to and with the said Henry Walker, his executours, administratours and assignes, and every of them, by theis presentes, that hee, the said William Shakespeare, his heires, executours, administratours or assignes, shall and will cleerlie acquite, exonerate and discharge, or from tyme to tyme, and at all tymes hereafter, well and sufficientlie save and keepe harmles the said Henry Walker, his executours, administratours and assignes, and every of them, and the said premisses by theis presentes dimised, and every parcell thereof, with th'appur-tenaunces, of and from all and al manner of former and other bargaynes, sales, guiftes, grauntes, leases, joyntures, dowers, intailes, statutes, recognizaunces, judgmentes, execucions, and of and from all and every other charges, titles, trobles and incum-braunces whatsoever by the said William Shakespeare, William Johnson, John Jackson and John Hemmyng, or any of them, or by their or any of their meanes, had, made, committed or donne, before th'ensealing and delivery of theis presentes, or hereafter

C 2

before the said nyne and twentith day of September next comming after the date hereof, to bee had, made, committed or donne, except the rentes and services to the cheefe lord or lordes of the fee or fees of the premisses, for or in respect of his or their seigniorie or seigniories onlie, to bee due and donne. In witnesse whereof the said parties to theis indentures interchaungablie have sett their seales. Yeoven the day and yeares first above written. 1612.—*Wm. Shakspere.—Wm. Johnson.—Jo: Jackson.*— Sealed and delivered by the said William Shakespeare, William Johnson, and John Jackson, in the presence of Will: Atkinson; Ed: Ouery; Robert Andrewes, scr.; Henry Lawrence, servant to the same scr.

XIII. Articles of Agreement between Shakespeare and William Replingham, 1614, by which the latter agrees to compensate the poet should loss accrue to him by enclosures which were then contemplated. The following is taken from a contemporary transcript entitled—"Coppy of the articles with Mr. Shakspeare."

Vicesimo octavo die Octobris, anno Domini 1614. Articles of agreement indented made⑤ betweene William Shackespeare, of Stretford in the county of Warwicke, gent., on the one partye, and William Replingham, of Greete Harborowe in the Countie of Warwicke, gent., on the other partie, the daye and yeare abovesaid.—Item, the said William Replingham, for him, his heires, executours and assignes, doth covenaunte and agree to and with the said William Shackespeare, his heires and assignes, that he, the said William Replingham, his heires or assignes, shall, upon reasonable request, satisfie, content and make recompence unto him, the said William Shackespeare or his assignes, for all such losse, detriment and hinderance as he, the said William Shacke- speare, his heires and assignes, and one Thomas Greene, gent., shall or maye be thought, in the viewe and judgement of foure indifferent persons, to be indifferentlie elected by the said William and William, and their heires, and in default of the said William Replingham, by the said William Shackespeare or his heires onely, to survey and judge the same to sustayne or incurre for or in respecte of the increasinge⑤ of the yearelie value of the tythes they the said William Shackespeare and Thomas doe joyntlie or severallie hold and enjoy in the said fieldes, or anie of them, by reason of anie inclosure or decaye of tyllage there ment and intended by the said William Replingham; and that the said William Replingham and his heires shall procure such sufficient securitie unto the said William Shackespeare, and his heires, for the perform- ance of theis covenauntes, as shal bee devised by learned counsell. In witnes whereof the parties abovsaid to theis presentes interchangeablie their handes and seales have put, the daye and yeare first above wrytten. Sealed and delivered in the presence of us,—Tho: Lucas; Jo: Rogers; Anthonie Nasshe; Mich: Olney.

XIV. A Deed transferring the Legal Estate of the Blackfriars property, 10 February, 1617-8, in trust to follow the directions of Shakespeare's will, subject only to the remaining term of a lease granted by the poet to one John Robinson. From the original preserved at Hollingbury Copse.

This indenture made the tenth day of February, in the yeres of the reigne of our sovereigne Lord James, by the grace of God kinge of England, Scotland, Fraunce and Ireland, defendor of the faith, &c., that is to say, of England, Fraunce and Ireland the fifteenth, and of Scotland the one and fiftith; between John Jackson and John Hemynge, of London, gentlemen, and William Johnson, citizen and vintiner of London, of thone part, and John Greene, of Clementes Inn in the county of Midd., gent., and Mathew Morrys, of Stretford-upon-Avon in the county of Warwick, gent., of thother part; witnesseth that the said John Jackson, John Hemynge and William Johnson, as well for and in performance of the confidence and trust in them reposed by William Shakespeare, deceased, late of Stretford aforesaid, gent., and to thend and intent that the landes, tenementes and hereditamentes, hereafter in theis presentes mencioned and expressed, may be conveyed and assured according to the true intent and meaning of the last will and testament of the said William Shakespeare, and for the some of fyve shillinges of lawfull money of England to them payd, for and on the behalf of Susanna Hall, one of the daughters of the said William Shakespeare, and now wife of John Hall of Stretford aforesaid, gent., before thensealling and delivery of theis presentes, have aliened, bargained, sold and confirmed, and by theis presentes doe, and every of them doth, fully, cleerely and absolutely alien, bargaine, sell and confirme unto the said John Greene and Mathew Morry, their heires and assignes for ever, All that dwelling-howse or tenement with thappurtenaunces scituat and being within the precinct, circuite and compase of the late Blackfriers, London, sometymes in the tenure of James Gardyner, esquior, and since that in the tenure of John Fortescue, gent., and now or late being in the tenure or occupacion of one William Ireland, or of his assignee or assignes, abutting upon a street leadinge downe to Puddle Wharfe on the east part, right against the kinges Majesties Warderobe, part of which tenement is erected over a great gate leading to a capitall messuage which sometymes was in the tenure of William Blackwell, esquior, deceased, and, since that, in the tenure or occupacion of the right honourable Henry, earle of Northumberland ; and also all that plot of ground on the west side of the said tenement which was lately inclosed with boordes on twoe sides thereof by Anne Bacon, widdow, soe farr and in such sort as the same was inclosed by the said Anne Bacon, and not otherwise, and being on the third side inclosed with an ould brick wall ; which said plot of ground was sometymes parcell and taken out of a great peece of voyd ground lately used for a garden; and also the soyle whereupon the said tenement standeth ; and also the said brick wall and boordes which doe inclose the said plot of ground, with free entry, accesse, ingres, egres and regres, in, by and through the said great gate and yarde there unto the usuall dore of the said tenement ; and also all singuler® cellers, sollars, roomes, lightes, easementes, profittes, comodyties and hereditamentes whatsoever to the said dwelling-howse or tenement belonging or in any wise apperteyning, and the revercion and revercions whatsoever of all and singuler the premisses and of every parcell thereof ; and also all rentes and yerely profittes whatsoever reserved, and from henceforth to grow due and payable, upon whatsoever lease, demise or graunt, leases, demises or grauntes, made of the premisses, or any parcell thereof ; and also all thestate, right, title, interest, property, use, clayme and demaund whatsoever, which they, the said John Jackson, John Hemynge and William Johnson, now have, or any of them hath, or of right may, might, shoold or ought to have in the premisses ; to have and to holde the said dwelling-howse or tenement, lights, cellers, sollars, plot of ground, and all and singuler other the premisses above by theis presentes mencioned to be bargained and sold, and every part and parcell thereof, with thappurtenaunces, unto the said John Green and Mathew Morrys, their heires and assignes, for ever, to the use and behoofes hereafter in theis presentes declared, mencioned, expressed and lymitted, and to none other use, behoofe, intent or purpose ; that is to say, to the use and behoofe of the aforesaid Susanna Hall for and during the terme of her naturall life, and after her decease to the use and behoofe of the first sonne of her body lawfully yssueing, and of thé heires males of the body of the said first sonne lawfully yssueing ; and, for want of such heires, to the use and behoofe of the second sonne of the body of the said Susanna lawfully yssueing, and of the heires males of the body of the said second sonne lawfully yssueing ; and, for want of such heires, to the use and behoofe of the third sonne of the body of the said Susanna lawfully yssueing, and of the heires males of the body of the said third sonne lawfully yssueing ; and, for want of such heires, to the use and behoofe of the fowerth, fyveth, sixt and seaventh sonnes of the body of the said Susanna lawfully yssueing, and of the severall heires males of the severall bodyes of the said fowerth, fiveth, sixt and seaventh sonnes, lawfully yssueing, in such manner as it is before lymitted to be

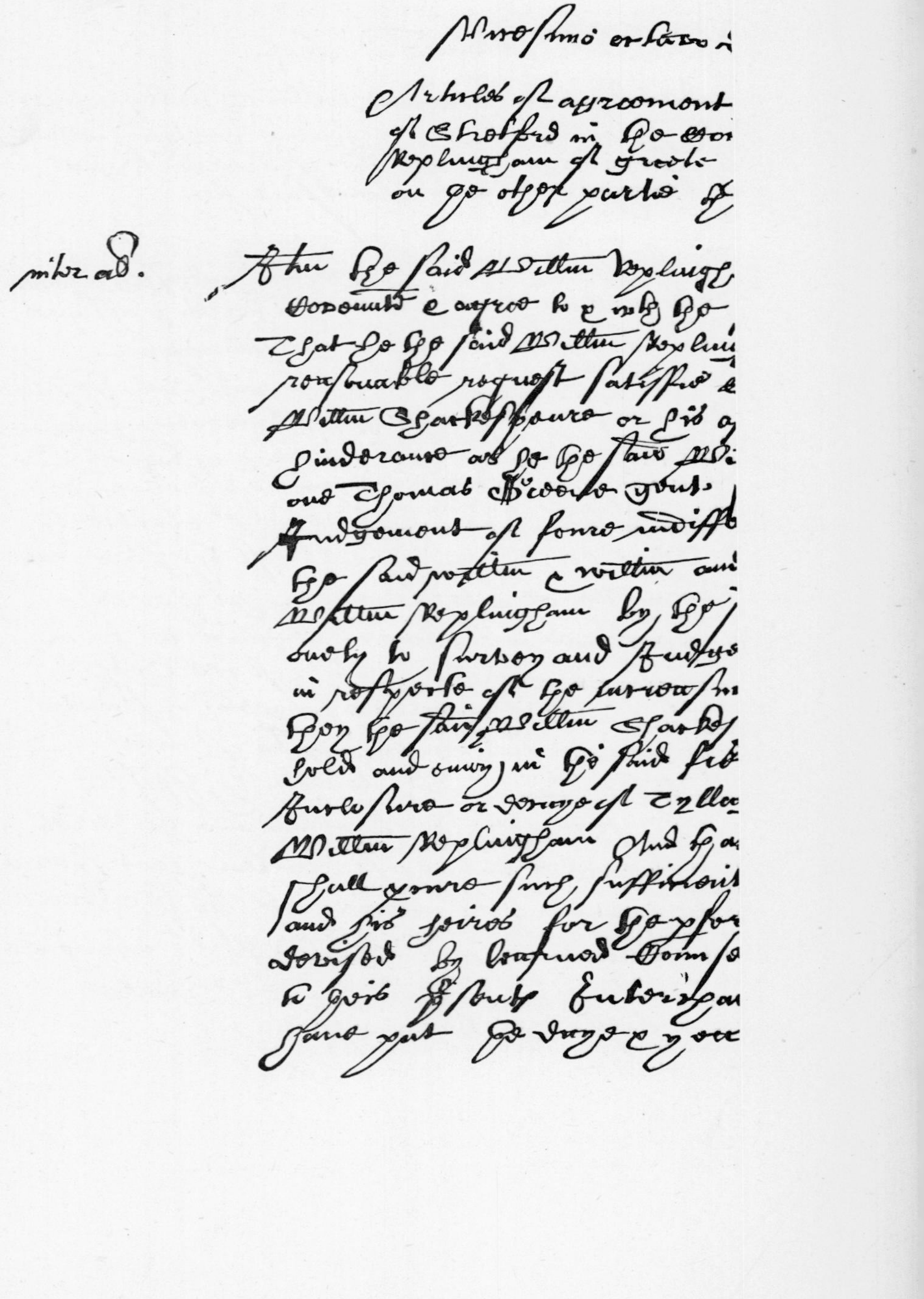
Vicesimo octavo d
Articles of agreement
of Stratford in the Coun
Replingham of Greate
on the other partie
Item the said William Replingh
Covenauntes & agreeth to & with the
That he the said William Replin
reasonable request satisfie
William Shackespeare or his a
hinderance as he the said Wi
and Thomas Greene gent.
Judgement of foure indiff
the said parties written and
William Replingham by the
onely to survey and judge
in respecte of the inclosur
Upon the said William Shakes
holde and enjoy in the said fie
furlonge or groundes of Tylla
William Replingham And tha
shall yeve such sufficient
and his heires for the per
devised by learned Couns

xxio octobris Anno Dni 1614

and remeyne to the first, second, and third sonnes of the body of the said Susanna lawfully yssueing, and to their heires males as aforesaid ; and, for default of such heires, to the use and behoofe of Elizabeth Hall, daughter of the said Susanna Hall, and of the heires males of her body lawfully yssueing ; and, for default of such heires, to the use and behoofe of Judyth Quiney, now wife of Thomas Quiney, of Stretford aforesaid, vintiner, one other of the daughters of the said William Shakespeare, and of the heires males of the body of the said Judyth lawfully yssueing ; and, for default of such yssue, to the use and behoofe of the right heires of the said William Shakespeare for ever. And the said John Jackson, for himself, his heires, executours, adminis- tratours and assignes, and for every of them, doth covenaunt, promise and graunt, to and with the said John Green and Mathew Morrys, and either of them, their and either of their heires and assignes, by theis presentes, that he, the said John Jackson, his heires, executours, administratours or assignes, shall and will, from-tyme to tyme and at all tymes hereafter, within convenient tyme after every reasonable request to him or them made, well and sufficiently save and keepe harmeles the said bargained premisses, and every part and parcell thereof, of and from all and all manner of former bargaines, sales, guiftes, grauntes, leases, statutes, recognizaunces, joynctures, dowers, intayles, uses, extentes, judgementes, execucions, annewyties, and of and from all other charges, titles and incombraunces whatsoever, wittingly and willingly had, made, comitted or done by him, the said John Jackson alone, or joynctly with any other person or persons whatsoever ; except the rentes and services to the cheiffe lord or lordes of the fee or fees of the premisses from henceforth to be due, and of right accustomed to be done, and except one lease and demise of the premisses with thappurtenaunces heretofore made by the said William Shakespeare, together with them, the said John Jackson, John Hemynge and William Johnson, unto one John Robinson, now tennant of the said premisses, for the terme of certen yeres yet to come and unexpired, as by the same whereunto relacion be had at large doth appeare. And the said John Hemynge, for himself, his heires, executours, administratours and assignes, and for every of them, doth covenaunt, promise and graunt, to and with the said John Greene and Mathew Morrys, and either of them, their and either of their heires and assignes, by theis presentes, that he, the said John Hemynge, his heires, executours, administratours or assignes, shall and will from tyme to tyme and at all tymes hereafter, within convenient tyme after every reasonable request, well and sufficiently save and keepe harmeles the said bargained premisses, and every part and parcell thereof, of and from all and all manner of former bargaines, sales, guiftes, grauntes, leases, statutes, recognizaunces, joynctures, dowers, intayles, uses, extentes, judgementes, execucions, annewyties, and of and from all other charges, titles and incombraunces whatsoever, wittingly and willingly had, made, comitted or done by him, the said John Hemynge alone, or joynctly with any other person or persons whatsoever, except the rentes and services to the cheiffe lord or lordes of the fee or fees of the premisses from henceforth to be due and of right accustomed to be done, and except one lease and demise of the premisses with thappurtenaunces heretofore made by the said William Shakespeare, togeither with them the said John Jackson, John Hemyng and William Johnson, unto one John Robinson, now tennant of the said premisses, for the terme of certen yeres yet to come and unexpired, as by the same whereunto relacion be had at large doth appeare. And the said William Johnson, for himself, his heires, executours, administratours and assignes, and for every of them, doth covenaunt, promise and graunt, to and with the said John Green and Mathew Morrys, and either of them, their and either of their heires and assignes, by theis presentes, that he, the said William Johnson, his heires, executours, adminis- tratours or assignes, shall and will, from tyme to tyme and at all tymes hereafter within convenient tyme after every reasonable request, well and sufficiently save and keepe harmeles the said bargained premisses, and every part and parcell thereof, of and from all and all manner of former bargaines, sales, guiftes, grauntes, leases, statutes, recognizaunces, joynctures, dowers, intayles, uses, extentes, judgementes, execucions, annewyties, and of and from all other charges, titles and incombraunces whatsoever, wittingly and willingly had made comitted or done by him, the said William Johnson alone, or joyntly with any other person or persons whatsoever, except the rentes and services to the cheiff lord or lordes of the fee or fees of the premisses from henceforth to be due and of right accustomed to be done, and except one lease and demise of the premisses with thappurtenaunces heretofore made by the said William Shakespeare, togeither with them, the said John Jackson, John Hemynges, and William Johnson, unto one John Robynson, now tennant of the said premisses, for the terme of certen yeres yet to come and unexpired, as by the same whereunto relation be had at large doth appeare. In witnes whereof the parties aforesaid to theis presente indentures have interchaungeably sett their handes and sealls. Yeoven the day and yeres first above written, 1617.—*Jo: Jackson.*—*John Heminges.*—*Wm. Johnson.* Sealed and delyvered by the within named John Jackson in the presence of Ric. Swale ; John Prise. Sealed and delyvered by the withinamed William Johnson in the presence of Nickolas Harysone ; John Prise. Sealed and delyvered by the withinamed John Hemynges in the presence of Matt : Benson ; John Prise. Memorand. that the xj.^{th} daye of Februarye in the yeres within written, John Robynson, tenant of the premysses withinmencioned, did geve and delyver unto John Greene withinnamed, to the use of Susanna Hall within-named, sixe pence of lawefull money of England, in name of attornement, in the presence of Matt : Benson ; John Prise. *Per me Rychardum Tyler.*

THE DAVENANT SCANDAL.

In illustration of what has been advanced in the text respecting the mythical character of this disreputable anecdote, it is desirable to give in chronological order the versions of it which have obtained currency during the last two centuries. They evince for the most part the fashionable aversion either to diminish the probability, or arrest the progressive development, of a nice bit of scandal. Added to these are a few pieces which will be found useful in the general argument. The following extracts are taken from—

1.—Wit and mirth chargeably collected out of Tavernes, &c., 1629 ; here given from the reprint in All the Workes of John Taylor, the Water-Poet, 1630.—A boy, whose mother was noted to be one not overloden with honesty, went to seeke his godfather, and enquiring for him, quoth one to him, Who is thy godfather? The boy repli'd, his name is goodman Digland the gardiner. Oh, said the man, if he be thy godfather he is at the next alehouse, but I feare thou takest Gods name in vaine.

2. Aubrey's Lives of Eminent Persons, a manuscript in the Bodleian Library completed in the year 1680. Towards the close of the last century an attempt was made by some one to erase the passages which are here given in Italics, but, with the exception of one word, they can still be distinctly read when placed under a magnifying-glass. That word is here printed trader, *but the true reading may be a coarse synonym, either term signifying a woman of very loose character. It should also be noticed that, in line 16, the word* seemed *is written over* was, *neither being marked for omission.*— Sir William Davenant, knight, poet-laureate, was borne about the end of February in . . . Street in the city of Oxford, at the Crowne taverne; baptized 3. of March, A. D. 1605–6. His father was John Davenant, a vintner there, a very grave and discreet citizen; his mother was a very beautifull woman, and of a very good witt, and of conversation extremely agreable. They had three sons, viz., Robert, William, and Nicholas, an attorney.—Robert was a fellow of St. John's Coll. in Oxon, then preferd to the vicarage of West Kington by Bp. Davenant, whose chaplaine he was,—and two handsome daughters, one m. to Gabriel Bridges, B. D. of C. C. C., beneficed in the Vale of White Horse; another to Dr. Sherburne, minister of Pembridge in Heref. and a canon of that church. Mr. William Shakespeare was wont to goe into Warwickshire once a yeare, and did commonly in his journey lye at this house in Oxon., where he was exceedingly respected. *I have heard Parson Robert say that Mr. W. Shakespeare has given him a hundred kisses.* Now Sir Wm. would sometimes, when he was pleasant over a glasse of wine with his most intimate friends, e. g., Sam : Butler, author of Hudibras, etc., say that it seemed to him that he writt with the very spirit that Shakespeare⑤, and was contented enough to be thought his son; he would tell them the story as above. *Now, by the way, his mother had a very light report. In those days she was called a trader.* He went to schoole at Oxon. to Mr. Charles Silvester, wheare F. Degorii W. was his schoole-fellowe; but I feare he was drawne from schoole before he was ripe enough. He was preferred to the first Dutches of Richmond to wayte on her as a page. I remember he told me she sent him to a famous apothecary for some unicornes horne, which he was resolved to try with a spider, which he empaled in it, but without the expected successe; the spider would goe over, and thorough and thorough, unconcerned.

3. *Gildon's edition of Langbaine's work on the Dramatic Poets, 1699.*—Sir William D'avenant, the son of John D'avenant, vintner of Oxford, in that very house that has now the sign of the Crown near Carfax ; a house much frequented by Shakespear in his frequent journeys to Warwickshire ; whither for the beautiful mistress of the house, or the good wine, I shall not determine.

4. *Hearne's manuscript pocket-book for 1709, preserved in the Bodleian Library.*— 'Twas reported by tradition in Oxford that Shakespear, as he us'd to pass from London to Stratford-upon-Avon, where he liv'd and now lies buried, always spent some time in the Crown tavern in Oxford, which was kept by one Davenant, who had a handsome wife, and lov'd witty company, tho' himself a reserv'd and melancholly man. He had born to him a son, who was afterwards christen'd by the name of William, who prov'd a very eminent poet and was knighted by the name of Sir William Davenant, and the said Mr. Shakespear was his god-father and gave him his name. In all probability he got him. 'Tis further said that one day, going from school, a grave doctor in divinity met him, and ask'd him,—Child, whither art thou going in such hast ? To which the child reply'd,—O, sir, my god-father is come to town, and I am going to ask his blessing. To which the Dr. said,—Hold, child ! You must not take the name of God in vaine.

5. *Jacob's Poetical Register, 1719, i. 58, reprinted in 1723.*—Sir William D'Avenant was son to Mr. John D'Avenant, a vintner of Oxford. He was born in the year 1605, and his father's house being frequented by the famous Shakespear, in his journeys to Warwickshire, his poetical genius in his youth was by that means very much encourag'd ; and some will have it that the handsome landlady, as well as the good wine, invited the tragedian to those quarters.

6. *Conversations of Pope in the year 1730, thus recorded by Spence.*—That notion of Sir William Davenant being more than a poetical child only of Shakespeare was common in town, and Sir William himself seemed fond of having it taken for truth.

7. *Spence's Anecdotes, the following being one said to have been related by Pope in the year 1744.*—Shakespeare, in his frequent journeys between London and his native place, Stratford-upon-Avon, used to lie at Davenant's, at the Crown in Oxford. He was very well acquainted with Mrs. Davenant ; and her son, afterwards Sir William, was supposed to be more nearly related to him than as a godson only.—One day, when Shakespeare was just arrived and the boy sent for from school to him, a head of one of the colleges, who was pretty well acquainted with the affairs of the family, met the child running home, and asked him whither he was going in so much haste ? The boy said, " to my god-father Shakespeare "—" Fie, child," says the old gentleman, " why are you so superfluous ? have you not learnt yet that you should not use the name of God in vain."

8. *Chetwood's General History of the Stage, from its origin in Greece down to the present Time, 8vo. Lond. 1749.*—Sir William Davenant was, by many, supposed the natural son of Shakespear. He succeeded Ben. Johnson as poet-laureat in 1637, and obtained a patent for a company of comedians from King Charles, and was knighted by that monarch. His works are printed in folio, 1673, which contains seventeen dramatic pieces besides his poems, with his head crowned with laurel. The features seem to resemble the open countenance of Shakespear, but the want of a nose gives an odd cast to the face.

9. *The Manuscript Collections of Oldys, written probably about the year 1750, and first printed by Steevens in 1778.*—If tradition may be trusted, Shakspeare often baited at the Crown Inn or Tavern in Oxford in his journey to and from London. The landlady was a woman of great beauty and sprightly wit, and her husband, Mr. John Davenant, afterwards mayor of that city ; a grave melancholy man ; who, as well as his wife, used much to delight in Shakspeare's pleasant company. Their son, young Will Davenant, afterwards Sir William, was then a little school-boy in the town

of about seven or eight years old, and so fond also of Shakspeare that, whenever he heard of his arrival, he would fly from school to see him. One day an old townsman, observing the boy running homeward almost out of breath, asked him whither he was posting in that heat and hurry. He answered, to see his god-father Shakspeare. There's a good boy, said the other, but have a care that you don't take God's name in vain. This story Mr. Pope told me at the Earl of Oxford's table upon occasion of some discourse which arose about Shakspeare's monument then newly erected in Westminster Abbey ; and he quoted Mr. Betterton the player for his authority. I answered that I thought such a story might have enriched the variety of those choice fruits of observation he has presented us in his preface to the edition he had published of our poet's works. He replied, There might be in the garden of mankind such plants as would seem to pride themselves more in a regular production of their own native fruits, than in having the repute of bearing a richer kind by grafting ; and this was the reason he omitted it.

10. The British Theatre, containing the Lives of the English Dramatic Poets, 8vo. Dublin, 1750.—Sir William Davenant was the son of a vintner in Oxford, where he was born in the year 1605, and admitted a member of Lincoln College in the year 1621. He is said to have been much encouraged in his poetic genius by the immortal Shakespear, and, in some accounts of that author's life, he is supposed to be his natural son.

11. Manuscript Notes written by Oldys on the margins of his copy of Langbaine, 1691, preserved in the library of the British Museum.—The story of Davnant's godfather Shakespeare, as Mr. Pope told it me, is printed among the jests of John Taylor, the water-poet, in his Works, folio, 1630, but without their names, and with a seeming fictitious one of the boy's godfather, vizt., Goodman Digland the gardener, I suppose of Oxford, for Taylor tells other jests that he pick'd up at Oxford in the same collection.

12. The Lives of the Poets, 1753, vol. ii. pp. 63–64.—All the biographers of our poet (Sir William Davenant) have observed that his father was a man of a grave disposition and a gloomy turn of mind, which his son did not inherit from him, for he was as remarkably volatile as his father was saturnine. The same biographers have celebrated our author's mother as very handsome, whose charms had the power of attracting the admiration of Shakespear, the highest compliment which ever was paid to beauty. As Mr. Davenant, our poet's father, kept a tavern, Shakespear, in his journies to Warwickshire, spent some time there, influenced, as many believe, by the engaging qualities of the handsome landlady. This circumstance has given rise to a conjecture that Davenant was really the son of Shakespear, as well naturally as poetically, by an unlawful intrigue between his mother and that great man.

13. A Description of England and Wales, 1769, vol. vii. p. 238.—William D'Avenant, poet laureat in the reigns of Charles the First and Charles the Second, was born in Oxford in the year 1605. His father, Mr. John D'Avenant, a vintner of that place, was a man, it is said, of a very peaceable disposition, and his mother a woman of great spirit and beauty ; and as their house was much frequented by the celebrated Shakespeare, this gave occasion to a report that the tragedian stood in a nearer relation than that of a friend to our author.

14. Notes by Warton in Malone's supplement to Shakespeare, 1780, i. 69, in which there is a gratuitous insinuation of the possibility of an extension of the scandal.—Antony Wood is the first and original author of the anecdote that Shakspeare, in his journies from Warwickshire to London, used to bait at the Crown-inn on the west side of the corn-market in Oxford. I will not suppose that Shakspeare could have been the father of a Doctor of Divinity who never laughed : but it was always a constant tradition in Oxford that Shakspeare was the father of Davenant the poet, and I have seen this circumstance expressly mentioned in some of Wood's papers. Wood was well qualified to know these particulars : for he was a townsman of Oxford, where he was born in 1632.

15. Letter to Malone from J. Taylor, of the Sun Office, written in August, 1810. — On re-perusing your history of the English stage and your anecdotes of Shakespeare and Davenant, I see no allusion to a story which I copied in early life from a manuscript book, and which, many years afterwards, when I became connected with the public press, I inserted in a newspaper. It is very probable that you have heard the story, though perhaps you did not think it was established on a sufficient tradition for notice in your work. I assure you upon my honour I found it there, and, if this could be doubted, I am ready to make oath of the accuracy of my statement. The manuscript-book was written by Mr. White, a very respectable gentleman who was a reading-clerk to the House of Lords. He died about the year 1772, and his property chiefly descended to a Miss Dunwell, his niece. He lived upon Wandsworth Common in a very good house. That house and other property was bequeathed by Miss Dunwell to a Mrs. Bodman, a very old acquaintance of my family, and who knew me from my birth. All Mr. White's books and manuscripts came into Mrs. Bodman's possession, and most of them, I believe, were sold by auction. The book to which I allude consisted chiefly of observations and anecdotes written by Mr. White himself, and were gleanings of conversations at which he was present. He was well acquainted with Mr. Pope, and often dined in company with him, and many of the observations and anecdotes had Mr. Pope's name at the bottom of them, indicating the source whence Mr. White derived them. What became of the book I know not. After all this preface, you will perhaps exclaim, *parturiunt montes, &c.*, but, as it relates to Shakespeare, it must be interesting. The story was to the following purport. It was generally supposed or whispered in Oxford that Shakespeare, who was the godfather of Sir William Davenant, was in reality the father. The story mentioned that Shakespeare used to come to London every two years, and always stayed a night or two, going and coming, at the Crown. On such occasions the boy was always sent for from school to pay his respects to Shakespeare. On one of these occasions, as the child was running along the street, he was met by one of the heads of the colleges, who asked where he was going. The child said,—to see my godfather Shakespeare. What ! said the gentleman, have they not taught you yet not to use the Lord's name in vain ?

16. Will of John Davenant, of Oxford, vintner, proved on October 21st, 1622. From the recorded copy in the Registry of the Prerogative Court of Canterbury. — It hathe pleased God to afflict me these four monethes rather with a paine then a sickenes which I acknowledge a gentle correction for my former sinnes in having soe faire a time to repent, my paines rather daily encreasing then otherwise. And for soe much as many wise men are suddenly overtaken by death, by procrastinateing of their matters concerning the settling of their estates, I thincke it fitt, though mine be of noe great value, considering the many children I have, and the mother dead which would guide them, as well for the quietnes of my owne mind when I shall depart this life as to settle a future amity and love among them, that there may be noe strife in the division of those blessinges which God hath lent me, to set downe my mind in the nature of my laste will and testament, both for the disposeing of the same, as also how I would have them order themselves after my decease till it shall please God to order and direct them to other courses. First, I committ my soule to Almighty God, hopeinge by my Redeemer Christ Jesus to have remission of my sinnes ; my body I committ to the earth to be buryed in the parish of St. Martins in Oxford as nere my wife as the place will give leave where shee lyeth. For my funeralls and obsequies, if I dye in the yeare of my marolty⁽ˢ⁾, I desire should be in comely manner, neither affecting pompe nor to much sparing, leaving the same to my executors discretion, whom I name to be as followeth, hartily desiring these five following whom I name to be my overseers to take paines not only in that but alsoe in any other matter of advice to my children concerning the settling of their estates, which five are these, Alderman Harris, Alderman Wright, Mr. John Bird, Mr. William Gryce, Mr. Thomas Davis. Item, I will that my debts be paid by my executors which I owe either by bond, bill or booke, which I have made within the compasse of this two yeares. Item, I give and bequeath to my three daughters, Elizabeth, Jane, and Alice, two hundred pound a-peece to be payd out of my estate within one yeare after my buriall. Item, I give to my four sonnes one hundred fiftie pound a-peece to be payd' them within a yeare after my buriall. Item, I give to my sonne Nicholas my house at the White Beare in Dettford, which is lett to Mr. Haines, schoolemaster of Marchant Tailers Schoole. Item, I give to my sonne Robert my seale-ring. Item, my will is that my houshold stuffe and plate be sold to the best value within the compasse of a yeare, excepting such necessaryes as my executors and overseers shall thinck fitt for the furnishing of my house, to goe towardes the payment of my childrens portions. Item, my will is that my house shall be kept still as a taverne, and supplied with wines continually, for the bringing up and entertainment of my children, untill such time as Thomas Hallom, my servant, comes out of his yeares, and the yearly profitt thereof, necessary expenses of rent, reparacion and housekeeping being deducted, to retorne at the time of his comeing forth of his yeares to my seaven children in equall portions, together with the stocke in the seller and debtes, or to the survivors, if any happen to dye in the meane tyme. And that this may be the better effected according to my will and intent, I will that my servant Thomas have the managing thereof duringe his apprentishipp, and that he shall give a true account of his dealing unto my executors and overseers four times in the yeare ; alsoe that George be kept here still in the house till his yeares come forth, at which time my will is that he be made free of the Marchant Tailers in London, and have five pound given him when he comes out of his yeares. And to the intent that this my devise of keeping my house as a taverne for the better releefe of my children may take the better effect, according to my meaning, in consideracion that my three daughters, being maidens, can hardly rule a thing of such consequence, my will is that my sister Hatton, if it stand with her good liking, may come with her youngest sonne, and lye and table at my house with my children till Thomas Hallom comes out of his yeares, for the better comfort and countenancing of my three daughters, and to have her said dyett free, and five pound a yeare in money, knowing her to have bin alwaies to me and my wife loving, just and kind. Alsoe my will is that twoe of my youngest daughters doe keepe the barre by turnes, and sett doune every night under her hand the dayes taking in the veiwe of Thomas Hallom, my servant, and that this booke be orderly kept for soe long time as they shall thus sustaine the house as a taverne, that, if need be, for avoiding of deceite and distrust there may be a calculation made of the receites and disbursementes. Now if any of my daughters marry with the consent of my overseers, that her porcion be presently paid her, and shee that remaineth longest in the house either to have her porcion when Thomas Hollome comes out of his yeares, or if he and shee can fancy one another, my will is that they marry together, and her porcion to be divided by itselfe towardes the maintenance of the trade ; and the one halfe of my two youngest sonnes stockes shal be in his the said Thomas his handes, payeinge or allowing after twenty nobles per hundred, giving my said two sonnes or my overseers security sufficient for the same to be paid at their cominge to twenty-one yeares of age, the other halfe to be putt forth for their best profitt by the advise of my overseers ; my will is also that my sonne William, being now arrived to sixteen yeares of age, shall be put to prentice to some good marchant of London or other tradesman by the consent and advise of my overseers, and that there be forty pound given with him to his master, whereof 20*li.* to be payd out of his owne stocke, and 20*li.* out of my goodes, and double apparrell, and that this be done within the compasse of three moneths after my death, for avoyding of inconvenience in my house for mastershippe when I am gone. My will is alsoe concerning the remainder of the yeares in my lease of my house, the taverne, that if Thomas and any of my daughters doe marry together, that he and she shall enjoy the remainder of the yeares, be it five or six more or lesse, after he comes out of his yeares, paying to my sonn Robert over and above the rent to Mr. Huffe yearely soe much as they two shall agree uppon, my overseers beinge umpires betwixt them, whereof the cheefest in this office I wish to be my frende Mr. Grice ; provided alwaies my meaning is that neither the gallery nor chambers, or that floore nor cockelofts over, nor kitchin, nor lorther nor little sellar, be any part of the thing demised, but those to remaine to the use of my sonne Robert, if he should leave the universitie, to entertaine his sisters if they should marry, &c., yet both to have passage into the wood-yard, garden and house of office. My will is alsoe that my sonne Robert shall not make nor meddle with selling or trusting of wyne, nor with any thing in the house, but have entertanement as a brother for meale tydes and the like, or to take phisicke in sicknes, or if he should call for wine and the like with his friendes and acquaintance, that he presently pay for it or be sett downe uppon his name to answeare the same out of his part, my meaning being that the government shall consist in my three daughters and in my servant Thomas, whom I have alwaies found faithfull unto me ; and to reward his vertue the better and to putt him into more encouragement, I give him twenty pound to be payd him when he comes out of his yeares. Alsoe, my will is that my sonne Robert for his better allowance in the university have quarterly paid him fifty shillinges and twenty shillinges to buy him necessaryes out of the provenew of the profitt of wyne, till Thomas comes out of his yeares, besides the allowance of the interest of his stocke ; and in the meane time, yf I dy before he goes out Bacheler, his reasonable apparell and expences of that degree to be payd out of my goodes, provided alwaies if it be done with the advice of Mr. Turr. My will is that Nicholas be kept at schoole at Bourton till he be fifteen yeares old, and his board and apparell be payd for out of the profitt of selling of the wyne ; and for John my will is he be kept halfe an yeare at schoole if my overseers thinke good, and his brothers and sisters, and after put to prentice and have thirty pound given with him x.*li.* out of his owne stocke and twenty pound out of the profitt of selling of wyne. Alsoe my will is that within twenty-four houres after my funerall, the wynes of all sortes and condicions be filled up, and reckon how many tunnes of Gascoyne wine there is, which I would have rated at twenty-five pound per tunne, and how many butts and pipes of sweet wynes there are, which I would have rated at twentie pound per ceece, both which drawne into a summe are to be sett downe in a booke. Alsoe the next day after, a schedule of the debtes which are oweing me in the debt-booke, the sperate by themselves and the desperate by themselves them alsoe sett downe, the ordinary plate to drincke in the taverne to be wayed and valued, the bondes and billes in my study to be lookt over and sett downe, in all which use the opinion of Mr. Gryce ; accompt with any marchant that I deale withall betimes, and aske my debtes with as much speede as may be. Lastly, take an inventory of all the utensells in my house, and let them be praysed ; in that use the advise of my overseers ; and what money shal be in caishe more then shal be needfull for the present to pay my debtes or buy wyne with, let it be putt foorth to the best advantage.

    17. A poem "on Mr. Davenantt, who died att Oxford in his Maioralty a fortnight after his wife." From a very curious manuscript volume of miscellanies, of the time of Charles the First, preserved in the library of the Earl of Warwick, the text being verbally corrected in a few places by the aid of a transcript made by Haslewood from another manuscript.—Well, sceince th'art deade, if thou canst mortalls heare, = Take this just tribute of a funerall teare ; = Each day I see a corse, and now no knell = Is more familiare then a passing-bell ; = All die, no fix'd inheritance men have, = Save that they are freeholders to the grave. = Only I truly greive, when vertues brood =

Becomes wormes meate, and is the cankers foode. = Alas, that unrelenting death should bee = At odds with goodnesse ! Fairest budds we see = Are soonest cropp't ; who know the fewest crimes, = Tis theire prerogative to die bee-times, = Enlargd from this worlds misery ; and thus hee, = Whom wee now waile, made hast to bee made free. = There needes no loud hyperbole to sett him foorth, = Nor sawcy elegy to bellowe his worth ; = His life was an encomium large enough ; = True gold doth neede no foyles to sett itt off. = Hee had choyce giftes of nature and of arte ; = Neither was Fortune wanting on her parte = To him in honours, wealth or progeny : = Hee was on all sides blest. Why should hee dye ? = And yett why should he live, his mate being gone, = And turtle-like sigh out an endlese moone ? = No, no, hee loved her better, and would not = So easely lose what hee so hardly gott. = Hee liv'd to pay the last rites to his bride ; = That done, hee pin'd out fourteene dayes and died. = Thrice happy paire ! Oh, could my simple verse = Reare you a lasting trophee ore your hearse, = You should vie yeares with Time ; had you your due, = Eternety were as short-liv'd as you. = Farewell, and, in one grave, now you are deade, = Sleepe ondisturb'ed as in your marriage-bed.

18. Another Poem " on the Same," preserved in the Manuscript which contains the verses printed in the last article.—If to bee greate or good deserve the baies, = What merits hee whom greate and good doth praise ? = What meritts hee ? Why, a contented life, = A happy yssue of a vertuous wife, = The choyce of freinds, a quiet honour'd grave, = All these hee had ; What more could Dav'nant have ? = Reader, go home, and with a weeping eie, = For thy sinns past, learne thus to live and die.

19. An Account of the English Dramatick Poets, by Gerard Langbaine. 8vo. Oxford, 1691.—Sir William Davenant, a person sufficiently known to all lovers of poetry, and one whose works will preserve his memory to posterity. He was born in the city of Oxford, in the parish of St. Martins, vulgarly call'd Carfax, near the end of February in the year 1605, and was christned on the third of March following. He was the mercurial son of a saturnine father, Mr. John D'Avenant, a vintner by profession, who liv'd in the same house which is now known by the sign of the Crown.

20. Wood's Athenæ Oxonienses, an Exact History of all the Writers and Bishops who have had their Education in the most ancient and famous University of Oxford. Fol. Lond. 1692, ii. 292.—William D'Avenant made his first entry on the stage of this vain world in the parish of S. Martin within the city of Oxford, about the latter end of the month of Febr., and, on the third of March following, anno 1605-6, he received baptism in the church of that parish. His father, John Davenant, was a sufficient vintner, kept the tavern now known by the name of the Crown, wherein our poet was born, and was mayor of the said city in the year 1621. His mother was a very beautiful woman, of a good wit and conversation, in which she was imitated by none of her children but by this William. The father, who was a very grave and discreet citizen,—yet an admirer and lover of plays and play-makers, especially Shakespeare, who frequented his house in his journies between Warwickshire and London,—was of a melancholic disposition, and was seldom or never seen to laugh, in which he was imitated by none of his children but by Robert his eldest son, afterwards Fellow of S. John's College and a venerable Doctor of Divinity. As for William, whom we are farther to mention, and may justly stile the sweet Swan of Isis, was educated in grammar learning under Edw. Sylvester, whom I shall elsewhere mention, and in academical in Lincoln College under the care of Mr. Dan. Hough, in 1620, 21, or thereabouts, and obtained there some smattering in logic ; but his genie, which was always opposite to it, lead him in the pleasant paths of poetry, so that tho' he wanted much of University learning, yet he made as high and noble flights in the poetical faculty, as fancy could advance, without it. After he had left the said college wherein, I presume, he made but a short stay, he became servant to Frances, the first Dutchess of Richmond, and afterwards to Foulk, Lord Brook, who being poetically given, especially in his younger days, was much delighted in him. After his death, anno 1628, he, being free from trouble and attendance, betook himself to writing of plays and poetry, which he did with so much sweetness and grace, that he got the absolute love and friendship of his two patrons, Endimyon Porter and Hen. Jermyn afterwards Earl of S. Alban's; to both which he dedicated his poem, which he afterwards published, called Madagascar. Sir John Suckling also was his great and intimate friend.

———————————

THE STRATFORD REGISTER.

The earliest register preserved in the Church of the Holy Trinity, the only one in which there are entries respecting the great dramatist, is a narrow and thick folio consisting of leaves of vellum held in a substantial ancient binding, the latter being protected by metal at the outer corners. This inestimable volume bears on its original leather side the date of 1600, in which year all the entries from 1558 were transcribed into it from then existing records, the contents of each page being uniformly authenticated by the signatures of the vicar and the church-wardens. After this attested transcript had been made, the records of the later occurrences, taken probably from the sexton's notes, were entered into the book, and their accuracy officially therein certified, at frequent but unsettled intervals, a system that continued in vogue for many years; so that there is not one amongst the following extracts which, in the manuscript, is more than a copy or an abridgment of a note made at the time of the ceremony. In these extracts, which are here given in chronological order, baptisms are denoted by the letter B, marriages by M, and funerals or burials by F, these forming three separate divisions in the register.

1558. B.—September 15. Jone Shakspere, daughter to John Shaxspere.

1562. B.—December 2. Margareta, filia Johannis Shakspere.

1563. F.—April 30. Margareta, filia Johannis Shakspere.

1564. B.—April 26. Gulielmus, filius Johannes⑤ Shakspere.

1566. B.—October 13. Gilbertus, filius Johannis, Shakspere.

1569. B.—April 15. Jone, the daughter of John Shakspere.

1571. B.—September 28. Anna, filia magistri Shakspere.

1573-4. B.—March 11. Richard, sonne to Mr. John Shakspeer.

1579. F.—April 4. Anne, daughter to Mr. John Shakspere.

1580. B.—May 3. Edmund, sonne to Mr. John Shakspere.

1583. B.—May 26. Susanna, daughter to William Shakspere.

1584-5. B.—February 2. Hamnet and Judeth, sonne and daughter to William Shakspere.

1588-9. B.—February 26. Thomas, sonne to Richard Queeny.

1589-90. F.—March 6. Thomas Green alias Shakspere.

1593. B.—June 20. Thomas, filius Anthonii Nash gen.

D 2

1596. F.—August 11.   Hamnet, filius William Shakspere.

1600. B.—August 28.   Wilhelmus, filius Wilhelmi Hart.

1601. F.—Septemb. 8.   Mr. Johannes Shakspeare.

1603. B.—June 5.   Maria, filia Willielmi Hart.

1605. B.—Julii 24.   Thomas, fil. Willielmi Hart, hatter.

1607. M.—Junij 5.   John Hall, gentleman, and Susanna Shaxspere.

1607. F.—Decemb. 17.   Mary, dawghter to Willyam Hart.

1607-8. B.—Februar. 21.   Elizabeth, dawghter to John Hall, gen.

1608. F.—Sept. 9.   Mayry Shaxspere, wydowe.

1608. B.—Sept. 23.   Mychaell, sonne to Willyam Hart.

1611-2. F.—February 3.   Gilbertus Shakspeare, adolescens.

1612-3. F.—February 4.   Rich. Shakspeare.

1615-6. M.—Feabruary 10.   Tho. Queeny tow Judith Shakspere.

1616. F.—Aprill 17.   Will. Hartt, hatter.

1616. F.—Aprill 25.   Will. Shakspere, gent.

1616. B.—November 23.   Shaksper, fillius Thomas Quyny, gent

1617. F.—May 8.   Shakspere, fillius Tho. Quyny, gent.

1617-8. B.—February 9.   Richard, fillius Thomas Quinee.

1618. F.—November 1.   Micael, fil. to Jone Harte, widowe.

1619-20. B.—Januarie 23.   Thomas, fili. to Thomas Queeny.

1623. F.—August 8.   Mrs. Shakspeare.

1626. M.—April 22.   Mr. Thomas Nash to Mrs. Elizabeth Hall.

1635. F.—November 26.   Johannes Hall, medicus peritissimus.

1638-9. F.—January 28.   Thomas, filius Thomæ Quiney.

1638-9. F.—February 26.   Richardus, filius Tho. Quiney.

1639. F.—March 29.   Willielmus Hart.

DOMESTIC RECORDS.

I. The Will of Robert Arden, Shakespeare's maternal grandfather, November, 1556. From the original in the Registry Court of Worcester.

In the name of God, Amen, the xxiiij.th daye of November, in the yeare of our Lorde God, 1556, in the thirde and the forthe yeare of the raygne of our soveragne lorde and ladye, Phylipe and Marye, kyng and quene, &c., I, Robart Arden, of Wyllmecote in the parryche of Aston Caunntlowe, secke in bodye and good and perfett of rememberence, make this my laste will and testement in maner and forme folowyng.—Fyryste, I bequethe my solle to Allmyghtye God and to our bleside Laydye, Sent Marye, and to all the holye compenye of heven, and my bodye to be beryde in the churchyarde of Seynt Jhon the Babtyste in Aston aforsayde. Allso I give and bequethe to my youngste dowghter Marye all my lande in Willmecote, cawlide Asbyes, and the crop apone the grounde sowne and tyllide as hitt is ; and vj.*li.* xiij.*s.* iiij.*d.* of monye to be payde orr ere my goodes be devydide. Allso I gyve and bequethe to my dowghter Ales the thyrde parte of all mye goodes, moveable and unmoveable, in fylde and towne, after my dettes and leggeses be performyde, besydes that goode she hathe of her owne att this tyme. Allso I gyve and bequethe to Annes my wife vj.*li.* xiij.*s.* iiij.*d.* apone this condysione, that shall℗ sofer my dowghter Ales quyetlye to ynyoye halfe my copye-houlde in Wyllmecote dwryng the tyme of her wyddowewhodde ; and if she will nott soffer my dowghter Ales quyetlye to ocupye halfe with her, then I will that my wyfe shall have butt iij.*li.* vj.*s.* viij.*d.* and her gintur in Snyterfylde. Item, I will that the resedowe of all my goodes, moveable and unmoveable, my funeralles and my dettes dyschargyde, I gyve and bequethe to my other cheldren to be equaleye devidide amongeste them by the descreshyon of Adam Palmer, Hugh Porter of Snytterfylde, and Jhon Skerlett, whome I do ordene and make my overseres of this my last will and testament, and they to have for ther peynes-takyng in this behalfe xx.*s.* apese. Allso I ordene and constytute and make my full exceqtores Ales and Marye, my dowghteres, of this my last will and testament, and they to have no more for ther peynes-takyng now as afore geven them. Allso I gyve and bequethe to every house that hathe no teme in the parryche of Aston, to every howse iiij.*d.*—Thes beyng wyttnesses,—Sir Wylliam Borton, curett ; Adam Palmer ; Jhon Skerlett ; Thomas Jhenkes ; Wylliam Pytt ; with other mo.—Probatum fuit, &c., Wigorn., &c., xvj.º die mensis Decembris, anno Domini 1556.

II. The Ynventory of all the goodes, moveable and unmoveable, of Robart Ardennes of Wyllmecote, late desseside, made the ix.th day of December, in the thyrde and the forthe yeare of the raygne of our soveraygne lorde and ladye, Phylipe and Marye, kyng and quen, &c. 1556.

Imprimis, in the halle, ij. table-bordes, iij. choyeres, ij. formes, one cobbowrde, ij. coshenes, iij. benches and one lytle table with shellves, prisede att viij.*s.*—Item, ij. peyntide-clothes in the hall and v. peyntid-clothes in the chamber, vij. peare of shettes, ii. cofferes, one which, priside at xviiij.*s.*—Item, v. borde-clothes, ij. toweles and one dyeper towelle, prisid att vj.*s.* viij.*d.*—Item, one fether-bedde, ij. mattereses, viij. canvases, one coverlett, iij. bosteres, one pelowe, iiij. peyntide-clothes, one whyche, prisid att xxvj.*s.* viij.*d.*—Item, in the kechen iiij. panes, iiij. pottes, iij. candell-stykes, one bason, one chafyng-dyche, ij. cathernes, ij. skellettes, one frying-pane, a gredyerene, and pott-hanginges with hookes, prisid att lj.*s.* viij.*d.*—Item, one broche, a peare of cobbardes, one axe, a bill, iiij. nagares, ij. hachettes, an ades, a mattoke, a yren crowe, one fatt, iiij. barrelles, iiij. payles, a quyrne, a knedyng-trogh, a lonng sawe, a hansaw, prisid at xx.*s.* ij.*d.*—Item, viij. oxen, ij. bollokes, vij. kyne, iiij. wayning caves, xxiiij.*li.*—Item, iiij. horses, ij. coltes, prisid att viij.*li.*—Item, l.ti shepe, prisid att vij.*li.*—Item, the whate in the barne and the barley, prisid at xviiij.*li.* —Item, the heye and the pease, ottes and the strawe, prised att iij.*li.* vj.*s.* viij.*d.*— Item, ix. swyne, prisid att xxvj.*s.* viij.*d.*—Item, the bees and powltrye, prised att v.*s.* —Item, carte and carte-geares, and plogh and plogh-geares with harrowes, prised att xl.*s.*—Item, the wodd in the yarde, and the baken in the roffe, prisid att xxx.*s.*—Item, the wheate in the fylde, prisid att vj.*li.* xiij.*s.* iiij.*d.*—Summa totalis, lxxvij.*li.* xj.*s.* x.*d.*

III. *The Will of Agnes Arden, step-mother to John Shakespeare's wife, and thus intimately connected with the poet's ancestry, 1579. From the original in the Registry Court of Worcester.*

In the name of God . . . . . yeare of our Lorde God 1579, and in the . . . . yeare of the raigne off our Soveraigne . . Queene Elyzabethe, by the grace off . . . Fraunce and Irlande, Queene, deffendris of the faythe, &c., I, Agnes Ardenne, of Wylmcote in the perishe of Aston Cantlowe, wydowe, do make my laste wyll and testamente in manner and forme followinge. First, I bequethe my soule to Almighty God, my maker and redeemer, and my bodie to the earthe. Item, I geve and bequethe to the poore people and inhabitaunce of Bearley iiij.*s.* Item, I geve and bequeth to the poore people inhabited in Aston perishe x.*s.*, to be equallie devided by the discrecion of my overseers. Item, I geve and bequeth to everi one of my god-children xij.*d.* a-peece. Item, I give and bequeth to Averie Fullwod ij. sheepe, yf they doe lyve after my desease. Item, I give and bequeth to Rychard Petyvere j. sheepe, and to Nycolas Mase j. sheepe, and Elizabeth Gretwhiche and Elyzabethe Bentley eyther of them one shepe. Item, I geve and bequeeth to everie off Jhon Hills children everi one of them one sheep, and allso to John Fullwodes children everi one of them one shepe. My wyll is that they said sheepe soe geven them shall goe forward in a stocke to they use of they sayd children untyll the come to the age of discrecion. Item, I geve and bequethe to John Payge and his wyfe, the longer liver off them, vj.*s* viij.*d.*, and to John Page his brother j. strike of wheat and one strike of maulte. I geve to John Fullwod and Edwarde Hill my godchilde, everi one of them, one shipe more. Allso I geve to Robarte Haskettes iij.*s.* iiij.*d.* Also, I geve to John Peter ij.*s.*, and allso to Henrie Berrie xij.*d.* Item, I give to Jhohan Lamberde xij.*d.*, and to Elizabethe Stiche my olde gowne. Item, and⑨ bequeth to John Hill, my sonne, my parte and moitie of my croppe in the fieldes, as well wheate, barley and pease, painge for the same half the lordes rente and dueties belonginge to the same, so that my wyll is the sayd John Hill shall have the nexte croppe uppon the grounde after my desease. I geve to the said Jhon Hill my best platter of the best sorte, and my best platter of the second sorte, and j. poringer, one sawcer, and one best candlesticke. And also I geve to the said John two paire of sheetes. I give to the said Jhon Hill my second potte, my best panne. Item, I geve and bequeth to Jhon Fullwod, my sonne-in-lawe, all the rest of my housholde stuffe. Item, I give and bequeth to John Hill, my sonne, one cowe with the white rumpe. And also I geve to John Fullwod j. browne steare of the age of two yeares olde. Item, I give and bequeth to my brother Alexander Webbes children, everi one of them, xij.*d.* a-peece. The rest of all my goodes, moveables and unmoveables, not bequevid, my bodie brought home, my debtes and legacies paid, I geve and bequeth to John Fullwod and to John Hill, to the use and behalf of the said John Fullwodes and

John Hilles children, to be delivered unto them and everie of them when the come to age of discrecion. Yf any of the said children doe die before they recover their partes so geven by me, their partes deseased shall remain to the other so levinge with the said John Fullwod and John Hill, I℈ do ordaine and make my full executors of this, my last, wyll. Allso I ordeyne and make my overseers, Addam Palmer, George Gibbes. These beinge witnesses,—Thomas Edkins, Richarde Petifere, with others.

Probatum fuit hoc presens testamentum coram magistro Richardo Cosin, legum doctore, reverendi in Christo patris et domini Johannis permissione divina Wigorn. episcopi etcetera ; apud Warwicum ultimo die mensis Martii, 1581. Exhibuit inventarium ad summam xlv. *li.*

IV. The inventorie of all the goodes, moveable and unmoveable, of Annes Ardenne of Wylmcote deseased, praised by Thomas Boothe, Addam Palmer, George Gibbes, Thomas Edkins thelder, Thomas Edkins the younger, the xix.th day of Januarye, anno regni Elizabethæ reginæ xxiij.—1581.

Inprimis, in the halle, twoe table-bordes with a cobbarde and a painted-clothe, three coshens with shilves, other formes and benches, viij.*s.*—Item, three pottes of brasse, ij. calderons, ij. brasse pannes, ij. peeces of pewter, with iij. candelstickes, with two saltes, xvj.*s.*—Item, ij. broches, j. payre of cobbardes, j. fireshovell, with pott-hokes and linkes for the same, xvj.*d.*—Item, in the chambers her apparrell, l.*s.*— Item, the beddinge and bedstides with apreeware in the said chambers, iij.*li.* iij.*s.* iij.*d.*—Item, three coffers with a peece of woollen clothe, xv.*s.*—Item, the cowperie ware, with a maulte-mylle, one knedinge-troughe with syves, and a stryke, x.*s.*—Item, fowre oxenne, fowre kyne, ij. yearlinge-calves, xij.*li.* xiij.*s.* iij.*d.*—Item, xxxviij.th sheepe, iij.*li.*—Item, three horses and one mare, iiij.*li.*—Item, five score pigges, xiij.*s.* iiij.*d.*—Item, wayne and wayne-geares, plowe and plow-geres, carte and cart-geares, xxx.*s.*—Item, the wheate in the barne her parte, iiij.*li.*—Item, her part of barly in the barne, iij.*li.*—Item, her parte of hey in the barnes, xiiij.*s.*— Item, the wheate one grounde in the fieldes her parte, v.*li.*—Item, her parte of peason, iij.*li.* vj.*s.* viij.*d.* —Somma totalis, xlv.*li.*

V. The Bond against Impediments which was exhibited at Worcester, in November, 1582, in anticipation of the marriage of Shakespeare and Anne Hathaway. From the original preserved in the Bishop's Registry.

Noverint universi per presentes nos, Fulconem Sandells de Stratford in comitatu Warwicensi, agricolam, et Johannem Rychardson, ibidem agricolam, teneri et firmiter obligari Ricardo Cosin, generoso, et Roberto Warmstry, notario publico, in quadraginta libris bone et legalis monete Anglie solvendis eisdem Ricardo et Roberto, heredibus, executoribus vel assignatis suis, ad quam quidem solucionem bene et fideliter faciendam obligamus nos et utrumque nostrum, per se pro toto et in solidum, heredes, executores et administratores nostros, firmiter per presentes sigillis nostris sigillatas. Datum 28 die Novembris, anno regni domine nostre Elizabethe, Dei gratia Anglie, Francie et Hibernie regine, fidei defensoris, etc., 25°.—The condicion of this obligacion ys suche that, if herafter there shall not appere any lawfull lett or impediment, by reason of any precontract, consanguitie, affinitie, or by any other lawfull meanes whatsoever, but that William Shagspere one thone partie, and Anne Hathwey, of Stratford in the dioces of Worcester, maiden, may lawfully solennize matrimony together, and in the same afterwardes remaine and continew like man and wiffe, according unto the lawes in that behalf provided ; and, moreover, if there be not at this present time any action, sute, quarrell or demaund moved or depending before any judge, ecclesiasticall or temporall, for and concerning any suche lawfull lett or impediment ; and, moreover, if the said William Shagspere do not proceed to solemnizacion of mariadg with the said Anne Hathwey without the consent of hir frindes ; and also if the said William do, upon his owne proper costes and expenses, defend and save harmles the right reverend Father in God, Lord John Bushop of Worcester, and his offycers, for licencing them the said William and Anne to be maried together with once asking of the bannes of matrimony betwene them, and for all other causes which may ensue by reason or occasion therof, that then the said obligacion to be voyd and of none effect, or els to stand and abide in full force and vertue.

VI. Draft of a Grant of Coat-Armour proposed to be conferred on Shakespeare's Father in the year 1596. From the original manuscript preserved at the College of Arms, the interlineations being denoted by Italics. The number of the regnal year, which is here erroneous, is correctly given in another draft of the same contemplated grant.

Non sanz droict. Shakespere, 1596.—To all and singuler noble and gentillmen of what estate or degree bearing arms to whom these presentes shall come, William Dethick, alias Garter, principall king of arms, sendethe greetinges ; Knowe yee that whereas, by the authorite and auncyent *pryvelege and* custome *perteyning to* my *said* office *of principall king of arms from* the Quenes most exc. majeste, and her highnes most noble and victorious progenitors, I am to take generall notice and record, and to make publique demonstracion and testemonie, for all causes of arms *and matters of* gentrie thoroughe out all her Majestes kingdoms and domynions, principalites, isles and provinces, to thend that, . . as some by theyre auncyent names, famelies, kyndredes and descentes, have and enjoye sonderie ensoignes and . . . . . of arms, so other for theyre valiant factes, magnanimite, vertue, dignites, and descertes, maye have suche markes and tokens of honor and worthinesse, whereby theyr name and good fame shal be . . . . . and divulged, and th.yre children and posterite *in all vertue to the service of theyre prynce and contrie.* Being *therefore* solicited and . . credible report informed *that* John Shakespeare, of Stratford-uppon-Avon in the counte of Warwick, whose *parentes and late* antecessors were for theyre valeant and faithefull service advaunced and rewarded by the most pruden⑤ prince King Henry the Seventh of famous memorie, sythence whiche tyme they have contiweed⑤ *at those partes* in good reputacion and credit ; *and that the said John having maryed Mary, daughter and one of the heyres of Robert Arden of Wilmcote, in the said counte, gent.* In consideration wherof, and for encouragement of his posterite, *to whom theyse achiwmentes maie desend by the auncient custom and lawes of armes,* I have *therfore* assigned, graunted, *and by these presentes confirmed,* this shield or cote of arms, viz., Gould on a bend sable a speare of the first, *the poynt steeled, proper,* and for his creast or cognizance, a faulcon, *his winges displayed, argent,* standing on a wrethe of his coullors, supporting a speare gould steled *as aforesaid,* sett uppon a healmett with mantelles and tasselles as *hathe ben accustomed and* more playnely appearethe depicted on this margent. Signefieng hereby that it shal be lawfull for the sayd John Shakespeare gent. and for his children, yssue and posterite, *at all tymes convenient, to make shewe of* and to beare the same *blazon atchevement* on *theyre* shield or escucheons, *cote of arms, creast, cognizance or* seales, ringes, signettes, *penons, guydons, edefices, utensiles, lyveries, tombes or monumentes,* or otherwyse, *at all tymes* in all lawfull warrlyke factes or civile use and exercises, *according to the lawes of armes,* without lett or interruption of any *other* person or persons. Yn wittnesse wherof I have hereunto subscribed my name, and fastened the seale of my office endorzed with the signett of my arms, at the Office of Arms, London, the xx.te daye of October, in the xxxix.te yeare of the reigne of our Soveraigne Lady Elizabeth, by the Grace of God Quene of England, France and Ireland, Defender of the Faithe, &c., 1596.

VII. A Letter from Abraham Sturley to his brother-in-law, Richard Quincy, 24 January, 1597-8, in which a reference is made to Shakespeare's contemplated purchase of land at Shottery. The name of the addressee, which is not given in the original, is ascertained from passages in another letter by the same writer. Although it is not biographically requisite to print this and the two other similar letters in full, yet they are so given as interesting examples of the domestic correspondence of the Stratfordians in the time of the poet.

Most loving and belovedd in the Lord, in plaine Englishe we remember u in the Lord, and ourselves unto u. I would write nothinge unto u nowe, but come home. I prai God send u comfortabli home. This is one speciall remembrance from ur fathers motion. Itt semeth bi him that our countriman, Mr. Shaksper, is willinge to disburse some monei upon some od yarde land or other att Shotterie or neare about us ; he thinketh it a veri fitt patterne to move him to deale in the matter of our tithes. Bi the instruccions u can geve him thereof, and bi the frendes he can make therefore, we thinke it a faire marke for him to shoote att, and not unpossible to hitt. It obtained would advance him in deede, and would do us muche good. Hoc movere, et quantum in te est permovere, ne necligas, hoc enim et sibi et nobis maximi erit momenti. Hic labor, hic opus esset eximie et gloriæ et laudis sibi.—U shall understande, brother, that our neighbours are growne with the wantes they feele throughe the dearnes of corne, which heare is beionde all other countries that I can heare of deare and over deare, malecontent. Thei have assembled togeather in a great nomber, and travelld to Sir Tho. Luci on Fridai last to complaine of our malsters ; on Sundai to Sir Foulke Gre. and Sir Joh. Conwai. I should have said on Wensdai to Sir Ed. Grevll first. Theare is a metinge heare expected to-morrowe. The Lord knoweth to what end it will sorte ! Tho. West, returninge from the ij. knightes of the woodland, came home so full that he said to Mr. Baili that night, he hoped within a weeke to leade some of them in a halter, meaninge the malsters ; and I hope, saith Jho. Grannams, if God send mi Lord of Essex downe shortli, to se them hanged on gibbettes att their owne dores.—To this end I write this cheifli, that, as ur occasion shall suffer u to stai theare, theare might bi Sir Ed. Grev. some meanes made to the Knightes of the Parliament for an ease and discharge of such taxes and subsedies wherewith our towne is like to be charged, and I assure u I am in great feare and doubte bi no meanes hable to paie. Sir Ed. Gre. is gonne to Brestowe, and from thence to Lond., as I heare, who verie well knoweth our estates, and wil be willinge to do us ani good.—Our great bell is broken, and Wm. Wiatt is mendinge the pavemente of the bridge.—Mi sister is chearefull, and the Lord hath bin mercifull and comfortable unto hir in hir labours, and, so that u be well imploied, geveth u leave to followe ur occasions for j. weeke or fortnight longer. I would u weare furnisht to pai Wm. Pattrike for me xj. *li.* and bring his quittance, for I thinke his specialtie is in Jho. Knight hand, due on Candlls. daie.—Yestrdai I spake to Mr. Sheldon att Sir. Tho. Lucies for the staie of Mr. Burtons suite, and that the cause might be referred to Mr. Walkrs of Ellyngton ; he answered me that Mr. Bur. was nowe att Lond., and, with all his harte and good will, the suite should be staied, and the matter so referred. I have here inclosed a breife of the reckoninge betwene him and me, as I would have it passe, and as in æqitie it should passe, if hē wil be but as good as his faith and promise. —Good brother, speake to Mr. Goodale that there be no more proceadinge in tharches bi Mr. Clopton, whom I am content and most willinge to compounde withall, and have bin ever since the beginninge of the laste terme, and thearefore much injured bi somebodie, that I have bin put to an unnecessarie charge of xx.*s.* and upwardes that terme ; wheareas I had satisfied Mr. Clopton, as I was credibli made beleve by some of his servantes. I was allso assured of the staie of suite bi Mr. Barnes in the harvest, and bi Mr. Pendleburi the latter end of the terme. Mi brothr Woodwarde commeth up att the latter end of this weeke, who will speake with Mr. Clopton himselfe to that purpose.—U understand bi mi letter I sent bi our countriman Burnell that masse Brentt dispatchd 50*l.* for u. Jh. Sdlr bounde alone as yeat.—Because Mr. Brbr might not have it for 12. moneths, he would none att all, wherebi I lost mi expectation, and leafte⑨, I assure u, in the greatest neede of 30*l.* that possibli maie be. In truth, brother, to u be it spoken and to nonne els, for want thereof knowe skarce wc. wai to turne me. Det Deus misericordiæ dominus exitum secundum bene placitum suum. —Ur fathr with his blessinge and comendation, mi sister with her lovinge remem· brance, comendes hir ; in health both, with all ur children and houshold : ur fathr, extraordinari hartie, chearefull and lustie, hath sent u this remembrance innclosed. —It maie be u knowe him his executr and brother, I meane of whom our brother Whte borowed for me the 80*l.* paihable att Mai next ; his name I have not att hand. He dwelleth in Watlinge Streate. If 40*l.* thereof might be procured for 6. monethes more, it would make me whole. I knowe it doeth u good to be doinge good, and that u will do all the good u can.—I would Hanlett weare att home, satisfied for his paines taken before his cominge, and so freed from further travell. Nunc Deus omnipotens, opt. max., pater omnimodæ consolationis, benedicat tibi in viis tuis, et secundet te in omnibus tuis, per Jhesum Christum, Dominum nostrum ; Amen ! Dum ullus sum tuis tum.—Stretfordiæ, Januarii 24.—*Abrah. Strl.*—Commend me to Mr. Tom Bur'll, and prai him for me and mi bro. Da. Bakr. to looke that J. Tub maie be well hooped, that he leake not out lawe to our hurte for his cause ; quod partim avidio non nihill suspicor et timeo.

Receved of Mr. Buttes :—

In beanes 23 qrs., att 3*s.* 4*d.* the strike - - -	30*l.*	13*s.*	4*d.*
Barlei 8 qrs., and 4 str., att 4*s.* the str. - - -	13*l.*	12*s.*	0*d.*
Wheate 4 qrs. 4 str., att 6*s.* 8*d.* the str. - - -	12*l.*	0*s.*	0*d.*
	56*l.*	5*s.*	4*d.*

I have paid and sowed theareof, 52*l.* 11*s.* 8*d.*—Mi Lad. Gre. is run in arreages with mi sister for malt, as it semeth, which hindreth and troubleth hir not a littell.

VIII. A Return of the Quantities of Corn and Malt held in February, 1598, by the inhabitants of the ward in which New Place was situated.

Stratforde Burrowghe, Warrwicke.—The noate of corne and malte taken the iiij.th of Febrwarij, 1597, in the xl.th yeare of the raigne of our moste gracious soveraigne ladie Queen Elizabethe, &c.

Chapple Street Warde.—Frauncys Smythe jun., iij. quarters.—Jhon Coxe, v. quarters.—Mr. Thomas Dyxon, xvij. quarters.—Mr. Thomas Barber, iij. quarters.— Mychaell Hare, v. quarters.—Mr. Bifielde, vj. quarters.—Hughe Aynger, vj. quarters. —Thomas Badsey, vj. quarters, bareley j. quarter.—Jhon Rogers, x. str.—Wm. Emmettes, viij. quarters.—Mr. Aspinall, aboutes xj. quarters.—Wm. Shackespere, x. quarters.—Julij Shawe, vij. quarters.

Straingers.—Ryc : Dyxon hathe of Sir Tho : Lucies, xvj. quarters.—of Sir Edw. Grevyles x. quarters —of Edw. Kennings, iiij. quarters.—Mr. Bifielde of hys systers, iiij. quarters.—Hughe Ainger of hys wyves systers, one quarter.—William Emmettes of one Nickes of Whatcoate, iiij. quarters, di.; of Frauncys Tibballs, vj. str.

IX. A Letter from Adrian Quiney, to his son Richard, undated, but, from a comparison of it with other correspondence, it is all but certain that it was written either late in the year 1598 or early in 1599. It is addressed,—" To my lovynge sonne, Rycharde Qwyney, at the Belle in Carter Leyne deliver thesse in London," and includes a notice of Shakespeare.

Yow shalle, God wyllyng, receve from youre wyfe by Mr. Baylye, thys brr, asowrance of x.*s.*, and she wold have yow to bye some grocerye, yff hyt be resonable ;

yow maye have carryage by a woman who I wyllyd to com to you. Mr. Layne by reporte hath receved a great summ of money of Mr. Smyth of Wotten, but wylle not be knowyn of hyt, and denyd to lende your wyff any, but hys wyff sayd that he had receved v. *li* which was gevyn hyr, and wysshd hym to lent that to your wyff, which he dyde ; she hopyth to mayk provyssyon to paye Mr. Combes and alle the rest. I wrot to yow concerning Jhon Rogerss ; the howsse goythe greatlye to dekaye ; ask secretli therin, and doo somewhat therin, as he ys in doubt that Mr. Parsonss wylle not paye the 3*li*. 13*s*. 4*d*. Wherfor wryte to hym, yff yow maye have carryage, to bye some such warys as yow may selle presentlye with profet. Yff yow bargen with Wm. Sha. . or receve money therfor, brynge youre money homme that yow maye ; and see howe knite stockynges be sold ; ther ys gret byinge of them at Aysshome. Edward Wheat and Harrye, youre brother man, were both at Evyshome thys daye senet, and, as I harde, bestow 20*li*. ther in knyt hosse ; wherefore I thynke yow maye doo good, yff yow can have money.

    X. A Letter from Abraham Sturley to Richard Quiney, 4 November, 1598, at the commencement of which there is an allusion to Shakespeare.

All health, happines of suites and wellfare, be multiplied unto u and ur labours in God our Father bi Christ our Lord. Ur letter of the **25**. of Octobr came to mi handes the laste of the same att night per Grenwai, which imported a stai of suites bi Sr. Ed. Gr. advise, untill &c., and that onli u should followe on for tax and sub. presentli, and allso ur travell and hinderance of answere therein bi ur longe travell and thaffaires of the Courte ; and that our countriman Mr. Wm. Shak. would procure us monei, which I will like of as I shall heare when, and wheare, and howe ; and I prai let not go that occasion if it mai sorte to ani indifferent condicions. Allso that if monei might be had for 30 or 40*l*., a lease, &c., might be procured. Oh howe can u make dowbt of monei, who will not beare xxx. tie or xl.*s*. towardes sutch a match ! The latter end of ur letter which concerned ur houshold affaires I delivered presentli. Nowe to ur other letter of the 1° of Novmbr received the 3d. of the same. I would I weare with u ; nai, if u continue with hope of those suietes u wrighte of, I thinke I shall wt. concent ; and I will most willingli come unto u, as had u but advise and compani, and more monei presente, much might be done to obtaine our charter enlargd, ij, faires more, with tole of corne, bestes and sheepe, and a matter of more valewe then all that ; for (sai u) all this is nothinge that is in hand, seeinge it will not rise to 80*l*., and the charges wil be greate. What this matter of more valewe meaneth I cannot undrstand ; but me thinketh whatsoever the good would be, u are afraid of want of monei. Good thinges in hand or neare hand can not choose but be worth monei to bringe to hand, and, beinge assured, will, if neede be, bringe monei in their mouthes, there is no feare nor dowbte. If it be the rest of the tithes and the College houses and landes in our towne u speake of, the one halfe weare aboundantli ritch for us ; and the other halfe to increase Sr. Ed. riallties would both beare the charge and sett him sure on ; the which I take to be your meaninge bi the latter parte of ur letter, where u write for a copie of the particulars, which allso u shall have accordingli. Oh howe I feare when I se what Sr. Ed. can do, and howe neare it sitteth to himselfe, leaste he shall thinke it to good for us, and procure it for himselfe, as he served us the last time ; for it semeth bi ur owne wordes theare is some of hit in ur owne conceite, when u write if Sr. Ed. be as forward to do as to speake, it 'will be done ; a dowbt I assure u not without dowbt to be made ; whereto allso u ad, notwithstandinge that dowbt, no want but monei. Somewhat must be to Sr. Ed. and to each one that dealeth somewhat and great reason. And me thinketh u need not be affraid to promise that as fitt for him, for all them, and for urselfe. The thinge obtained no dowbte will pai all. For present advise and encouragmente u have bi this time Mr. Baili, and for monei, when u certifie what u have done and what u have spent, what u will do, and what u wante ; somewhat u knowe we have in hand, and God will provide that wc. shall be sufficient.   Be of good cowrage.   Make fast Sr. Ed. bi all meanes, or els all our hope and ur travelles be utterli disgraced. Consider and advise if Sr. Ed. will be faste for us, so that bi his goodwill to us and his meanes for us these thinges be brought about.   What weare it for the fee-farme of his riallties, nowe not above xij. or xiiij. *l.*, he weare assured of the dowble, when these thinges come to hande, or more, as the goodnes of the thinge procured proveth.   But whi do i travell in these thinges, when I knowe not certainli what u intende, neither what ur meanes are, nor what are ur difficulties preciseli and bi name, all which must be knowen bi name, and specialli with an estimate of the charge before ani thinge can be added either for advise or supplie.   I leave these matters therefore unto the Allmighties mercifull disposition in ur hand, untill a more neare possibilite or more leisure will encourage u or suffer u to write more plainli and particularli.   But withall the Chancell must not be forgotten, which allso obtained would yeald some pretti gub of monei for ur present busines, as I thinke.   The particulars u write for shalle this morninge be dispatched and sent as soone as mai be.   All is well att home ; all ur paimentes made and dispatchd ; mi sister saith if it be so that u can not be provided for Mrs. Pendllbur, she will, if u will, send u up x. *l.* towardes that bi the next after, or if u take it up, pai it to whom u appointe.—Wm. Wallford sendeth order and monei per Wm. Court nowe cominge, who hathe some cause to feare, for he was neweli served with proces on Twsdai last att Alcr. per Roger S.—Mr. Parsons supposeth that Wenlock came the same dai with Mr. Baili that u writt ur letter.   He saith he supposeth u mai use that x. *l.* for our brwinge matters.   Wm. Wiatt answered Mr. Ba., and us all, that he would neither brwe himselfe, nor submitt himselfe to the order, but bi those veri wordes make against it with all the strength he could possibli make, yeat we do this dai begin Mr. Bar. and miselfe a littell for assai.   My bro. D. B. att Shrewsburi or homeward from thence.   But nowe the bell hath runge mi time spent.   The Lord of all power, glori, merci, and grace and goodnes, make his great power and mercie knowen towardes us in ur weakenes.   Take heed of tabacco whereof we heare per. Wm. Perri ; against ani longe journei u mai undertake on foote of necessiti, or wherein the exercise of ur bodi must be imploied, drinke some good burned wine, or aqavitæ and ale strongli mingled without bread for a toste, and, above all, kepe u warme.   Farewell, mi dare harte, and the Lord increase our loves and comfortes one to another, that once it mai be sutch as becometh Christianiti, puriti, and sinceriti, without staine or blemishe.   Fare ye well ; all ur and ours well.   From Stretford, Novem. 4th, 1598.   Urs in all love in the best bond,—*Abrah. Sturlei.*—Mrs. Coomb, when Gilbert Charnocke paid them their monei, as he told me, said that if ani but he had brought it, she would not receve it, because she had not hir gowne ; and that she would arrest u for hit as soone as u come home, and much twattell ; but att the end, so that youe would pai 4*l.* toward hit, she would allowe u xx.*s*, and we shall heare att some leasure howe fruictes are, and hoppes, and sutch knakkes.   Att this point came Wm. Sheldon, the silke man, with a warrant to serve Wm. Walford againe upon a trespasse of 500*l.*

To his most lovinge brother, Mr. Richard Quinei, att the Bell in Carterlane att London, geve these.   Paid 2d.

XI.   Draft of a Grant of Coat-Armour proposed to be conferred on Shakespeare's Father in the year 1599.   From the original manuscript preserved at the College of Arms, the interlineations being denoted by Italics.   A few words near the end of the paper, which were in a corner now lost, have been supplied from an old transcript.

To all and singuller noble and gentelmen of all estates and degrees bearing arms to whom these presentes shall com, William Dethick, Garter, Principall King of Arms of England, and William Camden, alias Clarentieulx, King of Arms, for the sowth, east and weste partes of this realme, sendethe greetinges. Knowe yee that in all nations and kingdoms the record and remembrances of the valeant factes and verteous dispositions of worthie men have ben made knowen and divulged by certeyne shieldes of arms and tokens of chevalrie, the grant and testemonie wherof apperteynethe unto us by vertu of our offices from the Quenes most exc. majeste, and her highenes most noble and victorious progenitors; wherfore being solicited, and by credible report informed, that John Shakespere, nowe of Stratford-uppon-Avon in the counte of Warwik, gent., whose parent, *great grandfather*, and *late* antecessor, for his faithefull and approved service to *the late most prudent prince* King H. 7. of famous memorie, was advaunced and rewarded with landes and tenementes geven to him in those partes of Warwikeshere, where they have continewed bie *some* descentes in good reputacion and credit; *and for that* the said John Shakespere having maryed the daughter and one of the heyrs of Robert Arden of Wellingcote in the said countie, and also produced *this his* auncient *cote* of arms heretofore assigned to him whilest he was *her Majesties officer* and baylefe of that towne, In consideration *of the premisses*, and for the encouragement of his posterite, unto whom suche blazon of arms *and atchevementes of inheritance* from theyre *said* mother by the auncyent custome and lawes of arms maye *lawfullie* descend, We, the said Garter and Clarentieulx, have assigned, graunted and confirmed, *and, by these presentes, exemplefied*, unto the said John Shakespere and to his posterite, that shield and cote of arms, viz., in a field of gould uppon a bend sables a speare of the first the poynt upward hedded argent; and for his creast or cognizance a falcon with his wynges displayed standing on a wrethe of his coullers supporting a speare *armed* hedded *or* and steeled *sylver*, fyxed uppon a helmet with mantelles and tasselles, as more playnely *maye* appeare depicted on this margent; and we have *lykewise uppon on other escucheone* impaled the same with the auncyent arms of *the said* Arden of Wellingcote, signefeing thereby that it *maye and* shal be lawefull for the said John Shakespere, gent., to beare and use the same *shieldes of arms*, single or impaled as aforesaid, during his naturall lyffe; and that it shal be lawfull for his children, *yssue*, and posterite, lawfully begotten, to beare, use, and quarter *ana shewe forthe* the same with theyre dewe differences *in* all lawfull warlyke factes and cevele use or exercises, according to the lawes of arms and custome that to gent. belongethe, without let or interruption of any person or persons for use or per bearing the same. In wyttnesse and testemonye wherof we have subscribed our names and fastened the seales of our offices. Yeven at the Office of Arms, London, the . . . day of . . in the xlij. te. yeare of the reigne of our most gratious soveraigne Elizabeth, by the Grace of God, Quene of Ingland, France and Ireland, Defender of the Faythe, &c., 1599.

XII. The Will of John Hall, Shakespeare's Son-in-law, from the recorded copy in the Registry of the Prerogative Court of Canterbury, where it is entitled, Testamentum nuncupativum Johannis Hall.

The last Will and Testament nuncupative of John Hall of Stratford-upon-Avon in the county of Warwick, gentleman, made and declared the five and twentith of November, 1635. Imprimis, I geve unto my wife my house in London. Item, I geve unto my daughter Nash my house in Acton. Item, I geve unto my daughter Nash my meadowe. Item, I geve my goodes and money unto my wife and my daughter Nash, to be equally devided betwixt them. Item, concerning my study of bookes, I leave them, sayd he, to you, my sonn Nash, to dispose of them as yow see good. As for my manuscriptes, I would have given them to Mr. Boles, if hee had been here; but forasmuch as hee is not heere present, yow may, son Nash, burne them, or doe with them what yow please. Wittnesses hereunto,—*Thomas Nash. Simon Trapp.*

*XIII. The Will of Lady Barnard, Shakespeare's grand-daughter, January, 1670,
proved at London in the following March.   From a contemporary transcript.*

In the name of God, Amen, I, Dame Elizabeth Barnard, wife of Sir John Barnard of
Abington in the county of Northampton, knight, being in perfect memory,—blessed
be God!—and mindfull of mortalitie, doe make this my last will and testament in
manner and forme following.   Whereas by my certaine deed or writeing under my
hand and seale dated on or about the eighteenth day of Aprill, 1653, according to a power
therein mencioned, I, the said Elizabeth, have lymitted and disposed of all that my
messuage with th'appurtenances in Stratford-upon-Avon, in the county of Warwicke,
called the New Place, and all that foure yard land and a halfe in Stratford, Welcombe
and Bishopton in the county of Warwick, after the decease of the said Sir John
Bernard and me, the said Elizabeth, unto Henry Smith of Stratford aforesaid, gent.,
and Job Dighton of the Middle Temple, London, esquire, sithence deceased, and
their heires, upon trust that they and the survivor of them, and the heirs of such
survivor, should bargaine and sell the same for the best value they can gett, and the
money thereby to be raised to bee imployed and disposed of to such person and
persons, and in such manner, as I, the said Elizabeth, should by any writing or note
under my hand, truly testified, declare and nominate, as thereby may more fully
appeare.   Now my will is, and I doe hereby signifie and declare my mynd and meaning
to bee that the said Henry Smith, my surviving trustee, or his heires, shall with all
convenient speed after the decease of the said Sir John Bernard, my husband, make
sale of the inheritance of all and singuler the premisses, and that my loving cousin,
Edward Nash, esq., shall have the first offer or refusall thereof according to my
promise formerly made to him ; and the moneys to be raised by such sale I doe give,
dispose of and appoint, the same to be paid and distributed as is hereinafter expressed,
that is to say, to my cousin Thomas Welles of Carleton, in the county of Bedford,
gent., the somme of fifty pounds to be paid him within one yeare next after such sale ;
and if the said Thomas Welles shall happen to dye before such time as his said legacy
shall become due to him, then my desire is that my kinsman, Edward Bagley, cittizen
of London, shall have the sole benefitt thereof.   Item, I doe give and appoint unto
Judith Hathaway, one of the daughters of my kinsman, Thomas Hathaway, late of
Stratford aforesaid, the annuall somme of five pounds of lawfull money of England, to
be paid unto her yearely and every yeare from and after the decease of the survivor of
the said Sir John Bernard and me, the said Elizabeth, for and during the naturall life
of her, the said Judith, att the two most usuall feasts or dayes of payment in the yeare,
videlicet, the feast of the Annunciacion of the Blessed Virgin Mary and St. Michaell
the Archangell, by equall porcions, the first payment thereof to beginne at such of the
said feasts as shall next happen after the decease of the survivor of the said Sir John
Bernard and me the said Elizabeth, if the said premisses can be soe soone sold, or
otherwise soe soone as the same can be sold ; and if the said Judith shall happen to
marry, and shal be mynded to release the said annuall somme of five pound, and
shall accordingly release and quitt all her interest and right in and to the same after it
shall become due to her, then and in such case I doe give and appoynte to her the
somme of forty pounds in liew thereof, to bee paid unto her at the tyme of the
executing of such release as aforesaid.   Item, I give and appointe unto Joane, the
wife of Edward Kent, and one other of the daughters of the said Thomas Hathaway, the
somme of fifty pounds to be likewise paid unto her within one yeare next after the
decease of the survivor of the said Sir John Bernard and me the said Elizabeth, if the
said premisses can be soe soone sold, or otherwise soe soone as the same can bee sold
and if the said Johan shall happen to die before the said fiftie pounds shal be paid to
her, then I doe give and appoynt the same unto Edward Kent, the younger, her sonne,
to be paid unto him when he shall attayne the age of one-and-twenty yeares.   Item, I
doe alsoe give and appoynt unto him, the said Edward Kent, sonne of the said Johan,

the somme of thirty pounds towards putting him out as an apprentice, and to be paid and disposed of to that use when he shall be fitt for it. Item, I doe give, appoynte, and dispose of unto Rose, Elizabeth and Susanna, three other of the daughters of my said kinsman, Thomas Hathaway, the somme of fortie pounds a-peece to be paid unto every of them at such tyme and in such manner as the said fiftie pounds before appointed to the said Johan Kent, their sister, shall become payable. Item, all the rest of the moneys that shal be raised by such sale as aforesaid I give and dispose of unto my said kinsman, Edward Bagley, except five pounds only, which I give and appoint to my said trustee, Henry Smith, for his paines ; and if the said Edward Nash shall refuse the purchase of the said messuage and foure yard land and a halfe with the appurtenances, then my will and desire is that the said Henry Smith, or his heires, shall sell the inheritance of the said premisses and every part thereof unto the said Edward Bagley, and that he shall purchase the same ; upon this condicion, nevertheles, that he, the said Edward Bagley, his heyres, executors or administrators, shall justly and faithfully performe my will and true meaning in making due payment of all the severall sommes of money or legacies before-mencioned in such manner as aforesaid. And I doe hereby declare my will and meaning to be that the executors or administrators of my said husband, Sir John Bernard, shall have and enjoy the use and benefit of my said house in Stratford, called the New Place, with the orchard, gardens and all other thappurtenances thereto belonging, for and dureing the space of six monthes next after the decease of him, the said Sir John Bernard. Item, I give and devise unto my kinsman, Thomas Hart, the sonne of Thomas Hart, late of Stratford-upon-Avon aforesaid, all that my other messuage or inne, situate in Stratford-upon-Avon aforesaid, commonly called the Maydenhead, with the appurtenances, and the next house thereunto adjoyning, with the barne belonging to the same now or late in the occupacion of Michaell Johnson or his assignes, with all and singuler the appurtenances, to hold to him, the said Thomas Hart, the sonne and the heires of his body ; and for default of such issue, I give and devise the same to George Hart, brother of the said Thomas Hart, and to the heires of his body ; and for default of such issue, to the right heires of me, the said Elizabeth Bernard, for ever. Item, I doe make, ordayne, and appoynte my said loving kinsman, Edward Bagley, sole executor of this, my last will and testament, hereby revokeing all former wills ; desireing him to see a just performance hereof according to my true intent and meaning. In witnes whereof I, the said Elizabeth Bernard, have hereunto sett my hand and seale the nyne-and-twentieth day of January, anno domini one thousand six hundred sixty-nyne.—*Elizabeth Barnard.*—Signed, sealed, published and declared to be the last will and testament of the said Elizabeth Bernard, in the presence of—John Howes, rector de Abington, Francis Wickes.

Mr. WILLIAM

SHAKESPEARES

COMEDIES, HISTORIES, & TRAGEDIES.

Published according to the True Originall Copies.

LONDON

Printed by Isaac Iaggard, and Ed. Blount. 1623.

THE FIRST FOLIO.

The earliest collective edition of the dramatic writings of Shakespeare was entered in the registers of the Stationers' Company on November the 8th, 1623, and was published under the title of,—"Mr. William Shakespeares Comedies, Histories and Tragedies.—Published according to the True Originall Copies.—London—Printed by Isaac Jaggard, and Ed. Blount. 1623." At the commencement of this valuable work are the following prefixes, which, it is scarcely necessary to observe, were written by Shakespeare's friends and contemporaries, and are of extreme value and interest in connexion with the history of the poet's literary career.

To the Most Noble and Incomparable Paire of Brethren, William, earle of Pembroke, &c., Lord Chamberlaine to the Kings most Excellent Majesty, and Philip, earle of Montgomery, &c., Gentleman of his Majesties Bed-chamber, both Knights of the most Noble Order of the Garter, and our singular good lords.

Right Honourable,—Whilst we studie to be thankful in our particular for the many favors we have received from your L.L., we are falne upon the ill fortune to mingle two the most diverse things that can bee, feare and rashnesse ; rashnesse in the enterprize, and feare of the successe. For when we valew the places your H.H. sustaine, we cannot but know their dignity greater then to descend to the reading of these trifles ; and, while we name them trifles, we have depriv'd ourselves of the defence of our Dedication. But since your L.L. have beene pleas'd to thinke these trifles some-thing heeretofore, and have prosequuted both them, and their authour living, with so much favour, we hope, that (they out-living him, and he not having the fate, common with some, to be exequutor to his owne writings) you will use the like indulgence toward them, you have done unto their parent. There is a great difference whether any booke choose his patrones, or finde them. This hath done both. For so much were your L.L. likings of the severall parts, when they were acted, as, before they were published, the volume ask'd to be yours. We have but collected them, and done an office to the dead to procure his orphanes guardians ; without ambition either of selfe-profit or fame, onely to keepe the memory of so worthy a friend and fellow alive, as was our Shakespeare, by humble offer of his playes to your most noble patronage. Wherein, as we have justly observed, no man to come neere your L.L. but with a kind of religious addresse, it hath bin the height of our care, who are the presenters, to make the present worthy of your H.H. by the perfection. But there we must also crave our abilities to be considerd, my Lords. We cannot go beyond our owne powers. Country hands reach foorth milke, creame, fruites or what they have : and many nations (we have heard) that had not gummes and incense, obtained their requests with a leavened cake. It was no fault to approch their gods by what meanes they could, and the most, though meanest, of things are made more precious when they are dedicated to temples. In that name, therefore, we most humbly consecrate to your H.H. these remaines of your servant Shakespeare ; that what delight is in them may be ever your L.L., the reputation his, and the faults ours, if any be committed by a payre so carefull to shew their gratitude both to the living and the dead as is—Your Lordshippes most bounden,—*John Heminge.—Henry Condell.*

To the great Variety of Readers.—From the most able to him that can but spell ;—there you are number'd. We had rather you were weighd, especially when the fate of all bookes depends upon your capacities, and not of your heads alone, but of your purses. Well ! It is now publique, and you wil stand for your priviledges wee know; to read and censure. Do so, but buy it first. That doth best commend a booke, the stationer saies. Then, how odde soever your braines be, or your wisedomes, make your licence the same and spare not. Judge your sixe-pen'orth, your shillings worth, your five shillings worth at a time, or higher, so you rise to the just rates, and welcome. But, whatever you do, buy. Censure will not drive a trade or make the jacke go. And though you be a magistrate of wit, and sit on the stage at Black-Friers or the Cock-pit to arraigne playes dailie, know, these playes have had their triall alreadie, and stood out all appeales, and do now come forth quitted rather by a Decree of Court then any purchas'd letters of commendation.

It had bene a thing, we confesse, worthie to have bene wished, that the author himselfe had liv'd to have set forth and overseen his own writings ; but since it hath bin ordain'd otherwise, and he by death departed from that right, we pray you do not envie his friends the office of their care and paine to have collected and publish'd them ; and so to have publish'd them, as where (before) you were abus'd with diverse stolne and surreptitious copies, maimed and deformed by the frauds and stealthes of injurious impostors that expos'd them ; even those are now offer'd to your view cur'd and perfect of their limbes, and all the rest absolute in their numbers as he conceived them ; who, as he was a happie imitator of Nature, was a most gentle expresser of it. His mind and hand went together ; and what he thought, he uttered with that easinesse that wee have scarse received from him a blot in his papers. But it is not our province, who onely gather his works and give them you, to praise him. It is yours that reade him. And there we hope, to your divers capacities, you will finde enough both to draw and hold you : for his wit can no more lie hid then it could be lost. Reade him, therefore ; and againe and againe ; and if then you doe not like him, surely you are in some manifest danger not to understand him. And so we leave you to other of his friends, whom, if you need, can bee your guides. If you neede them not, you can leade yourselves and others ; and such readers we wish him.—*John Heminge.*—*Henrie Condell.*

To the memory of my beloved, the author, Mr. William Shakespeare, and what he hath left us.—To draw no envy (Shakespeare) on thy name, = Am I thus ample to thy booke and fame ; = While I confesse thy writings to be such, = As neither man nor muse can praise too much, = 'Tis true, and all mens suffrage. But these wayes = Were not the paths I meant unto thy praise ; = For seeliest ignorance on these may light, = Which, when it sounds at best, but eccho's right ; = Or blinde affection, which doth ne're advance = The truth, but gropes and urgeth all by chance ; Or crafty malice might pretend this praise, = and thinke to ruine where it seem'd to raise. = These are, as some infamous baud or whore = Should praise a matron. What could hurt her more ? = But thou art proofe against them, and indeed = Above th'ill fortune of them, or the need. = I, therefore, will begin.—Soule of the age ! = The applause ! delight ! the wonder of our stage ! = My Shakespeare, rise ; I will not lodge thee by = Chaucer or Spenser, or bid Beaumont lye = A little further, to make thee a roome ; Thou art a moniment without a tombe, = And art alive still while thy booke doth live, = And we have wits to read and praise to give. = That I not mixe thee so my braine excuses, = I meane with great, but disproportion'd muses, = For if I thought my judgement were of yeeres, = I should commit thee surely with thy peeres, = And tell how farre thou didstst our Lily out-shine, = Or sporting Kid, or Marlowes mighty line. = And though thou hadst small Latine and lesse Greeke, = From thence to honour thee I would not seeke = For names, but call forth thund'ring Æschilus, = Euripides and Sophocles to us, =

Paccuvius, Accius, him of Cordova dead, = To life againe, to heare thy buskin tread = And shake a stage ; or, when thy sockes were on, = Leave thee alone, for the comparison = Of all that insolent Greece or haughtie Rome = Sent forth, or since did from their ashes come. = Triúmph, my Britaine, thou hast one to showe, = To whom all scenes of Europe homage owe. = He was not of an age, but for all time ! = And all the Muses still were in their prime, = When, like Apollo, he came forth to warme = Our eares, or like a Mercury to charme ! = Nature herselfe was proud of his designes, = And joy'd to weare the dressing of his lines, = Which were so richly spun and woven so fit, = As, since, she will vouchsafe no other wit. = The merry Greeke, tart Aristophanes, = Neat Terence, witty Plautus, now not please, = But antiquated and deserted lye = As they were not of Natures family. = Yet must I not give Nature all ; thy art, = My gentle Shakespeare, must enjoy a part ; = For though the poets matter Nature be, = His art doth give the fashion ! and that he, = Who casts to write a living line, must sweat, = Such as thine are, and strike the second heat = Upon the Muses anvile ; turne the same, = And himselfe with it, that he thinkes to frame ; = Or for the lawrell he may gaine a scorne, = For a good poet's made as well as borne, = And such wert thou. Looke how the fathers face = Lives in his issue ; even so, the race = Of Shakespeares minde and manners brightly shines = In his well-torned and true-filed lines, = In each of which he seemes to shake a lance, = As brandish't at the eyes of ignorance. = Sweet Swan of Avon ! what a sight it were = To see thee in our waters yet appeare, = And make those flights upon the bankes of Thames, = That so did take Eliza and our James ! = But stay, I see thee in the hemisphere = Advanc'd, and made a constellation there ! = Shine forth, thou Starre of Poets, and with rage = Or influence, chide or cheere the drooping stage ; = Which, since thy flight from hence, hath mourn'd like night, = And despaires day but for thy volumes light.—*Ben : Jonson.*

Upon the Lines and Life of the Famous Scenicke Poet, Master William Shakespeare. —Those hands, which you so clapt, go now and wring, = You Britaines brave, for done are Shakespeares dayes ; = His dayes are done that made the dainty playes, = Which made the Globe of heav'n and earth to ring. = Dry'de is that veine, dry'd is the Thespian spring, = Turn'd all to teares, and Phœbus clouds his rayes ; = That corp's, that coffin, now besticke those bayes, = Which crown'd him poet first, then poets king. = If tragedies might any Prologue have, = All those he made would scarse make one to this ; = Where Fame, now that he gone is to the grave, = Deaths publique tyring-house, the Nuncius is. = For though his line of life went soone about, = The life yet of his lines shall never out.—*Hugh Holland.*

To the Memorie of the deceased Authour, Maister W. Shakespeare.—Shake-speare, at length thy pious fellowes give = The world thy Workes,—thy Workes, by which out-live = Thy tombe thy name must ; when that stone is rent, = And Time dissolves thy Stratford moniment, = Here we alive shall view thee still. This booke,—When brasse and marble fade, shall make thee looke = Fresh to all ages ; when posteritie = Shall loath what's new, thinke all is prodegie = That is not Shake-speares ; ev'ry line, each verse, = Here shall revive, redeeme thee from thy herse. = Nor fire, nor cankring age, as Naso said, = Of his, thy wit-fraught booke, shall once invade. = Nor shall I e're beleeve, or thinke thee dead, = Though mist untill our bankrout stage be sped, = Impossible, with some new straine t' out-do = Passions of Juliet and her Romeo ; = Or till I heare a scene more nobly take, = Then when thy half-sword parlying Romans spake. = Till these, till any of thy volumes rest = Shall with more fire, more feeling, be exprest, = Be sure, our Shake-speare, thou canst never dye, = But, crown'd with lawrell, live eternally.—*L. Digges.*

E 2

To the memorie of M. W. Shake-speare.—Wee wondred (Shake-speare) that thou
went'st so soone=From the worlds stage to the graves tyring-roome.=Wee thought
thee dead, but this, thy printed worth,=Tels thy spectators that thou went'st but forth=
To enter with applause.   An actors art=Can dye, and live, to acte a second part.=
That's but an exit of mortalitie,=This, a re-entrance to a plaudite.—I, M.

*The Workes of William Shakespeare, containing all his Comedies, Histories, and
Tragedies, truely set forth according to their first Originall.—The names of the Princi-
pall Actors in all these playes.*—William Shakespeare ; Richard Burbadge ; John
Hemmings ; Augustine Phillips ; William Kempt ; Thomas Poope ; George Bryan ;
Henry Condell ; William Slye ; Richard Cowly ; John Lowine ; Samuell Crosse ;
Alexander Cooke ; Samuel Gilburne ; Robert Armin ; William Ostler ; Nathan
Field ; John Underwood ; Nicholas Tooley ; William Ecclestone ; Joseph Taylor ;
Robert Benfield ; Robert Goughe ; Richard Robinson ; John Shancke ; John Rice.

*A Catalogue of the severall Comedies, Histories, and Tragedies contained in this
Volume.*—COMEDIES. The Tempest, folio 1 ; the Two Gentlemen of Verona, 20 ; The
Merry Wives of Windsor, 38 ; Measure for Measure, 61 ; The Comedy of Errours, 85 ;
Much adoo about Nothing, 101 ; Loves Labour lost, 122 ; Midsommer Nights Dreame,
145 ; The Merchant of Venice, 163 ; As you Like it, 185 ; The Taming of the Shrew,
208 ; All is well that Ends well, 230 ; Twelfe-Night, or what you will, 255 ; The
Winters Tale, 304.—HISTORIES. The Life and Death of King John, fol. 1 ; the Life
and Death of Richard the Second, 23 ; the First Part of King Henry the Fourth, 46 ;
The Second Part of K. Henry the fourth, 74 ; The Life of King Henry the Fift,
69 ; The First part of King Henry the Sixt, 96 ; The Second part of King Hen. the
Sixt, 120 ; The Third part of King Henry the Sixt, 147 ; The Life and Death of
Richard the Third, 173 ; The Life of King Henry the Eight, 205.—TRAGEDIES. The
Tragedy of Coriolanus, fol. 1 ; Titus Andronicus, 31 ; Romeo and Juliet 53 ; Timon
of Athens, 80 ; The Life and death of Julius Cæsar, 109 ; The Tragedy of Macbeth,
131 ; The Tragedy of Hamlet, 152 ; King Lear, 283 ; Othello, the Moore of Venice,
310 ; Anthony and Cleopater, 346 ; Cymbeline King of Britaine, 369.

BIOGRAPHICAL NOTICES.

I. From Ben Jonson's—" Timber, or Discoveries made upon Men and Matter, as they have flow'd out of his daily Readings, or had their refluxe to his peculiar Notion of the Times," fol. Lond. 1641. The following remarks were no doubt written long before their author's death in 1637.

De Shakespeare nostrat.—I remember, the players have often mentioned it as an honour to Shakespeare that, in his writing, whatsoever he penn'd, hee never blotted out line. My answer hath beene, would he had blotted a thousand ;—which they thought a malevolent speech. I had not told posterity this, but for their ignorance who choose that circumstance to commend their friend by wherein he most faulted ; and to justifie mine owne candor,—for I lov'd the man, and doe honour his memory, on this side idolatry, as much as any. Hee was, indeed, honest, and of an open and free nature ; had an excellent phantsie ; brave notions and gentle expressions ; wherein hee flow'd with that facility that sometime it was necessary he should be stop'd ;—*sufflaminandus erat*, as Augustus said of Haterius. His wit was in his owne power ;—would the rule of it had beene so too ! Many times hee fell into those things, could not escape laughter ; as when hee said in the person of Cæsar, one speaking to him,—*Cæsar thou dost me wrong ;* hee replyed,—*Cæsar did never wrong but with just cause ;* and such like ; which were ridiculous. But hee redeemed his vices with his vertues. There was ever more in him to be praysed then to be pardoned.

II. Lines on the Familiar Names given to Shakespeare and his contemporaries, from Heywood's Hierarchie of the Blessed Angells, 1635.

Our moderne poets to that passe are driven, = Those names are curtal'd which they first had given ; = And, as we wisht to have their memories drown'd, = We scarcely can afford them halfe their sound. = Greene, who had in both academies ta'ne = Degree of Master, yet could never gaine = To be call'd more than Robin ; who, had he = Profest ought save the Muse, serv'd and been free = After a seven yeares prentiseship, might have, = With credit too, gone Robert to his grave. = Marlo, renown'd for his rare art and wit, = Could ne're attaine beyond the name of Kit ; = Although his Hero and Leander did = Merit addition rather. Famous Kid = Was call'd but Tom. Tom Watson, though he wrote = Able to make Apollo's selfe to dote = Upon his muse, for all that he could strive, = Yet never could to his full name arrive. = Tom Nash, in his time of no small esteeme, = Could not a second syllable redeeme. = Excellent Bewmont, in the formost ranke = Of the rar'st wits, was never more than Franck. = Mellifluous Shakespeare, whose inchanting quill = Commanded mirth or passion, was but Will. = And famous Johnson, though his learned pen = Be dipt in Castaly, is still but Ben. = Fletcher and Webster, of that learned packe = None of the mean'st, yet neither was but Jacke. = Deckers but Tom ; nor May, nor Middleton. = And hee's now but Jacke Foord, that once were⑧ John.

III. From Fuller's History of the Worthies of Warwickshire, forming part of his History of the Worthies of England, fol. Lond. 1662. This was a posthumous work, the author having died in 1661, and the following notice was doubtlessly written several years previously to that event.

William Shakespeare was born at Stratford-on-Avon in this county, in whom three eminent poets may seem in some sort to be compounded,—1. Martial in the warlike sound of his sur-name, whence some may conjecture him of a military extraction, hasti-vibrans or Shake-speare.—2. Ovid, the most naturall and witty of all poets, and hence it was that Queen Elizabeth, coming into a grammar-school made this extemporary verse,—" Persius a crab-staffe, bawdy Martial, Ovid a fine wag."—3. Plautus, who was an exact comædian yet never any scholar, as our Shake-speare, if alive, would confess himself. Adde to all these that, though his genius generally was jocular and inclining him to festivity, yet he could, when so disposed, be solemn and serious, as appears by his tragedies ; so that Heraclitus himself, I mean if secret and unseen, might afford to smile at his comedies, they were so merry, and Democritus scarce forbear to sigh at his tragedies, they were so mournfull.—He was an eminent instance of the truth of that rule, *poeta non fit sed nascitur,*—one is not made but born a poet. Indeed, his learning was very little, so that, as Cornish diamonds are not polished by any lapidary, but are pointed and smoothed even as they are taken out of the earth, so nature itself was all the art which was used upon him. Many were the wit-combates betwixt him and Ben Johnson, which two I behold like a Spanish great gallion and an English man-of-war. Master Johnson, like the former, was built far higher in learning, solid, but slow in his performances. Shake-spear, with the English man-of-war, lesser in bulk, but lighter in sailing, could turn with all tides, tack about, and take advantage of all winds, by the quickness of his wit and invention. He died anno Domini 16 . ., and was buried at Stratford-upon-Avon, the town of his nativity

IV. Notes respecting Shakespeare extracted from an original memoranda-book of the Rev. John Ward, Vicar of Stratford-on-Avon. They were written either in 1662 or 1663, as appears from the following entry,—" this booke was begunne Feb. 14, 1661, and finished April the 25, 1663, att Mr. Brooks his house in Stratford-uppon-Avon."

Shakspear had but two daughters, one whereof Mr. Hall, the physitian, married, and by her had one daughter, to wit, the Lady Bernard of Abbingdon.—I have heard that Mr. Shakespeare was a natural wit, without any art at all ; hee frequented the plays all his younger time, but in his elder days livd at Stratford, and supplied the stage with two plays every year, and for that had an allowance so large that hee spent att the rate of a thousand a yeer, as I have heard.—Shakespear, Drayton, and Ben Jhonson, had a merry meeting, and, itt seems, drank too hard, for Shakespear died of a feavour there contracted.—Remember to peruse Shakespears plays and bee versed in them, that I may not bee ignorant in that matter.

V. A biographical notice of Shakespeare, from Aubrey's Lives of Eminent Men, a manuscript completed in the year 1680. The marginal notes of the original are here denoted by Italics.

Mr. William Shakespear was borne at Stratford-upon-Avon in the county of Warwick ; his father was a butcher, and I have been told heretofore by some of the neighbours that, when he was a boy, he exercised his fathers trade, but when he kill'd a calfe, he would doe it in a high style and make a speech. There was at that time another butchers son in this towne, that was held not at all inferior to him for a naturall witt, his acquaintance and coetanean, but dyed young. This Wm., being inclined naturally to poetry and acting, came to London I guesse about 18, and was an actor at one of the play-houses, and did act exceedingly well. Now B. Johnson was never a good actor, but an excellent instructor. He began early to make essayes at dramatique poetry, which at that time was very lowe, and his playes tooke well. He was a handsome well shap't man, very good company, and of a very readie and pleasant smooth witt. The humur of . . . ., the cunstable in a Midsomers Night's Dreame, he happened to take at Grenden in Bucks, which is the roade from London to

Stratford, and there was living that constable about 1642, when I first came to Oxon. *I thinke it was Midsomer night that he happened to lye there.* Mr. Jos. Howe is of the parish and knew him. Ben Johnson and he did gather humours of men dayly where-ever they came. One time, as he was at the tavern at Stratford-super-Avon, one Combes, an old rich usurer, was to be buryed ; he makes there this extemporary epitaph,—" Ten in the hundred the devill allowes, = But Combes will have twelve he sweares and vowes ; = If any one askes who lies in this tombe, = Hoh ! quoth the devill, tis my John o'Combe !"—He was wont to goe to his native country once a yeare. I thinke I have been told that he left 2 or 300 *li.* per annum there and thereabout to a sister. I have heard Sir Wm. Davenant and Mr. Thomas Shadwell, who is counted the best comœdian we have now, say that he had a most prodigious witt (*v. his Epitaph in Dugdale's Warw.*), and did admire his naturall parts beyond all other dramaticall writers. He (*B. Johnsons Underwoods*) was wont to say that he never blotted out a line in his life ; sayd Ben Johnson,—I wish he had blotted out a thousand. His comœdies will remaine witt as long as the English tongue is understood, for that he handles *mores hominum ;* now our present writers reflect so much upon particular persons and coxcombeities, that 20 yeares hence they will not be understood. Though, as Ben Johnson sayes of him, that he had but little Latine and lesse Greek, he understood Latine pretty well, for he had been in his younger yeares a schoolmaster in the countrey. *From Mr. . . . Beeston.*

VI. Notes on Shakespeare, those in Roman type having been made before the year 1688 by the Rev. William Fulman, and those in Italics being additions by the Rev. Richard Davies made previously to 1708. From the originals preserved at Corpus Christi College, Oxford. There is no evidence in the manuscript itself that the interesting additions were made by Davies, but the fact is established by the identity of the handwriting with that in one of his autographical letters preserved in the same collection.

William Shakespeare was born at Stratford-upon-Avon in Warwickshire about 1563-4. *Much given to all unluckinesse in stealing venison and rabbits, particularly from Sr . . . Lucy, who had him oft whipt and sometimes imprisoned, and at last made him fly his native country to his great advancement; but his reveng was so great that he is his Justice Clodpate, and calls him a great man, and that in allusion to his name bore three lowses rampant for his arms.* From an actor of playes he became a composer. He dyed Apr. 23, 1616, ætat. 53, probably at Stratford, for there he is buryed, and hath a monument (Dugd. p. 520), *on which he lays a heavy curse upon any one who shal remoove his bones. He dyed a papist.*

VII. Anecdotes respecting Shakespeare, from a little manuscript account of places in Warwickshire by a person named Dowdall, written in the year 1693.

The first remarkable place in this county that I visitted was Stratford-super-Avon, where I saw the effigies of our English tragedian, Mr. Shakspeare ; parte of his epitaph I sent Mr. Lowther, and desired he would impart it to you, which I finde by his last letter he has done ; but here I send you the whole inscription.—Just under his effigies in the wall of the chancell is this written.—" Judicio Pylum, genio Socratem, arte Maronem, = Terra tegit, populus mœrett, Olympus habet. = Stay, passenger, why goest thou by soe fast ? = Read if thou canst, whome envious death hath plac't = Within this monument ; Shakspeare, with whome = Quick nature dyed ; whose name doth deck the tombe = Far more then cost, sith all that he hath writt = Leaves liveing art but page to serve his witt.—Obiit A. Dni. 1616.—Ætat. 53, Die. 23 Apr."—Neare the wall where his monument is erected lyeth a plaine free-stone, underneath which his bodie is buried with this epitaph made by himselfe a little before his death,—" Good friend, for Jesus sake forbeare = To digg the dust inclosed here ! = Bles't be the man that spares these stones, = And curs't be he that moves my bones !"—The clarke that shew'd me this church is above 80 years old ; he says that this Shakespear was formerly in this towne bound apprentice to a butcher, but that he run from his master to London, and there was received into the play-house as a serviture, and by this meanes had an opportunity to be what he afterwards prov'd. He was the best of his family, but the male line is extinguishd. Not one for feare of the curse abovesaid dare touch his grave-stone, tho his wife and daughters did earnestly desire to be layd in the same grave with him.

VIII. An Extract from a Letter written in the year 1694, by William Hall, an Oxford graduate, to his intimate friend, Edward Thwaites, an eminent Anglo-Saxon scholar. From the original Manuscript in the Bodleian Library.

I very greedily embrace this occasion of acquainting you with something which I found at Stratford-upon-Avon. That place I came unto on Thursday night, and the next day went to visit the ashes of the great Shakespear which lye interr'd in that church. The verses which, in his lifetime, he ordered to be cut upon his tomb-stone, for his monument have others, are these which follow,—" Reader, for Jesus's sake forbear= To dig the dust enclosed here ;= Blessed be he that spares these stones,= And cursed be he that moves my bones."—The little learning these verses contain would be a very strong argument of the want of it in the author, did not they carry something in them which stands in need of a comment. There is in this Church a place which they call the bone-house, a repository for all bones they dig up, which are so many that they would load a great number of waggons. The poet, being willing to preserve his bones unmoved, lays a curse upon him that moves them, and haveing to do with clarks and sextons, for the most part a very ignorant sort of people, he descends to the meanest of their capacitys, and disrobes himself of that art which none of his co-temporaries wore in greater perfection. Nor has the design mist of its effect, for, lest they should not onely draw this curse upon themselves, but also entail it upon their posterity, they have laid him full seventeen foot deep, deep enough to secure him. And so much for Stratford, within a mile of which Sir Robinson lives, but it was so late before I knew, that I had not time to make him a visit.

IX. Extracts from Rowe's Account of the Life of Shakespeare, 1709. The portions of this essay which are here omitted consist mainly of remarks on the plays and are of no biographical value.

It seems to be a kind of respect due to the memory of excellent men, especially of those whom their wit and learning have made famous, to deliver some account of themselves, as well as their works, to posterity. For this reason, how fond do we see some people of discovering any little personal story of the great men of antiquity, their families, the common accidents of their lives, and even their shape, make, and features have been the subject of critical enquiries. How trifling soever this curiosity may seem to be, it is certainly very natural ; and we are hardly satisfy'd with an account of any remarkable person 'till we have heard him describ'd even to the very cloaths he wears. As for what relates to men of letters, the knowledge of an author may sometimes conduce to the better understanding his book ; and tho' the works of Mr. Shakespear may seem to many not to want a comment, yet I fancy some little account of the man himself may not be thought improper to go along with them.—He was the son of Mr. John Shakespear, and was born at Stratford-upon-Avon, in Warwickshire, in April, 1564. His family, as appears by the register and publick writings relating to that town, were of good figure and fashion there, and are mention'd as gentlemen. His father, who was a considerable dealer in wool, had so large a family, ten children in all, that, tho' he was his eldest son, he could give him no better education than his own employment. He had bred him, 'tis true, for some time at a free-school, where 'tis probable he acquir'd that little Latin he was master of ; but the narrowness of his circumstances, and the want of his assistance at home, forc'd his father to withdraw him from thence, and unhappily prevented his further proficiency in that language.—Upon his leaving school, he seems to have given intirely into that way of living which his father propos'd to him; and, in order to settle in the world after a family manner, he thought fit to marry while he was yet very young. His wife was the daughter of one Hathaway, said to have been a substantial yeoman in the neighbourhood of Stratford. In this kind of settlement he continu'd for some time, 'till an extravagance that he was guilty of forc'd him both out of his country and that way of living which he had taken up; and tho' it seem'd at first to be a blemish upon his good manners, and a misfortune to him, yet it afterwards happily prov'd the occasion of exerting one of the greatest genius's that ever was known in dramatick poetry. He had, by a misfortune common enough to young fellows, fallen into ill company; and amongst them, some that made a frequent practice of deer-stealing engag'd him with them more than once in robbing a park that belong'd to Sir Thomas Lucy of Cherlecot, near Stratford. For this he was prosecuted by that gentleman, as he thought, somewhat too severely; and in order to revenge that ill usage, he made a ballad upon him. And tho' this, probably the first essay of his poetry, be lost, yet it is said to have been so very bitter that it redoubled the prosecution against him to that degree, that he was oblig'd to leave his business and family in Warwickshire for some time, and shelter himself in London.—It is at this time, and upon this accident, that he is said to have made his first acquaintance in the play-house. He was receiv'd into the company then in being at first in a very mean rank; but his admirable wit, and the natural turn of it to the stage, soon distinguish'd him, if not as an extraordinary actor, yet as an excellent writer. His name is printed, as the custom was in those times, amongst those of the other players, before some old plays, but without any particular account of what sort of parts he us'd to play; and tho' I have inquir'd, I could never meet with any further account of him this way than that the top of his performance was the ghost in his own Hamlet. I should have been much more pleas'd to have learn'd, from some certain authority, which was the first play he wrote; it would be without doubt a pleasure to any man, curious in things of this kind, to see and know what was the first essay of a fancy like Shakespear's. Perhaps we are not to look for his beginnings, like those of other authors, among their least perfect writings. Art had so little, and nature so large a share in what he did, that, for ought I know, the performances of his youth, as they were the most vigorous, and had the most fire and strength of imagination in 'em, were the best. I would not be thought by this to mean that his fancy was so loose and extravagant as to be independent on the rule and government of judgment; but that what he thought was commonly so great, so justly and rightly conceiv'd in itself, that it wanted little or no correction, and was immediately approv'd by an impartial judgment at the first sight. Mr. Dryden seems to think that Pericles is one of his first plays; but there is no judgment to be form'd on that, since there is good reason to believe that the greatest part of that play was not written by him; tho' it is own'd some part of it certainly was, particularly the last act. But tho' the order of time in which the several pieces were written be generally uncertain, yet there are passages in some few of them which seem to fix their dates. So the chorus in the beginning of the fifth Act of Henry V., by a compliment very handsomly turn'd to the Earl of Essex, shows the play to have been written when that lord was general for the queen in Ireland; and his elogy upon Q. Elizabeth, and her successor K. James, in the latter end of his Henry VIII., is a proof of that play's being written after the accession of the latter of those two princes to the crown of England. Whatever the particular times of his writing were, the people of his age, who began to grow wonderfully fond of diversions of this kind, could not but be highly pleas'd to see a genius arise amongst 'em of so pleasurable, so rich a vein, and so plentifully capable of furnishing their favourite entertainments. Besides the advantages of his wit, he was in himself a good-natur'd man, of great sweetness in his manners, and a most agreeable companion ; so that it is no wonder if, with so many good qualities, he made himself acquainted with the best conversations of those times. Queen Elizabeth had several of his plays acted before her, and without doubt gave him many gracious marks of her favour. It is that maiden princess plainly whom he intends by—"a fair vestal, throned by the west." And that whole passage is a compliment very properly brought in, and very handsomly apply'd to her. She was so well pleas'd with that admirable character of Falstaff in the two parts of Henry the Fourth, that she commanded him to continue it for one play more, and to shew him in love. This is said to be the occasion of his writing the Merry Wives of Windsor. How well she was obey'd, the play it self is an admirable proof. Upon this occasion it may not be improper to observe, that this part of Falstaff is said to have been written originally under the name of Oldcastle ; some of that family being then remaining, the Queen was pleas'd to command him to alter it ; upon which he made use of Falstaff. The present offence was indeed avoided ; but I don't know whether the author may not have been somewhat to blame in his second choice, since it is certain that Sir John Falstaff, who was a Knight of the Garter, and a lieutenant-general, was a name of distinguish'd merit in the wars in France in Henry the Fifth's and Henry the Sixth's times. What grace soever the Queen confer'd upon him, it was not to her only he ow'd the fortune which the reputation of his wit made. He had the honour to meet with many great and uncommon marks of favour and friendship from the Earl of Southampton, famous in the histories of that time for his friendship to the unfortunate Earl of Essex. It was to that noble lord that he dedicated his Venus and Adonis, the only piece of his poetry which he ever publish'd himself, tho' many of his plays were surrepticiously and lamely printed in his lifetime. There is one instance so singular in the magnificence of this patron of Shakespear's, that, if I had not been assur'd that the story was handed down by Sir William D'Avenant, who was probably very well acquainted with his affairs, I should not have ventur'd to have inserted ; that my Lord Southampton at one time gave him a thousand pounds to enable him to go through with a purchase which he heard he had a mind to. A bounty very great, and very rare at any time, and almost equal to that profuse generosity the present age has shewn to French dancers and Italian eunuchs.—What particular habitude or friendships he contracted with private men I have not been able to learn, more than that every one who had a true taste of merit, and could distinguish men, had generally a just value and esteem for him. His exceeding candor and good nature must certainly have inclin'd all the gentler part of the world to love him, as the power of his wit oblig'd the men of the most delicate knowledge and polite learning to admire him. Amongst these was the incomparable Mr. Edmond Spencer, who speaks of him, in his Tears of the Muses, not only with the praises due to a good poet, but even lamenting his absence with the tenderness of a friend. The passage is in Thalia's complaint for the decay of dramatick poetry, and the contempt the stage then lay under. —I know some people have been of opinion that Shakespear is not meant by Willy in the first stanza of these verses, because Spencer's death happen'd twenty years before Shakespear's. But, besides that the character is not applicable to any man of that time but himself, it is plain by the last stanza that Mr. Spencer does not mean that he was then really dead, but only that he had with-drawn himself from the publick, or at least with-held his hand from writing, out of a disgust he had taken at the then ill taste of the town, and the mean condition of the stage. Mr. Dryden was always of opinion these verses were meant of Shakespear, and 'tis highly probable they were so, since he was three and thirty years old at Spencer's death, and his reputation in poetry must have been great enough before that time to have deserv'd what is here said of him. His acquaintance with Ben Johnson began with a remarkable piece of humanity and good nature ;—Mr. Johnson, who was at that time altogether unknown to the world, had offer'd one of his plays to the players in order to have it acted; and the persons into whose hands it was put, after having turn'd it carelessly and superciliously over, were just upon returning it to him with an ill-natur'd answer that it would be of no service to their company, when Shakespear luckily cast his eye upon it, and found something so well in it as to engage him first to read it through, and afterwards to recommend Mr. Johnson and his writings to the publick. After this they were profess'd friends; tho' I don't know whether the other ever made him an equal return of gentleness and sincerity. Ben was naturally proud and insolent, and, in the days of his reputation, did so far take upon him the supremacy in wit, that he could not but look with an evil eye upon any one that seem'd to stand in competition with him. And if at times he has affected to commend him, it has always been with some reserve, insinuating his uncorrectness, a careless manner of writing, and want of judgment; the praise of seldom altering or blotting out what he writ, which was given him by the players who were the first publishers of his works after his death, was what Johnson could not bear; he thought it impossible, perhaps, for another man to strike out the greatest thoughts in the finest expression, and to reach those excellencies of poetry with the ease of a first imagination, which himself with infinite labour and study could but hardly attain to. Johnson was certainly a very good scholar, and in that had the advantage of Shakespear; tho' at the same time I believe it must be allow'd that what nature gave the latter was more than a ballance for what books had given the former; and the judgment of a great man upon this occasion was, I think, very just and proper. In a conversation between Sir John Suckling, Sir William D'Avenant, Endymion Porter, Mr. Hales of Eaton, and Ben Johnson; Sir John Suckling, who was a profess'd admirer of Shakespear, had undertaken his defence against Ben Johnson with some warmth; Mr. Hales, who had sat still for some time, hearing Ben frequently reproaching him with the want of learning and ignorance of the antients, told him at last that, " if Mr. Shakespear had not read the antients, he had likewise not stollen anything from 'em " (a fault the other made no conscience of);—and that, " if he would produce any one topick finely treated by any of them, he would undertake to shew something upon the same subject at least as well written by Shakespear." Johnson did indeed take a large liberty, even to the transcribing and translating of whole scenes together; and sometimes, with all deference to so great a name as his, not altogether for the advantage of the authors of whom he borrow'd. And if Augustus and Virgil were really what he has made 'em in a scene of his Poetaster, they are as odd an emperor and a poet as ever met. Shakespear, on the other hand, was beholding to no body farther than the foundation of the tale; the incidents were often his own, and the writing intirely so. There is one play of his, indeed, the Comedy of Errors, in a great measure taken from the Menœchmi of Plautus. How that happen'd I cannot easily divine, since I do not take him to have been master of Latin enough to read it in the original, and I know of no translation of Plautus so old as his time.—'Tis not very easie to determine which way of writing he was most excellent in. There is certainly a great deal of entertainment in his comical humours; and tho' they did not then strike at all ranks of people, as the satyr of the present age has taken the liberty to do, yet there is a pleasing and a well-distinguish'd variety in those characters which he thought fit to meddle with. Falstaff is allow'd by every body to be a master-piece; the character is always well-sustain'd, tho' drawn out into the length of three plays; and even the account of his death given by his old landlady Mrs. Quickly, in the first act of Henry V., tho' it be extremely natural, is yet as diverting as any part of his life. If there be any fault in the draught he has made of this lewd old fellow, it is that, tho' he has made him a thief, lying, cowardly, vainglorious, and in short every way vicious, yet he has given him so much wit as to make him almost too agreeable; and I don't know whether some people have not, in remembrance of the diversion he had formerly afforded 'em, been sorry to see his friend Hal use him so scurvily when he comes to the crown in the end of the second part of Henry the Fourth. Amongst other extravagances, in the Merry Wives of Windsor, he has made him a dear-stealer, that he might at the same time remember his Warwickshire prosecutor under the name of Justice Shallow; he has given him very near the same coat of arms which Dugdale, in his Antiquities of that county, describes for a family there, and makes the Welsh parson descant very pleasantly upon 'em.—Hamlet is founded on much the same tale with the Electra of Sophocles. In each of 'em a young prince is engag'd to revenge the death of his father, their mothers are equally guilty, are both concern'd in the murder of their husbands, and are afterwards married to the murderers. I cannot leave Hamlet without taking notice of the advantage with which we have seen this master-piece of Shakespear distinguish itself upon the stage by Mr. Betterton's fine performance of that part. A man who, tho' he had no other good qualities, as he has a great many, must have made his way into the esteem of all men of letters by this only excellency. No man is better acquainted with Shakespear's manner of expression, and indeed he has study'd him so well, and is so much a master of him that whatever part of his he performs, he does it as if it had been written on purpose for him, and that the author had exactly conceiv'd it as he plays it. I must own a particular obligation to him for the most considerable part of the passages relating to his life which I have here transmitted to the publick; his veneration for the memory of Shakespear having engag'd him to make a journey into Warwickshire on purpose to gather up what remains he could of a name for which he had so great a value.—The latter part of his life was spent, as all men of good sense will wish theirs may be, in ease, retirement, and the conversation of his friends. He had the good fortune to gather an estate equal to his occasion, and, in that, to his wish; and is said to have spent some years before his death at his native Stratford. His pleasurable wit and good nature engag'd him in the acquaintance, and entitled him to the friendship of the gentlemen of the neighbourhood. Amongst them it is a story almost still remember'd in that country, that he had a particular intimacy with Mr. Combe, an old gentleman noted thereabouts for his wealth and usury. It happen'd that, in a pleasant conversation amongst their common friends, Mr. Combe told Shakespear, in a laughing manner, that he fancy'd he intended to write his epitaph if he happen'd to out-live him, and since he could not know what might be said of him when he was dead, he desir'd it might be done immediately; upon which Shakespear gave him these four verses,—"Ten-in-the-Hundred lies here ingrav'd,=\'Tis a hundred to ten, his soul is not sav'd;=If any man ask, who lies in this tomb?=Oh! ho! quoth the Devil, 'tis my John-a-Combe."—But the sharpness of the satyr is said to have stung the man so severely that he never forgave it.—He dy'd in the 53d year of his age, and was bury'd on the north side of the chancel, in the great Church at Stratford, where a monument is plac'd in the wall. On his grave-stone underneath is,—"Good friend, for Jesus sake, forbear=To dig the dust inclosed here.=Blest be the man that spares these stones,=And curst be he that moves my bones."—He had three daughters, of which two liv'd to be marry'd; Judith, the elder, to one Mr. Thomas Quiney, by whom she had three sons, who all dy'd without children; and Susannah, who was his favourite, to Dr. John Hall, a physician of good reputation in that country. She left one child only, a daughter, who was marry'd first to Thomas Nash, esq., and afterwards to Sir John Bernard of Abbington, but dy'd likewise without issue. This is what I could learn of any note either relating to himself or family. The character of the man is best seen in his writings. But since Ben Johnson has made a sort of an essay towards it in his Discoveries, tho', as I have before hinted, he was not very cordial in his friendship, I will venture to give it in his words,—"I remember the players," &c.

PECUNIARY LITIGATION.

The following evidences of the Stratford Court of Record are the only existing ones of that tribunal which relate to proceedings in which Shakespeare was involved. The register of the Court being unfortunately imperfect, the only information which they yield respecting the poet is the negative fact that he did not appear as one of its litigants between 20 January, 1585, and 7 October, 1601.

I. *A Declaration filed by Shakespeare's Orders, in the year 1604, to recover the value of malt sold by him to a person of the name of Rogers. There is an obvious error in the first mention of the regnal year, and it should also be noticed that the word modios is incorrectly given in every instance in which it occurs in the original document.*

Stretford Burgus.—Phillipus Rogers sommonitus fuit per servientem ad clavam ibidem ad respondendum Willielmo Shexpere de placito quod reddat ei triginta et quinque solidos decem denarios quos ei debet et injuste detinet, et sunt plegii de prosequendo Johannes Doe et Ricardus Roe, etc., et unde idem Willielmus, per Willielmum Tetherton attornatum suum, dicit quod cum predictus Phillipus Rogers, vicesimo septimo die Marcii, anno regni domini nostri Jacobi regis, nunc Anglie, Francie et Hibernie, primo, et Scocie tricesimo-septimo, hic apud Stretford predictam, ac infra jurisdiccionem hujus curie, emisset de eodem Willielmo tres modios brasii pro sex solidis de predictis triginta et quinque solidis decem denariis ; ac etiam quod cum predictus Phillipus Rogers, decimo die Aprillis, anno regni dicti domini regis nunc Anglie, etc., secundo, hic apud Stretford predictam ac infra jurisdiccionem hujus curie, emisset de eodem Willielmo quatuor modios brasii pro octo solidis de predictis triginta et quinque solidis decem denariis ; ac etiam quod cum predictus Phillipus, vicesimo quarto die dicti Aprillis, anno regni dicti domini regis nunc Anglie, etc., secundo, hic apud Stretford predictam, infra jurisdiccionem hujus curie, emisset de eodem Willielmo alios tres modios brasii pro sex solidis de predictis triginta et quinque solidis decem denariis ; ac etiam quod cum predictus Phillipus, tercio die Maii anno regni dicti domini regis nunc Anglie, etc., secundo, hic apud Stretford predictam, ac infra jurisdiccionem hujus curie, emisset de eodem Willielmo alios quatuor modios brasii pro octo solidis de predictis triginta et quinque solidis decem denariis ; ac etiam quod cum predictus Phillipus, decimo-sexto die Maii, anno regni dicti domini regis nunc Anglie, etc., secundo, hic apud Stretford predictam, infra jurisdiccionem hujus curie, emisset de eodem Willielmo alios quatuor modios brasii pro octo solidis de predictis triginta et quinque solidis decem denariis ; ac etiam quod cum predictus Phillipus, tricesimo die Maii, anno regni dicti domini regis nunc Anglie, etc., secundo, hic apud Stretford predictam, ac infra jurisdiccionem hujus curie, emisset de eodem Willielmo duas modios brasii pro tres solidis decem denariis de predictis triginta et quinque solidis decem denariis ; ac etiam quod cum predictus Phillipus, vicesimo quinto die Junii, anno dicti domini regis nunc Anglie, etc., hic apud Stretford predictam, ac infra jurisdiccionem hujus curie, mutuatus fuisset duos solidos legalis monete, etc., de predictis triginta et quinque solidis decem denariis residuos, solvendos eidem Willielmo cum inde requisitus fuisset. Que omnia separales somme attingunt se in toto ad quadraginta et unum solidos decem denarios. Et predictus Phillipus Rogers de sex solidis inde eidem Willielmo postea satisfecisset. Predictus tamen Phillipus, licet sepius requisitus, predictos triginta et quinque solidos decem denarios residuos eidem Willielmo nondum reddidit, sed illos ei huc usque reddere contradixit et adhuc contradicit, unde dicit quod deterioratus est et dampnum habet ad valencian decem solidorum. Et inde producit sectam, etc.

II. *Orders and Papers in an Action brought by Shakespeare against John Addenbrooke, 1608-1609, for the Recovery of a Debt.*

i. Stratford Burgus.—Preceptum est servientibus ad clavam ibidem quod capiant, seu etc., Johannem Addenbrooke, generosum, si etc., et eum salvo etc., ita quod habeant corpus ejus coram ballivo burgi predicti, ad proximam curiam de recordo ibidem tenendam, ad respondendum Willielmo Shackspeare, generoso, de placito debiti, et habeant ibi tunc hoc preceptum. Teste Henrico Walker, generoso, ballivo ibidem, xvij. die Augusti, annis regni domini nostri Jacobi, Dei gratia regis Anglie, Francie et Hibernie, sexto, et Scotie quadragesimo.⑧ *Greene.*—Virtute istius precepti cepi infranominatum Johannem, cujus corpus paratum habeo prout interius mihi precipitur. Manucaptor pro defendente, Thomas Hornebye. Gilbertus Charnock, serviens.

ii. Stratford Burgus.—Preceptum est servientibus ad clavam ibidem quod habeant, seu etc., corpora Philippi Greene, Jacobi Elliottes, Edwardi Hunt, Roberti Wilson, Thome Kerby, Thome Bridges, Ricardi Collyns, Johannis Ingraham, Danielis Smyth, Willielmi Walker, Thome Mylls, Johannis Tubb, Ricardi Pincke, Johannis Smyth pannarii, Laurencii Holmes, Johannis Boyce, Hugonis Piggen, Johannis Samvell, Roberti Cawdry, Johannis Castle, Pauli Bartlett, Johannis Yeate, Thome Bradshowe, Johannis Gunne, juratorum summonitorum in curia domini regis hic tenta coram ballivo ibidem, ad faciendum quandam juratam patrie inter Willielmum Shackspeare, generosum, querentem, et Johannem Addenbrooke, defendentem, in placito debiti, et habeant ibi tunc hoc preceptum. Teste Francisco Smyth juniore, generoso, ballivo ibidem, xxj. die Decembris, annis regni domini nostri Jacobi, Dei gratia regis Anglie, Frauncie et Hibernie, sexto, et Scotie quadragesimo secundo. *Greene.*—Executio istius precepti patet in quodam panello huic precepto annexo. Gilbertus Charnock, serviens.

iii. Nomina juratorum inter Willielmum Shakespere, generosum, versus Johannem Addenbroke de placito debiti.—Philippus Greene ; Jacobus Elliott ; Edwardus Hunte ; Robertus Wilson ; Thomas Kerbye ; Thomas Bridges ; Ricardus Collins ; Johannes Ingraham ; Daniell Smyth ; Willielmus Walker ; Thomas Mills ; Johannes Tubb ; Ricardus Pincke ; Johannes Smyth, draper ; Laurencius Holmes ; Johannes Boyce ; Hugo Piggon ; Johannes Samwell ; Robertus Cawdry ; Johannes Castle ; Paulus Bartlett ; Johannes Yeate ; Thomas Bradshowe ; Johannes Gunne.—Quilibet jurator predictus, pro se separatim, manucaptus est per plegios, Johannem Doo et Ricardum Roo.

iv. Stratford Burgus.—Preceptum est servientibus ad clavam ibidem quod distringant, seu etc., Philippum Greene, Jacobum Elliottes, Edwardum Hunt, Robertum Wilson, Thomam Kerbey, Thomam Bridges, Ricardum Collins, Johannem Ingraham, Danielem Smyth, William Walker, Thomam Mylls, Johannem Tubb, Ricardum Pincke, Johannem Smyth, pannarium, Laurencium Holmes, Johannem Boyce, Hugonem Piggin, Johannem Samwell, Robertum Cawdry, Johannem Castle, Paulum Bartlett, Johannem Yate, Thomam Bradshawe, et Johannem Gunne, juratores summonitos in curia domini regis de recordo hic tenta inter Willielmum Shackspeare, querentem, et Johannem Addenbroke, defendentem, in placito debiti, per omnes terras et cattalla sua in balliva sua, ita quod nec ipsi nec aliquis per ipsos ad ea manum apponant, donec aliud inde a curia predicta habuerint preceptum, et quod de exitibus eorundem de curia predicta respondeant. Et quod habeant corpora eorum coram ballivo burgi predicti ad proximam curiam de recordo ibidem tenendam, ad faciendum juratam illam et ad audiendum judicium suum de pluribus defaltis ; et habeant ibi tunc hoc preceptum. Teste Francisco Smyth juniore, generoso, ballivo ibidem, xvº. die Februarii, annis regni domini nostri Jacobi, Dei gratia regis Anglie, Francie et Hibernie, sexto, et Scotie quadragesimo-secundo. *Greene.*—Executio istius precepti patet in quodam panello huic precepto annexo.—Franciscus Boyce, serviens.

v. Nomina juratorum inter Willielmum Shackspere, querentem, et Johannem Addenbrooke, de placito debiti.—Philippus Greene ; Jacobus Elliottes egrotat ; Edwardus Hunt ; Robertus Wilson, juratus ; Thomas Kerby ; Thomas Bridges ; Ricardus Collyns, juratus ; Johannes Ingraham, juratus ; Daniel Smyth, juratus ; Willielmus Walker, juratus ; Thomas Mills, juratus ; Johannes Tubb, juratus ; Ricardus Pincke, juratus ; Johannes Smyth, pannarius, juratus ; Laurencius Holmes ; Johannes Boyce ; Hugo Piggin, juratus ; Johannes Samvell ; Robertus Cawdrey, juratus ; Johannes Castle ; Paulus Bartlett ; Johannes Yate, juratus ; Thomas Bradshawe et Johannes Gunne. Quilibet juratorum predictorum, per se separatim, attachiatus est per plegios, Johannem Doo et Ricardum Roo. Exitus cujuslibet eorum per se, vj.*s.* viij.*d.* Juratores dicunt pro querente ; misas, iiij.*d.* ; dampna, ij.*d.*

vi. Stratford Burgus.—Preceptum est servientibus ad clavam ibidem quod capiant, seu etc., Johannem Addenbrooke, si etc., et eum salvo etc., ita quod habeant corpus ejus coram ballivo burgi predicti, ad proximam curiam de recordo ibidem tenendam, ad satisfaciendum Willielmo Shackspeare, generoso, tam de sex libris debiti quas predictus Willielmus in eadem curia versus eum recuperavit quam de viginti et quatuor solidis qui ei adjudicati fuerunt pro dampnis et custagiis .suis quos sustinuit occacione detencionis debiti predicti, et habeant ibi tunc hoc preceptum. Teste Francisco Smyth juniore, generoso, ballivo ibidem, xv. die Marcii, annis regni domini nostri Jacobi, Dei gracia regis Anglie, Francie et Hibernie sexto, et Scotie xlijº. *Greene.*— Infranominatus Johannes non est inventus infra libertatem hujus burgi. Franciscus Boyce, serviens.

vii. Stratford Burgus.—Preceptum est servientibus ad clavam ibidem quod cum quidam Willielmus Shackspeare, generosus, nuper in curia domini Jacobi, nunc regis Anglie, burgi predicti, ibidem tenta virtute literarum patentium domini Edwardi, nuper regis Anglie, sexti, levavit quandam querelam suam versus quendam Johannem Addenbrooke de placito debiti, cumque eciam quidam Thomas Horneby de burgo predicto in eadem querela devenit plegius et manucaptor predicti Johanne, scilicet, quod si predictus Johannes in querela illa legitimo modo convincaretur quod idem Johannes satisfaceret prefato Willielmo Shackspeare tam debitum in querela illa per prefatum Willielmum versus predictum Johannem in curia predicta recuperandum quam misas et custagia que eidem Willielmo in querela illa per eandem curiam adjudicata forent versus eundem Johannem, vel idem se redderet prisone dicti domini regis Jacobi nunc, burgi predicti, ad satisfaciendum eidem Willielmo eadem debitum misas et custagia ; et ulterius quod si idem Johannes non satisfaceret eidem Willielmo debitum et misas et custagia, nec se redderet predicte prisone dicti domini regis nunc ad satisfaciendum eidem Willielmo in forma predicta, quod tunc ipse idem Thomas Horneby debitum sic recuperandum et misas et custagia sic adjudicata eidem Willielmo satisfacere vellet. Cumque eciam in querela illa taliter processum fuit in eadem curia quod predictus Willielmus in loquela illa, per judicium ejusdem curie, recuperabat versus predictum Johannem tam sex libras de debito quam viginti et quatuor solidos pro decremento misarum et custagiorum ipsius Willielmi in secta querela illius apposito. Super quo preceptum fuit servientibus ad clavam ibidem quod capiant, seu etc., predictum Johannem, si etc., et eum salvo etc., ita quod habeant corpus ejus coram ballivo burgi predicti, ad proximam curiam de recordo ibidem tenendam, ad satisfaciendum predicto Willielmo de debito predicto sic recuperato, quam de viginti et quatuor solidis pro predictis dampnis et custagiis adjudicatis; unde Franciscus Boyle, tunc et nunc serviens ad clavam, ad diem retorni inde mandavit quod predictus Johannes non est inventus in balliva sua, unde idem Willielmus, ad predictam curiam dicti domini regis, supplicaverit sibi de remedio congruo versus predictum manucaptorem in hac parte provideri, super quod preceptum est servientibus ad clavam ibidem quod per probos et legales homines de burgo predicto scire faciant, seu etc., prefatum Thomam quod sit coram ballivo burgi predicti, ad proximam curiam de recordo in burgo predicto tenendam, ostensurus si quid et⑧ se habeat vel dicere sciat quare predictus Willielmus execucionem suam versus eundem Thomam de debito et misis et custagiis illis habere non debeat, juxta vim, formam et effectum manucapcionis predicti, si sibi viderit expedire, et ulterius facturus et recepturus quod predicta curia dicti domini regis consideret in ea parte, et habeant ibi tunc hoc preceptum. Teste Francisco Smyth juniore, generoso, ballivo ibidem, septimo die Junii, annis regni domini nostri Jacobi, Dei gracia regis Anglie, Francie et Hibernie, septimo, et Scotie xlij°. *Greene.*—Virtute istius precepti mihi directi per Johannem Hemynges et Gilbertum Chadwell, probos et legales homines burgi infrascripti, scire feci infranominatum Thomam Hornebye, prout interius mihi precipitur. Franciscus Boyce, serviens.

THEATRICAL EVIDENCES.

In this section will be found some of the most interesting contemporary notices of Shakespearean performances, as well as a few pieces of a later date which may be considered to include personal recollections of them during the poet's own time. Other allusions to early representations will be observed in the title-pages of the quartos, and in the extracts from the Stationers' Registers.

I. Notice of the Performance of the First Part of Henry the Sixth, from Nash's Pierce Penilesse, printed by Jeffes, 1592. This was a very popular work, two editions appearing in that year, and two more in the next.

How would it have joyed brave Talbot (the terror of the French) to thinke that, after he had lyen two hundred yeare in his toomb, he should triumph againe on the stage, and have his bones new embalmed with the teares of ten thousand spectators at least, at severall times, who, in the tragedian that represents his person, imagine they behold him fresh bleeding.

II. Satirical Verses upon a great Frequenter of the Curtain Theatre, from Marston's Scourge of Villanie, 1598, a work entered at Stationers' Hall on May 27th. The same lines, a few literal errors being corrected, are in the second edition of 1599.

Luscus, what's playd to day? faith, now I know ;＝I set thy lips abroach, from whence doth flow＝Naught but pure Juliat and Romio.＝Say, who acts best? Drusus or Roscio?＝Now I have him that nere of ought did speake,＝But when of playes or plaiers he did treate;＝H'ath made a common-place booke out of plaies,＝And speakes in print, at least what ere he sayes＝Is warranted by Curtaine plaudeties. ＝If ere you heard him courting Lesbias eyes,＝Say, curteous sir, speakes he not movingly＝From out some new pathetique tragedie?＝He writes, he railes, he jests, he courts,—what not?＝And all from out his huge long-scraped stock＝Of well penn'd playes.

III. From the Third Part of—Alba, the Months Minde of a Melancholy Lover, divided into three parts: By R. T. Gentleman.—At London. Printed by Felix Kyngston for Matthew Lownes. 1598,—a very small 8vo.

Loves Labor Lost, I once did see a play＝Ycleped so, so called to my paine,＝Which I to heare to my small joy did stay,＝Giving attendance on my froward dame ; ＝My misgiving minde presaging to me ill,＝Yet was I drawne to see it gainst my will.

This play no play but plague was unto me,＝For there I lost the love I liked most ; ＝And what to others seemde a jest to be,＝I that (in earnest) found unto my cost.＝ To every one (save me) twas comicall,＝Whilst tragick-like to me it did befall.

Each actor plaid in cunning wise his part,＝But chiefly those entrapt in Cupids snare ;＝Yet all was fained, twas not from the hart ;＝They seemde to grieve, but yet they felt no care ;＝Twas I that griefe (indeed) did beare in brest ;＝The others did but make a show in jest.

Yet neither faining theirs, nor my meere truth,＝Could make her once so much as for to smile ;＝Whilst she (despite of pitie milde and ruth)＝Did sit as skorning of my woes the while.＝Thus did she sit to see Love lose his Love,＝Like hardned rock that force nor power can move.

IV. An Extract from the Diary of John Manningham, a barrister of the Middle Temple, London, 1601-2 ; from the original in the British Museum, MS. Harl. 5353.

Febr : 1601.—2.—At our feast wee had a play called Twelve Night, or what you will, much like the Commedy of Errores, or Menechmi in Plautus, but most like and neere to that in Italian called Inganni. A good practise in it to make the steward beleeve his lady widdowe was in love with him, by counterfayting a letter as from his lady in generall termes, telling him what shee liked best in him, and prescribing his gesture in smiling, his apparaile, &c., and then, when he came to practise, making him beleeve they tooke him to be mad, &c.

V. Licence to Fletcher, Shakespeare, and others, to play comedies, &c., 17 May, 1603. Bill of Privy Signet ; endorsed, "The Players Priviledge." The King's Licence is given in the same terms in the Writ of Privy Seal dated on May the 18th, as well as in the Patent under the Great Seal issued on the following day.

By the King.—Right trusty and wel beloved Counsellour, we greete you well, and will and commaund you that, under our Privie Seale in your custody for the time being, you cause our lettres to be directed to the Keeper of our Greate Seale of England, comaunding him that under our said Greate Seale he cause our lettres to be made patentes in forme following.—James, by the grace of God King of England, Scotland, Fraunce and Irland, Defendor of the Faith, &c., to all justices, maiors, sheriffes, constables, hedboroughes, and other our officers and loving subjectes greeting. Know ye that we, of our speciall grace, certaine knowledge and meere motion, have licenced and authorized, and by these presentes doo licence and authorize, these our servantes, Lawrence Fletcher, William Shakespeare, Richard Burbage, Augustine Phillippes, John Henninges®, Henry Condell, William Sly, Robert Armyn, Richard Cowlye and the rest of their associates, freely to use and exercise the arte and facultie of playing comedies, tragedies, histories, enterludes, moralles, pastoralles, stage-plaies, and such other, like as they have already studied or heerafter shall use or studie, as well for the recreation of our loving subjectes as for our solace and pleasure when we shall thinke good to see them, during our pleasure. And the said comedies, tragedies, histories, enterludes, morall®, pastoralles, stage-plaies and such like, to shew and exercise publiquely to their best commoditie, when the infection of the plague shall decrease, as well within their now usuall howse called the Globe within our countie of Surrey, as also within any towne-halles or mout-halles, or other convenient places within the liberties ánd freedome of any other cittie, universitie, towne or borough whatsoever within our said realmes and dominions, willing and comaunding you and every of you, as you tender our pleasure, not only to permitt and suffer them heerin without any your lettes, hinderances, or molestacions during our said pleasure, but also to be ayding and assisting to them, yf any wrong be to them offered, and to allowe them such former courtesies as hath bene given to men of their place and qualitie. And also, what further favour you shall shew to these our servantes for our sake we shall take kindely at your handes. In witnes whereof &c. And these our lettres shall be your sufficient warrant and discharge in this behalf. Given under our Signet at our Mannor of Greenwiche the seavententh day of May in the first yeere of our raigne of England, Fraunce and Irland, and of Scotland the six and thirtieth.— Ex : per Lake.—To our right trusty and wel beloved Counsellour, the Lord Cecill of Esingdon, Keeper of our Privie Seale for the time being.

VI. A Letter, now preserved at Hatfield, from Sir Walter Cope, addressed—"from your library.—To the right honorable the Lorde Vycount Cranborne at the Courte." It is endorsed 1604, that is, 1604-5, the Queen having been entertained by Lord Southampton in the January of the latter year.

Sir,—I have sent and bene all thys morning huntyng for players juglers and such kinde of creaturs, but fynde them harde to fynde ; wherfore, leavinge notes for them to seeke me, Burbage ys come, and sayes ther ys no new playe that the Quene hath not seene, but they have revyved an olde one cawled *Loves Labore lost*, which for wytt and mirthe he sayes will please her excedingly. And thys ys apointed to be playd to-morowe night at my Lord of Sowthamptons, unless yow send a wrytt to remove the corpus cum causa to your howse in Strande. Burbage ys my messenger ready attendyng your pleasure.—Yours most humbly,—*Walter Cope.*

VII. In the play of the Return from Parnassus, written in the winter of 1601-2, but not printed till 1606, Burbage and Kemp are discovered instructing two Cambridge students, Philomusus and Studioso, in the histrionic art. Kemp has taught Philomusus a long speech, when Burbage thus addresses the latter.

Bur. I like your face and the proportion of your body for Richard the 3. I pray, M. Phil., let me see you act a little of it.

Phil. Now is the winter of our discontent
Made glorious summer by the sonne of Yorke.

Bur. Very well, I assure you. Well, M. Phil. and M. Stud., wee see what ability you are of. I pray, walke with us to our fellows and weele agree presently.

VIII. The Preface to the First Edition of Troilus and Cressida, 1609. It was most likely written, at the request of the publishers, by some well-known author of the day.

A never writer to an ever reader,—Newes.--Eternall reader, you have heere a new play, never stal'd with the stage, never clapper-clawd with the palmes of the vulger, and yet passing full of the palme comicall ; for it is a birth of your⑨ braine that never under-tooke any thing commicall vainely ; and were but the vaine names of commedies changde for the titles of commodities, or of playes for pleas, you should see all those grand censors, that now stile them such vanities, flock to them for the maine grace of their gravities ; especially this authors commedies, that are so fram'd to the life that they serve for the most common commentaries of all the actions of our lives ; shewing such a dexteritie and power of witte, that the most displeased with playes are pleasd with his commedies. And all such dull and heavy-witted worldlings as were never capable of the witte of a commedie, comming by report of them to his representations, have found that witte there that they never found in themselves, and have parted better-wittied then they came ; feeling an edge of wit e set upon them more then

F 2

Fac-simile of a Notice of Love's Labour Lost in the year 1605.

ever they dreamd they had braine to grinde it on.   So much and such savored salt of witte is in his commedies, that they seeme, for their height of pleasure to be borne in that sea that brought forth Venus.   Amongst all there is none more witty then this ; and had I time I would comment upon it, though I know it needs not, for so much as will make you thinke your testerne well bestowd, but for so much worth as even poore I know to be stuft in it.   It deserves such a labour as well as the best commedy in Terence or Plautus, and beleeve this, that when hee is gone, and his commedies out of sale, you will scramble for them, and set up a new English Inquisition.   Take this for a warning, and, at the perrill of your pleasures losse and judgements, refuse not, nor like this the lesse for not being sullied with the smoaky breath of the multitude ; but thanke fortune for the scape it hath made amongst you ; since, by the grand possessors wills, I beleeve you should have prayd for them℗ rather then beene prayd. And so I leave all such to bee prayd for (for the states of their wits healths) that will not praise it.— *Vale*

IX. From the original manuscript Journal of the Secretary to the German embassy to England in April, 1610.

Lundi, 30.—S. E. alla au Globe, lieu ordinaire ou l'on joue les commedies ; y fut représenté l'histoire du More de Venise.

X. In the Ashmole collection of manuscripts is a small folio pamphlet of fourteen leaves, nine of which are unwritten upon, but the remaining five contain,—" The Bocke of Plaies and Notes therof per Formans for common pollicie." This little tract, which

is in the autograph of the celebrated Dr. Simon Forman, consists of his accounts of the representations of four plays, three relating to dramas by Shakespeare and a fourth to one by another writer on the subject of Richard the Second. The former only are here given.

In the Winters Talle at the Glob, 1611, the 15 of Maye, Wednesday.—Observe ther howe Lyontes, the Kinge of Cicillia, was overcom with jelosy of his wife with the Kinge of Bohemia, his frind, that came to see him, and howe he contrived his death, and wold have had his cupberer to have poisoned, who⑤ gave the King of Bohemia warning therof and fled with him to Bohemia.—Remember also howe he sent to the orakell of Appollo, and the aunswer of Apollo that she was giltles, and that the king was jelouse, &c., and howe, except the child was found againe that was loste, the kinge shuld die without yssue; for the child was caried into Bohemia, and there laid in a forrest, and brought up by a sheppard, and the Kinge of Bohemia his sonn maried that wentch; and howe they fled into Cicillia to Leontes, and the sheppard, having showed the letter of the nobleman by whom Leontes sent a⑤ was that child, and the⑤ jewells found about her, she was knowen to be Leontes daughter and was then 16 yers old.—Remember also the rog that cam in all tottered like Coll Pipci, and howe he feyned him sicke and to have bin robbed of all that he had, and howe he cosoned the por man of all his money; and after cam to the shep-sher with a pedlers packe, and ther cosoned them again of all their money; and howe he changed apparrell with the Kinge of Bomia his sonn, and then howe he turned courtiar, &c.   Beware of trustinge feined beggars or fawninge fellouse.

Of Cimbalin King of England.—Remember also the storri of Cymbalin, King of England in Lucius tyme; howe Lucius cam from Octavus Cesar for tribut, and, being denied, after sent Lucius with a greate armi of souldiars, who landed at Milford Haven, and affter wer vanquished by Cimbalin, and Lucius taken prisoner; and all by means of three outlawes, of the which two of them were the sonns of Cimbalin, stolen from him when they were but two yers old by an old man whom Cymbalin banished, and he kept them as his own sonns twenty yers with him in a cave; and howe of⑤ of them slewe Clotan, that was the quens sonn, goinge to Milford Haven to sek the love of Innogen, the kinges daughter, whom he had banished also for lovinge his daughter; and howe the Italian that cam from her love conveied himself into a cheste, and said yt was a chest of plate sent from her love and others to be presented to the kinge; and in the deepest of the night, she being aslepe, he opened the cheste, and came forth of yt, and vewed her in her bed, and the markes of her body, and toke awai her braslet, and after accused her of adultery to her love, &c., and in thend howe he came with the Romains into England, and was taken prisoner, and after reveled to Innogen, who had turned herself into mans apparrell, and fled to mete her love at Milford Haven, and chanchsed to fall on the cave in the wodes wher her two brothers were; and howe, by eating a sleping dram, they thought she had bin deed, and laid her in the wodes, and the body of Cloten by her in her loves apparrell that he left behind him; and howe she was found by Lucius, etc.

In Mackbeth at the Glob, 1610, the 20 of Aprill, Saturday, ther was to be observed, firste, howe Mackbeth and Bancko, two noble men of Scotland, ridinge thorowe a wod, the⑤ stode before them three women feiries or nimphes, and saluted Mackbeth, sayinge three tyms unto him, Haille, Mackbeth, King of Codon; for thou shall be a kinge, but shall beget no kinges, etc.   Then said Bancko, what all to Mackbeth, and nothing to me?   Yes, said the nimphes, haille to thee, Banko, thou shall beget kinges, yet be no kinge; and so they departed and cam to the courte of Scotland to Dunkin, King of Scotes, and yt was in the dais of Edward the Confessor. And Dunkin bad them both kindly wellcom, and made Mackbeth forthwith Prince of Northumberland, and sent him hom to his own castell, and appointed Mackbeth to provid for him, for he wold sup with him the next dai at night, and did soe.   And Mackebeth contrived to kill Dunkin, and thorowe the persuasion of his wife did that night murder the kinge in his own castell, beinge his guest; and ther were many prodigies seen that night and the dai before.   And when Mack Beth had murdred the kinge, the blod on his handes could not be washed of by any means, nor from his wives handes, which handled the bluddi daggers in hiding them, by which means they became both moch amazed and affronted.   The murder being knowen, Dunkins two sonns fled, the on to England, the (other to) Walles, to save them selves.   They beinge fled, they were supposed guilty of the murder of their father, which was nothinge so. Then was Mackbeth crowned kinge; and then he, for feare of Banko, his old companion, that he should beget Kinges but be no kinge him self, he contrived the death of Banko, and caused him to be murdred on the way as he rode. The next night, beinge at supper with his noble men whom he had bid to a feaste, to the which also Banco should have com, he began to speake of noble Banco, and to wish that he wer ther. And as he thus did, standing up to drinck a carouse to him, the ghoste of Banco came and sate down in his cheier be-hind him. And he, turninge about to sit down again, sawe the goste of Banco, which fronted him so, that he fell into a great passion of fear and fury, utteringe many wordes about his murder, by which, when they hard that Banco was murdred, they suspected Mackbet. Then Mack Dove fled to England to the kinges sonn, and soe they raised an army and cam into Scotland, and at Dunstonanyse overthrue Mackbet. In the mean tyme, whille Macdove was in England, Mackbet slew Mackdoves wife and children, and after in the battelle Mackdove slewe Mackbet. Observe also howe Mackbetes quen did rise in the night in her slepe, and walke and talked and confessed all, and the docter noted her wordes.

XI. From the Accounts of moneys expended by Lord Stanhope, Treasurer of the Chamber, between Michaelmas, 1612, and Michaelmas, 1613, from the original manuscript in the Bodleian Library, Rawl. A. 239.

Item, paid to John Heminges uppon the Cowncells warrant dated att Whitehall xx.° die Maij, 1613, for presentinge before the Princes Highnes, the Lady Elizabeth and the Prince Pallatyne Elector, fowerteene severall playes, viz., one playe called Filaster, one other called the Knott of Fooles, one other Much adoe abowte nothinge, the Mayeds Tragedy, the merye dyvell of Edmonton, the Tempest, A kinge and no kinge, the Twins Tragedie, the Winters Tale, Sir John Falstafe, the Moore of Venice, the Nobleman, Cœsars Tragedye, and one other called Love lyes a bleedinge, all which playes weare played within the tyme of this accompte, viz., paid the some of iiij.ˣˣ xiij.*li.* vj.*s.* viij.*d.*

Item, paid to the said John Heminges uppon the lyke warrant, dated att Whitehall xx°. die Maij, 1613, for presentinge six severall playes, viz :, one playe called a badd beginininge⑤ makes a good endinge, one other called the Capteyne, one other the Alcumist, one other Cardenno, one other the Hotspurr, and one other called Benedicte and Betteris, all played within the tyme of this accompte, viz :, paid fortie powndes, and by waye of his Majesties rewarde twentie powndes. In all, lx.*li.*

XII. Extract from an account of a visit to Bosworth Field, given in an itinerary by Bishop Corbet, here taken from the edition in his Poems, ed. 1647. This pleasant narrative was written long before the date of publication, while the recollections of the host of the Leicester inn are obviously meant to extend to a period antecedent to the year 1619.

Mine host was full of ale and history, = And, on the morrow, when he brought us nigh = Where the two Roses joyned, you would suppose = Chaucer nere writ the Romant of the Rose. = Heare him,—See yee yond' woods? there Richard lay = With his whole army. Looke the other way, = And loe where Richmond in a bed of grosse⑤ = Encamp'd himselfe o're night with all his force. = Upon this hill they met. Why, he could tell = The inch where Richmond stood, where Richard fell; = Besides what of his knowledge he could say, = Hee had authentique notice from the play, = Which I might guesse by's mustring up the ghosts, = And policies not incident to hosts; = But chiefly by that one perspicuous thing = Where he mistooke a player for a king, = For when he would have said, King Richard dy'd, = And call'd a horse, a horse, he Burbage cry'd.

XIII. The commencement of an elegy—" On Mr. Richard Burbidg, an excellent both player and painter"—from a manuscript of the time of Charles I., preserved in the library of the Earl of Warwick.   The line given in Italics, wanting in that volume, is supplied from another copy.   This addition is necessary to the context, but otherwise the original is carefully followed, a single text in these cases being more authoritative than an eclectic one.   The first word of l. 17 is of course an error for oft, *and two various readings are worth special notice,—in l. 19* mad *for* sad, *and in l. 21* his *for* this.   *Five transcripts of the elegy, all of them in seventeenth-century manuscripts of undoubted genuineness, are known to exist, viz.—one at Warwick Castle, two at Thirlestane House, and two (one in octavo and one in folio) formerly belonging to Haslewood and now in the library of Mr. A. Huth.   The lines referring to Hamlet, Lear, and Othello, are found in all but one, the octavo Haslewood of these manuscripts, the solitary omission being no doubt accidental.   It must also be observed that the poem is termed in one of the Huth manuscripts,—" A Funerall Ellegye on the death of the famous actor, Richard Burbedg, who dyed on Saturday in Lent the 13 of March, 1618,"—and as it may fairly be assumed that so precise a title was derived from one that was given soon after the actor's death, the composition of the elegy may be assigned to the year 1619.*

Some skillful limmer aid mee ; if not so, = Som sad tragœdian helpe to express my wo ; = But, oh ! hee's gone, that could the best both limme = And act my greif ; and it is only him = That I invoke this strang assistance to it, = And on the point intreat himself to doe it ; = For none but Tully Tully's prais can tell, = And as hee could no man could doe so well = This part of sorrow for him, nor here shew = So truly to the life this mapp of woe, = That greifs true picture which his loss hath bred. = Hee's gone, and with him what a world is dead, = Which hee reviv'd ; to bee revived so = No more :—young Hamlet, old Hieronimo, = Kind Leir, the greived Moor, and more beside, = That livd in him, have now for ever died. = Ought⊛ have I seene him leape into the grave, = Suiting the person (that hee seemd to have) = Of a sad lover with so true an eie, = That then I would have sworn hee meant to die. = *Oft have I seene him play this part in jeast* = So lively, that spectators and the rest = Of his sad crew, whilst hee but seemd to bleed, = Amazed thought ev'n that hee died indeed. = And did not knowledg cheke mee, I should sweare = Even yet it is a fals report I heare, = And think that hee that did so truly faine = Is still but dead in jest, to live againe ; = But now hee acts this part, not plaies, tis knowne ; = Others hee plaid, but acted hath his owne.

XIV. Verses prefixed to—" Poems written by Wil. Shakespeare, gent.," a small octavo volume printed at London in 1640.   Leonard Digges, the author of these lines, was an Oxford scholar, whose earliest printed work appeared in the year 1617, and who died at that university in 1635.   The following poem was evidently written soon after the opening of the second Fortune Theatre in 1623, and it bears every appearance of having been intended for one of the Commendatory Verses prefixed to the first folio, perhaps that for which his shorter piece in that volume may have been substituted.   It is superscribed as being " upon Master William Shakespeare, the deceased authour, and his poems."

Poets are borne not made,—when I would prove = This truth, the glad rememberance I must love = Of never dying Shakespeare, who alone = Is argument enough to make that one. = First, that he was a poet none would doubt, = That heard th' applause of what he sees set out = Imprinted ; where thou hast—I will not say, = Reader, his Workes, for to contrive a play = To him twas none,—the patterne of all wit, = Art without Art unparaleld as yet. = Next Nature onely helpt him, for looke thorow = This whole booke, thou shalt find he doth not borrow = One phrase from Greekes, nor Latines imitate, = Nor once from vulgar languages translate, = Nor plagiari-like from others gleane;=Nor begges he from each witty friend a scene=To peece his Acts with;—all that he doth write,=Is pure his owne ; plot, language exquisite. =But oh ! what praise more powerfull can we give=The dead, then that by him the Kings Men live,=His players, which, should they but have shar'd the⑤ fate,=All else expir'd within the short termes date,=How could the Globe have prospered, since, through want=Of change, the plaies and poems had growne scant?=But, happy verse, thou shalt be sung and heard, =When hungry quills shall be such honour bard. =Then vanish, upstart writers to each stage,=You needy poetasters of this age ;=Where Shakespeare liv'd or spake, vermine, forbeare,=Least with your froth you spot them, come not neere ;=But if you needs must write, if poverty=So pinch, that otherwise you starve and die,=On Gods name may the Bull or Cockpit have=Your lame blancke verse, to keepe you from the grave :=Or let new Fortunes younger brethren see,=What they can picke from your leane industry. =I doe not wonder when you offer at=Blacke-Friers, that you suffer : tis the fate=Of richer veines, prime judgements that have far'd=The worse, with this deceased man compar'd. =So have I seene, when Cesar would appeare,=And on the stage at halfe-sword parley were,= Brutus and Cassius, oh how the audience=Were ravish'd ! with what wonder they went thence,=When some new day they would not brooke a line=Of tedious (though well laboured) Catiline ;=Sejanus too was irkesome ; they priz'de more=Honest Iago, or the jealous Moore.=And though the Fox and subtill Alchimist,=Long intermitted, could not quite be mist,=Though these have sham'd all the ancients, and might raise=Their authours merit with a crowne of bayes,=Yet these sometimes, even at a friends desire=Acted, have scarce defrai'd the seacoale fire=And doore-keepers : when,let but Falstaffe come,=Hall, Poines, the rest,—you scarce shall have a roome,=All is so pester'd : let but Beatrice=And Benedicke be seene, loe, in a trice=The cockpit, galleries, boxes, all are full=To hear Malvoglio, that crosse-garter'd gull. =Briefe, there is nothing in his wit-fraught booke,=Whose sound we would not heare, on whose worth looke,=Like old coynd gold, whose lines in every page=Shall passe true currant to succeeding age.=But why doe I dead Sheak-speares⑤ praise recite, =Some second Shakespeare must of Shakespeare write ;=For me tis needlesse, since an host of men=Will pay, to clap his praise, to free my pen.— *Leon. Digges.*

SHAKESPEARE'S NEIGHBOURS.

Few particulars have been discovered respecting the persons who resided in Shakespeare's immediate neighbourhood, and none at all of the terms on which he lived with them. Although it is known that he had a wide circle of acquaintances in his native town, it is by the merest accident that even the names of any of them have been recorded. Amongst the latter the only one of his neighbours was Julius Shaw, who, having been invited to witness the execution of the poet's will, may be reasonably assumed to have been a somewhat intimate friend. There is, however, an interest in what details can be given of the inhabitants and residences in the vicinity of New Place, and it will be afterwards observed that some of this information is of great value in the determination of the western boundaries of Shakespeare's gardens. In the case of Nash's House, its history is so inextricably connected with those boundaries that it has been continued to the present day; but it need scarcely be added that no similar prolixity has been necessary in other instances.

The name of Shakespeare's next-door neighbour in Chapel Street, the inhabitant of the tenement now, and as early as the year 1674, known as Nash's House, has not been ascertained. There was a building here at least as early as 37 Henry VIII., then mentioned as the tenement of William Phillips, and one Henry Norman seems to have resided in it in 1618, for in that year his name appears as contributing three shillings for its Church-rate. Thomas Nash, in his will dated August 25th, 1642, proved in 1647, devised to his wife Elizabeth, for her life, "all that messuage or tenemente with thappurtenaunces scituate, lyeinge and beinge in Stratford-uppon-Avon in the county of Warwicke, in a streete there called or knowen by the name of the Chappell Streete, and nowe in the tenure, use and occupacion of one Johane Norman, widowe;" and, after the death of the said Elizabeth, to his kinsman, Edward Nash, in fee. The house thus became the property of Shakespeare's grand-daughter from 1647 until her death in 1670, when it devolved upon the relative just mentioned. Edward Nash's will is dated in March, 1678, but, owing to the testator referring to, without quoting, a deed of settlement executed three days previously, there is no mention of the house, which must have been in some way settled upon his grand-daughter Jane, who afterwards married Franklyn Miller, of Hyde Hall, co. Hertford. This gentleman sold it to Hugh Clopton in May, 1699, when it was described as "all that messuage or tenement with the appurtenances scituate, lying and being, in the Chappell Street within the burrough of Stratford-upon-Avon, wherein Samuell Phillipps did late inhabitt, and now in the tenure of Edward Clopton, esq.," and, in the foot of the fine levied on the occasion, it is mentioned as being "one messuage and one garden with the appurtenances in Stratford-upon-Avon," Fin. Term. Trin. 11 Gul. III. It appears, however, from a declaration, made in the following October, that Hugh Clopton's name in the deed of 1699 was used in trust for his brother Edward, the latter continuing to be the occupier of the house until March, 1705–6, when 342 he sold it, together with the Great Garden of New Place, a piece of land then also in his occupation, to Aston Ingram, of Little Woolford, the husband of his sister Barbara. In the agreement for this purchase, dated in the preceding January, there is the following interesting description of the properties,—" all that messuage or tenement scituate and being in Stratford-upon-Avon, wherein the said Edward Clopton now dwells, togeather with the yard, garden, backside, outhouses and appurtenances to the same belongeinge, and alsoe the hangins that are in the chamber over the kitchin, the two furnises in the brewhouse, and the coolers there ; and alsoe all that peece of ground to the said messuage belongeing, called the Greate Garden, heretofore belongeing to New Place, and alsoe the barne, stables, outhouses and appurtenances to the said Greate Garden belongeing."

Aston Ingram, in his will, 1710, devises Nash's House to his wife Barbara in fee, subject to portions to younger children, which were subsequently paid by the sale of the house and the Great Garden. The latter is not specifically named in that will, but that it was included in the devise is certain from the wording of the release of his sons to their mother in March, 1728–9, who sold the premises in that year to Frances Rose of Stratford, the Great Garden being expressly excluded from the parcels conveyed to the latter. That piece of land had then been recently purchased by Hugh Clopton, and thenceforth restored to the New Place grounds. In 1738, the estate purchased by Rose was transferred to Philip Hatton, who devised it in 1740 to his wife Grace for her life, with remainders to his sons, Philip and Joseph, and to his son-in-law, Thomas Mortiboys, to be equally divided between the three. Joseph Hatton, by will dated shortly before his decease in 1745, devised his share of the property to his brother Philip ; and in July, 1760, the latter conveyed to Thomas Mortiboys his two undivided third parts, the whole, subject of course to Mrs. Hatton's life-interest, thus becoming the property of Thomas Mortiboys, who, by his will, dated in 1779, devised it to his daughter Susanna. This lady made a will, but it was not sufficient to pass real estate, as it merely disposed of personalty ; and, after her death, Nash's House descended to Fanny Mortiboys, who, in March, 1785, conveyed it to Charles Henry Hunt. In 1790, Mr. Hunt became also the owner of New Place, and, at some time prior to 1800, the boundaries of the Nash garden were removed, the two estates then becoming one property. In May, 1807, the whole was sold by him to Battersbee and Morris as tenants in common, but a few years afterwards the Great Garden again became a separate holding. In this new division, there was taken from the latter, to be added to the western premises, a slip of land, about twenty feet in width, which extended from Chapel Lane to the northern end of the garden belonging to Nash's House.

In 1827, the slip of land above mentioned and all the New Place estate that lay to the westward of it, together with Nash's House and garden, found their next purchaser in Miss Lucy Smith of Coventry, after whose death they were bought, in 1836, by Mr. David Rice. Upon the decease of the latter in 1860, they again came into the market, and, in the following year, they were purchased by me with moneys collected by public subscription, becoming then and for ever the property of the Corporation of Stratford-on-Avon. No representation of the original house is known to exist, but from existing remains of the upper outside part of its ancient southern end, it is seen that its roof was higher than that of Shakespeare's residence, its gable end overhanging the latter, and the purlines projecting about eleven or twelve inches from the face of the wall. From the appearance of the framing of the timbers, there is every reason to believe that this gable is in the same condition as when it was originally constructed. The front of the house has been twice rebuilt since the time of the great dramatist, and the interior has been greatly modernized, but the massive timbers, the immense chimneys and the principal gables at the back, are portions of the ancient building, and part of the original large opening of the chimney adjoining New Place can still be observed. The foundations appear to have been of sandstone, very similar in quality to that used in the construction of the Guild Chapel.

The house adjoining Nash's on the north side, now as formerly belonging to the Corporation of Stratford, is one of considerable interest, for here resided in Shakespeare's time, at the next house but one to New Place, Julius Shaw, one of the poet's testamentary witnesses in 1616. This house is mentioned in the time of Henry the Eighth as occupied by Thomas Fylle, a glover, and in 1591 it was held from the Corporation for a long term by Robert Gybbes, whose interests having been purchased by Shaw in 1597, a new lease was then granted to the latter for twenty-five years. "July Shawe holdeth one tenemente with a garden, yearly rent xij.*s*.," Rent Roll, January, 1597-8. The property is also described as a tenement and garden in a survey taken in 1582; more particularly in the same document in the following terms,—"a house, tenure of Robert Gybbes, sufficiently repayered save a lyttelle outt-house lackethe tyllying, and a pese of a baye is thatched which was tyled, but before hys tyme ;" and yet at greater length, as it appeared in the poet's days, in a survey of 1599, in which it is noted as "a tenemente in the strete ij. baies tiled, on the backside a barne of ij. baies, with either side a depe lentoo thatched; more inward, another crosse-backhouse of ij. baies thatched; betwene that and the stret house a range of j. baie thatch and ij. baies tiled, and a garden answerable in bredth to the house, in length as John Tomlins," that is, the same length as the garden of Tomlins, Shaw's next-door neighbour on the north.   The frontage and interior of these premises are now modernized, but nearly the whole of the outside walls at the back, and the main structure generally except the front, are of framed timber work apparently as old as Shakespeare's time, and in the straggling outhouses adjoining the residence lying on the southern side of the yard or garden is some more framed timber work supported by a stone basement.   The eastern terminus of this property is divided from the Great Garden of New Place by a substantial brick wall of considerable age, but one which is extremely unlikely to have formed the boundary in the days of Julius Shaw.

It appears from the vestry-book that Shaw contributed six shillings for his proportion of a church-rate levy on this house in 1617, eight shillings being paid at the same time by Mr. Hall for New Place.   It would seem from this circumstance that Shaw's house must have been a substantial residence, or there would have been a wider difference between the two amounts paid.   When the Corporation leased the premises to him in the year 1626, we are told that " the bredth thereof on the streete side is twenty-six foote ; item, the bredth thereof at the est end is thirtie ffoote ; item, the length thereof is nyne score ffoote." The existing dimensions are as follows,—street frontage, twenty-six feet ; length, one hundred and seventy-nine feet, three inches ; width at east end, twenty-four feet ; but the discrepancy of the few inches in the length may readily be accounted for by assuming that the shorter length was taken along the centre of the premises.   The difference in the width of the eastern limit is not so readily explained, but as the present measurement of the same boundary of the next house, also belonging to the town, is several feet in excess of the ancient computation, it may be assumed that at some period one garden received an augmentation from the other.   Fortunately, the question of length as to these premises is the only one of importance in the investigation of the boundaries of Shakespeare's Great Garden.

Julius Shaw, who was born in the year 1571, was the son of a wool-driver of Stratford-on-Avon, one Ralph Shaw, who died when Julius was about twenty years of age.   The latter continued his father's business,

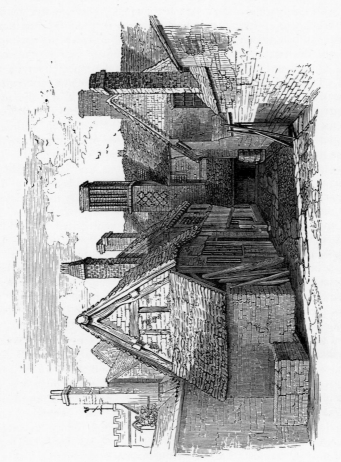

THE BACK OF JULIUS SHAW'S HOUSE, AS IT APPEARED IN THE YEAR 1862.

marrying Anne Boyes in 1594. His position in the following year is thus described—"Julye Shawe usethe the trades of buyinge and sellinge of woll and yorne, and malltinge, and hathe in howse xviij. quarter and halfe of mallte and x. quarters of barley, whereof xx. tie stryke of the mallte is Mr. Watkyns, Mr. Grevylls mans, and v. quarters of one Gylbardes of Reddytche, and the reste his owne; there are in howshold iij. persons," MS. Presentments, 1595. He is mentioned as holding seven quarters of corn at his house in Chapel-street in February, 1598, and like many other provincial tradesmen of the time, he appears to have been a kind of general dealer. At all events he is mentioned several times in the chamberlains' accounts as the seller of wood, tiles and other building materials, to the Corporation. He was elected a member of the Town Council in 1603, and acted as one of the chamberlains for 1610, an alderman in 1613 and bailiff in 1616. Having prospered in business, in the year last mentioned he purchased land from Anthony Nash for the then considerable sum of £180. He was re-elected bailiff in 1627, and died in June, 1629. He appears to have been much respected, his colleagues in 1613 speaking of " his honesty, fidelity" and their "good opinion of him," MS. Council Book.

Shaw's next-door neighbour on the northern side in 1599 was one John Tomlins, whose residence is thus described in a survey of that date,—"a tenemente in the strete-side ij. baies tiled, from the stret-house to the garden v. baies thatched, his garden in length about xvj. yerdes; in the old buildinge on Juli Shaues yarde there is a coller-poste broke, and silles wantinge, and an ill gutter; warninge must be geven for these defaultes, according to his lease." The dimensions of the garden, as here given, must be erroneous, for when the Corporation granted his widow a lease of the premises in 1619, a former one of 1608 to her being then surrendered, the following schedule is attached,— "Imprimis, the bredth therof one the streete syde is thirtie two foote; item, the bredth of the est end is thirtie foote; the length therof from the streete to the est end is eight score and seventeene foote." The same dimensions are given in the Corporation leases up to the year 1774, although, according to the plan attached to one of that date, the street frontage was thirty-two feet five inches, the length one hundred and eighty-five feet nine inches, and the width at the eastern boundary thirty-three feet four inches. These premises, which are mentioned in 1630 (MS. Orders, 2 April) as being then in a very dilapidated state, were leased in 1646 to Henry Tomlins, who covenanted to refront the house within six years, that is, before 1652, to about which period, and not to the Shakespearean, the modernized but still antiquated face of the present structure must be referred. Some of the main features, such as the overhanging upper storey and the covered passage, may have been reproduced, but little, if any, of the original work of the sixteenth

It may be fairly assumed that Julius Shaw was one of the poet's most intimate Warwickshire friends, for otherwise his name would hardly have been found next to that of the solicitor in the attesting clause of the will. His autograph and seal, here engraved, are attached to the counter-part of the lease of 1597, in which the "bailiffe and burgesses, in consideracion of and for the somme of seaven poundes of good and lawfull money of Englonde by the seide Julianus Shawe well and trulye contented and paide, demysed, graunted, sett and to farme lett unto the seide Julinus Shawe, all that tenemente with thappertenaunces scituate and beinge in a streete called the Chappell Streete, late in the tenure of one Robert Gybbes . . . . —in witnes whereof to thone parte of this indenture remayninge with he, the seide Julinus Shawe, the seide bailiffe and burgesses have putt their common seale, and to thother parte of the same indenture, remayninge with the seide bayliffe and burgesses, the seide Julinus Shawe hathe putt his seale the daye and yeare firste above written. — *Julyles Shawe.* Selyd and delyvered in the presence of Abraham Sturley, bayliffe, Thomas Barber, principall alderman, John Jeffereys, stuard there, William Wilson, Thomas Rogers, Henry Wylson, Richard Quyney, John Smythe, et aliorum." Shaw penned his baptismal name in a great variety of uncouth forms, but he had nevertheless the advantage of his immediate neighbour, Henry Norman, who was unable to write at all.

century is now to be traced. This house was long erroneously considered to have formerly been the residence of Julius Shaw.

The next house towards the north is described in 1620 as a "tenement and garden in the occupaccion of George Perrye." In 1647 it belonged to one Richard Lane, who, in the April of that year, sold it to "Thomas Hathway of Stratford-uppon-Avon joyner," under the title of "all that messuage or tenement, backside and garden, in Stratford aforesaide, in a streete there called the Chappell Streete." It was then in the occupation of this Thomas Hathaway, the same person who is mentioned in Lady Barnard's will as her kinsman, and who was therefore connected with the Shakespeare family. He died in January, 1654-5, when the premises became the property of his widow, Jane Hathaway, who, in 1691, was presented at the sessions "for not repaireing the ground before her house in Chappell Street." This lady continued to reside in the house until the time of her death in October, 1696, but some years previously, namely in September, 1692, her grand-daughter Susannah sold the reversion in fee accruing to her on Jane's death to Richard Wilson of Cripplegate, London, who, in May, 1698, conveyed the estate to Edward Clopton in a deed in which it is described as "all that messuage or tenement with the appurtenances thereunto belonging, situate and being in the Chappell Street in the said borough of Stratford-upon-Avon, being late the messuage or tenement of one Jane Hathaway, widow, and lyes between a messuage or tenement of one Richard Holmes on the north part, and a messuage or tenement late of one William Baker, gentleman, deceased, on the south part." These premises, afterwards known by the sign of the Castle, were rebuilt by Edward Clopton, and now contain no vestiges of the architectural work of the Shakespearean period.

The determination of the western boundaries of the New Place estate has been alone rendered possible by a careful enquiry into the measures of the spaces occupied by the properties above described. Although the boundary marks of the garden formerly attached to Nash's House have long been removed, their positions can be ascertained with nearly mathematical exactitude. That Shakespeare's garden was originally, as it is now, contiguous to the eastern limits of the other properties, is shown decisively by the terms of a nearly contemporary lease of the third house from New Place; and, as those premises have belonged to the Corporation from the sixteenth century to the present time, it is all but impossible that their boundaries should have been changed without a record of the fact having been made. No evidence of any such alteration is to be discovered amongst the town muniments. The lease referred to was granted to Mary Tomlins in 1619, the house being therein described as,—"all that messuage or tenement and garden with thappurtenances wheerin the said Marye now dwelleth, scittuate and beinge in Stratford aforesaide in a certaine place or streete there called Chappell Streete, betweene the tenement and garden of the saide Bayliffe and Burgesses in the occupaccion of Julyus Shawe one the south parte, the tenement and garden in the occupaccion of George Perrye one the north parte, *the garden or orchard of Mr. John Hall one thest parte,* and the saide streete one the west." Another testimony to the same effect occurs in the conveyance of the house and garden in Chapel Street from Richard Lane to Thomas Hathaway in 1647, in which the property sold is described as consisting of, "all that messuag or tenement, with the backside and garden, and all other thappurtenaunces thereunto belonging, scittuate, lyeing and being in Stratford aforesaide, in a street there called the Chappell Streete, betweene the dwelling howse of John Loach on the north side, and the howse of Henry Tomlins on the south, *the land of Mrs. Hall on the east,* and the said streete on the west partes thereof, and now in the occupaccion of the said Thomas Hathway."

Opposite to New Place, on the south-west end of Chapel Street and at the corner of Scholar's Lane, was, in Shakespeare's time, a private residence, which was afterwards, some time between the years 1645 and 1668, converted into a tavern distinguished by the sign of the Falcon. At the last-mentioned date, it was kept by one Joseph Phillips, who issued a token in that year, the sign, a falcon, being in the centre. It

was probably this individual who first used the house as an inn, and the sign, there can hardly be a doubt, was adopted in reference to Shakespeare's crest, even if it be a mere conjecture that the landlord was descended from William Phillips, the maternal grandfather of Thomas Quiney, and in that way remotely connected with the poet's family. The most ancient title-deed yet discovered which refers to this house is dated in 1640, and the premises are therein described as consisting of a house and garden "latelie in the tenure, use and holdinge of Mrs. Katherine Temple, and nowe in the use and occupation of Joseph Boles, gent." It was then evidently a private house, and it is similarly described in a deed of 1645. In 1681 it is mentioned as "all that messuage or tennement with the apurtenances called by the name of the Falcon;" in 1685, as "comonly called by the name of the Falcon house;" and in 1687, as " all that messuage, or tenement, or inne, comonly called or knowne by the name of the Falcon, scituate and beinge in a certaine street there comonly called or knowne by the name of the Chappell Street, and now in the occupacion of Joseph Phillips." The Falcon has been twice modernized within the last hundred years, and no reliable representation of it in its original state is known to be preserved. The view given by Ireland in 1795, with lattice-windows on the ground floor, is at all events inaccurate, if not chiefly fanciful, and the same observation will apply to engravings of the ancient tavern in more recent works. That writer speaks of the house as " built of upright oak timbers with plaister," and there is no doubt, from the structural indications visible even in its present altered condition, that it was originally a post-and-pan edifice of three stories, the fronts of the two upper ones overhanging the ground-floor rooms. Ireland adds the unfounded statements that it was kept, in Shakespeare's days, by Julius Shaw, and that the poet, passing much time there, had "a strong partiality for the landlord, as well as for his liquor," Views on the Warwickshire Avon, 1795, p. 204. It may be just worth mentioning that there is still preserved a shovel-board table, sixteen feet and a half in length, which is asserted to have belonged to the Falcon Inn in olden times, and at which Shakespeare is said to have often played. That the table came from the Falcon there is no doubt, but as to its implied age there is much uncertainty, while the tradition connecting it with the poet is unquestionably a modern fabrication.

THE HISTORY OF NEW PLACE.

There is a vellum roll, which was written in the year 1483, in which a tenement at Stratford-upon-Avon is described as being *juxta Capellam modo Hugonis Clopton generosi;* but the earliest distinct notice of the large house in that town, situated at the corner of Chapel Street and Chapel Lane, generally referred to in the old records as the New Place, the term *place* being used in old English in the sense of residence or mansion, occurs in the will of Sir Hugh Clopton, an eminent citizen and mercer of London in the fifteenth century. In that document, which was proved in October, 1496, very shortly after the testator's death, the building is devised in the following terms,—"to William Clopton I bequeith my grete house in Stratford-upon-Avon, and all other my landes and tenementes being in Wilmecote, in the Brigge Towne and Stratford, with reversion and servyces and duetes thereunto belonginge, remayne to my cousin William Clopton, and, for lak of issue of hym, to remayne to the right heires of the lordship of Clopton for ever being heires mailes." That the "grete house" refers to New Place clearly appears from the inquisition upon Sir Hugh Clopton's death, taken at Stratford-upon-Avon in 1497, in which he is described as being seized "de uno burgagio jacente in Chapell Strete in Stretforde predicta *ex oposito Capelle ex parte boriali.*" Sir Hugh had previously granted a life-interest in the estate to one Roger Paget, in whose posses-sion it was vested in 1496. The William Clopton, to whom the rever-sion in fee was bequeathed in the same year, was the son of John, and the grandson of Thomas, the brother of Sir Hugh. Livery of seizin in respect to New Place was granted to him in July, 1504, probably after the death of Paget ; Rot. Pat. 19 Hen. VII. He died in 1521, leaving a will in which he bequeathed all his lands and tenements in Stratford-upon-Avon to his wife Rose for her life, and in the inquisition taken on his death, held in September, 1521, he was found to be possessed of one tenement in Chapel Street situated to the north of the Chapel of the Guild,—"necnon de et in uno burgagio jacente in strata vocata Chapel Strete in Stratford-super-Avene ex parte boriali Capelle Sancte Trinitatis in Stratford predicta," Inq. 13 Henry VIII. In the same will he leaves "all such maners, londes, and tenementis, which were sumtyme of thenheritance of myne auncettours havyng the name and names of Clopton, to those of the heirez males of my body commyng, and for defaulte of suche heire male of my body comyng, to the use of the heires malez of my said auncettours of the name of the Cloptones, accordyng to the old estates of intaylez and willis hertofore therof had, made and declared by my said auncettours, or any of theym." This devise seems to include New Place, otherwise there would be no provision for its descent after the death of Rose in 1525, when it became the property of William Clopton, son of the above-named William. It is alluded to as his freehold estate in an inquisition taken on his death in 1560, and as then consisting of one tenement with the appurtenances in Chapel Street in the tenure of William Bott,—Escheat. 2 Eliz.

Leland, who visited Stratford-upon-Avon about the year 1540, describes New Place as an elegant house built of brick and timber. His words are,—"there is a right goodly chappell, in a fayre street towardes the south ende of the towne, dedicated to the Trinitye; this chappell was newly re-edified by one Hugh Clopton, major of London; this Hugh Clopton builded also by the north syde of this chappell a praty house of bricke and tymbre, wherin he lived in his latter dayes and dyed." Leland perhaps means that upright and cross pieces of timber were used in the construction of the house, the intervening spaces being filled in with brick. This writer appears, however, to have been misinformed when he made the statement that Sir Hugh resided at New Place in the latter part of his life, and that he died there. It seems evident, from his remains having been interred at St. Margaret's in Lothbury, as recorded by Stow, that he died in London, for he expressly stipulates in his will that, if Stratford was the place of his death, he should be buried in that town. New Place, as previously mentioned, was not even in Sir Hugh's possession at that period, it having been sold or given by him to one Roger Paget for the life of the latter; so that, in fact, the house did not revert to the Cloptons until after the death of that tenant. It may be doubted if any members of the Clopton family lived there in the sixteenth century, for they are generally spoken of as residing at Clopton, and in no record of that period yet discovered is there any evidence that they were inhabitants of Stratford. In November, 1543, William Clopton let New Place on lease for a term of forty years to Dr. Thomas Bentley, who had been more than once President of the College of Physicians in its very early days, the Doctor paying for the house, including some lands in the neighbourhood, a yearly rent of ten pounds. Some time afterwards this lease was surrendered, and a new one granted at the same rental to continue in force during the lives of Dr. Bentley and his wife Anne, or during her widowhood should she survive her husband. Dr. Bentley died in or about the year 1549, leaving New Place *in great ruyne and decay and unrepayryd*. His widow married one Richard Charnocke, and the lease by this event being forfeited, Clopton entered into possession of the premises, a circumstance which was the occasion of a law-suit, the result of which is not stated, but there can be little doubt that it terminated in some way in favour of the defendant, who devised his estates at Stratford-upon-Avon to his son, William Clopton, in 1560. This bequest was encumbered with a number of heavy legacies, in consequence of which the testator's son was compelled to part with some of the estates, which he did in 1563 to one William Bott, who had previously resided at New Place and in that year became its owner. It may be assumed that the latter was living there in 1564, when his name occurs in the Council-book of Stratford as contributing more than any one else in the town to the relief of the poor. His transactions with Clopton were mysterious and extensive, but there is no good reason for a supposition that New Place was obtained in other than an honourable manner. Clopton's embarrassments appear to have arisen from his father burdening his estates with legacies of unusual magnitude, hence arising the necessity for a recourse to a friendly capitalist.

During the time that Bott was in possession of New Place he brought an action of trespass against Richard Sponer, accusing the latter of entering into a close in Chapel Lane belonging to Bott called the *barne yarde nigh le New Place gardyn*, and taking thence by force twelve pieces of squared timber of the estimated value of fourty shillings. This act is stated to have been committed on June 18th, 1565, and the spot referred to was clearly an enclosed space of ground in which stood a barn belonging to New Place, a little way down Chapel Lane next to the garden of that house. Sponer was a painter living at that time in Chapel Street in the third house from New Place and on the same side of the way, a fact which appears from a lease granted by the Corporation on May 28th, 1563, to "Rychard Sponer of Stratford peynter" of "a tenement wyth appurtenaunces scytuate and beinge in the borrough of Stratford aforseid, in a strete there callyd the Chapell Strete, nowe in the tenure and occupacion of the seid Richard, and also a gardyn and bacsyde adjoynynge to the seid tenemente now lykwyse in the tenure and occupacion of the seid Richard." It appears from an endorsement that the house was the same which was afterwards held by Tomlins, the garden of which extended to the western side of what was afterwards the Great Garden of New Place. "John Tomlins holdeth one tenemente with thappurtenaunces late in the tenure of Richard Sponer," Rent-roll, January, 1597-8. Now, in all probability, the timber was taken by Sponer from a spot close to his own garden, the division between the premises being in those days either a hedge or a mud-wall, not a fence of a nature which would have rendered the achievement a difficult one. In his defence he admits having taken away six pieces of timber, but asserts that the plaintiff had presented the same to one Francis Bott, who had sold them to the defendant. This statement is declared by William Bott to be false, but it is reiterated by Sponer in the subsequent proceedings. The result of the action is not recorded, but it was settled, probably by compromise, at the close of the year. Several papers respecting this suit have been preserved, but the only one of interest in connexion with New Place is the following plea which Bott filed against Sponer on September 12th, 1565,—"Willielmus Bott queritur versus Ricardum Sponer de placito transgressionis, et sunt plegii de prosequendo, videlicet, Johannes Doo et Ricardus Roo, unde idem Willielmus, per Jacobum Woodward, attornatum suum, dicit quod predictus Ricardus, xviij. die Junii, anno regni domine Elizabethe Dei gracia Anglie Francie et Hibernie regine, fidei defensoris, etc., septimo, vi et armis, etc., clausum ipsius Willielmi Bott vocatum *le barne yarde*, jacens et existens in Stretford predicta juxta *le newe place gardyn*, in quodam⊛ venella vocata Dede Lane apud Stretford predictam, infra jurisdiccionem hujus curie, fregit et intravit, et duodecim pecias de meremiis vocatas *xij. peces of tymber squaryd and sawed* precii quadraginta solidorum, de bonis cattallis⊛ ipsius Willielmi Bott adtunc et ibidem inventas, cepit et asportavit, unde idem Willielmus dicit quod deterioratus est et dampnum habet ad valenciam centum solidorum, et unde producit sectam, etc." The first mention of there being a garden attached to New Place occurs in this document; but there could not have been a very large one belonging to the house during the early part of the century, for a portion, if not the whole, of what was afterwards called the Great Garden belonged to the Priory of Pinley up to the year 1544. In deeds of 12 and 21 Henry VI., the Clifford Charity estate is described as adjoining the *land* of the Prioress of Pinley; but, in 12 Edward IV., that term is changed into *tenement*,—"inter tenementum Abbathie de Redyng ex parte una et tenementum priorisse de Pynley, nunc in tenura Johannis Gylbert, ex parte altera." From this period until some time after 1544, the probability is that there were a cottage and garden between New Place and the Clifford estate. As to the exact period when the cottage was pulled down, and its site with the garden attached to New Place, it would be in vain now to conjecture.

In July, 1567, the New Place estate was sold by William Bott and others to William Underhill for the sum of £40, being then described as consisting of one messuage and one garden; and in a return to a commission issued out of the Exchequer for the survey of the possessions of Ambrose earl of Warwick, made in 1590, it is stated that "Willielmus Underhill generosus" held in fee a house called *the Newe Place* with its appurtenances at an annual court-rent of twelve-pence. The estate continued in the hands of the Underhill family until the year 1597, when it was purchased by Shakespeare, being then described as consisting of one messuage, two barns, and two gardens. The following is a copy of the foot of the fine levied on this occasion,—"Inter Willielmum Shakespeare, querentem, et Willielmum Underhill, generosum, deforciantem, de uno mesuagio, duobus horreis, et duobus gardinis, cum pertinenciis, in Stratford-super-Avon, unde placitum convencionis summonitum fuit inter eos in eadem curia, Scilicet quod predictus Willielmus Underhill recognovit predicta tenementa cum pertinenciis esse jus ipsius Willielmi Shakespeare, ut illa que idem Willielmus habet de dono predicti Willielmi Underhill, et illa remisit et quietumclamavit de se et heredibus suis predicto Willielmo Shakespeare et heredibus suis imperpetuum ; et preterea idem Willielmus Underhill concessit, pro se et heredibus suis, quod ipsi warantizabunt predicto Willielmo Shakespeare et heredibus suis predicta tenementa cum pertinenciis imperpetuum ; et pro hac recognicione, remissione, quieta clamancia, warantia, fine et concordia idem Willielmus Shakespeare dedit predicto Willielmo Underhill sexaginta libras sterlingorum," Pasch. 39 Eliz. A facsimile of the exemplification of this fine, that which was held by Shakespeare with his title-deeds, is here given. Another one was levied on New Place in 1602, for the same property is unquestionably referred to, notwithstanding the addition of the words, *et duobus pomariis*, in the foot of the fine,—"Inter Willielmum Shakespeare, generosum, querentem, et Herculem Underhill, generosum, deforciantem, de uno mesuagio, duobus horreis, duobus gardinis, et duobus pomariis cum pertinenciis, in Stretford-super-Avon ; unde placitum convencionis summonitum fuit inter eos in eadem curia, Scilicet quod predictus Hercules recognovit predicta tenementa cum pertinenciis esse jus ipsius Willielmi, ut illa que idem Willielmus habet de dono predicti Herculis, et illa remisit et quietumclamavit de se et heredibus suis predicto Willielmo et heredibus suis imperpetuum ; et preterea idem Hercules concessit, pro se et heredibus suis, quod ipsi warantizabunt predicto Willielmo et heredibus suis predicta tenementa cum pertinenciis contra predictum Herculem et heredes suos imperpetuum ; et pro hac recognicione, remissione, quieta clamancia, warantia, fine et concordia idem Willielmus dedit predicto Herculi sexaginta libras sterlingorum," Mich. 44 & 45 Eliz. In the absence of the deed which would explain the object of this fine, it can only be conjectured that, after Shakespeare had bought New Place, it was discovered that Hercules Underhill had some contingent interest in the property which was conveyed to the poet by this second transaction.

There is evidence, in the list of corn and malt owners, dated a few months after Shakespeare's purchase of New Place, that he was then the occupier of that residence, and there is no doubt that it continued to be in his possession until his death in 1616. In the latter year he devised "all that capitall messuage or tenemente, with thappurtenaunces, called the Newe Place, wherein I nowe dwell," to his daughter Susanna Hall for life, remainders to her male issue in strict entail, remainder to his grand-daughter, Elizabeth Hall, then a little girl of eight years of age, and her male issue, remainder to his daughter Judith and her male issue,

THE EXEMPLIFICATION OF THE FINE THAT WAS LEVIED WHEN SHAKESPEARE

PURCHASED THE ESTATE OF NEW PLACE FROM UNDERHILL IN THE YEAR 1597.

remainder to the testator's own heirs for ever.   No further dealings with the estate took place until the early part of the year 1639, when, on the death of the two surviving sons of Judith Quiney, that lady herself being then fifty-four years of age, the poet's devise of remainders to her children was accepted as void.   Within a few weeks after this unexpected occurrence, Susanna Hall joined with Mr. and Mrs. Nash in making a new settlement of the Shakespeare entails.   Under a deed of May 27th, 1639, New Place and the other settled estates were confirmed "to the onelie use and behoofe of the said Susan Hall for and during the terme of her naturall life, and after her decease to the use and behoofe of the said Thomas Nash and Elizabeth his wife for and during the terme of their naturall lives, and the life of the longest liver of them, and after their deceases, to the use and behoofe of the heires of the bodies of the said Thomas Nash and Elizabeth his wife betweene them lawfullie begotten or to bee begotten, and for default of such issue, to the use and behoofe of the heires of the bodie of the said Elizabeth lawfullie begotten or to bee begotten, and, for default of such issue, to the use and behoofe of the said Thomas Nash and of his heires and assignes for ever, and to none other use or uses, intent or purpose whatsoever."   The estate tail and remainders appear to have been barred by this settlement, the fine and recovery under it having been duly enrolled in the latter part of the same year.

In the month of July, 1643, New Place was the temporary residence of Queen Henrietta Maria in the course of her triumphant march from Newark to Keinton.   This fact, which there is no reason to dispute, rests upon a tradition told by Sir Hugh Clopton to Theobald early in the last century, and the anecdote exhibits a continuation in the family of the sincere loyalty which the favours of previous sovereigns must have riveted to the poet's own affections.   According to the last-named editor the Queen "kept her Court for three weeks in New Place," preface to his edition of Shakespeare, ed. 1733, p. xiv.   She was, however, at Stratford only three days, arriving there on July 11th with upwards of two thousand foot and a thousand horse, about a hundred waggons, and a train of artillery.   This was a memorable day for Stratford, for here the Queen was met by Prince Rupert at the head of another body of troops, the most stirring event of the kind the ancient town has ever witnessed.   The Corporation bore at least some of the expense of entertaining Henrietta, who left Stratford on the 13th of the same month, meeting the King in the vale of Keinton, near the site of the battle of Edgehill.

The entertainment of the royal visitor at New Place may be fairly considered a testimony to the local importance that was attached to the mansion ; and some indication of its powers of accommodation may be seen in a hearth-tax return made in the year 1663, preserved amongst

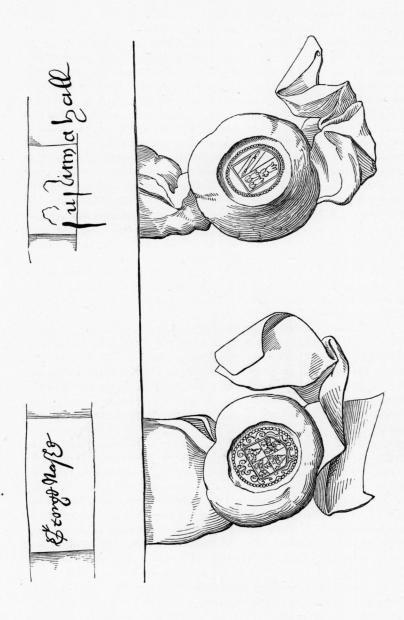

the county manuscripts at Warwick, from which it appears that there were at that time no fewer than ten fire-places of one kind or other in the building.   The number of apartments was no doubt greatly in excess of that of the hearths, it being all but impossible that a house, originally erected in the fifteenth century, could have been furnished with such luxuries throughout its whole extent ; and when it is borne in mind that it had a frontage of more than sixty feet, while its breadth in some parts was at least seventy, and its height over twenty-eight feet, there is no difficulty in assuming that, in those days of low ceilings, Mrs. Hall and the Nashes were perfectly at their ease, so far as space was concerned, in their reception of the Queen and her personal attendants.   The elevation of the building at the northern end,—twenty-eight feet two inches above the level of the ground-floor,—is ascertained by the still visible traces of the gable in the places where it rested against what was formerly the extreme southern wall of Nash's House.   The upper part and some of

the foundations of that wall are all of it that now exist, the intervening portions having been removed when the dwelling was enlarged at the time of the erection of the second New Place in 1702.   That the upper and lower walls *a—a*, the situations of which are indicated in the annexed plans, originally belonged to one and the same piece of work-manship, is proved by a vertical line dropped from *x—x* on the attic story falling to *x—x* in the basement; and this fact, viewed in connexion with the position of the older gable, distinctly shows that the outer line, *a—a*, was contiguous to the poet's estate, raising also a high probability that the old work, *c—c,* is another relic of its ancient boundary.

The dotted lines in the annexed section exhibit the manner in which the northern gable-end of the Poet's mansion rested against the higher southern wall of Nash's House. That wall was no doubt a subsequent erection that was constructed to adjoin, at all

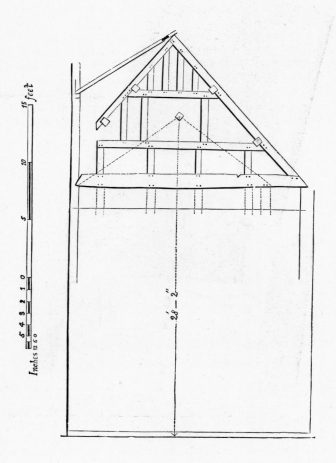

events in the upper story, the neighbouring building, for in it is still imbedded (at the top of the lower gable) a scantlet of the New Place ridge that the demolishers found it easier or more desirable to leave than to remove.

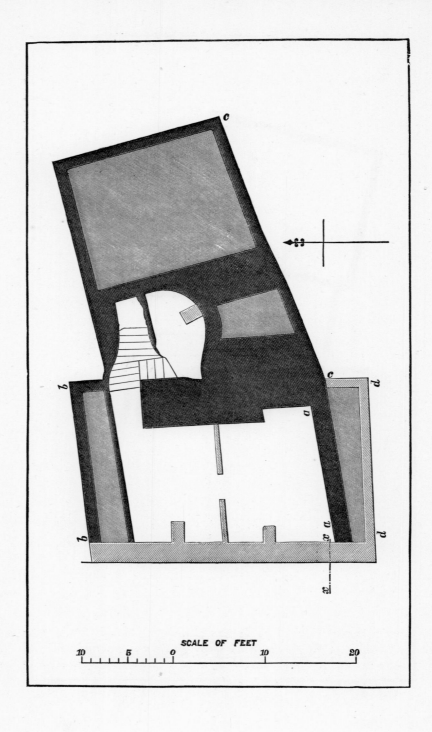

SCALE OF FEET

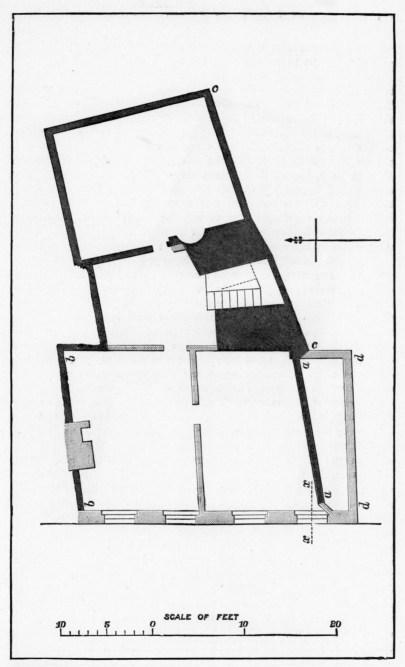

SCALE OF FEET

10   5   0   10   20

Thomas Nash appears to have considered the settlement of 1639 as one entitling him to dispose of Shakespeare's estates by will, perhaps on the supposition that he would outlive his mother-in-law, and a period at which it was unlikely for her daughter to have issue. There was also the exonerative fact that the terms of the devise in his will would merely have conveyed the reversion of the fee, and would not have affected the life-interest of his wife as secured by that settlement. It is, at all events, certain that, in 1642, he devised three of the estates, viz., New Place, the Combe arable land, and the Blackfriars house, to his kinsman Edward Nash, just as if they were his own property,—"item, I geve, dispose and bequeath unto my kinsman, Edward Nash, and to his heires and assignes for ever, one messuage or tenement with the appurtenances comonly called or knowne by the name of the New Place, scituate, lieinge and beinge in Stratford-upon-Avon, in a streete there called or knowne by the name of the Chappell Streete, together alsoe with all and singuler howses, out-howses, barnes, stables, orchardes, gardens, easementes, proffittes and comodities to the same belonginge or in anie wise appertayning, or reputed, taken, esteemed or enjoyed as thereunto belonginge, and now in the tenure, use and occupacion of mee, the sayd Thomas Nashe ; and also fowre yard land of arrable land, meadowe and pasture, with the appurtenances, lieinge and beinge in the common fields of Old Stratford, together with all easmentes, profittes, commons, commodities and hereditaments to the same fowre yard lands or any of them belonginge or in any wise appertayning, now in the tenure, use and occupacion of mee, the sayd Thomas Nash ; and also one other messuage or tenement with the appurtenances, scituate, lieing and beinge in the parishe of . . . . in London, and called or knowne by the name of the Wardropp, and now in the tenure, use and occupacion of one . . . Dickes." It would seem from the omission of the name of the parish, and from the erroneous title given to the house, that the testator had but a hazy knowledge of the Blackfriars estate. In a nuncupative codicil, made very shortly before his death on April the 4th, 1647, he declares that the land given in the will to Edward Nash, including doubtlessly the reversion to New Place, should be by him settled, after his decease, upon Edward's son Thomas. He was clearly a man of very considerable wealth, which is even specifically alluded to in the lines inscribed on his tombstone in the chancel of Stratford church. Shakespeare's grand-daughter Elizabeth was his sole executrix and residuary legatee, but most of the other terms of the will indicate a partiality in favour of his own relatives, the disposition to whom of the poet's estates does not appear to be equitable. The codicil mentions the then handsome legacy of £50 to his mother-in-law, Shakespeare's daughter ; and it also exhibits him on friendly terms with other members of his wife's family, there being several bequests to the Hathaways and Quineys.

So full of civil troubles were those days that, at the very time of her husband's death, Mrs. Nash had soldiers quartered upon her at New Place, one of whom was implicated in a robbery of deer from the park of Sir Greville Verney, an occurrence which took place on the last day of April, 1647. She duly proved her husband's will in the following June, but the entail of New Place having been barred in 1639, and re-settled on her and her issue, and as she, at her husband's decease, was not thirty-nine years of age, she declined to carry out Nash's will so far as that estate and the two others were concerned. She therefore without delay,—in fact, within two or three weeks after her husband's decease,— joined with her mother in levying a fine (Easter Term, 23 Car. I.) on the entailed property, and re-conveying it on June 2nd, 1647, "to the onlie use and behoofe of the said Susan Hall for and duringe the terme of her naturall life, and after her decease, to the use and behoofe of the said Elizabeth Nash, and the heires of her body lawfully begotten or to be begotten, and, for default of such issue, to the use and behoofe of the right heires of the said Elizabeth Nash for ever." It is worth mentioning that Mrs. Nash was not present when the will was signed at New Place on August the 25th, 1642, and unless the devise of that estate were made with her full knowledge and consent, she might reasonably have felt herself at liberty to endeavour to secure control over a residence associated with the memories of her father and grandfather.

Edward Nash, naturally anxious to sustain his interests, filed a bill in Chancery on February the 12th, 1647–8, against Elizabeth Nash and other legatees, to compel them to produce and execute the provisions of his uncle's will. The defendant, in her answer, admits its contents, but denies that the testator had the power to dispose of any of the poet's entails, asserting that they could not legally be so devised, because they were the inheritance of William Shakespeare, her grandfather, who was seized thereof in fee simple long before her marriage with Nash, bequeathing them to Susanna Hall, the daughter and coheir of the said William, for her life, and after her death to her and her issue. She then proceeds to mention that Mrs. Hall, to whom the property was bequeathed by Shakespeare, was yet living and enjoying the same; that she and her mother, after Nash's death, levied a fine and recovery on the estate to the use of Susanna for life, remainder to herself; and that she only disputed that portion of her husband's will which had reference to New Place, the arable land, and the house in London. Mrs. Nash also admits that she "hath in her hands or custodie many deeds, evidences, writings, charters, escripts and muniments which concerne the lands and premises which the defendant claymeth as her inheritance, and other the lands which are the defendant's joynture, and are devised to her by the said Thomas Nash." Amongst these were the title-deeds of New Place.

The answer of Elizabeth Nash was taken by commission at Stratford, no doubt at New Place, in April, 1648, and on June 10th, process of duces tecum having been previously awarded against the defendants "to bringe into this Court the will, evidences and writinges confessed by their answere to be in their custody, or att the retourne thereof to shewe unto this Courte good cause to the contrary," it was ordered "that the will be brought into this Court to the end the plaintiff may examine witnesses therupon, and then to be delivered back to the defendant, and that the defendant shall allsoe bring the said evidencies and writinges into Court upon oath the first day of the next terme there to remaine for the equall benefitt of both parties, and shall within ten daies after notice deliver unto the plaintiff a true schedule thereof." The will of Thomas Nash was produced before the examiners in Chancery in November, and Michael Johnson, one of the witnesses, was examined at length as to its authenticity; but it seems that Elizabeth Barnard defied altogether the above-named order in respect to the title-deeds of the estates in dispute. It appears from the affidavit filed at the Six Clerks' Office in December, 1649, that the writ of execution of the order of the tenth of June was personally served upon her on July the sixth, and there is a note in the books of the same office, dated November the 20th, to the effect that she had paid no attention to the order or to the writ. There was clearly an indisposition to allow the evidences in her possession respecting the property to be deposited in Court, and if the plaintiff had not been made acquainted with the terms of the settlement of 1639, it is possible that she was desirous of avoiding the production of a document the terms of which might have raised legal questions as to the validity of the subsequent arrangement of 1647. The litigation apparently terminated in the latter part of the year 1650. It appears from the books in the Six Clerks' Office that no replication was ever filed, and no decree in the suit can be found; but an order for the publication of the evidence was granted in November, so it is clear that after that date the pleadings were closed, and henceforth no more is heard of the suit. The terms of the compromise can only be conjectured, but as Lady Barnard, in her will, in directing her trustees to dispose of New Place and the Combe land, provides "that my loving cousin Edward Nash, esq., shall have the first offer or refusal thereof, *according to my promise formerly made to him*," it may be presumed that the dispute was amicably adjusted, that assurance having probably been elicited on the occasion.

A few weeks previously to the termination of the suit between the Nashes, a fine, dated in 1650, was levied on New Place, the only effect, however, of which seems to have been to place John Barnard and

Henry Smith as trustees of the settlement of 1647 in the stead of Richard Lane, whose colleague, William Smith of Balsall, appears to have been dead. This explanation is offered, however, with hesitation, fines being as a rule merely auxiliary to deeds explaining their object, one which otherwise can often only be conjectured. In 1652, another fine was levied, and a settlement made whereby New Place and the Combe land were confirmed " to the use of John Barnard and Elizabeth his wife for and dureing theire naturall lives, and the life of the longest liver of them, and to the heires of the body of the said Elizabeth lawfully begotten or to be begotten, and for defaulte of such issue, to the use of such person or persons, and for such estate and estates, as the said Elizabeth by any writeing either purporteing her last will or otherwise, sealed and subscribed in the presence of two or more credible witnesses, shall lymitt and appoint; and from and after such nominacion or appointment, or in defaulte of such nominacion or appointment, to the use and behoofe of the right heires of the survivor of them, the said John and Elizabeth, for ever." In pursuance of this power, Mrs. Barnard, in April, 1653, executed a deed conveying the two estates, after the death of her husband and the decease of herself without issue, to trustees, who were directed to sell them and apply the proceeds " in such manner, and by such some or somes, as I, the said Elizabeth, shall by any wrighting or noate under my hand, truly testified, declare and nominate."

John Barnard, who was knighted by Charles the Second in 1661, owned the manor of Abington, near Northampton, at which place he and his wife resided at the time of her death in 1670. How long after their marriage they occupied New Place does not appear, but it is mentioned as in his tenure in 1652, and, from the names of the witnesses, it may be perhaps assumed that Mrs. Barnard was living at Stratford when she executed the deed of 1653. From a list of fire-hearths made in 1663, it would seem that Francis Oldfield, gentleman, was then living in the house, and he continued to occupy it until at least 1670, being followed in his tenancy by Mrs. Frances Greene. Sir John Barnard was presented for a nuisance in Chapel Lane in 1670, but probably as owner, not as occupier. Oldfield, there is reason to believe, removed from New Place in or soon after that year, for on June 16th, 1671, he requested to be released from being an alderman " in respect he hath removed his habitacion into another county, and liveth att that distance from this burrough that hee is incapacitated to doe that respect and duty which belongs to his said office or place of alderman, as formerly hee hath done," a request, however, which was not complied with until September, 1672. The usual place of residence of Sir John and Lady Barnard, during the later years of their lives, appears to have been at the chief mansion in the small and retired village of Abington.

The house, which is situated very near the church, still remains, but in a modernised state, the only relics of the Barnards consisting of carved oak panelling in the old dining-room, and a fine hall of the sixteenth century, the latter remaining in the original state, with the exception that some modern village carpenter has added pieces of wood placed cross-wise between the spaces of the original work. No tradition respecting the family has been preserved in the neighbourhood, as I ascertained many years ago from careful enquiries amongst the then old inhabitants. Lady Barnard executed her will there on January 29th, 1669–70, being probably in a delicate state of health, for she died in the following month, and was buried at Abington on February 17th. "Madam Elizabeth Bernard, wife of Sir John Bernard kt., was buried 17° Febr., 1669," Abington register. In her will she requests her surviving trustee, after the death of her husband, to sell New Place to the best bidder, and to make the first offer of it to Edward Nash. She also directs that

the executors or administrators of Sir John Barnard "shall have and enjoy the use and benefit of my said house in Stratford, called the New Place, with the orchards, gardens, and all other the appurtenances thereto belonging, for and during the space of six months next after the decease of him the said Sir John Barnard." There is a little bit of traditional evidence leading to the not at all improbable conclusion that this will gave dissatisfaction to the Harts. "I have been told by Thomas Hart," says Jordan, in one of his manuscripts, "his great-grand-father George attempted to recover New Place by virtue of his great uncle's (the poet's) will." If George Hart meditated, which is not unlikely, an attempt of the kind, it probably never came into court, the entail having been too successfully barred to lead us to believe that material progress could have been made in any legal proceedings that may have been instituted in his favour.

No sepulchral monument of any description was erected in com-memoration of the last descendant of Shakespeare. The memory of her husband, who died at Abington early in 1674, was not so neglected, but his remains, with probably those of Lady Barnard, have long since disappeared, for beneath his memorial slab is now a vault belonging to another family.   Administration of his effects was granted to his son-in-law, Henry Gilbert of Locko, co. Derby, the husband of his daughter Elizabeth, and to his two other surviving daughters.   By these, or some of these, New Place was no doubt kept possession during the six months named by Lady Barnard.

Edward Nash not purchasing the estate, it was sold by Lady Barnard's surviving trustee to Sir Edward Walker, at one time Secretary at War to Charles the First, and then Garter King at Arms.   In the conveyance, dated May 18th, 1675, it is described as "all that capitall messuage or tenement, with appurtenances, scituate and being in Stratford-upon-Avon, comonly called or knowne by the name of the New Place, scituate in part in a street there called Chappell Street, and in part in a lane there called Chappell Lane, and all gardens, orchards, courts, yards, outlets, backsides, barnes, stables, outhowses, buildings, walls, mounds and fences to the same belonging, or in any wise of right apperteyning or therwithall formerly comonly used or enjoyed, or reputed as parcell or member therof, or belonging therunto."   It appears from the Stratford records and from Dugdale's Diary that Sir Edward did not reside at New Place, when he was in Warwickshire, but at Clopton House, an ancient mansion which, of course, externally at least, must have been familiar to Shakespeare, although no reliance is to be placed on the recently asserted, and most likely fictitious, tradition that he visited there.   The house, which has long been modernized, was a large rambling gabled edifice said to have been originally moated.   It is situated on the brow of the Welcombe Hills, amidst land of trivial undulation, within two miles of Stratford-on-Avon.

Sir Edward Walker did not long retain the enjoyment of his Shake-spearean purchase.   He died in 1677, devising New Place to his daughter Barbara, wife of Sir John Clopton, for her life, with remainder to the testator's senior grandson, Edward Clopton; but the rental of the premises was to be reserved for ten years "towards raising portions for my female grandchildren, Agnes and Barbara Clopton."   The terms of the bequest to his daughter and grandson are,—"I give unto my said deare daughter after the expiracion of tenn yeares the house called the New Place, with the gardens, barnes, &c., lying in the borough of Stratford, during her naturall life, and then to come to my eldest grand-sonn, Edward Clopton and his heires."   Barbara died in 1692, when the estate devolved on her son Edward, who became the occupier of New Place about two years afterwards, previously to which time the premises had been tenanted successively by persons named Joseph Hunt 343 and Henry Browne.   It appears from a deed previously quoted that

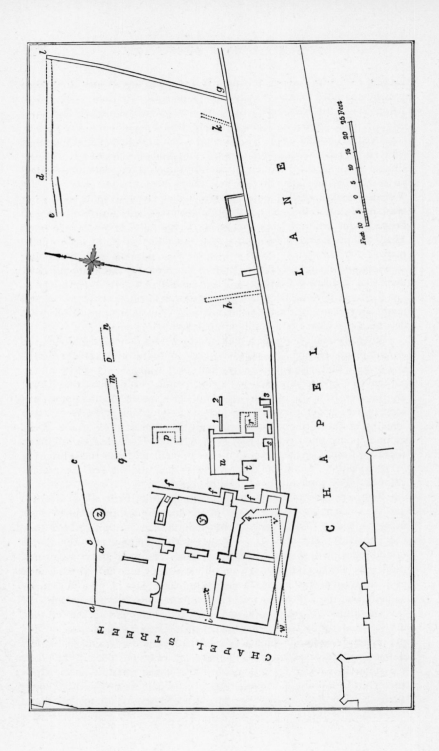

CHAPEL STREET

CHAPEL LANE

Feet 10 5 0 5 10 15 20 25 Feet

Edward Clopton removed to Nash's House some time before May, 1699, continuing, nevertheless, to hold the Great Garden that belonged to New Place. In November, 1698, he had given the rest of the latter estate to his father, Sir John Clopton, who, in January, 1699–1700, conveyed to himself for life "all that messuage or tenement and premises, with the appurtenances, situate, lying and being in Chapel Street and Chapel Lane in the borough of Stratford-upon-Avon, commonly called or known by the name of the New Place, then in the tenure of John Wheeler, gent.," with remainder to the use of Hugh Clopton in fee. It was shortly after this period that Sir John pulled down the original building, for when, in September, 1702, he settled New Place upon Hugh Clopton and his intended wife, in anticipation of the former's marriage with Elizabeth Millward, it was described as "one new house standing and being in Stratford-upon-Avon, which house is intended for them, the said Hugh Clopton and Elizabeth his intended wife, to live in, but the same haveing been lately built is not finished, or fitted up, and made convenient for them to inhabitt in." All these transactions were no doubt the results of a family arrangement.

When Sir John Clopton rebuilt the poet's residence he modified the ground-plan, erecting the northern and southern walls at a different angle with the eastern boundary-line of Chapel Street, most of the garden side of the new mansion being parallel with the latter. It will also be seen from the opposite diagram that the ancient building was in some places wider than the modern one, the positions of the eastern remains of the former, which are nearly level with the surface of the ground, being shown at p, u, t and r, and a general view of these, engraved from a sketch taken by Blight immediately after their discovery in 1862, will be found on the reverse of the title-page of the present volume. The remnant at p, most likely part of a bay-window, is constructed of rough stones laid in with clay, the front being about two feet and the sides about twenty inches in thickness, the former nine feet six inches in width. Of an exactly similar formation, but not so broad, are the imperfect walls at u, the floorings within them bearing evidences of their having been constructed of stone, and here were discovered numerous vestiges of charcoal. A hollow place at r and a small nook at t are paved with the same material, both of them being undoubtedly ancient, but the other remains in this immediate locality, namely, the brickwork marked 3 to s, 1, 2, and a separate fragment to the left of t, are of modern date, the first-named piece being built across an old pebbled walk. The basement-floor of the new house was about ten feet below the street-level, and that there was at least one cellar in the poet's day, there being then no underground kitchens at Stratford, is shown by the depth of the original foundations still remaining at w. Erected on the cellar floor from i to x, is a piece of brickwork, apparently belonging to the earlier structure, and extending a few inches beyond the present wall to the virgin soil on the left. The only portions of the ancient building that were discovered on the west of f are the foundations from w to v, i to x and v to 4, the last quoted numeral indicating the spot where the modern fire-place crosses over the old stonework ; and as to the vestiges of structures on the extreme right, h, k and g may be assigned to the Shakespearean, and the two others to the Queen Anne period. The remains at w are roughly constructed of pieces of Wilmecote stone laid in clay. They are four feet in height and three in width at the corner, that which is represented at the lower part of the opposite engraving. From e to d and from d to l are underground

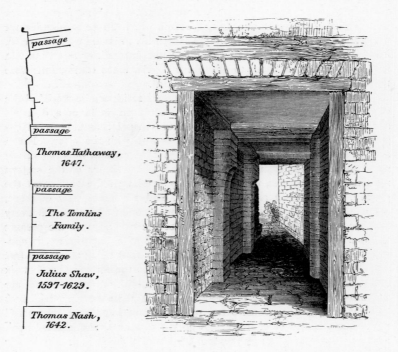

remnants of walls that probably mark the situation of the old boundary between the gardens of Nash's House and New Place, a boundary that no doubt extended in some form or other from e to c.

It appears nearly certain, from their parallel direction in respect to the southern boundary of the original mansion, that the remnants of foundations between q and n belonged to a structure of some kind, but perhaps only a wall, that was attached to Shakespeare's premises. The

Remains of the Foundations at the South-Western corner of the Poet's mansion at New Place, now preserved under the surface at the top of Chapel Lane. The road was formerly narrower at this spot than it is at present, a slip of land of about four feet in

width, of gradual decrease towards the east, having been divorced from the Shakespearean estate in the year 1806 for the purpose of widening the lane.

ancient well at *z*, now under one of the modern outer walls of the adjoining residence, was no doubt in the poet's court-yard, and near what was in all probability the eastern termination of one of those open passages under the first-floor that were once all but universal at Stratford. That there was anciently one at Nash's House may be surmised from the plan of its foundations, and a like mode of construction was followed in all the buildings that were situated between that dwelling and the Town Hall. The annexed example of one of these inlets, all of them that were in this row being on the north of the several premises to which they belong, is engraved from a sketch taken by Blight in 1862. That the upper part of the northern end of the poet's residence abutted upon Nash's House is evident from the position of the gable traces, there being no doubt also that the upper end of New Place absolutely joined the other building, the whole of the wall and timbers above those traces having been pointed and obviously long exposed to the influences of the weather, while the portions of them beneath the boundaries of the lower gable, although unpointed, are in sound condition.

When the rebuilding of New Place was completed and it was fitted for residence in 1703, it was occupied by Hugh Clopton with the small back garden and premises attached to it, while his brother Edward occupied the adjoining house and garden, together with the Great Garden. They continued neighbours until 1706, when Nash's House, together with the large garden, became, as has been previously noticed, the property of Aston Ingram. Hugh Clopton did not re-annex the Great Garden to New Place until March 21st, 1728–9, when, in the conveyance from his sister Barbara, the widow of Ingram, as recited in an old abstract of title, it is described as "all that piece or parcel of ground lying and being within the borough of Stratford-upon-Avon called the Great Garden, and which did formerly belong to New Place, the house wherein he the said Hugh Clopton did then inhabit and dwell and was near adjoining to the said house and backside thereof, which said garden contained by estimation three quarters of an acre more or less, together also with all barns, stables, outhouses, brick walls, edifices, buildings, ways, waters, &c., to the same premises belonging." The word *near* used in this description must not be understood to imply that the Great Garden did not actually join the back premises of New Place, for in the conveyance of Nash's House from Ingram to Rose, 1729, the former is described as "the plot or peice of ground called or knowne by the name of the Great Garden, being or being reputed three quarters of an acre, bee the same more or less, with the yard, barnes, stables, and outhouses to the same belonging, standing, lyeing and being on the east side the house called the New Place, now in the possession of the said Hugh Clopton, and some years since belonged to or was a part of that house or premisses thereunto belonging."

In June, 1732, Hugh Clopton settled New Place and its grounds to himself for life, with various remainders over. He died in 1751, and, in 1756, the then owners of the estate under that settlement conveyed to the Rev. Francis Gastrell in fee, "all that capital messuage or mansion house called the New Place, situate and being in Chapel Street and Chapel Lane within the borough of Stratford-upon-Avon in the county of Warwick, with the kitchen garden heretofore purchased of William Smith, gentleman, as also the Great Garden and yard thereto adjoining, together with the buildings erected thereon, some time since purchased of Barbara Ingram, widow, now in the tenure of the said Henry Talbott, and also all the pews and seats in the Church and Chapel of Stratford-upon-Avon aforesaid usually held and enjoyed by the said Sir Hugh Clopton and his domesticks as appurtenant to the said messuage; and also all the fixtures and ornaments fixed to and belonging to the said capital messuage, with their incidents and appurtenances." It was this Gastrell who pulled the modern non-Shakespearean house down to the ground in the year 1759.

In the settlement of 1732, the estate is particularly described as "all that capitall messuage called the New Place, scituate in Chappel Street, adjoyning to Chappel Lane, within the Burrough of Stratford-upon-Avon, in the county of Warwick, together with the kitchin garden heretofore purchased of William Smith, gent., as also the Great Garden and yard thereto adjoyning, together with the buildings erected thereon, and lately purchased of Barbara Ingram, widdow, together with all outhouses, edifices, buildings, barns, stables, and edifices thereunto belonging, or in anywise appertaining, or therewith usually held, occupied or enjoyed, and now in the occupation of the said Hugh Clopton." Mention is here first made of the kitchen garden formerly belonging to William Smith, but it appears from another document that this piece of ground had been bought by Hugh Clopton about the year 1707, that it was altogether unconnected with New Place, and that it adjoined land belonging to the vicarage on the other side of Chapel-lane. It was not, therefore, as might have been surmised from the above descriptions of parcels, an annex to the Great Garden, and there is no reason for doubting that the northern boundary-line of the original Shakespeare estate has been unaltered to the present day. Had any change been made, the fact could hardly have escaped notice in the title-deeds, but no absolute evidence is at present accessible, the most anxious search having failed to unearth the old indentures referring to the property between that line and Sheep Street, the only records that would be likely to enable us to arrive at a definite conclusion.

The Great Garden of New Place was bounded on the east by a slip of land which, long before the time of Shakespeare, and for many generations afterwards, belonged to the trustees of the Charity of Clifford

Chambers, a village near Stratford. It had been given to the parish of Clifford for eleemosynary purposes by Hugh Chesenale, who was the priest of that village in the time of Henry the Seventh. This little estate measured only sixty feet in length by thirty in width, and is described in a deed of the year 1472 as, "burgagium cum suis pertinenciis scituatum in vico vocato Dede Lane in Stratford, inter tenementum Abbathie de Redyng ex parte una et tenementum priorisse de Pynley, nunc in tenura Johannis Gylbert, ex parte altera." In 1572, it is mentioned as consisting of a barn and garden, and a lease was granted in that year by the trustees, amongst whom was one named in the deed John Shaxber, to Lewis ap Williams of Stratford, ironmonger, of "one barne with a garden to the same belonginge in Stretforde aforesaied, in a lane ther commonlye caled Deadd lane alias Walker stret, nowe in the tenure and occupation of Robarte Bratte or his assignes," such lease to commence at the expiration of one formerly granted to Robert Bratte. The annual rental was five shillings and ninepence, Williams covenanting to keep the barn and garden in good order, and to pay all chief-rents and other outgoings. This barn is mentioned in 1590 in a return to a commission issued out of the Exchequer for the survey of the possessions of Ambrose earl of Warwick,—"inhabitantes de Clyfford, unum horreum vj.*d*," the sixpence being the chief-rent paid to the Lord of the Manor In 1619, the estate was occupied by one John Beesly alias Coxe, carpenter, who in or shortly before that year pulled down the barn, in the place of which he erected a small cottage of two bays, and, in defiance of orders then in vogue at Stratford, roofed the tenement with thatch. On the back of the lease above-named is an endorsement that may be assigned to the period of the first James, which contains one of the very few contemporary written notices of the great poet, and it is important as proving decisively that the Great Garden of New Place was occupied by Shakespeare himself. The memorandum is as follows,—"the barne on the west sid bounds by Mr. William Shaxpeare of Pynley Holt, and

the est sid on the Kinges land William Wyatt of Stratford yoman." This means that the western side of the Clifford estate was bounded by property of William Shakespeare which had belonged to the Priory of Pinley Holt, and the eastern side by Crown land belonging to William Wyatt of Stratford.

Another evidence that the western side of this small estate adjoined the Great Garden of New Place is contained in a lease dated March the

25th, 1622, between the Clifford trustees and the above-named John Beesley, in which it is witnessed that the former, "for and in consideration that the said John Beesley alias Cox hath alreadie at his owne proper costes and charges newlie erected and builte up two bayes of new buyldinges, and for diverse other good causes and consideracions them especiallie moveing, have demised, sett and to farme lett, and by theise presentes doe graunte, demise, sett and to farme lett, unto the saide John Beesley alias Cox, all that now cottage or tenemente newlie erected by the said John Beesley alias Cox, containinge by estimacion two bayes, with a backside or garden plotte to the same belonging, contayninge in length three score yardes, and in breadth tenn yardes, all which lie in a streete called Deade Lane or Chappell Lane, and now Walkers Streete, in Stratforde aforesaide, *and is bounded on the weste side with the now land of John Hawle, gent.*, sometyme the lande of the dissolved Priorie of Pynley Houlte, and on the easte side with the lande sometyme belonging to the Abbie of Reading, and now the land of William Wyate, gent." In August, 1758, Gastrell, having then just previously bought the land on the eastern side of this estate, induced the trustees of Clifford Chambers to give the latter up to him in exchange for a more valuable holding in Sheep Street, after which transaction he was the owner of all the land on the north side of the lane that extended from New Place to the western boundary of the Corporation property.

The slip of land which was between the Clifford estate and the town property on the east belonged in 1434, and probably long previously, to the Abbey of Reading. It is described in 1622 as "the lande sometyme belonging to the Abbie of Reading, and now the land of William Wyate, gent.;" and, in 1656, as "the land sometyme belonging to the Abbey of Reading, and now or late the land of Nicholas Ryland, gent." There is no evidence to show that Wyat's property extended on the north beyond the boundaries of that belonging to Clifford, but in all probability it did, and, including a larger piece of land on the north-east, reached from Chapel Lane to Sheep Street. At all events, it is certain that Nicholas Ryland owned such an estate, which, in 1681, he or his son sold for £153 to Thomas Maides of Stratford-upon-Avon, felmonger, and which is described in the conveyance recited in an old abstract of title as "all that messuage or tenement and malthouse, with the gardens, orchard and backside thereunto belonging, situate, lying and being in Stratford-upon-Avon, in a certain street called the Sheep Street, and one piece or parcel of ground belonging to the said messuage and lying behind and southward from the same, then lately planted with hopps, and was then in the tenure of Joseph Hunt, gent., all which premises was then in the tenure or occupation of the said Thomas Maides, his assigns or undertenants; and also all that barn to the said messuage belonging, situate, lying and being in Stratford-upon-Avon aforesaid, in a certain street called Walkers Street or Chapel Lane, then in the tenure or occupation of one William Greenway or his undertenants." This proves decisively that the barn on the Ryland estate stood in Chapel Lane, but the "one piece or parcel of ground then (1681) lately planted with hopps" was not included in the portion of the estate sold to Spurr in 1707. It was situated at the back of the premises in Sheep Street, a portion of it most likely adjoining the northern boundary of the ancient Clifford estate in Chapel Lane. This appears from the following description of the Sheep Street estate, when it passed from Michael Goodrich to Joseph Smith in 1709,—"all that messuage or tenement and malthouse with th'appurtenences, scituate lyeing and being in Stratford-upon-Avon, in a certaine streete there called the Sheepe Streete, late in the severall occupacions of the said Michaell Goodrich, Jane Washbrooke and Frances Williams, or some or one of them; and alsoe all that peece or parcell of ground lyeing behind the said messuage, and southward from the same, formerly planted with hopps." All the property here described was bought by Gastrell in 1758 of Elizabeth Barodale, who inherited from the Smiths. It was then divided into three tenements, two of which, those lying to the eastward, were given by Gastrell to the Clifford Trustees, in the same year, in exchange for their small estate in Chapel Lane.

In December, 1692, Mary, the widow of the above-named Thomas Maides, with other parties, conveyed the Ryland estates to Michael Goodrich the younger. They are then described as consisting of "all that messuage or tenement and maulthouse with thappurtenances, scituate and being in Stratford-upon-Avon, in a certaine streete there called the Sheep Streete, and one peece or parcell of ground belongeing to and lyeing behind the said messuage and southward from the same, formerly planted with hopps, and then in the tenure of Joseph Hunt, gen., and all that barne to the said messuage belongeing scituate in Stratford afore-said, in a certaine streete there called the Walkers Streete or Chappell Lane, formerly in the tenure of one William Greenway, all which premises were heretofore purchased by the said Thomas Maides of one Nicholas Ryland; and such interest, title, estate, use and advantage as the said Thomas Maides formerly had or might have into out of and through the gatehouse belongeing to one Samuell Ryland, formerly in the occupacion of one John Izod, glazior, adjoyneing to the west side of the said messuage." This gatehouse did not form part of the Goodrich estate, but a right of way under it, through Izod Yard, to the premises at the back of his property in Sheep Street, was always carefully provided for. In the year 1704, at the back of the house adjoining this gateway on the east was first a yard, then a newly erected barn, then a garden called the Little Garden, which latter was divided from another called the Great Garden, this Great Garden adjoining the northern boundaries of the Clifford Chapel Lane estate and the yard afterwards sold by Goodrich to Spurr. The passage under the gateway and through Izod Yard is now an alley, and, as traces of seventeenth-century work are yet visible in the adjoining houses, it may be as well to observe that they do not include a vestige of construction that can be judiciously assigned to the Shakespearean period.

The barn in Chapel Lane occupied by William Greenway in 1681, with a back yard, were sold by Michael Goodrich, the son, probably, of the Michael above named, to Edward Spurr in October, 1707. The yard extended to the southern boundary of Goodrich's garden attached to his premises in Sheep Street, from which garden it was divided by a hedge. The barn and yard are described as then, 1707, "having the tenement now in the tenure of the said Edward Spurr on the west side and the barne of Richard Tyler, gent., now in the occupacion of John Hunt, gent., on the east side thereof," and further as, "all and singuler the said recited barne and yard, as the same is now devided from the garden belonging to the messuage of the said Michaell Goodrich by an old quicksett hedge, togeather with the passage att the end of the said barne leading out of the said streete called Walkers Streete alias Chappell Lane into the said yard lying behind the said barne, which said barne and yard are now in the tenure or occupacion of Thomas Woolmore, gent., and John Hunt, gent., and are scituate in the said streete called Walkers Streete alias Chappell Lane, and were purchased by Michaell Goodrich, deceased, father of the said Michaell Goodrich, party to these presents, to him and his heires, of one Mary Maides, widdow of Thomas Maides, late of Stratford, felmonger, deceased." The yard and barn continued with the Spurrs until April, 1758, when John, the eldest son of Edward Spurr, in consideration of £30, conveyed to the Rev. Francis Gastrell in fee, "all that barn and yard situate and being in a certain street or lane in Stratford-upon-Avon called Walkers Street alias Chappell Lane, together with the passage at the end of the said barn leading out of the said street called Walkers Street alias Chappell Lane into the said yard lying behind the said barn, which said yard and barn were heretofore in the tenure of Thomas Woolmore, gentleman, and John Hunt, gentleman, and are now in the possession of the said Francis Gastrell." The barn no doubt adjoined Chapel Lane, for in the year 1694 Michael Goodrich was "presented for not reparing the ground before his barne in the Chappel' Lane," Court Leet MS.

To the east in Chapel Lane of the slip of land sold by Michael Goodrich to Edward Spurr in 1707, were three estates belonging to the Corporation, the only one which is of importance in the present enquiry being of course that nearest to New Place. It adjoined the property of Goodrich, and is said in a deed of 1723 to have measured one hundred and eighty feet on that, its western side, but in a later one of 1763, as one hundred and eighty-two feet eight inches. These premises are described in 1599 as "all that barne and backside thereunto belonginge with thappurtenaunces whatsoever scituate, lienge and beinge in Stretforde aforeseyd, in a certeyne lane there called the Chappell Lane or Walkers Strete, and nowe in the tenure or occupacion of Abraham Strelley or his assignes." Early in the seventeenth century they were occupied by William Mountford, and when leased in 1619 to Richard Mountford, they were described as consisting of a barn, garden and workhouse, although from another document of the same date it is certain that the barn had then been recently destroyed. Some time after the destruction of the latter, a smaller one was erected which occupied a portion only of the frontage in Chapel Lane, leaving an open plot of land between the new barn and the one on the Corporation estate on the east side, so that the latter is described in 1689 as bounded by "*the land* of Samuell Tyler, gent." William Greeneway, who occupied the adjoining barn, afterwards Spurr's, in 1681, also at that time rented the estate formerly Mountford's, which latter was in 1682 demised by the Corporation to Samuel Tyler. The person last-named died in May, 1693, and the premises were occupied by Richard Tyler at and after this date, the latter being succeeded in the occupation by John Hunt in or before 1707. In a poor-rate levy made in July, 1697, "Mr. Tiler his barne and garden" are valued at £3 per annum. In the year 1723 these premises were leased by the Corporation to John Hunt, gentleman, and were then described as consisting of "all that their barne, plotts of ground and workehouse to the same belonging, scituate lyeing and being in a certaine lane there called the Chappell Lane, heretofore in the tenure or occupacion of Samuel Tyler, gent., but now in the tenure or occupacion óf the said John Hunt, his assignes or under-tenants, and is abutted and bounded as hereinafter mencioned, viz., the breadth towards the street eastward goeing bevell ninteen yards and a halfe and one inch, the length from the barne to the end of Richard Hulls ground eight and fifty yards, the length from the lane next the barne now in the possession of Thomas Woolmer, gent., to the ground of Mr. John Woolmer of Gainsburrough on the other side thereof sixty yards, and the breadth on the lane side ninteen yards and one foote." This description is important, because it proves that Thomas Woolmer's barn adjoined this property, thus removing all doubt as to the locality of the one conveyed by Goodrich to Spurr in the year 1707.

It is deeply to be regretted that the dimensions of the small estate sold by Goodrich in 1707 are not given in any of the deeds referring to it. Its exact size must, therefore, be a matter of conjecture; but the frontage in Chapel Lane could not have been extensive, for the barn is referred to as adjoining the Corporation property on the east, while, on the western side, between the barn and the Clifford land, there was only a passage leading to the back-yard. It is extremely unlikely that, if this yard was very wide towards the north-east end, the whole property could have been sold in 1707 for the small sum of £24, or in 1758 for £30, the purchase moneys paid respectively by Spurr and Gastrell. It may, therefore, be assumed that it consisted of a long narrow slip of land, the average width being that required for a barn and side-passage. Taking this width at the lowest estimate of thirty feet,—it was probably rather more,—and bearing in mind that the Clifford estate was only ten yards in breadth, it follows that on the east of the New Place estates as thrown into one property by Gastrell there is a strip of land *at least* sixty feet in width, which certainly neither belonged to Shakespeare, nor was ever in his occupation.

The history of New Place after the death of Gastrell remains to be told. By his will dated in 1768, and proved in 1772, he devised to his wife all his estates in Stratford-upon-Avon. In March, 1775, his widow conveyed to William Hunt, of that town, gentleman, "all that large garden or parcel of land near the Chappel, upon part of which a capital messuage lately stood, as the same is now walled in, together with the barn and dovehouse standing thereupon;" this description, although it has been otherwise stated, certainly including the Clifford and Spurr properties. The trustees of this last owner sold the estate in September, 1790, to Charles Henry Hunt, who, in May, 1807, conveyed it to Messrs. Battersbee and Morris as tenants in common. At the time of this latter purchase, there were, in Chapel Lane and on the New Place ground, two cottages which had been formed some years previously out of a large barn that had been one of the appendages to the Shakespeare property in the time of the second Hugh Clopton.

In 1819, all the estates above-mentioned were submitted to auction in a number of lots, but none of the purchases were completed until 1827, when, as previously stated, Nash's House and garden, with the site of New Place and some of its adjoining grounds, were purchased by a Miss Smith, and afterwards became vested in the Corporation of Stratford-on-Avon. At the same time all the remainder, with the exception of the two cottages and their small back-gardens, was sold to Edward Leyton of that town. One of these cottages was purchased by the same gentleman in 1834, and the other in 1838 ; but in April, 1827, he had sold a small piece of ground abutting on Chapel Lane, upon which an ugly building, occasionally used for theatrical entertainments, was afterwards erected. In 1844, all the estate, with the exception of the land just alluded to, was settled by him upon his daughter, Mrs. Loggin, and from her trustee it was purchased by me in October, 1861, with moneys collected by public subscription. Some years afterwards I

I 2

had the satisfaction of reversing the divorce of April, 1827, in respect to the fragment of land which had then been separated from the rest. Thus, after a number of intricate vicissitudes, the whole of Shakespeare's estate of New Place once more became an individual property, to be held for ever in memory of the great dramatist by the Corporation of his native town.

————

The foregoing essay is practically an abridged version of a previous compilation of mine on the same history, a work that appeared in 1864 in a folio volume in which the subject was treated at greater prolixity than would here be either necessary or desirable. During the interval which has since elapsed I have more than once re-studied the whole of the evidences, correcting in this way several important oversights and errors of judgment. The latter have been found to be most conspicuous in those portions which relate to the brick and stone vestiges, and amongst these misconceptions must be specially noticed the attribution of an impost of the former article to the earlier Cloptonian period, the ground-plan of the new house rendering it altogether impossible that it could have belonged to the ancient structure. This is the concurrent opinion of two experienced architects, both of whom are, moreover, convinced, from the rigid adherence to a modern style which pervaded the building of 1702, that, with the possible and uncertain exception of a number of bricks, none of the materials of the old edifice were used in the construction of its successor; and a glance at the character of the latter, as seen on the left-hand in the opposite engraving, will unfold better than a written description the extreme improbability of its director having introduced fifteenth or sixteenth century work into any portion of his design.

With respect to the poet's domestic movables, the conditions under which his residence was destroyed, and the later transactions with the site, render it impossible that any of them could have been lodged amidst the rubbish that was thrown into the new basement when Gastrell demolished the second house in 1759. A few articles of that character, as well as two or three coins, have been discovered near the surface of the ground, but so many explanations of their deposit can be suggested, their ascription to a special period or individuality of owner-ship is beyond the limits of sober biography. A similar observation is applicable to a number of pieces of fashioned stone, some of which were too hastily assumed to have been remnants of the older edifice,

A BRIEF ACCOUNT OF NEW PLACE AS IT APPEARED AT THE END OF THE SEVENTEENTH CENTURY.

Facsimile of a Memorandum in the somewhat peculiar handwriting of the Rev. Joseph Greene, M.A., master of the local Grammar-school. It is prefaced by the following note:— October the 24th, 1767, I visited Richard Grimmitt, formerly a shoemaker in Stratford, who

was born in the latter end of January, 1682–3." By the expression,—plain windows,—Grimmitt most likely meant windows set in frames, the adjuncts of which were destitute of stonework or ornamentation.

but our utter ignorance of the details of its workmanship above the foundations excludes the only reliable guide to identification, while there is not one of those relics of such manifest antiquity that it could not have been originally prepared for the mansion that was erected by Sir John Clopton. Their general appearance, indeed, favours the opinion that they all belong to the later period, and, from what has been recorded by Leland and Grimmitt, it would seem most probable that the stonework in the early dwelling was restricted to the basement and foundations. It should also be observed that a partial reconstruction of Nash's House was made to effect its junction with the modern New Place when the latter was in course of erection in 1702, both estates then belonging to the same family, and all the new arrangements doubtlessly in the hands of one builder, circumstances that are in themselves sufficient to arrest judicious overtures respecting the history of the isolated relics that have been found in either locality.

OLD BUILDINGS ADJOINING SHAKESPEARE'S GREAT GARDEN, 1862.

SHAKESPEARE THE CORVIZER.

John Shakespeare, a corvizer or shoemaker, was the only namesake of the poet's father who was a contemporary resident with the latter at Stratford-on-Avon. Arriving in that town in or very shortly before 1584, being then a young man, he succeeded, after an undetermined interval, to the business, vacant by death, of one Thomas Roberts, who was the father, most likely, of the damsel that he married in the November of that year; and he left the neighbourhood altogether in or about 1594. Nearly all of the little that is known of his history, during his brief career in the locality, leads to the belief that he was a trustworthy and unembarrassed tradesman. But this individual would hardly have been entitled to a line of biography were it not that his presence in the borough has been the occasion of doubts which have arisen respecting the true identification of the John Shakespeare who is so frequently mentioned in the registry of the Court of Record. It is unnecessary, however, to entertain grave misgivings on the subject. The officers of that Court made a practice, so far as can be ascertained, of noting distinctions in all cases of the kind in which mistakes might otherwise have been reasonably anticipated; and it is all but certain that, once at least in the records of every action in which he was engaged, the sutorial John would have been termed either corvizer, or shoemaker, or *cordionarius*, the last title being twice appended to his name in a declaration of 1591. The following notices, arranged in chronological order, may be useful for reference.

1584. The earliest notice of this person which has yet been discovered is in the record of his marriage, an event which took place in the autumn of this year. "November 25, John Shakspere and Margery Roberts," Stratford Register of Marriages.

1585. At a town-council held on September the 2nd he was elected one of the tasters, and was sworn into office with his colleague in the following month,—"tasters juratus, John Shaxpere, Humfry Brace," MS. register, 1 Oct. The name of alderman John Shakespeare is introduced in the lists as a non-attendant on each of these occasions.

1586. "Receved of Shackespere for his fredome the xix.th of Januarie, xxx.s," Chamberlains' Accounts from Christmas, 1585, to Christmas, 1586. "Reseved of Shakspeare the shumaker for his fredom the xix.th day of Jeanuarey, xxx.s," duplicate copy of the same account. It appears from these entries that he had paid £3 on his admission into the Company of Shoemakers and Sadlers, the Corporation being entitled to one half, and it is worthy of remark that he was enabled to furnish this sum, one of no little moment at that period, on the very day that the poet's father was pronounced to be in a state bordering upon insolvency. It is gathered from "the constitucions, ordinances and decrees of the mistrie or craft," 1578, that the large amount of this entrance-fee is a decisive proof that the new freeman was not a native of Stratford. He was chosen one of the petty constables in the autumn of 1586, having been sworn in with Humphrey Brace at the council-meeting at which his namesake is especially mentioned as an absentee.

1587. "Thomas Okens money was delivered to the personnes whose names are underwritten, to be emploied accordinge to the last will and testament of the saide Thomas, ... John Shaxpere, v. *li.*, his suerties, Richard Sponer et Roberte Yonge," register of the council, 17 February, 1587. This transaction may merely indicate that Shakespeare the Corvizer wanted a then important sum for the efficient conduct of his business, not necessarily that he was at all embarrassed ; the latter theory being, moreover, an improbable one, loans under Oken's gift having been restricted to young tradesmen who were likely to make a good commercial use of the temporary assistance. Thomas Oken of Warwick, in his will dated Nov. 24th, 1570, gave £40 to Stratford-on-Avon, "to bestowe and deliver the said somme of fourtie poundes to divers yong occupiers of the same towne of Stretford-upon-Avon in lone, in maner and forme following, that is to say, unto eight such honest yong men dwelling within the same towne that bee of some honest mistery or craft, and householders within the same towne, being also of good name fame and conversacion with their neighbors in the same towne, that is to say, to every such one of the said eight yong men the somme of five poundes by the waye of loane to be occupied by him and them in their said craftes or mysteryes during the space of foure yeres,"—MS. Black Book in the Corporation Archives, Warwick. These conditions were formally accepted in 1575, and it should be mentioned that every borrower had to pay interest on the loan at the rate of eightpence in the pound and to find two sureties for the repayment of the principal.

Shakespeare the Corvizer was re-elected one of the petty constables on September the 6th, 1587, losing his wife in the following month. "October 29, Margery, wife to John Shakspere," Stratford burial-register.   But he did not remain a widower for any length of time if, as is most probable, the following baptismal entries in the same volume refer to his children,—1588-9.   March 11, Ursula, daughter to John Shakspere.—1590.   May 24, Humphrey, sonne to John Shakspere.— 1591.   September 21, Phillippus, filius Johannes® Shakspere.   They most likely accompanied their father in his departure from the town, no further notice of them appearing in the local records.

1588.   He consented, in the October of this year, to be trustee and guardian for two of the sons of the before-named Thomas Roberts. "At this halle Mr. Abraham Sturley hathe delyverd thre severall ob-ligacions to the use of the children of one Thomas Robertes, decessed, videlicet, one bande made to Thomas Robertes, one of the sonnes of Thomas Robertes, decessed, of fyftie poundes, wheryn Richard Masters of Mylverton, yoman, and John Shaxspere of Stratford, corvizer, stand bounde for the bredinge of the seyd Thomas Robertes and the payment of xxxij.*li.*, accordinge to the condycions of the seyd bande, whiche bande berithe date quarto die Octobris, anno tricesimo Elizabethe Regine ; and one other bande beringe date tercio die Octobris, anno xxx.   Elizabethe Regine, of fyftie poundes, made from John Laurence of Studley, husbandman, Edmunde Edes of the Holte in the parishe of Audley, husbandman, and William Bowkeley of Studley, tanner, to John Robertes, one other of the sonnes of the seyd Thomas Robertes, for the payment of the somme of xxvj.*li.*, accordinge to the condicion of the same bande ; and also one other bande from John Shaxspere of Stratford, corvizer, and Edwarde Busshell de eisdem, wolsted-wever, in lx.*li.*, for the bredinge of Richard Robertes, the yongest sonne of the seyd Thomas, and also for payment of suche money as ys conteyned in the condicion of the same bande bearinge date tercio die Octobris, anno xxx.° Elizabethe regine,"—MS. register of Council-meetings, 9 January, 1590.   The bonds in which Shakespeare the Corvizer was an obligor were cancelled in 1604,—MS. ibid., 27 July, 2 James I.   It may be worth adding that in June, 1588, *John Shaksper, corvizer*, was one of the witnesses to the execution of the lease of a cellar in the Middle Row.

1590. *Johannes Shaxspere, shumaker*, is mentioned in this year as a bail for the defendant in a suit in the Court of Record.

1591. "*Johannes Shaksper, cordionarius*, summonitus fuit per ser-vientem ad clavam ibidem ad respondendum Ricardo Tyler de placito quod reddat ei quatuor libras, quas ei debet et injuste detinet," declaration filed in the Court of Record, MS.   There is nothing to lead us to believe that the suit of Tyler v. Shaxpere, commenced on January the 10th, 1593, had any connexion with the one last mentioned.

1592. " A note of Mr. Oken's money and to whom yt ys lent, and the names of theire suerties, and also of Bakers money . . . . *Bakers money.* Thomas Fourde, shuemaker, in v.*li.* for l.*s.*, and Henrie Rogers, butcher, and John Shaxpere, shuemaker, his suerties . . . . *Okens money.* Philipus Grene in x.*li.* for v.*li.*, Henrie Rogers, butcher, and John Shaxpere, shuemaker, his suerties," register of the Council meetings, 29 March, 1592. " Item, Jhon Shackespere, Mr. of the Companie of Shoemakers, paid to the same Henrye Wyllson, for the moitee of Ryc. Fletcher, the sadler, hys freedome, xx.*s.*, whiche saied xx.*s.* is dwe to the chamber, and soe paied," ibid., 30 June, 1592. " Of John Shackesper for Richard Fletcher, xx.*s*," accounts of moneys received by the chamberlains in the year last mentioned. These entries merely record that Shakespeare the Corvizer, in his official capacity as master of the society, paid over half the sum that they had received from Fletcher on his admission.

Thomas Roberts, the shoemaker who has been more than once previously mentioned, lived on the north side of Back Bridge Street, holding extensive premises there under a lease from the Corporation that had been granted to him in 1578 for thirty-one years at the annual rental of twelve shillings. At some unascertained period after the death of this individual in September, 1583, the house was occupied by Shakespeare the Corvizer, who was certainly the tenant a few years afterwards, his name occurring in a list, drawn up in October, 1589, of those who had paid three quarters of their annual rents, in his case nine shillings out of twelve,—" Jhon Shackespere, ix.*s.*, . . . xij.*s.*" He is also noted in another manuscript as having regularly discharged the quarterly claim for the tenement in Bridge Street throughout the year 1590 ; Misc. Doc. i. 109. " Brydge Strett Warde, John Shaxpere, xij.*s.*," manuscript list dated January, 1590-1. After June, 1592, he is heard of no more in the records of Stratford, and he appears to have left the neighbourhood at some time before 1595, in which year his dwelling is noticed in an official rental as tenanted by another person.

THE CHAPEL LANE.

This narrow road, known also formerly as Walker Street or Dead Lane, skirted one end of Shakespeare's house and the longest side of his garden. Evidences of the insalubrious state of the lane in the poet's time are, therefore, of interest in estimating the probable cause of his fatal illness. Its appearance was then essentially different from that now to be observed, for, with the single but important exception of the Guild Chapel, there is not a vestige left of its ancient character or surroundings. Passing through it was a streamlet, the water of which turned a mill that is alluded to in rentals of the town property dated in 1545 and 1604, as also in the Ministers' Accounts, co. Warw., 2 Edw. VI. The sanitary condition of the lane was execrable, and with its bad road, fetid gutters, dunghills, pigsties, mud-walls and thatched barns, it must have presented an extremely squalid appearance. The "gutteres or dyches" are mentioned as requiring to be cleansed in a record dated as early as 1553,—Item, "that every tenaunt in Chapell lane or Ded lane do scour and kep cleane ther gutteres or dyches in the same lane befor thassencyon day, and so from thensfurthe from tyme to tyme to kepe the same, in peyn of every offender to forfet for every deffalt iij.*s.* iiij.*d.*, and that every tenaunt do ryd the soyelles in the stretes of logges and blokes ther lyenge and beynge to the noysaunce of the kynges leage people by the same day in lyke peyne." A comparison of this entry with others in the same manuscript would lead to the belief that Chapel Lane was then one of the, if not the, dirtiest locality in the town. In 1558, William Clopton, residing at New Place was fined for not keeping clean "the gutter alonge the Chappell in Chappell Lane;" and in the following year, 1559, it was ordered that no inhabitant of the ward "dwellynge neer unto the Chappell from hensfurthe use to ley eny muk in eny other place in the Chappell Lanes, but only in the gravell pyt in the Chappell Lane," under a penalty of three shillings and four pence for each offence. The following entries respecting the former state of the lane are extracted from the records of Stratford and from the rolls of the manor-court:—"1554. That every the tenauntes or ther famyly from hensfurthe do carry ther mucke to the commen dunghylles appwntyd, or elles into Meychyn's yard or in the gravell pyttes in Chappell Lane.—1556. Thomas Godwyn, fletchar, Sir William Brogden, clericus, for not scouryng ther gutter in Ded Lone they be amersyd.—1558. That non dyg from hensfurthe eny gravell in the gravell pyttes in Chappell Lane under the peyne vj.*s.* viij.*d.*—That the chamburlens do ryd the mukhyll in Chappell Lane, nye unto the Chappell at the goodwyf Walker's hous end, before the Assensyon day under the peyn of vj.*s.* viij.*d.*—1560. That every tenaunt in Ded Lone do scoure and kep cleane ther dyches and the lane before ther soylles from tyme to tyme.—1561. John Sadler, mylner, for wynnowyng his peas in Ded lane and levyng the chaf in the lane, and bryngeynge hys swyne into the same lane, and not scourynge the dyche ther, he stands amerced, xvj.*d.*—that every tenaunt kep cleene ther gutturs and dyches as well in the strets as in Ded lane under pene vj.*s.* viij.*d.*—1605. It is agreed that the Chamberlaines shall gyve warning to Henry Smyth to plucke downe his pigges-cote which is built nere the chapple wall and the house-of-office there, and that hee forbeare to kepe anie swine about the house which hee holdeth of Mr. Aspinall or the Chapple yard, and this to be done before the next hall.—1605-6. Henrye Smythe [presented] for nott makinge cleane the water couarsse before his barne in Chapple Laine.—Johne Perrie for a muckhill in the Chapple Laine." It will be observed from some of these notices that even the surroundings of the Guild Chapel itself were no exceptions to the general squalidity. The only later notices of the state of the lane in the poet's time which have been discovered relate to a pigsty which John Rogers, the vicar, had commenced to erect, about the year 1613, immediately opposite the back court of New Place. Some of the inhabitants, most probably including Shakespeare, the person most interested in the suppression of the impending nuisance, had complained of this addition to the engendering causes of a villanous compound of bad smells, and the vicar accordingly besought the Corporation that they "would consent to the finishinge of that small plecke which I have begunne in the lane, the use whereof was noe other but to keepe a swine or two in, for about my howse there is noe place of convenience without much annoyance to the Chappell, and how farre the breedeinge of such creatures is needefull to poore howskeepers I referre myselfe to those that can equall my charge ; moreover the highway will be wider and fayrer, as it may now appeare."

The original streamlet of Chapel Lane appears to have gradually undergone deterioration until it became a shallow fetid ditch, an open receptacle of sewerage and filth. There is a curious account of this ditch, as it appeared in the last century, in a letter written for the purposes of a law-suit in 1807, and, although of so recent a date, it is worth giving as confirmatory, notwithstanding the changes that had taken place in the interval, of some of the early notices of the lane. " I very well remember," says the writer, " the ditch you mention fourty-five years, as after my sister was married, which was in October, 1760, I was very often at Stratford, and was very well acquainted both with the ditch and the road in question ;—the ditch went from the Chapel, and extended to Smith's house ;—I well remember there was a space of two or three feet from the wall in a descent to the ditch, and I do not think any part of the new wall was built on the ditch ;—the ditch was the receptacle for all manner of filth that any person chose to put there, and was very obnoxious at times ;—Mr. Hunt used to complain of it, and was determined to get it covered over, or he would do it at his own expence, and I do not know whether he did not ;—across, the road from the ditch to Shakespeare Garden was very hollow and always full of mud, which is now covered over, and in general there was only one waggon tract along the lane, which used to be very bad, in the winter particularly ;—I do not know that the ditch was so deep as to overturn a carriage, and the road was very little used near it, unless it was to turn out for another, as there was always room enough." Thomas Cox, a carpenter, who lived in Chapel Lane from 1774, deposed to remembering the open gutter from the Chapel to Smith's cottage, " that it was a wide dirty ditch choaked with mud, that all the filth of that part of the town ran into it, that it was four or five feet wide and more than a foot deep, and that the road sloped down to the ditch." According to other witnesses, the ditch extended to the end of the lane, where, between the road-way and the Bancroft, was a narrow creek or ditch through which the overflow from Chapel Lane no doubt found a way into the river.

Smith's house, above alluded to, was on the site of the Getley copyhold tenement which had once belonged to Shakespeare. On the south of the ditch, on the side opposite to New Place, between the Getley estate and the Guild Chapel, there was originally a mud-wall, such a one having been on that site at least as early as 1590, and it is occasionally alluded to in the local records of the last century. About the year 1807, the Corporation, having taken in a small piece of waste ground when they filled in the ditch and built a new wall, subjected themselves to an action on the plea that they had exceeded their strictly legal rights. In their defence, they assert that,—" about twenty years ago this lane was a narrow and almost impassable road, and very little used ;—there was a wide open ditch running from the Chapel to a house in the tenure of Samuel Smith, and so on to the bottom of the lane on the south side thereof, which was generally filled up with mud and stagnant water, and became the receptacle for all the filth and rubbish of the town ; and on the side of this ditch, between that and the mud-wall, heaps of manure, ashes, and broken crockery-ware were continually thrown by the inhabitants ;—the space between the ditch and the old mud-wall was between two or three feet, and went sloping to the edge of the ditch, and was the lord's waste, and never was part of the road, and the ditch itself was so bad that no carriage could safely go within

two feet of the brink or edge of it on the lane side," that being on
account of the ground sloping down towards the ditch.   The evidences
differ as to the exact time when the ditch was covered over, but the
work was probably executed about the year 1780.   The "lord's waste"
seems to have been an indefinite slip of land on either side of the lane,
probably all that was not actually used by vehicles passing through,
presumed to belong to the lord of the manor, and continually subjected
to encroachments by the owners of the adjoining properties.

In Shakespeare's time, Chapel Lane ran almost exclusively through
gardens and barns, the latter being the storehouses for corn so numerous
in Stratford before the various enclosures of the common lands in the
neighbourhood.   On the New Place side, there was first the poet's
garden, and then the barn in which, in February, 1598, he had stocked
ten quarters of corn.   This building is thus mentioned in 1590, in a
return to a commission issued out of the Exchequer for the survey of
the possessions of Ambrose earl of Warwick,—"Willielmus Underhill
generosus tenet libere unum horreum, viij.*d.*," *vicus voc. Walkers
Streete*, nine other barns being mentioned in the same list as being
in Chapel Lane.   On the site of Shakespeare's barn stood in 1556 a
tenement that had belonged to the priory of Pinley ; Warw. Survey,
Longbridge MS.   Immediately adjoining the Great Garden of New
Place was the barn on the Clifford Charity estate, which was pulled
down about the year 1619.   There then appears to have been, in the
poet's time, a small plot of land, afterwards Spurr's, unbuilt upon ; but
on the Corporation estate adjoining this on the east there was a barn
attached to each of three holdings.   Next to Spurr's estate, divided
from it by a quickset hedge, the usual kind of fence about here in the
days of Shakespeare, was a slip of land, on which stood a barn, leased
by the Corporation to Abraham Strelley in 1599 for twenty-one years.
This little estate was previously described in 1582 as "a barne with
backesyd in tenure of Nicholas Barnshurst, sufficiently repayred, and
j. ellme groweing thereon."   It was thatched and of four bays, occupying
the entire frontage in Chapel Lane ; and in the back premises was a
thatched hovel of two bays, in many of the deeds termed a workhouse,
and sometimes a wood-house.   This barn and two others on the east had
been destroyed by fire shortly before the year 1619.   Their history may
to some extent be gathered from a lease granted in that year to Alice
Smith, widow, of the premises in the middle of the three holdings into
which the property was divided.   In this deed it is recited that, in
consideration of the surrender of a former lease, and "that the saide
Alice Smith hath at her owne costes and charges newlie erected, built
and tyled, the saide barne, the same beinge heertofore consumed by
fyer," the Corporation grant her, for a period of sixty years, "all that
barne and garden with thappurtenaunces, scituate and beinge in Dead

Lane alias Walkers Streete, betweene a garden and plott of grownd wheron late stood a barne of the said bayliffe and burgesses late in the occupation of William Mountford, deceased, one the west parte, and the garden and plott of grownd wherone late stood a barne of the saide bayliffe and burgesses in the occupaccion of Mr. Tyler one the est parte, and the gardens of the said bayliff and burgesses in the occupacions of Charles Rooke and William Byddle one the north, and the said streete or lane one the south." Next to these premises were a barn and piece of land, which were leased by the Corporation in 1591 to Richard Tyler for twenty-one years. " Richard Tiler, a barne of v baies thatchd, a backside in bredth answerable, in length about liij. yerdes," survey dated 1599. This barn having been destroyed, the ground was leased to William Shawe in 1623 on the condition that he should, within three years, build "a good, substantiall and sufficient well-tymbered barne conteineing foure bayes, and cover the same with tyles or slates." Sketches of one or two of the later barns of Chapel Lane have been preserved, but none of those of the Shakespearean period are known to exist.

———

OLD HOUSES AT THE RIVER END OF CHAPEL LANE, 1840.

CONTEMPORARY NOTICES.

This division is restricted to those allusions to the great dramatist *by name* which have been discovered in the printed literature of his own time, those which are attached to recognised quotations or poems being excluded. It has not been considered necessary to form a corresponding selection of innominate references to him, or of the occasional authentic or travestied quotations from, or imitations of, passages in his works; but those that are of real practical use for the illustration of facts or theories are referred to either in the text or notes. Let it be observed that it is sometimes impossible to decide whether certain similarities are to be attributed to recollections of Shakespeare, or if they be prototypes of his own language or thought; in which cases of uncertainty they are obviously of no argumentative value.

I. The commencing verses of a laudatory address prefixed to— Willobie his Avisa, or the true Picture of a modest Maid and of a chast and constant Wife, 4to. Lond. 1594, a work entered at Stationers' Hall on September the third in that year, and reprinted in 1596, 1605, and 1609.

> In Lavine land though Livie bost,
> There hath beene seene a constant dame;
> Though Rome lament that she have lost
> The gareland of her rarest fame,
> > Yet now we see that here is found
> > As great a faith in English ground.
>
> Though Collatine have deerely bought
> To high renowne a lasting life,
> And found that most in vaine have sought,
> To have a faire and constant wife,
> > Yet Tarquyne pluckt his glistering grape,
> > And Shake-speare paints poore Lucrece rape.

II. The second nominated allusion to Shakespeare in our printed literature occurs on the margin of a curious volume entitled,—" Polimanteia, or the meanes lawfull and unlawfull, to judge of the fall of a Common-wealth, against the frivolous and foolish conjectures of this age," 4to., Cambridge, 1595. The author is eulogising in his text the poets of England as superior to those of foreign nations, but the two side-notes

—one consisting of three and the other of two words,—in which references are made to the early poems of Shakespeare, appear to be merely illustrative examples in support of the author's main position. They seem to be isolated, and altogether unconnected with the other marginalia. The following extract, here printed V. L., exhibits the exact manner in which they are placed in the original work, the first portion being at the bottom of one page and the four concluding lines at the top of the next.

Let o-
ther countries (sweet *Cambridge*) enuie,
All praise (yet admire) my *Virgil*, thy petrarch, di-
worthy. uine *Spenser*. And vnlesse I erre, (a thing
Lucrecia easie in such simplicitie) deluded by
Sweet Shak- dearlie beloued *Delia*, and fortunatelie
speare. fortunate *Cleopatra ; Oxford* thou maist
Eloquent extoll thy courte-deare-verse happie
Gaueston. *Daniell*, whose sweete refined muse, in
contracted shape, were sufficient a-
mongst men, to gaine pardon of the *Wanton*
sinne to *Rosemond*, pittie to diftressed *Adonis.*
Cleopatra, and euerliuing praise to her *Watsons*
louing *Delia.* *heyre.*

III. From Barnfield's Encomion of Lady Pecunia, 1598, the same lines, with a verbal error, occurring in the second edition of that work, 1605. In both editions the following verses conclude,—" A Remembrance of some English Poets."

And Shakespeare thou, whose hony-flowing vaine,
Pleasing the world, thy praises doth obtaine ;
Whose *Venus*, and whose *Lucrece*, sweete and chaste,
Thy name in fames immortall booke have plac't,—
Live ever you, at least in fame live ever ;
Well may the bodye dye, but fame dies never.

IV.—The following extracts are from a treatise entitled,—"A com-parative Discourse of our English poets with the Greeke, Latine and Italian poets"—which is near the end of a thick little volume called,— " Palladis Tamia. Wits Treasury, being the Second part of Wits Commonwealth. By Francis Meres, Maister of Artes of both Universities. Viuitur ingenio, cætera mortis erunt.—At London.—Printed by P. Short for Cuthbert Burbie, and are to be solde at his shop at the Royall Exchange, 1598." There can be no doubt that this chapter was written in the summer of 1598, the work itself having been entered at Stationers' Hall on the 7th of September in that year, aud there being in the Discourse a notice of Marston's Satires registered on the previous 27th of May. The date of publication is a fact of so much interest that a facsimile of the copyright entry to Burby is here subjoined.

1598 Anno 40mo Re

xiijo September

Entred for his copie vnder the
wardons handes and mr
Hartwell a booke called
wittes Treasury.
being the second parte of
wittes Common wealth

As the Greeke tongue is made famous and eloquent by Homer, Hesiod, Euripedes, Aeschilus, Sophocles, Pindarus, Phocylides and Aristophanes; and the Latine tongue by Virgill, Ovid, Horace, Silius Italicus, Lucanus, Lucretius, Ausonius and Claudianus; so the English tongue is mightily enriched and gorgeouslie invested, in rare ornaments and resplendent abiliments, by Sir Philip Sidney, Spencer, Daniel, Drayton, Warner, Shakespeare, Marlow and Chapman.—As the soule of Euphorbus was thought to live in Pythagoras, so the sweete wittie soule of Ovid lives in mellifluous and hony-tongued Shakespeare; witnes his Venus and Adonis, his Lucrece, his sugred Sonnets among his private friends, &c.—As Plautus and Seneca are accounted the best for comedy and tragedy among the Latines, so Shakespeare among the English is the most excellent in both kinds for the stage; for comedy, witnes his Gentlemen of Verona, his Errors, his Love labors lost, his Love labours wonne, his Midsummers night dreame, and his Merchant of Venice; for tragedy, his Richard the 2, Richard the 3, Henry the 4, King John, Titus Andronicus and his Romeo and Juliet.—As Epius®

Stolo® said that the Muses would speake with Plautus tongue, if they would speake Latin ; so I say that the Muses would speak with Shakespeares fine filed phrase, if they would speake English.—As Ovid saith of his worke ;—Jamque opus exegi, quod nec Jovis ira, nec ignis, =Nec poterit ferrum, nec edax abolere vetustas. And as Horace saith of his ; Exegi monumentum ære perennius ; regalique situ pyramidum altius ; quod non imber edax, non aquilo impotens possit diruere ; aut innumerabilis annorum series et fuga temporum ; so say I severally of sir Philip Sidneys, Spencers, Daniels, Draytons, Shakespeares and Warners workes,—Non Jovis ira, imbres, Mars, ferrum, flamma, senectus,=Hoc opus unda, lues, turbo, venena ruent.=Et quanquam ad pulcherrimum hoc opus evertendum tres illi dii=Conspirabunt, Cronus, Vulcanus, et pater ipse gentis,=Non tamen annorum series, non flamma, nec ensis, =Æternum potuit hoc abolere decus.—As Pindarus, Anacreon and Callimachus, among the Greekes, and Horace and Catullus among the Latines, are the best lyrick poets ; so in this faculty the best among our poets are Spencer, who excelleth in all kinds, Daniel, Drayton, Shakespeare, Bretton.—As these tragicke poets flourished in Greece, Aeschylus, Euripedes, Sophocles, Alexander Aetolus, Achæus Erithriæus, Astydamas Atheniensis, Apollodorus Tarsensis, Nicomachus Phrygius, Thespis Atticus and Timon Apolloniates ; and these among the Latines, Accius, M. Attilius, Pomponius Secundus and Seneca ; so these are our best for tragedie, the Lorde Buckhurst, Doctor Leg of Cambridge, Doctor Edes of Oxforde, maister Edward Ferris, the authour of the Mirrour for Magistrates, Marlow, Peele, Watson, Kid, Shakespeare, Drayton, Chapman, Decker and Benjamin Johnson.—The best poets for comedy among the Greeks are these, Menander, Aristophanes, Eupolis Atheniensis, Alexis Terius, Nicostratus, Amipsias Atheniensis, Anaxandrides Rhodius, Aristonymus, Archippus Atheniensis and Callias Atheniensis ; and among the Latines, Plautus, Terence, Nævius, Sext. Turpilius, Licinius Imbrex and Virgilius Romanus ; so the best for comedy amongst us bee Edward Earle of Oxforde, Doctor Gager of Oxforde, Maister Rowley, once a rare Scholler of learned Pembrooke Hall in Cambridge, Maister Edwardes, one of her Majesties Chappell, eloquent and wittie John Lilly, Lodge, Gascoyne, Greene, Shakespeare, Thomas Nash, Thomas Heywood, Anthony Mundye, our best plotter, Chapman, Porter, Wilson, Hathway and Henry Chettle.—As these are famous among the Greeks for elegie, Melanthus, Mymnerus Colophonius, Olympius Mysius, Parthenius, Nicæus, Philetas Cous, Theogenes Megarensis and Pigres Halicarnassæus ; and these among the Latines, Mecænas, Ovid, Tibullus, Propertius, T. Valgius, Cassius Severus and Clodius Sabinus ; so these are the most passionate among us to bewaile and bemoane the perplexities of Love,—Henrie Howard, earle of Surrey, Sir Thomas Wyat the elder, Sir Francis Brian, Sir Philip Sidney, Sir Walter

Rawley, Sir Edward Dyer, Spencer, Daniel, Drayton, Shakespeare, Whetstone, Gascoyne, Samuell Page, sometimes fellowe of Corpus Christi Colledge in Oxford, Churchyard, Bretton.

V. Verses on Shakespeare, inscribed, "Ad Gulielmum Shakespeare," from John Weever's "Epigrammes in the oldest cut and newest fashion," 8vo. Lond. 1599.

Honie - tong'd Shakespeare, when I saw thine issue,=I swore Apollo got them and none other,=Their rosie-tainted features cloth'd in tissue,=Some heaven-born goddesse said to be their mother ;= Rose-checkt⑧ *Adonis* with his amber tresses,=Faire fire-hot *Venus* charming him to love her,=Chaste *Lucretia*, virgine-like her dresses,= Prowd lust-stung *Tarquine* seeking still to prove her ;=*Romea⑧, Richard ;* more whose names I know not,=Their sugred tongues and power attractive beuty=Say they are Saints, althogh that Sts they shew not,= For thousands vowes to them subjective dutie ;=They burn in love ; thy children, Shakespear, het them ;=Go, wo thy muse ; more nymphish brood beget them.

VI. From—"Bel-vedere, or the Garden of the Muses,—Imprinted at London," 1600. This work, a collection of poetical extracts, was entered at Stationers Hall the same year on August the 11th.

Now that every one may be fully satisfied concerning this Garden, that no one man doth assume to him-selfe the praise thereof, or can arrogate to his owne deserving those things which have been derived from so many rare and ingenious spirits, I have set down both how, whence and where these flowres had their first springing till thus they were drawne togither into the *Muses Garden*, that every ground may challenge his owne, each plant his particular, and no one be injuried in the justice of his merit. . . . . Edmund Spencer ; Henry Constable esquier ; Samuell Daniell ; Thomas Lodge, Doctor of Physicke ; Thomas Watson ; Michaell Drayton ; John Davies ; Thomas Hudson ; Henrie Locke esquier ; John Marstone ; Christopher Marlow ; Benjamin Johnson ; William Shakspeare ; Thomas Churchyard esquier ; Thomas Nash ; Thomas Kidde ; George Peele ; Robert Greene ; Josuah Sylvester ; Nicholas Breton ; Gervase Markham ; Thomas Storer ; Robert Wilmot ; Christopher Middleton ; Richard Barnefield ; *these being moderne and extant poets that have liv'd togither ; from many of their extant workes, and some kept in privat.*

VII. Verses from—"A Mournefull Dittie entituled Elizabeths Losse, together with a Welcome for King James," a very rare ballad in the library of S. Christie-Miller, Esq., of Britwell House, Burnham.

You poets all, brave Shakspeare, Johnson, Greene,
Bestow your time to write for Englands Queene.
Lament, lament, lament, you English peeres ;
Lament your losse, possest so many yeeres.

VIII. From "Epigrames, served out in 52 severall Dishes for every man to tast without surfeting. By I. C. Gent.," 12mo. Lond. There is no date to this rare little volume, but it was entered in the Stationers Registers on May the 22nd, 1604, and is there ascribed to J. Cooke gent.

Who er'e will go unto the presse may see=The hated fathers of vilde balladrie ;=One sings in his base note the river Thames=Shal sound the famous memory of noble King James ;=Another sayes that he will, to his death,=Sing the renowned worthinesse of sweet Elizabeth ;=So runnes their verse in such disordered straine,=And with them dare great majesty prophane ;=Some dare do this ; some other humbly craves=For helpe of spirits in their sleeping graves,=As he that calde to Shakespeare, Johnson, Greene,=To write of their dead noble Queene.

IX. From—"Daiphantus, or the Passions of Love. Comicall to Reade, but tragicall to act ; as full of Wit as Experience ; by An. Sc. gentleman," 4to. Lond. 1604. The author, supposed to be one Anthony Scoloker, observes, in a quaint dedication, that an Epistle to the Reader—

should be like the never-too-well read Arcadia, where the prose and verce, matter and words, are like his mistresses eyes, one still excelling another, and without corivall ; or to come home to the vulgars element, like friendly Shake-speares tragedies, where the commedian rides, when the tragedian stands on tiptoe ; Faith, it should please all, like Prince Hamlet. But, in sadnesse, then it were to be feared he would runne mad. In sooth, I will not be moonesicke to please ; nor out of my wits, though I displeased all.

X. From Camden's Remaines of a Greater Worke concerning Britaine, 1605, ii. 8, the Epistle Dedicatorie to Sir Robert Cotton bearing the date of June, 1603. The following passage is repeated in ed. 1614, p. 324.

These may suffice for some poeticall descriptions of our auncient poets; if I would come to our time, what a world could I present to you out of Sir Philipp Sidney, Ed. Spencer, Samuel Daniel, Hugh Holland, Ben: Johnson, Th. Campion, Mich. Drayton, George Chapman, John Marston, William Shakespeare, and other most pregnant witts of these our times, whom succeeding ages may justly admire.

XI. From criticisms on the English poets in a drama written in the winter of 1601-2, but not printed until 1606, in which latter year two editions appeared under the title of,—The Returne from Pernassus, or the

Scourge of Simony, publiquely acted by the Students in Saint Johns Colledge in Cambridge." It was entered at Stationers' Hall in October, 1605. A character named Ingenioso, a university student, asks another, one Judicio, the opinions of the latter on various writers, each name being supposed to be preceded by the words,—"What's thy judgment of "—. In one edition of this play the word lazy in the fifth line is omitted.*

> *Ing.* William Shakespeare.
> *Jud.* Who loves Adonis love, or Lucre's rape,
> His sweeter verse containes hart-robbing life ;
> Could but a graver subject him content,
> Without loves foolish lazy languishment.

XII. In a later part of the drama last mentioned, the Returne from Pernassus, the celebrated actors, Burbage and Kemp, appear as instructors of their art to two university students, previously to which the following dialogue takes place between them.

Bur. Now, Will Kempe, if we can intertaine these schollers at a low rate, it wil be well ; they have oftentimes a good conceite in a part.—*Kempe.* Its true, indeede, honest Dick, but the slaves are somewhat proud, and, besides, it is a good sport in a part to see them never speake in their walke but at the end of the stage, just as though, in walking with a fellow, we should never speake but at a stile, a gate or a ditch, where a man can go no further. I was once at a comedie in Cambridge, and there I saw a parasite make faces and mouths of all sorts on this fashion.—*Bur.* A little teaching will mend these faults, and it may bee, besides, they will be able to pen a part.—*Kemp.* Few of the university pen plaies well : they smell too much of that writer Ovid, and that writer Metamorphosis, and talke too much of Proserpina and Juppiter. Why, heres our fellow Shakespeare puts them all downe, I, and Ben Jonson too. O that Ben Jonson is a pestilent fellow ! he brought up Horace giving the poets a pill, but our fellow Shakespeare hath given him a purge that made him beray his credit.—*Bur.* Its a shrewd fellow, indeed.—I wonder these schollers stay so long ; they appointed to be here presently that we might try them ; oh, here they come.

XIII. The conclusion of "Mirrha, the Mother of Adonis, or Lustes Prodegies, by William Barksted," 8vo. Lond. 1607, a work entered at Stationers' Hall on the twelfth of November in that year.*

But stay, my Muse, in thine owne confines keepe,=And wage not warre with so deere lov'd a neighbor ;=But having sung thy day-song, rest and sleepe ;=Preserve thy small fame and his greater favor.=His song was worthie merrit ;—Shakspeare, hee=Sung the faire blossome, thou, the withered tree ;=Laurell is due to him ; his art and wit=Hath purchast it ; cypres thy brow will fit.

XIV. From—"The Scourge of Folly, consisting of satyricall Epigramms and others in honor of many noble and worthy Persons of our Land," by John Davies of Hereford, 8vo., Epig. 159, pp. 76, 77. This curious little volume is undated, but it was entered at Stationers' Hall on October the 8th, 1610. The following verses are addressed "To our English Terence, Mr. Will: Shake-speare."

Some say, good Will, which I, in sport, do sing,=Had'st thou not plaid some kingly parts in sport,=Thou hadst bin a companion for a king,=And beene a King among the meaner sort.=Some others raile ; but, raile as they thinke fit,=Thou hast no rayling, but a raigning wit ;= And honesty thou sow'st, which they do reape,=So to increase their stocke which they do keepe.

XV. The conclusion of the Dedication to Webster's White Divel, or the Tragedy of Paulo Giordano Ursini, 4to. Lond. 1612.

Detraction is the sworne friend to ignorance. For mine owne part, I have ever truly cherisht my good opinion of other mens worthy labours, especially of that full and haightned stile of maister Chapman, the labor'd and understanding workes of maister Johnson, the no lesse worthy composures of the both worthily excellent Maister Beamont and Maister Fletcher, and lastly, without wrong last to be named, the right happy and copious industry of M. Shake-speare, M. Decker, and M. Heywood, wishing what I write may be read by their light ; protesting that, in the strength of mine owne judgement, I know them so worthy, that, though I rest silent in my owne worke, yet to most of theirs I dare (without flattery) fix that of Martiall,—non norunt, Hæc monumenta mori.

XVI. From—"The Excellencie of the English tongue by R. C. of Anthony, esquire," printed in Camden's Remaines, ed. 1614, pp. 43, 44. The initials stand for the name of Richard Carew, whose earliest published work appeared in 1598, but the date of the composition of the present essay is unknown.

The long words that we borrow, being intermingled with the short of our owne store, make up a perfect harmonie, by culling from out which mixture with judgement you may frame your speech according to the matter you must worke on, majesticall, pleasant, delicate or manly, more or lesse, in what sort you please. Adde hereunto that, whatsoever grace any other language carrieth in verse or prose, in tropes or metaphors, in ecchoes and agnominations, they may all bee lively and exactly represented in ours. Will you have Platoes veine ?—reade Sir Thomas

Smith. The Ionicke?—Sir Thomas Moore. Ciceroes?—Ascham. Varro?—Chaucer. Demosthenes?—Sir John Cheeke, who, in his treatise to the Rebels, hath comprised all the figures of rhetorick. Will you reade Virgill?—take the Earle of Surrey. Catullus?—Shakespheare and Barlowes® fragment. Ovid?—Daniell. Lucan?—Spencer. Martial?—Sir John Davies and others. Will you have all in all for prose and verse—take the miracle of our age, Sir Philip Sidney.

XVII. From the Second Part of a work entitled,—" Rubbe and a great Cast, Epigrams by Thomas Freeman, gent.," 4to. Lond., 1614; entered at Stationers' Hall on June the 30th. The following epigram is addressed " to Master W: Shakespeare."

Shakespeare, that nimble mercury, thy braine,=Lulls many hundred Argus-eyes asleepe,=So fit for all thou fashionest thy vaine;=At th' horse-foote fountaine thou hast drunk full deepe;=Vertues or vices theame to thee all one is;=Who loves chaste life, there's Lucrece for a teacher;=Who list read lust, there's Venus and Adonis,=True modell of a most lascivious leatcher.=Besides in plaies thy wit windes like Meander,=When® needy new-composers borrow more=Thence® Terence doth from Plautus or Menander.=But to praise thee aright I want thy store;=Then let thine owne works thine owne worth upraise, =And help t' adorne thee with deserved baies.

XVIII. From—" The Annales or Generall Chronicle of England, begun first by maister John Stow, and after him continued and augmented, with matters forreyne and domestique, auncient and moderne, unto the ende of this present yeere, 1614, by Edmond Howes, gentleman," fol., Lond., 1615, p. 811. The following are amongst the observations of Howes on the writers that flourished in the reign of Elizabeth.

Our moderne and present excellent poets, which worthely florish in their owne workes, and all of them in my owne knowledge, lived togeather in this Queenes raigne; according to their priorities, as neere as I could, I have orderly set downe, viz.,—George Gascoigne, esquire; Thomas Church-yard, esquire; Sir Edward Dyer, knight; Edmond Spencer, esquire; Sir Philip Sidney, knight; Sir John Harrington, knight; Sir Thomas Challoner, knight; Sir Frauncis Bacon, knight; and Sir John Davie, knight; Master John Lillie, gentleman; Maister George Chapman, gentleman; M. W. Warner, gentleman; M. Willi. Shakespeare, gentleman; Samuell Daniell, esquire; Michaell Draiton, esquire of the bath; M. Christopher Marlo, gen.; M. Benjamine Johnson, gentleman; John Marston, esquier; M. Abraham Frauncis, gen.; master Frauncis Meers, gentle.; master Josua Silvester, gentle.; master Thomas Deckers, gentleman; M. John Flecher, gentle.; M. John Webster, gentleman; M. Thomas Heywood, gentleman; M. Thomas Middelton, gentleman M. George Withers.

THE ROTHER MARKET.

This street, which extended from the northern side of Poor's Close to the western end of Meer Pool Lane, was the longest one in the poet's native town, and at the latter boundary also the widest. It was also known under the title of the Rother Street. In the time of "Adreane Quyny, capytall alderman, John Taylor and John Shakspeyr, chamburlens," 1563, it is mentioned as the *Roder Streate*, while in an indenture of the previous year we hear of the *Rather Merkett*, and, at a later period, of "the Rother Street otherwise called the Rother Market." The name was derived from the old English word *rother*, a term which was applied to horned cattle and which has only become obsolete within the present century.

The Rother Market must formerly, with its streamlet, its half-timbered houses, its mud-walled cottages and its thatched hovels, have exhibited at all events a quaint if not a picturesque appearance. The rivulet has long since vanished, but it was to be seen in the latter part of the eighteenth century, the only view of it known to exist being preserved in a rude sketch of the locality which was taken about the year 1780. An engraving of this sketch will be found near the commencement of the present volume, but it should be mentioned that the little bridge which is therein exhibited does not belong to the Shakespearean period. The stream, after passing through Meer Pool Lane, crossed Henley Street into the Guildpits, finally emptying itself into the Avon near the stone bridge.

The old house in the Rother Street, a view of which is here given, is one of the most perfect and interesting examples of the domestic architecture of Shakespeare's time that are now to be met with in the town. The main features of the building are certainly in their original state, and the annexed sketches of two of its rooms may perhaps convey as faithful an idea of an Elizabethan Stratford interior as is now within our reach.

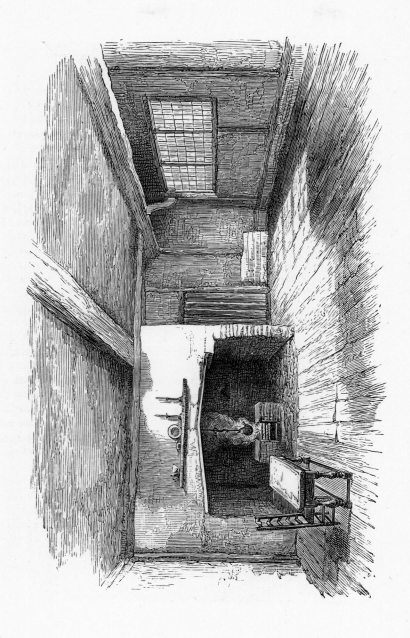

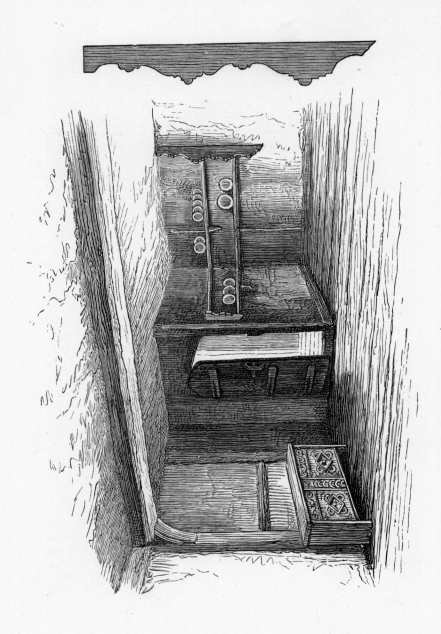

PLAYS AT COURT, 2 JAMES I.

One of my main endeavours in the compilation of this work is to place the student who resides in a distant land, and who may never have the opportunity of investigating for himself the reliability of the Shakespearean evidences, as far as possible on a level, in respect to his security from deception, with the critic who dwells in their midst. The task is not an easy one, for literature has been afflicted for many generations by the reception of unscrupulous forgeries that have corrupted nearly every branch of enquiry which relates to the life or works of the great dramatist. The rigid elimination of these is of course my paramount object, but the separation would probably be imperfect were not every fragment of documentary evidence brought to the initial test of an adverse surmise. Instead of being contented with the mere absence of suspicious indications, the first duty in every instance is to anxiously consider if there is even a remote possibility of fraud; and the next, if such a possibility can be rationally imagined, to submit the case to the decision of skilled paleographers—of those who have passed their lives in the study and examination of ancient documents, and have thus obtained that decisive insight in such matters which a lengthened and continuous experience can alone bestow. This is the system which has been followed throughout the construction of the present volume, and it may be confidently affirmed that, excepting where reasons for hesitation have been distinctly set forth, there has not been a single document heretofore printed or quoted upon the authenticity of which the slightest doubt can be entertained by a qualified critic.

This perception of absolute surety is at length unfortunately interrupted. In the year 1842 there appeared a collection of extracts from the old manuscript accounts of the Court Revels that were then preserved at the Audit Office, and included in the volume, in "the Accompte of the Office of the Revelles of this whole yeres charge in anno 1604 untell the last of Octobar, 1605," is a register mentioning by name some of the dramas that were acted before Royalty during that period. The whole of this last-mentioned record, a copy of which is given on the next page, is unquestionably a modern forgery, and if this had been all the evidence on the subject, there would obviously have been no

A List of Theatrical Performances from a work entitled, "Extracts from the Accounts of the Revels at Court in the Reigns of Queen Elizabeth and King James I., from the original Office Books of the Masters and Yeomen," 8vo. Lond. 1842, a few oversights in transcription being here corrected.

The Plaiers.	1604.	The Poets which mayd the plaies.
By the kings Ma^{tis} plaiers.	Hallamas Day being the first of Nouembar A play in the Banketinge house att Whithall called the Moor of Venis.	
By his Ma^{tis} plaiers.	The Sunday ffollowinge A Play of the Merry Wiues of Winsor.	
By his Ma^{tis} plaiers.	On S^t. Stiuens Night in the Hall A Play caled Mesur for Mesur.	Shaxberd.
	On S^t. Jhons Night A Maske wth musike presented by the Erl of Penbrok the Lord Willowbie ꝺ 6 Knightes more of ye Court.	
By his Ma^{tis} Plaiers.	On Inosents Night The Plaie of Errors.	Shaxberd.
By the Queens Ma^{tis} plaiers.	On Sunday ffollowinge A plaie How to larne of a woman to wooe	Hewood.
The Boyes of the Chapell.	On Newers Night A playe cauled: All Fouelles.	By Georg Chapman.
By his Ma^{tis} plaiers.	Betwin Newers Day and Twelfe day A Play of Loues Labours Lost.	
	On Twelfe Night the Queens Ma^{tis} Maske of Moures w^h Aleven Laydies of honno^r to accupayney her ma^{tie} wch cam in great showes of devises wch thay satt in wth exselent musike.	
By his Ma^{tis} plaiers.	On the 7 of January was played the play of Henry the fift.	
By his Ma^{tis} plaiers.	The 8 of January A play cauled Euery on out of his Umor.	
By his Ma^{tis} plaiers.	On Candelmas night A playe Euery one in his Umor.	
	The Sunday ffollowing A playe provided and discharged.	
By his Ma^{tis} plaiers.	On Shrousunday A play of the Marchant of Venis.	Shaxberd.
By his Ma^{tis} plaiers.	On Shroumonday A Tragidye of The Spanishe Maz:	
By his Ma^{tis} players.	On Shroutusday A play cauled The Martchant of Venis againe comanded by the Kings Matie.	Shaxberd.

alternative but to dismiss it entirely from consideration. There are, however, substantial reasons for believing that, although the manuscript itself is spurious, the information which it yields is genuine.

In the year 1791 Sir William Musgrave, the First Commissioner of the Board of Audit, made arrangements for Malone's inspection of the ancient manuscripts then in his office, these including what he termed "records of the Master of the Revels" for 1604 and 1605. These facts are derived from explicit notes that will be found in the variorum Shakespeare, ed. 1821, iii. 363, 361. That Malone availed himself of the opportunity, and visited Somerset House for the express purpose of examining the whole collection of the documents that pertained to the Office of the Revels, is evident from his own statement in the work just quoted, iii. 361; and amongst the papers that came with that portion of his library which was added to the treasures of the Bodleian in 1821 is a leaf which contains the following memoranda, no clue, however, being given to the source whence they were derived,—

1604 & 1605—Ed^d. Tylney—Sunday after Hallowmas—Merry Wyves of Windsor perf^d by the K's players—Hallamas—in the Banquetting ho^e. at Whitehall the Moor of Venis—perf^d by the K's players—On S^t. Stephens Night—Mesure for Mesur by Shaxberd—perf^d. by the K's players—On Innocents night Errors by Shaxberd perf^d. by the K's players—On Sunday following "How to Learn of a Woman to wooe by Hewood, perf^d. by the Q's players—On New Years Night—All fools by G. Chapman perf^d. by the Boyes of the Chapel—bet New y^{rs}. day & twelfth day—Loves Labour lost perf^d by the K's p:^{rs}—On the 7th Jan. K. Hen. the fifth perf^d. by the K.'s P^{rs}—On 8th Jan—Every one out of his humour—On Candlemas night Every one in his humour—On Shrove sunday the Marchant of Venis by Shaxberd—perf^d by the K's P^{rs}—the same repeated on Shrove tuesd. by the K's Comm^d.

Although the contents of this leaf are not in Malone's handwriting, there is no doubt whatever that it belonged to his collection of materials, it being one with others of an analogous character that were in a loose bundle of scraps which formed part of the original gift to the Bodleian, and had remained uncatalogued and inaccessible to students until they were bound in recent years under the direction of Mr. H. S. Harper, one of the officials of that library. The leaf containing the abridged transcript just given is now preserved in MS. Mal. 29, and Mr. Harper, who well recollects arranging the papers for the formation of that volume, assures me that there is no possibility of any of its contents having been acquired subsequently to the reception of the Malone collection in 1821.

There is nothing either in the character of the handwriting, or in the form of this transcript, to justify the faintest suspicion that it is in itself a forgery. It has, on the contrary, every indication of being a faithful abridgement, sent most probably to Malone from the Audit Office, of the list which was printed in 1842. There now arises the crucial enquiry for the period at which Malone became acquainted with the information yielded by that list, for, unless he met with the latter for the first time nearly at the end of his career, it is incredible that he should have accepted the genuineness of any of its important details without a personal examination of the original. Such an assumption is incompatible with the numerous traces of the unwonted assiduity that pervaded his Shakespearean researches. Now although there is at present no direct evidence of the fact, the little that is known favours the belief that he was in possession of the contents of the existing forgery within a few years after his invitation to the Audit Office in 1791, while nothing has been produced which is in the slightest degree inconsistent with that opinion. Let the following intimations be carefully weighed.—The material novelties that are introduced into that forgery are restricted to the dates therein given of the performances of Othello and Measure for Measure, and the entries respecting these are the only items that Malone would have been absolutely compelled to notice in his dissertation upon the order of Shakespeare's plays. With respect to the first, he took the new chronological fact for granted when he made the following decisive statement,—" we *know* it (Othello) was acted in 1604 and, I have therefore placed it in that year,"—important words that were penned before his death in 1812 (variorum Shakespeare, ed. 1821, ii. 404); and there can hardly be a reasonable doubt that he was relying on the same testimony when he observed in another work, —"I formerly thought that Othello was one of our great dramatick poet's latest compositions, but I now know, from indisputable evidence, that was not the case," note to a passage in Dryden's Grounds of Criticism, ed. 1800, pp. 258, 259. If the former work, the variorum of 1821, had not been impaired by the disadvantages attending its posthumous compilation, it being the product of Malone's imperfectly revised text and essays, the confirmation of his assertion respecting the date of the tragedy would no doubt have been given; and to the same unfortunate accident must be imputed the circumstance of his observations on the date of Measure for Measure in that edition being a mere reprint of those which had appeared in 1790.

It is altogether impossible that so experienced a record-student as Malone could have been even transiently deceived by the forgery which is now in existence, while the character of its ink encourages the suspicion that it could not have been perpetrated until long after his death in 1812. The latter opinion is to some extent supported by its entries not belonging to the more graphic species of literary frauds that were current before that period. Then there is the extreme improbability that Malone should have lighted upon two documents each of them yielding the unexpected information of the early date of Othello, while his acknowledged rigid integrity excludes the very thought that he could have been accessory to a deception in the matter. It may, therefore, on the whole be fairly presumed that he had access in or before 1800 to a genuine manuscript that included in some form the entries that are given in the abridged transcript; for we may feel sure that he would never have used the words "indisputable evidence" in respect to one of them until he had made a personal scrutiny of the original, even if his residence had not been, as it was, within less than an hour's walk from the Audit Office. There appears to be only one solution that reconciles all the known facts of the case. It is that the forger had met with, and reproduced in a simulated form, trustworthy extracts from a genuine record that had disappeared from that office. This view of the case is essentially supported by what is, in respect to the present inquiry, the important discovery at Hatfield of the note of Sir Walter Cope which mentions the revival of Love's Labour's Lost by the King's Company in or shortly before January, 1605, an evidence that could not have been known to the impostor, and one of a fact that would have been beyond even the remote proba-bility of a successful conjecture. On the other hand, with the single exception of the day assigned for the performance of that comedy, there are no questionable indications of any kind in the contents of the fabricated list, nothing that cannot be either explained or corro-borated. The only other feature that could really justify a suspicion is the quaint orthography of the poet's name, but this is no doubt to be ascribed to the illiteracy of the original scribe, and it may be added that similar forms were in provincial use, e.g., *Shaxber*, Chapel-lane deed, 1572, and Stratford MS., 1704; *Shaxbere*, Henley-street con-veyance, 1573; *Shaxbeer*, Stratford MS., 1737.

The following passages, all but one of which are confirmatory of the facts stated in the printed list of 1842, must now be given.—1. "For makeinge readie the greate chamber at Whitehalle for the Kinges majestie to see the plaies, by the space of twoe daies mense Novembris, 1604, xxxix. *s.* iiij. *d.*", accounts of the Treasurer of the Chamber, MS.—2. "For makeinge readie the Banquetinge House at Whitehalle for the Kinges Majestie againste the plaie, by the space of iiij.ᵒʳ daies mense Novembris, 1604, lxxviij.*s.* viij.*d.*", MS. ibid.—3. "To John Hemynges, one of his Majesties players, uppon the Counselles warraunte dated at the Courte at Whitehalle, xxj.ᵐᵒ die Januarij, 1604, for the paines and expences of himselfe and his companie in playinge and presentinɣe of six enterludes or plaies before his Majestie, viz., on All Saintes daie at nighte, the Sonday at nighte followinge beinge the iiij.th of November, 1604, St. Stephens daie at nighte, Innocentes day at nighte, and on the vij.th and viij.th daies of Januarie, for everie of the saide plaies accord-inge to the usualle allowaunce of vj.*li.* xiij.*s.* iiij.*d* the peece, xl.*li.*, and lxvj.*s.* viij.*d* for everie plaie by waie of His Majesties rewarde, xx.*li.*, in all the some of lx.*li.*", MS. ibid.—4. "On St. Johns day we had the marriage of Sir Philip Herbert and the Lady Susan performed at Whitehall with all the honour could be done a great favourite ;—at night there was a mask in the hall, which for conceit and fashion was suitable to the occasion ; the actors were the Earle of Pembrook, the Lord Willoby, Sir Samuel Hays, Sir Thomas Germain, Sir Robert Cary, Sir John Lee, Sir Richard Preston and Sir Thomas Bager," letter of January, 1604–5, ap. Winwood's Memorials, 1725, ii. 43.—5. "To John Duke, one of the Quenes Majesties plaiers, uppon the Counselles warraunte dated at the Courte at Whitehalle, xix.ⁿᵒ die Februarij, 1604, for the expenses of himselfe and the reste of his companie for presentinge one interlude or plaie before his Majestie on Sundaye nighte, the xxx.th daie of December, vj.*li.* xiij.*s.* iiij.*d.*, and to them by waie of his Majesties rewarde, lxvj.*s.* viij.*d.*, in all x.*li.*," Treas. Chamb. MS.—6. "To Samuell Daniell and Henrie Evans, uppon the Counselles warraunte dated at the Courte at Whitehalle xxiiij. to die Februarij, 1604, for twoe enterludes or plaies presented before the Kinges majestie by the Quenes Majesties Children of the Revelles, the one on Newyers daie at nighte, 1604, and the other on the third daie of Januarie followinge, xiij.*li.* vj.*s.* viij.*d.*, and by waye of his Highnes rewarde, vj.*li.* xiij.*s.* iiij.*d.*, in all xx.*li.*," MS. ibid.   The Children of the Revels, previously to the reconstruction of the company in 1604, were generally known as the Children of her Majesty's Chapel.—7. "On Twelfth Day at night we had the Queen's maske in the Banquetting House, or rather her pagent ;—there was a great engine at the lower end of the room which had motion, and in it were the images of sea-horses, with other terrible fishes, which were ridden by Moors," letter of January, 1604–5, ap. Winwood, ii. 43–44. This was the Masque of Blacknesse by Ben Jonson, who gives the names of the eleven ladies in his Workes, ed. 1616, p. 899.—8. "To John Heminges, one of his Majesties plaiers, uppon the Counselles warraunte dated at the Courte at Whitehalle xxiiij.to die Februarij, 1604, for himselfe and the reste of his companie, for iiij.ᵒʳ interludes or plaies presented by them before his Majestie at the Courte, viz., on Candlemas daie at nighte, on Shrovesundaye at nighte, Shrovemundaye at nighte and Shrovetuesdaie at nighte, 1604, at vj.*li.* xiij.*s.* iiij.*d.* for everie plaie, and lxvj.*s.* viij.*d.*, by waye of his Majesties rewarde for each playe, in all the some of xl.*li.*," Treas. Chamb. MS.

It would appear from these notices either that the fabricator had not before him a complete list of the plays that had been acted, or that he intentionally omitted a number of entries.   Whatever may have been the exact nature of his proceedings, it is certain that the particulars of the forgery were not based upon the defective information given in the official accounts of the Treasurer of the Chamber.   If that had been the case, it would be necessary to assume that he went recklessly out of his way to insert a fictitious notice of a performance on a day that was not sanctioned by those accounts, the high probability of the accuracy of that solitary discrepancy having, moreover, been lately revealed by the discovery of an evidence to which he could not have had access. This singular coincidence may fairly be held to outweigh the suspicion attending the omission in the treasurer's ledger, an oversight of a very unusual character, and yet an error infinitely more likely to occur than the preternatural ratification of what would have been by itself an extravagant conjecture. Upon a balance of probabilities there can thus hardly be a doubt that Love's Labour's Lost was revived at Court very early in the January of 1605 in a representation that was not honoured by the presence of the Queen. When, therefore, a play was to be selected almost immediately afterwards for the entertainment of her Majesty at Lord Southampton's, it was natural that Burbage, who had only one day's notice of the intended performance, should have recommended a drama which his company had just then in hand, and which at the same time would have been a novelty to the only spectator whose approval was regarded.

SHAKESPEARE'S WILL.

The alterations to which this instrument was subjected previously to its execution render it difficult to give a complete idea of the original through the medium of typography; but if the reader will carefully bear in mind that, in the following transcript, *all the Italics represent interlineations*, he will be able to obtain a tolerably clear impression of this valuable record.

Vicesimo quinto die ~~Januarii~~ *Martii,* anno regni domini nostri Jacobi, nunc regis Anglie, &c. decimo quarto, et Scotie xlix° annoque Domini 1616.

T. Wmi. Shackspeare.—In the name of God, amen! I William Shackspeare, of Stratford-upon-Avon in the countie of Warr. gent., in perfect health and memorie, God be praysed, doe make and ordayne this my last will and testament in manner and forme followeing, that ys to saye, First, I comend my soule into the handes of God my Creator, hoping and assuredlie beleeving, through thonelie merittes of Jesus Christe, my Saviour, to be made partaker of lyfe everlastinge, and my bodye to the earth whereof yt ys made. Item, I gyve and bequeath unto my ~~sonne in L~~ daughter Judyth one hundred and fyftie poundes of lawfull English money, to be paied unto her in manner and forme followeing, that ys to saye, one hundred poundes *in discharge of her marriage porcion* within one yeare after my deceas, with consideracion after the rate of twoe shillinges in the pound for soe long tyme as the same shal be unpaied unto her after my deceas, and the fyftie poundes residewe thereof upon her surrendring *of,* or gyving of such sufficient securitie as the overseers of this my will shall like of to surrender or graunte, all her estate and right that shall discend or come unto her after my deceas, or *that shee* nowe hath, of, in or to, one copiehold tenemente with thappurtenaunces lyeing and being in Stratford-upon-Avon aforesaied in the saied countie of Warr., being parcell or holden of the mannour of Rowington, unto my daughter Susanna Hall and her heires for ever. Item, I gyve and bequeath unto my saied daughter Judith one hundred and fyftie poundes more, if shee or anie issue of her bodie be lyvinge att thend of three yeares next ensueing the daie of the date of this my will, during which tyme my executours to℗ paie her consideracion from my deceas according

to the rate aforesaied ; and if she dye within the saied terme without
issue of her bodye, then my will ys, and I doe gyve and bequeath
one hundred poundes thereof to my neece Elizabeth Hall, and the
fiftie poundes to be sett fourth by my executours during the lief of my
sister Johane Harte, and the use and proffitt thereof cominge shal be
payed to my saied sister Jone, and after her deceas the saied l.ⁱⁱ· shall
remaine amongst the children of my saied sister equallie to be devided
amongst them ; but if my saied daughter Judith be lyving att thend
of the saied three yeares, or anie yssue of her bodye, then my will ys
and soe I devise and bequeath the saied hundred and fyftie poundes
to be sett out *by my executours and overseers* for the best benefitt of her
and her issue, and *the stock* not *to be* paied unto her soe long as she
shalbe marryed and covert baron ~~by my executours and overseers~~ ;
but my will ys that she shall have the consideracion yearelie paied
unto her during her lief, and, after her deceas, the saied stock and
consideracion to bee paied to her children, if she have anie, and if not,
to her executours or assignes, she lyving the saied terme after my
deceas, Provided that if such husbond as she shall att thend of the
saied three yeares be marryed unto, or att anie after⑤, doe sufficientle⑤
assure unto her and thissue of her bodie landes awnswereable to the
porcion by this my will gyven unto her, and to be adjudged soe by
my executours and overseers, then my·will ys that the saied cl.ⁱⁱ· shalbe
paied to such husbond as shall make such assurance, to his owne use.
Item, I gyve and bequeath unto my saied sister Jone xx.ⁱⁱ· and all
my wearing apparrell, to be paied and delivered within one yeare after
my deceas ; and I doe will and devise unto her *the house* with thappurtenaunces in Stratford, wherein she dwelleth, for her naturall lief, under
the yearelie rent of xij.ᵈ· Item, I gyve and bequeath unto her
three sonns, William Harte, ... Hart, and Michaell Harte, fyve
poundes a peece, to be pay̆ed within one yeare after my deceas ~~to be
sett out for her within one yeare after my deceas by my executours, with
thadvise and direccions of my overseers, for her best proffitt untill her
marriage, and then the same with the increase thereof to be paied unto
her~~ . Item, I gyve and bequeath unto ~~her~~ *the saied Elizabeth Hall* all
my plate *except my brod silver and gilt bole*, that I now have att the date
of this my will. Item, I gyve and bequeath unto the poore of Stratford
aforesaied tenn poundes ; to Mr. Thomas Combe my sword ; to Thomas
Russell esquier fyve poundes, and to Frauncis Collins of the borough of
Warr. in the countie of Warr., gent., thirteene poundes, sixe shillinges,
and eight pence, to be paied within one yeare after my deceas. Item,
I gyve and bequeath to ~~Mr. Richard Tyler thelder~~ *Hamlett Sadler*
xxvj.ˢ· viij.ᵈ· to buy him a ringe ; *to William Raynoldes, gent., xxvj.ˢ·
viij.ᵈ· to buy him a ring* ; to my god-son William Walker xx.ˢ· in gold ;
to Anthonye Nashe gent. xxvj.ˢ· viij.ᵈ·, and to Mr. John Nashe xxvj.ˢ·

viij.ᵈ ~~in gold~~ ; *and to my fellowes, John Hemynges, Richard Burbage, and Henry Cundell, xxvj.ˢ viij.ᵈ a peece to buy them ringes.* Item, I gyve, will, bequeath and devise, unto my daughter Susanna Hall, *for better enabling of her to performe this my will, and towardes the performans thereof,* all that capitall messuage or tenemente, with thappurtenaunces, *in Stratford aforesaied,* called the Newe Place, wherein I nowe dwell, and twoe messuages or tenementes with thappurtenaunces, scituat lyeing and being in Henley streete within the borough of Stratford aforesaied ; and all my barnes, stables, orchardes, gardens, landes, tenementes and hereditamentes whatsoever, scituat, lieing and being, or to be had, receyved, perceyved, or taken, within the townes, hamlettes, villages, fieldes and groundes of Stratford-upon-Avon, Oldstratford, Bushopton, and Welcombe, or in anie of them in the saied countie of Warr. And alsoe all that messuage or tenemente with thappurtenaunces wherein one John Robinson dwelleth, scituat lyeing and being in the Blackfriers in London nere the Wardrobe; and all other my landes, tenementes, and hereditamentes whatsoever, To have and to hold all and singuler the saied premisses with their appurtenaunces unto the saied Susanna Hall for and during the terme of her naturall lief, and after her deceas, to the first sonne of her bodie lawfullie yssueing, and to the heires males of the bodie of the saied first sonne lawfullie yssueinge, and for defalt of such issue, to the second sonne of her bodie lawfullie issueinge, and ~~of~~ to the heires males of the bodie of the saied second sonne lawfullie yssueinge, and for defalt of such heires, to the third sonne of the bodie of the saied Susanna lawfullie yssueing, and of the heires males of the bodie of the saied third sonne lawfullie yssueing, and for defalt of such issue, the same soe to be and remaine to the fourth ~~sonne~~, fyfth, sixte, and seaventh sonnes of her bodie lawfullie issueing one after another, and to the heires males of the bodies of the saied fourth, fifth, sixte, and seaventh sonnes lawfullie yssueing, in such manner as yt ys before lymitted to be and remaine to the first, second and third sonns of her bodie, and to their heires males, and for defalt of such issue, the saied premisses to be and remaine to my sayed neece Hall, and the heires males of her bodie lawfullie yssueing, and for defalt of such issue, to my daughter Judith, and the heires males of her bodie lawfullie issueinge, and for defalt of such issue, to the right heires of me the saied William Shackspeare for ever. *Item, I gyve unto my wiefe my second best bed with the furniture.* Item, I gyve and bequeath to my saied daughter Judith my broad silver gilt bole. All the rest of my goodes, chattels, leases, plate, jewels, and household stuffe whatsoever, after my dettes and legasies paied, and my funerall expences discharged, I gyve, devise. and bequeath to my sonne-in-lawe, John Hall, gent., and my daughter

Susanna, his wief, whom I ordaine and make executours of this my last will and testament. And I doe intreat and appoint *the saied* Thomas Russell, esquier, and Frauncis Collins, gent., to be overseers hereof, and doe revoke all former wills, and publishe this to be my last will and testament. In witnes whereof I have hereunto put my ~~seale~~ *hand* the daie and yeare first above written.—By me William Shakspeare.

Witnes to the publishing hereof,—Fra: Collyns; Julius Shawe; John Robinson; Hamnet Sadler; Robert Whattcott.

THE SNITTERFIELD ESTATES.

The extent of Robert Arden's property at Snitterfield cannot be definitely given, it being impossible to completely reconcile the varying descriptions of parcels, but it appears to have included two farm-houses and about a hundred acres of land. In the year 1550 he made one settlement of a messuage and land on his three daughters, Agnes, Jane and Katherine, and another of a messuage, three quartrons of land, a meadow, a cottage, a garden and orchard, on three other daughters, Margaret, Joyce and Alice, both of these dispositions being subject to the life-interest of Agnes Arden. These estates, each of them held under a chief-rent of four shillings, one cock and two hens, are the only freehold possessions of Robert Arden within the boundaries of Snitterfield that are mentioned in a nearly contemporary manorial roll in the Longbridge collection. In what manner his two other daughters, Elizabeth Scarlet and Mary Shakespeare, became entitled to portions of them is unknown, but that this was the case is shown by the conveyances to Robert Webbe, the inheritor of one and the purchaser by degrees of all the other shares.—A large number of documents respecting these estates have been preserved, but the following selection from them (numbers one to five) includes all that are necessary to be given in elucidation of the history of the reversionary interest that fell into the hands of the Shakespeares.

I. Sciant presentes et futuri quod ego, Robertus Ardern de Wylmecote in parochia de Aston Cantlowe in comitatu Warwici, husbandman, dedi, concessi, et hac presenti carta mea tripartiter indentata confirmavi, Ade Palmer de Aston Cantlowe predicta, et Hugoni Porter de Snytterfylde in comitatu predicto, totum illud mesuagium meum, cum suis pertinenciis, in Snytterfylde predicta, que nunc sunt in tenura cujusdam Ricardi Shakespere, ac omnia illa mea terras, prata, pascuas et pasturas, cum suis pertinenciis in Snytterfylde predicta eidem mesuagio spectantia et pertinentia, que nunc sunt in tenura predicti Ricardi Shakespere,— habendum et tenendum omnia predicta mesuagium, terras, prata, pascuas et pasturas, cum suis pertinenciis, predictis Ade Palmer et Hugoni Porter, heredibus et assignatis suis, ad usum et opus mei, predicti Roberti Ardern et Agnetis, nunc uxoris mee, pro termino vite nostrum, eorundem Roberti et Agnetis, ac diucius viventis nostrum, et post decessum diucius viventis nostrum, predictorum Roberti Ardern et

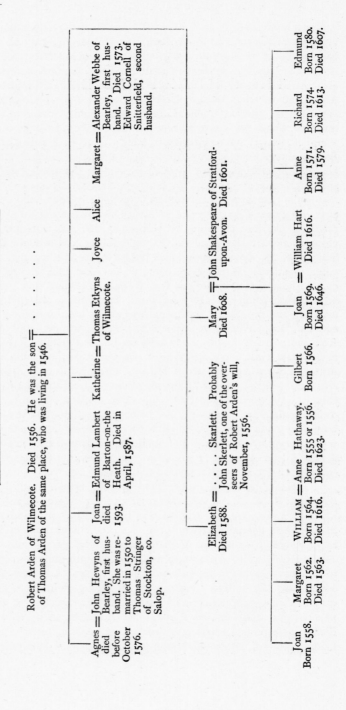

Robert Arden of Wilmecote. Died 1556. He was the son of Thomas Arden of the same place, who was living in 1546.

Agnes = John Hewyns of Bearley, first husband. She was remarried in 1550 to Thomas Stringer of Stockton, co. Salop. Died before October 1576.

Joan = Edmund Lambert of Barton-on-the Heath. Died in April, 1587. died 1593.

Katherine = Thomas Etkyns of Wilmecote.

Joyce

Alice

Margaret = Alexander Webbe of Bearley, first husband. Died 1573. Edward Cornell of Snitterfield, second husband.

Elizabeth = ... Skarlett. Probably John Skerlett, one of the overseers of Robert Arden's will, November, 1556. Died 1588.

Mary = John Shakespeare of Stratford-upon-Avon. Died 1601. Died 1608.

Joan Born 1558.

Margaret Born 1562. Died 1563.

WILLIAM = Anne Hathaway. Born 1564. Born 1555 or 1556. Died 1616. Died 1623.

Gilbert Born 1566.

Joan = William Hart Born 1569. Died 1616. Died 1646.

Anne Born 1571. Died 1579.

Richard Born 1574. Died 1613.

Edmund Born 1580. Died 1607.

Agnetis, nunc uxoris mee, tunc ad usus et opus sequentia,—scilicet, unam terciam partem omnium predictorum mesuagii, terrarum, pratorum, pascuarum et pasturarum, cum suis pertinenciis, ad usum et opus Agnetis Strynger, nunc uxoris Thome Strynger, ac nuper uxoris Johannis Hewyns, dudum de Bereley, modo defuncti, filie mei predicti Roberti Ardern, ac heredum et assignatorum ejusdem Agnetis Strynger imperpetuum; et alteram terciam partem omnium eorundem mesuagii, terrarum, pratorum, pascuarum et pasturarum, cum suis pertinenciis, ad usum et opus Johanne Lambert, nunc uxoris Edwardi Lambert de Barton-super-lez-Hethe, alie filie mei, predicti Roberti Ardern, ac heredum et assignatorum ejusdem Johanne Lambert imperpetuum; aliamque terciam partem omnium predictorum mesuagii, terrarum, pratorum, pascuarum et pasturarum, cum suis pertinenciis, ad usum et opus Katerine Etkyns, nunc uxoris Thome Etkyns de Wylmecote predicto, alie filie mei, predicti Roberti Ardern, ac heredum et assignatorum ejusdem Katerine Etkyns imperpetuum, de capitalibus dominis feodi illius per servicia inde prius debita et de jure consueta;—et ego vero, predictus Robertus Ardern, et heredes mei, omnia predicta mesuagium, terras, prata, pascuas et pasturas, cum suis pertinenciis, prefatis Ade Palmer et Hugoni Porter, heredibus et assignatis suis, ad usus et opus supradicta, contra omnes gentes warantizabimus et imperpetuum defendemus per presentes. Sciatis insuper me, predictum Robertum Ardern, plenam et pacificam possessionem et seisinam de et in predictis mesuagio terris, pratis, pascuis et pasturis, cum suis pertinenciis, prefatis Ade Palmer et Hugoni Porter ad usus et opus superius specificata, secundum vim, formam, tenorem et effectum hujus presentis carte mee tripartiter indentate inde eis, confecte in propria persona mea tradidisse et liberasse. In cujus rei testimonium cuilibet parti hujus, presentis carte mee, tripartiter indentate, sigillum meum apposui. Datum decimo-septimo die Julii, anno regni domini Edwardi Sexti, Dei gracia Anglie, Francie et Hibernie regis fidei, defensoris, et in terra ecclesie Anglicane et Hibernie supremi capitis, quarto.

II. Sciant presentes et futuri quod ego, Robertus Ardern de Wylme-cote in parochia de Aston Cantlowe, in comitatu Warrewicensi, husband-man, dedi, concessi, et hac presenti carta mea tripartita indentata con-firmavi, Ade Palmer de Aston Cantlowe predicta, et Hugoni Porter de Snytterfylde in comitatu predicto, totum illud mesuagium meum et tres quartronas terre, cum prato eisdem pertinente, cum suis pertinenciis, in Snytterfylde predicta, que nunc sunt in tenura cujusdam Ricardi Henley, ac totum illud cotagium meum cum gardino et pomario adja-centibus, cum suis pertinenciis, in Snytterfyld predicta, que nunc sunt in tenura predicti Hugonis Porter,—habendum et tenendum omnia pre-dicta mesuagium, cotagium, gardinum, pomarium, terram, pratum, et cetera premissa, cum suis pertinenciis, predictis Ade Palmer et Hugoni

Porter, heredibus et assignatis suis, ad usum et opus mei, predicti Roberti Ardern, et Agnetis nunc uxoris mee, pro termino vite nostrum, eorundem Roberti et Agnetis, ac diucius viventis nostrum, et post decessum diucius viventis nostrum, predictorum Roberti Ardern et Agnetis, nunc uxoris mee, tunc ad usus et opus sequentes,—scilicet, unam terciam partem omnium predictorum mesuagii, cotagii, gardini, pomarii, terre, prati, et ceterorum premissorum, cum suis pertinenciis, ad usum et opus Margarete Webbe, nunc uxoris Alexandri Webbe de Bereley, filie mei, predicti Roberti Ardern, ac heredum et assignatorum ejusdem Margarete Webbe imperpetuum ; et alteram terciam partem omnium eorundem mesuagii, cotagii, gardini, pomarii, terre, prati, et ceterorum premissorum, cum suis pertinenciis, ad usum et opus Jocose Ardern, alie filie mei, predicti Roberti Ardern, ac heredum et assignatorum ejusdem Jocose Ardern imperpetuum ; aliamque terciam partem omnium predictorum mesuagii, cotagii, gardini, pomarii, terre, prati, et ceterorum premissorum, cum suis pertinenciis, ad usum et opus Alicie Ardern, alie filie mei, predicti Roberti Ardern, ac heredum et assignatorum ejusdem Alicie Ardern imperpetuum, de capitalibus dominis feodi illius per servicia inde prius debita et de jure consueta. Et ego vero, predictus Robertus Ardern et heredes mei, omnia predicta mesuagium, cotagium, gardinum, pomarium, terram, pratum, et cetera premissa, cum suis pertinenciis, prefatis Ade Palmer et Hugoni Porter, heredibus et assignatis suis, ad usus et opus supradictos contra omnes gentes warantizabimus et imperpetuum defendemus per presentes. Sciatis insuper me, predictum Robertum Ardern, plenam et pacificam possessionem et seisinam de et in predictis mesuagio, cotagio, gardino, pomario, terra, prato, et ceteris premissis, cum suis pertinenciis, prefatis Ade Palmer et Hugoni Porter ad usus et opus superius specificatos, secundum vim, formam, tenorem et effectum hujus, presentis carte mee, tripartite indentate inde eis confecte, in propria persona mea tradidisse et liberasse. In cujus rei testimonium cuilibet parti hujus, presentis carte mee, tripartite indentate, sigillum meum apposui. Datum decimoseptimo die Julii, anno regni domini Edwardi Sexti, Dei gracia Anglie, Francie et Hibernie regis, fidei defensoris, et in terra ecclesie Anglicane et Hibernice supremi capitis quarto.

III. Hec est finalis concordia facta in curia domine Regine apud Westmonasterium a die Pasche in quindecim dies anno regnorum Elizabethe, Dei gracia Anglie, Francie et Hibernie regine, fidei defensoris, etc., a conquestu vicesimo-secundo, coram Jacobo Dyer, Thoma Meade et Francisco Wyndame, justiciariis, et aliis domine regine fidelibus tunc ibi presentibus,—inter Robertum Webbe, querentem, et Johannem Shackspere et Mariam uxorem ejus, deforciantes, de sexta parte duarum partium duorum mesuagiorum, duorum gardinorum, duorum pomariorum, sexaginta acrarum terre, decem acrarum prati, et triginta acrarum jampnorum et bruere, cum pertinenciis, in tres partes dividendorum in Snitterfylde; unde placitum convencionis summonitum fuit inter eos in eadem curia, scilicet, quod predicti Johannes et Maria recognoverunt predictam sextam partem, cum pertinenciis, esse jus ipsius Roberti; et concesserunt pro se, et heredibus ipsius Marie, quod predicta sexta pars, cum pertinenciis, quam Agnes Arden, vidua, tenet ad terminum vite sue de hereditate predicte Marie die quo hec concordia facta fuit, et que, post decessum ipsius Agnetis, ad predictam Mariam et heredes suos debuit reverti, post decessum ipsius Agnetis integre remanebit predicto Roberto et heredibus suis, tenendum de capitalibus dominis feodi illius per servicia que ad predictam sextam partem pertinent imperpetuum; et predicti Johannes et Maria, et heredes ipsius Marie, warantizabunt predicto Roberto et heredibus suis predictam sextam partem, cum pertinenciis, sicut predictum est, contra predictos Johannem et Mariam, et heredes ipsius Marie, imperpetuum; et pro hac recognicione, concessione, warantia, fine et concordia idem Robertus dedit predictis Johanni et Marie quadraginta libras sterlingorum. *The indenture leading the uses of this fine has not been discovered.*

IV. Warr :—In onere Georgii Digbie, armigeri, vicecomitis comitatus predicti, de anno vicesimo-tercio Regine Elizabethe; fines de Banco anno vicesimo-secundo regine Elizabethe pro termino Pasche.—De Roberto Webbe, pro licencia concordandi cum Johanne Shackespeare et alia de placito convencionis de sexta parte duarum partium duorum messuagiorum, duorum gardinorum, duorum pomariorum, sexaginta acrarum terre et aliorum, cum pertinenciis, in Snytterfeild, vj.*s.* viij.*d.* Recepta per me, Johannem Cowper, subvicecomitem.

V. This indenture made the xxj.th daye of Maie, in the seconde yeare of the reigne of our soveraigne Lady Elyzabeth, by the grace of God Quene of Englande, Fraunce and Irelande, defender of the faith, &c., betwene Agnes Arderne of Wylmecote, in the countie of Warr :, wydowe, on the one partie, and Alexander Webbe of Bereley, in the same countie, husbandeman, on the other partie, wytnessyth that the said Agnes Arderne, for dyverse and sondry consyderations, hath demysed, graunted, sett and to ferme lett, and by these presentes demyseth, graunteth, setteth and to ferme letteth, unto the said Alexander Webbe, and to his assignes, all those her two measuages with a cottage, with all and singuler their appurtenaunces in Snytterfeld, and a yarde and a halfe of ayrable lande therunto belongyng, with all landes, medowes, pastures, commons, profettes and commodities in any wyse therunto apperteynynge, scituate, lying and beyng in the towne and fyldes of Snytterfeild afforsaid, all whiche now are in the occupation of Richarde Shakespere, John Henley, and John Hargreve,—to have and to holde the said two measuages or tenementes and cottage, wyth their appurtenaunces, a yarde and a half of lande arrable and all other the premysses, with all and synguler their appurtenaunces, unto the said Alexander Webbe, his executors and assignes, from the feast of thannuncyacion of our Lady next ensuyng the date hereof untyll the ende and terme of fourtie yeares next and ymmediatly folowyng, fully to be completed and ended, yff the said Agnes Arderne so longe do lyve, yeldynge and paying therfore yearely duryng the said terme unto the said Agnes Arderne, or her assignes, fourtie shillynges of lawfull money of Englande, to be payde at two termes in the yeare, that is to saye, at the feast of Saynt Michaell tharchaungell and the annunciation of our Ladye by equall portions ; and the said Alexander Webbe covenaunteth by these presentes to dyscharge, paye and save harmeles, the said Agnes Arderne, of all maner of chieff rentes and suete of court dewe to the lorde of the fee, and all other charges belongyng to the forsaid measuages or tenementes ; and yf it happen the said rent of fourtie shillynges to be byhynde unpayde in parte or in all after any of the said feastes or dayes of payment at whiche it ought to be payde as is afforsaid by the space of one moneth, beyng laufully asked or demaunded, and no sufficient distres can or may be founde in and upon the premysses by the space of syxe wekes next after any of the sayde feastes, that then it shall be laufull to the said Agnes Arderne and her assignes to re-entre and have agayn the premysses, and every parcell thereof, as in her first estate, and the said Alexander Webbe, his executers and assignes, therof to expell and putt owt, any thynge herein contayned to the contrary in any wyse notwythstandynge. Also the said Agnes covenaunteth and graunteth to and wyth the said Alexander, and his assignes, that he, the said Alexander, his executors and assignes, shall have, enjoy and take, duryng all the said terme, sufficient housebote, ploughbote, cartbote and hedgebote, wyth loppes and shredes growyng and beyng in and upon the premysses, or any parcell therof, for the defense and use of the same howses and clousures withowt doyng any wast. Also the said Alexander Webbe covenaunteth by these presentes yearely to repayre, maynteyne and keape, all and all maner of necessary reparacions perteynyng and belongeinge to the forsayd tenementes, cottage, havyng sufficient tymbre on the forsaid groundes, yf any be there to be hadd for the same. And the said Agnes Arderne and her assignes the saide two measuages or tenements, with the said cotage, a yarde and a halfe of lande, and all other the premysses, with their appurtenaunces, unto the said Alexander Webbe, his executers and assignes, for the said yearely rent in maner and fourme afforsaid, agaynst her and her assignes shall awarrant and defende duryng the said terme of xl^{ti} yeares, if she live so longe. In wytnes wherof the parties afforsaid to these present indentures enterchaungeably have putt to their seales, the day and yeare above wrytten.—Selyd and de-lyveryd in the presentes of John Somervyle, and Thomas Osbarston, and others.

All that is known respecting the interests of Mary Arden in her father's Snitterfield estates may be gathered from the preceding documents, but it appears that her husband had an individual share in two messuages in that village, and that he parted with it in 1579 for the comparatively insignificant sum of £4. The latter facts are exhibited in the following conveyance from John and Mary Shakespeare to Robert Webbe, the wife's name being no doubt merely introduced with the view of barring dower, the terms of the warranty proposed for the covenanted fine being inconsistent with the supposition that she was joining in a conveyance of her own property. In this last case that warranty would have been from Johannes et Maria, et heredes ipsius Marie.

VI. This indenture made the fyftenthe daye of Octobar, in the yeare of the raigne of our soveraigne ladye Elyzabethe, bye the grace of God, of England, Fraunce and Ireland Quene, defendor of the faithe, &c., the twentythe and one, betwene John Shackspere of Stratford-uppon-Avon, in the countye of Warwicke, yoman, and Marye his wyeffe, on the one partye, and Robert Webbe of Snytterfylde, in the same countye, yoman, on the other partye; wittnessethe that the said John Shackspere and Marye his wieffe, for and in consideracion of the somme of foure poundes of goode and lawfull Englishe money by the aforesaid Roberte Webbe unto the said John Shackspere, and Marye his wyeffe, before the delyverie of these presentes well and trulye contented and paied, of the which said somme the said John Shackspere, and Marye his wyeffe, doe acknowledge themselves fully satisfyed, contented and paied, and thereof and of everye parte thereof the said Robert Webbe, his heires, executors, administrators and assignes doe fullye freely and cleerelye acquyte, exonerate and dyscharge for ever, by these presentes have gyven, graunted, bargayned and solde, and by these presentes doe gyve, graunte, bargayne and sell, unto the said Robart Webbe, his heires and assignes, for ever, all that theire moitye, parte and partes, be yt more or lesse, of and in twoo messuages or tenementes, with thappurte-naunces, sett, lyenge and beynge in Snitterfield aforesaid, in the said county of Warwicke, and of all and singular houses, edifices, barnes, stables, gardens, orchardes, medowes, lesues, pastures, feedinges, commons, furzes, brushewoodes, underwoodes, waters, landes, tene-mentes, hereditamentes, profyttes, commodyties, whatsoever or where-soever in any wise to the said twoo messuages or tenementes, or any of them, belonginge or apperteininge, or occupied with the same, in whose tenure or occupacion soever they or any of them, or any parte or parcell of them, nowe be; and furthermore, the revertion and revertions, remaynder and remaynders of the same, and the rentes, dutyes, profyttes and commodyties whatsoever to the said revertion or revertions, re-maynder or remaynders, in any wyse belonginge, incident or apper-teyninge, or excepted or reserved uppon any manner of graunte or demyse

M 2

thereof heretofore had or made, or of any of the graunted premisses, together with all and singular deedes, cherters, evydences, wrytynges and mynimentes whatsoever towchinge and concerninge onely the foresaid twoo messuages or tenementes, or all or any of thaforesaid premisses which theye the foresaid John Shackspere, or Marye his wyeffe, or eyther of them, or anye other person or persons, eyther by theyre or any of theyre delyverie, or by theire or eyther of theire knowledge, nowe have or ought to have ;—to have and to holde theire said moitye, parte and partes, of the said twoo messuages or tenementes, and of all and singular the graunted premisses, with theire and everye of theire appurtenaunces, unto thaforesaide Roberte Webbe, his heires and assignes, for ever, to his and theire onelye proper use and behoofe ; all which theire said moitye, parte and partes, of the said twoo messuages or tenementes, with thappurtenaunces, and of all and singular the graunted premisses, with theire and everye of theire appurtenaunces, thafforesayd John Shackspere and Marye his wyeffe, for them and theire heires, and the heires of eyther of them, by these presentes to thafforesaid Robert Webbe his heires and assignes doe warrante and promysse to defende against the said John and Marye his wiffe, and theire heires and the heires of eyther of them, for ever by these presentes. And the saide John Shackspere and Marye his wyeffe, for the consideracion aforesaid, for them, theire heires and the heires of eyther of them, theire executors, administrators and assignes, and everye of them, doe covenaunt, promysse and graunte to and with the said Roberte Webbe, his heires, executors, administrators and assignes, and everye of them, by these presentes, that theire said moitye, parte and partes, of thafforesaide twoo messuages or tenementes, and of all and singular the graunted premisses with theire appurtenaunces, att all tyme and tymes henceforth, after the delyverie of these presentes, maye and shall lawfully and rightfully come be and remayne unto thaforesaid Robert Webbe, his heires and assignes, accordinge to the true tenour and effecte of the graunte thereof before made in these presentes, free cleere and voyde, or otherwise well and sufficientlie saved harmelesse, by the foresaid John Shackspere and Marye his wyeffe, theire heires and the heires of eyther of them, and theire assignes, of and from all and singular bargaines, sales, feoffmentes, grauntes, intayles, joyntures, dowars, leases, willes, uses, rent-charge, rent-sectes, arrereges of rentes, recognizaunce, statute marchant and of the staple, obligacions, judgementes, executions, condempnacions, yssues, fynes, amercementes, intrusions, forfaitures, alienacions without lycens, and of and from all other charges, troubles and incumbraunces whatsoever heretofore had made or done by the foresaid John Shackspere and Marye his wieffe, or eyther of them, or of theire heires or the heires of eyther of them, or by any other person or persons by, thorough or under theire or any of theire right, tytle or interest, acte, consent or procurement,—the rentes, customes and services due to the chieffe lord or lordes of the fee or fees onely excepted and foreprised ; and that theye, the foresaid John Shackspere and Marye his wyeffe, and all and everye other person and persons, except before excepted, nowe havinge, claiminge or pretendinge to have, or that hereafter shall have, claime or pretend to have, any manner of lawfull and just right, tytle and intereste, of, in, to or out of theire said moitye, parte and partes, of the foresaid twoo messuages or tenementes, and of all or any of the graunted premisses with theire appurtenaunces, in, by or thoroughe, the right, tytle or intereste of the said John Shackspere and Marye his wyeffe and theire heires, and the heires of eyther of them, at all tyme and tymes hereafter, from and after the delyverie of these presentes, from tyme to tyme, uppon lawfull warninge and request made by the said Robert Webbe, his heires and assignes, unto thaforesaid John Shackspere and Mary his wyeffe, and theire heires and the heires of eyther of them, at the proper costes and charges in the lawe of the said Robert Webbe, his heires or assignes, shall and wyll doe, cause and suffer to be done, all and everye reasonable and lawfull acte and actes, thinge and thinges, devyse and devyses, for the more better and perfect assuraunce and sure makenge in the lawe of thaforesaid moitye, parte and partes, of the said twoo messuages or tenementes, and of all and singular the graunted premisses with theire appurtenaunces, to the said Robert Webbe, his heires and assignes, to his and theire onely use and behoofe, be yt by fyne, feoffment, recovery with single or double voucher, deedes inrolled, inrollement of these presentes, or by any or by all of them, or by any other wayes or meanes whatsoever, with warranty against them, the said John Shackspere and Marye his wyeffe, and theire heires, and the heires of eyther of them, as shal be advised or devised by the said Robert Webbe, his heires and assignes, or by his or theire councell learned in the lawe. And furthermore that the said John Shackspere and Marye his wyeffe, and theire heires, and the heires of eyther of them and theire assignes, shall and wyll delyver, uncanceled and undefaced, unto the said Roberte Webbe, his heires or assignes, before the feast of Easter next ensuenge the date of these presentes, all and singular the cherters, deedes, evidences, wrytinges and mynimentes, before in these presentes bargained and sold, which theye may come by without suite in the lawe, and that of all other cherters, evydences, wrytinges and mynimentes which theye, the said John Shackspere and Marye his wyeffe, hath, or that theye, theire heires, executors or assignes, at any tyme hereafter maye lawfully come by, without suite in the lawe, towchinge and concerninge thaforesaid twoo messuages or tenementes, or the before bargained premisses or any of them, they the said John Shackspere and Mary his wyeffe, or one of them, uppon lawfull request of the said Roberte Webbe his heires and assignes, at his and theire proper costes and charges, unto them the said John and Marye, theyre heires and assignes, had and made, shall deliver or cause to be delyvered to the said Robart Webbe, his heires and assignes, the true and perfecte coppie and coppies at all tyme and tymes hereafter. In wittnesse whereof the parties abovesaid to these present indentures interchangeblie have putte theire handes and seales the daye and yeare fyrst above wrytten.—*The marke* + *of John Shackspere.*—*The marke* + *of Marye Shacksper.*—Sealed and delivered in the presens of Nycholas Knooles, vicar of Auston, of Wyllyam Maydes and Anthony Osbaston, with other moe.

VII. Noverint universi per presentes nos, Johannem Shackspere de Stratford-uppon-Avon in comitatu Warwici, yoman, et Mariam, uxorem ejus, teneri et firmiter obligari Roberto Webbe de Snitterfielde in comitatu predicto, yoman, in viginti marcis bone et legalis monete Anglie, solvendis eidem Roberto aut suo certo attornato, executoribus, administratoribus, vel assignatis suis ; ad quam quidem solucionem bene et fideliter faciendam obligamus nos heredes, executores, et administratores nostros firmiter per presentes sigillo nostro sigillatas. Datum decimo-quinto die mensis Octobris, anno regni domine Elizabethe, Dei gracia Anglie, Francie et Hibernie regine, fidei defensoris, etc., vicesimo-primo.—The condition of this obligacion is such that, if thabove bounden John Shackspere and Marye his wyeffe, theire heires and the heires of eyther of them, theire executors, administrators and assignes, and everye of them, doe well and trulye observe, performe, fulfyll and keepe all and singular covenantes, grauntes, artycles and agreementes which on theire partes are to be observed, performed, fulfylled and kepte, contayned, comprised and specified in one paire of indentures, bearinge date the daye of the date of this present obligacion, made betwene the abovenamed Robarte Webbe on the one partye and thabove bound John Shackspere and Marie his wieffe on the other partye, that then this present obligacion to be utterlye voyde and of none effecte, or ells to stande, remayne and be in full power, strengthe, force and vertue.—*Signum Joannis* + *Shaxpere.* + *Signum Mariæ Shacksper.*—Sealed and delyvered in the presens of Nycholas Knooles, vicar of Auston, Wyllyam Maydes, and Anthonye Osbaston, with other moe.

THE HATHAWAY FAMILIES.

It is impossible, with our present means of information, to unravel the mystery that surrounds the descent of the poet's wife, nothing whatever being known for certain respecting her parents beyond the fact that their surname was Hathaway. The oft-repeated notion that they resided at Luddington may be summarily dismissed, there not being the faintest shadow of evidence in its favour, while the so-called tradition that her marriage took place in that hamlet is unquestionably a modern invention. But the more favourite, as well as the more plausible, theory is that they were inhabitants of Shottery, and although the reasons that are given in support of this latter theory are undoubtedly equivocal, they are yet of sufficient importance to justify a predilection in its favour. The leading features of the case, as it now stands, may thus be briefly stated, it being as well, however, to premise that the marriage-bond of November, 1582, includes the only evidences respecting Anne Hathaway during her maidenhood that have yet been discovered.

1. In that document Anne is described as belonging to Stratford, but so are also the two bondsmen, Fulk Sandells and John Richardson, and it is known that the latter resided at Shottery, one of the several hamlets that were included in what was generally termed the parish of Old Stratford.

2. Fulk Sandells, one of the husbandmen who are named as sureties in the marriage-bond, was an inhabitant of Shottery, and on friendly terms with Richard Hathaway in 1581, being one of the "supervisors" of his will and introduced therein as "my trustie frende and neighbour." He is mentioned several times in the local records as engaged with others in the preparation of testamentary inventories, and was no doubt one of the godfathers to the " Fowlke, filius Johannis Richardson de Shottery" whose burial is recorded under the date of November the 1st, 1595. "One messuage, one barne, one yard land and a halfe, one closse called or knowen by the name of the Barne Closse, one other closse called or knowen by the name of the Brooke Closse, in the towne and fields of Shotterye aforesaid, nowe or late in the tenure or occupacion of the said Foulke Sandells," indenture of 1616. Land in the holding of " Fowlk Sandles of Shotterye" is also mentioned in a Chancery paper written before the year 1621 ; Misc. Chanc. Proc., 1. 236.

3. The second bondsman, John Richardson, husbandman, was also doubtlessly an inhabitant of Shottery, but there appear to have been two persons of that name residing in the hamlet, one a large farmer who was returned in 1594 as having died possessed of numerous contemporary domestic luxuries and an unusually valuable agricultural stock, the other an individual whose goods, limited to wearing apparel and a few cattle, were assessed in 1605 at £11. Fulk Sandells was one of the appraisers on each of these occasions, and it is impossible to say for certain which of the John Richardsons witnessed Richard Hathaway's will in 1581. Then there was a John Richardson, perhaps a son of one of the last-named, who is mentioned as " of Shottery within the parishe of Olde Stratford, husbondman," in a deed of 1610. "Elizabetha Smythe, vidua, attachiata fuit per servientes ad clavam ad respondendum Roberto Parrett in placito debiti, Johannes Richardson de Shottrey et Fulcus Sandells, de Shottrey predicta, manucaptores pro predicta Elizabetha," proceedings in the Court of Record, April, 1587.

4. There were at least three families of the name of Hathaway belonging to Shottery during the maidenhood of the poet's wife, one of them, each of its members being generally here distinguished by the literal prefix of A. H. C., inhabiting the house now known as Anne Hathaway's Cottage.

5. One of the seals attached to the marriage-bond is impressed by 292 the letters R. H., and there was an A. H. C. Richard Hathaway who had

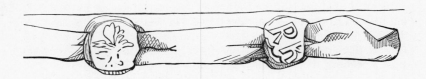

died in September, 1581, having a few days previously made a will in which he bequeathed " unto Agnes, my daughter, sixe poundes, thirtene shillinges, fower pence, to be paide unto her at the daie of her marriage." There is no seal to the copy of the will that was admitted to probate, and there is now probably no means of ascertaining whether the one used at the execution of the bond had belonged to the testator of 1581.

6. It does not follow from the terms of the above-quoted bequest to Agnes that her marriage was in contemplation, the phrase respecting it being an ordinary legal formula which the testator again introduces in a subsequent paragraph respecting his daughter Catherine.

7. The Christian names of Agnes and Anne were sometimes convertible. "Annys, propyr name, Agnes," Prompt. Parv., c. 1440. Agnes Arden, so called in her will and in numerous other documents,

is styled *Annes* by her husband in 1556 and in the inventory of her goods taken in 1581. Thomas Hathaway's daughter Agnes of Richard's will, 1581, is Anne in the only two instances in which her name occurs in the parish-register. "Thomas Greene and Agnes his wife," register of Bishopton, near Stratford-on-Avon, 1598-9, 1602; "Thomas Greene and Anne his wife," ibid., 1605. The wife of Phillip Henslowe, who is mentioned by himself in his will under the name of Agnes, is termed Anne in the entry of her funeral at Dulwich College, 1617, and also, according to Aubrey's Natural History of Surrey, 1719, i. 198, in the inscription on her grave-stone. And there was a tourist of the seventeenth century who, when transcribing one of the inscriptions in the church at Stratford, thus unconsciously deviates from the original,— "here lyeth the bodyes of William Clopton, esquier, and Anne his wife, daughter of Sir George Griffyth, knight, which William deceased the 18 of Aprill, 1592; the said Agnes deceased 17 of September, 1596," MS. Harl. 6072. "*Nancy*, the name substituted for Agnes, although some view it as belonging to Anne," Jamieson's Supplement to the Dictionary of the Scottish Language, 1825, ii. 146. "*Nancy*, Anna mea," Coles's Dictionary English-Latin, ed. 1679. It may be as well to observe that Annys, Annes, Anneys, Annyce, &c., are merely old forms of Anne.

8. The Thomas Hathaway who, with his daughters, Agnes and Elizabeth, are mentioned in Richard's will, 1581, does not appear to have been even distantly related to the A. H. C. family. He was a resident of Shottery, and the father of the person thus named in the will of John Cocks of Stratford-on-Avon, husbandman, 27 May, 1600,— "item, I geve unto Thomas Hathway, sonne to Margret Hathway of Old Stratford, a chylver shepe, and to the same Margrets thre dawghters xij.*d.* a-peece of them, and to the same Margret I geve lykewyse xij.*d.*" He is again introduced in the previously cited will of Thomas Whittington, 1601,—"item, I geve to Thomas Hathaway, sonne to the late decessed Margret Hathway, late of Old Stratford, xij.*d.*," Worcester MS. "October 16, Thomas Hathaway, and Margret Smith," Stratford marriages, 1575. "September 29, Anne, daughter to Thomas Hathaway," baptisms, 1577. "December 29, Elizabeth, daughter to Thomas Hathaway," ibid., 1579. "November 1, Rose, daughter to Thomas Hathaway," ibid., 1582. "September 21, Thomas, sonne to Thomas Hathaway," ibid., 1586. "September 5, Anne, filia Margret Hathaway," burials, 1600. "September 7, Margret Hathaway," ibid., 1600. "Januarie 23, Margareta et Elizabetha, filie Rose Hathaway, bastardes," baptisms, 1602. "Januari 29, Margaret, daughter to Rose Hathway, bastard," burials, 1602. "Januari 30, Elizabeth, filia Rose Hathway, bastard," ibid., 1602. It may be well to observe that, although the special hamlet in which a person resided is frequently added to the name in the Church

register, it is clear from numerous entries that the distinction was not always observed.

9. It appears from the papers of the Court of Record, filed in 1566, that the poet's father, John Shakespeare, was then on intimate terms with a Richard Hathaway, but the identification of the latter with the A. H. C. Richard is a matter of considerable uncertainty. There was a Richard Hathaway who was a plaintiff in the same court in July, 1596, and another, or the same, who was one of the constables in 1605, but whether either or both were the individual who was baptized in 1559 is unknown. The first is not likely to have been Richard 293 Hathaway, the baker, who was for some years a leading member of the Corporation, whose house in Bridge Street is frequently mentioned in the local records, and who died in 1636. The last-named individual would have been under ten years of age in 1596, if, as is almost certain, his brother John, born in 1586, was the eldest son of Bartholomew Hathaway. Neither is it likely that the baker was the constable of 1605, for he filled that post for two years from September, 1613, and re-elections to minor offices of the kind were not usual after so long an interval.

10. The poet's wife was on friendly terms with one Thomas Whittington of Shottery, the person mentioned as "my sheepherd" by Richard Hathaway in 1581. This individual died in April, 1601, and in a will drawn up in the previous month he bequeathed "unto the poore people of Stratford xl.*s.* that is in the hand of Anne Shaxspere, wyfe unto Mr. Wyllyam Shaxspere, and is due debt unto me, beyng paid to mine executor by the sayd Wyllyam Shaxspere or his assignes according to the true meanyng of this my wyll."

11. In an unpublished version of Rowe's Life of Shakespeare, written before the year 1766, MS. Addit. 4225, John is given as the Christian name of Anne Shakespeare's father, and Jordan, in one of his manuscripts, mentions her as the daughter of Samuel Hathaway. It is not likely that there was satisfactory evidence for either of these nominal ascriptions.

12. John Hall, the poet's son-in-law, was on friendly terms with the A. H. C. Hathaways, for Bartholomew appointed him an overseer to his will in 1621, and he was one of the trustees in 1625 under the marriage settlement of Isabel, the daughter of Richard Hathaway of Bridge Street, and the grand-daughter of Bartholomew.

13. Although Anne Shakespeare was living at the time that the will of Bartholomew Hathaway was drawn up, there is no mention of her in that document, but it is unsafe to draw an inference of any kind from such an omission, and it is to be observed that the testator's bequests are restricted to his children and grandchildren. Bear in mind also the facts stated in the preceding note.

14. The first published notice of Anne's surname appears in Rowe's Life of Shakespeare, 1709, wherein he states that she "was the daughter of one Hathaway, *said to have been a substantial yeoman in the neighbourhood of Stratford.*" The concluding words show that, when Betterton was collecting his materials, the locality of Anne's parentage was not currently known at Stratford, and this could hardly have been the case if she had been definitely allied to the A. H. C. Hathaways, some of whom were residing in the town in the days of Rowe, others being at the same period the chief inhabitants of Shottery. There was, moreover, an acknowledged member of her family, Jane Hathaway, who was living at Stratford so recently as 1696.

15. Richard Hobbyns and George Hatheweye held for their lives, by Copy of Court dated 12 April, 1543, unum messuagium, unum toftum, et duas virgatas terre, cum suis pertinenciis, in Shoterey, nunc in tenura Ricardi Hobbyns, at a rental of xxj.*s.* iiij.*d.*, with fine and heriots,— Warwickshire Survey, 1556, MS. Longbridge. "May 18, Henry Smith of Banbury to Ales Hathaway of Shattry," marriages, 1572. Nothing for certain is known respecting the genealogical position of either of these Hathaways.

16. "Januari 17, William Wilsonne and Anne Hathaway of Shotterye," marriage-register, 1579. There is nothing in the local records that indicates the family to which this namesake of Shakespeare's Anne belonged.

17. There was a family of the name of Hathaway alias Gardner residing at Shottery, temp. Elizabeth, connected most probably with Bartholomew Hathaway alias Garner of Tysoe, husbandman, to whom the lease of a house in Ely Street had been granted by the Quineys in 1581. "March 29, Richardus, filius Ricardi Hathway alias Gardner," burials, 1561, an entry repeated on April the 1st. "January 4, Richardus, filius Richardi Hathaway alias Gardner," baptisms, 1562. "October 22, Caterina, filia Richardy Hathaway alias Gardner," baptisms, 1563." "May 9, Johanna filia Richardi Hathaway alias Gardner de Shotery," ibid., 1566. "Item, of Richard Hathewaye alias Gardyner of Shotterey, six poundes, viij.*s.* iiij.*d.*," in list of "debtes which are owinge unto me, Roger Saddeler," 1578.

18. Families of the name of Hathaway were to be found dispersedly in various parts of England, especially in the counties of Warwick, Gloucester, Oxford, and Worcester, throughout the sixteenth and seventeenth centuries, and there was a cluster of them during that period in Stratford on-Avon and its immediate neighbourhood. A history of the latter, even if the defective and perplexing nature of the evidences had not rendered its satisfactory compilation an impossibility, would be beyond the scope of the present enquiry ; but perhaps the following additional early notices of Hathaways who belonged either to the borough or parish, chronologically arranged, may be worth giving.—"April 13, John, sonne

to William Hathaway," burials, 1558. " June 4, Ales Hathaway," ibid.,
1560. " Januari 1, William, sonne to William Hathaway de Bishopton,"
ibid., 1561. "June 13, Thomas, filius Gulielmi Hathaway de Bushopton,"
baptisms, 1562. " Februari 13, W. Hathaway," burials, 1566. "January
13, Lawrencius Walker et Phillippa Hathway," marriages 1567. "August
22, Sibbilla Hathaway, vidua, de Bushopton," burials, 1568. "March 11,
Thomas, filius Wilhelmi Hathway of Byshopton," ibid., 1569. Bishopton,
a hamlet in the parish of Old Stratford, has a chapel of its own, but no
notice of the Hathaways is to be found in its ancient register. "October
22, Georg Hathaway and Anne Heaton of Loxley," marriages, 1570.
"September 5, a child of goodman Hathwayes," burials, 1572, the
epithet indicating that he belonged to a somewhat inferior grade of
society. "December 14, Richard sonne to John Hathway," baptisms,
1573. "September 25, George Hathaway," burials, 1573. "October 14,
Margery, daughter to Georg Hathaway," ibid., 1573. "August 18,
Francis, daughter to Thomas Hathaway," ibid., 1576. "March 17,
Margret, daughter to William Hathaway," baptisms, 1577. "June 22,
David Jones and Francis Hathaway," marriages, 1579. "Paid to
Thomas Hatheweye for a peece of tymber, vj.*s*. viij.*d*.," chamb. acc.,
Mich. 1580 to Mich. 1581. "Robertus Gibbes queritur versus Willielmum Holmes, Annaniam Nason et Thomam Hathawaie, in placito
transgressionis super casum," proceedings of the Court of Record, 28
September, 1586. The names of Thomas and John Hathaway are found
in the same register in various entries belonging to the years 1586 and
1587. "John Hathwaye, in goodes, iij.*li*.," subsidy-roll for Old Stratford,
1593. "Willielmus Greene summonitus fuit per servientes ad clavam
ad respondendum Willielmo Hathwaye de placito quod reddat ei viginti
libras quas ei debet, et injuste detinet," Court of Record MS., 1601.
"Johannes Wheeler summonitus fuit per servientes ad clavam ad
respondendum Johanni Hathwaye de placito quod reddat ei viginti
libras quas ei debet, et injuste detinet," MS. ibid., 1601. "Julij 2,
Gilbart Clarke to Elizabeth Hathway," marriages, 1609.

The preceding evidences favour on the whole the opinion that the
Anne of the marriage-bond was a native of Shottery, but, if this be the
case, there are reasons for believing that the heads of the family to
which she belonged must have left that hamlet at some unrecorded
period after her marriage, and removed to a locality that was outside the
boundaries of the parish of Stratford. The facts are these.—In Lady
Barnard's will, 1670, the bequests to the Hathaways are restricted to
294 very handsome legacies to six individuals who, it may be fairly assumed,
were then the chief if not the only representatives of the ancestors of the
testator's grandmother. Now five of these legatees are described by her
295 ladyship as "daughters of my kinsman, Thomas Hathaway, late of
Stratford," that is, of Stratford lately deceased, the remaining one being

his grandson, and this Thomas, whose descendants are thus so affection-
ately remembered, came to reside in that town in or shortly before the
year 1636, arriving there from some place that was beyond the limits of
the borough or parish, the latter fact appearing from the amount of the
fee, £2. 10s., that he paid for his admission into the local company of
joiners, the Corporation gracefully returning to him more than half of
the share to which they were entitled. "Tho. Hathewaye, joyner, paid
for his freedome to the company, 2*li*. 10*s*.,—20*s*. is given him backe;
10*s*. is given to Richard George, and 5*s*. to Braye, and the other 15*s*. is
delivered to William Higgins, Chamberlyne," 25 March 1636. "Received
of Thomas Hathway for his fredom, oo. 15. o," chamb. acc., 1636.

The joiner here mentioned, who was occasionally employed by the 296
town-council, was living in Chapel Street, a few doors from New Place, 297
in 1647, in a house that was afterwards occupied by his widow Jane 298
from the time of his death in 1655 to that of her own in 1696, the
last-named event terminating the connexion of the poet's Hathaways
with Stratford and its neighbourhood. There can be no reasonable
doubt of the identity of this Thomas Hathaway with the person of the
same name who is mentioned in Lady Barnard's will, "William Hathaway
of Weston-upon-Avon, in the county of Glocester, yeoman, and Thomas
Hathway of Stratford-upon-Avon, joyner," being parties to the New Place
settlement of 1647, a circumstance which encourages the hope that an
entire solution of the present genealogical mystery may one day be found
amongst the records of Weston. The early registers of that village are,
however, unfortunately lost, and all endeavours to trace the history of its
William Hathaway have hitherto failed.

There is unhappily no tradition indicating the birth-place of Shakespeare's Anne upon which the least reliance can be placed. The
earliest notice of its presumed locality is in an unpublished version of
Rowe's biography that was compiled about the year 1750 by the Rev.
Joseph Greene, then master of the grammar-school at Stratford, in which,
as originally written, occurs the following paragraph,—"his (Shakespeare's) wife was the daughter of one Hathaway, a substantial yeoman
in the neighbourhood of Stratford, probably *of a* place about a mile from
thence call'd *Luddington*, where a *substantial* family of *that name and* 299
occupation still reside," the manner in which the name of that hamlet is
introduced showing that the attribution was conjectural. That this was
the case is also apparent from revisions that were afterwards made by

Greene, who erased the italicized words in the concluding sentences of the above quotation rewriting them in these terms,—"probably *at that* place about *half* a mile from thence call'd *Shotteriche*, where a *creditable* family of *the name aforemention'd 'till within these few years resided*." The retention of the word *probably* appears to exclude what might otherwise have been the inference, that the alterations were the result of a more careful investigation ; but the same writer, nevertheless, in a subsequent memorandum accepts the Shottery theory as an established fact,—"as Shakespear, the poet, married his wife Hathaway from Shottery, a village near Stratford-upon-Avon, possibly he might become possessor of a remarkable house there as part of her portion, and, jointly with his wife, convey it as part of their daughter Judith's portion to Thomas Queeny ;—it is certain that one Queeny, an elderly gentleman, sold it to . . . Harvey esq., of Stockton, near Southam, Warwickshire, father of John Harvey Thursby, esq., of Abington, near Northampton, and that the aforesaid Harvey sold it again to Samuel Tyler, Esq., whose sisters, as his heirs, now enjoy it," note by Greene written on July the 4th, 1770. This Quiney hypothesis is disproved by the passages in Shakespeare's will that refer to Judith, and there is no probability that he was ever the owner of the house here mentioned, and which, it is hardly necessary to observe, is not the Anne Hathaway Cottage of the present day.

The house now known under the last-mentioned appellation is the one which is mentioned in the old records as attached to land called Hewland or Hewlands. "Johannes Hathewey tenet, per copiam curie datam xx. die Aprilis, anno regni nuper regis Henrici Octavi xxxiiij.to, unum messuagium et dimidiam virgatam terre, jacentem in Shotterey, vocatam Hewland, et unum messuagium et unam virgatam terre nuper in tenura Thome Perkyns, ac unum toftum et dimidiam virgatam terre vocatam Hewlyns, cum suis pertinenciis, ibidem habendum sibi et suis secundum consuetudinem manerii predicti, reddendo inde per annum xxxiij.*s.* viij.*d.*, sectam curie et finem, ac herriettum cum acciderit," survey dated October, 1556, MS. Longbridge. The tenant here mentioned was probably the "John Hathewey, archer," whose name is found in a list of the "abell men" of Shottery in a muster-roll of 28 Henry VIII. In the inquisition on the possessions of the Earl of Warwick, taken in 1590, it is stated that "Johanna Hatheway, vidua, tenet per copiam unum messuagium, et duas virgatas terre et dimidiam, cum pertinenciis, per redditum per annum xxxiij.*s.* iiij.*d.*, finem et harriotum," the customary rent here named being the same amount that is given in the latest manor-book that has come under my notice, one that is dated from 1769 to 1783. But it was not until 1610 that the Hathaways became the owners of the estate, Bartholomew purchasing it in that year, subject to the last-named chief-rent, from William Whitmore and John Randoll, to whom the manor of Old Stratford had been granted by the Crown by letters-patent of 7 James I. The deed of conveyance, which was executed on 1st April, 8 James, confirmed " unto the said Bartholomew Hathaway, all that theire messuage and tenemente and one yarde land, 303 with thappurtenaunces, scituate and being in Shottery aforesaid, in the said countie of Warwicke, sometyme in the tenure or occupacion of Thomas Perkins, and now or late in the possession or occupacion of the said Bartholomew Hathaway, or of his assignee or assignes ; and all that theire mesuage and tenemente, and one other yarde land, with theire appurtenaunces, called or knowne by the name of Hewlands, scituate and being in Shotterie aforesaid, in the said countie of Warwick, now or late in the tenure or possession of the said Bartholomew Hathaway, or of his assignee ; and also all that their tofte and half yarde land, with thappurtenaunces, called or knowne by the name of Hewlyns, scituate, lyeing and being in Shotterie aforesaide, in the said countie of Warwicke, now or late in the possession or occupacion of the saide Bartholomew Hathaway, or of his assignee or assignes ; and also all those theire three closes, with theire and every of theire appurtenaunces, whereof one is called or knowne by the name of Hewland Close, one other called or knowne by the name of Hewlyns Close, and thother called or knowne by the name of Palmers Close, which said three closes are scituate, lying and being in Shottery aforesaide, in the said countie of Warwicke, and now are or late were in the possession or occupacion of the said Bartholomew Hathaway, or of his assignee or assignees." Upon the death of Bartholomew Hathaway in October, 1624, the Shottery property that he had acquired in 1610 came, under the terms of his will, into the hands of his son John, 304 and although there was more than one partial alienation of the estate in the last century, a portion of it, including the house above-mentioned, remained in the possession of the family until 1838, the male line, however, having become extinct on the death of a later John in 1746.

The earliest reference to the present Anne Hathaway's Cottage under that title is that found in Ireland's Picturesque Views on the Warwickshire Avon, 1795, in which work there is an engraving of the dwelling introduced by the following observations,—" the cottage in which she is said to have lived with her parents is yet standing, and although I have doubts as to the truth of the relation, I have yet given a faithful representation of it in the annexed view ;—it is still occupied by the descendants of her family, who are poor and numerous ;—to this same humble cottage I was referred, when pursuing the same inquiry, by the late Mr. Harte of Stratford," the person last named, who died in 1793, being a descendant from the poet's sister. With the exception of an inferior lithograph circulated by Green about the year 1820, no further notice cf the house appears to have been submitted to the public until 1828, in which year excellent views of it were issued by Rider, and the 305 late R. B. Wheler, in a manuscript note written about 1830, speaks of the then "generally believed tradition" that it was "the identical one from which Shakespeare married Anne Hathaway," adding in confirmation that "the Hathaway's family certainly resided at Shottery at that period." This latter writer, however, does not mention such a belief in either his History of Stratford, 1809, or in his Guide, 1814, while from 306 a notice of Shottery, compiled from his memoranda and published in 1820, it is obvious that he had personally no faith in its validity.

The farm-house that was inhabited by Richard Hathaway in 1581 must have undergone very considerable alteration since that period, but the history of the various changes that have occurred is necessarily incomplete. Two pieces of new work were introduced in the closing years of the seventeenth century, one a chimney which still bears the inscription—I.H., 1697—on a stone let into the outside brickwork at the top, the initials being those of the then owner of the property, John Hathaway; the other the latticed door of a bacon cupboard in the left-hand recess of a large open fire-place, the intermediate cross-bar of that door being thus lettered,—I.H., E.H., I.B., 1697. It is most likely that John Hathaway renovated at the same time other parts of the building, but that its original structural form was preserved may be gathered from a comparison of the inventory taken after Bartholomew's death in 1624 with one that was attached to the will of Robert Hathaway in 1728. Not only are the same kind of rooms mentioned in each, but the names of several of them and their uses are identical, the Little Chamber, for example, still holding at the latter date "one bed and other odd things." So many variations, however, have been effected in the interior arrangements since these lists were compiled, it is impossible for us to determine with certainty the localities therein mentioned, and even the main entrance is said to have been originally in what is now the back of the house. The conversion of the dwelling in the later part of the eighteenth century into two, and at a subsequent period into three, tenements, must also necessarily have been the occasion of a variety of mutations in the details of the structure. We may nevertheless assume, without much risk of error, that the original kitchen was the apartment on the right of the present entry and that the hall was the one on its left.

The name of Anne Hathaway's Cottage, that by which this lengthy domicile has been known for so many years, is misleading, it being really a substantial thatched farm-house of the Elizabethan period. It was built on a slope, and thus it happens that parts of the ground-floor, resting on walls of unequal height, are nearly level with the ground on one side and several feet above it on the other. There is still much of the old work to be traced in various portions of the building, on the exterior the framed timbers erected on foundations of lias shale, the gables and the small dormer windows, and in the interior the ancient roomy fire-places with their quaint recesses, the rude stone floors, the massive oaken beams and rafters. It should be mentioned that the upper rooms were open to the thatch until within a comparatively recent period, and that the centre passage was floored with globular stones. There is, indeed, no portion of the inside of the building that has not suffered from modifications of one kind or other, the apartment in which they have interfered the least with our realization of its original state being the ancient dairy. This half-timbered annex is at the upper end of the house, and, in spite of the late introduction of a fire-place and chimney, it gives the visitor a determinate idea of the appearance that it must have presented in the sixteenth century. The ponderous stone-bench is, or was at least in 1864, the identical ledge that once supported the milk-pans of Richard Hathaway, and the bottom of a cheese-press, now a part of the stone flooring, is most likely a remnant of the one that belonged to his son Bartholomew in 1624.

HATHAWAY RECORDS.

I. The Will of Richard Hathaway of Shottery, 1581, from the recorded copy in the Registry of the Prerogative Court of Canterbury.

In the name of God, amen ; the firste daie of September, in the yeare of oure Lorde God one thowsande fyve hundred eightie one, and in the three and twentithe yeare of thee raigne of oure soveraigne ladye Elizabethe, by the grace of God queene of Englande, Fraunce, and Irelande, defender of the faithe, etc., I, Richard Hathway of Shottree in the parrishe of Stratforde-uppon-Avon in the countie of Warwicke, husband-man, beinge sicke in bodye but of perfecte memorye, I thancke my Lord God, doe ordaine and make this my last will and testamente in manner and forme followinge. Firste, I bequeathe my sowle unto Allmightie God, trustinge to be saved by the merittes of Christes Passion, and my bodye to be buried in the churche or churche-yarde of Stratforde aforesaide. Item, I give and bequeathe unto Thomas, my sonne, six poundes thirtene shillinges fower pence, to be paide unto him at the age of twentie yeares. Item, I give and bequeathe unto John, my sonne, six poundes thirtene shillinges fower pence, to be paide unto him at the age of twentie yeares. Item, I give and bequeathe unto William, my sonne, tenne poundes to bee paide unto him at the age of twentie yeares. Item, I give and bequeathe unto Agnes, my daughter, six poundes thirtene shillinges fower pence, to be paide unto her at the daie of her marriage. Item, I give and bequeathe unto Catherine, my daughter, six poundes thirtene shillinges fower pence, to be paide unto her at the daie of her marriage. Item, I give and bequeathe unto Margaret, my daughter, six poundes thirtene shillinges fower pence, to be paide unto her at the age of seaventeene yeares. And if it fortune that any of my said sonnes or daughters before named, that is to saie, Thomas, John, William, Agnes, Catherine, or Margarett, to decease before theie receyve theire legacies, then my will is that the legacies of he or she so deceased to remayne equallie amonge the rest, and so unto the longest lyvers of theme. Item, my will is, withe consente of Jone, my wife, that my eldiste sonne Barthellmewe shall have the use, commoditie and profytt, of one halfe yearde lande withe all pastures and meadowinge therto belonginge, withe the appurtenaunces, to be tilled, mucked, and sowed at the charges of Joane, my wyffe, he onelie findinge seede, duringe the naturall life or widdowehode of the same Johan, my wife, to be severed from the other of my lande for his commoditie and profitte. And my will is that he, the same Bartholomewe, shal be a guide to my saide wife in hir husbandrye, and also a comforte unto his bretherne and sisters to his power. Provided alwaies that if the saide Joane, my wife, shall at anye tyme or tymes at-after my decease goe aboute to disanull or to take awaye from my saide sonne Bartholomewe the foresaide half yarde lande withe the appurtenaunces, so that he doe not enjoye the commoditye and proffitte of the same, according to the trewe meaninge of this my last will and testamente, then my will is that the sayde Joane, my wief, shall gyve delyver and paye unto my saide sonne Bartholomewe, within one yeare after any suche deniall or discharge, the somme of fortie poundes of lawfull Englishe monneye. Item, my will is that all the seelinges in my hall-howse, withe twoe joyned-beddes in my parlor, shall contynewe and stande unremoved duringe thee naturall liffe or widowhode of Jone, my wyffe, and the naturall lief of

Bartholomewe, my sonne, and John, my sonne, and the longest lyver of theme. Item, I gyve and bequeathe unto everie of my god-childrenne fower pence a peece of theme. Item, I gyve and bequeathe unto Agnes Hathway and Elizabethe Hathway, daughters unto Thomas Hathway, a sheepe a-peece of theme. This bequeast donne, debts paide, and legacies leavied, and my bodye honestlie buried, then I gyve and bequeathe all the rest of my goodes, moveable and unmoveable, unto Joane, my wief, whome I make my sole executrixe to see this my last will and testament trulye performed. And I desier my trustie frende and neighbours, Stephen Burman and Fowlke Sandelles, to be my supervisors of this my last will and testamente, and theie to have for theire paynes therin to be taken twelve-pence a-peece of theme. Witnesses, sir William Gilbarde, clarke and curate in Stretforde, Richarde Burman, John Richardson, and John Hemynge, withe others. Signum + Richardi Hathwaie testatoris.—*Debtes to be paide.* Inprimis, I doe owe unto my neighbour, John Pace, fortye shillinges. Item, I owe unto John Barber thirtie six shillinges fower pence. Item, I owe unto Thomas Whittington, my sheepherd, fower poundes six shillinges eight pence. Item, I owe unto Edwarde Hollyocke for woode twenty shillinges.—Probatum &c. apud London. nono die mensis Julii, 1582.

II. *The Will of Bartholomew Hathaway, from the copy that was exhibited in the Peculiar Court of Stratford-on-Avon, 1624.*

In the name of God, amen, the sixteenth day of September, Anno Domini 1621, I, Bartholomew Hathaway of Shottery in the parrish of Olde Stratford, in the cownty of Warwick, yeoman, being in my good and prosperous health, and of sownd and perfect memorie, thanks be given to Almighty God, doe ordeine and make this my last will and testament in manner and forme followeing, that is to say,—first, I bequeath my soule to the handes of Almighty God, my maker, and by fayth in the merittes and passion of his sone, Jesus Christ, I beleeve and hope to be saved, and my body to therth from whence yt came to be burryed in the Christian burriall of the parrish church of Olde Stratford aforesaid, hopeing to arise at the latter day, and to receive the reward of his ellect; and for my worldly goodes I bequeath them as followeth, that is to say,—Imprimis, I give and bequeath to Richard Hathaway, my sone, the some of twenty shillinges of lawfull English money to be paide unto him within one yeire next after my decease. Item, I give and bequeath unto Isabell Hathaway, my graundchilde, daughter of the saide Richard, one chilver shipp. Ittem, I give and bequeath unto my sone, Edmonde Hathaway, my third sone, the whole some of one hundred and twenty powndes of lawfull English monye to be paide unto him, the said Edmond, within seaven yeires next after my decease, that is to say, the some of twenty powndes a yeire for the first five yeires next after my decease, and the other twenty powndes to be paide tenne powndes a yeire the next two yeires followeinge, after the saide terme of five yeires, in full satisfaccion of the saide summe of one hundred and twenty powndes. Item, I further give unto my saide sone Edmonde my yongest gray mare, and my best cowe soe two, and my elme cart and the wheeles belonging to yt, which mare, cart and wheeles, he hath alredy in possession; togither alsoe with my best fether bedd, my best heiling, two paire of sheetes, and one payre of my best blankettes, and my best bowlster, and one of my best pillowes, my second brass pott, and one of the bedsteedes in the over-chamber. Ittem, I give and bequeath unto my daughter, Anne Edwardes, the now wyfe of Richard Edwardes, the summe of thirty shillinges to buy her a gowne, and to her seven⊚ children, Avery, Bartholomew, Alice, Thomas, Richard, and Ursula Edwardes, I give unto each of them severally the severall sums of six shillinges eight pence apeece to be paide unto them within one yeire next after my decease. Ittem, I give and bequeath unto my sone, John Hathaway, his children, Alice Hathaway, Richard, Anne and Ursula Hathaway, and to each ot them one of my best ewes a-peece. Ittem, I give and bequeath unto my said sone,

John Hathaway, and to the heires males of his body lawfully begotten, or to be begotten, all that my messuage or tenement, orchard, garden and backside, with thappertenaunces, scituate, lyeing and being in Shottery aforesaid, togither alsoe with two yard land and a half earable, meddow, comon and pasture, with two closses therunto belonging, scituate, lyeing and beinge within the towne, hamlettes and feildes of Shottery and Olde Stratford, with theire and every of theire appertenaunces ; and for want of such issue of the said John Hathaway, I give and bequeath the said messuage or tenement, two yard land and a half, with thappertenaunces, unto the saide Edmond Hathaway, my . . . . lawfully to (be) begotten, and for want of such issue of the saide Edmonde Hathaway, I give and bequeath the saide messuage or tenement . . . . aunces unto my sone, Richard Hathaway, and to the heires males of his body lawfully begotten, or to be begotten, and for want of such issue of the said Richard, then to remaine to the right heires of me, the said Bartholmew Hathaway, for ever. Ittem, I give and bequeath towards the repaire of the parish church of Olde Stratford the some of tenn shillings. Ittem, I give and bequeath unto the poore of the said parrish the some of thirteene shillinges foure pence to be distributed amongst them at my funerall. All the rest of my goodes and cattell and chattelles whatsoever unbequeathed, my deptes and legacyes being paide, and funerall exspences discharged, I wholly give unto my said sone, John Hathaway, whome I doe ordeine and make my whole and executor of this my last will and testament. Overseers of this my last will and testament I doe make choyse of John Hall of Stratford aforesaide, gentleman, and Stephen Burman of Shottery aforesaide, yeoman, and for theire paines therein to be taken I do give unto eache of them two shillinges six-pence a-peece. In wytnesse wherof to this my last will and testament I have heerunto sett my hand and seale in the presence of these wittnesses heerunder written.—Witnesses heerunto,—William Court, junior ; Clement Burman ; Stephen Burman ; William Richardson.

III. An Inventory of the Goodes, Chatelles and Credites, of Bartholmew Hathway of Shotery, in the Cownty of Warr:, deceased, taken as they were praysed by Steven Burman, William Richardsons, and John Edwardes, the xxvij.th day of October, 1624.

Imprimis, in chamber where he lay.—His weareing apparell and mony, iij.*li.* Item, one joyned-bedsteed, one fether-bed, one bolster, one pillow, one coverlit, one pere blanketes, two pere sheetes, iij.*li.* Item, four paire sheetes, ij. napkins, j. hurden bordcloth, j.*li.* iiij.*s.* Item, three bordclothes and vj. napkins, x.*s.* One chest, ij.*s.* vj.*d.*

In the Broode Soller or Chamber.—One half hed-bedsteed, j. bed bolster pillow, one pere sheetes, blanketes and coverlit, j.*li.* Item, in cheese, aples, tow, yarne and oatmeale, and old bordes and botles, and buter, lard and talloe, ij.*li.* x.*s.*

In the Butrye.—Two barelles and one powtherin-tubb, x.*s.*

In the Litle Chamber.—A bedsteed and press, v.*s.*

In the Hall.—One table, ij. cheires, two formes, ij. stooles, ij. cushions, x.*s.* viij. peeces pewter, j. brass candlestick, j. chafing-dish, x.*s.* j. pere links, j. pere belloes, ij.*s.* ij. brass potes, ij. ketles, j.*li.* vj.*s.* viij.*d.*

In the Kitchin.—ij. loomes, ij. kives, payles, tubes and other implementes, xij.*s.* j. spit, coberd, and dripan, and a peale, iij.*s.* iiij.*d.*

In the Chamber over the Kitchin.—One heire-clothe, one wheele, j. stryke, ij. sives, iiij. stryke malt and hurdes, and other ode trumpery, j.*li.* x.*s.*

In the Barnes and Backhowses.—One bay and more of barli vallued at xx. quarter, xvj.*li.* x. stryke wheate, ij.*li.* Powlse and hey, viij.*li.* A malt-mill, cheese-presse, with hemp and flax, xij.*s.*

In the Stable.—iij. horsses, viij.*li.*

In the Backside.—Six kyne and other bease, viij.*li.* xxxvij. sheepe, viij.*li.* vj. piges or swyne, ij.*li.*   Cartes, plowes, harrowes, harnes and geires, shippachs, and other implementes, iij.*li.* vj.*s.* viij.*d.*   Woode, lumber and trash, j.*li.* x.*s.*

Summe is lxxiiij.*li.* iiij*s.* ij.*d.*—Praysers,—signum Steven + Burman, John Edwardes, signum William + Richarsons.

IV. The Will of Richard, one of the Sons of Bartholomew Hathaway, 1 *September,* 1636. *From an Official Copy.*

In the name of God, amen, I, Richard Hathaway of Stratford-uppon-Avon, in the countie of Warwick, baker, beinge sicke in bodie, but of good and perfect memorie, doe make and ordaine this my last will and testament in manner and forme following, that is to say,—first, I bequeath my soule to Almightie God, trusting to be saved through the meritts of my Saviour, Jesus Christ, and my body to be buried in the parish Church of Stratford at the discrecion of my executrix hereafter named ; and for the messuages, lands and worldly goods which it hath pleased God to bestowe uppon mee, I give and dispose of them in manner and forme followinge, that is to say, my will is, and I doe by theis presents give and bequeath unto Priscilla, my deere beloved wife, all that messuage wherein I nowe live, and all those messuages, cottages or tenements situate and being in Stratford aforesaid, nowe or late in the severall tenures or occupacions of William Parker, malster, widow Durie, John Swan and John Burman, and five lands in the common feilds of Old Stratford, of which messuages, cottages, tenements and lands, except the messuage wherein I live, I, the said Richard Hathaway, am seised of an estate in fee simple, to have and to hold all the said messuages, cottages, five lands, the said messuage wherein I live, and all and singular the said premisses, unto the said Priscilla for and duringe the time of her naturall life ; and further my will is that, my debts and funerall discharged, the said Priscilla shall have all and singuler my goods and chattells, moveable and unmoveable whatsoever, as well reall as personall.   And of this my last will I do constitute and appointe the said Priscilla, my wife, my executrix, and Richard Castell overseer of the same.   In witnes whereof I have hereunto put my hand and seale the first day of September, in the twelveth yeare of the raigne of our Soveraigne Lord Charles, by the grace of God, &c.

THE ESTATE OF ASBIES.

Amongst the Shakespearean delusions that have too long mocked the enthusiasm of the unwary tourist, and amongst those which have elicited the larger measure of sentimental reflection, perhaps the most remarkable is the pretended identification of a certain old farmhouse at Wilmecote, on the sole authority of a notorious impostor, with that which was the birth-place and subsequently part of the dowry of Mary Arden. It was in the year 1794 that Jordan, ever anxious to increase his slender income by communicating new information to Malone and the elder Ireland, was corresponding with the latter respecting a drawing 326 of the house in question, the victim acknowledging that he had never heard of its presumed interesting character during his artistic rambles in the district in the summer months of 1792 and 1793. Ireland, in his Picturesque Views, issued in 1795, takes no notice of the statement that had been made to him in the previous year, but, after a while, the fabricated story, emancipated from its origin, came to be accepted as a genuine tradition, this stage in progressive credulity being followed by its reception as an established fact.

Two of Jordan's rude sketches of the locality have been preserved, one noted by him as a "view of the house at Wilmcotte where Robert Arden resided, whose daughter Mary was married to John Shakespeare;" the other as "a view of the publick house at Wilmcotte where Robert Arden, esq., lived, whose daughter Mary was married to John Shakespere, by whom she had issue the immortal William Shakespere;" and from all that can now be ascertained, the genuineness of these ascriptions rests entirely upon the slippery basis of the draughtsman's veracity. In the absence, however, of a distinct refutation, the truthfulness of these positive assertions might still be considered a possibility, but fortunately for the interests of truth, there is yet preserved the history of what must be termed the pseudo-Asbies from the year 1561 to the present time, a history that is altogether inconsistent with the theory that it was ever possessed either by the Shakespeares or the Lamberts. This pseudo-Asbies belonged in the middle of the sixteenth century to the Fyndernes, who sold it, with the manor and other estates at Great Wilmecote, to Adam Palmer and George Gibbes, and the fine levied on the occasion of the transfer was enrolled in Easter Term, 4 Elizabeth. These two purchasers held it as tenants in common until 1575, in the June of which year there was a partition made under which Gibbes took, in absolute lieu of his share,—" the small messuage and all houses and buildings, with their appurtenances, which he then dwelt in and occupied, and the orchards, gardens, poles, ponds, and the close on the backside the said

327 messuage extending to the fyld called Sheloyle, and one close called Berry Hill adjoining to the Queens highway, with all the trees and wood growing and standing upon the same; and the half part of one plow called the Meadow-Piece adjoining to Shelfyll, and extending to the merestones then newly set for the division of the same; and half seven lees ends adjoining to the closes of Thomas Edkins the elder on the east side, and the close of John Fullwood on the other side; and two yard-land and a half containing nyne score sellions, lees, ridges, pikes, parcels of meadow-ground, with all woods, &c., to the said messuage belonging," old abstract of title.

This property continued in the hands of George Gibbes and his descendants until August, 1704, when it was purchased by one Matthew Walford, and it subsequently became vested in his daughter, Margaret Nanfan, in fee simple, at whose death it came into the possession of the Webbs. Its identity with the pseudo-Asbies is shown by the following description of parcels in a Walford family indenture of 1790, the same description, with a few immaterial variations, occurring in a release of it from Elias Webb to John Whitehead, 1807,—" all that messuage or tenement, with the yard, garden, orchard and appurtenances thereto belonging, situate, standing and being in the hamlet of Wilmcoate, in the parish of Aston Cantlowe, then in the occupation of John Checketts or his undertenants; and also all those several closes, pieces or parcels of arable, meadow, and pasture land, situate, lying and being in the hamlet of Wilmcoate aforesaid, and then in the tenure or occupation of the said John Checketts or his undertenants, and called or known by the several names following, that is to say,—house close; stone-pit close; eight-acre close; dovehouse close next the lane; wheat hill; middle-ground, otherwise redland; barn-piece, otherwise rough-ground; the piece beyond them divided into two closes, one of them meadow ground and next the turnpike road, and the other of them arable land; the old pasture ground then divided into two parts, one part thereof being meadow, and the other part coppice; the meadow adjoining to mott orchard and to a cottage; berry-hill and chapel-close, or by whatsoever other name or names the same then or then late were better known or distinguished; and also all those two cottages, gardens and orchards, called mott orchard, with the appurtenances, then late in the respective occupations of . . . . . . and then untenanted; and also all those five leys lying in upper stone-pit field in Wilmcoate aforesaid; and all those six leys lying in lower stone-pit field in Wilmcoate aforesaid in the occupation of the said John Checketts," old abstract of title.

Although, however, these notices cannot refer to the Shakespearean estate, the dwelling which has been erroneously accepted as Mary Arden's birth-place is yet an object of considerable interest, being one of the very few buildings now remaining in Wilmecote which retain any of the characteristics of a farm-house of the kind in which her girlhood must have been passed. Its singularly massive beams are alone good evidences of its antiquity, and there was in the kitchen until recent years a very large open fire-place under a roof of carved wood-work. There was also a long carved wooden bench under the window, and an upper room, with its timber-framed walls, oaken floor and ancient fire-place, is still, or was at least in 1863, in nearly its original condition. The exterior of the house and its outbuildings appear to have been subjected to greater changes, and that Featherbed Lane, in which the premises are situated, now a fairly good road, was formerly in a very different condition, may be gathered from the following note which has been kindly transmitted by an old Stratford friend,—" when my father was married in November, 1804, he brought my mother in a post-chaise to the top of this lane, intending to drive through it into the village, but it was so soft, adhesive and muddy, that he found it impossible to do so ;—it runs through Starve-all Farm, which then possessed the same kindred qualities, and I have heard that its name originated in its tendency to starve all who sought to obtain a living upon it, but all this is now altered, the land having years ago been thoroughly drained and put into good order." This narrative is one of the many evidences that show how complete has been the transformation in the face of this part of England since the days of the Ardens.

The exact site of the real Asbies is unknown, but it must have been within a very short distance of the above-named farm. Amongst the lands assigned to Palmer in the division of 1575 was "one parcel of meadow and lees called the Meadow-Piece, adjoining to the close of John Shakesperes of the west side," old abstract of title, the original deed having unfortunately been lost ; and included in Gibbes's share was "the half part of one plow called the Meadow-Piece adjoining to Shelfyll," the last-named field not necessarily being the one which is now termed Shelshill, and which is on the south-eastern side of Featherbed Lane, nearly opposite the house of the pseudo-Asbies. All endeavours to ascertain the locality of the Meadow-Piece have hitherto failed, but that it was near the village may be inferred from a deed of conveyance, 1656, of "all that cottage or tenement wherein the said William Edkins alias Atkins then or late dwelt, situate in Wilmcot aforesaid, with the garden, orchard, backside, and one little close called the Meadow-Piece unto the said cottage or tenement adjoining and belonging," old abstract of title, a similar description occurring in a number of later indentures of the seventeenth and eighteenth centuries.

The estate of Asbies was lost for ever to the Shakespeares when, on November the 14th, 1578, they unfortunately passed it over to Edmund Lambert as a security for an advance of £40, the latter receiving no interest for his money, but taking in its stead the "rents and profits" of the farm.   Previously to the completion of this arrangement, at some time before the Feast of St. Martin, 20 Elizabeth, they seem to have granted a lease of the whole of the property, the house only excepted, to one George Gibbes, for twenty-one years from Michaelmas, 1580, at the annual rental of "the moiety of one quarter of wheat and the moiety of one quarter of barley," favourable terms which lead to the suspicion that a premium was received from the lessee.   A copy of the fine that passed on this occasion is here annexed.—

Wilmecote Fine, Hilary Term, 21 Eliz.—*Hec est finalis concordia facta in curia domine Regine apud Westmonasterium, in crastino sancti Martini, anno regnorum Elizabethe, Dei gracia Anglie, Francie et Hibernie regine, fidei defensoris, etc., a conquestu, vicesimo, coram Jacobo Dyer, Rogero Manwoode, Roberto Mounsone et Thoma Meade, justiciariis, et postea in octabis Sancti Hillarii, anno regnorum ejusdem Regine Elizabethe vicesimo primo, ibidem concessa et recordata coram eisdem justiciariis et aliis domine Regine fidelibus tunc ibi presentibus,—inter Thomam Webbe et Humfridum Hooper, querentes, et Johannem Shakespere et Mariam, uxorem ejus, et Georgium Gybbes, deforciantes, de septuaginta acris terre, sex acris prati, decem acris pasture et communia pasture pro omnimodis averiis, cum pertinenciis, in Wylmecote, unde placitum convencionis summonitum fuit inter eos in eadem curia, scilicet, quod predicti Johannes et Maria et Georgius recognoverunt predicta tenementa et communiam pasture, cum pertinenciis, esse jus ipsius Thome, ut illa que iidem Thomas et Humfridus habent de dono predictorum Johannis et Marie et Georgii, et illa remiserunt et quietumclamaverunt de ipsis, Johanne et Maria et Georgio, et heredibus suis, predictis Thome et Humfrido, et heredibus ipsius Thome, imperpetuum; et preterea iidem Johannes et Maria concesserunt, pro se et heredibus ipsius Marie, quod ipsi warantizabunt predictis Thome et Humfrido et heredibus ipsius Thome, predicta tenementa et communiam pasture, cum pertinenciis, contra omnes homines imperpetuum; et pro hac recognicione, remissione quietaclamancia, warantia, fine et concordia, iidem Thomas et Humfridus concesserunt predicto Georgio predicta tenementa et communiam pasture, cum pertinenciis, et illa ei reddiderunt in eadem curia, habenda et tenenda eidem Georgio a festo sancti Michaelis Archangeli quod erit in anno Domini millesimo quingentesimo et octogesimo, usque finem termini viginti et unius annorum extunc proximo sequentium et plenarie complendorum, reddendo inde annuatim predictis Thome et Humfrido, et heredibus ipsius Thome, medietatem unius quarterii tritici et medietatem unius quarterii ordei ad festum Natalis Domini annuatim solvendas; et si contingat predictum redditum medietatis unius quarterii tritici et medietatis unius quarterii*

ordei, aut aliquam inde parcellam, aretro fore in parte vel in toto post
festum predictum quo ut prefertur solvi debeat non solutum per spatium
viginti dierum, quod tunc bene licebit predictis Thome et Humfrido, et
heredibus ipsius Thome, in predicta tenementa et communiam pasture,
cum pertinenciis, intrare et distringere, districcionesque sic ibidem captas et
habitas licite abducere, asportare et effugare, ac penes se retinere quousque
de predicto redditu medietatis unius quarterii tritici et medietatis unius quar-
terii ordei, cum arreragiis ejusdem, si que fuerint, plenarie fuerit satisfactum
et persolutum; concesserunt etiam predicti Thomas et Humfridus predictis
Johanni et Marie revercionem tenementorum et communie pasture predic-
torum, cum pertinenciis, ac predictum redditum superius reservatum, et illa
eis reddiderunt in eadem curia, habenda et tenenda eisdem Johanni et Marie,
et heredibus ipsius Marie, de capitalibus dominis feodi illius per servicia que
ad predicta tenementa et communiam pasture pertinent imperpetuum.

The above interpretation of the contents of this document appears
to be the most feasible, but it is unsafe to speak positively in the matter,
its terms being peculiar and the indenture leading its uses not having
been discovered. It might even be that Gibbes was a trustee for the
Shakespeares, such arrangements having often been made privately and
not expressed in any of the written instruments. See the second part of
West's Symbolæographie, ed. 1594, Chanc. Sect., 94,128. However
that may be, the mortgage-loan was made repayable at the Michaelmas
at which the lease commenced to run, and the bare legal denial of John
Lambert, based probably on family hearsay, does not appear to be a
sufficient reason for doubting the circumstantial assertion made in the
replication of 1598, one that had been previously given in nearly the
same terms in the bill of the previous year, that the poet's father travelled
on that Michaelmas-day to the mortgagee's residence at Barton-on-the-
Heath, a retired village on the southern borders of Warwickshire, "and
then and there tendered to paie unto him the said Edmunde Lambert
the said fortie poundes, which he was to paie for the redempcion of the
said premisses ; which somme the said Edmunde did refuse to receyve,
sayinge that he owed him other money, and unles that he, the said John,
would paie him altogether, as well the said fortie poundes as the other
money, which he owed him over and above, he would not receave the
said fortie poundes." So absolute was the law of forfeiture on such
occasions that the Shakespeares would hardly have ventured upon an
expensive litigation had they not felt that there were reasonable grounds
for the course they adopted, the probability being that Edmund Lambert,
at the above-mentioned interview, had verbally guaranteed the surrender
of the estate at any time at which his conditions were fulfilled. This
would explain the absence of litigation during the life-time of the original
mortgagee, and, after the failure of the negociations with his successor,
want of means no doubt hindered further action until the subject was

revived under the poet's sanction and influence in 1597. That strenuous efforts were then made to recover possession of the estate appears from the Chancery papers that are given in the Estate Records, No. 4, and from the following Orders of the Court.—

I. July the 5th, 1598.—*Quinto die Julij. John Shackspere and Mary, his wief, plaintiffes, John Lamberte, defendant. A commission ys awarded to examyne witnesses on bothe partes, directed to Richard Lane, John Combes, Thomas Underhill and Fraunces Woodward, gentlemen, iij. or ij. of them, returnable octavis Michaelis, by assente of the attorneyes, Powle and Hubard, and the plaintiefes to geve xiiij. daies warninge.*

II. July the 10th, 1598.—*Lune, decimo die Julii. John Shackespere and Marye, his wief, plaintiffes; John Lambert, defendant.—A commission ys awarded to examyne witnesses on both partes, directed to Richard Lanne, John Combes, Thomas Underhill and Frances Woodward, gentlemen, or two of them, returnable octavis Michaelis, by the assent of the attorneys, Powle and Hubard, and the plaintiffes to give xiiij. dayes warninge.*

III. May the 18th, 1599.—*xviij.° die Maij. John Shakespeare, plaintiff; John Lambard, defendant.—Forasmuch as this Cowrt was this presente day ynformed by Mr. Overbury, beinge of the defendantes councell, that the plaintiff did fyrst exhibyte a bill unto this Cowrt against the defendant, as well by his owne name as in the name of his wyef, to be relyved towchinge a mortgage of certene landes lyinge in the county of Warr. made to the defendantes father, whose heyre the defendant is, and afterwardes exhibyted a bill in his owne name only concerninge such matter in substaunce as the former bill doth; and althoughe the plaintiff hath taken owt two severall commisyones upon the later bill, yet he hath not examyned any wytnesses thereupon. It is therfore ordered that, yf Mr. D. Hunt, one of the Masters of this Cowrt, shall, upon consideracion of the said bills, fynde and report that bothe the said billes doe in substaunce conteyne one matter, then the defendant ys to be dismissed from one of the said billes, with such costes as the said Mr. D. Hunt shall tax and asseasse; and the plaintiff ys to procede to the hearinge thereof withe effect, and the defendant shal be at lyberty to chaunge his commissyones, yf he will, and the plaintiffes attorney is to be warned hereof.* There is a duplicate entry of this Order, the only variation worthy of notice being the words *another bill* instead of *a bill* in l. 8.

IV. June the 27th, 1599.—*xxvij.° die Junij. John Shackspeere and Margaret®, his wief, plaintiffes; John Lamberte, defendant.—A commission ys awarded to examine witnesses on bothe partes, directed to Richard Lane, John Combes, William Berry and John Warne, gentlemen, iij. or ij. of them, returnable octavis Michaelis, by assente of the attorneyes, Powle and Hubard, and the plaintiffes to geve xiiij. daies warninge.* In the contemporary index to the Orders, under Trin. Term. 41 Eliz., there is the entry,—*Shackspeere contra Lambert, 896*,—but the end of the volume which did contain that leaf is unfortunately missing.   The lost note was most probably a duplicate of the Order here given.

V. October the 23rd, 1599.—*Martis, xxiij.° die Octobris.   John Shakespere and Mary, his wief, plaintiffes; John Lamberte, defendant.— Yf the defendant shewe no cawse for stay of publicacion by this day sevenight, then publicacion ys graunted.*—There is a duplicate of this entry in which the surname of the plaintiffs appears in the form of *Shakesbere.*

The continuous descent of the Asbies estate after the time of the Lamberts is unknown, but it is found in the latter part of the seventeenth century in the hands of one Clement Edkins, who owned "three quarters of one yard-land, and *one messuage and one yard-land and four acres,*" at Wilmecote in 1699, these two properties being then described as "the lands late of one John Smith, deceased."   It appears from an indenture of 1725 that the three quarters of the yard-land had been purchased by Smith in 1668 from Adam Edkins, and hence it may be inferred that the other estate, the description of which is identical with that given of Asbies in 1589 and 1597, had also belonged to the last-named individual.

THE ANCESTRAL FAMILIES.

Robert Arden, Shakespeare's maternal grandfather, was the son of a Thomas Arden who was residing at Wilmecote in the year 1501. "Sciant presentes et futuri quod ego, Johannes Mayowe de Snytterfeld, dedi, concessi, et hac presenti carta mea confirmavi Roberto Throkmerton, armigero, Thome Trussell de Billesley, Rogero Reynoldes de Heenley-in-Arden, Willielmo Wodde de Wodhouse, Thome Ardern de Wylmecote et Roberto Ardern, filio ejusdem Thome Ardern, unum mesuagium, cum suis pertinenciis, in Snytterfeld," commencement of a deed, May, 16 Hen. VII. This is the earliest indisputable notice of the poet's family on the mother's side that has yet been discovered, and the history of the father's descent is in a yet more unsatisfactory condition. The most elaborate researches have hitherto failed to unearth a fragment of direct evidence respecting the career of John Shakespeare previously to his arrival at Stratford-on-Avon, but there is a high probability, amounting nearly to a certainty, that he was the brother of one Henry of Snitterfield. There is no mention in the local records or neighbouring registers of any other person at all likely to have been the *Henricus* 331 *Shaxpere, frater Johannis*, who is named in one of the papers of the Court of Record, 1587, and, as far as can be gathered from the papers at our disposal, there is nothing whatever to disturb a belief in the identity. So far, moreover, from there being an indication of adverse testimony, the little that is known favours the opinion that the two brothers were natives of Snitterfield, and this theory derives no inconsiderable degree of support from the conveyance-deed of October, 1579. Under the impression that no reasonable doubt can be entertained on the subject, and that the immediate ancestors of the great dramatist were established in that village, the following notes on persons of his name who were resident there in the sixteenth century are here given.

Richard Shakespeare.—"Item, presentant quod Ricardus Meydes (xij.*d*), et Ricardus Shakespere (xij.*d*), superoneraverunt communem pasturam cum averiis suis, contra ordinacionem curie;—idio ipsi in misericordia," visus Franci Plegii, 1 October, 1535. "Unto Richarde Shakespere of Snytfelde my foure oxen which are nowe in his keping," will of Thomas Atwode alias Tailor of Stratforde-uppon-Aven, 1543. "Totum illud mesuagium cum suis pertinenciis in Snytterfylde, que nunc sunt in tenura cujusdam Ricardi Shakespere, ac omnia illa mea terras, prata, pascuas, et pasturas, cum suis pertinenciis in Snytterfylde predicta, eidem mesuagio spectantia et pertinentia, que nunc sunt in tenura predicti Ricardi Shakespere," settlement of an estate made by Robert Arden in 1550. "All those her two measuages with a cottage, with all and singuler their appurtenaunces, in Snytterfeld, and a yarde and a halfe of ayrable lande therunto belongyng, with all landes, medowes, pastures, commons, profettes and commodities, in any wyse therunto apperteynynge, scituate, lying and beyng in the towne and fyldes of Snytterfeild afforsaid, all whiche now are in the occupation of Richarde Shakespere, John Henley, and John Hargreve," lease from Agnes Arden to her brother, Alexander Webbe, of her Snitterfield estates, May, 1560. Richard Shakespeare most probably died either in this or the following year, there being no allusion to him in the parish-register, commencing in 1561, nor in any of the subsequent records. The latest notices of him that I have met with occur in an account of the proceedings of a View of Frank Pledge held at Snitterfield on October the 3rd, 1560,— "imprimis, that every tenaunte for his parte doe make his hedges and ditches betwixt the end of the lane of Richard Shakespere, and the hedge called Dawkins hedge, before the feast of St. Luke, sub pene iij.*s.* iiij.*d*," paines and orders made att the Courte there holdene the third day of October in the secound yeare of Queene Eliz. "Item, presentant Ricardum Shakespere (iiij.*d*), et Margeriam Lyncecombe (iiij.*d*), et Richardum Maydes (iiij.*d*), quia custodierunt animalia sua super *le leez*, contra ordinacionem inde factam ; item, preceptum cuilibet tenentium quod quilibet pro parte sua debet facere sepem et fossatum inter finem venelle Ricardi Shakespere et sepem vocatam *Dawkyns hedge*, scilicet, ante festum sancti Luce, sub pena iij.*s.* iiij.*d*," visus Franci Plegii, 3 October, 1560. As there was a field termed Dawkins Close at the back of the farmhouse of the Old, now known as the Wolds, and the hedge could not have been in the open fields, where there were more than one Dawkins Furlong, it may be assumed that Richard's land, or at least a portion of it, lay somewhere on the north of Warwick Way, anciently called Warwick Lane ; but the allusions in the presentation are too indefinite to sanction a more absolute inference. The locality of his residence is unknown, and no reliance must be placed on the so-called tradition respecting it, those who were years ago the oldest inhabitants of the Green, a part of the village near the Wolds, having assured me that the subject had never been mentioned in their early days. "The Rev. Donald Cameron, vicar of Snitterfield, informs me that, about four or five years ago, two poor cottages were pulled down on the left hand of the green which were reported to have once belonged to the Shaksperes, but he knows not that the tradition had any solid foundation," Tweddell's Shakspere, 8vo., Bury, 1842, p. 45.

Henry Shakespeare.—It will be observed, from some of the following evidences, that Henry Shakespeare's farm was one of considerable importance, and that it included two fields, called Burman and Red Hill, that were separated by a ditch, the latter circumstance showing that they were old enclosures. These extensive fields, which are still known under those names, are at a short distance from the Church on the right-hand side of the highway proceeding towards Luscombe; and there is an old house at the corner of the former one which may very likely occupy the site of Henry's residence. No fragment of the more ancient dwelling is now to be seen, but one of the oldest inhabitants of Snitterfield told me, in 1881, that he had assisted many years previously in the removal of a neighbouring barn in which there were, to use his own words, "a lot of turned posts a little carved at the top," and these were possibly the last-surviving relics of the farm-house at which the poet was most likely, in his youthful days, a frequent visitor.—"Et quod Henricus Shakespere (iij.*s.* iiij.*d.*) et Edwardus Cornewaile (ij.*s.*) invicem affraiam fecerunt, et idem Henricus traxit sanguinem super predictum Edwardum, ad injuriam dicti Edwardi, et contra pacem domine regine," visus Franci Plegii, 12 October, 1574, a day on which he was fined twopence for being absent from the Court. "That he this jurate had in the yeare libellated of wheate, maslin and rye, aboutes five wane-loodes, and of barley and ootes aboutes five wane-loodes, and of pease aboutes five wane-loodes, . . . that every wane-lode of wheate, maslin and rye, did extent⑨ and was worth by this jurates estimacion vj.*s.* viij.*d*, and every of the loodes of barley and ootes was worth aboutes v.*s.* and every wane-loode of pease afore by him deposid was worth by this jurates estimacion to the summe of v.*s.* . . . that the simple value of the halff of the tythe wheate, maslin and rie, did extende to xx.*d.*, and the triple value thereof to v.*s.* . . . that the simple value of the halffe of the tythe of the barley and ottes afore by him deposid did extende to xv.*d*, and the triple value thereof to iij.*s.* ix.*d*, and that the simple value of the tythe of the one halff of the pease afore by him deposid did extende to xv.*d*, and the triple value thereof to iij.*s.* ix.*d.* . . . that he payed no tythes to the sayd Sheldon and Bewfoe, bycause, as he sayeth, he compounded with Mr. Rich. Brokes of Warwike for the sayd moitie, who this jurate did beleve was owner thereof," *responsiones personales Henrici Saxspere de Snytterfild* in a tithe-suit, 22 November, 1580. "Ad quintum articulum libelli dicit that Henry Shagspere had and convertid to his owne use of wheate, mongcorn and rie, in the yere libellatid, x. carte-lodes comminge and growinge in the parishe of Snitterfild, and had and convertid to his owne use, in the yere libellatid, of barley and otes x. carte-lodes by this deponentes estimacion, and of peese he had and convertid to his owne use x. carte-lodes, or thereaboutes, comminge and growinge within the parishe of Snitterfild;—ad sextum, septimum et octavum articulos libelli dicit that every lode of wheate, mongcorn and rie, did extend or was worth on with another xvj.*s.* a lode by this deponentes estimacion, and every lode of barley and otes was worth x.*s.* a lode on with another; and every carte-lode of peese on with another was worth by this deponentes estimacion ix.*s.* a carte-lode on with another, had bj the said Shagspere;—ad nonum et decimum articulos libelli dicit that the simple value of the on half of the tythe of the wheate, mongcorn and rie, had by the said Henry Shagspere, in the yere libellated, did extend to vij.*s*, or thereaboutes, by this deponentes estimacion, and the tripell value therof to xxj.*s.*—ad undecimum articulum dicit that the simple value of the on halfe of the tythe of the barley had bj the said Shagspere, in the yere libellatid, within the parishe of Snitterfild, did extend to v.*s.*, or thereaboutes, and the simple value of thon halff of the otes to v.*s.*—ad duodecimum articulum dicit that the simple value of the on halfe of the tythe of the peese had by the said Shagspere, in the yere libellatid, did extend to iiij.*s.* vj.*d.*, or thereaboutes," depositions of John Sheldon, 14 March, 1580–1. "Willielmus Totnolle de Warwico, yoman, etatis xl. annorum, aut circiter, pro parte Thome Sheldon et Johannis Beawfo contra Henricum Shagspere, dicit quod dictos firmarios per tantum tempus predictum, et dictum Henricum Shagspere de facie per vj. annos ultimo preteritos, novit, aliter non novit.—ad quintum articulum libelli dicit that Henry Shagspere had and convertid to his owne use in the yere libellatid x. carte-loades of wheate, mongcorn, and rie, and of barley and otes x. carte-loodes, and of peese he had and convertid to his owne use x. carte-loodes, or thereaboutes, by this deponentes estimacion, comminge and growinge in and upon the groundes by him occupyed in the parishe of Snitterfild in the dioces of Worcester.—ad sextum articulum libelli dicit that every carte-lode of the wheate, mongcorn and rie afore by him deposid was worth, by this deponentes estimacion, xv.*s.* a lode on with another.—at septimum articulum libelli dicit every loode of barley and otes, afore by this deponent deposid, did extend, by this deponentes estimacion, to ix.*s.* a lode on with another.—ad octavum articulum libelli dicit that every carte-lode of the pease, afore by him deposed, was worth, by this deponentes estimacion, viij.*s.* a lode on with another.—ad nonum articulum libelli dicit that the simple value of the tythe of the on halfe of the wheate, mongcorn and rie, afore by him deposid and had by the said Henry Shagspere, did extend to vij.*s.* vj.*d.*, or thereaboutes.—ad decimum articulum libelli dicit that the tripell value of the tythe of the on halfe of the wheate, mongcorn, and rie, afore by him deposid, had by the said Henry Shagspere in the yere libellatid, did extend to xxij.*s.* vj.*d.*, or thereaboute," deposition, 14 March, 1580–1. "Iidem firmarii contra Henricum Shagspere in causa subtraccionis decimarum.— Shagspere, excommunicatio ut supra, et similiter Richardson certificavit de denunciatione dicti Shagspere in ecclesia de Snitterfild quinto die mensis Novembris," 21 November, 1581. "Dominus Thomas Robbins, vicarius de Hampton-in-Arden, Coventrensis et Lichefeldensis diocesis, contra Henricum Shagspere de Snitterfild in causa subtraccionis deci-marum;—Shagspere est contumax; reservata pena ut supra; dominus ad petitionem suam pronunciavit eum excommunicatum, pena reservata etc.," 22 May, 1582. There are a number of other papers connected with these tithe-suits, in which the name of Henry Shakespeare is mentioned, but the above extracts include everything respecting him that appears to be of the slightest interest. "Wytnesses to be examynyd for Robert Webbe and others, defendauntes,—Adam Palmer, John Henley, William Perkes, Hary Shakspere, William Betson," a memo-randum in the suit of Mayowe v. Webbe, 1582, leading us to infer that the poet's uncle was familiarly known as Harry Shakespeare.

"Of Henry Shackesper, viij.*d*, for not havinge and wearinge cappes on Sondayes and hollydayes to the Churche, according to the forme of the statute; of Henry Shackesper, ij.*d*, for not doinge there sute at this courte," fines levied by order of a court-leet held at Snitterfield on October the 25th, 1583, entries to the same effect occurring in a con-temporary report given in Latin. "The 4 day of September was baptysed Henry Townsend, the sonn (of) John Townsend and Darrity, his wyff,—William Meaydes, Henry Shexsper, Elizabeth Perkes, pledges," parish-register, 1586. "Item, Henry Shaxspere of Snytterfild oweth me v.*li*. ix.*s*," memorandum attached to the will of Christopher Smyth alias Court of Stratford-on-Avon, yeoman, 2 November, 1586. For notices of Henry Shakespeare in the following year see the Annals of his brother John, the poet's father, under 1587. "Ricardus Ange narrat versus Henricum Shakespere in placito transgressionis super casum," register of the Court of Record, 22 September, 1591. "Henricus Shakspere attachiatus fuit ad sectam Ricardi Ange in placito transgres-sionis super casum, et defendens remanet in prisona," ibid., 8⊕ September, 1591. "Henricus Shaxspere nichill dicit ad narracionem Ricardi Ange in placito transgressionis super casum;—ideo fiat preceptum ad

O 2

inquirendum que dampna predictus Ricardus sustinuit occasione," ibid., 20 October, 1591. "Henricus Shackespere attachiatus fuit per servientes ad clavam ibidem ad sectam Johannis Tomlyns in placito debiti; Henricus Wylson manucepit pro defendente," register of the Court of Record, 29 September, 1596. "Stratford burgus,—preceptum est servientibus ad clavam ibidem quod capiant, seu etc., Henrye Shackspere, si etc., et eum salvum etc., ita quod habeant corpus ejus coram ballivo burgi predicti ad proximam curiam de recordo ibidem tenendam ad respondendum John Tomlenes de placito debiti, et hoc etc.," 29 September, 1596. "Continuatur accio inter Johannem Tomlyns, querentem, et Henricum Shaxpere, defendentem, in placito debiti," 13 October, 1596. "Johannes Tomlyns narravit versus Henricum Shaxpere in placito debiti," erased note dated 27 October, 1596. It may be inferred from the absence of Henry Shakespeare's name in the later proceedings of the Court that these entries of September and October, 1596, relate to the poet's uncle. Of Henry Shaxper, iiij.*d*, for not doing his sute at this daye, being resiaunt within the precinct of this leete ; of Henry Shaxper, ij.*s*. vj.*d*, for not laboring with teemes for the amending of the Queenes highe-wayes at the dayes appointed, according to the forme of the statute ; of Henry Shaxper, ij.*s*, for having a diche betweene Redd Hill and Burman in decaye for want of repayringe," fines levied by order of a court-leet held at Snitterfield on October the 22nd, 1596. "Henrey Sakspere was bureyd the xxix.th day of December, anno 1596," parish-register. "Margret Sakspere, widow, being times the wyff of Henry Shakspere, was bured ix. Feb.," ibid., 1596–7.

Thomas Shakespeare.—This person must have been a considerable holder of land, his annual rental being given at £4 in a record of 1563. "Thomas Shakespeare is a comon forstaller and ingrosser of bareley, wheate, and rye, against the forme of the statute and an evill example of other subjectes of our soveraigne Lady, the Queene," presentment made at a Snitterfield Court held in April, 1575. Thomas Shaxper was one of the jurors at a Visus Franci Plegii ultimo die Marcii, 23 Eliz. "Baptizatus fuet John, filius Thome Shaxper, the x.th of March, 1581," register of Snitterfield parish, the year not being put for 1581–2. "Et quod Thomas Rounde (iiij.*d*) et Thomas Shaxper (iiij.*d*) incurrant penam predicte ordinacionis pro superoneracione commune predicte cum averiis et anseribus suis; item dicunt quod Thomas Shaxper (iiij.*d*) est communis forstallator et ingrossator granorum, ordei, frumenti et siliginis, contra formam statuti et in malum exemplum aliorum subditorum dicte domine regine; item dicunt quod Thomas Shaxper (iiij.*d*) . . . incurrant penam statuti pro defectu arcium et sagittarum ; Thomas Shaxper, Robertus Webbe, electi decenarii, et sunt jurati," visus Franci Plegii, 31 March, 1581. "Of Thomas Shackespere, vj.*d*, for not havinge and exercisinge bowes and arrowes, according to the forme of the statute; of Thomas Shackesper, iiij.*d*, for not havinge and wearinge cappes on sondayes and hollydayes to the Churche, according to the forme of the statute; of Thomas Shackesper, xij.*d*., for sufferinge swyne to goe in the common feildes unringed, against the order of the Courte," fines levied by order of a Court held at Snitterfield on October the 25th, 1583, Thomas Shackesper being one of the jurors on the occasion. There is no evidence that this individual was the person of the same name who is occasionally mentioned in the Stratford records, 1578–1586, nor that either was the " Thomas Green alias Shakspere " who was buried in that town on March the 6th, 1589–90. The term *alias* between two surnames almost invariably originated with a bride, the first being her maiden and the second her husband's name; and the last mentioned Thomas was, therefore, in all probability, either the son or the descendant of a Green who had married a Shakespeare. Thomas Greene, who was the town-clerk of Stratford in the early part of the following century, speaks of the poet as his cousin, a term then applied to nearly any kind of distant or collateral relationship, but the manner in which the connection between the two families arose has not at present transpired.

John Shakespeare.—" Juratores ibidem presentant quod Johannes Shakespere (xij.*d*), Margeria Lyncecombe (xij.*d*), William Rounde (xij.*d*), non fecerunt sepes suas secundum ordinacionem sibi adjunctam," visus Franci Plegii held at Snitterfield, 1 October, 1561. This is the only notice of a John Shakespeare that I have met with in the records of this manor, and it is possible that the scribe may have committed an error in the form of the Christian name. See the entry quoted in the next paragraph.

Joan Shakespeare.—" Johanna Shaxspere mortua est, et sepulta Januarii quinto, anno 1595," *i.e.*, 1595–6, parish-register.

Anthony Shakespeare.—The name of " Anthonye Shaxpere " occurs in the list of the "bilmen" of "Snyterfield" in the Warwickshire Muster-Book of 1569.

The Affeerors of October, 1559.

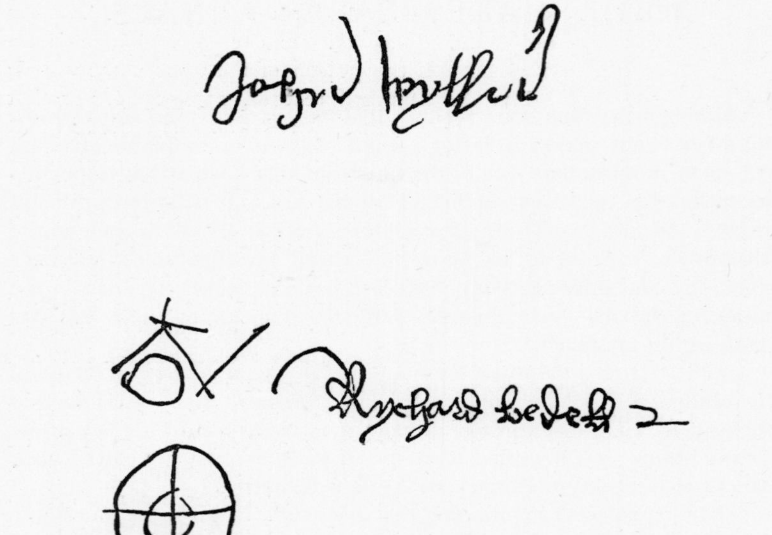

JOHN SHAKESPEARE.—ANNALS.

Although the numerous records that mention this individual throw but a faint light upon his history, some of them are valuable auxiliary evidences in more than one of the questions that have arisen respecting occurrences in the career of his illustrious son. It is, indeed, difficult to say what notices of John Shakespeare are too trivial to exclude the feasibility of their being useful to the critical investigator of the poet's biography, and under this impression I have collected together, in the following Annals, every definite particular concerning him that has come within my reach.

1552. "Item juratores presentant super sacramentum suum quod Humfridus Reynoldes, xij.*d*, Adrianus Quyney, xij.*d*, et Johannes Shakyspere, xij.*d*, fecerunt sterquinarium in vico vocato Hendley Strete contra ordinacionem curie; ideo ipsi in misericordia, ut patet," visus franci plegii, Stratford Burgus, 29 April, 6 Edward VI.

1555. It is worth mentioning that his name is not to be found in a list of the members of the Corporation which was drawn up on April the 20th, 1 and 2 Philip and Mary, and inserted in a lease of that date.

1556. He was summoned on a Court of Record jury on 21 March. "Thomas Siche de Arscotte, in comitatu Wigorniensi, queritur versus Johannem Shakyspere de Stretforde, in comitatu Warwicensi, glover, in placito quod reddat ei octo libras, etc.," proceedings of the Court of Record, 17 June. "Ad hanc curiam venit Johannez Shakyspere in propria persona sua, et defendit vim et juriam® quando etc., et petit licenciam interloquendi hic usque ad proximam curiam, etc., et habet etc.," ibid., 15 July. "Ad hanc curiam venit Thomas Siche, per Willielmum Courte, consiliarium ad barram, et petit diem ad emenda-cionem declaracionis predicti Thome Siche ad proximam curiam, et ei conceditur, etc.," ibid., 29 July. "Ad hanc curiam Johannez® Shakyspere, per Thomam Martene, consiliarium ad barram, et petit judicium versus Thome® Siche quia non protulit accionem que® habuit versus predictum Johannem Shakyspere, et habet judicium cum expensis," ibid., 12 August. This suit occupied, therefore, just about two months, John Shakespeare obtaining judgment in his favour with costs. On 12 August he was summoned on a Court of Record jury, and on September the 23rd one Layne brought an action against a person of the name of Rodes, and the latter was essoined *per Shakyspere*. "Item presentant quod Georgius Turnor alienavit Johanni Shakespere, et heredibus suis, unum tenementum cum gardino et crofto, cum pertinenciis, in Grenehyll Strete, tenta de domino libere per cartam per redditum inde domino per annum vj.*d*, et sectam curie, et idem Johannes, presens in curia, fecit domino fidelitatem pro eisdem," visus franci plegii, Stratford-super-Avon, 2 October. This tenement in Greenhill Street, with its garden, croft, and appurtenances, the last descriptive term probably including a barn, is not mentioned in any of the later documents. " Edwardus West alienavit predicto Johanni Shakespere unum tenementum, cum gardino adjacente, in Henley Stret, per redditum inde domino per annum vj.*d*, et sectam curie, et idem Johannes, presens in curia, fecit fidelitatem," visus franci plegii, ibid., 2 October. " Johannes Shakysper queritur versus Henricum Fyld in placito quod reddat ei xviij. quarteria ordei que ei injuste detinet, etc.," proceedings of the Court of Record, 19 November, with the note of an order for summoning the defendant. " Accio inter Brace et Rawson committitur Rogero Myller et Johanni Shakysper usque proximam curiam," ibid., 19 November. " Accio inter Johannem Shakispere et Henricum Fyld continuatur ex consensu parcium usque ad proximam curiam," ibid., 2 December. " Accio inter Shakysper et Henricum Fyld continuatur ulterius usque proximam® curiam," ibid., 16 December. It is worthy of remark that this suit respecting the quarters of barley, the termination of which does not appear to be recorded, was commenced not only before John Shakespeare's marriage, but also before the death of Robert Arden.

1557. Johannes Shakespere was put on the list of a manorial jury on 30 April, but it appears, from a cancel of his name, that he did not serve. " De Johanne Shakysper, uno testatorum servicie burgi, quia non venit ad exequendum officium suum per iij. curias ; ideo in misericordia viij.*d*," proceedings of the Court of Record, 2 June. " Johannes Shakespere queritur versus Ricardum Wagstaff in placito debiti x.*s*," ibid., 22 September, with the order, *summoneatur*, against the defendant. John Shakspeyre was one of the jurors in a View of Frank Pledge, 1 October. " Ricardus Wagstaffe essoniatur, ad hunc diem ad sectam Johannis Shakespere in placito debiti, videlicet, per Radulphum Chester," proceedings of the Court of Record, 6 October. " Johannes Shakespere queritur versus Willielmum Rychardson de placito transgressionis," ibid., 6 October,—summoneatur. " Willielmus Rychardson ad hunc diem comparuit ad sectam Johannis Shakespere, et querens habet ulteriorem diem ad narrandum," ibid., 20 October. " Johannes Shakespere queritur versus Johannem Asshell in placito debiti super demandam xlij.*s*," ibid., 20 Ocotober. " Radulphus Cawdrey queritur versus Willielmum Wynkfyld de placito debiti super demandam . . . plegii de prosequendo, Ricardus Byddyll et Johannes Nevell ; dictus defendens traditur in ballium Johanni Shakspere et Willielmo

Smythe, haberdassher, usque ad finem placiti," ibid., 20 October. "Ad hanc curiam venit Johannes Asshell in propria persona, et fatetur accionem Johannis Shakspeyr xlij.*s*, et datus est dies dicto deffendenti ad solvendum dictam solucionem modo et forma sequentibus, videlicet, ad festum Sancti Andree Apostoli proximo sequens hujus curie⊛ xx.*s*, et ad festum Naturtatis Domini ex tunc proximo sequens xxij.*s*, et si defectus fiat in parte solucionis, vel in toto, ad aliquod festum festorum predictorum ad quod solvi debeat, quod tunc fiet execucio pro toto, etc.," ibid., 17 November. "Ad hanc curiam venit Ricardus Wagstaf in propria persona, et fatetur accionem Johannis Shakspeyr, videlicet, x.*s*, et datus est dies dicto deffendenti ad solvendum dictos x.*s* ante festum Natalis Domini proximo sequens hujus curie, ac pro misis et custagiis circa curiam etc. x.*d*, et si defectus fiat in parte solucionis predicte, vel in toto, ad festum predictum quod⊛ solucionem debeat, quod tunc fiet execucio pro toto, etc.," ibid., 17 November. "Miseri- cordia ij.*d*, p.—De Willielmo Rychardson pro licencia concordandi cum Johanne Shakespere in placito transgressionis," ibid., 1 December. "Willielmus Wyngfyld traditur in ballium Johanni Shakespere et Johanni West, videlicet, predicti Johannes et Johannes manuceperunt pro dicto Willielmo Wyngfyld, quod si contigerit eum convinci in aliqua accione ad sectam Radulphi Cawdrey, quod tunc predictus Willielmus solvet et contentabit omnia hujusmodi debita et dampna in quibus contigerit eum convinci, aut se prisone infra burgum predictum submittet, alioquin ipsi predicti Johannes et Johannes manuceperunt solvere predicto Radulpho Cawdrey debita et dampna predicta pro predicto Willielmo Wyngfyld, etc.," ibid., 1 December. The probability is that John Shakespeare was chosen one of the burgesses towards the end of this year, there having been four vacancies at Michaelmas, but the exact period has not been recorded, and the position of his name in the earliest lists in which it occurs is not a safe guide to the order of his election. He is not noticed in an official enumeration of the members of the Corporation that was registered on September the 29th.

1558. Johannes Shakespere was summoned on a Court of Record jury, 23 February. "Fraunces Harbadge, master bely that now ys, Adreane Quyny, Mr. Hall, Mr. Clopton for the gutter alonge the Chappell in Chappell Lane, John Shakspeyr (iiij.*d*), for not kepynge ther gutters cleane they stand amerced," view of frank-pledge, April. "Adrianus Quenye et Thomas Knyght queruntur versus Johannem Shakespere de placito debiti super demandam vj.*li*," proceedings of the Court of Record, 19 April, a summoning order against the defendant being duly granted. "Adreanus Quyny et Thomas Knyght petunt distringas versus Johannem Shakspeyr in placito debiti," ibid., 6 May, and an order of distringas was given. "Willielmus Malpas queritur versus Johannem Shakspeyr in placito debiti super demandam viij.*s*," ibid., 6 May,—summoneatur. "Ad hanc curiam venit Johannes Shakspeyr, et fatetur accionem Adreani Quyny et Thome Knyght, videlicet, vj.*li.*,—ideo consideratum est per curiam quod querentes recuperent debitum predictum et xvj.*d* pro misis et custagiis ; ideo fiat levari facias," the latter part of this entry originally appearing as follows,— " datus est dies dicto diffendenti ad concordandum se citra proximam curiam, datis plegiis," ibid., 6 May. "Adrianus Queny et Thomas Knyght petunt distringas versus Johannem Shakespere in placito debiti pro vj.*li*," ibid., 5 June, a cancelled entry respecting this suit, the probability being that the debt and costs were paid on this day. "Willielmus Malpas ad hunc diem petit distringas versus Johannem Shakespere in placito debiti pro viij.*s*," ibid., 5 June, and the order of distringas was given. "Johannes Shakespere opponit se versus Willielmum Malpas in placito debiti, et querens petit diem ad narrandum usque proximam curiam," ibid., 13 July. "Misericordia ij.*d*, non pros.,—de Willielmo Malpas quia non prosequitur accionem suam versus Johannem Shakespere in placito debiti," ibid., 27 July. "September 15, Jone Shakspere, daughter to John Shaxspere," baptismal register. "Johannes Shakespere, jur.," view of frank-pledge, 30 September, in a list of jurors. "The xij. men have ordenyd ther trysty and wel-belovyd Humfrey Plymley, Roger Sadler, John Taylor and John Shakspeyr (jur.), constabulles," ibid., 30 September. "Franciscus Herbage queritur versus Johannem Shakespere de placito debiti super demandam x.*s*," proceedings of the Court of Record, 9 November. "Johannes Shakespere ad hunc diem essoniatur per Robertum Lock ad sectam Francisci Herbage," ibid., 23 November. "Misericordia ij.*d*, p.,—de Francisco Herbage, quia non prosequitur accionem suam versus Johannem Shakesper in placito debiti," ibid., 21 December.

1559. "Johannes Shakespere queritur versus Matheum Bramley de placito debiti," proceedings of the Court of Record, 1 February,— summoneatur. "Misericordia ij.*d*., non pros.,—de Johanne Shakespere, quia non prosequitur accionem suam versus Matheum Bramley in placito debiti," ibid., 15 February. "Adreanus Quyny et Thomas Knyght petunt capias satisfaciendum⑨ versus Johannem Shakspeyr pro quinque libris," ibid., 26 April, an entry originally written as follows,— "Adreanus Quyny et Thomas Knyght queruntur versus Johannem Shakspeyr de placito debiti super demandam v.*li*.,—plegii de prosequendo Rogerus Sadler et Ricardus Harenton," ibid. "Accio,— Johannes Shakspeyr queritur versus Ricardum Court in placito debiti vj.*s*. viij.*d*," ibid., 5 July. "Accio,—Johannes Shakspeyr queritur versus Ricardum Court in placito detencionis," ibid., 5 July. "Accio inter Johannem Shackspere et Ricardum Court ponitur ad Radulfum Cawdrye et Johannem Ichyver ad audiendum et terminandum aliter ad certificandum ad proximam curiam," ibid., 19 August. "Accio continuatur ex assensu partium," marginal note appended to the last entry. He was summoned on a Court of Record jury on 6 September. "Accio,—Johannes Shakespere queritur versus Matheum Bromley (essoniatum per Johannem Mors) in placito debiti," proceedings of the Court of Record, 20 September. "Johannes Shakspere queritur versus Aliciam Nevell vidicam in placito debiti,—non prosecutus est querens, ideo in misericordia ij.*d*.," ibid., 4 October. "Johne Taylor, Johne Shakspeyr, William Tyler, William Smythe, habardassher, constabulles, jur.," view of frank-pledge, 6 October. John Shakspeyr was also one of the affeerors who were sworn into office on the same day, 6 October, at a meeting of the court-leet, his mark, formed something like a pair of compasses, appearing in the record at a short distance on the left of his name. "Ad istam curiam Matheus Bromley confessus est se debere Johanni Shakespere xxx.*s*., quos promysit solvere ad dies sibi per ballivum et aldermannos . . . ad proximam curiam," proceedings of the Court of Record, 17 October, an entry described in the margin as—confessio debiti, ac dies datus est ad solucionem. "Accio detencionis inter Edwardum Bate, querentem, et Cristoferum Smythe ponitur Ricardo Bidill, Johanni Wheler, Ricardo Hill et Johanni Shakspere, ad audiendum et terminandum ante proximam curiam, aliter ad sertificandum ad dictam curiam, etc.," ibid., 15 November, with the marginal note—ponitur in arbitrium.

1560. Johannes Shakespere is in a list of jurors that were appointed at a view of frank-pledge held at Stratford-on-Avon on October the 5th, but it appears, from a cancel of his name, that he did not serve.

1561. "Robertus Locke queritur versus Johannem Shackspere in placito debiti," proceedings of the Court of Record, 16 April, the note *extra* being inserted over the defendant's name. He was elected one of the chamberlains on Michaelmas-day, and in this year also he was once more sworn in as one of the affeerors under the Leet.

1562. He was re-elected one of the chamberlains at Michaelmas for the official year that terminated on the same day in 1563. "Leywys ap Wylliams, hye bayly, Robert Perotte, capitall aldermane, Johne Tayler and Johne Shackespere, chamburlens," lease of 3 October. "December 2, Margareta, filia Johannis Shakspere," baptismal register, most likely named after her aunt, the wife of Alexander Webbe of Bearley, but there was also a Margaret at Snitterfield, the wife of the Henry who is believed to have been the poet's uncle. "Adreane Quyny, capytall alderman, John Shakspeyre and John Tayler chaumburlens," lease of 26 December. The seal attached to this last-quoted document is impressed with a scroll that adorns the initials W.S., those of William Smith, a haberdasher.

1563. It was either in this year, or at some time after Michaelmas, 1562, that he sold the Corporation a piece of timber. "Item, payd to

NOTICES OF JOHN SHAKESPEARE FROM THE REGISTER OF THE TOWN COUNCIL FOR THE YEARS 1563 & 1564.

A halle holden in the Counsell Chamber of Stratford-uppon-Avon the xx.ti day of December, —1563.

Shakspeyr for a pec tymbur, iij.*s.*," chamb. acc. drawn up in January, 1564. "Adreane Quyny, capytall alderman, John Taylor and John

Shakspeyr, chamburlens," lease of 20 January. "Johannes Shakspere queritur versus Ricardum Court in placito debiti," proceedings of the Court of Record, 20 January,—extra. "Thaccount of John Tayler and John Shakspeyre, chamburlens, made the xxiiij.t day of January, in the v.th yere of the reigne of sovereigne® lady Elyzabethe, by the grace of God of Englond, Fraunce and Irelond, quene, defender of the feithe, etc., for on wholl yer endyng at the feest of Sent Mychaell tharchaungell now last past," title of the statement of receipts and expenditure. Neither of these chamberlains could write, and from John Shakespeare's mark being the only one found in what may be termed the declaration of the accounts, it may be presumed that he was the chief, if not the only, official who attended to their preparation. Two separate marks are found on the reverse of the document, the cross being that of the poet's father, and the other no doubt one of the symbols that were used by his colleague. "Accio debiti inter Johannem Shackspere (extra) et Ricardum Court concordata fuit per arbitramentum, et dismissa fuit extra curiam," proceedings of the Court of Record, 3 February. "Adrean Quyny, capytall alderman, Johne Taylere and Johne Shakspeyr, chamberlens," lease of 20 February. "John Tayler and John Shakspeyre, chamburlens," another lease of the same date. "Humfrey Plymley, bayliffe, Adryan Quynye, highe alderman, Johne Shackspere and Johne Tayler, chamberleyns," lease of 26 April. "April 30, Margareta, filia Johannis Shakspere," burial register. "John Taylor and John Shakspere, chamberleyns," lease of 27 May. "Adryan Quyney, highe alderman, John Taylor and John Shakspere, chamberleyns," lease of 28 May. "Accio,—Johannes Shakspere queritur versus Ricardum Careles in placito debiti," proceedings of the Court of Record, 1 September. "Datus est dies Johanni Shakspere usque proximam curiam ad narrandum versus Ricardum Careles in placito debiti," ibid., 26 Sept. "John Taylor and Shakspere, chamberleyns," lease of 3 November. John Shaxspere is noticed as amongst the "burgesys beyng then present" at a meeting of the Town Council that was held on 20 December, no earlier report of any of the proceedings of the Corporation being known to exist.

1564. On 10 January John Shakespeare and his colleague, John Tayler, delivered in their accounts of the receipts and expenditure of the

Chamont

Corporation from Michaelmas, 1562, to Michaelmas 1563. "Thaccompt of John Tayler and John Shakspeyr, chamburlens, made the x.th day of January, in the syxt yere of the reigne of our sovereigne Lady Elyzabethe, by the grace of God quene of Englond, Fraunce and Irelond, defendor of the feyth, &c., ut sequitur," title of the account. "Sic remaynythe *v.s.* ix.*d*, whyche ys delyverd into the handes of William Tylar and William Smythe, newe chamburlens, so that they befor-namyd John Tayler and John Shakspeyr have made a trw and a lawfull accompt for ther tyme, beyng chamburlens,—et sic quieti sunt, Johannes Tayler et Johannes Shak-speyr," conclusion of the same account. "Accio,—Johannes Shakspere queritur versus Humfridum Gadcliffe in placito debiti," proceedings of the Court of Record, 19 January. "At a hall holden the xxvj.th day of January the chambur ys found in arrerage and ys in det unto John Shakspeyr xxv.*s.* viij.*d.*," a balance that was subsequently repaid, this fact being gathered from a cancel in the original document. "April 26, Gulielmus, filius Johannes® Shakspere," baptismal register. "Accio,— Johannes Shakspere queritur versus Humfridum Gadcley (misericordia iiij.*d*) in placito debiti," proceedings of the Court of Record, 6 June. "Humfridus Gadcley solempniter exactus ad respondendum Johanni Shakspere in placito debiti, et non venit,—ideo ipse in misericordia, et dictus Johannes petit preceptum de distringas, et ei conceditur,—ideo, etc.," ibid., 5 July, with the marginal order, fiat distringas. "Preceptum est Ricardo Sharppe, servienti ad clavam, quod distringat Humfridum Gadcley, per bona et catalla sua, ad respondendum Johanni Shakspere in placito debiti ad proximam curiam, etc.," order of 5 July. In a list of "moneye paid towardes the releffe of the poure at the hall holldyn in oure garden the 30 daye of Auguste, anno 1564," is the entry, "Jhon Shacksper, xij.*d*," proceedings of the Council, the meeting being held in the garden on account of the plague that was then raging in Stratford. There were five donors, including John Shakespeare, giving twelve-pence each, fourteen others subscribing a greater and six a lesser amount. The largest sum given was four shillings, subscribed by William Botte, the then owner of New Place. The bailiff gave three shillings and fourpence, the chief alderman two shillings and eightpence, four gave two and sixpence each, six gave two shillings each, four gave eightpence each, and three individuals gave respectively sixteen pence, sixpence and fourpence. Amongst the "burgesys presente at the haulle holdyn the 6 daye of September" was Jhon Shacksper, and there being on this occasion "money gethyryd towardes the releyff of thosse that be vysytyd," that is, by the plague, he was one of five who gave sixpence each, one out of the remaining nine subscribers giving one-and-sixpence, six giving twelve-pence each, and two others fourpence and twopence respectively. Jhon Shackspere was amongst the "burgesys presente" on 20 September. On 27 September there was a subscription for the relief of the poor, and out of sixteen donors eight, including John Shakespeare, gave sixpence each, seven gave twelvepence each, and one gave fourpence. He was present at a meeting of the Corporation that was held on the same day, 27 September, his name occurring in a formal list given in the Council-book and distinguished by his compass-mark. On October the 20th there was another subscription for the relief of the poor collected

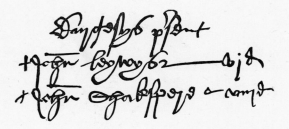

from those members of the Town-council who were present at the meeting held on that day. On this occasion the bailiff gave sixteen-pence, nine aldermen twelvepence each, one alderman fourpence, six burgesses, including John Shakespeare, eightpence each, and five other burgesses sixpence each. It is worthy of remark that he was one of a minority of the donors, exceeding only slightly a third of the entire number, whose name is found in each of the four subscription-lists above-named.—In the chamberlains' accounts of expenses incurred between Michaelmas, 1564, and Michaelmas, 1565, is the following entry,—"item, payd to Shakspeyr for a rest of old det, iij.*li.* ij.*s.* vij.*d.* ob." This statement is important,

not only as proving that John Shakespeare was in affluent circumstances about this period, but that he was the leading director of the accounts that were passed on 21 March, 1565, those which pertained to the receipts and expenditure from Michaelmas, 1563, to Michaelmas, 1564. The sum above-named, £3. 2. 7½, was then declared to be owing to the chamberlains, Tyler and Smythe, so it is clear that the financial management was in the hands of John Shakespeare, and that he advanced the money out of his own pocket.

1565. The name of John Shakspere is in a list of "burgesyes beyng then present" at a meeting of the Town-council held on 16 January, and again at another on 15 February. "Thaccompt of William Tyler and William Smythe, chamburlens, made by John Shakspeyr and John Tayler, xxj.te day of Marche anno Elizabethe regine vij. mo, for one wholl yere endynge at the feest of Sent Mychell th' archaungell now last past," title of accounts passed on 21 March. John Shakespeare is mentioned in the lists of the burgesses present at the meetings of the Council that were held on 22 March, and on 2 and 9 May. "Johannes Shakspere queritur versus Johannem Mille (misericordia, iiij.*d.*) in placito debiti," proceedings of the Court of Record, 6 June, the note *fiat distringas* having been subsequently added in the margin. An alderman of the name of Botte, who was then the owner of New Place, having been expelled from the Council in May, John Shakespeare was chosen for the vacant office at a meeting that was held on 4 July. He is accordingly mentioned on that day firstly in the list of "burgesez present," and secondly in that of "aldermen present," his election being noted in the following words,—"at thys hall John Shakspeyr ys appwntyd an alderman." On 15 August he was on a Court of Record jury, and he

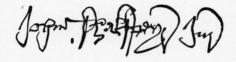

was sworn in as alderman on 12 September,—"Johne Shakspeyr, jur." At a meeting of the Council held on 27 October he is noted amongst the "aldermen abcent."

1566. The chamberlain's accounts from Michaelmas, 1564, to Michaelmas, 1565, were placed under John Shakespeare's individual superintendence, as appears from the following heading to them when they were submitted to the Corporation on 15 February, a day on which he is noted amongst the aldermen present,—"the accompt of William Tylor and William Smythe, chamburlens, made by John Shakspeyr the xv th day of February, in the eight yere of the reigne of our sovereigne Lady Elyzabeth, by the grace of God of Englond, Fraunce and Irelond, quene, defendor of the feith, etc., for one yere endyng at the feest of Sent Mychell tharchaungell now last past." We are told that "in thys accompt the chaumbur ys in det unto John Shakspeyr, to be payd unto hym by the next chamburlein, vij.*s.* iij.*d.*," an entry which was cancelled upon the repayment in January, 1568. In September, becoming bail and perhaps security for a Richard Hathaway in two actions that had been brought against the latter in the Court of Record, his name was

substituted in the later proceedings for that of the defendant. "Johannes Page queritur versus Ricardum Hatheway de placito detencionis, etc., ad valenciam octo librarum," register of the Court of Record, 11 September. "Johanna Byddoll queritur versus Ricardum Hatheway de placito detencionis, etc., ad valenciam xj. librarum," ibid., 11 September; a distringas against the defendant having been ordered in both these suits, and afterwards withdrawn. "Johannes Whelar, justiciarius de pace ac ballivus infra burgum predictum, Humfridus Plymley, justiciarius de pace ac capitalis-alderman infra burgum predictum, Willielmo Butlar et Henrico Russell, servientibus ad clavam, salutem, vobis precipimus et mandamus quod capiatis, seu unus vestrum capiat, per corpus suum Ricardum Hatheway, ita quod habeatis corpus ejus coram nobis, justiciariis predictis, apud proximam curiam de recordo tentam ibidem, ad respondendum Johannem Page de placito detencionis, etc.—plegiis de prosequendo, Willielmo Reve et Johanni Stone ;—dictus diffendens traditur in ballio Johanni Shakyspeyr usque ad finem placiti ;—per me Henricum Hygford, senescallum ibidem," undated order to which is attached the following memorandum,—cepimus infra-nominatum corpus⑧ suum Ricardum Hatheway, prout nobis preceptum, *William Butlar, Henricus Russell.* "Preceptum est servientibus ad clavam quod distringant, seu unus vestrum distringat, Johannem Shakespere, per omnia bona et cattalla sua, ita quod sit apud proximam curiam de recordo tentam ibidem, ad respondendum Johanne⑧ Pagge de placito debiti," precept issued by Henry Hygford, the Steward of the Court, 11 September. "Preceptum est servientibus ad clavam quod distringant, seu unus vestrum distringat, Johannem Shakespere, per omnia bona et cattalla sua, ita quod sit apud proximam curiam de recordo tentam ibidem, ad respondendum Johanni Byddele de placito debiti," precept similarly issued 11 September. "October 13, Gilbertus, filius Johannis Shakspere," baptismal register.

1567. He was assessed on goods of the value of £4 to a subsidy that was levied in 9 Elizabeth,—"John Shakespere, in bonis, iiij.*li.*— iij.*s.* iiij.*d,*" roll for Stratford, MS. Longbridge ; and he is again mentioned in the record of another collection under the same Act,—"John Shakespere, in bonis, iij.*li.*—ij.*s.* vj.*d.*" He was present at the meetings of the Town Council that were held on 8 and 19 January, 16 July, and 3 September, being one of the three persons who, on the day last-named, were "nominatyd for the belyf."

1568. On 12 January he was repaid the sum of vij.*s.* iij.*d.* that had been owing to him by the chamberlains ever since Michaelmas, 1565. On 4 September the Corporation "procedyd to thellectione of theire balyf for the next yere," and John Shakespeare was the chosen one out of the three who were nominated,—"the names whereof one to be balyf, Mr. John Shakysper, Mr. Robert Perrot, Robert Salusburye." He presided as High Bailiff at a meeting of the Council held on the 1st of

October, and at the Court of Record on the 6th and 20th of the same month. In precepts that he issued in December he is termed, justiciarius de pace ac ballivus infra burgum.

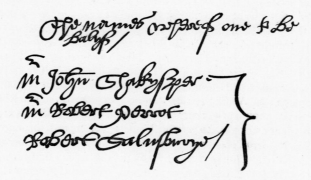

1569. On 26 January the accounts of the chamberlains were taken "before Mr. John Shakyspere," High Bailiff, to whom, on this occasion, there was, under some unknown conditions, an "allowaunce" of fourteen shillings,—"item, to Mr. Balyf that nowe ys, xiiij.*s.*" On 12 February

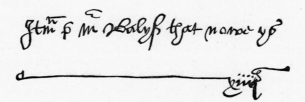

Thomas Stringer, who held the third part of an estate in Snitterfield, an interest that had devolved to him from his wife Agnes, one of the daughters of Robert Arden, granted a contingent lease of it to Alexander Webbe, and the indenture, as well as a bond of even date for the performance of the covenants, was witnessed, amongst others, by *John Shaxpere*, the name in each instance being in the handwriting of the scrivener and without a mark. The known intimacy that existed between Webbe and the poet's father renders it almost certain that the latter was the individual who was then present. "April 15, Jone, the daughter of John Shakspere," baptismal register, Stratford-on-Avon. On 2 November he was chosen one of the arbitrators in a suit between Henry Bragge and John Ball,—"Johannes Shakyspere, Lewes ap Wyllyams, deligantur ex parte Henrici Bragge ad arbitrandum materiam inter eos," proceedings of the Court of Record. In his capacity of High

Bailiff he presided at meetings of the Council held on 20 April, 7 and 9 September; and at those of the Court of Record on 26 January, 9 March, 20 April, 1, 15, and 19 June, 23 August, 7 and 21 September.

1570.   He was present at the meetings of the Council that were held on 27 January, 20 April, 23 August, and 6 September.   The chamberlains, in their account of the receipts and expenditure of the Corporation from Michaelmas, 1569, to Michaelmas, 1570, "praye allowaunce of money delivered to Mr. Shaxpere at sundrie times, vj.*li.*"

1571.   On 5 September he was elected Chief Alderman, a position that he held till 3 September, 1572, but for some unnoticed reason he was not formally recognised in that office until some time between the 5th and the 10th of October, 1571.   "At a hall there holden the v.th day of September, Mr. John Shakespere was elected alderman for the yere to come, and ys sworne ut supra, etc.," that is, "according to the custome of the borrowgh," council-book.   "September 28, Anna, filia magistri Shakspere," baptismal register.   He was present at the meetings of the Corporation that were held on 24 January, 7 February, 2 May, 11 July, 5 September, 10 and 24 October, and 28 November.

1572.   "At this hall yt is agreed, by the asent and consent of the aldermen and burgeses aforeseid, that Mr. Adrian Queny, now baylif, and Mr. John Shakespere shall at Hillary terme next ensuinge deale in the affayres concerninge the commen wealthe of the borroughe accordinge to theire discrecions," register of a Council meeting held on 18 January. On 3 September his year of office as Chief Alderman terminated.   He was amongst the aldermen present at the meetings of the Corporation that were held on 18 January, 7 February, 2, 9 and 18 April, 28 May, and 3 September.

1573.   On 28 August John Shaxbere, for so the name was that day spelt by Walter Roche, ex-master of the Stratford grammar-school, was a witness to the conveyance of a piece of land near the Birth-Place from William Wedgewood to Richard Hornbee, both of whom were resident in Henley Street. He was present at the Council meetings that were held on 9 January and 9 September.

1574. "March 11, Richard, sonne to Mr. John Shakspeer," baptismal register. He was present at the meetings of the Council that were held on 17 February, 1 September, 4 November, and 29 December.

1575. On 20 September his neighbour, William Wedgewood, sold to Edward Willis for £44 "all those his towe tenementes or burgages lying together and beinge in Stretford, in a street there commonly called Henley Streete, which now ar in the use occupatyon and possessyon

of the sayd William Wedgewood, betwyne the tenement of Richard Hornebe of the east part, and the tenement of John Shakesper, yeoman, of the west parte, and the streete aforesaid of the sowthe parte, and the Quenes highway called the Gillpittes of the north parte, together with all gardens, edyfices, buildinges, and other commodytyes whatsoever to the sayd tow tenementes or burgages belonging, or in any wyse now appertayninge." This indenture was witnessed by John Shakesper, but it is scarcely necessary to observe that the name is not an autograph.

In October he gave £40 for two houses at Stratford, and a copy of the fine that was levied on the occasion will be seen in the notes on the Birth-Place. He was amongst the aldermen who were present at the meetings of the Council that were held on 7 September, 7 October, and 23 November.

1576. He was amongst the aldermen who were present at the meetings of the Council that were held on 5 September, 5 October, and 5 December.

1577. Six meetings of the Town Council are registered under this year, but there is only one, that held on 4 October, at which it can be stated for certain that he was present. He was absent on 23 January, 8 May, 24 July, and on the two remaining occasions, 6 November and

4 December, there are no marks either of attendance or non-attendance to any of the names.

1578. At a meeting of the Town Council held on 29 January there was a levy upon the inhabitants of the town for the purchase of military accoutrements, and the note of this taxation is preceded by the following resolution,—"at this hall yt ys agreed that every alderman, except suche under-wrytten excepted, shall paye towardes the furniture of the pikemen, ij. billmen, and one archer, vj.*s.* viij.*d*, and every burgese, except suche under-wrytten excepted, shall pay iij.*s.* iiij.*d*," the favoured aldermen being, "Mr. Plumley, v.*s.*—Mr. Shaxpeare, iij.*s.* iiij.*d*." The excepted burgesses were,—"John Walker, ij.*s.* vj.*d*.—Robert Bratt, nothinge in this place.—Thomas Brogden, ij.*s.* vj.*d*.—William Brace, ij.*s.*—Anthony Tanner, ij.*s.* vj.*d*." In a list of "debtes which are owinge unto me, Roger Saddeler," a baker of Stratford, appended to his will of 14 November, 1578, is the following entry,—"item, of Edmonde Lambarte and . . . Cornishe, for the debte of Mr. John Shaksper, v.*li*. This note would appear to indicate that the poet's father had been unable to borrow the money until he had provided himself with two securities, one of them being the brother-in-law whose pecuniary loans to him are else-where mentioned as having been unpaid in 1580 ; and the transaction indicates that John Shakespeare's circumstances were not as flourishing in 1578 as they were in 1564, for he had been able in the latter year, and obviously without inconvenience, to advance over £3 to the chamberlains. There is a more striking testimony to the same effect in the following resolution that was passed in his absence at a meeting of the Town Council held on 19 November, a few days after the mortgage on Asbies had been effected,—"item, yt ys ordened that every alderman shall paye weekely towardes the releif of the poore iiij.*d*, savinge Mr. John Shaxpeare and Mr. Robert Bratt, who shall not be taxed to pay anythinge." This Robert Bratt, who was a weaver, seems to have been one of the poorest members of the Corporation, his subscriptions in the plague year of 1564, although he was then an alderman, being, with a single exception, the lowest of all in amount. Nine meetings of the Council are recorded for this year, at eight of which he was an absentee, those held on 15 and 29 January, 5 and 18 June, 3 and 24 September, 3 October, 19 November ; and in the case of the remaining one,—15 January,—there are no marks either of attendance or non-attendance to any of the names. On 3 September there were only two other aldermen who were not present, one of them having leave of absence and the other being fined twenty shillings.

1579. In the notes on the Estate of Asbies will be found a copy of a fine that was levied in Hilary Term inter Thomam Webbe et Humfridum Hooper, querentes, et Johannem Shakespere et Mariam, uxorem ejus, et Georgium Gybbes, deforciantes. On 11 March, in an account of money levied on the inhabitants for the purchase of armour and defensive weapons, his name is found amongst the defaulters,—" John Tonge, iiij.*d.*— George Badger, xij.*d.*—Thomas Ward, vj.*d.*—Mr. Shaxpeare, iij.*s.* iiij.*d.*—Mr. Nashe, iij.*s.* iiij.*d.*—Mr. Raynoldes, iij.*s.* iiij.*d.*—William Brokes, ij.*s.*—Basill Burdet, iiij.*d.*—Hugh Pyggin, vj.*d.*—wydow Bell, iiij.*d.*—these somes are unpayd and unaccompted for," register of council-meeting. "April 4, Anne, daughter to Mr. John Shakspere," burial register. In Easter Term John and Mary Shakespeare levied a fine on Asbies, a step that was the necessary result of the mortgage that had been effected in the previous year, and on 15 October they conveyed his interest in a Snitterfield estate to Robert Webbe, the purchase-money being only £4. Ten meetings of the Town-Council are registered under this year, at seven of which John Shakespeare is noted amongst the absentees, and of the names of those who were present or not at the other three there is no record. On 2 August he was the only alderman who did not attend, and on the day of the official elections, 2 October, there was only one other who was absent.

1580. "May 3, Edmund, sonne to Mr. John Shakspere," baptismal register. On 29 September he paid a visit to his brother-in-law, Edmund Lambert, at Barton-on-the-Heath. In "a booke of the names and dwelling-places of the gentlemen and freeholders in the county of Warwicke, 1580," in the Hundred de Barlichway, and under Stretford-upon-Aven, occurs the name of John Shaxper. He was absent from every one of the eight council-meetings that are recorded for this year,— 20 January, 9 March, 3 August, 7 and 30 September, 19 October, 14 and 22 December.

1581. He was not present at any of the six meetings of the Town-Council that were registered for this year,—26 January, 22 February, 17 May, 6 and 20 September, and 6 October.

1582. In May he was one of the witnesses who were cited to appear personally before a Warwickshire commission that had been issued by the Court of Chancery to take depositions in a suit that had been originally brought by Thomas Mayowe in 1580 against Edward Cornwell, Agnes Arden, and Robert Webbe ; the person last-named

being now, however, the chief defendant. This Mayowe alledged that he was entitled, under the conditions of an old entail, to a large portion of the Arden-Snitterfield estates, but the result of the proceedings is un-known, and no record of the nature of John Shakespeare's evidence has

been discovered.   At a meeting of the Corporation held on 5 September Johannes Shaxper was present and voted for John Sadler, the successful candidate for the office of bailiff, but he did not attend any of the other ten councils that are registered under this year,—31 January, 2 May, 10 and 19 September, 5 October, four meetings in November and one on 12 December.

1583.   Fourteen meetings of the Town-Council are registered under this year, and he was absent from every one of them,—11, 23 and 25 January, 1 February, 13 March, 17 April, 7 and 15 May, 12 and 26 June, 21 August, 4 September (the only alderman not present), 4 and 16 October.

1584.   Nine meetings of the Town-Council are registered under this year, no record of attendances being given in the notice of one that was held on 11 January, and John Shakespeare not being present at any of the remaining eight,—5 February, 10 April, 20 May, 4 September, 2 October, 11 and 18 November, and 9 December.

1585.   "Johannes Browne queritur versus Johannem Shakesper, deffendentem, de placito debiti," proceedings of the Court of Record, 27 October.   "Fiat distringas versus Johannem Shaxpeare ad sectam Johannis Browne in placito debiti," ibid., 10 November.   "Fiat alias distringas versus Johannem Shaxpeare ad sectam Johannis Browne in placito debiti," ibid., 24 November.   Ten meetings of the Town-Council are registered under this year, no record of attendances being given in the notice of one that was held on 20 January, and John Shakespeare not being present at any of the remaining nine,—13 January, 17 February, 17 March, 28 April, 23 June, 7 July, 2 September, 1 and 27 October.

1586.   "Ad hunc diem servientes ad clavam burgi predicti retornaverunt precipe de distringas eis directum versus Johannem Shackspere ad sectam Johannis Browne, quod predictus Johannes Shackspere nihil habet unde distringi potest; ideo fiat capias versus eundem Johannem Shackspere ad sectam predicti Johannis Browne, si petatur," proceedings of the Court of Record, 19 January.   There is unfortunately no account in the Stratford records of the mode of procedure that was adopted in this Court, but there can be no doubt whatever that the words,—*quod predictus Johannes Shackspere nihil habet unde distringi potest,*—are not to be taken literally, and that they merely belong to a formula that was in use when a writ of distringas failed in enforcing an appearance. "Fiat capias versus Johannem Shaxkspere ad sectam Johannis Browne in placito debiti," ibid., 16 February.   "Fiat alias capias versus Johannem Shaxspere ad sectam Johannis Browne in placito debiti," ibid., 2 March. To the first of the two entries just quoted the words *non solutum* are added in the margin, and to the second, *non solutum per Browne,* allusions probably to the Court fees, and nothing more is heard of the suit.   John Shakespeare was placed upon Court of Record juries on 25 May and 20 July.   On 4 June he had a conference with Nicholas

Lane at Stratford respecting moneys due from his brother Henry to that individual (see further under 1587). On 19 July he went over to Coventry and appeared before a magistrate of that city to become one of the bail for the due appearance, in the ensuing Michaelmas term at the Queen's Bench, of one Michael Pryce, who had been indicted for felony,—"venerunt Michaell Pryce de Stretford-super-Avon, in comitatu Warrewicensi, tinker, Johannes Shakespere de eisdem villa et comitatu, glover, et Thomas Jones de eisdem villa et comitatu, copper-smythe, personaliter constituti," Controlment Roll, 29 Eliz. On 6 September there was an "eleccion of newe aldermen," and "at thys halle William Smythe and Richard Courte are chosen to be aldermen in the places of John Wheler and John Shaxspere, for that Mr. Wheler dothe desyre to be put owt of the companye, and Mr. Shaxspere dothe not come to the halles when they be warned, nor hathe not done of longe tyme." Previously to the day on which this resolution was carried, there were five meetings of the town-council that are registered under this year, 1586, at four of which John Shakespeare was an absentee,—16 and 30 March, 25 May, and 6 July. In the notice of the remaining one, that held on 31 August, the name of alderman Johannes Shaxpere is marked with a dot of presence, but that the symbol was placed there by mistake is distinctly established by the terms of the order that was passed a few days afterwards.

1587. In the early part of this year John Shakespeare was tormented by an action that had been brought against him in the Court of Record by Nicholas Lane, who averred that, in a conference they had held in the previous June, the former had made himself responsible for £10 in the event, subsequently realized, of his brother Henry not paying that sum on Michaelmas Day, 1586, part of a debt of £22 that was owing to Lane. Judgment was no doubt given in favour of the plaintiff, the suit having been removed by certiorari at the instance of the defendant. "Johannes Shakspere attachiatus fuit per servientes ad clavam, secundum consuetudinem burgi, ad respondendum Nicholao Lane de placito transgressionis super casum, etc., et sunt plegii de prosequendo, Johannes Doe et Willielmus Roe, etc.,—et unde idem Nicholaus Lane, per Thomam Trussell, attornatum suum, dicit quod cum quarto die Junii, anno regni domine nostre Elizabethe, Dei gratia Anglie Francie et Hibernie regine, fidei defensoris, etc., vicessimo octavo, hic apud Stretford predictam, ac infra juresdictionem hujus curie, quoddam colloquium tractatum et habitum fuit inter prefatum Johannem Shakesper et dictum Nicholaum Lane de quodam debito viginti et duorum librarum legalis monete Anglie, in quibus Henricus Shakspere, frater dicti Johannis, debito modo indebitatus fuit prefato Nicholao Lane ; et super colloquium illud aggreatum et concordatum fuit, et postea, scillicet, die et anno supradictis, hic apud Stretford predictam, et infra juresdictionem hujus curie, pro et in consideracione premissorum, ac pro et in consideracione quatuor denariorum legalis, etc., prefato Johanni ad tunc et ibidem per prefatum Nicholaum pre manibus solutorum, super se assumpsit et prefato Nicholao ad tunc et ibidem fideliter promisit quod, si dictus Henricus Shaksper non solveret prefato Nicholao decem libras, parcellam dicte somme viginti et duorum librarum, in feasto sancti Michaelis archangelli ex tunc proxime sequente, quod tunc ipse idem Johannes Shaksper dictam sommam decem librarum, parcellam etc., prefato Nicholao bene et fideliter solvere et contentare vellet, cum inde eum hoc requisitum fuerit etc.—et predictus Nicholaus dicit in facto quod predictus Henricus Shacksper non solvebat prefato Nicholao Lane dictam sommam decem librarum, parcellam etc., in festo sancti Michaelis archangelli predicto, seu unquam antea vel postea ; unde actio accrevit prefato Nicholao Lane ad habendum et exequendum de prefato Johanne Shaksper dictam sommam decem librarum, parcellam etc., secundum assumptiones et fideles promissiones suas predictas, etc.—predictus tamen Johannes Shaksper, assumptiones et fideles promissiones suas predictas quo ad dictas decem libras, parcellam etc., minime curans vel ponderans, sed machinans ipsum Nicholaum in hac parte callide et deceptive decipere et defraudare dictam sommam decem librarum, parcellam etc., prefato Nicholao Lane, non dum solvit, seu aliquo modo contentavit, sed illam ei hucusque solvere aut contentare omnino contradixit, et adhuc contradicit, licet sepius ad hoc secundum assumptiones et fideles promissiones suas predictas requisitus fuit ; unde dictus Nicholaus Lane dicit quod deterioratus est et dampnum habet ad valenciam viginti librarum, et inde producit sectam," undated pàper. "Johannes Shaxpere attachiatus fuit per servientes ad clavam ibidem ad respondendum Nicolao Lane in placito transgressionis super casum, et Ricardus Hyll manucaptor pro deffendente, etc.," proceedings of the Court of Record, 18 January.   "Preceptum est servientibus ad clavam ibidem quod capiant, seu unus eorum capiat, Johannem Shackspere, si etc., et eum salvum etc., ita quod habeant corpus ejus coram ballivo burgi predicti ad proximam curiam de recordo ibidem tenendam ad respondendum Nicholao Lane, generoso, de placito transgressionis super casum, et hoc etc.," 25 January.   "Nicolaus Lane narrat versus Johannem Shaxpere in placito transgressionis super casum, et defendens licenciam⊛ loquendi," 1 February. "Johannes Shakesper, per Willielmum Courte, venit etc., et dicit quod non assumpsit prefato Nicolao Lane modo et forma prout predictus Nicholaus versus eum narravit," proceedings, 1 March. "Et predictus Johannes Shakesper, per Willielmum Court, attornatum suum, venit et defendit vim et injuriam, quando etc., et dicit quod predictus Nicholaus Lane actionem suam inde versus eum habere non debet, quia dicit quod narracio predicti Nicholai minus sufficiens in lege existit ad quam ipse necesse non habet, nec per legem terre, tenetur respondere, protestando quod predictus Henricus Shakesper, in narracione ipsius Nicholai specificatus per scriptum suum obligatorium, concessisset se teneri prefato Nicholao Lane in . . . libris pro solucione viginti et duarum librarum, videlicet, in festo Sancti Michaelis archangeli ultimo preterito debito modo decem librarum, et in festo Sancti Michaelis archangeli ex tunc proximo futuro duodecim libras, de predictis viginti et duarum librarum residuarum, et non cognoscendo aliquam in narracione predicti Nicholai fore vera, sed pro placito idem Johannes Shakesper dicit quod predictus Nicholaus Lane non solvebat prefato Johanni Shakesper quatuor denarios legalis etc. in consideracione assumpcionis et promissionis dicti Johannis ; ac salvis sibi omnibus advantagiis tam ad narracionem quam ad querelam predicti Nicholai, dicit ulterius quod ipse non assumpsit modo et forma prout idem Nicholaus Lane in narracione sua predicta superius versus eum narravit ; et de hoc ponit se super patriam, etc.," undated paper. "Johannes Shakesper protulit breve domine Regine de habeas corpus cum causa coram domina regina, retornabile Mercurii℈ proxima post xviij. Pasce," 29 March. On 26 September, in an interview held at Stratford, he made the ineffective arrangement with John Lambert for the surrender of Asbies.

1588. "Johannes Shaxpere queritur versus Johannem Tomson in placito debiti," proceedings of the Court of Record, 20 June, an entry originally inserted in the record of a previous Court held on 22 May. "Continuatur accio inter Johannem Shaxpere, querentem, et Johannem Tompson, defendentem, ex assensu partium," ibid., 3 July. "De Johanne Shackspere, quia non prosequitur," ibid., 17 July. It is worthy of remark that he was the plaintiff not merely in this suit, but in all the three which are recorded in the following year. On 1 September he paid a visit to John Lambert at Barton-on-the-Heath, with the hope of inducing him to carry out a proposed arrangement for the surrender of Asbies to the latter.

1589. "Johannes Shakespere queritur versus Willielmum Grene de placito debiti," proceedings of the Court of Record, 23 April,—concordati sunt. In the autumn of this year he brought an action in the Court of Queen's Bench against Lambert, respecting a pecuniary arrangement that had been made for the surrender of Asbies, and it is ascertained, from an interesting passage in his Bill of Complaint (see Estate Records, No. 2), that he was still engaged in commercial speculations. The bill was filed early in October, and the cause put down for trial at the commencement of the following Hilary Term, 1590, but the litigation seems to have been abandoned, there being no further record of the suit. "Johannes Shaxpere queritur versus Johannem Tompson in placito debiti," proceedings of the Court of Record, 22 October. "Johannes Shaxpere queritur versus Ricardum Sutton in placito debiti," ibid., 22 October. "Fiat distringas versus Johannem Tompson ad sectam Johannis Shaxpere in placito debiti," ibid., 5 November. "Fiat distringas versus Ricardum Sutton ad sectam Johannis Shaxpere in placito debiti," ibid., 5 November. "Johannes Tompson essoniatur ad sectam Johannis Shaxpere in placito debiti," ibid., 19 November. "Johannes Tompson defaltam fecit super essonium ad sectam Johannis Shaxpere in placito debiti," ibid., 3 December. "Judicium redditum est versus Johannem Tompson ad sectam Johannis Shax(pere in placito debiti), tam pro x.*s.* debiti quam pro iij.*s.* iiij.*d.* pro misis et custagiis suis," ibid., 17 December.

1590. His estate in Henley Street described in the inquisition on the lands of the Earl of Warwick, 6 October. He served on a Court of Record jury, 16 December.

1591. "Adrianus Quiney, Humfridus Plumley, et Ricardus Hyll, queruntur versus Johannem Shaxsper in placito debiti," proceedings of the Court of Record, 24 February. "Fiat distringas versus Johannem Shaxspere ad sectam Adriani Quyney et aliorum in placito debiti," ibid., 10 March. "Fiat capias pro corpore Johannis Shaxspere et Ricardi Sponer ad sectam Adriani Quyney, Humfridi Plumley et Ricardi Hyll, in placito debiti," ibid., 24 March. "Johannes Shaxspere essoniatur ad sectam Adriani Quyney et aliorum in placito debiti," ibid., 7 April. "Johannes Shaxspere defaltam fecit super essonium ad sectam Adriani Quyney, et aliorum, in placito debiti," ibid., 21 April. "Johannes Shaxsper queritur versus Robertum Jones de placito debiti ix.*s.* j.*d.* ob.," ibid. "Accio inter Adrianum Queeney et alios, querentes, versus Johannem Shaxsper, deffendentem, est in respectu usque proximam curiam," ibid.,

19 May. "Thomas West, defendens, profert hic in curia unum *de le cawtherin* ad sectam Johannis Shacksper, etc., et finita est accio," ibid., 19 May, and on the same day there was the following entry,—"Johannes Shaxpere queritur versus Thomam West in placito transgresionis super casum." The officials appear to have blundered in this instance, the note last given probably belonging to 21 April, when it is stated that John Shakespeare complained against West in a plea, the nature of the suit being omitted. The phrase *de le cawtherin* is obscurely expressed, but that a caldron was the object that was brought into Court may be gathered from the form of that word in Robert Arden's inventory, 1556, —ij. cathernes. "Robertus Jones comparuit ad accionem Johannis Shaksper querentis, de placito debiti, etc.,—querens petit diem ad

narrandum," proceedings of the Court of Record, 19 May. "Transgressio super casum, etc., Johannes Shakspere manucepit pro deffendente, et Thomas Grene manucepit pro querente," ibid., 19 May. "Joannes Shaxpere queritur versus Robertum Yonge in placito transgressionis super casum," ibid., 19 May. "Johannes Shaxpere defaltam fecit super essonium ad sectam Adriani Quyney, Humfridi Plumley et Ricardi Hylle, in placito debiti," ibid., 2 June. "Johannes Shaxpere narrat versus Robertum Jones in placito debiti," ibid., 2 June. "Robertus Jones nichil dicit ad accionem Johannis Shaxpere in placito debiti; ideo consideratum est per curiam quod predictus Johannes recuperet debitum suum, et pro misis, etc.," ibid., 30 June. "Judicium redditum est versus Robertum Jones pro . . . . pro misis et custagiis Johannis Shaxsper que sibi adjudicata fuerunt," ibid., 22 September. "Johannes Shaxspere et Robertus Jones concordati sunt," ibid., 20 October. He served on a Court of Record jury, 16 December.

    1592. It was necessary after a person's decease, and previously to the distribution of his estate, that his goods " be particularly valued and praised, by some honest and skilfull persons, to be the just value thereof in their judgements and consciences, that is to say, at such price as the same may be solde for," Swinburn on Testaments, ed. 1590, fol. 220. John Shakespeare was engaged in this way on two occasions in this present year, 1592, the first compilation to which his attention was directed being entitled,—" the true and perfect inventory of Ralph Shawe of Stratford-upon-Avon, in the county of Warwycke, woll-dryver, decessed, taken the xxiiij.th day of Julye, in the xxxiiij.th yeare of the rayngne of our soverayngne lady Elizabeth, by the grace of God of Eyngland, Fraunce and Ireland, Queene, defender of the feyth, &c., by the discretyon of Mr. John Shaxspere, Mr. Willyam Wilson and Valentyne Tant, with others." The other one is described as,—" a trew and a perfecte inventory of the goodes and cattells which were the goodes and cattells of Henry Feelde, late of Stretford-uppon-Avon, in the cownty of Warwyke, tanner, now decessed, beynge in Stretford aforsayd the xxj.the daye of Auguste, anno Domini 1592, by Thomas Trussell, gentyllman, Mr. John Shaksper, Richard Sponer, and others," the entire document, with the exception of the attestation of Richard Sponer, being in Trussell's handwriting, and John Shakespeare, here denominated *John Shaksper senior*, using his cross-mark. It is difficult to understand why the poet's father should have been termed *senior*, but perhaps the writer was under the impression that he had a son who bore the same Christian-name.—It was probably in the summer of this year that Sir Thomas Lucy and other commissioners were engaged in the preparation of a list of the recusants of Warwickshire, their report on the subject being dated 25 September, 1592. Amongst those whom they found had been " hearetofore presented " at Stratford-on-Avon " for not comminge monethlie to the Churche according to hir Majesties lawes" were "Mr. John Shackespere" and eight others, to whose names, however, they annex the following note,—"it is sayd that these laste nine coom not to Churche for feare of processe for debtte." In the original presentment from which the commissioners derived their information, and which is unfortunately without a date, the memorandum respecting these individuals is given in the following terms,— "wee suspect theese nyne persons next ensuinge absent themselves for feare of processes,—Mr. John Wheeler; John, his sonne; Mr. John Shackspeare; Mr. Nycholas Barnehurste; Tho: James alias Giles; William Baynton; Rychard Harington; William Fluellen; George Bardell."

1593. "Ricardus Tyler queritur versus Johannem Shaxpere in placito debiti," proceedings of the Court of Record, 10 January. "Fiat distringas versus Johannem Shaxpere ad sectam Ricardi Tyler in placito debiti," ibid., 24 January. "Ricardus Tyler narrat versus Johannem Shaxpere in placito debiti, et defendens licenciam⊕ loquendi," ibid., 21 February. "Johannes Shaxpere attachiatus fuit per servientes ad clavam ibidem ad respondendum Henrico Wilson in placito transgressionis," ibid., 21 February. "Johannes Shaxpere nichill dicit ad accionem Ricardi Tyler in placito debiti," ibid., 21 March.

1595. "Adrianus Quyney et Thomas Barber versus Philippum Grene, chaundeler, Henricum Rogers, butcher, et Johannem Shaxspere, in placito debiti v.*li.*," proceedings of the Court of Record, 19 March. The somewhat peculiar form of this entry, John Shakespeare being the only one of three defendants whose name is given without the addition of a trade, seems to be an indication that he was at that time out of business, and that he did not indulge, during the remainder of his life, in his former love for speculation may perhaps be gathered from the circumstance of the present being his last appearance in the register of the Court of Record. It is impossible to ascertain the exact history of the suit, none of the pleas or declarations having been preserved, but there being no notice of him in the entries of the proceedings after its commencement on 19 March, Quiney and Barber continuing the litigation against the other two parties only, it is clear that he was released in some way or other from further liability in the matter.

1596. In this year a marriage was arranged between Robert Fulwood of Little Alne and Elizabeth, the sister of Richard Hill, rector of Hampton Lucy. This Robert was the grandson of Agnes Arden, the line of descent being exhibited in the annexed table. Endorsed on the marriage-settlement, which bears the date of October the 10th, 1596, and refers to several properties in Warwickshire, are memoranda of three deliveries of seisin, one of which, relating to premises at Lapworth, was witnessed by four persons including a John

Shakespeare, that name being in the handwriting of the scrivener, and unfortunately without a mark,—"full and peaceable possession and seisin of that messuage at Lapworth, with thappurtenaunces, within named, was taken in the presence of these persones whose names are here subscribed,—Thomas Warde, Thomas Fulwood his marke +, Wylliam Peytoe, John Shaxpere." It might naturally at first sight be considered that this individual must have belonged to the family of the Shakespeares of that village, but this conclusion will be found on examination

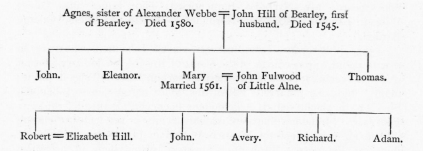

to be disputable. The three deliveries concerned estates at Aston Cantlowe, Lapworth and Tanworth, and as *each* of these transactions was witnessed *on the same day*, November the 5th, 38 Elizabeth, by a person named Warde and by Thomas Fulwood, it is extremely improbable that the localities of the properties were identical in all cases with those of the seisin. It is inconceivable that the parties would have voluntarily given themselves the unnecessary trouble of meeting such conditions. The site of the legal formalities cannot of course be absolutely indicated, but in all probability they were completed at the family residence in Little Alne, a hamlet of Aston Cantlowe, and, if this were the case, there cannot be much doubt that the John Shakespeare above-mentioned was the poet's father. We know on indisputable evidence that he was intimately acquainted with one of the bridegroom's uncles, and, in those days of elastic family recognitions, he was most likely considered by the Fulwoods to be one of their relatives.

1597. On 26 January he parted with a narrow strip of land, a scantling that laid on the extreme west of his Henley-street freeholds, to his neighbour, George Badger, for the sum of £2. 10s., and in or about this year he sold a fragment of ground on the east of the same estate, the latter plot being situated at the back of the Wool-shop. The Bill and Answer in the suit that was brought by his wife and himself against John Lambert, and which are printed at length in the Estate Records No. 4, were filed in Chancery on 24 November.

1598.   On 4 February a return was made of those inhabitants of Stratford who had the good fortune to be holders of corn, an article which was then at a famine price, but the name of John Shakespeare does not occur in the list that was taken for the Henley-street Ward. His son, however, had at this time accumulated ten quarters at New Place.   This was one of the years of the Asbies litigation, the particulars of which are elsewhere given.

1599.   The Orders that were filed this year in the cause of the Shakespeares v. Lambert, dated in May, June and October, will be found at the end of the observations on the Estate of Asbies.

1601.   In the early part of this year an action was brought by Sir Edward Greville against the Corporation respecting the toll-corn, and John Shakespeare assisted, in company with four other persons, including Adrian Quiney, in the preparation of suggestions for the use of Counsel for the defendants.   This is the latest contemporary notice of the worthy old glover that has yet been discovered, and it is an interesting evidence that longevity had neither extinguished his capacity for business nor its appreciation by his fellow-citizens.   The suggestions above-mentioned are without a date, but they were certainly written before September, the funeral of " Mr. Johannes Shakspeare " having taken place upon the eighth of that month.   And here terminates the fragmentary history of the poet's father.   No record of the site of his grave has been discovered, and all traces of a sepulchral memorial, if one were ever to be seen either within or without the Church, have long disappeared.

ILLUSTRATIVE NOTES.

No. 1. Or his emotions.—It is difficult to treat with seriousness the opinion that the great master of imagination wrote under the direct control of his varying personal temperaments. In this way it is implied that he was merry when he wrote a comedy, gloomy when he penned a tragedy, tired of the world when he created Prospero, and so on. It would thence follow that, when he was selecting a plot, he could have given no heed either to the wishes of the managers or the inclination of the public taste, but was guided in his choice by the necessity of discovering a subject that was adapted for the exposition of his own transient feelings. One wonders, or, rather, there is no necessity for conjecturing, what Heminges and Condell would have thought if they had applied to Shakespeare for a new comedy, and the great dramatist had told them that he could not possibly comply with their wishes, he being then in his Tragic Period.

No. 2. Æsthetic criticism.—It is not easy to define the present meaning of this term, but it seems to be applied, without reference to quality, to observations on the characteristics of the Shakespearean personages and on the presumed moral or ethical intentions of the great dramatist. It is already an immense literature in itself, and as all persons of ordinary capacity can, and many do, supply additions to it by the yard, its probable extent in the future is appalling to contemplate. This is not said in depreciation of all such efforts in themselves, for they occasionally result in suggestions of value ; and so subtle are the poet's theatrical uses, as well as so exhaustless his mental sympathies, there are few who could diligently act or study one of his characters without being able to propound something new that was at least worthy of respectful consideration. This unlimited expanse of æsthetic criticism stifles its practical utility, each day removing us further from the possibility of mastering its better details. The latter unfortunately cannot be readily dissociated from the main bulk, that which at present consists either of the pompous enunciation of matters that are obvious to all, or of the veriest twaddle that ever deceived the unwary in its recesses amidst the wilds of dreary verbiage and philosophical jargon.

No. 3. Of greater certainty.—It has been one of the missions of the æsthetic critics to discover, in the works of the great dramatist, a number of the author's subtle designs in incidents that are found, on examination, to have been adopted from his predecessors.   There is, for instance, the little episode of Rosaline, one which is closely taken, both in substance and position, from the foundation-tale.   According, however, to Coleridge, " it affords a strong instance of the fineness of Shakespeare's insight into the nature of the passions, that Romeo is introduced already love-bewildered."   A glance at the original narrative will show that, if there was a preconceived recondite design in the invention of the first love, the merits of the adaptation must be conceded to the wretched poetaster who put the old story into rhyme in 1562. Equal if not greater perception is exhibited in making the icy and un-conquerable apathy of Rosaline do so much in clearing the way to Juliet, but this, like the other " fine insight," may be observed in the elder romance.   The probability is that, in this play as in some others, Shakespeare was merely exercising his unrivalled power of successfully adapting his characters to a number of preformed events that he did not feel inclined to alter.   So homely an explanation is not likely to satisfy the philosophical critics, who will have it that there is some mysterious contrast between the qualities of Romeo's two infatuations.   " Rosaline," observes Coleridge, " was a mere creation of his fancy ; and we should remark the boastful positiveness of Romeo in a love of his own making, which is never shown where love is really near the heart," Notes and Lectures, ed. 1875, p. 147.   But the impetuosity of Romeo's passion is seen, so far as circumstances admit, as much in one case as in the other ; and as for the " boastful positiveness," it is difficult to understand that an expressed belief in the perfection of his mistress's beauty can be an evidence of a lover's insincerity.   It could more fairly be said that Romeo's despondency, under the treatment he experienced at the hands of his first love, is a testimony in the opposite direction.

No. 4.   Visited Stratford-on-Avon.—Aubrey himself refers to "some of the neighbours " in that town as his authority for the calf anecdote, and a notice of the poet's effigy, apparently given from ocular inspec-tion, is found in his Monumenta Britannica, MS.   A few brief notes respecting this undoubtedly honest, though careless, antiquary, who was born in 1626 and died in 1697, may be worth giving.   Educated at first in his native county of Wilts and afterwards at Blandford in Dorset, he was entered at the University of Oxford in 1642, but his sojourns at the last-named place were brief and irregular.   A love for the study of archæology exhibited itself even in his boyish days, and a large portion of his life was expended in itinerant searches after antiquities and all kinds of curious information.

No. 5.   From his own recollections of them.—Thus, in making the statement respecting Mrs. Hall, he says,—" I think I have been told," —as, indeed, he must have been in one way or other, although the word *sister* is erroneously put for daughter.   Amongst his most favourite phrases are "I think" and "I guess," both, as a rule, attached to the merest conjectures. It is not known when his memoir of Shakespeare was written, but it was evidently compiled from scraps gathered from a variety of informants. The Grendon notice would appear to have been derived from a recollection of what was told him at Oxford in 1642 by Josias Howe of Trinity College, a native of the former place. This gentleman, a son of the rector of Grendon, was an excellent authority for the village tradition, but Aubrey has contrived to record it in such an embarrassing hotchpot that it is useless to attempt to recover the original story.

No. 6. All through the seventeenth century.—The poet's sister and her descendants inhabited the birth-place from the time of his death to the year 1806; and his younger daughter lived at Stratford-on-Avon until her death in 1662. Then there were Hathaways, who were members of his wife's family, residing in Chapel Street from 1647 to 1696. His godson, William Walker, who died in the same town in 1680, must have been one of the last survivors of personal acquaintance-ship.

No. 7. The printed notices.—The best of these is the one in Fuller's Worthies, 1662, but that writer was not even at the pains to ascertain the year of the poet's decease. What there is of novelty in the sub sequent publications of Phillips, Winstanley, Langbaine, Blount and Gildon, is all but worthless. Dugdale, in his Antiquities of Warwick-shire, 1656, gives a valuable account of the sepulchral monuments, but adds no information respecting the poet himself.

No. 8. Thomas Betterton.—This actor, who was born in West-minster in 1635, appeared on the stage at the Cockpit in Drury-Lane in 1660. He attained to great eminence in his profession, but lost the first collection of his well-earned savings through a commercial enter-prise that he joined in 1692. In 1700 he acted in Rowe's first tragedy, a circumstance which may have led to his acquaintance with that dramatist. He died in London in April, 1710, having very nearly completed his seventy-fifth year. The precise time of his visit to Strat-ford-on-Avon is unknown, but it is hardly likely to have occurred in his declining years, and towards the close of his life he was afflicted with a complaint that must have rendered any of the old modes of travelling exceedingly irksome. He is mentioned, however, as having in 1709 a country house at Reading,—Life, ed. 1710, p. 11. That town would certainly have been nearer to Stratford than from London, but still at what was for those days an arduous cross-country journey of seventy miles or thereabouts.

No. 9. A farmer named Shakespeare.—This name probably arose in the thirteenth century, when surnames derived from personal occupa-tions first came into general use in this country, and it appears to have rapidly become a favourite patronymic. The origin of it is sufficiently obvious. Some, says Camden, are named "from that which they commonly carried, as Palmer, that is, Pilgrime, for that they carried palme when they returned from Hierusalem; Long-sword, Broad-speare, Fortescu, that is, Strong-shield, and in some such respect, Break-speare, Shake-speare, Shot-bolt, Wagstaffe," Remaines, ed. 1605, p. 111. "Breakspear, Shakspear, and the lyke have bin surnames imposed upon the first bearers of them for valour and feates of armes," Verstegan's Restitution of Decayed Intelligence, ed. 1605, p. 294. Shakeshaft and Drawsword were amongst the other old English names of similar formation. The surname of the poet's family was certainly known as early as the thirteenth century, there having been a John Shakespere, living, apparently in Kent, in the year 1279, who is mentioned in Plac. Cor. 7 Edw. 1 Kanc. From this time the Shakespeares are found dispersedly in gradually increasing numbers until the sixteenth and seventeenth centuries, when they were to be met with in nearly every part of England. It cannot be said that during the latter periods the surname was anywhere an excessively rare one, but from an early date Shakespeares abounded most in Warwickshire. In the fifteenth century they were to be discovered in that county at Coventry, Wroxhall, Balsall, Knowle, Meriden and Rowington; in the sixteenth century, at Berkswell, Snitterfield, Lapworth, Haseley, Ascote, Rowington, Packwood, Beausal, Temple Grafton, Salford, Tanworth, Barston, Warwick, Tachbrook, Haselor, Rugby, Budbrook, Wroxall, Norton-Lindsey, Wolverton, Hampton-in-Arden, Knowle, Hampton Lucy and Alcester; and in the seventeenth century, at Weston, Bidford, Shrewley, Haseley, Henley-in-Arden, Kenilworth, Wroxhall, Nuneaton, Tardebigg, Charlecote, Kingswood, Knowle, Flenkenho, Coventry, Rowington, Sherbourn, Packwood, Hatton, Ansley, Solihull, Lapworth, Budbrook, Arley, Packington, Tanworth, Warwick, Longbridge, Kington, Fillongley, Little Packington, Meriden, Long Itchington, Claverdon and Tachbrook. It is not probable that this list, which has been compiled almost exclusively from records inspected by myself, is by any means a complete one, but it is sufficiently extensive to show how very numerous formerly were Shakespeares in Warwickshire, and how dangerous it must be, in the absence of direct evidence, to assume that early notices of persons of that name relate to members of the poet's family. Thus it has happened that more than one John Shakespeare has been erroneously identified with the father of the great dramatist. There was an agriculturist of that name, who, in 1570, was in the occupation of a small farm, situated in the parish of Hampton Lucy near Stratford-on-Avon, which was described as "one other meadowe with thappurtenaunces called or knowen by the name of Ingon alias Ington meadowe, conteynynge by estymacion fouretene acres, be it more or lesse, then or late in the tenure or occupacion of John Shaxpere or his assignes," Rot. Claus. 23 Eliz. This individual has always been considered to have been the John Shakespeare of Henley Street, but that he was a different person who resided at Ingon appears from the following entry in the Hampton Lucy register under the date of 1589,—" Joannes Shakespere of Yngon was buried the xxv. th of September." He was in all probability at one time the owner of a field which bordered on Ingon Lane, and which is described in the will of John Combe, 1613, as Parson's Close alias Shakespeare's Close. It has also been supposed that the poet's father resided about the year 1583 at Clifford, a village at a short distance from Stratford-on-Avon, but that this conjecture is groundless may be confidently inferred from the fact of the John Shakespeare of Clifford having been married there in 1560 to a widow of the name of Hobbyns. " 1560, 15 Octobris, John Shaxspere was maryed unto Julian Hobbyns, vidua," MS. Register. Even when there are documents which yield notices referring apparently to one individual in one locality, identification should not be assumed in the absence of corroborative evidence or at least of circumstances inducing a high degree of probability ; but when, as in the instances just discussed, there are merely the facts of persons of the same Christian and surname living about the same period in neighbouring but different parishes, conjecture of identity, without such confirmation, ought to be inadmissible. Neither would interest attach to the volumes which might be compiled on the numerous ancient branches of the Shakespeares, and at the same time be destitute of a single morsel of real evidence to connect them in any degree of consanguinity with those of Stratford-on-Avon.

No. 10. At Snitterfield.—Richard Shakespeare was residing in that village as lately as 1560, but the conjecture that he removed some time after that year to Rowington, and was the same person as the Richard Shakespeare of the latter village, who died in or about 1592, is one of those gratuitous speculations which unfortunately embarrass most discussions on genealogical subjects. Richard had been a Christian name in the Rowington family at least as early as the time of Henry the Eighth, as appears from the subsidy-rolls of that reign, and it frequently occurs in the Rowington Shakespeare documents from that period to the close of the seventeenth century. There is no reason for believing that any person of the name migrated to Rowington after the year 1560, much less any evidence that he arrived there from Snitterfield. It is not probable, however, that the idea of a connexion between the Shakespeares of Rowington and the poet's family would have arisen, had it not been assumed, from the fact of Shakespeare having been a copyholder under the manor, that he was also connected with the parish. This was not necessarily the case. Singularly enough, there were two very small properties at Stratford-on-Avon held under the

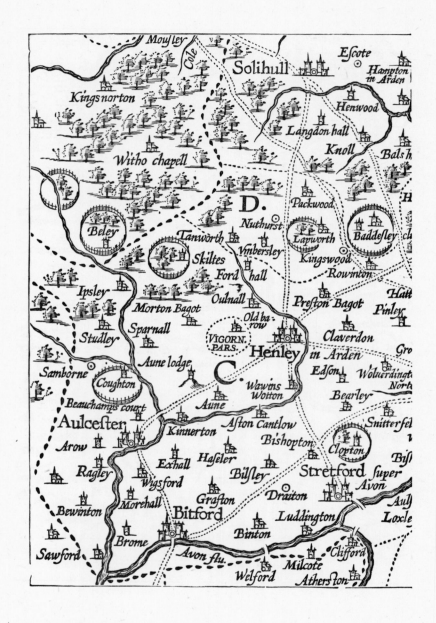

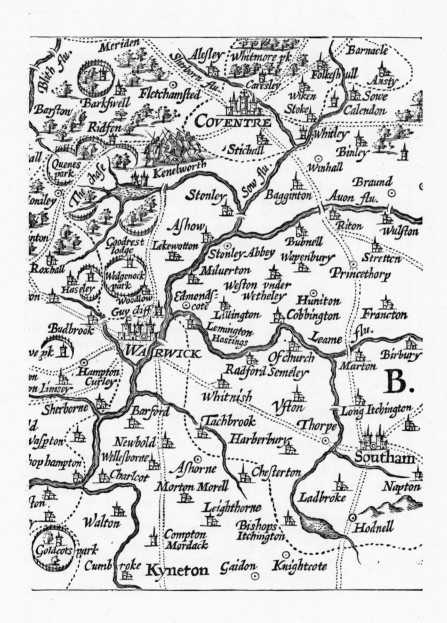

manor of Rowington, but it does not follow, from the mere circumstance of Shakespeare purchasing one of those estates, that he was connected in any way with that village, or that he was ever there with the exception of one attendance at the manorial court.　One of these Stratford copyholds was located in Church Street, and the other was the one in Chapel Lane, that which was surrendered to the poet in 1602. Rowington and Stratford-on-Avon are in the same Hundred, but they were about twelve miles distant from each other by the nearest road, and there was very little communication between the two places in Shakespeare's time.　Their relative situations will be best observed in the map of Warwickshire engraved in 1603, in which the indirect roads between them are delineated.　More than one person of the name of William Shakespeare was living at Rowington in the times of Elizabeth and the first James. Richard Shakespeare of that village, who died in 1560, mentions his son William in a will dated in the same year; and it appears from the will of another inhabitant of the same name, 1591, that his youngest son was also named William.　There was another William, who signs his name with a mark, something like a small letter *a*,—"the mark of William Shakespere"—in a roll of the customs of the manor which were confirmed in 1614, this person being one of the jury sworn on that occasion. The eldest son of a Richard Shakespeare of Rowington, who died in 1614, was also called William, as appears from his will and from the papers of a Chancery suit of 1616.　This individual may or may not have been the marksman of the customs roll, but he was over forty years of age in 1614, as is ascertained from the Chancery records just mentioned.　Legal proceedings were commenced at Worcester in 1614 " per Willielmum Shakespeare, filium naturalem Elizabethe Shakespeare, nuper de Roweington," respecting her will; MS. Episc. Reg.　Which of these William Shakespeares was the trained soldier of Rowington in the muster-roll of 1605 is a matter of no consequence, it being certain that the latter was not the great dramatist, who, in such a list, would undoubtedly have been described as belonging to Stratford-on-Avon, not to a place in which he never resided.　A reference to the original muster-roll will set the question at rest, a list of the trained soldiers at Stratford-on-Avon appearing not only in a different part of the manuscript, but in another division of the Hundred, and including no person of the name of Shakespeare.　There is no doubt that, amongst the multitude of Shakespeare families who were settled in Warwickshire in the sixteenth and seventeenth centuries, the Shakespeares of Rowington are those most frequently noticed in the records of those times.　It is no exaggeration to say that at least a hundred pages of this work could be filled even with the materials regarding them which have been collected by myself, and these are certainly not exhaustive.　If any connexion, however slight, had existed between the Shakespeares of

Rowington and those of Stratford-on-Avon during that period, it is all but impossible that some indication of the fact should not be discovered in one or other of the numerous wills, law papers and other documents relating to the former.   There is nothing of the kind.

No. 11.   Only six.—There is supposed to be a possibility, derived from an apparen treference to it in Weever's Mirror of Martyrs, that the tragedy of Julius Cæsar was in existence as early as the year 1599, for although the former work was not published till 1601, the author distinctly tells his dedicatee that " this poem, which I present to your learned view, some two yeares agoe was made fit for the print."   The subject was then, however, a favourite one for dramatic composition, and inferences from such premises must be cautiously received.   Shakespeare's was not, perhaps, the only drama of the time to which the lines of Weever were applicable ; and the more this species of evidence is studied, the more is one inclined to question its efficacy.   Plays on the history of Julius Cæsar are mentioned in Gosson's Schoole of Abuse, 1579; the Third Blast of Retrait from Plaies, 1580; Henslowe's Diary, 1594, 1602; Mirrour of Policie, 1598; Hamlet, 1603; Heywood's Apology for Actors, 1612.   There was a French tragedy on the subject published at Paris in 1578, and a Latin one was performed at Christ Church, Oxford, in 1582.   Tarlton, who died in 1588, had appeared as Cæsar, perhaps on some unauthorised occasion, a circumstance alluded to in the Ourania, 1606.   A play called Cæsars Tragedye, acted before Prince Charles, the Lady Elizabeth, and the Elector Palatine, in the earlier part of the year 1613, is reasonably considered to have been Shakespeare's drama, the great popularity of which is recorded by Digges in 1623.

No. 12.   Cannot admit of a reasonable doubt.—There is no absolute evidence on this subject, nor was there likely to be, but it is unreasonable to require early written testimony on such a point, or to assume it credible that Shakespeare did not witness scenes that were then, in all probability, familiar to every lad at Stratford-on-Avon.   We have no evidence that the poet ever saw a maypole, yet we know perfectly well that he must have met with many a one in the course of his life, and the persuasion that he was a spectator at some of the mysteries rests on exactly similar, though less cogent, deductive impressions.   Had the representations of those primitive dramas been of very exceptional occurrence, it would of course have been a different matter.

No. 13.   The Boar's Head Tavern.—It is a singular circumstance that there is no notice of this celebrated tavern in any edition of Shakepeare previously to the appearance of Theobald's in 1733, but that the locality is there accurately given from an old and genuine stage-tradition is rendered certain by an allusion to " Sir John of the Boares-Head in Eastcheap" in Gayton's Festivous Notes, 1654, p. 277.   Shakespeare never mentions that tavern at all, and the only possible allusion to it is in the Second Part of Henry the Fourth, where the Prince asks, speaking of Falstaff,—"doth the old boar feed in the old frank?" The Boar's Head was an inn at least as early as 1537, when it is expressly demised in a lease as all that tavern called the Bores Hedde "cum cellariis, sollariis et aliis suis pertinentiis in Estchepe, in parochia Sancti Michaelis predicti, in tenura Johanne Broke, vidue." About the year 1588 it was kept by one Thomas Wright, a native of Shrewsbury. "George Wrighte, sun of Thomas Wrighte of London, vintener, that dwelt at the Bore's Hed in Estcheap," Liber Famelicus of Sir James Whitelocke, sub anno 1588. In 1602, the Lords of the Council gave permission for the servants of the Earls of Oxford and Worcester to play at this house. There were numerous other tenements in London and the country, including five taverns in the City, known by the name of the Boar's Head, but the one in Eastcheap was totally destroyed in the great fire of 1666, and no genuine representation of it is known to exist.

No. 14.   Macbeth.—If Dryden may be trusted, there are speeches in this drama which were not liked by Rare Ben. "In reading some bombast speeches of Macbeth, which are not to be understood, he (Jonson) us'd to say that it was horrour, and I am much afraid that this is so," Essay on the Dramatique Poetry of the last Age, 1672.

No. 15.   Was acted.—In the little thin folio manuscript pamphlet which Forman calls, "the bock of plaies and notes therof per Formans, for common pollicie," there are notes of the performances of four plays, namely,—1. Cymbeline, undated; 2. Macbeth, on Saturday, April the 20th, 1611; 3. A play on the history of Richard the Second, on Tuesday, April the 30th, 1611; 4. The Winter's Tale, on Wednesday, May the 15th, 1611. In the original manuscript, the year 1610 is given as the date of the second theatrical visit, but, as there must be an oversight either in the note of the year or in that of the day of the week, it seems most likely that all the dramas above mentioned were seen by Forman about the same time, and that the error lies in the former record.

No. 16.   A graphic account.—This is the earliest distinct notice of the tragedy which has been discovered, so that it must have been written at some time between March, 1603, and April, 1611, for there is the all but certainty that it was produced after the accession of James. The allusion to the "two-fold balls and treble sceptres," and the favourable delineation of the character of Banquo, appear sufficient to establish the accuracy of this conclusion. It may also be thought probable that Macbeth was written and acted before the year 1607, from an apparent reference to Banquo's ghost in the comedy of the Puritan, 1607,— "we'll ha' the ghost i' th' white sheet sit at upper end o' th' table." All deductions, however, of this kind are to be cautiously received, for it is of course possible that the incident referred to may have been originally introduced in the older play on the subject. A similar observation will apply to a passage in the Knight of the Burning Pestle, 1611, where the probability of the allusion is somewhat marred by the reference to a whispering tale. The story of Macbeth had been introduced on the English stage at least as early as 1600, for, in that year, Kemp, the actor, in his Nine Daies Wonder performed in a Daunce from London to Norwich, thus alludes to some play on the subject,—"still the search continuing, I met a proper upright youth, onely for a little stooping in the shoulders all hart to the heele, a penny poet, whose first making was the miserable stolne story of Macdoel, or Macdobeth, or Macsomewhat, for I am sure a Mac it was, though I never had the maw to see it." The concluding words clearly imply that Kemp alluded to some piece that had been represented on the stage, one whence Shakespeare may have derived the legend of the murder and other incidents. It is at all events worth notice, in reference to the feasibility of this suggestion, that when Lady Macbeth says,—"nor time nor place did then adhere, and yet you would make both,"—there seems to be an allusion to some incident which was in the author's recollection, and which, in the hurry of composition, he had forgotten was inconsistent with his own treatment of the subject.

No. 17. On horseback.—Rude models of horses, the bodies made of canvas dilated with hoops and laths, were familiar objects on the early English stage. "Enter a spruce courtier a-horse-backe," stage-direction in MS. play of Richard the Second, c. 1597. "One great horse with his leages," list of theatrical properties, 1599. Many actors of the Shakespearean period were dexterous in their management of these hobby-horses, and it would seem that there was at least one troupe composed entirely of that class of performers. "Payed Mr. Maior that hee gave to the Princes hobyehorse plaiores, ij.*s*. vj.*d*.," Reading Corporation MSS., 1608.

No. 18. Cymbeline.—The tragedy is called "Cymbeline King of Britaine" in the list prefixed to the first folio, 1623. It may be just worth notice that a cavern near Tenby, that might be passed in a walk to Milford, known as Hoyle's Mouth, has been suggested as the prototype of the cave of Belarius.

No. 19. When that eccentric astrologer, Dr. Forman, died suddenly. —The day of his burial is thus recorded in the beautifully written ancient register of St. Mary's, Lambeth,—"A.D. 1611, September 12 ; Simon Forman, gent."

No. 20. The Midsummer Night's Dream.—It has been plausibly suggested that this title was derived from the circumstance of its having been originally produced at Midsummer, as otherwise the name would be inappropriate ; and the graceful compliment paid in it to Elizabeth would appear to indicate that the comedy was written with a view to its representation before that sovereign. The Lord Chamberlain's servants were not in the habit of acting plays before Royalty in the summer time, but when there was one intended for ultimate performance before the Court, it was their usual custom to produce it in the first instance at the theatre. In this way, by means of what may be termed public rehearsals, the actors were trained for a more effective representation before the Queen than would otherwise have been attainable. "Whereas licence hath bin graunted unto two companies of stage-players to use and practiçe stage-playes, whereby they night be the better enhabled and prepared to shew such plaies before her Majestie as they shal be required at tymes meete and accustomed," Privy Council Register, 1598.

No. 21. Mentioned for the first time.—There seems to be a probability that Shakespeare, in the composition of the Midsummer Night's Dream, had in one place a recollection of the sixth book of the Faerie Queene, published in 1596, for he all but literally quotes the following line from its eighth canto,—" *Through hils and dales, through bushes and through breres,*" ed. 1596, p. 640. As the comedy was not printed until the year 1600, and it is impossible that Spenser could have been present at any representation of it before he had written the sixth book of his celebrated poem, it may fairly be concluded that Shakespeare's play was not composed at the earliest before the year 1596, in fact, not until some time after January the 20th, 1595-6, on which day the Second Parte of the Faerie Queene was entered on the Stat. Reg. The sixth book was probably composed as early as 1592 or 1593, no doubt in Ireland and at some time before the month of November, 1594, the date of the entry of publication of the Amoretti, in the eightieth sonnet of which it is distinctly alluded to as having been written previously to the composition of the latter work.

No. 22. One little fragment.—A curious stage-artifice, which was originally practised in the workmen's interlude, is thus mentioned in Sharpham's comedy of the Fleire, published in 1607,—"*Kni.* And how lives he with 'am ?—*Fle.* Faith, like Thisbe in the play, 'a has almost kil'd himselfe with the scabberd." Another little vestige of the old performance is accidentally recorded in the first folio, 1623, where a man named Tawyer is introduced as heading the procession of the actors as trumpeter. This person was a surbordinate in the pay of Hemmings, his burial at St. Saviour's in June, 1625, being thus noticed in the sexton's MS. note-book,—"William Tawier, Mr. Heminges man, gr. and cl., xvj.*d.*"

No. 23. In plain and unobtrusive language.—Life is not breathed into a skeleton by attiring it in fancy gauze, and thus the climax of dullness has been reached by those who, blending the real with the ideal, have hitherto attempted to produce a readable Life of Shakespeare. A foolish desire to avoid the title of Dryasdusts has driven them into the ranks of the larger family of Drierthandusts. It is not every subject that can legitimately be made attractive to the lazy, or, as it is the fashion to term him, the general reader. In the entire absence of materials that reveal the poet's living character, the selection really lies between the acceptance of romance and that of a simple narrative of external facts. We have not even the consolation of expecting that narrative to be ever interwoven with an absolutely faithful representation of contemporary life,—a life with all the infinite variations from that of the present day many of which necessarily elude the most assiduous research.

No. 24. Titus Andronicus.—The actors who were enlisted under the banner of the Earl of Sussex were playing at the Rose from December the 27th, 1593, to February the 6th, 1594, the last-mentioned day being that of the third performance of this drama and also that of the entry of its copyright by Danter at Stationers' Hall. It is clear, however, from the actorial notices on the title-page of the edition of 1594, that the tragedy itself could not have been published for some weeks, if not months, after the latter transaction. No copy of that impression is now known to exist, but it had been seen by Langbaine, who, in his Account of the English Dramatick Poets, 1691, p. 464, says,—"this play was first printed 4°. Lond. 1594, and acted by the Earls of Derby, Pembroke and Essex, their Servants." That Essex is here a misprint for Sussex is evident from the title-page of the 1600 edition, and also from the half-title on the first page of text in that of 1611. Those two later impressions were published by Edward White, but neither he nor Danter had aught to do with any of the subsequent productions of Shakespeare, while the assignment of "Titus and Andronicus" from Millington to Pavier in 1602 may refer to a prose history, in the same way that the "book called Thomas of Reading," named in the same entry, certainly does. In the note of the transfer of the copyright from Mrs. Pavier to Brewster and Bird, 1626, Titus Andronicus is not included in the "right in Shakesperes plaies or any of them," but is inserted in company with the prose Hamlet. Whether the interest of the Paviers was in the history or in the drama is, however, a question of no great moment, the title-pages of the old editions of the latter showing that an acting copy of it was in the repertoire of Shakespeare's company during the later years of the reign of Elizabeth and in the early part of that of James the First.

No. 25. Having been successfully produced.—Its immediate popularity on the stage is evidenced, not merely by its timely publication and the large receipts at the theatre, but also by the circumstance of its having been performed by several different companies within a brief time after its production in 1594. It is also worth notice that Danter entered the copyright of a ballad on the history of the play at the same time that he registered the latter, and this **is** another testimony in a like direction. In Father Hubburds Tales, 1604, the action of a man with one arm is compared to that of "old Titus Andronicus," the reference being probably to the tragedy, and one which, it is clear, was assumed to have been familiar to readers of the day. A drama called Andronicus, which is noted as having been twice acted at Newington in June, 1594, was most likely another production, and the one which is mentioned, under that single title, and as being a very old play in 1614, in Ben Jonson's Induction to his Bartholomew Fair. It is improbable that Henslowe's three titles recorded in January and February, 1594, should vary so distinctly from the two given in the following June, had the same play been intended in all the entries.

No. 26. The authenticity of Shakespeare's earliest tragedy.—An alteration of Titus Andronicus by Edward Ravenscroft, a dramatist of the Restoration period, was produced on the stage in or about the year 1678, when it was heralded by a prologue that included the following lines,—"To day the poet does not fear your rage,=Shakespear by him reviv'd now treads the stage ;=Under his sacred lawrels he sits down= Safe from the blast of any cricks frown.=Like other poets, he'll not proudly scorn=To own that he but winnow'd Shakespear's corn ;=So far he was from robbing him of 's treasure,=That he did add his own to make full measure." But when the work itself was published in 1687, under the title of "Titus Andronicus or the Rape of Lavinia, acted at the Theatre Royall, a tragedy alter'd from Mr. Shakespears Works by Mr. Edw. Ravenscroft," the adapter makes this curious state-ment,—"I have been told by some anciently conversant with the stage that it was not originally *his*, but brought by a private author to be acted, and *he* only gave some master-touches to one or two of the principal parts or characters," the words *his* and *he* referring to the great dramatist. Ravenscroft adds that the original prologue had then been lost, but Langbaine, who has preserved the lines above quoted in his Account of the English Dramatick Poets, 1691, p. 465, seems to question the truth of that assertion, plainly holding the opinion that the former writer was not distinguished for his literary integrity. How-ever that may be, it is clear that so late a tradition respecting the authorship of the earlier play cannot fairly be held to outweigh the decisive testimonies of Shakespeare's own contemporaries.

No. 27. In the Christmas holidays.—The performance here men-tioned took place on the evening of December the 26th, at Whitehall. "1604 and 1605—Edmund Tylney—on St. Stephens night Mesure for Mesur by Shaxberd, performed by the King's players," old notes of the Audit Records taken for Malone about the year 1800. "For makeinge readie the halle at Whitehalle for the Kinge, for the plaies againste

Christmas, by the space of iiij.ᵒʳ daies in the same moneth, lxxviij.*s.* viij.*d.*"
MS. Accounts of the Treasurer of the Chamber, 1604.

No. 28. A great dislike.—James the First had long exhibited a taste
for seclusion. As early as the year 1586, a contemporary alludes to "his
desire to withdraw himself from places of most access and company, to
places of more solitude and repose, with very small retinue." A similar
feeling pervaded his movements after he had ascended the throne of
these realms, and in his progress from Edinburgh to London, "he was
faine," observes the writer of A True Narration of the Entertainment of
his Royall Majestie, 1603, "to publish an inhibition against the in-
ordinate and dayly accesse of peoples comming." In his "publick
appearance," observes Wilson, "especially in his sports, the accesses of
the people made him so impatient that he often dispersed them with
frowns, that we may not say with curses."

No. 29. Merely out of deference.—There seems to be no other
solution of the problem at all feasible. The trivial historical allusions,
if they are to be seriously received as evidences of the date of action,
would place the comedy between the two parts of Henry the Fourth
and the drama of Henry the Fifth ; but its complete isolation from those
plays offers the best means of deliverance from the perplexity created by
those references. Arguments on any other basis will only land us, to
use the words of Mrs. Quickly, "into such a canaries as 'tis wonderful."
This woman, she of the Merry Wives of Windsor, is an essentially
different character from her namesake of the historical plays, and is
positively introduced into the former as a stranger to Sir John, without
the slightest reference to the memories of the Boar's Head tavern.
All this leads to the inference that the small connexion to be traced
between the comedy and the historical plays is to be attributed to the
necessity of at least a specious compliance with the wishes of the
Queen, and this is as much as can fairly be said even in regard to the
love-adventures of Falstaff. Then, again, there are traces in the play
itself of its composition having been subjected to external influence.

No. 30. At the desire of the Queen.—With respect to the degree of
credibility to be given to Rowe's version of the Falstaff anecdote, much
will depend upon the importance to be attached to the subsequent
discovery of a confirmatory fact which was unknown to that biographer.
There is no reason to believe that the first edition of the Merry Wives
had been seen by any writers of the eighteenth century until a copy of
it came into the hands of Theobald about the year 1731. See a letter
from that critic to Warburton in MS. Egerton 1956. According to the
title-page of that edition, the comedy, in 1602, had "bene divers times
acted by the Right Honorable my Lord Chamberlaines Servants, both
before her Majestie and elsewhere." This is the only known contemporary evidence that it was ever performed before Queen Elizabeth,

although the internal references to Windsor Castle in connexion with that Sovereign would suggest the probability of its having been written with a view to its performance before the Court.

No. 31. In the brief space of a fortnight.—This tradition was first recorded by Dennis in the dedication to the Comical Gallant, 1702, in which he says, referring to the Merry Wives of Windsor and Queen Elizabeth—"this comedy was written at her command, and by her direction, and she was so eager to see it acted that she commanded it to be finished in fourteen days; and was afterwards, as tradition tells us, very well pleas'd at the representation," and in the prologue, he repeats the assertion that Shakespeare's comedy was written in the short space of fourteen days. Rowe, in 1709, speaking of Queen Elizabeth, says, —"she was so well pleased with that admirable character of Falstaff in the two parts of Henry the Fourth, that she commanded him (Shakespeare) to continue it for one play more, and to show him in love; this is said to be the occasion of his writing the Merry Wives of Windsor." This evidence was followed by that of Gildon, who, in his Remarks, 1710, p. 291, observes that "the fairys in the Fifth Act makes a handsome complement to the Queen, in her palace of Windsor, who had oblig'd him to write a play of Sir John Falstaff in love, and which I am very well assured he perform'd in a fortnight; a prodigious thing, when all is so well contriv'd and carry'd on without the least confusion." Gildon here says nothing of the incentive created by the original attractions of the theatrical Falstaff, but Elizabeth could not very well have commanded a portrayal of the fat knight in love if she had not been previously introduced to him in another character. Pope, Theobald, and later editors, appear to have taken their versions of the tradition second-hand from their predecessors. Rowe's version of the anecdote is, as usual with him, the one most cautiously written, and therefore that to be preferred; but still there is no reason for disbelieving the assertions of the others to the extent that the play was written with great celerity. So much can be accepted, without absolutely crediting the asserted short limit of the fortnight; and Dennis's authority on that point must be considered to be somewhat weakened by the fact that, in his Letters, ed. 1721, p. 232, he reduces the period to ten days. It is at the same time to be remembered that extreme rapidity of composition was not unusual with the dramatists of the Shakespearean period.

No. 32. Brevity of time.—The wording of the entries is somewhat obscure, but it would seem, from two in Henslowe's Diary, that in August, 1598, Munday undertook to write a play for the Court, and Drayton gave "his worde for the boocke to be done within one fortnight." On the third of December, 1597, Ben Jonson apparently had only the plot of one of his dramas ready, and yet he engaged to complete it before the following Christmas, that is, in three weeks.

No. 33. *A catchpenny publisher.*—It is worthy of remark that, in the title-page of the quarto, Parson Evans is termed in error *the Welch Knight,* a mistake which could hardly have emanated from any one acquainted with the play, and shows that the title was probably compiled, in all its attractive dignity, by the publisher. There is no other contemporary edition of any of the plays of Shakespeare in the title-page of which so many flattering notices of characters are introduced.

No. 34. *A very defective copy.*—The first edition, in every respect an irregular performance, is considered by some critics to be an imperfect copy of a very hastily written original sketch of the comedy. Were this the case, surely there would be found passages unmistakeably derived from Shakespeare's pen, adapted solely to that original, and intentionally omitted in a reconstruction of the play ; but, instead of this, the quarto consists for the most part of imperfect transcripts of speeches that are found in the authentic drama. The few re-written portions are of very inferior power, and it would be difficult to imagine that they could not have been the work of some other hand. One of these, where Falstaff is tormented by the pretended fairies in Windsor Park, the most favourable of the pieces which are clearly derived from another source, exhibits few, if any, traces of genius. As for the other original fragments in the quarto, they are hardly worthy of serious consideration, and some of the lines in them are poor and despicable. There are indications that the botcher was fully acquainted with Shakespeare's play of Henry the Fourth, several phrases being evidently borrowed from it. "When Pistol lies, do this," is a line found in Johnson's quarto and in the Second Part of Henry the Fourth, but not in the perfect copy of the Merry Wives. The same may also be said of such expressions as *woolsack* and *iniquity,* as applied to Falstaff, neither of which are to be traced in the first folio. Sometimes, also, Shakespeare's own expressions are employed in wrong places to suit the editor's purpose ; and oversights, some of the greatest magnitude, occur in nearly every page. The succession of scenes, however, is exactly the same as in the larger play, although not so divided, with the exception of the fourth and fifth scenes of the third act, which are transposed. The first scene of the fourth act, and the first four scenes of the fifth act in the folio edition, are entirely omitted in the quarto. Amongst the numerous other indications of an imperfect publication, attention may be drawn to the introduction of Bardolph in the second stage-direction, while he is entirely omitted in the business of the scene ; and to the incident of the Doctor's sending a challenge to Evans being altogether inexplicable without the assistance derived from the more perfect version. Several other speeches and devices are of so extremely an inartificial and trivial a character, it can scarcely be imagined but that some inferior writer of the time was concerned with the publication.

No. 35.   Written before the production of Henry the Fifth.—The foreign swindlers, who are facetiously termed cousin-germans by Parson Evans in ed. 1623, are alluded to in ed. 1602 as "three sorts of cosen *garmombles*," the last word being reasonably conjectured to be an allusion in some way by metathesis to Count *Mompelgard*, the second title of the Duke of Wirtemberg.   This nobleman paid a visit to England in 1592, being then known under the former designation, for he did not succeed to the dukedom until the following year.   He was ceremoniously received by Queen Elizabeth at Reading, leaving that place for Windsor escorted by a person of rank who was specially deputed by her Majesty to show him every mark of attention.   He remained only two days in the latter town, proceeding thence, under the guidance of one or more members of the royal household, to the palace at Hampton Court.   There was clearly no opportunity during these excursions between Reading and Hampton Court for the perpetration of the garmomble rogueries, and the same remark will apply to the conditions under which he travelled from London through Colebrook and Maidenhead.   From the minute account of these occurrences, which was published at Tubingen in 1602, it seems that the Queen sent one of her own carriages expressly to London for the use of the distinguished stranger, and that he had driven in it to Reading "with several post-horses," but not a word is said respecting his having then had an authority for engaging them without payment.   Even if there had been such an exercise of tyrannical privilege, it was of far too usual a kind to have elicited the references in the Merry Wives of Windsor, and that the Count himself would have sanctioned a disreputable personal fraud is, under the circumstances, altogether incredible; the rather also from the fact of his having been accompanied the whole distance by one of the Queen's pages of honour.   If, as is most probable, Shakespeare alludes to real events, it may be concluded that, on some other occasion, three Germans, staying at the Garter Inn as retainers of a Duke Mompelgard, pretended that they had to meet him in his progress from London towards the Court, and, by that stratagem, managed to run off with the poor innkeeper's horses, defrauding him at the same time of his charges for a week's luxurious maintenance.   Now it seems that when Breuning was the special ambassador to this country from Wirtemberg in 1595, he ascertained that one Stammler had previously appeared with fictitious credentials before the Queen as an envoy from the Duke.   This impudent knave, who was ultimately "banished the kingdom on account of his discreditable tricks," was still in England in the latter part of that year, and was evidently suspected of indulging in nefarious equine transactions.   It appears that Breuning, having received private information that Stammler was making enquiries respecting a horse with an ostensible view to its purchase, consulted La Fontaine on the matter, and, by his advice, "employed some one to watch him, giving orders that he should be arrested if he showed any signs of an intention to levant." Some of these particulars will be found in Rye's England as seen by Foreigners, 1865, and others are given by Herr Kurz in his Altes und Neues, zu Shakspeare's Leben und Schaffen, 1868. La Fontaine arrived in England in October, 1595, as Chargé des affaires du Roi en l'absence d'Ambassadeur ; App. Publ. Rec. Rep., xxxvii., 187. No exact record of Stammler's delinquencies has come to light, but it is by no means impossible that he may have been the ringleader in the deceptions practised on mine Host of the Garter. Whether this were the case or not, no legitimate inference respecting the date of Shakespeare's composition is to be drawn from the allusions to the transactions of the Germans. When the great dramatist was at Windsor he may have heard a full account of the story in the form in which it is introduced into the comedy, for it should be remembered that, in those days of restricted intercourse, unusual incidents of all kinds would continue to be subjects of local gossip for years after their occurrence.

No. 36. A new drama.—This fact is ascertained from Henslowe's Diary, the letters N.E., that is, New Enterlude, being attached to the note of the performance, which realised the then large sum of three pounds sixteen shillings and five pence.

No. 37. On unquestionable authority.—That of Robert Greene who, in his Groatsworth of Wit, written in or shortly before August, 1592, mentions Shakespeare as an *upstart crow*, a phrase altogether inconsistent with the opinion that the authorial career of the latter had been initiated any length of time previously to the appearance of that work.

No. 38. Month of July.—Nash's Pierce Penilesse, the work here alluded to, was entered on the registers of the Stationers' Company on August the 8th, 1592. The words of Nash, those in which he calls Talbot the Terror of the French, viewed in connection with the entries in Henslowe's Diary, not only prove that he refers to the drama which was produced in March, but that the latter was, in all probability, the First Part of Henry the Sixth ; that is to say, if it be conceded that Greene quotes from the Third Part in the Groatsworth of Wit published in the following September.

No. 39. Collective Edition of 1623.—The omissions, discrepancies, transpositions, and repetitions, found in this edition of the Second and Third Parts, merely show that the latter was printed from theatrical copies in which there were numerous erasures and alterations. Both plays, in reference to these peculiarities, should be considered together. In one instance, at least, a speech which occurs in the First Part of the Contention and in the Second Part of Henry the Sixth is repeated nearly word for word in the Third Part of the latter, but is not inserted in the True Tragedie,—" Hold, Warwick, seek thee out," &c., 2 Henry VI., act v. sc. 2.   The careless manner in which the folio copies have been edited is perhaps nowhere more clearly seen than in the lines respecting the Castle Tavern, a speech which in that edition is obviously an imperfect transcript.   Malone, referring to the obviously incorrect repetitions in ed. 1623, considers that they arose " from Shakespeare's first copying his original as it lay before him, and afterwards, in subsequent passages, added to the old matter, introducing expressions which had struck him in preceding scenes."   This deduction is not sustained on a careful examination, for repetitions also occur in the quartos.   It is unsafe to rest arguments either on these or on verbal indications, but one of the latter, *fore-spent* in the edition of 1623, printed *sore spent* in that of 1595, may possibly imply the priority of the text of the former.

No 40.   A garbled and spurious version.—This theory appears to present fewer difficulties than any other that has been advanced to meet the singular perplexities of the case.   As some of this version was probably taken in short-hand at the theatre, and that in the folio printed from a theatrical copy that had been tampered with, it is most likely that some lines of Shakespeare's are peculiar to the former.   There are several that he could hardly have rejected had he been merely composing an alteration of the First Part of the Contention.   The internal evidence is strongly in favour of the Second Part of Henry the Sixth, although of course it may have been retouched by the author after its first production, being one of Shakespeare's earliest plays.   That part of young Clifford's speech commencing, " Meet I an infant of the house of York," is in itself almost decisive as to this point, while it is an essential portion of a noble harangue, the other lines of which may or may not have been subject to revision.   It is also worth notice that there are a larger number of decided archaisms in the Second Part of Henry the Sixth than there are in the First Part of the Contention ; and as there are good reasons for believing that the manuscript of the Third Part of Henry the Sixth was in existence in 1594, it is most extremely unlikely, in such a case, that copies of the other parts, as written by Shakespeare, were not in the actors' hands at the same period.

No. 41.   By Millington.—Both parts of the Contention had been assigned by Millington to Pavier in April, 1602, the latter entering them upon the books of the Stationers' Company on that occasion, *salvo jure cujuscunque*, as " the first and second parte of henry the vi.t, ii. bookes ;" a mistake for the First and Second Parts of the Contention.   There appears to be something mysterious in the Latin words, and it is curious that Pavier should have kept the two plays till the year 1619 without a republication.   The entry is, however, important, for it clearly shows that, as early as 1602, the present title of Henry the Sixth had superseded the older one. Pavier's first edition appeared as "the Whole Contention betweene the two famous Houses, Lancaster and Yorke."

No. 42. The earliest record.—Taking Greene's words in their contextual and natural sense, he first alludes to Shakespeare as an actor, one "beautified with our feathers," that is, one who acts in their plays, then to the poet as a writer just commencing to try his hand at blank verse, and, finally, to him as not only engaged in both those capacities but in any other in which he might be useful to the company. If Greene had intended, as some think, to accuse Shakespeare of pilfering from his works, or from those of other contemporaries, it may be assumed that he would have made the charge in far more direct terms. *Moreover, the particular satire, which was evidently aimed at Shakespeare, would have lost its significance if the words of any other writer had been travestied.* The attack of Greene's, plainly interpreted, is a decisive proof of Shakespeare's authorship of the line, and hence, by fair inference, of the speech in which it occurs.

No 43. A surreptitious and tinkered version of the Third Part.— There is almost conclusive evidence that the first folio text of the Third Part of Henry the Sixth was in existence at least as early as the year 1594, and, therefore, before the publication of the True Tragedie, Gabriel Spencer and Humphrey Jeffes, two of the subordinate actors in the former, having continued in the Lord Admiral's Company after that period. It is obviously most unlikely that the manuscript of the play should have been left with that company after Shakespeare had joined the Lord Chamberlain's, there being every reason for believing that those two companies acted altogether independently of each other after the year 1594. Gabriel acted the Messenger in the second scene of the first act, as appears from the text of ed. 1623. It seems that he was popularly known by his Christian name, being so noticed in a list of the Lord Admiral's Company in October, 1597, by Henslowe in 1598, and again in the complimentary reminiscences of deceased players in Heywood's Apology for Actors, 1612. On October the 2nd, 1597, a warrant was issued "to the keeper of the Marshalsea, to release Gabriell Spencer and Robert Shaa, stage-players, out of prison, who were of late committed to his custodie," most probably for debts. Although Gabriel had an interest in the profits of the company to which he belonged, it appears that in the later part of his career he was in pecuniary difficulties, being compelled to be constantly borrowing money on his promissory notes, and once at least on the pawn of a jewel. He met with an untimely death in 1598, when, having challenged Ben Jonson, he was killed by the latter in a duel. This unfortunate event took place in the fields near Hoxton, then a straggling country village, and the regret of Henslowe at his loss is thus expressed in a letter to Allen dated on the 26th of September,—"sence yow weare with me I have loste one of my company, which hurteth me greatley, that is, Gabrell, for he is slayen in Hogesden fylldes by the hands of Bengemen Jonson, bricklayer," Dulwich MS. The poor actor's burial is thus recorded in the register of St. Leonard's, Shoreditch,—"Gabriell Spencer, being slayne, was buryed the xxiiij.th of September," a note adding that his residence was in Hog Lane, a street in the vicinity of the northern theatres. Two other actors, Humphrey and Sinklow, undertook the parts of the two Keepers in the first scene of the third act of the Third Part of Henry the Sixth, their names being attached to the speeches of those characters in the edition of 1623. Humphrey Jeffes, the person here alluded to, acted, in or before the year 1592, in a drama called the First Part of Tamber Can, and he was one of the Lord Admiral's Company acting in Peele's Battle of Alcazar about the year 1594. Henslowe mentions him as a half-sharer in the same company in 1598, he and his brother Anthony having one share between them. He was one of the actors in the play of the Six Yeomen of the West in 1601, and in that year he appears to have been residing in Southwark,—"Marye Jeffes, d. of Humphrey, a player," Baptisms, St. Saviour's, Southwark, 25 Jan. 1600-1. When most of the Lord Admiral's actors transferred their services to Prince Henry in 1603, Humphrey Jeffes and his brother were members of the new company, and they marched in the procession of James the First through London, 1604; Lord Chamberlain's MS. Early in the year 1613, a few weeks after the death of the Prince, whose funeral he attended, Humphrey became one of the servants of the Elector Palatine, in which company he remained until two or three years before his death. "Humphrie Jeffes, plaier," Burials at St. Giles's, Cripplegate, 21 August, 1618. It may be just worth a note to add that he was one of the players summoned before the Privy Council in March, 1616, for joining in stage-performances during Lent. Little, however, as there is known of the history of this actor, still less has been discovered respecting his fellow-player, Sinklow, who is generally, and perhaps rightly, presumed to be the John Sincler, one of the performers with Burbage and others in the Second Part of the Seven Deadly Sins, a drama originally produced some time before September, 1588. Sinklow was a subordinate member of the Lord Chamberlain's Company at least as early as the year 1600, for he is introduced into the first edition of the Second Part of Henry the Fourth as having enacted the part of a Beadle in that drama, and he was one of the company of itinerant players in the Induction to the Taming of the Shrew, no doubt acting in the comedy itself. He appears also in the Induction to the Mal-content, 1604, where he is introduced with several of the King's Players, and takes the part of a rich gallant who wishes to indulge in the dignity of having a stool on the stage. With respect to his capabilities as an actor, nothing can safely be inferred from the graceful compliment paid by the Lord to the Second Player in the Induction to the Taming of the Shrew, for it is of course possible that Shakespeare had written that episode before he knew the distribution of the parts. The character of Soto, therein alluded to, was probably one in an early drama which is no longer in existence, certainly not the personage so named who is introduced in Fletcher's Women Pleased.

No. 44.   The Earl of Pembroke's Servants.—And no doubt produced by that company. It is to be observed that, however occasionally mendacious in other respects, the title-pages of the earliest impressions of old quartos are generally excellent authorities for the names of the companies by whom the plays were first acted.

No. 45.   Had outlived the possibility.—Mr. Swinburne, in an eloquent criticism, is of opinion that the lines which open the fourth act of the Second Part, and are not to be found in the version of 1594, are indisputably by Marlowe. "It is inconceivable," he observes, "that any imitator but one should have had the power so to catch the very trick of his hand, the very note of his voice, and incredible that the one who might would have set himself to do so," a Study of Shakespeare, 1880, p. 52. But if Shakespeare, as is most probable, wrote those lines in the year 1592, he may not at that time have outlived the possibility referred to in the text. It is worth notice that there are a few striking coincidences of language, especially in the passage respecting the wild Oneil, to be traced in Marlowe's Edward the Second and the Contention plays of 1594 and 1595 ; and also that a line from the Jew of Malta is found in the Third Part of Henry the Sixth, but not in the True Tragedie. The transference of occasional lines from one writer by another was, however, too common a practice of the day to prove much in the way of authorship, or to involve a serious charge of plagiarism.

No. 46.   The quarto editions.—"The old copies," observes Dr. Johnson, "are so apparently imperfect and mutilated, that there is no reason for supposing them the first draughts of Shakespeare ; I am inclined to believe them copies taken by some auditor who wrote down, during the representation, what the time would permit, then perhaps filled up some of his omissions at a second or third hearing, and, when he had, by this method, formed something like a play, sent it to the printer." This auditor would have taken down his notes in short-hand. In plain words, the quartos are jumbles composed of parts of the original play made up with other matter supplied by some wretched hack, the whole abounding in obvious inaccuracies. An endeavour to unravel the precise history of such relics, printed in those days of commonplace books compiled from short-hand notes taken at the theatres, must necessarily be futile. Some of the trifling additions to and variations from the texts of 1594 and 1595, found in the editions of 1600 and 1619, may perhaps be attributed to the use of such materials.

These additions appear for the most part to be such as might be the work of the poorest of botchers, but there is one line, peculiar to ed. 1619,—" Under pretence of outward seeming ill,"—which is greatly in Shakespeare's manner.

No. 47. Blundering.—Some of the evidences which have been adduced to show that the quartos were either very early productions of Shakespeare, or the works of elder writers, are really instances of unskilful and obtuse attempts to supply the place of imperfect notes or recollections.

No 48. A secondary title.—If so, All's Well that Ends Well, a comedy first heard of under that title in 1623, would seem to have the fairest claim, but it is not likely to have been written so early as 1598. Assuming that the mysterious letter E of the first folio refers to Ecclestone, All's Well must have been produced some time before August the 29th, 1611, on which day he is mentioned as belonging to a company with which Shakespeare had no connexion. It has been plausibly suggested that Cowley was another of the original performers in this drama, and that Parolles jocularly alludes to his name when he addresses the Clown as "good monsieur Lavatch," meaning, probably, *la vache.* The latter was an ancient English surname, " Sire Phylype la Vache knyht " being mentioned in a document of 1404 printed in Blount's Law Dictionary, ed. 1717, in v. *Will.*

No. 49. Richard the Third.—A Latin drama on the subject of Richard the Third, written by Dr. Thomas Legge, was acted at St. John's College, Cambridge. as early as the year 1579, and long continued in favour with scholastic audiences; but the earliest known English play on this reign, probably one only of several, is entitled the True Tragedie of Richard the Third, which was published in 1594. There is only one line in this production,—"a horse, a horse, a fresh horse,"—which bears a great resemblance to any in Shakespeare's, but, if the great dramatist adapted his from a previous work, it is possible that he remembered what the Moor says in Peele's Battle of Alcazar, 1594,—"a horse, a horse, villaine, a horse!" Another piece on the same history, one which has unfortunately long since perished, is thus alluded to in a little volume of excessive rarity entitled, A New Booke of Mistakes, or Bulls with Tales and Buls without Tales, but no lyes by any meanes, 1637,—" In the play of Richard the Third, the Duke of Buckingham, being betraid by his servant Banister, a messenger, comming hastily into the presence of the King to bring him word of the Duke's surprizall, Richard asking him, what newes?, he replyed,—My leige, the Duke of *Banister* is tane,=And *Buckingham* is come for his reward." The high probability of Shakespeare's drama having been founded on an anterior one encourages the belief that the first of the lines just given belonged, in its genuine form, to the older play. The former work was most likely produced in 1597, for, according to the title-page of the first quarto, which was entered at Stationers' Hall in October, it had then been "*lately* acted by the Right Honourable the Lord Chamberlaine his servants," and the company did not re-assume the title until the April of that year. The first edition is without the author's name, but the second appeared in 1598 as a drama written "by William Shakespeare," both published by Wise, who issued other editions in 1598 and 1602, and the copyright remained in his hands until June, 1603, when it was transferred to Matthew Law, who pub-lished the subsequent quartos of 1605 and 1612. Few plays of the time attained a greater popularity, and, amongst the evidences of this, may be specially noticed one in a poem entitled the Ghost of Richard the Third, 1614, in which the author makes the King refer to Shake-speare in the following elegant panegyric,—"To him that impt my fame with Clio's quill,=Whose magick rais'd me from oblivions den,=That writ my storie on the Muses' hill,=And with my actions dignifi'd his pen ;=He that from Helicon sends many a rill,=Whose nectared veines are drunke by thirstie men ;=Crown'd be his stile with fame, his head with bayes,=And none detract, but gratulate his praise."

No. 50. Dick Burbage.—Manningham, writing in the early part of the year 1602, alludes to Burbage's impersonation of Richard the Third, and in the Return from Parnassus, composed about the same time, he is introduced as selecting the character for an exercise to enable him to test the tragic powers of a Cambridge student. See the extracts from that play in the collection of Theatrical Evidences.

No. 51. Satirized.—That this was his intention would appear from an allusion in the Whipping of the Satyre, 1601,—"But, harke, I heare the cynicke satyre crie,=A man, a man, a kingdome for a man." In Parasitaster, 1606, Marston introduces, with slight variations, the line,—"Plots have I laid, inductions dangerous,"—evidently with an intention of ridiculing it.

No. 52. One of the first dramas.—The first appearance of a "new ballad" on the subject of a popular drama is a probable indication of its following shortly after the production of the latter on the stage. Edward White entered "a newe ballad of Romeo and Juliett" on the books of the Stationers' Company on August the 5th, 1596, the ballad having in all probability been written and published in consequence of the success of Shakespeare's drama produced in the early summer of that year. No copy of the former is now known to exist, but it seems that one came under the notice of Warton about the middle of the last century, as appears from the following note by that critic in the Appendix to the first volume of Johnson's edition of Shakespeare, 1765, —"a ballad is still remaining on the subject of Romeo and Juliet, which, by the date, appears to be much older than Shakespeare's time.

It is remarkable that all the particulars in which that play differs from the story in Bandello are found in this ballad."

No. 53.　Which was produced at the Curtain Theatre.—With respect to the evidences for the date of the production of the tragedy it is important to exclude that which has been supposed to be gathered from a notice in Weever's Epigrammes, 1599. It is stated by the author that these poems were written before he had attained the age of twenty,—"that twenty twelve months yet did never know,"—that is to say, before 1596 or 1597, as may be gathered from a note in Stow's Survey of London, ed. 1633, p. 900. This statement of early authorship must, however, be taken with some qualification, for one of the pieces, an elegy on the death of Spenser, could not have been composed before the date of publication, 1599. As Weever does not particularize which of the poems were written at the earlier period to which he refers, it is obvious that the elegy may not be the only one of a later date, and that it would be unsafe to conclude that the verses addressed to Shakespeare were amongst the former.

No. 54.　The play of the season.—It is scarcely necessary to observe that this notion is chiefly founded upon the well-known lines of Marston in the Scourge of Villanie, 1598. Then there is also the direct assertion of Danter, in 1597, that the tragedy had then been *often* played with " great applause," a statement which may be readily trusted, for otherwise that shifty publisher would not have incurred the risk and trouble attendant on the production of a surreptitious copy ; and it is worth notice that there is no other instance of the use of the word *often* in the title-pages of the life-time editions.

No. 55.　Several early allusions.—One telling line in the tragedy is quoted nearly literally by Porter in a drama acted in the same year,— " Ile rather have her married to her grave," Two Angrie Women of Abington, 1599. Allot, in his Englands Parnassus, 1600, cites Romeo and Juliet much oftener than he does any other of Shakespeare's plays ; but it may be worth observing that there are sophistications of the text in some of his extracts. Bodenham, in his Bel-vedere, also published in 1600, gives several quotations, and Nicholson, in the same year, in his Acolastus his After-Witte, 1600, garbles a line as follows,—" Thrust in a frozen corner of the North." The notion of Jove laughing at lovers' perjuries became a favourite idea. It is quoted in the comedy of How a Man may Choose a Good Wife from a Bad, 1602, and again by Day, in his Humour out of Breath, 1608. Romeo and Juliet is cited more than once in Decker's Satiro-Mastix, 1602, and other quotations from it are to be found in Blurt Master Constable, 1602, Achelley's Massacre of Money, 1602, and in Marston's Malcontent, 1604. There likewise appear to be some recollections of the tragedy in Ram Alley, first printed in 1611.

No. 56. As You Like It.—The comedy is not mentioned by Meres in 1598, and the earliest notice of it by name occurs in one of the volumes of the Stationers' registers, on a leaf which does not belong to the proper series of the registers, but contains irregular entries, prohibitions, &c. In this leaf, between two other notes, the first dated in May, 1600, and the other in January, 1603, is a notice of As You Like It, under August the 4th, "to be staied," this memorandum no doubt to be referred to the year 1600, Shakespeare's plays of Henry the Fifth and Much Ado about Nothing, and Ben Jonson's Every Man in his Humour, the only other plays noticed in that entry, having been licensed in the same month of that year. It is improbable that the prohibition would have been applied for or recorded after the publication of those dramas, and it may reasonably be concluded that the objection was removed shortly after the date of the entry, it being possibly of such doubtful validity that the clerk did not consider it advisable to make a formal note of it in the body of the register.

No 57. One of its ditties.—Although Morley does not expressly claim his title to the words that are set to music in his First Booke of Ayres, 1600, he neither in his dedication or preface insinuates that he had borrowed a single line, while the song of the "lover and his lass" is of the same description with others found in that work. This latter fact, taken by itself, would have thrown grave doubts on the Shakespearean authorship of that song, but that it was written by the great dramatist for the comedy is shown by its analogy to one found near the conclusion of the foundation-tale, Euphues Golden Legacie.

No. 58. This interesting plan.—There are numerous engravings which are stated to be plans of the metropolis as it existed in the latter part of the reign of Queen Elizabeth, but Norden's is the only one of undoubted accuracy. It was engraved by Pieter Vanden Keere in 1593, and that the survey was executed, or at least completed, in the same year, appears from the following memorandum,—*Joannes Norden Anglus descripsit anno* 1593,—being inserted after the list of references. The copy of the plan given in the text has been carefully taken from a fine example of the original engraving, but there have been several imitations of it, and one so-called facsimile, all of which are inaccurate and worthless. Underneath the engraving is the following list of streets and buildings,—*a.* Bushops gate streete; *b.* Papie; *c.* Alhallowes in the wall; *d.* S. Taphyns; *e.* Sylver streete; *f.* Aldermanburye; *g.* Barbican; *h.* Aldersgate streete; *i.* Charterhowse; *k.* Holborne Conduct; *l.* Chauncery lane; *m.* Temple barr; *n.* Holbourn; *o.* Grayes Inn lane; *p.* S. Androwes; *q.* Newgate; *r.* S. Jones; *s.* S. Nic. shambels; *t.* Cheap syde; *u.* Bucklers burye; *w.* Brodestreete; *x.* The stockes; *y.* The Exchannge; *z.* Cornehill; 2.® Colmanstreete; 3. Bassings hall; 4. Honnsditche; 5. Leaden hall; 6. Gratious streete; 7. Heneage

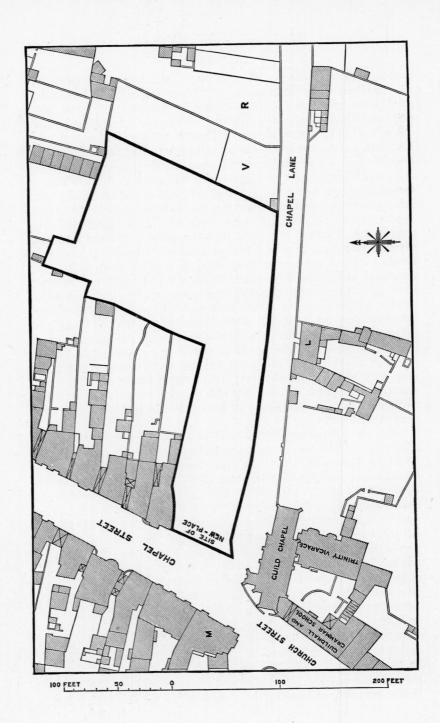

CHAPEL LANE

R

V

CHAPEL STREET

SITE OF
NEW - PLACE

M

CHURCH STREET

GUILD CHAPEL

TRINITY VICARAGE

GUILDHALL AND
GRAMMAR SCHOOL

100 FEET   50   0   100   200 FEET

house; 8. Fancshurche; 9. Marke lane; 10. Minchyn lane; 11. Paules; 12. Eastcheape; 13. Fleetstreete; 14. Fetter lane; 15. S. Dunshous; 16. Themes streete; 17. London stone; 18. Olde Baylye; 19. Clerkenwell; 20. Winchester house; 21. Battle bridge; 22. Bermodsoy⑧ streete. There are but two other surveys of London belonging to the reigns of Elizabeth and James which can be considered to be of any authority. One of these is a very large one of uncertain date, executed on wood and generally attributed to Aggas, which was first issued in the time of Queen Elizabeth and reproduced in the reign of her successor. The other plan is an engraving on a much smaller scale, published by Braun at Cologne in 1572 from a survey evidently made before 1561, the steeple of St. Paul's, destroyed in that year, being introduced. Neither of these maps appear to be copies of absolutely original surveys taken for the object of publication, there being indications which lead to the conclusion either that they are alterations of a plan which was executed some years previously, or that the latter was used in their formation. Aggas's is the only one of the time which represents the City with minuteness of detail, and it is unfortunate that its value should be impaired by this uncertainty. That there is much, however, in it on the fidelity of which reliance can be placed is unquestionable, but the survey of the locality in which the Theatre and Curtain were situated must have been taken before 1576, the year in which the former was erected, for the artist engaged in a plan on such a large scale could not have failed to have introduced so conspicuous a building, had it then been in existence.

No. 59. The absence of a genuine sketch of New Place.—The engraving of this house, as it is said to have existed in 1599, and published by Malone in 1790 as taken "from a drawing in the margin of an ancient survey made by order of Sir George Carew, afterwards Baron Carew of Clopton and Earl of Totness, and found at Clopton near Stratford-upon-Avon in 1786," is either a modern forgery, or at least no representation of Shakespeare's residence. Neither the Carews nor the Cloptons had any kind of interest in New Place in the latter part of the sixteenth century, and it is in the highest degree improbable that a representation of it should have been attached in 1599 to a plan of an estate that was situated in another locality. Malone's copy of the view was not taken from the original, but from a drawing furnished by Jordan, from whom another one, published by Ireland in 1795, was also derived. Although the latter has several important variations from the other, it is clearly meant for a copy of the same view, for Ireland describes it as having been taken "from an old drawing of one Robert Treswell's made in 1599 by order of Sir George Carew, afterwards Baron Carew of Clopton and Earl of Totness; it was found in Clopton House in 1786, and was in the possession of the late Mrs. Patriche, who was the last of the antient family of the Cloptons; the drawing, I am informed, is since lost or destroyed," Picturesque Views on the Avon, 1795, p. 197. The fact of such an early drawing being in existence in 1786 rests entirely on Jordan's vulnerable testimony, "diligent enquiries" instituted by the late R. B. Wheler a few years afterwards yielding no collateral evidence in support of his assertions. There was, however, at Clopton House a large plan of the family estates delineated by Robert Treswell alias Somersett in April, 1599, which in all probability suggested the pretended discovery of a con- temporary drawing of New Place on the margin of such a survey. It is an interesting map of those Clopton estates which were situated on the eastern side of the Avon, and could never have included the representa- tion of a house in Chapel Lane.

No. 60. Its continued popularity.—This may be concluded, not merely from the lines of Digges, but from the familiar quotations from the comedy in Heywood's Fayre Mayde of the Exchange, 1607, and in several other contemporary plays. It appears, from the title-page of the quarto edition, that Much Ado about Nothing had been performed by the Lord Chamberlain's company either in or before the year 1600; but the only early notice of the performance of the comedy yet dis- covered is that in the accounts of Lord Stanhope, in which it is stated that it was one of the dramas performed at Court in the year 1613. From a subsequent entry of the same date we learn that the comedy was also played under the appellation of Benedick and Beatrice. Digges alludes to those characters as the special favourites of the public, and there can be no doubt but that their adventures, and the ludicrous representation of the process of their conversion to mutual affection, attract the principal attention both of the reader and the audience, and that the impression made even by the inimitable blundering of the constables is but secondary.

No. 61. The constables.—Kemp was the original representative of Dogberry, and Cowley of Verges, as appears from the prefixes to a number of speeches in ed. 1600. Kemp, who is termed in a manuscript diary of February, 1600, "a player in interludes, and partly the Queenes Majesties-jester," appears to have left Shakespeare's company some time before the following August, his successor being another favourite clown, Robert Armin. That the latter at one time acted Dogberry is clear from the following passage in the Dedication to his Italian Taylor and his Boy, 1609,—"pardon, I pray you, the boldnes of a begger who hath been writ downe for an asse in his time, and pleades under *forma pauperis* in it still, notwithstanding his constableship and office."

No. 62. The eccentric biographer.—Aubrey, whose nature it was to blunder, had forgotten the names both of the character and the play, and speaks of 'the constable in a Midsummer's Night's Dream," adding

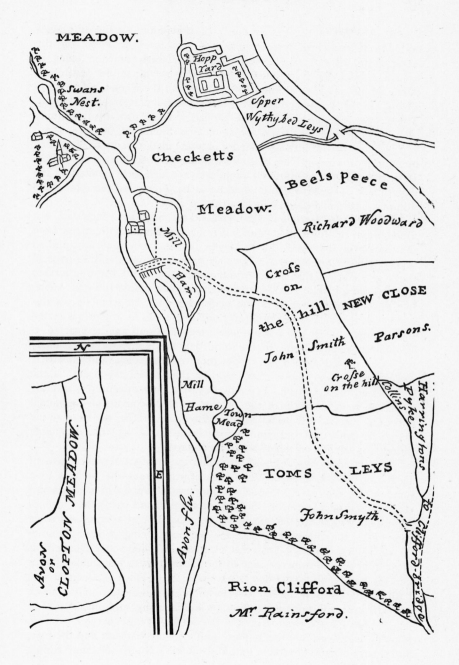

the gratuitous observation,—" I think it was Midsummer Night that he (Shakespeare) happened to lie there."

No. 63.   Taken from an old farce.—The earliest notice of this play yet discovered occurs in the register of the Stationers' Company for May the 2nd, 1594, when there was entered to a printer named Short, "a booke intituled a plesant conceyted hystorie called the Tayminge of a Shrowe," the published work bearing the title of,—" A Pleasant Conceited Historie called the Taming of a Shrew, as it was sundry times acted by the Right honorable the Earle of Pembrook his servants," 1594.   A reprint of this edition was published by Burby in 1596, in which year the play is thus alluded to by Sir John Harington, —"for the shrewd wife, read the booke of Taming a Shrew, which hath made a number of us so perfect, that now every one can rule a shrew in our country save he that hath her," Metamorphosis of Ajax, 1596. Burby retained his interest in the comedy until January the 22nd, 1607, when the copyright was transferred to Ling, the latter shortly afterwards, that is to say, in the following November, assigning it to John Smeth-wick, who never seems to have considered it worth a reprint.   It is certain that the note of the 22nd of January refers to the old play, a third edition of it having been published by Ling in 1607, and the Taming of *a* Shrew is also the title in both of the copyright entries made in 1642, after Smethwick's decease.   When that publisher issued Shakespeare's drama in 1631, the fact merely shows that he preferred it to the other, for in those days it is not likely that there would have been any one to interfere, and it is, moreover, not impossible that the proceeding had the sanction of his colleagues, the proprietors of the first folio.   The omission of the Taming of *the* Shrew in the copyright entry of 1623 can be plausibly accounted for.   If Hemmings and Condell had submitted at the Hall a list of the plays in their folio edition, and the registration had been confided to an official who had no special acquaintance with dramatic literature, and who merely went through the books to ascertain which of the pieces had already been entered, nothing would have been more natural than a mistake in regard to two works all but identical in title, or than his conclusion that the Third was the only Part of Henry the Sixth that had not been registered.

No. 64.   Some time before.—There is a passage in Greene's Menaphon, 1589, nearly identical with a line in the Taming of a Shrew, but simi-larities of this description are rarely of value in a question of date.   It is obvious to be as likely for the author of the comedy to have had Greene's words in his recollection, as for the latter to have quoted from the play.

No. 65.   Solely of conjecture.—It is true that Rowlands, in his Whole Crew of Kind Gossips, 1609, makes a would-be Petruchio say, in reference to his wife,—" The chiefest Art I have I will bestow— About a worke cald taming of the Shrow," but the language does not appear sufficiently precise to warrant the conclusion that the author intended a reference to Shakespeare's comedy. If he had contemplated such an allusion, it is most probable that the name of the play would have been given in Italics, the titles of songs alluded to in the same poem being so distinguished. Another possible test for the date of the Taming of the Shrew occurs in the edition of 1623, the speech of a person who is introduced as a Messenger being therein marked as delivered by one *Nicke*, Tooley being the only actor in the King's company to whom that sobriquet can be referred. He is first mentioned as belonging to that company in May, 1605, but the slight part to which his name is attached may have been undertaken by him when, if ever, he was one of the subordinate actors whose names would not be found in the list of 1603.

No. 66. The Merchant of Venice.—The earliest notice which has yet been discovered of this comedy is that in the Stat. Reg. of July, 1598. No tangible reason for assigning its composition to an earlier year has been produced, but it may be mentioned that there are passages in the drama of Wily Beguiled which bear considerable similarity to others in the Merchant of Venice. Then arises the usual difficulty, in those instances at least in which resemblances can hardly be accidental, of determining the priority of composition; and there is no reliable evidence that the former play was anterior to Shakespeare's. There is not, however, in Wily Beguiled a thought or expression of such peculiar excellence that any dramatist of the time could not have adopted it from recollection, unconsciously or otherwise, without incurring the smallest risk of a plagiarical imputation.

No. 67. The earliest editions.—The comedy was first printed in 1600 by Roberts, who, on October the 28th, transferred his interest in the copyright to Hayes, the latter issuing a second edition in the same year.

No. 68. Was produced in the season of 1601-2.—The obvious fact that the play was new to Manningham hardly bears on the question of date, for although he had evidently seen a performance of the Comedy of Errors, it would appear from his Diary that he was not an habitual frequenter of the theatres. As a rule, however, the dramas that were selected for representation at the Court and at the legal inns were pieces that had been recently introduced on the public stage. Shakespeare's comedy was certainly written not very long before the performance at the Middle Temple, as may be gathered from the use which Shakespeare has made of the song,—" Farewell, dear love,"—a ballad which had first appeared in the previous year in the Booke of Ayres composed by Robert Jones, fol., Lond. 1601. Jones does not profess to be the author of the words of this song, for he observes,—"If the ditties dislike thee, 'tis my fault that was so bold to publish the private contentments of divers gentlemen without their consents, though, I hope, not against their wils;" but there is every reason to believe that the verses referred to in Twelfth Night were first published in this work, a collection of new, not of old songs. As the tune and ballad were evidently familiar to Shakespeare, the original of the portion to which he refers in the comedy is here given,—"Farewel, dear love, since thou wilt needs be gon,=Mine eies do shew my life is almost done;—Nay, I will never die,=so long as I can spie;=There be many mo,=though that she do go.=There be many mo, I feare not;=Why, then, let her goe, I care not.—Farewell, farewell, since this I finde is true,=I will not spend more time in wooing you;=But I will seeke elswhere,=if I may find her there.=Shall I bid her goe?=What and if I doe?=Shall I bid her go and spare not?=Oh, no, no, no, no, I dare not."

No. 69. Most probably on January the Fifth.—That is, on Twelfth Night, 1602, a circumstance, however, which was thought so insufficient for the adoption of the title that liberty of substitution was freely offered. It is curious that Marston in 1607 should have chosen the second title of Twelfth Night for the appellation of one of his own comedies.

No. 70. In their beautiful hall.—The erection of the present hall, the interior of which measures a hundred by forty feet, was completed about the year 1577, the work occupying a long time, having been commenced at least as early as 1562. The exterior has undergone numerous changes since the time of Shakespeare, the old louvre having been removed many years ago, the principal entrance or porch rebuilt, and the whole exposed to a series of repairs and alterations. The main features of the interior, however, bear practically the same appearance which they originally presented. It is true that some of the minor accessories are of modern date, but the beautiful oaken screen and the elegant wood-carved roof suffice to convey to us a nearly exact idea of the room in which the humours of Malvolio delighted an Elizabethan audience.

No. 71. Leonard Digges.—This writer would seem to have blundered if he implies that Malvolio was in the same play with Benedick and Beatrice, as his words appear to indicate, but such an oversight on his part is almost incredible. It may be worth mentioning that Twelfth Night was acted, by the company to which the author had belonged, in February, 1623, under the title of Malvolio, and that it was performed at the Blackfriars Theatre after the children had left that establishment. The latter fact is gathered from its being included by Sir William Davenant amongst "some of the most ancient playes that were playd at Blackfriers," MS. dated in 1660, a list which also includes the Tempest, Measure for Measure, Much Ado about Nothing, Romeo and Juliet, Henry the Eighth, Lear, Macbeth and Hamlet.

No. 72. Love's Labour's Lost.—It appears from the title-page of the first edition of this comedy, 1598, that it was acted before Queen Elizabeth in the Christmas holidays of the previous year, and the locality of the performance is ascertained from the following entry in the accounts of the Treasurer of the Chamber,—" to Richard Brakenburie, for altering and making readie of soundrie chambers at Whitehall against Christmas, and for the plaies, and for making readie in the hall for her Majestie, and for altering and hanging of the chambers after Christmas daie, by the space of three daies, mense Decembris, 1597, viij.*li.* xiij.*s.* iiij.*d.*" The original impression of 1598 is not mentioned in the registers of the Stationers' Company, but, from the words "this last Christmas" on the title, it may be inferred that it was published early in that year. No notice of the copyright is found in those records until January, 1607, when it was transferred by Burby to Ling, who, in the following November, parted with the copyright to Smethwick, one of the proprietors of the first folio. This last-named publisher, however, seems to have preserved an independent ownership in the comedy, for it was published separately, under his auspices, in the year 1631, with the statement that it had been "acted by his Majesties Servants at the Blacke-Friers and the Globe."

No. 73. Had not been re-written.—If it had been, the fragments of the earlier drama could not have been found in the impression of 1598, which was evidently printed from a corrected manuscript of the first version, a copy in which altered lines might have been written on the margins and the additions inserted on paper slips. The dramatists of the Shakespearean period frequently amended their plays for special occasions, but with rare exceptions it was not their custom to re-write them. Love's Labour's Lost was probably retouched in anticipation of its performance before Queen Elizabeth in 1597, but the extent of the alterations then made was probably of a very limited character, for otherwise more traces of them might be expected to be found in the printed copy. In the following year Chettle was engaged in "mending" his play of Robin Hood "for the Court."

No. 74. Is mentioned by Tofte.—The earliest incidental notice of Shakespeare's comedy occurs in this writer's Alba, 1598.—" I *once* did see a play ycleped so." The term *once* does not here mean *formerly*, but merely, at some time or other. It does, nevertheless, imply that the representation of Love's Labour's Lost had been witnessed some little time before the publication of Alba in 1598, but the notice, however curious, is of no value in the question of the chronology, as we are left in doubt whether it was the original or the amended play that was seen by him. The poor fellow had escorted his lady-love to the theatre and, for some unexplained reason, she had taken an opportunity, during their visit, to reject his addresses. Tofte alludes to the comedy as Loves Labor Lost, and other early forms of the title are here given V.L.,—Loues labors lost, Loues Labor's lost, ed. 1598; Loue labors lost, Meres, 1598; Loves Labore lost, Cope's letter, 1605; Loues labour lost, Stat. Reg., 1607; Loues Labour lost, Catalogue in ed. 1623; Loues Labour's lost, head-lines ibid. It should be added that, although the early printers sometimes used the apostrophe unmeaningly, such a practice was altogether exceptional.

No. 75. Some years previously.—As a rule it is unsafe to pronounce a judgment on the period of the composition of any of Shakespeare's dramas from internal evidence, but the general opinion that the Two Gentlemen of Verona is one of the author's very earliest complete dramatic efforts may be followed without much risk of error. Admitting its lyrical beauty, its pathos, its humour, and its infinite superiority to the dramas of contemporary writers, there is nevertheless a crudity in parts of the action, one at least being especially unskilful and abrupt, which would probably have been avoided at a later period of composition. The only sixteenth-century notice of the play yet discovered is that given by Meres in his Palladis Tamia, 1598, where he alludes to it as the Gentlemen of Verona. It is not impossible that the last-mentioned title was the original designation of the comedy, one by which it was generally known in the profession : and, at a later period, Kirkman, who was intimately connected with the stage, inserts it, with a similar title, in a catalogue which first appeared in 1661.

No. 76. A Comedy of Errors.—The notice given in the text of the performance of this drama in the year 1594 is taken from a contemporary account of the Gray's Inn Revels which was published many years afterwards, 1688, under the title of the Gesta Grayorum. It appears, from the dedication, that this tract was printed exactly from the original manuscript, from which, observes the editor, it was "thought necessary not to clip anything, which, though it may seem odd, yet naturally begets a veneration upon account of its antiquity;" nor is there, indeed, the slightest reason for suspecting its authenticity. There is no evidence that any one but Shakespeare ever wrote a play bearing the exact title of the one named in this Gesta. The comedy is next mentioned, so far as is yet known, in the list given by Meres in 1598, where it is referred to under the abbreviated title of Errors; and there was a Historie of Error performed by the Children of Pauls in 1577, which latter has been generally considered, on the merest conjecture, to have been the play from which Shakespeare derived his knowledge of the incidents. It may be added that Manningham, in 1602, alludes to the Comedy of Errors as then familiar to play-goers, and that other references to it occur in Decker's Satiro-Mastix, 1602, in the same author's Newes from Hell, 1606, and in Anton's Philosophers Satyrs, 4to. Lond. 1616.

No. 77. The latter in probably that of 1595.—There being no record of Shakespeare's use of any particular impression, it follows that verbal tests are the only means of its identification. These are necessarily indefinite in all cases in which the variations between two editions could have been independently adopted by the poet himself. Thus, in the Life of Antonius, ed. 1595, p. 983, there is the genuine archaism, *gables*, which is altered to *cables* in eds. 1603 and 1612; but it is obvious to be likely that Shakespeare might have preferred the latter form when he adopted some of Plutarch's words in the speech of Menas to Pompey in Antony and Cleopatra, act ii., sc. 7. Again, in the life of Coriolanus, in the famous speech of Volumnia,—"how much more *unfortunately* then all the women living," eds. 1595 and 1603, Shakespeare has merely put the line into a blank verse, one which almost necessitates the alteration of the fourth word to *unfortunate*, which adjective happens to be found instead of the adverb in the 1612 edition of Plutarch. Such examples as these are assuredly indecisive. What is required is an expression, peculiar to Shakespeare and to certain editions of the translation of Plutarch, one which could not be reasonably attributed to the independent fancy of the great dramatist. There is such an expression in the 1579 and 1595 editions of the Life of Coriolanus,—"if I had feared death, I would not have come hither to have put my life in hazard, but prickt forward with *spite*, and desire I have to be revenged of them that thus have banished me." Whoever compares this passage with the speech of Coriolanus in the tragedy, act iv., sc. 5, and is told that the word *spite* is omitted in all the later Plutarch editions, may be convinced that Shakespeare must have read either the impression of 1579 or that of 1595, and probably the latter, which was one of the speculations of his fellow-townsman, the printer of the first edition of Venus and Adonis.

No. 78. Although successful.—This fact may be inferred from the entry in the Stationers' Registers of 1608, to Edward Blount of "his copie by the lyke aucthoritie, a booke called Anthony and Cleopatra." The "like authority" refers to the sanction of Sir George Buck and the company, as appears from the previous entry in the register, so that Blount was no doubt in possession of the copyright of the authentic play. If he printed it in 1608, no copy of the impression is now known to exist, the earliest edition which has been preserved being that in the collective work of 1623, of which Blount was one of the publishers; and although it is included in the list of tragedies "as are not formerly entred to other men" in the notice of the copyright of the folio, it is still not impossible that an earlier separate edition was issued by him.

There are indications that the list of non-entered plays was carelessly drawn up.

No. 79.   Did not equal.—This may be gathered from the rarity of contemporary allusions to it.   The only extrinsic notice of the tragedy during the author's life-time appears to be a curious one in Anton's Philosophers Satyrs, 1616, where the latter poet blames ladies for encouraging the performance of so vicious a drama by their presence.

No. 80.   King John.—Little is known respecting the external history of this drama.   It is noticed by Meres in 1598, and that it continued to be popular till 1611 may be inferred from the re-publication in that year of the foundation-play, the Troublesome Raigne of King John, as "written by W. Sh.," a clearly fraudulent attempt to pass off the latter in the place of the work of the great dramatist.   Shakespeare's King John was first printed in the folio of 1623, and it is worthy of remark that it is his only authentic play which is not named in any way in the registers of the Stationers' Company.   It is not even mentioned in the list of his dramas, amongst "soe manie of the said copies as are not formerly entred to other men," which is inserted under the date of November, 1623.   The older history of King John had appeared in the previous year with Shakespeare's name in full on the title, but it is not likely that so glaring an imposition could have led to the withdrawal of the genuine play from the above-mentioned list. The omission was probably accidental, the issues of the Troublesome Raigne in 1611 and 1622 leading to the inference that no copy of the more recent drama on the subject had then escaped from the theatre.

No. 81. Perhaps the best version.—The earliest record of the anecdote which is known to be extant is a manuscript note preserved in the University Library, Edinburgh, written about the year 1748, in which the tale is narrated in the following terms,—"Sir William Davenant, who has been call'd a natural son of our author, us'd to tell the following whimsical story of him;—Shakespear, when he first came from the country to the play-house, was not admitted to act; but as it was then the custom for all the people of fashion to come on horseback to entertainments of all kinds, it was Shakespear's employment for a time, with several other poor boys belonging to the company, to hold the horses and take care of them during the representation;—by his dexterity and care he soon got a great deal of business in this way, and was personally known to most of the quality that frequented the house, insomuch that, being obliged, before he was taken into a higher and more honorable employment within doors, to train up boys to assist him, it became long afterwards a usual way among them to recommend themselves by saying that they were Shakespear's boys." These latter may have been grown-up men, occasional helpers in such duties who are of any age being to this day called stable-boys, but the reference to the poet himself as a young lad is clearly erroneous. The next account in order of date is the following one in the Lives of the Poets, 1753, i. 130-1,—"I cannot forbear relating a story which Sir William Davenant told Mr. Betterton, who communicated it to Mr. Rowe; Rowe told it Mr. Pope, and Mr. Pope told it to Dr. Newton, the late editor of Milton, and from a gentleman who heard it from him 'tis here related. Concerning Shakespear's first appearance in the playhouse;—When he came to London, he was without money and friends, and being a stranger he knew not to whom to apply, nor by what means to support himself. At that time, coaches not being in use, and as gentlemen were accustomed to ride to the playhouse, Shakespear, driven to the last necessity, went to the playhouse door, and pick'd up a little money by taking care of the gentlemen's horses who came to the play. He became eminent even in that profession, and was taken notice of for his diligence and skill in it; he had soon more business than he himself could manage, and at last hired boys under him, who were known by the name of Shakespear's boys. Some of the players, accidentally conversing with him, found him so acute and master of so fine a conversation that, struck therewith, they and⊗ recommended him to the house, in which he was first admitted in a very low station, but he did not long remain so, for he soon distinguished himself, if not as an extraordinary actor, at least as a fine writer." This form of the story is nearly identical with that given in the text, the latter having been first printed by Dr. Johnson in 1765 as "a passage which Mr. Pope related as communicated to him by Mr. Rowe." There is yet another variation of the tale in an account furnished by Jordan in a manuscript written about the year 1783,— "some relate that he had the care of gentlemen's horses, for carriages at that time were very little used; his business, therefore, say they, was to take the horses to the inn and order them to be fed until the play was over, and then see that they were returned to their owners, and that he had several boys under him constantly in employ, from which they were called Shakespear's boys." It may be doubted if this be a correct version of any tradition current at the time it was written, Jordan having been in the habit of recording tales with fanciful additions of his own. Gentlemen's horses in Shakespeare's days were more hardy than those of modern times, so that stables or sheds for them, during the two hours the performance then lasted, were not absolute necessities; but it is worth recording that there were taverns, with accommodation for horses, in the neighbourhood of the Shoreditch theatres. A witness, whose deposition respecting some land in the immediate locality was taken in 1602, states that he recollected, in years previously, " a greate ponde wherein the servauntes of the earle of Rutland, and diverse his neighbours, inholders, did usually wasshe and water theire horses, which ponde was commonly called the earles horsepond." Another and much simpler version of the anecdote was published as follows in 1818,—" Mr. J. M. Smith said he had often heard his mother state that Shakspeare owed his rise in life, and his introduction to the theatre, to his accidentally holding the horse of a gentleman at the door of the theatre on his first arriving in London ; his appearance led to enquiry and subsequent patronage ;" Monthly Magazine, February, 1818, repeated in Moncrieff's Guide, eds. 1822, 1824. This form of the tradition is as old as 1785, the mother of J. M. Smith having been Mary Hart, who died in that year, and was a lineal descendant from Joan Shakespeare, the poet's sister.

No. 82. Horse-stealing.—Whoever it was, tavern-keeper or other, that, in those days, first entrusted Shakespeare with the care of a horse, must have seen honesty written in his face. The theatres of the suburbs, observes a puritanical Lord Mayor of London in the year 1597, are " ordinary places for vagrant persons, maisterless men, thieves, *horse-stealers*, whoremongers, coozeners, conycatchers, contrivers of treason and other idele and daungerous persons to meet together, and to make theire matches, to the great displeasure of Almightie God and the hurt and annoyance of her Majesties people, which cannot be prevented nor discovered by the governors of the Citie for that they ar owt of the Citiees jurisdiction," City of London MSS.

No. 83. In a very humble capacity.—A gentleman who visited the Church of the Holy Trinity at Stratford-on-Avon early in the year 1693 gives the following interesting notice of the traditional belief, then current in the poet's native county, respecting this incident in his life,— " the clarke that shew'd me this church is above eighty years old ; he says that this Shakespear was formerly in this towne bound apprentice to a butcher, but that he run from his master to London, and there was received into the play-house as a serviture, and by this meanes had an oppertunity to be what he afterwards prov'd." Although the parish-clerk was not so old as is here represented, William Castle, who was then clerk and sexton (Stratford Vestry-book), having been born in the year 1628 (Stratford Register), there can be no hesitation in receiving his narrative as the truthful report of a tradition accepted in the neighbourhood at the time at which it was recorded. Rowe, in his Account of the Life of Shakespear, published in 1709, assigns a special reason for the poet's departure from Stratford, but agrees with the clerk in the point now under consideration ; and a similar evidence appears in a later biographical essay of less authority and smaller value, published in a newspaper called the London Chronicle in 1769,—" his first admission into the playhouse was suitable to his appearance ; a stranger, and ignorant of the art, he was glad to be taken into the company in a very mean rank ; nor did his performance recommend him to any distinguished notice.' '

No. 84. With tapestries.—The Smiths' Company in 1440 paid three shillings and sixpence halfpenny for "cloth to lap abowt the pajent." On another occasion sixpence was invested in "halfe a yard of Rede Sea," Smiths' accounts, 1569, Coventry, MS. Longbridge. Two "pajiont clothes of the Passion" are mentioned in an inventory of the goods of the Cappers' company in the time of Henry the Eighth, and in a list of the theatrical appliances of another trading company, 1565, are included "three paynted clothes to hang abowte the pageant." Some of the pageant accounts include payments "for curten ryngus." It is probable that curtains were sometimes placed across the stage, so that a new scene might by their withdrawal be instantaneously presented to the audience. "Payd for makyng of the hooke to hang the curten on, iiij.*d.*," Accounts 2 Edward VI., MS. ibid.

No. 85. Hell-mouth.—"The little children were never so afrayd of hell mouth in the old plaies painted with great gang teeth, staring eyes and a foule bottle nose," Harsnet's Declaration, 1603. "Item, payd for payntyng hell hede newe, xx.*d.*; payde for kepynge hell hede, viij.*d.*; item, payd for kepyng of fyer at hell mothe, iiij.*d.*; payd to Jhon Huyt for payntyng of hell mowthe, xvj.*d.*; payd for makyng hell mowth and cloth for hyt, iiij.*s.*," accounts of the Drapers' pageant at Coventry, 1554–1567, printed in Sharp's Dissertation, 1825, pp. 61, 73. It may be observed that hell-mouth was one of the few contrivances in use in the ancient mysteries which were retained on the metropolitan stage in the time of Shakespeare, it being in the list of properties belonging to the Lord Admiral's Servants in 1599.

No. 86. Decorated sentry-boxes.—Noah's Ark must have been a magnificent example of this class of properties, as may be gathered from the following stage-direction in the Chester mystery of the Flood,— "then Noy shall goe into the arke with all his famylye, his wife excepte; the arke must be borded rounde about, and upon the bordes all the beastes and fowles hereafter rehearsed must be painted, that there wordes maye agree with the pictures," MS. Harl. 2013, fol. 23.

No. 87. The garments of skins.—"Adam and Eve aparlet in whytt lether," stage-direction in the old Cornish mystery of the Creation of the World. "Two cotes and a payre hosen for Eve stayned; a cote and hosen for Adam steyned," inventory of pageant costumes, 1565.

No. 88. Herod.—It would seem that the actor of this part wore a painted mask, there being several entries of payments in the accounts of the guilds for mending and painting his head. "Item, to a peyntour for peyntyng the fauchon and Herodes face, x.*d.*," accounts of the Smiths' company, 1477, MS. Longbridge. "Item, payd to a peynter for peyntyng and mendyng of Herodes heed, iiij.*d.*," costes on Corpus Christi day, 1516, MS. ibid. "Paid to John Croo for menddyng of Herrode hed and a mytor and other thynges, ij.*s.*," costes on Corpus

Crysty day, 1547, MS. ibid. "Payd to John Hewet, payntter, for dressyng of Errod hed and the faychon, ij.*s.*," paymentes for the pagent, 1554, MS. ibid. The faychon here mentioned was a painted sword, in addition to which Herod carried a sceptre and had an ornamented helmet and crest.

No. 89.   As far as costume.—"Item, paid for a gowen to Arrode, vij.*s.* iiij.*d.* ; item, paid for peynttyng and stenyng theroff, vj.*s.* iiij.*d.* ; item, paid for Arrodes garment peynttyng that he went a prossassyon in, xx.*d.* ; item, paid for mendyng off Arrodes gauen to a taillour, viij.*d.* ; item, paid for mendyng off hattes, cappus and Arreddes creste, with other smale geyr belongyng, iij.*s.*," accounts of the Smiths' company, 1490, MS. Longbridge. "Item paid for iij. platis to Heroddis crest of iron, vj.*d.* ; item, paid to Hatfeld for dressyng of Herodes creste, xiiij.*d.*," Smiths' accounts, 1495, MS. ibid. "Item, paid for colour and coloryng of Arade, iiij.*d.*," costes of Corpus day Christi, 1508, MS. ibid.

No. 90.   Painting the faces.—"Item, paid for gloves to the pleyares, xix.*d.* ; item, paid for pyntyng⊛ off ther fasus, ij.*d.*," accounts of the Smiths' Company, 1502, MS. Longbridge. "Payd to the paynter for payntyng the players facys, iiij.*d.*," paymentes on Corpus Crysty day, 1548, MS. ibid. The Longbridge manuscripts, so frequently cited in the present work, were erewhile preserved at the ancient seat of the Staunton family near Stratford-on-Avon, and were part of the largest and most valuable Warwickshire collection ever formed. This celebrated and important assemblage of rare volumes, engravings and drawings, all relating to that county, has now unfortunately been destroyed by fire. In many former years, through the kind liberality of its possessor,— John Staunton, esq., of Longbridge House,—every possible facility was given me for consulting those treasures, and I have at least the consolation of believing that they included no fact of interest, bearing on the history of the poet's life, that could have eluded my researches.

No. 91.   Appeared with sooty faces.—"The Black or Damned Souls had their faces blackened, and were dressed in coats and hose ; the fabric of the hose was buckram or canvas, of which latter material nineteen ells were used, nine of yellow and ten of black, in 1556, and probably a sort of party-coloured dress was made for them, where the yellow was so combined as to represent flames," Sharp's Dissertation on the Coventry Mysteries, 1825, p. 70. The following notices of these singular personages are taken from the accounts of the Coventry Guilds as quoted in the same work,—" 1537. Item, for v. elnes of canvas for shyrts and hose for the blakke soules at v.*d.* the elne, ij.*s.* j.*d.* ; item, for coloryng and makyng the same cots, ix.*d.* ; item, for makyng and mendynge of the blakke soules hose, vj.*d.*" In 1556, there is an entry of a payment which was made " for blakyng the sollys fassys."

No. 92. *Offered for sale.*—It was issued to the public some time previously to June the 12th, the following entry occurring in a manuscript diary quoted in Malone's Inquiry, 1796, p. 67,—" 12th of June, 1593, for the Survay of Fraunce, with the Venus and Athonay per Shakspere, xij.*d.*"

No. 93. *Its voluptuous character.*—" I have convay'd away all her wanton pamphlets, as Hero and Leander, Venus and Adonis," A Mad World my Masters, 1608. Davies, in his Papers Complaint, which will be found in his Scourge of Folly, 1610, makes Paper admit the superlative excellence of Shakespeare's poem, but at the same time censure its being " attired in such bawdy geare." It is also stated that " the coyest dames in private read it for their closset-games." In the Dumbe Knight, 1608, the lawyer's clerk is represented as terming it " maides philosophie." The stanza commencing with the word *fondling*, ll. 229–234, is quoted in the play last named and also in Heywood's Fayre Mayde of the Exchange, 1607.

No. 94. *Favourably received.*—The second edition appeared before June the 25th, 1594, on which day Field assigned the copyright to Harrison. It was reprinted oftener in Shakespeare's lifetime than any one of the plays, but there was no such edition as that of Harrison's, 1600, registered in some lists on the erroneous authority of a manuscript title-page of the last century. There are numerous early allusions to Venus and Adonis, as well as occasional quotations from it, but the most considerable number of the latter will be found in Bodenham's Belvedere, 1600, and in the Englands Parnassus of the same year.

No. 95. *A ready and natural defence.*—As in Spenser's dedication of Mother Hubberds Tale to the Lady Compton in 1591, probably the most analogous to Shakespeare's of all compositions of the kind,— " having often sought opportunitie by some good meanes to make knowen to your ladiship the humble affection and faithfull duetie which I have alwaies professed, and am bound to beare, to that house from whence yee spring, I have at length found occasion to remember the same by making a simple present to you of these my idle labours; which, having long sithens composed in the raw conceipt of my youth, I lately amongst other papers lighted upon, and was by others, which liked the same, mooved to set them foorth. Simple is the device, and the composition meane, yet carrieth some delight, even the rather because of the simplicitie and meannesse thus personated. The same I beseech your ladiship take in good part, as a pledge of that profession which I have made to you, and keepe with you untill with some other more worthie labour I do redeeme it out of your hands, and discharge my utmost dutie."

No. 96. *Made the largest purchase.*—The original conveyance, as well as an intermediate draft of it, are preserved at Stratford. In the latter document, which is written on thirteen large sheets of pot-paper, the final covenant is omitted, and the variations from the engrossment are either trivial or erroneous.

No. 97. Nor is there a probability.—The mere circumstance of there having been a Fool introduced into the play then in course of representation is of course a decisive proof that it was not Shakespeare's Henry the Eighth, and there are other incidental passages that lead to the same conclusion. If it had been, the fire must have commenced before the termination of the first act, and there would almost certainly have been, amongst the elaborate stage-directions of ed. 1623, some reference to "the matting of the stage," which is so specially noticed by Wotton as then being an extraordinary novelty. Then, again, it is to be inferred, from the records of the calamity, that the acting copies of the play then in hand could hardly have been rescued from the flames.

No. 98. The new drama.—Wotton, in a letter written only three days after the fire, speaks of it as "a new play called *All is True,* representing some principal pieces of the raign of Henry 8." It is mentioned in two other accounts of the calamity as "the play of Henry the 8th," the latter being most likely a second title, one that may have originally followed the terms of that given by Rowley to When You See Me You Know Me,—"The famous Chronicle Historye of King Henry the Eighth." It clearly appears, from the burden of the sonnet that was written on the occasion, that Wotton gave the main title correctly.

No. 99. Some of the historical incidents.—Several dramas on historical events of the reign of Henry the Eighth were produced in England in the time of Shakespeare. In the years 1601 and 1602 the subject attained a singular popularity in the hands of Henslowe's company. In June of the former year Henry Chettle was occupied in "writtinge" a play entitled Cardinal Wolsey's Life, which was produced with great magnificence so far as regards the apparel of the performers, by the Earl of Nottingham's players, in the following August. An entry of £21 for velvet, satin, and taffeta, proves, regard being had to the then value of money, how expensively the characters in the play were attired. This drama was so successful that it was immediately followed by another entitled the Rising or the First part of Cardinal Wolsey, in the composition of which no fewer than four writers, Drayton, Chettle, Munday, and Wentworth Smith, were engaged. It seems to have been licensed in September, 1601, as "the remainder of Carnowlle Wollseye," words which imply that it was considered supplementary to Chettle's first play on the subject. The amendment of the first part in 1602 was immediately followed by the appearance of a continuation in which Will Summers, the celebrated jester, was introduced. The name of the author of this second part is not stated, but it is not impossible that it was written by Samuel Rowley, who had been attached to Henslowe's company as early as the year 1599. Certain it is that the character of Summers is a prominent one in that author's vulgar comedy of When You See Me You Know Me, published by Butter in 1605, and entered on the registers of the Stationers' Company in February, 1604–5, as "the enterlude of K. Henry the 8th." Butter's several reprints, his interest in the copyright until 1639, taken in conjunction with the statement in those registers under the date of November the 8th, 1623, decisively prove that the entry last quoted does not refer to Shakespeare's play. According to a manuscript on the state of Ireland, written about the year 1604, "the earle of Kildare dyed in prison in England, where he lyved a longe tyme, and his brothers and eldest sonne deprived of their lyves by the synister practizes of Cardynall Wolsey, sett forth at lardge in the Irishe Chronicle, and of late acted publiquely upon the stage in London, in the tragidie of the life and death of the said Wolsey, to tedious to be reported to your Majestie." This enumeration of dramas on the incidents of the same reign may be concluded with a notice of the Chronicle History of Thomas Lord Cromwell, which was first published as "written by W. S." in 1602. It had then most likely been recently produced by Shakespeare's company, an entry of the copyright in the August of that year mentioning the play "as yt was lately acted by the Lord Chamberleyn his servantes." An assignment of the copyright was entered in December, 1611, the second impression, however, not appearing till 1613, the author of the play in both instances being denoted by the above-mentioned initials. The drama of Lord Cromwell was attributed to Shakespeare by the publisher of the third folio in 1664, but it is hardly necessary to observe that it has no pretensions to the claim of so high a distinction.

No. 100. Any other resemblance.—Excepting that both were framed with a view to spectacular display, as appears from the accounts of the fire, and from the elaborate stage-directions in the first edition of Shakespeare's drama, the somewhat irregular construction of the latter may be attributed to the circumstance of some of the incidents being practically subservient to the accessories of the stage.

No. 101. The two last being so dilatory.—The words of the ballad admit of several interpretations, and it is difficult, if not impossible, to ascertain the writer's exact meaning. That which occurs in the text is not given with undue confidence, but it is in a measure supported by the contemporary evidence of the risk that was incurred by those who were in the theatre at the time of the conflagration. The appearance of a fool in the represented play is, however, the only point of the slightest importance, and that fact seems to be decisively established by the lines in question. So far from there being evidence that the Globe was one of those theatres in which a Fool was a regular appendage, the very contrary may be inferred from a dialogue in Greene's Tu Quoque.

No. 102. The Prologue.—It has been suggested that there is here an allusion to Rowley's production on the same reign, a drama in which no regard is paid to chronological order or accuracy. In the latter play, certainly a "merry bawdy one," Summers, the jester, a prominent character, is a "fellow in a long motley coat, guarded with yellow," and the noise of targets was heard in a street brawl in which the King is vigorously engaged in combat with a ruffian named Black Will. As, however, this piece belonged to a rival establishment, it is more likely that the prologue refers to one containing similar incidents, perhaps that which was in the course of performance on the day of the fire. A second edition of the former play appeared in 1613, and it may then have been revived at the Fortune.

No. 103. This theory of a late date.—There does not appear to be a sufficient reason for attributing the composition of Henry the Eighth to the reign of Elizabeth. The main reason for that opinion is found in the termination of Cranmer's prophecy, the sudden reversion in which to his eulogy on Elizabeth has elicited the impression that the portion of his harangue which refers to James was an insertion that was written some years after the play originally appeared. But it should be observed that the whole of that portion is a ramification from the introductory encomium on the Queen, the sentiments in the latter having in all probability been framed with a view to gratify the King by their subsequent application to him and without reference to the author's own views. By the obliquity of the panegyric the poet adroitly softened and naturalized its intrinsic extravagance. The prophecy was evidently composed for the ear of one of those sovereigns, and very unlikely for that of Elizabeth, who would hardly have considered the subsequent notice of an aged princess neutralised by the previous flattery, or have complacently endured the reference to her own decease. The known character of that sovereign leads us to believe that either of these allusions would have been most distasteful to her. Again, that the play, as we now have it, was not written until 1606, may be gathered from the reference to the new nations, which is believed to relate to the American colonies, the settlement and chartering of which had but then commenced. There is another possible evidence in the allusion to the strange Indian. In 1611, Harley and Nicolas, the commanders of two vessels in an expedition to New England, returned to this country, bringing with them five savages. One of these, who was named Epenow, remained in England until 1614, was distinguished for his stature, and publicly exhibited in various parts of London.

No. 104. By this disagreeable innovation.—There are several critics who take another view, and, relying in a great measure on metrical percentages, would have us believe that all speeches redolent with this peculiarity must have been written by one or other of those later contemporaries of Shakespeare who were specially addicted to its use. Under this direction it follows that Wolsey's celebrated farewell to all his greatness, as well as a large part of the scene in which it occurs, are henceforth to be considered the composition of some other author. So also, by the like process of reasoning, must the last speeches of Buckingham, as exquisitely touching as any in Shakespeare, the death-scene of Katharine, the magnificent dialogue between Wolsey and Cromwell, as well as Cranmer's prophecy, be eliminated from his works. As to the theories recently promulgated, that some contemporary dramatist could, and that Shakespeare could not, have written those passages, neither one nor the other is likely to be ultimately sustained. It is true that in Henry the Eighth there is much unwelcome variation from the poet's usual diction, but surely the play as a whole will commend itself to most readers as one that could only have emanated from Shakespeare's laboratory. This much can be admitted without ignoring the unavoidable suspicion that the drama, in the form in which it has come down to us, has been tampered with by the players or their confederates. But there is no tangible evidence to show the precise extent or nature of the modifications that may thus have been induced, and, in its absence, individual opinions can never be decisive. The latter, moreover, rest too frequently upon the treacherous foundation of a belief in the power of assigning a definite limit to the writer's mutations in style and excellence.

No. 105. Old Mr. Lowin.—It would seem, from a dialogue in the comedy of Knavery in all Trades, 1664, that Taylor and Pollard acted with Lowin in Henry the Eighth at an early period, but the notice must refer to the performances of it which took place some time after the death of the author. Neither of the two first-named actors joined the King's company until after the year 1616.

No. 106. Told by Fuller.—In his Worthies, ed. 1662. "A company of litle boyes were by their schoolmaster not many years since appointed to act the play of King Henry the Eighth, and one who had no presence, but an absence rather, as of a whyning voyce, puiling spirit, consumptionish body, was appointed to personate King Henry himselfe onely because he had the richest cloaths, and his parents the best people of the parish : but when he had spoke his speech rather like a mouse then a man, one of his fellow actors told him,—If you speake not Hoh with a better grace, your Parliament will not give you a penny of mony," old jest-book, MS. Sloane 384. There is another copy of the anecdote in the Fragmenta Aulica, 1662, and the vigour of the exclamation long continued to be one of the professional traditions. "Like our stage Harry the Eighth, cry out Hough! Hough!", Memoirs of Tate Wilkinson, ed. 1790, i. 195, referring to a period some time about the year 1758.

No. 107. Where it is recorded.—"Item, paid to the players of Coventrie by the commaundement of Mr. Mayer and thaldremen, x.*s.*," Bristol Corporation MSS., December, 1570. They were at Abingdon in the same year and at Leicester in 1569 and 1571, but there is no record of the nature of their performances. Those at Coventry were no doubt of a more impressive character, the players there having the advantage of elaborate appliances. "Item, paide at the commaundiment of master mayor unto Mr. Smythes players of Coventree, iij.*s.*," Abingdon Corporation MSS., 1570. There can be little doubt that *Mr.* in this last extract is an error for *the.*

No. 108. To live another age.—In a subsequent verse Lucrece is represented as "acting her passions on our stately stage," so that it may be that Drayton is referring to some drama on the subject, although both previously and afterwards he is speaking exclusively of poems. Heywood, in his Apology for Actors, 1612, sig. G, most likely refers to a play older than his own time on the Rape of Lucrece. Drayton's lines are not found in any copies of the Matilda published after the year 1596, a circumstance which has been the occasion of several conjectures; but no inference can be safely deduced from the omission, that writer having been in the constant habit of making extensive alterations in his texts for new editions.

No. 109. It was received.—"Who loves chaste life, there's Lucrece for a teacher;=Who lis't read lust there's Venus and Adonis," Freeman's Runne and a Great Cast, 1614. There are numerous quotations from Lucrece in Bodenham's Belvedere and the England's Parnassus in 1600, as well as several in Nicholson's Acolastus published in the same year. Notices of the poem occur in Barnfield's Poems in Divers Humors, 1598; Palladis Tamia, 1598; Weever's Epigrammes, 1599; England's Mourning Garment, 1603; and in the Return from Parnassus, 1606. That which Sir John Suckling, in the time of Charles the First, calls his "Supplement of an imperfect Copy of Verses of Mr. Wil. Shakespears," appears to commence with his own alterations of two stanzas in Lucrece, the rest being stated by himself to be entirely new compositions.

No. 110. Christopher Sly.—The Christian as well as the surname of this personage are taken from the older play, but there was a Christopher Sly who was a contemporary of Shakespeare's at Stratford-on-Avon, and who is mentioned in Greene's manuscript diary under the date of March the 2nd, 1615–16. This is a singular coincidence, even if it be not considered a slight indication that the author of the Taming of a Shrew may have been a Warwickshire man.

No. 111. The author.—Heywood here appears to take it for granted that Shakespeare was the author of the whole of the Passionate Pilgrim, but he does not appear to have examined the volume with any degree of care. Had he done so, he would hardly have refrained from enhancing his complaint against Jaggard by observing that, independently of the two epistles, the latter had also appropriated five other poems from the Troia Britanica.

No. 112. The Earls of Derby and Pembroke.—Henslowe, a great buyer of original plays, was in the habit of lending them to various bodies of performers. Thus the Jew of Malta, one of his stock pieces, was acted by at least three separate and two conjunctive companies previously to the departure of the Lord Chamberlain's servants from his theatres in June, 1594. As Henslowe's Diary is not a perfect record of his theatrical doings, it is not improbable that the players of Lords Derby and Pembroke were acting at the Rose or at Newington, under some arrangement with him, in the spring of that year.

No. 113. Or in any other.—According to Aubrey, that most unreliable of all the early biographers, Shakespeare "understood Latine pretty well, for he had been in his younger yeares a schoolmaster in the countrey." It is very unlikely that there can be any truth in this unsupported statement, and it is, indeed, inconsistent with what Aubrey himself previously observes respecting Shakespeare's early life.

No. 114. Was not extended.—There is no positive evidence of this fact, but it is one which is found to be the case at this time in so many other towns that its accuracy in respect to Stratford-on-Avon may be fairly assumed, supported, as it is, by local probabilities. It is, for instance, almost impossible that the players of Lord Chandos, who were continually performing in the neighbourhood, should have visited that town merely on the single recorded occasion in the autumn of 1582.

No. 115. In the history.—This narrative is or was preserved in a manuscript written by Sadler's daughter, but it is here taken from extracts from the original which were published in the Holy Life of Mrs. Elizabeth Walker, 1690.

No. 116. That of a glover.—This appears not only from the often quoted entry in the Corporation books of June, 1556, but from a recognizance in the Controlment Roll of the twenty-ninth of Elizabeth, the latter showing that John Shakespeare was known in Stratford-on-Avon as a glover thirty years afterwards, 1586.

No. 117. One hundred and seven acres of land.—It may be that this acquisition is referred to by Crosse in his Vertues Common-wealth, 1603, when he speaks thus ungenerously of the actors and dramatists of the period,—" as these copper-lace gentlemen growe rich, purchase lands by adulterous playes, and not fewe of them usurers and extortioners, which they exhaust out of the purses of their haunters, so are they puft up in such pride and selfe-love as they envie their equalles and scorne theyr inferiours." Alleyn had not at this time commenced his purchases of land at Dulwich.

No. 118.   Was soon forgotten.—Otherwise he would have been at the pains to have made arrangements for having the offensive allusions in the Groatsworth of Wit cancelled in the second edition of that work in 1596.   Unfortunately no copy of the first edition is now known to exist, and we can only infer, from Chettle's apology and from the subsequent impressions containing invidious references to Shakespeare and others, that there is a high probability of Greene's tract having been reprinted without alteration.

No. 119.   Nicholas Rowe.—This author, who was born in 1673, was educated at Highgate and Westminster.   He afterwards entered at the Middle Temple, but in a few years, on his accession to a competent fortune, the study of the law was gradually superseded by his taste for dramatic composition.   He had a great esteem for Betterton, and wrote an epilogue on the occasion of that venerable actor's celebrated benefit in 1709, the same year in which the Life of Shakespeare appeared.   The second edition of the last-named work was published in 1714, but it is unfortunately a mere reprint of the first.   Rowe died in 1718.

No. 120.   Who consider it decorous or reasonable.—No one likes to admit the genuineness of either Titus Andronicus or the First Part of Henry the Sixth, and, with the view of removing the former from consideration, I ventured to suggest, many years ago, that the text which has been preserved is that of an earlier drama on the same history. This theory, as I now see, is foolish and untenable.

No. 121.   This Gilbert.—In the Coram Rege rolls, 1597, Gilbert Shackspere, who appears as one of the bail in the amount of £19 for a clockmaker of Stratford, is described as a haberdasher of the parish of St. Bridget ; but as his name does not occur in the subsidy lists of the period, it is not unlikely that he was either a partner with, or assistant to, some other tradesman of the same occupation.   It was not unusual in former days to refer to an assistant in a shop under the trading appellation of his employers.   Gilbert was at Stratford on May the 1st, 1602, on which day he received the acknowledgment of an important conveyance of land on behalf of his brother, a fact which may be held to show that he enjoyed the poet's confidence.   He is next heard of as the witness to a local deed of 1609, one in which his signature appears so ably written that it may be safely concluded that he had been educated at the Free-School.   In the Stratford register of 1612 is the notice of the burial of " Gibertus Shakspeare, adolescens," but although the last term is of somewhat indefinite application, it is not likely that a person over forty-five years of age would have been so designated, and the entry refers probably to a son.   If the latter theory be correct, it should be observed that the form of the entry warrants a doubt of legitimacy.   Scarcely any particulars have reached us respecting

A Signature of the Poet's Brother, with others of his Relatives, Connexions and Friends.

Shakespeare's brothers and sisters. Joan being the only one of them mentioned in his will, it is generally assumed that none of the óthers were living when that document was prepared, and, from the number of memorials given to personal friends, it would have been strange if relatives had been overlooked. But the "second-best bed" was an afterthought, and such deductions are to be received with hesitation. Gilbert, however, could at any rate have been then the only unmentioned survivor, and Malone, who seldom or never speaks at random, but relying no doubt on substantial evidence, stated in 1790 that he "certainly died before his son." A few claims on the parts of modern families to descent from one of Shakespeare's brothers have been proffered, but they are unsupported by allegations worthy the name of evidence. It is, moreover, most probable that if any of them, or any of their issue, had been living at the time of the death of Judith Quiney's only surviving child in 1639, the fact would have transpired in one or other of the subsequent transactions respecting the legal rights under the terms of the last devise of estates in the poet's will.

No. 122. The Winter's Tale.—In the office-book of Sir Henry Herbert is the following curious and interesting entry,—"For the king's players;—an olde playe called Winters Tale, formerly allowed of by Sir George Bucke, and likewyse by mee on Mr. Hemmings his worde that there was nothing prophane added or reformed, thogh the allowed booke was missinge; and therefore I returned itt without a fee, this 19 of August, 1623," ap. Malone, ed. 1790, p. 226. Now Sir George Buck obtained a reversionary grant of the office of the Master of the Revels in 1603, expectant on the death of Tylney, who died in October, 1610; but he did not really succeed to the office, as is shown by documents at the Rolls, before August, 1610, in short, a few weeks previously to the decease of Tylney. Sir George, as Deputy to the Master, licensed dramas for publication long before the year last-mentioned, as appears from several entries in the books of the Stationers' Company; and that he could also have passed them for acting would seem clear from the above entry, the words "likewyse by mee" showing that the comedy had been allowed by Herbert before he had succeeded to the office of Master. In the absence of direct evidence to the contrary, it seems, however, unnecessary to suggest that the Winter's Tale was one of the dramas that passed under Buck's review during the tenancy of Tylney in the office; and it may fairly, at present, be taken for granted that the comedy was not produced until after the month of August, 1610. This date is sanctioned, if not confirmed, by the allusion to the song of *Whoop, do me no harm, good man,* the music to which was published by William Corkine, as one of his "private inventions," in his Ayres to Sing and Play to the Lute and Basse Violl, fol., Lond., 1610. It would seem from Wilson's Cheerful Ayres,

1660, that he was the original composer of the music to the Lawn song, another evidence for the late date of the play, that celebrated musician having been born in June, 1595. See Wood's Fasti, fol., Lond., 1691, col. 725.

No. 123. By Decker and Chettle.—It is their play which is most likely alluded to in the following passage in Cawdray's Treasurie or Store-house of Similies, ed. 1600, p. 380,—"as an actor in a comedie or tragedy, which sometimes resembleth Agamemnon, somtimes Achilles, somtimes their enemie Hector, sometimes one mans person, sometimes another; even so an hypocrite wil counterfeit and seeme sometimes to be an honest and just man, sometimes a religious man, and so of al conditions of men, according to time, persons and place." Decker and Chettle's play of Troilus and Cressida, afterwards termed Agamemnon, is thus mentioned in Henslowe's Diary,—"Lent unto Thomas Downton, to lende unto Mr. Dickers and Harey Cheattell, in earneste of ther boocke called Troyeles and Creassedaye, the some of iij.*li.*, Aprell 7 daye, 1599.—Lent unto Harey Cheattell and Mr. Dickers, in parte of payment of ther boocke called Troyelles and Cresseda, the 16 of Aprell, 1599, xx.*s.*—Lent unto Mr. Dickers and Mr. Chettell the 26 of Maye, 1599, in earneste of a boocke called the tragedie of Agamemnon, the some of xxx.*s.*—Lent unto Robarte Shawe the 30 of Maye, 1599, in full paymente of the boocke called the tragedie of Agamemnone, to Mr. Dickers and Harey Chettell, the some of iij.*li.* v.*s.*—Paid unto the Master of the Revelles man for lycensynge of a boocke called the tragedie of Agamemnon the 3 of June, 1599, vij.*s.*" It is clear from these entries that in this play, as in Shakespeare's, Chaucer's story was combined with the incidents of the siege of Troy. The allusion to the interchange of presents between Troilus and Cressida in the old comedy of Histriomastix, first published in 1610 but written before the death of Elizabeth, may refer to an episode that had been rendered popular by its treatment in the above-named play. At all events, no allusive inference can be safely drawn from the probably accidental use of the words *shakes* and *speare*.

No. 124. Is not likely to refer.—There is a strong confirmation of this in the following all but positive allusions to three of Shakespeare's works, including Troilus and Cressida, in a rare poem entitled Saint Marie Magdalens Conversion, 1603,—"Of Helens rape and Troyes beseiged towne,=Of Troylus faith, and Cressids falsitie,=Of Rychards stratagems for the english crowne,=Of Tarquins lust and Lucrece chastitie,=Of these, of none of these my muse nowe treates,=Of greater conquests, warres and loves she speakes." The preface to the Conversion is dated "this last of Januarie, 1603," but, as the book itself bears the date of that year, it may be fairly assumed that 1603, not 1603-4, is intended.

No. 125.   Appear to exult.—That the manuscript was obtained by some artifice may be gathered from the use of the word *scape* in the preface to the first edition.

No. 126.   The printers had received.—That the second impression is the one referred to in the registers of the Stationers' Company of January the 28th, 1609, may, perhaps, also be inferred from the omission in both of the word *famous.*

No. 127.   Originally known under the title of the Moor of Venice.—This appears from the entries of 1604 and 1610, hereafter quoted, and from the record of the performance of the tragedy at Whitehall on May the 20th, 1613.   The author of the elegy on Burbage speaks of that famous actor as unrivalled in the character of "the grieved Moor," and the earliest instance of the double appellation occurs in the title-page of the first edition, here given V.L.,—"The Tragœdy of Othello, The Moore of Venice.   As it hath beene diuerse times acted at the Globe, and at the Black-Friers, by his Maiesties Seruants.   Written by William Shake-speare.   London, Printed by N. O. for Thomas Walkley, and are to be sold at his shop, at the Eagle and Child, in Brittans Bursse.   1622."   The second title was the one under which the play was usually acted during the whole of the seventeenth century.

No. 128.   Is first heard of.—It may be well to remark that a passage in the Newe Metamorphosis or a Feaste of Fancie, which has been adduced to support an earlier date for Othello, is of no critical value in the enquiry.   Although the date of 1600 appears on the title-page of that poem, the manuscript itself contains a distinct allusion by name to Speed's Theatre of Great Britaine, a work first published in 1611.   The first quarto contains several irreverent expressions which are either modified or omitted in the later editions, a proof, as Mr. Aldis Wright observes, "that the manuscript from which it was printed had not been recently used as an acting copy," that is to say, since 1606, when the Statute of James against profanity in stage-plays was enacted.

No. 129.   In 1604.—There are some faint reasons for conjecturing that the tragedy was not written before the nineteenth of March in this year. The twelfth Public Act which was passed in the first Parliament of James the First, some time between March 19th and July 7th, 1604, was levelled "against conjuration, witchcrafte and dealinge with evill and wicked spirits."   In the course of this Act it is enacted that, "if any person or persons shall, from and after the feaste of Saint Michaell the Archangell next comminge, take upon him or them, *by witchcrafte, inchantment, charme or sorcerie,* to tell or declare in what place any treasure of golde or silver should or might be founde or had in the earth or other secret places, or where goodes or thinges loste or stollen should be founde or be come, *or to the intent to provoke any person to unlawfull love,*" then such person or persons, if convicted, "shall for the said offence suffer imprisonment by the space of one whole yere without baile or maineprise, and once in everie quarter of the saide yere shall, in some markett towne upon the markett day, or at such tyme as any faire shal be kept there, stand openlie uppon the pillorie by the space of sixe houres, and there shall openlie confesse his or her error and offence." It seems probable that part of the first Act of Othello would not have assumed the form it does, had not the author been familiar with the Statute, in common with the public of the day, the Duke referring to such a law when he tells Brabantio that his accusation of the employment of witchcraft shall be impartially investigated. Although the offence named in the Statute refers not to the use of charms to make people love one another, but to the employment of them for the provocation of unlawful love, yet still this may be said to have an oblique application to the story of the tragedy in the surreptitious marriage of Othello. By the Act of James, a previous one, 5 Eliz. c. 16, of a similar character, was "utterlie" repealed, and the object of the second Act appears to have been to punish the same offence more severely.

No. 130. One William Bishop.—"Catherine and Dezdimonye, the daughters of William Bishoppe, were baptised the xiiij.th of September," Registers of St. Leonard's, Shoreditch, 1609. This is not the only instance of the adoption of a theatrical name. "Comedia, daughter of William Johnson, player," bur. reg. of St. Giles's, Cripplegate, 1592-3. The burial of Juliet, a daughter of Richard Burbage, is recorded in the Shoreditch register for 1608, but it clearly appears from other entries that her real name was Julia.

No. 131. The first performer of Iago.—According to Wright's Historia Histrionica, 1699, p. 4, Taylor was distinguished in this part, but probably not until after the death of Shakespeare. The insertion of Taylor's name in the list of the Shakespearean actors in ed. 1623 merely proves that he had been one of them in or before that year.

No. 132. A curious tradition.—"I'm assur'd, from very good hands, that the person that acted Iago was in much esteem of a comedian, which made Shakespear put several words and expressions into his part, perhaps not so agreeable to his character, to make the audience laugh, who had not yet learnt to endure to be serious a whole play,"—Gildon's Reflections on Rymer's Short View of Tragedy, 1694.

No. 133. The words of Meres.—Those who believe that the Sonnets, as we now have them, comprise two long poems addressed to separate individuals, must perforce admit that they are the "sugared" ones alluded to by Meres, for the celebrated lines on the two loves of Comfort and Despair are found in the Passionate Pilgrim of 1599. But copies of specially dedicated poems would most likely have been forwarded solely to the addressees, or, at all events, would not have been made subjects of literary notoriety through the adopted course recorded by

Meres. That writer, in all probability, would have used the words, *to his private friends*, if he had entertained the views now adopted by the personality theorists.

No. 134. Separate exercises.—Here and there is to be distinctly observed an absolute continuity, but a long uninterrupted sequence after the first seventeen can be traced only by those who rely on strained inferences, or are too intent on the establishment of favourite theories to condescend to notice glaring difficulties and inconsistencies. The opinion that the address to the "lovely boy" in 126 is the termination of a series, dedicated to one and the same youth, is, indeed, absolutely disproved by the language of 57. There are several other sonnets antecedent to 126 that bear no internal evidence of being addressed to the male sex, and it is difficult to understand the temerity that would gratuitously represent the great dramatist as yet further narrowing the too slender barriers which then divided the protestations of love and friendship.

No. 135. Their fragmentary character.—Two of the sonnets, those referring to Cupid's brand, are obviously nothing more than poetical exercises, and these lead to the suspicion that there may be amongst them other examples of iterative fancies. Here and there are some which have the appearance of being mere imitations from the Classics or the Italian, although of course it is not necessary to assume that either were consulted in the original languages. It is difficult on any other hypothesis to reconcile the inflated egotism of such a one as 55 with the unassuming dedications to the Venus and Lucrece, 1593 and 1594, or with the expressions of humility found in the Sonnets themselves, e.g., 32 and 38.

No. 136. In the generation immediately following.—In MS. Bright 190, now MS. Addit. 15, 226, a volume which may be of the time of Charles the First, or perhaps of a little earlier date, there is a copy of the eighth sonnet, there ascribed to Shakespeare, and entitled,—*In laudem musice et opprobrium contemptorii ejusdem.* In my copy of Benson's edition of 1640, some of the printed titles there given have been altered to others in a manuscript hand-writing which is nearly contemporary with the date of publication.

No. 137. From the arrangement.—And not only from the classification and titles given by Benson in his edition of 1640, but from the terms in which he writes of the Sonnets themselves. "In your perusall," he observes in his address to the reader, "you shall finde them seren, cleere, and elegantly plaine ; such gentle strains as shall recreate and not perplexe your braine ; no intricate or cloudy stuffe to puzzell intellect, but perfect eloquence such as will raise your admiration to his praise." These words could not have been penned had he regarded the Sonnets in any light other than that of poetical fancies.

No. 138. Five-pence.—In a manuscript account of payments, 1609, is a note by Alleyn, under the title of *howshowld stuff*, of "a book,

Shaksper sonettes, 5^{d.}" That this was the contemporary price of the work is confirmed by an early manuscript note, 5^{d.}, on the title-page of the copy of the first edition preserved in Earl Spencer's library at Althorp. On the last page of that copy is the following memorandum in a handwriting of the time,—"Commendacions to my very kind and approved frind, B. M."

No. 139. He dedicated the work.—To the "only begetter," that is, to the one person who obtained the entire contents of the work for the use of the publisher, the verb *beget* having been occasionally used in the sense of *get*. "I have some cossens Garman at Court, shall *beget* you the reversion of the Master of the King's Revels," Decker's Satiro-Mastix, 1602. Cf. Hamlet, iii. 2. The notion that *begetter* stands for *inspirer* could only be received were one individual alone the subject of all the poems ; and, moreover, unless we adopt the wholly gratuitous conjecture that the sonnets of 1609 were not those which were in existence in 1598, had not the time somewhat gone by for a *publisher's* dedication to that object ?

No. 140. Numerous futile conjectures.—There does not appear to be one of these which deserves serious investigation, but perhaps the climax of absurdity has been reached in the supposition that the initials represent William (Shakespeare) Himself. Scarcely less untenable are the various theories which assume that the publisher would have dared to address a person of exalted rank, under any circumstances, as Mr. W. H.,—this in days when social distinctions were so jealously exacted that a nobleman considered it necessary in the previous year, 1608, to vindicate his position by bringing an action in the Star-Chamber against a person who had orally addressed him as Goodman Morley. It is also worth notice that to a translation of the Manual of Epictetus, which appeared in 1616, there is prefixed a dedication from Thomas Thorpe to William, earl of Pembroke, in the course of which the writer parenthetically observes,—"pardon my presumption, great lord, from so meane a man to so great a person." The following passages from the commencement of that dedication were not penned in the spirit of one who had addressed a nobleman of high rank on terms of equality,— "it may worthily seeme strange unto your lordship out of what frenzy one of my meanenesse hath presumed to commit this sacriledge, in the straightnesse of your lordships leisure, to present a peece for matter and model so unworthy, and in this scribbling age wherein great persons are so pestered dayly with dedications."

No. 141. On good terms with the Halls.—When Thomas Quiney was in serious pecuniary difficulties in 1633, John Hall and Thomas Nash acted, with another connexion, as trustees for his estate ; and Nash, in a codicil to his will, 1647, leaves to Thomas Quiney and his wife, to each of them, "twentie shillinges to buy them rings."

No. 142. A small house on the west of the High Street.—Thomas Quiney, in December, 1611, arranged to purchase from the Corporation a twenty-one years' lease of these premises, which are thus described in a terrier of the High Street Ward, 1613,—"Thomas Quyney holdeth on tenement contaynyng on the strett sid sixteen foott and d., in length inwardes sixty feete, the bredhe backwardes sixteen foott and d." The front of this house, which is situated a few doors from the corner of Wood Street, has been modernized, but much of the interior, with its massive beams, oaken floors and square joists, remains structurally as it must have been in the days of Thomas Quiney.

No. 143. The Cage.—Quiney obtained the lease of this place, in the summer of 1616, from his brother-in-law, William Chandler, who gave it to him in exchange for his interests in the house on the other side of the way. He appears to have inhabited the Cage from the time it came into his hands until he removed from it shortly before November, 1652, when the lease was assigned to his brother Richard of London, the premises being then described as "lately in the tenure of Thomas Quiney," Stratford Council Book, MS. The house has long been modernized, the only existing portions of the ancient building being a few massive beams supporting the floor over the roof of the cellar.

No. 144. In which he was supported.—Occasional payments for wine supplied by him to the Corporation are entered in the local books at various periods from 1616 to 1650. In February, 1630-31, he mentions having been "for a long time" in the habit of purchasing largely from one Francis Creswick of Bristol, to which city he now and then repaired for the purpose of selecting his wines. According to his own account, about three years previously he had bought from this merchant several hogsheads, all of which had been tampered with before they reached Stratford-on-Avon, and this to so great an extent that he was not only dreadfully grumbled at, but lost some of his most important customers. He also seems to have dealt in tobacco and vinegar.

No. 145. Fined for swearing.—In "a note of what mony hath bine recovered since the 21 of September, 1630, for the poore for swearing and other defaults," are the following entries,—" item, of Mr. Quiny for swearing, 1*s.* 0*d.*; item, of Mr. Quiny for suffering townsmen to tippell in his houss, 1*s.* 0*d.*"

No. 146. His brother Richard.—In whose will, dated in August, 1655, is the following paragraph,—"I doe hereby give and devise unto my loving brother, Thomas Quiney, and his assignes, for and during the terme of his naturall life, one annuall or yearlie summe of twelve pounds of lawfull monie of England to be issuing and going out, and yearely to be receaved, perceaved, had and taken by the said Thomas

Quiney and his assignes out of, in and upon, all those my messuages and lands at Shottery, with the appurtenances, in the countie of Warwicke ; and at the time of the decease of my said brother, my executors to have, receive, perceive and take out of, in and upon, the said lands, the summe of five pounds, therewith to bear and defray the charges of my said brother's funerall." It is not likely that the concluding words would have been inserted, had not Thomas Quiney been then impoverished and in a precarious state of health. The testator left a numerous family, one of whom, Thomas, who subsequently held the lease of the Cage for many years, has often been mistaken for the poet's son-in-law.

No. 147.   The eldest, Shakespeare Quiney.—" May 8, Shakespeare, sonne to Thomas Queene," list of Stratford burials for 1617, Worcester MS.   " Receaved, for the great bell, at the deat⊕ of Thomas Quynis child, iiij.*d.*," Stratford Accounts, 1617.

No. 148.   The death of their mother.—Her burial is thus noted in the Stratford register for 1661-2,—" February 9, Judith, uxor Thomas Quiney, gent."   The introduction of the epithet *uxor* is no proof, as has been suggested, that her husband was then living.   Compare the epitaph on Shakespeare's widow.

No. 149.   In this case, at least.—That Jaggard would have yielded to remonstrances in 1599, had such then been made to him, may be inferred from the circumstance of his cancelling the title-page containing Shakespeare's name in the edition of 1612, and this apparently at the instigation of a minor writer.

No. 150.   Wincot.—The ancient provincial name of the small village of Wilmecote, about three miles from Stratford-on-Avon.   It is spelt both Wincott and Wilmcott in the same entry in the Sessions Book for 1642, MS. County Records, Warwick ; and Wincott in a record of 32 Elizabeth at Stratford-on-Avon.   In the parish of Clifford Chambers, and at about four miles from the poet's native town, is a very minute and secluded hamlet called Wincot.   It is described by Atkyns in 1712 as then containing only two houses, one of which, to judge from its present appearance, was in former days the substantial residence of a landowner, and a confirmation of this opinion will be found in a petition of one Robert Loggin, House of Lords' MSS., January, 1667 ; but it is extremely unlikely that here was to be found an alehouse of any kind, and there appears to be nothing beyond the mere name to warrant recent conjectures of this being the hamlet mentioned by Shakespeare.   Marian Hacket, the fat ale-wife, was probably a real character, as well as Stephen Sly, old John Naps, Peter Turf, and Henry Pimpernell.   The documentary evidence respecting the inferior classes of society, especially at so early a period, is at all times brief and difficult of access ; but the opinion here expressed with regard to

the truthfulness of the names referred to may be said to be all but confirmed by the discovery of contemporary notices of Stephen Sly, who is
described as a "servant to William Combe," and who is several times
mentioned in the records of Stratford-on-Avon as having taken an
active part in the disputes which arose on the attempted enclosures of
common lands, acting, of course, under the directions of his master. In
a manuscript written in 1615 he is described as a labourer, but he
seems to have been one of a superior class, for his house, "Steeven Slye
house," is alluded to in the parish register of Stratford of the same year,
as if it were of some slight extent.

No. 151. Mill.—This anecdote was first published by Capell in the
following terms,—"Wincot is in Stratford's vicinity, where the memory
of the ale-house subsists still; and the tradition goes that 'twas resorted
to by Shakespeare for the sake of diverting himself with a fool who
belong'd to a neighbouring mill," Notes to the Taming of the Shrew,
ed. 1780, p. 26. The fact of there having been a water-mill at this village
(Dugdale, ed. 1656, p. 617) in ancient times may be thought to give
some colour of possibility to the tradition. Warton merely says that
"the house kept by our genial hostess still remains, but is at present a
mill," Glossary to the Oxford edition of Shakespeare, 1770. According
to an unpublished letter written by Warton in 1790, he derived his
information from what was told him, when a boy, by Francis Wise, an
eminent Oxford scholar, who went purposely to Stratford-on-Avon
about the year 1740 to collect materials respecting the personal history
of Shakespeare. Warton's own words may be worth giving,—"my note
about Wilnecote I had from Mr. Wise, Radclivian librarian, a most
accurate and inquisitive literary antiquary, who, about fifty years ago,
made a journey to Stratford and its environs to pick up anecdotes about
Shakespeare, many of which he told me; but which I, being then very
young, perhaps heard very carelessly and have long forgott;—this I
much regrett, for I am sure he told me many curious things about
Shakespeare;—he was an old man when I was a boy in this college;—
the place is Wylmecote, the mill, or Wilnicote, near Stratford, not
Tamworth," 31 March, 1790. The anecdote, as related by Capell,
belongs to a series of traditions that show how wide-spread was the
belief in Warwickshire in the last century that the great poet was of a
jovial and simple disposition; and this is also assumed in the following
curious statement,—"the late Mr. James West of the Treasury assured
me that, at his house in Warwickshire, he had a wooden bench, once
the favourite accommodation of Shakespeare, together with an earthern
half-pint mug out of which he was accustomed to take his draughts
of ale at a certain publick house in the neighbourhood of Stratford
every Saturday afternoon," Steevens in Supplement to Shakespeare,
1780, ii. 369.

No. 152. And the Court.—That the Tempest was originally written with a view to its production before the Court may perhaps be gathered from the introduction of the Masque, and from the circumstance that Robert Johnson was the composer of the music to *Full Fathom Five* and *Where the Bee Sucks*, the melodies of which, though re-arranged, are preserved in Wilson's Cheerful Ayres or Ballads set for three Voices, 1660. Johnson is mentioned, in the Treasurer's accounts for 1612, as one of the royal musicians "for the lutes." There may be a suspicion that, when the author was engaged upon this drama, the company were short of actors, and that he was bearing this deficiency in mind when he made Ariel, in the midst of a "corollary" of spirits, unnecessarily assume the somewhat incongruous personality of Ceres. A similar observation will apply to his introduction as a harpy, neither transformation exactly harmonizing with the incipient delineation of his attributes.

No. 153. The evening of the first of November.—In the Booke of the Revells, extending from 31 October, 1611, to 1 November, 1612, a manuscript in the Audit Office collection, there is a page containing a list of plays acted during that period before the Court, two of Shakespeare's being therein mentioned in the following terms,—"By the Kings players Hallomas nyght, was presented att Whithall before the Kinges Majestie a play called the Tempest.—The Kings players the 5th of November, a play called the Winters Nightes Tayle." This list is considered by more than one experienced paleographer to be a modern forgery, but, if this be the case, the facts that it records were, in all probability, derived from a transcript of an authentic document. Speaking of the Tempest, in the Account of the Incidents, 1809, p. 39, Malone distinctly says,—"I *know* that it had a being and a name in the autumn of 1611;" and he was not the kind of critic to use these decisive words unless he had possessed contemporary evidence of the fact.

No. 154. With success.—Dryden gives us two interesting pieces of information respecting the comedy of the Tempest,—the first, that it was acted at the Blackfriars' Theatre; the second, that it was successful. His words are,—"the play itself had formerly been acted with success in the Black-Fryers," Preface to the Tempest or the Enchanted Island, ed. 1670. This probably means that the comedy was originally produced at the Blackfriars' Theatre after the Children had left that establishment, and it is alluded to in a list of "some of the most ancient playes that were playd at Blackfriers," a manuscript dated in December, 1660. It is not at all improbable that the conspicuous position assigned to this comedy in the first folio is a testimony to its popularity, for that situation is unquestionably no evidence of its place in the chronological order.

No. 155. In the year 1613.—It has been thought that Ben Jonson alludes to the Tempest and the Winter's Tale in the following passage in the Induction to his Bartholomew Fair, first acted in the year 1614, which is thus printed in the original edition of the play that appeared in 1631, the distinctions of italics and capital letters not being peculiar to this quotation, and therefore of little value in the consideration of the opinion respecting the allusion,—"if there bee never a *Servant-monster* i' the *Fayre*, who can helpe it, he sayes? nor a nest of *Antiques?* Hee is loth to make nature afraid in his *Playes*, like those that beget *Tales, Tempests*, and such like *Drolleries*." As the Tempest and the Winter's Tale were both acted at Court shortly before the production of Bartholomew Fair, and were probably then in great estimation with the public, there would be some grounds for the conjecture that Shakespeare's plays are here alluded to, were it not for the circumstance that Jonson can hardly be considered to refer to regular dramas. In the comedy of Bartholomew Fair he ridicules those primitive dramatic exhibitions which, known as motions or puppet-shows, were peculiar favourites with the public at that festival. In some of these tempests and monsters were introduced, as in the motion of Jonah and the Whale. The "nest of anticks," which is supposed to allude to the twelve satyrs who are introduced at the sheep-shearing festival, does not necessarily refer even to the spurious kind of drama here mentioned. The "servant-monster," and the "nest of anticks," may merely mean individual exhibitions. If the latter really does relate to a dramatic representation, it may very likely be in allusion to the fantastic characters so frequently introduced in the masques of that period; but the context seems to imply that Jonson is referring to devices exhibited at the fair.

No. 156. In the Spring.—This appears from the entry in the books of the Stationers' Company on July 26th, 1602, of "a booke called the

Revenge of Hamlett, Prince Denmarke⑧, as yt was *latelie acted* by the Lo: Chamberleyne his servantes." The tragedy is not noticed by Meres in 1598, and it could not have been written in its present form before the spring of the year 1600, the period of the opening of the Globe, there being a clear allusion to performances at that theatre in act ii. sc. 2.

No. 157. Our national tragedy.—There was an old English tragedy on the subject of Hamlet which was in existence at least as early as the year 1589, in the representation of which an exclamation of the Ghost, —"Hamlet, revenge!"—was a striking and well-remembered feature. This production is alluded to in some prefatory matter by Nash in the edition of Greene's Menaphon issued in that year, here given V.L.— "I'le turne backe to my first text, of studies of delight, and talke a little in friendship with a few of our triuiall translators. It is a common practise now a daies amongst a sort of shifting companions that runne through euery arte and thriue by none, to leaue the trade of *Nouerint* whereto they were borne, and busie themselues with the indeuors of art, that could scarcelie latinize their necke-verse if they should haue neede ; yet English *Seneca* read by candle light yeeldes manie good sentences, as *Bloud is a begger*, and so foorth : and if you intreate him faire in a frostie morning, he will affoord you whole *Hamlets*, I should say handfulls, of tragical speaches," Nash's Epistle to the Gentlemen Students of both Universities prefixed to Greene's Menaphon, 1589, first edition, the statement of there having been a previous one being erroneous. Another allusion occurs in Lodge's Wits Miserie, 1596, p. 56,—"and though this fiend be begotten of his fathers own blood, yet is he different from his nature, and were he not sure that jealousie could not make him a cuckold, he had long since published him for a bastard ;—you shall know him by this, he is a foule lubber, his tongue tipt with lying, his heart steeld against charity ; he walks for the most part in black under colour of gravity, and looks as pale as the visard of the ghost which cried so miserally at the Theator like an oister wife, *Hamlet, revenge.*" Again, in Decker's Satiromastix, 1602,—"*Asini.* Wod I were hang'd if I can call you any names but Captaine and Tucca.—*Tuc.* No, fye'st my name's *Hamlet, revenge :*—Thou hast been at Parris Garden, hast not?—*Hor.* Yes, Captaine, I ha plaide Zulziman there ;" with which may be compared another passage in Westward Hoe, 1607,—"I, but when light wives make heavy husbands, let these husbands play mad *Hamlet*, and crie *revenge.*" So, likewise, in Rowlands' Night-Raven, 1620, a scrivener, who has his cloak and hat stolen from him, exclaims,—"I will not cry, *Hamlet, revenge* my greeves." There is also reason to suppose that another passage in the old tragedy of Hamlet is alluded to in Armin's Nest of Ninnies, 1608, —"ther are, as Hamlet sayes, things cald whips in store," a sentence which seems to have been well-known and popular, for it is partially cited in the Spanish Tragedie, 1592, and in the First Part of the Contention, 1594. It seems, however, certain that all the passages above quoted refer to a drama of Hamlet anterior to that by Shakespeare, and the same which is recorded in Henslowe's Diary as having been played at Newington in June, 1594, by " my Lord Admeralle and my lorde Chamberlen men." This older play was clearly one of a series of dramas on the then favourite theme of revenge aided by the supernatural intervention of a ghost, and a few other early allusions to it appear to deserve quotation. " His father's empire and government was but as the poeticall furie in a stage-action, compleat, yet with horrid and wofull tragedies ; a first, but no second to any *Hamlet;* and that now *Revenge*, just *Revenge*, was comming with his sworde drawne against him, his royall Mother, and dearest Sister, to fill up those murdering sceanes," Sir Thomas Smithes Voiage and Entertainment in Rushia, 1605. "Sometimes would he overtake him and lay hands uppon him like a catch-pole, as if he had arrested him, but furious Hamlet woulde presently eyther breake loose like a beare from the stake, or else so set his pawes on this dog that thus bayted him that, with tugging and tearing one anothers frockes off, they both looked like mad Tom of Bedlam," Decker's Dead Terme, 1608. " If any passenger come by and, wondring to see such a conjuring circle kept by hel-houndes, demaund what spirits they raise ther, one of the murderers steps to him, poysons him with sweete wordes and shifts him off with this lye, that one of the women is falne in labour ; but if any mad Hamlet, hearing this, smell villanie and rush in by violence to see what the tawny divels are dooing, then they excuse the fact, lay the blame on those that are the actors, and, perhaps, if they see no remedie, deliver them to an officer to be had to punishment," Decker's Lanthorne and Candle-light, or the Bell-man's Second Nights Walke, 1608, a tract which was reprinted in 1609 and afterwards under more than one title. "A trout, Hamlet, with foure legs," Clarke's Parœmiologia Anglo-Latina, or Proverbs English and Latine, 1639, p. 71. The preceding notices may fairly authorize us to infer that the ancient play of Hamlet, —1. Was written by either an attorney, or an attorney's clerk, who had not received a university education.—2. Was full of tragical high-sounding speeches.—3. Contained the passage, "there are things called whips in store," spoken by Hamlet ; and a notice of a trout with four legs by one of the other characters.—4. Included a very telling brief speech by the Ghost in the two words,—Hamlet, revenge !—whence we may fairly conclude that the spectre in this, as in the later play, urged Hamlet to avenge the murder.—5. Was acted at the Theatre in Shoreditch and at the playhouse at Newington Butts.—6. Had for its principal character a hero exhibiting more general violence than can be attributed to Shakespeare's creation of Hamlet. It also appears that this older play was not entirely superseded by the new one, or, at all events, that it was long remembered by play-goers.

No. 158. The Revenge of Hamlet.—This title encourages the belief that Shakespeare's tragedy was to some unknown extent founded on the older drama, whence he probably obtained most of his incidents and a few bald hints for some of his dialogues, especially for those of the latter that are disfigured by unnecessary ribaldry. It may be suspected that Polonius would never have been called a fishmonger had there not been a cognate pleasantry in that scene of the earlier play in which there was an allusion to a trout, both terms being allied in meanings that are unworthy of explanation. Whether the compiler of ed. 1603 was indebted to it for any of his language is a point which, however probable, is not likely to be satisfactorily determined. The manuscript of the elder play of Hamlet no doubt belonged to the Lord Chamberlain's company, otherwise some notice of it would have appeared in Henslowe's diary after its performance in June, 1594, and this view is to some degree confirmed by the notice given by Lodge in 1596 of its performance in Shoreditch. It may be concluded, therefore, that Shakespeare had good opportunities for being well acquainted with the earlier piece.

No. 159. In course of representation.—It appears from a stage-direction in the quarto of 1603, that, in Burbage's time, Ophelia in act iv., sc. 5, came on the stage playing upon a lute, no doubt accompanying herself on that instrument when singing the snatches of the ballads. "Enter Ofelia playing on a lute, and her haire downe singing," ed. 1603. No such direction occurs in the other quartos, while the folio has merely,—"enter Ophelia distracted." It is also worth notice that, in the original performance, Hamlet appeared on one or more occasions without either coat or waistcoat,—" Puts off his cloathes; his shirt he onely weares, =Much like *mad-Hamlet;* thus as passion teares,"—Daiphantus, 1604.

No. 160. Recently composed.—Bishop Percy, who died in 1811, owned a copy of Speght's edition of Chaucer, 1598, with manuscript notes by Gabriel Harvey, a portion of one of them, as first printed by Steevens in 1773, being in the following terms,—"the younger sort take much delight in Shakespeare's Venus and Adonis, but his Lucrece and his tragedy of Hamlet, Prince of Denmarke, have it in them to please the wiser sort." The fate of this volume being unknown, there is no alternative but to give what seem to be the essential particulars of the case from the notes of Malone and Percy which occur in letters of 1803 in the Bodleian Library and in an essay in the variorum Shakespeare, ed. 1821, ii., 369.—Harvey's autograph in the book is followed by the date of 1598, and, in the same manuscript passage from which the above extract is taken, there is an allusion to Spenser and Watson as two of " our now flourishing metricians." It has been assumed from these facts, Spenser having died in January, 1599, that the Hamlet note must have been written in the previous year; but the death of Watson having occurred long before the 1598 edition of Chaucer appeared, it is clear that the words *now flourishing* are used in the sense of *now admired*. It is also certain that Harvey's manuscript date is only that of the time when he became possessed of the volume, for in one passage he speaks of *Translated Tasso*, and the first edition of Fairfax, which is doubtlessly alluded to, appeared in 1600.

No. 161. Its popularity.—This is shown by the direct evidence in Daiphantus, 1604,—" faith, it should please all, like Prince Hamlet." There is no question, as in some other notices, of the possibility of the reference being to the older drama, the author distinctly mentioning it as one of "friendly Shakespeare's tragedies." It may be observed that Hamlet is the only one of Shakespeare's plays which is noticed as having been acted in his life-time before the Universities of Oxford and Cambridge. The distinction was a rare one, as may be gathered from the terms in which Ben Jonson acknowledges the similar honour which was bestowed upon his comedy of Volpone.

No. 162. Until the Summer.—The edition of 1603, as appears from its title-page, could not have been published until after the nineteenth of May in that year, while the statement of the tragedy having been "*diverse times* acted by his Highnesse servants in the Cittie of London, as also in the two Universities of Cambridge and Oxford, and else-where," may probably lead to the conclusion that the book was not issued until late in the year. What share Trundell possessed in this edition is not known, but, as he was a young catch-penny tradesman of inferior position, it is not unlikely that he it was who surreptitiously obtained the imperfect and erroneous copy, placing it in the hands of some obscure printer who would have less fear of the action of the Stationers' Company than a man of higher character would have entertained. It was certainly printed by some one who had a very small stock of type, as is shown by the evident deficiency of some of the Italic capitals.

No. 163. Employed an inferior and clumsy writer.—The proposition here advanced seems to be the one that most fairly meets the various difficulties of an intricate problem, an interpretation explaining nearly all the perplexing circumstances which surround the history of the barbarously garbled and dislocated text of the first edition, and accounting for what is therein exhibited of identity with and variations from the characterization and dramatic structure of the authentic work. There is another theory which assumes that the quarto of 1603 is a copy, however imperfect, of Shakespeare's first sketch of the play. Were this the case, surely there would be found in it some definite traces of the poet's genius, sparkling in lines which belong to the variations above noticed, and which could not have found a place in the short-hand notes of the enlarged tragedy. There can scarcely be a doubt but that the unreasonable length of this drama led to all manner of omissions in the acting copies, and that these last were subjected to continual revision at the theatre. If this were so, it is not unlikely that the first edition may contain small portions, more or less fully exhibited, of Shakespeare's own work nowhere else to be found; but, taking that edition as a whole, excluding those parts of it which, either accurately or defectively rendered, are evidently derived from the genuine play, there is little beyond an assemblage of feeble utterances and inferior doggrel, the composition of which could not reasonably be assigned to any period, however early, of Shakespeare's literary career. The absolute indications of the hand of a very inferior dramatist are clearly visible in his original scene of the interview between the Queen and Horatio, and it is more easy to believe that such a writer could have made structural and characterical alterations which subtle reasoning may persuade itself are results of genius, than that Shakespeare could ever have written in any form that which no amount of logic can succeed in removing from the domain of balderdash. So wretched, indeed, is nearly the whole of the twaddle which has been cited as part of the first draft of the immortal tragedy, that one is inclined to suspect plagiarism in cases where anything like poetry is discovered. In one instance, at all events, in the lines beginning, "Come in, Ofelia," ed. 1603, sig. C. 2, there seems to be a palpable imitation of words of Viola in Twelfth Night.

No. 164. Scraps.—The exact mode in which all these fragments were obtained will ever remain a mystery, but some were clearly derived from memoranda taken in short-hand at the theatre. Independently of spurious words which may possibly be ludicrous misprints, there are errors that cannot easily be explained on any other hypothesis, as *right done* for *writ down* in the second scene of the first act. In act ii, sc. 2, *in venom steept* is printed *invenom'd speech*, and by a similar ear-mistake we have, "the law hath writ those are the only men." The uniform spelling of Ofelia in ed. 1603 may also be due to ear-notes. The celebrated "to be" speech appears to be a jumble formed out of insufficient memoranda, a conjecture supported by the circumstance of the word *borne* (bourn) being misunderstood and converted into *borne*, with another meaning. So in act iii., sc. 4, "most secret and most grave," is converted into, "I'll provide for you a grave;" and probably the short-hand for *inheritor* was erroneously read as *honor*, the sentence being arranged to meet the latter reading. The three beautiful lines commencing, "anon as patient as the female dove," are abbreviated most likely through short-hand to the single one, "anon as mild and gentle as a dove"; and there are numerous other instances of palpably bungling abridgments of the text. Some of the notes of lines taken at the play must have been imperfect, as, for example, in the Player-King's speech commencing, "I do believe," where the word *think* having been omitted in the notes, the line is incorrectly made up in ed. 1603 by the word *sweet*. In act i., sc. 2, "a beast that wants discourse of reason" is printed, "a beast devoid of reason." Again, the name of Gonzago is correctly given in one speech in ed. 1603, while in another it is printed Albertus, and there are other variations in the names of persons and localities which may possibly be due to the short-hand writing of such names being easily misinterpreted. Thus the town of Vienna appears as Guyana, this variation occurring in an erroneous text of one of the genuine Hamlet speeches so incorrectly printed that he is made to address his uncle as Father. To this short-hand cause may also be attributed the orthography of the names of Valtemand, Cornelius, Laertes, Rosencraus, Guyldensterne, and Gertrard in ed. 1604 being as follows in ed. 1603,—Voltemar, Cornelia, Leartes, Rossencraft, Gilderstone, Gertred. In some instances it would seem that the compiler had no memoranda of the names, and hence the omission of those of Barnardo and Francisco may be explained. Then, again, there is the important fact that the compiler of the edition of 1603 either was possessed of notes or had recollected portions of the folio copy as they were recited on the stage. See, for example, the garbled version of the sentence, "the clown shall make those laugh whose lungs are tickled o' the sere," which is altogether omitted in the other quartos. The expressive line,—"what, frighted with false fire,"—is peculiar to ed. 1603 and the folio, and is identical in both with the insignificant exception that the reading *fires* occurs in the former. The line, "that to Laertes I forgot myself," is found only in eds. 1603 and 1623, not in the other quartos. A trace of Hamlet's within speech, the repetitions of *mother* in act iii., sc. 4, in ed. 1623, not in ed. 1604, is found in ed. 1603; and the Doctor of ed. 1604 is correctly given as the Priest in eds. 1603, 1623. Mere verbal coincidences, of which there are several, are of less evidential value, but *French grave* in eds. 1603 and 1623 for the *friendly ground* of ed. 1604 are variations hardly to be accounted for excepting on the above hypothesis. It is thus perfectly clear that the text of the folio copy and that of the first edition are partially derived from the same version, and there can be little doubt that portions of the latter were taken from some copy of the genuine drama which was printed in the following year. It seems impossible to account otherwise for the identity of a large number of lines common to the editions of 1603 and 1604, that identity extending even sometimes to the spelling and the nearly textual copy of more than one speech, as, for instance, that of Voltimand in act ii. sc. 2, while a comparison of the first act in the two copies would alone substantiate this position. Some peculiar orthography may also be fairly adduced as corroborative evidence, e.g.,

Capapea in the quartos for the *cap-a-pe* of the folio, *strikt* for *strict, cost* for *cast, troncheon* for *truncheon, Nemeon* for *Nemian* (Nemean), *eager* for *aygre, Fortenbrasse* for *Fortinbras, penitrable* for *penetrable, rootes* for *rots,* and, especially, the unique verbal error *sallied.* This last is a strange perversion of the term *solid,* and one which appears to prove decisively that the quarto texts of the well-known speech in which it occurs were all derived in some way or other from one authority. It is, however, evident, from its corrupted form, that the speech in ed. 1603 was not copied from the manuscript used by the first printer of the enlarged work. At present the only feasible explanation of the difficulty is one suggested by Professor Dowden, who thinks that the compositor engaged on the second quarto may have found it convenient and useful to have by him a copy of the printed edition of 1603. If his manuscript had been obscurely written, a glance at that edition might have assisted him, and hence the misprints have been accidentally copied, the hand mechanically repeating the word that occupied his eye.

No. 165. Or other memoranda.—In the play of Eastward Hoe, printed in 1605, there is a parody on one of Ophelia's songs, which is of some interest in regard to the question of the critical value of the quarto of 1603, the occurrence of the word *all* before *flaxen* showing that the former word was incorrectly omitted in all the other early quartos. So, again, in 1606, when the author of Dolarnys Primerose made use of one of Hamlet's speeches, the recollection was either of the printed version of 1603, or, what is more probable, of the play as originally acted, as is evidenced by the use of the word *quirks,* which is peculiar to that edition. The latter theory may be supported by an apparent Hamlet reference in the Dutch Courtezan, 1605,—"wha, ha, ho, come, bird, come,"—the word *bird* in Shakespeare's tragedy first appearing in print in ed. 1623 ; and the certain quotation,—"illo, ho, ho, ho, art there, old truepeny,"—in the Malcontent, 1604, is far more likely to have been derived from a performance of Hamlet than from the contemporary printed edition, the word *old* not improbably belonging to the original text of the nobler drama.

No. 166. Abnormous variations.—The compiler of the edition of 1603 must have made use of some version of the story that originally appeared in the works of Saxo Grammaticus, that version, in all probability, being the one then current in the elder tragedy. Note, for example, the feelings and conduct of the Queen towards Hamlet at the end of her interview with him and afterwards, as also her solemn denial of any complicity in the murder. The change of the names of Corambis and Montano in ed. 1603 to those of Polonius and Reynaldo in ed. 1604 has not been satisfactorily explained. Corambis, a trisyllable, not only suits the metre in the mangled play, but also in the three instances in which the name of Polonius occurs in verse in

Shakespeare's own tragedy. Hence it may be concluded that the great dramatist did not alter the former name on his own judgment, but that, for some mysterious reason, the change was made by the actors and inserted in the play-house copy at some time previously to the appearance of the edition of 1604.

No. 167. Enlarged.—Although Roberts registered the copyright of the tragedy in 1602, he did not, so far as we know, print the work before 1604, and then with a note which appears to imply that the edition of 1603 was not "according to the true and perfect copy," but that the new one was "imprinted and enlarged to almost as much again as it was" *by the use of that copy.* This impression was re-issued in the following year, the title-page and a few leaves at the end, sigs. N and O being fresh printed, the sole alteration in the former being the substitution of 1605 for 1604. If the initials I. R. are those, as is most likely, of James Roberts, a printer frequently employed by Ling, there must have been some friendly arrangement between the two respecting the ownership of the copyright, which certainly belonged to the latter, as appears from the entry on the books of the Stationers' Company of November, 1607, when he transferred his interest to Smethwick.

No. 168. Admirably portrayed by Burbage.—This is ascertained from the very interesting and ably written elegy on Burbage, but there is no record of his treatment of the character, his delineation probably differing materially from that of modern actors. Stage tradition merely carries down the tricks of the profession, no actor entirely replacing another, and, in the case of Hamlet, hardly two of recent times but who are or have been distinct in manner and expression, and even in idea. The fact appears to be that this tragedy offers a greater opportunity than any other for a variety of special interpretations on the stage, those being created by the individual actor's elevation or depression of one or more of the hero's mental characteristics. According to Downes, Sir William Davenant, "having seen Mr. Taylor of the Black-Fryars company act it, who, being instructed by the author, Mr. Shaksepeur®, taught Mr. Betterton in every particle of it," Roscius Anglicanus, 1708. Shakespeare may have given hints to Burbage, but Taylor did not undertake the part until after the author's decease. See Wright's Historia Histrionica, 1699, p. 4.

No. 169. Hamlet leaping into Ophelia's grave.—"Leartes leapes into the grave,—Hamlet leapes in after Leartes," stage-directions in ed. 1603. When the author of the elegy on Burbage mentions having seen that actor play Hamlet *in jest,* the lines following do not necessarily allude to the scene in the grave, the words *this part* most likely referring to the character generally. It may here be observed that the presumed allusion to Kemp in the speech respecting the extempore wit of clowns is purely fanciful, while the conjecture that he

1607 · 5to Rs

19 · Novembr

Jo · Smythick · Entred for his copies vnder thandes of the wardens these bookes followinge Whiche dyd belonge to Nicholas Lynge · viz ·

6 a booke called Hamlett — vjd

9 The tamynge of A Shrewe — vjd

10 Romeo and Julett — vjd

11 Loves Labour Lost — vjd

undertook at any time the part of the First Gravedigger in Shakespeare's tragedy is contrary to all probability. There is no reliable evidence that Kemp was a member of Shakespeare's company either at or after the production of Hamlet.

No. 170.   The once popular stage-trick.—There is a graphic description of the incident in a Frenchman's account of the tragedy as performed at Covent Garden, in Kemble's time, 1811,—" it is enough to mention the grave-diggers to awaken in France the cry of rude and barbarous taste, and were I to say how the part is acted it might be still worse ;— after beginning their labour and breaking ground for a grave, a conversation begins between the two grave-diggers ;—the chief one takes off his coat, folds it carefully and puts it by in a safe corner ; then, taking up his pick-axe, spits in his hand, gives a stroke or two, talks, stops, strips off his waistcoat, still talking, folds it with great deliberation and nicety, and puts it with the coat, then an under-waistcoat, still talking, another and another ;—I counted seven or eight each folded and unfolded very leisurely in a manner always different, and with gestures faithfully copied from nature ;—the British public enjoys this scene excessively, and the pantomimic variations a good actor knows how to introduce in it are sure to be vehemently applauded." A similar artifice was formerly introduced in the performance of the Duchess of Malfi, certainly produced before March, 1619, for when the Cardinal tells the Doctor to put off his gown, the latter, according to the stage-direction in ed. 1708, "puts off his four cloaks one after another." Another old stage-trick was that of Hamlet starting to his feet, and throwing down the chair on which he had been sitting, in his consternation at the sudden appearance of his Father's spirit in act iii. sc. 4. This incident is pictured in the frontispiece to the tragedy in Rowe's edition of Shakespeare, 1709, and it is no doubt of much greater antiquity. It appears from this engraving that, in the then performance of Hamlet, the pictures referred to by the hero in that act were represented by two large framed portraits hung on the walls of the chamber, and this was probably the custom after the Restoration, the separate paintings taking the place of those in the tapestry, the latter accidental and imaginary. Hamlet on the ancient stage no doubt pointing to any designs in the arras in which figures were represented. It is clear from his speech in the genuine tragedy that the portraits were intended to be whole lengths, and this would be inconsistent with the notion of miniatures, to say nothing of the absurdity of his carrying about with him one of the " pictures in little " the rage for the possession of which he elsewhere disparages.

No. 171.   Not a native of that village.—For John Hall of Acton was married there on September the 19th, 1574, to Margaret Archer, and " Elizabeth Hall, the daughter of John, xxned the v.th of June, 1575."

The poet's son-in-law, in 1635, bequeathed "my house in Acton" to his daughter, who was possibly named after the lady above mentioned. All this is, however, suggested with diffidence, for Hall being one of the commonest of surnames, absolute identifications are hopeless in the absence of definite clues, and little assistance can be derived from the arms found on the gravestone of 1635. No record exists of the tinctures belonging to those arms, and the coat stands, in different colours, for various families of Hall. It should be observed that the registers of Maidstone negative a favourite conjecture that he was the son of an eminent physician of that town.

No. 172.   The Old Town.—" I have seen, in some old paper relating to the town, that Dr. Hall resided in that part of Old Town which is in the parish of Old Stratford," MS. of R.B. Wheler, c. 1814. If so, Hall's residence was not very near Church Street, and it must have been either one of the few houses on the north of Old Town or one on the small piece of land between the College grounds and the borough. It is not likely that it occupied the latter situation, the house that was standing there in 1769 being then described as having formerly consisted of three tenements, and these were, no doubt, in Hall's time merely small cottages.

No. 173.   New Place.—In the Vestry notes of October, 1617, he is mentioned as residing in the Chapel Street Ward, and " Mr. Hall at Newplace" is alluded to in a town record dated February the 3rd, 1617–18. Mrs. Hall continued to reside there until her death in 1649, and during some part, if not all, of the time of her widowhood, her daughter and son-in-law lived with her in the same house. Thomas Nash speaks of it as being in his own occupation in August, 1642, and in a manuscript dated 14 March, 1645–6, he alludes to "my mother-in-law, Mrs. Hall, who lives with me." He was, however, practically only a lodger, Mrs. Hall being not only at the time the legal owner of the estate but also the ratable occupier of the house. The latter fact is clear from the overseers' accounts of June, 1646, in which she is noted as being in arrears of rates to the amount of eight shillings and sixpence.

No. 174.   His advice was solicited.—These particulars are gathered from a rare little volume entitled,—" Select Observations on English Bodies, or Cures both Empericall and Historicall performed upon very eminent Persons in desperate Diseases, first written in Latine by Mr. John Hall, physician, living at Stratford-upon-Avon in Warwickshire, where he was very famous, as also in the counties adjacent, as appeares by these Observations drawn out of severall hundreds of his as choysest ; now put into English for common benefit by James Cooke, practitioner in Physick and Chirurgery," 12mo. Lond. 1657. A second edition appeared in 1679, re-issued in 1683 with merely a new title-page. In the original small octavo manuscript used by Cooke much of the Latin

VOL. II.

X

is obscurely abbreviated, and some of the translations appear to be paraphrased. The cases were selected from a large number of previous notes, and being mostly undated, without a chronological arrangement, it is impossible to be certain that some of them are not to be referred to the time of the poet. The earliest one to which a date can be assigned seems to be that of Lord Compton, at p. 91, who was attended by Hall previously to his lordship's departure with the King for Scotland in March, 1617. Hall was evidently held in much esteem by the Northampton family, whom he attended both at Compton Wynyates and at Ludlow.

No. 175. Strong religious tendencies.—He occasionally attended the vestries, most likely as often as regard for his professional duties warranted, and interested himself in all that related to the services of the parish church, to which he presented a costly new pulpit. He was selected one of the borough churchwardens in 1628, a sidesman in 1629, and he was exceedingly intimate with the Rev. Thomas Wilson, the vicar, a thorough-going puritan, who was accused of holding conventicles, and of having so little ecclesiological feeling that he allowed his swine and poultry to desecrate the interior of the Guild Chapel. When the latter individual, in 1633, brought a suit in Chancery against the town, Hall seems to have been nominated a churchwarden by the vicar on purpose that the latter might have an excuse for making him a party to the suit, which he accordingly did, although the nomination was subsequently cancelled. They were such great friends that the vicarial courts were sometimes held at New Place. Of Hall's religious sincerity a favourable opinion may be formed from a memorandum written by him after his recovery from a serious illness in 1632,—"Thou, O Lord, which hast the power of life and death, and drawest from the gates of death, I confesse without any art or counsell of man, but only from thy goodnesse and clemency, thou hast saved me from the bitter and deadly symptomes of a deadly fever, beyond the expectation of all about me, restoring me, as it were, from the very jaws of death to former health, for which I praise Thy name, O most Mercifull God, and Father of our Lord Jesus Christ, praying thee to give me a most thankfull heart for this great favour, for which I have cause to admire thee."

No. 176. Expelled in 1633.—He had for many years previously exhibited a great reluctance to serve on the Town Council, where his attendances would have interfered with the calls of his arduous profession. Elected a burgess in 1617 and again in 1623, he was on each occasion excused from undertaking the office, but in 1632 he was compelled to accept his election, non-attendances being punishable by fines, the payment of which the Corporation were determined to enforce. Serious disputes arose between the Council and himself respecting these fines and other matters, the differences culminating in the following almost unprecedented resolution which was passed at a meeting held in October, 1633,—"at this hall Mr. John Hall is displaced from beinge a Capitall Burgesse by the voices and consent of nineteene of the Company, as appeareth by the letter *r* at there names, for the breach of orders wilfully, and sundry other misdemenours contrary to the duty of a burgesse and the oath which he hath taken in this place, and for his continual disturbances at our halles, as will appeare by the particulars." The bad feeling that existed between Hall and the Corporation was prolonged by his appearance as one of the plaintiffs in the Chancery suit that was shortly afterwards brought against the latter.

No. 177. On the following day.—"November 26, Johannes Hall, medicus peritissimus," burial register for 1635. His tombstone bore the following inscription, thus given in Dugdale's Warwickshire Antiquities, ed. 1656, p. 518,—"Here lyeth the body of John Hall, gent.—he marr. Susanna, daughter and coheir of William Shakespere, gent.—he deceased November 25, anno 1635, aged 60 years.—Hallius hic situs est, medica celeberrimus arte,=Expectans regni guadia leta Dei.=Dignus erat meritis qui Nestora vinceret annis=In terris omnes, sed rapit æqua dies ;=Ne tumulo quid desit, adest fidissima conjux,=Et vitæ comitem, nunc quoque mortis, habet." The concluding lines of this epitaph would appear to indicate that it was composed after the death of the widow in the year 1649.

No. 178. The only interesting personal glimpse.—For it surely cannot profit us to be informed that on one occasion she was "miserably tormented with the collick," Select Observations, ed. 1657, p. 24. A similar observation will apply to Hall's notices of his daughter's illnesses, and none of these have been thought worthy of transcription.

No. 179. To whom she was warmly attached.—When he was afflicted with a dangerous illness in 1632, Mrs. Hall was so uneasy about him that, on her own responsibility, she secured the attendance of two physicians at New Place; v. Select Observations, ed, 1657, p. 229. It was doubtlessly at her wish that she was buried in her husband's grave, a fact that is gathered from the concluding lines of the epitaph on his tombstone, which give an evidence that must outweigh that of the record of her death on the adjoining one. The probability seems to be that the latter inscription, with its accompanying verses, were written with the intention of their being engraved on the physician's tomb, but that, for want of sufficient room, they were inscribed on another slab.

No. 180. On the grave-stone that records her decease.—The inscription here referred to having been tampered with in modern times, the following copy of it is taken from Dugdale,—"Here lyeth the body of Susanna, wife of John Hall, gent., the daughter of William Shakespere, gent.—She deceased the 2. day of July, anno 1649, aged 66 ;" the numeral *two* being an error for *eleven.* "July 16, Mrs. Susanna Hall,

X 2

widow," Stratford burial register for 1649. The verses given in the text were on the original stone under the above-named memorial, but, in the early part of the last century, they were removed to make space for a record of the death of one Richard Watts, who owned some of the tithes and so had the right of sepulture in the chancel. In 1844, the last-named inscription was erased for the restoration of the lines on Mrs. Hall, which had been fortunately preserved in the Warwickshire Antiquities, ed. 1656, p. 518.

No 181. *His father and uncle.*—Thomas Nash, the father of these persons, died suddenly at Aylesbury in the course of a journey from London, and was buried at the former place on June the 2nd, 1587. He left several children, including Anthony, his eldest born, afterwards described as of Welcombe and Old Stratford, who died in 1622, and John, his second son, a resident in the Bridge Street Ward, whose decease occurred in the following year. Both of these persons are remembered in the poet's will by gifts of rings, and Anthony, who busied himself very much in agricultural matters, was present in October, 1614, when Replingham signed the agreement respecting the enclosures. Thomas Nash, the husband of Shakespeare's grand-daughter, and the eldest son of this Anthony by Mary Baugh of Twining, co. Gloucester, was baptised at Stratford-on-Avon on June the 20th, 1593. He was executor under his father's will in 1622, the latter bequeathing him two houses and a piece of land near the bridge termed the Butt Close. It may be mentioned that amongst "the names of such persons within the burrough of Stratford-upon-Avon who by way of loane have sent in money and plate to the King and Parliament," 24 Sept., 1642, is found as by far the largest contributor,— " Thomas Nashe esq^r, in plate or money paid in at Warr :, 100*li*." There were other Nashes resident at Stratford, but the individuals above noticed belong to the family that was the highest in social position, one entitled to coat armour which, as well as the pedigree, were entered by Thomas Nash at the visitation of 1619.

No. 182. *Became a widow in 1647.*—Thomas Nash died at New Place on April the 4th, and was buried at Stratford on the next day. " Aprill 5, Thomas Nash, gent.," burial register for 1647. His tomb-stone in the chancel bore the following inscription, here taken from the copy in Dugdale's Warwickshire Antiquities, ed. 1656, p. 518,—" Here resteth the body of Thomas Nashe, esquier ;—he mar. Elizabeth, the daug. of John Hall, gentleman ;—he dyed April 4, anno 1647, aged 53. —Fata manent omnes ; hunc non virtute carentem, = Ut neque divitiis abstulit, atra dies = Abstulit, at referet lux ultima ; siste, viator, = Si peritura paras per mala parta peris." This monument was in a dilapidated condition at the end of the last century, and had probably further deteriorated before most of the Shakespeare family memorials were either tampered with, or replaced by new slabs, during the extensive alterations made in the church about the year 1836. Malone informs us that, in 1790, six words in the above elegy were then entirely obliterated, and Hunter speaks of the inscription in 1824 as being then "nearly perished."

No. 183. About two years afterwards.—She was married on June the 5th, 1649, at Billesley, a village about four miles from Stratford-on-Avon. The register is lost, and the accuracy of these facts rests on information given to Malone in a letter from Northampton written in the year 1788.

No. 184. Bardon Hill.—This hill, from the summit of which are to be seen exquisite views of the Cotswolds, is situated about a mile from Stratford-on-Avon, and overlooks the village of Shottery. Henry Cooper, a tradesman of Stratford-on-Avon, residing in Ely Street, in a letter to Garrick written in 1771, mentioning astroites, says,—"thees small stones which I have sent are to be found on a hill called Barn-hill within a mild® of Stratford, the road that Shakespear whent when he whent to see his Bidford topers; thees stones will swim in a delf-plate amongst viniger." In Shakespeare's day there was no carriage or wagon road over Bardon Hill, the route supposed to have been followed by the poet having been then no doubt a bridle-way. It may be observed that the word *topers* does not appear to have been in use, in the sense above intended, before the middle of the seventeenth century.

No. 185. Noted for its revelry.—But in a report on the state of Bidford in 1605, we are told that "alehowses keepe good order in them; roagues punyshed;" and, in another one for 1606, that "alehouses keepe good order," Warwick Corporation MSS. It is possible, however, that these may have been exceptional years, for at a later period there are different tales. In 1613, one John Darlingie was presented at Bidford "for keepinge ill rule in his house on the sabaoth in service time by sellinge of alle," MS. Episc. Reg. Wigorn. In 1646, six of the ale-house keepers were presented at the Warwick Sessions for pursuing their calling without licenses, and in the following year, 1647, "William Torpley of Bidford presented for sellinge of lesse then mesure, and for keeping disorders in his howse," Warwick County MSS.

No. 186. He happened to meet with a shepherd.—A gentleman who visited Stratford-on-Avon in 1762, relates how the host of the White Lion Inn took him to Bidford, "and shewed me in the hedge a crab-tree called Shakespear's Canopy, because under it our poet slept one night; for he, as well as Ben Johnson, loved a glass for the pleasure of society; and he, having heard much of the men of that village as deep drinkers and merry fellows, one day went over to Bidford to take a cup with them;—he enquired of a shepherd for the Bidford drinkers, who

replied they were absent, but the Bidford sippers were at home, and, I
suppose, continued the sheepkeeper, they will be sufficient for you ; and
so, indeed, they were ;—he was forced to take up his lodging under
that tree for some hours," British Magazine for June, 1762.   This is
the only traditional account which is of the slightest value, but a
ridiculous amplification of it is narrated by Jordan in a manuscript
written about the year 1770.   This manuscript, which was formerly in
Ireland's possession (Confessions, 1805, p. 34), and is now in my own
collection, is here printed V.L.,—" The following anecdote of Shakspeare is tho a traditional Story as well authenticated as things of this
nature generally are   I shall therefore not hesitate relating it as it was
Verbally delivered to me.   Our Poet was extremely fond of drinking
hearty draughts of English Ale, and glory'd in being thought a person of
superior eminence in that proffession if I may be alowed the phrase.
In his time, but at what period it is not recorded, There were two
companys or fraternitys of Village Yeomanry who used frequently to
associate to gether at Bidford a town pleasantly situate on the banks of
the Avon about 7 Miles below Stratford, and Who boasted themselves
Superior in the Science of drinking to any set of equal number in the
Kingdom and hearing the fame of our Bard it was determined to
Challenge him and his Companions to a tryal of their skill which the
Stratfordians accepted and accordingly repaired to Bidford which place
agreeable to both parties was to be the Scene of Contendtion.   But
when Shakespeare and his Companions arrived at the destined spot, to
their disagreeable disapointment they found the Topers were gone to
Evesham fair and were told that if they had a mind to try their strenght
with the Sippers, they were ther ready for the Contest, Shakespr and his
compainions made a Scoff at their Opponents but for want of better
Company they agreed to the Contest and in a little time our Bard and
his Compainions got so intollerable intoxicated that they was not able
to Contend any longer and acordingly set out on their return to
Stratford   But had not got above half a mile on the road e'er the
found themselves unable to proceed any farther, and was obliged to lie
down under a Crabtree which is still growing by the side of the road
where they took up their repose till morning when some of the
Company roused the poet and intreated him to return to Bidford
and renew the Contest he declined it saying I have drank with—
Piping Pebworth, Dancing Marston,=Haunted Hillborough, Hungry
Grafton,=Dadgeing Exhall, Papist Wicksford,=Beggarly Broom, and
Drunken Bidford,"—meaning, by this doggrel, with the bibulous com-
petitors who had arrived from the first-named seven villages, all of
which are within a few miles of Bidford.   A tinkered version of this
latter anecdote, in which it is for the first time classed amongst the
" juvenile levities " of Shakespeare, was sent by the writer to Malone in

the. year 1790 as one that was told him by George Hart who died in 1778, and who was a descendant from the poet's sister. It will be found in Malone's edition of Shakespeare, 1821, ii. 500-502; and two other accounts, those in the Gentleman's Magazine for December, 1794, and in Ireland's Views on the Warwickshire Avon, 1795, pp. 229-233, are known to have been constructed from materials furnished by Jordan. Another version, that printed in the Monthly Mirror for November, 1808, is obviously taken from the one of 1794. There is hearsay, but no other kind of evidence, that the story, as above given, was in circulation anterior to its promulgation by the Stratford rhymer, and until more satisfactory testimony can be adduced to that effect, it must remain under the suspicion of being one of his numerous fabrications. This seems, indeed, the only feasible explanation that can be given of the lines on the villages not appearing, if they had been then current, in the traditional account of 1762. They have the appearance of belonging to the tribe of rural doggrels of the kind that were formerly so popular in our country districts. They may be genuine, and yet of course have no real connection with the Shakespearean history, however cleverly they have been adapted to Bacchanalian utterances.

No. 187. Easily find the Sippers.—Long after the time of Jordan, some one, without the least authority, asserted that these gentlemen were discovered at the Falcon Inn at Bidford. It is scarcely credible, but it is nevertheless a fact, that a room in a large building once so called, though probably not a tavern at all in Shakespeare's time, has been unblushingly indicated as the scene of the revelry. It has also been pretended that an antique chair, said to have been in that building from time out of mind, was the identical seat occupied by the poet; and even the sign of the inn, a daub of the last century, has been considered worthy of respectful preservation.

No. 188. Sufficiently jolly.—The epigram on Wincot ale, printed in Sir Aston Cokain's Poems, 1658, having been produced in support of other versions of the story, it should be mentioned that it obviously has no connection with the Shakespearean tradition, even if it be a fact that the Falcon Inn at Bidford was kept, in the poet's time, by a person of the name of Norton. The latter statement is made in Green's Legend of the Crab-Tree, 1857, p. 14, but no evidence on the subject is adduced. It appears, however, from the parish register, commencing in 1664, that there was a Norton family residing in that village in 1687 and 1692. In the only other early documents that I have been able to consult, the manorial rolls from 1671 to 1681, there is no mention either of the Falcon Inn or of the Nortons.

No. 189. Under the branches of a crab-tree.—From a sketch which was made by Ireland either in 1792 or 1793, the fidelity of which was assured to me many years ago by persons who had seen the tree in their youthful days, it may be inferred that it was then of an unusual size and antiquity, and there is certainly no impossibility in the assumption that it was large enough in the poet's time to have afforded the recorded shelter. Early in the present century it began to decay, the foliage gradually disappearing until, in 1824, the only remaining vestiges, consisting of the trunk and a number of roots, all in an advanced stage of decay, were transferred to Bidford Grange.

No. 190. Early in the following morning.—Some of the later ramifications of the tale are sufficiently ludicrous. Thus we are told in Brewer's Description of the County of Warwick, 1820, p. 260, that "those who repeat the tradition in the neighbourhood of Stratford invariably assert that the whole party slept undisturbed from Saturday night till the following Monday morning, when they were roused by workmen going to their labour." According to an improved version of this form of the anecdote, so completely had the previous day been effaced from the sleeper's memory that, when he woke up, he rebuked a field labourer in the vicinity for his desecration of the sabbath.

No. 191. In corn and other articles.—There were other glovers at Stratford-on-Avon in Elizabeth's time, who did not restrict themselves to their nominal business. One of them dealt in wool, yarn, and malt, the last-named article seeming to be their usual additional trading material. "George Perrye, besides is glovers trade, usethe buyinge and sellinge of woll and yorne, and makinge of mallte," MS. dated 1595. "Roberte Butler, besides his glovers occupation, usethe makinge of mallte," MS. ibid. "Rychard Castell, Rother Market, usethe his glovers occupacion; his weiffe utterethe weekelye by bruynge ij. strikes of mallte," MS. ibid. In one of the copies of an inventory taken at Stratford after the death of Joyce Hobday, 1602, are the following entries,—"George Shacleton oweth me for woll. xxiiij.*s.*—Mr. Gutteridge oweth me for calves lether, iiij.*s.* viij.*d.*—John Edwards of Allveston, alias Allston, oweth me for two pere of gloves, viij.*d.*" Even in this century there were firms in the north who were glovers and dealers in wool, as well as dyers of leather and dressers of skins. In former days glovers were almost invariably fellmongers, the material furnished by the latter being well adapted for the production of coarse leather gloves, the only ones that, in John Shakespeare's time, were in general provincial use. "To Townsen, the glover, for two sheepe skines, vj.*s.* viij.*d.*," records of Rye, co. Sussex, 1604. "Butler of Puddle Wharfe, a glover, felmonger, or sheep-skin-dresser," Brian, 1637. There is, in the churchyard of Stratford-on-Avon, a tombstone of the latter part of the seventeenth century (1688-9) to the memory of "a fellmonger and glover."

No. 192. The concentration of several trades.—Thus it is recorded in 1595, that "Thomas Rogers. now baieliefe of this towne, besydes his butchers trade, which untill now of late hee allwaies used, hee ys a buyer and seller of corne for great somes, and withall usethe grazinge and buyinge and sellinge of cattell, and hathe in howshold xiij. persons ;" and in the same year we are told, under *Hyghe Streete*, that "Jhon Perrye usethe sometimes his butchers trade besides his husbandrye." When Aubrey states that John Shakespeare was a butcher, he either confused the father's occupation with that of the son, or was led to the assertion by the probable circumstance of the former having sometimes dealt in meat when he was the owner of Asbies. There can be little doubt that John Shakespeare, in common with other farmers and landowners, often killed his own beasts and pigs both for home consumption and for sale, but it is in the highest degree improbable that his leading business was ever that of a butcher. If that had been the case, there would assuredly have been some allusion to the fact in the local records. Two other examples of the combination of trades at Stratford-on-Avon are worth adding. "Mr. Persons hathe, besides his trade of draperye and lyvinge yeerely commynge in, of longe tyme used makinge of mallte and bruyinge to sell in his howse, and ys a common buyer and seller of corne," MS. dated 1595. "Peeter Davyes, besides his woolwynders occupacion, usethe the makinge of mallte and victuallinge," MS. ibid.

No. 193. The domination of a commercial spirit.—It is not at all probable that Shakespeare could have entertained, under the theatrical conditions that surrounded his work, the subtle devices underlying his art which are attributed to his sagacity by the philosophical critics, and some of which, it is amusing to notice, may be equally observed, if they exist at all, in the original plot-sources of his dramas. Amongst the most favourite and least tenable of these fancies is that he gratuitously permitted his art to be controlled by the necessity of blending a variety of actions in subjection to one leading moral idea or by other similar limitations. But the phenomenon of a moral unity is certainly not to be found either in nature or in the works of nature's poet, whose truthful and impartial genius could never have voluntarily endured a submission to a preconception which involved violent deviations from the course prescribed by his sovereign knowledge of human nature and the human mind.

No. 194. If this view.—It is well supported by the few accessible evidences. The poet was not a member of Lord Strange's company in May, 1593, or his name would assuredly have been included in the list of that date. If he was then one of Lord Pembroke's actors, there were ample reasons for his leaving them in the following autumn, when they are mentioned as having been in such deplorable straits that they were compelled to pawn their theatrical apparel. The company of actors under the patronage of the Earl of Sussex was disbanded in the spring of 1594, some of them in all probability joining those of the Lord

Chamberlain. There is, moreover, the corroborative fact that Shakespeare, throughout his subsequent career, was never known to write for any other managers but those with whom he was theatrically connected.

No. 195. A play on the subject of Henry the Fifth.—It would seem from the epilogue to the Second Part of Henry the Fourth that Shakespeare's original intention was to make his play on the subject of the following reign one of a more comic nature than that which ultimately appeared, one in which the dramatic construction would no doubt have harmonized with the previous design.

No. 196. It was favourably received.—The surreptitious editions may be fairly regarded as evidences of the popularity of Henry the Fifth, and it was performed at Court by the King's players early in the year 1605. This sovereign was probably a favourite character on the old English stage. There was not only the Famous Victories, which appeared either in or before 1594, but a new drama called Henry the Fifth was produced at one of the Surrey theatres in the following year. "The 28 of Novmbr, 1595, n.e., R. at Harey the v, iij.*li.* vj.*s*," Henslowe's Diary. The patriotic influences of one or more of the three dramas are noticed by Heywood in his Apology for Actors, 1612.

No. 197. Specially relished.—This may be gathered from the title-page of ed. 1600, and it would even seem that the play was sometimes known under the title of Ancient Pistol. In the reply of a decisive young lady to a boisterous lover, he is told,—" it is not your hustie rustie can make me afraid of your bigge lookes, for I saw the plaie of Ancient Pistoll, where a craking coward was well cudgeled for his knavery ; your railing is so neere the rascall that I am almost ashamed to bestow so good a name as the rogue uppon you,"—Breton's Poste with a Packet of Madde Letters, 1603, "newly inlarged," the tract having originally appeared in the preceding year. In the Scornful Lady, a comedy written before 1616, Beaumont introduces a character who is a poor imitation of Pistol.

No. 198. Of any of those.—These editions do not contain the choruses, and, as the latter were written as early as 1599, it is next to impossible that the quartos represent the author's imperfect sketch. The fact that Shakespeare wrote the play after he had completed the Second Part of Henry the Fourth, as appears from the epilogue to the latter, precludes the supposition that Henry the Fifth could have been a very early production ; and especially such a piece as would be suggested by the edition of 1600. It is, moreover, perfectly clear that some of the speeches in that impression are mere abridgments of others in the perfect version.

No. 199. The unity of character.—The definition given in the text conveys a sense different from that in which the term is used by the æsthetic critics. "The unity of feeling," observes Coleridge, "is everywhere and at all times observed by Shakespeare in his plays; read Romeo and Juliet,—all is youth and spring; it is one and the same feeling that commences, goes through, and ends the play; the old men are not common old men,—they have an eagerness, a heartiness, a vehemence, the effect of spring;—this unity of feeling and character pervades every drama of Shakespeare," Notes and Lectures, ed. 1875, p. 63. One may be permitted to suspect that this kind of individuality exists solely in the fancy, while it is very difficult to understand that it could be preserved throughout an entire drama without an undue limitation of the author's fidelity in his characterizations. The notion that the composition of one play was uniformly influenced by the geniality of youth and spring, that of another by the rigor of old age and winter, and so on;—this, in reference to the works of nature's great interpreter, is one of the most curious theories yet enunciated by the philosophical commentators.

No. 200. No fewer than a hundred and twenty-seven acres.—The præcipe of the fine is dated May the 28th, 1610,—" Willielmo Combe armigero, et Johanni Combe, generoso, quod juste &c. teneant Willielmo Shakespere, generoso, conventionem &c. de centum et septem acris terre, et viginti acris pasture, cum pertinentiis, in Old Stratford et Stratford-super-Avon." This property is mentioned in 1639 as "all those fower yards land and a halfe of arrable, meadowe and pasture, with thappurtenaunces, lying and being in the townes, hambletts, villages, feilds and grounds of Stratford-upon-Avon, Ould Stratford, Bishopton and Welcombe," and a like description is found in the later settlements. The extent of a yard land curiously varied even in the same localities of the same county, and the facts that a hundred and seven acres were taken as four of them in 1602, and twenty as a half of one of them in 1639, show that there was formerly no precise idea on the subject.

No. 201. With affectionate tributes.—At this period the funereal charges at Stratford included four-pence for ringing the bell, and the like sum for the use of the pall. The latter article was very frequently dispensed with, but both were ordered upon this occasion,—" item, for the bell and pall for Mr. Shaxpers dawghter, viij.*d.*" A payment

dictated by sentiment cannot reasonably be adduced in evidence respecting the circumstances of the parents, although even such comparatively insignificant amounts were of moment in those days to an embarrassed tradesman.

No. 202.   On that Saturday.—De Quincy was the first to conjecture that the 22nd of April, corresponding to our present 4th of May, is the real birthday.   The suggestion was derived from the circumstance of the poet's only grand-child having been married to Thomas Nash on the 22nd of April, 1626; and few things are more likely than the selection of her grandfather's birthday for such a celebration.   Only ten years had elapsed since his death, and that he had been kind to her in her childhood may be safely inferred from the remembrances in the will.   Whatever opinion may be formed respecting the precise interpretation of the record of the age under the monumental effigy, the latter is a certain evidence that Shakespeare was not born after the 23rd of April. It may also be fairly assumed that the event could not have happened many days previously, for it was the almost universal practice amongst the middle classes of that time to baptize children very shortly after birth.   The notion that Shakespeare died on his birthday was not circulated until the middle of the last century, and it is completely devoid of substantial foundation.   Had so unusual a circumstance occurred, it is all but impossible that it should not have been numbered amongst the early traditions of Stratford-on-Avon, and there is good evidence that no such incident was known in that town at the close of the seventeenth century.   There is preserved at the end of the parish register a few notes on the local celebrities headed,—" I finde these persons remarkable,"—written about the year 1690, and under the poet's name is this statement,—" born Ap. the 26th, 1564,"—a date obviously taken from the baptismal register, and proving that the writer had no other information on the subject.

No. 203.   With such celerity.—Shakespeare commenced to write for the stage in or shortly before the winter of 1591-1592, and prior to the summer of 1598 he had written at least fifteen plays, including several of his master-pieces.   In the course of the next four years he had produced, amongst others, Hamlet and Twelfth Night.   Having thus reached the summit of dramatic power in the middle of his literary career, an endeavour to classify or to study a large number of his works in an order of progressive ability would be manifestly futile.   Shakespeare is not to be judged by ordinary rules, and, although it is obvious that a few of his plays belong to the very early years of authorship, it is equally certain that he shortly afterwards exercised an unlimited control over his art.

No. 204.   Who had died some time previously.—This is the most probable view of the case, but the register of the first Joan's burial has not been discovered, being, in all probability, one of the omissions in the later transcript of the original entries.   It should be observed that, in the time of Elizabeth, and for long afterwards, the practice of giving a deceased child's first name to a successor was extremely common.   In this way Shakespeare's friend, Adrian Quiney, born in 1586, was preceded by a brother of the same name whose burial was recorded two years previously. It may also be worth mentioning that a Christian name was occasionally repeated in a family even in cases where the earlier holder of it was still living ; but the absence of all other notice of the first Joan renders this latter contingency somewhat improbable. Goodlacke Edwardes of Worcester, clothier, in his will of 1559, distinctly mentions two daughters of the name of Anne both living at the same time, and this baptismal practice was the occasional source of litigation.

No. 205. Joan was then so common a name.—It was frequently in those days considered synonymous with Jane. "Wray said, the names are both one, and so it had been adjudged before this time, upon conference with the grammarians, that Jane and Joane is one name," Croke's Reports for Easter Term, 32 Eliz., ed. 1683, i. 176.

No. 206. The great dramatist purchased.—One of the indentures of conveyance has the following endorsement,—"Combe to Shackspeare of the four yard land in Stratford field." These words have been thought to be in Shakespeare's handwriting, but they were indubitably written long after the poet's decease.

No. 207. In complete readiness for the purchaser's attestation.—With one label ready placed for one seal only, showing that the counterpart was intended for the poet's signature. The text of the duplicate indenture is practically identical with the one given in this work, the few variations that are found in it being of the most insignificant and accidental character.

No. 208. A long and tedious poem.—It was probably not a very successful publication, unsold copies having been re-issued in 1611 under the new title of,—"The Annals of great Brittaine ; or, a most excellent Monument, wherein may be seene all the antiquities of this Kingdome, to the satisfaction both of the Universities or any other place stirred with Emulation of long continuance."

No. 209. The recognized pieces of this latter series.—The character of the work, throughout the entire volume, should suffice to exclude the irrational conjecture that deception has been practised in any of these attributions. It is scarcely possible that the external testimony to their genuineness could have been more decisive, while the internal evidence in the case of Shakespeare's poem can only be regarded as unsatisfactory by those who are under the impression that his style was never materially influenced by contemporary emergencies.

No. 210. The amazing number of different characters.—It has been often remarked that some of Shakespeare's characters are germs of others that were brought on the stage at a later period of composition, but this is a notion that will not be sustained by a patient analysis, especially if the different circumstances by which they are surrounded are taken

Facsimile of the Title-page to the concluding portion of Chester's Loves Martyr or Rosalins Complaint, allegorically shadowing the Truth of Love in the constant Fate of the Phœnix and Turtle.

HEREAFTER
FOLLOVV DIVERSE
Poeticall Effaies on the former Sub-
iect; viz: the *Turtle* and *Phœnix.*

Done by the beft and chiefeft of our
moderne writers, with their names fub-
fcribed to their particular workes:
neuer before extant.

And (now firft) confecrated by them all generally,
to the loue and merite of the true-noble Knight,
Sir Iohn Salisburie.

Dignum laude virum Mufa vetat mori.

MDCI.

Facsimile of the Page of Chester's Loves Martyr, with the concluding Verses of Shakespeare's lines on the Phœnix and Turtle, from the original edition which was published in London in the year 1601.

Threnos.

Beautie, Truth, and Raritie,
Grace in all fimplicitie,
Here enclofde, in cinders lie.

Death is now the *Phœnix* neft,
And the *Turtles* loyall breft,
To eternitie doth reft.

Leauing no pofteritie,
Twas not their infirmitie,
It was married Chaftitie.

Truth may feeme, but cannot be,
Beautie bragge, but tis not fhe,
Truth and Beautie buried be.

To this vrne let thofe repaire,
That are either true or faire,
For thefe dead Birds, figh a prayer.

William Shake-fpeare.

fully into consideration. There are an infinite number of trivial variations a very few of which in themselves suffice to elicit a diversity between the natures of two persons, both of whom may yet be endowed with a large proportion of the same characteristics.

No. 211. Pericles.—No mention of this play has been discovered in any book or manuscript dated previously to the year 1608. The statement that an edition of Pimlyco or Runne Red-Cap was issued in 1596 is inconsistent with the original entry of that tract on the Registers of the Stationers' Company under the date of April the 15th, 1609.

No. 212. At the Globe Theatre.—George Wilkins, probably the dramatist of that name, made up a novel from Twyne's Patterne of Paineful Adventures, and from Pericles as acted at the Globe Theatre in 1608. It was published in that year under the title of,—"The Painfull Adventures of Pericles Prince of Tyre ; being the true History of the Play of Pericles, as it was lately presented by the worthy and ancient poet John Gower, 1608." This very rare and curious tract is printed in small quarto, and in the centre of the title-page is an interesting wood-cut of John Gower, no doubt in the costume in which he was represented at the theatre, with a staff in one hand and a bunch of bays in the other ; while before him is spread open a copy of the Confessio Amantis, the main source of the plot of the drama. Wilkins, in a dedication to Maister Henry Fermor, speaks of his work as "a poore infant of my braine ;" but he nevertheless copies wholesale from Twyne, adapting the narrative of the latter in a great measure to the conduct of the acting play. It appears from the circumstance of Wilkins frequently using passages obviously derived from the tragedy in the wrong places, and from his making unnecessary variations in some of the main actions, that he had no complete copy of Pericles to refer to, and that his only means of using the drama was by the aid of hasty notes taken in shorthand during its performance at the Theatre. At the end of the argument of the tale, he entreats "the reader to receive this historie in the same manner as it was under the habite of ancient Gower, the famous English poet, by the Kings Majesties Players excellently presented." Other evidences of the theatrical success of Pericles occur in the title-pages of ed. 1609, in Pimlyco or Runne Red-Cap, 1609, and in Tailor's Hogge Hath Lost his Pearle, 1614 ; and, notwithstanding occasional depreciations of it on the score of immorality, there are numerous testimonies to its continued popularity during the reigns of James and Charles the First, *insignis Pericles*, as it is called in some unpublished Latin verses of Randolph. The following little anecdote may possibly refer to a period anterior to the death of Shakespeare,— "two gentlemen went to see Pericles acted, and one of them was moved with the calamities of that prince that he wept, whereat the other laughed extreamely. Not long after, the same couple went to see the Major of

Qinborough, when he who jeered the other at Pericles now wept himselfe, to whom the other, laughing, sayd, what the divell should there
bee in this merry play to make a man weep? O, replied the other, who
can hold from weeping to see a magistrate so abused? The jest will
take those who have seene these two plaies," *Booke of Bulls* baited with
two Centuries of bold Jest and nimble Lies, 1636.

No. 213. The first edition.—Printed in 1609, "as it hath been
divers and sundry times acted by his Maiesties Servants at the Globe
on the Banck-side." It was published before the fifth of May in that
year, 1609, there existing a copy with an owner's autograph written on
that day. The copies of this edition vary from each other in some
important readings, and there are two impressions of 1609 distinguishable
from each other by having variations in the device of the first capital letter
in the text. A third edition was issued in 1611, "printed at London
by S.S.," a surreptitious and badly printed copy with numerous typographical errors. There is a rather curious peculiarity in the title-pages
of the two earliest editions, the Christian name of the author being
divided from his surname by a printer's device of two small leaves.

No. 214. The poet's share.—Dryden, writing about the year 1680,
expressly states that Pericles was the earliest dramatic production of our
national poet,—"Shakespear's own muse her Pericles first bore,=The
Prince of Tyre was elder than the Moore." If this were really the case,
the Globe play of 1608 must of course have been a revival of a much
earlier work; but Dryden, as appears from several of his notes, was very
imperfectly acquainted with the history of the Elizabethan drama, so
that his statement, or rather what may more judiciously be termed his
opinion, on this subject cannot be implicitly relied upon. Thus, for
example, in one place he decisively states Othello to have been Shakespeare's last play, whereas it is now well-known to have been in existence
more than eleven years before his death.

*No. 215. Inconsistent with the perfect unity and harmony of the
dramatic art.*—And so are the various theories which assume that
Shakespeare worked for the establishment of preconceived moral or
ethical intentions. Such views would have been beyond the theatrical
requirements of his age, and, considered as emanations from his own
temperament, is it credible that, if he had seriously desired to entertain
them as objects of his work, they could ever have been listlessly interrupted by a neglect to encounter the smallest trouble in their favour, as
when, for example, he adhered to the foundation-tale in the pardon of
so repulsive a villain as Angelo. It is certain that, as a rule, instead of
constructing his own plots, he followed almost literally the incidents of
stories already in existence. He then seems to have been enabled, by
the gift of a preternatural instinct, to create simultaneously, and interpret
the minds of, any required number of personages whose resultant

actions, under the various circumstances by which they were surrounded, and the powers with which they were invested, would harmonize with the general conduct of the tale, and lead naturally to its *adopted* dênouement.   In a drama written under such conditions, the combination of a special philosophical design of any kind with fidelity to nature in characterization would be clearly impossible.   And although the belief that the great dramatist wrote numerous speeches with an ethical purpose cannot be so distinctly refuted, yet even this modified theory is at best but a mere surmise.   The introduction of some of his treasures of wisdom may be due to a following of the dramatic practice of the day, and as to the remainder, it is surely not very wonderful that the instinctive metaphysician,—the unrivalled expositor of the human mind amidst its numberless permutations of conditions and influences,— should become on countless occasions an incidental moralist.

No. 216.   King Lear.—There was an old and popular ballad on the history of King Lear, the earliest known copy of which is preserved in the Golden Garland of Princely Pleasures and delicate Delights, wherein is conteined the Histories of many of the Kings, Queenes, Princes Lords, Ladies, Knights, and Gentlewomen of this Kingdome, 1620. This was the third edition of that little work, and although no earlier copy of it has been discovered, it is all but impossible that it could have been published before the appearance of Shakespeare's tragedy.

No. 217.   One or more.—There were at least two old plays on the subject in the dramatic repertory of the time, one which was printed under the title of the True Chronicle History of King Leir, and another, now lost, that bore probably more affinity to Shakespeare's drama.   The latter fact is gathered from an interesting entry in an inventory of theatrical apparel belonging to the Lord Admiral's Company in March, 1598-9, where mention is made of " Kentes woden leage," that is, stocks. A play of King Lear was acted in Surrey on April the 6th and 8th, 1594, by the servants of the Queen and the Earl of Sussex, who were then performing as one company.   The representation attracted liberal receipts, especially on the first of these occasions, but it is not mentioned by Henslowe as being then a new production.   In the May of that year there was entered to Edward White, on the books of the Stationers' Company, "a booke entituled the moste famous chronicle historye of Leire Kinge of England and his three daughters."   No impression of that date is known to exist, the earliest printed copy which has been discovered being one which appeared in 1605.   On the title-page of a copy of this last-named edition, preserved in the British Museum, are the following words in manuscript,—"first written by Mr. William Shakespeare."   This note is nearly obliterated, but it was certainly penned too long after the date of publication to be of value in a question of authorship.   Poor as this old play of King Leir undoubtedly is as a whole, it has passages of considerable merit, and it seems to have been popular in Shakespeare's time. According to the title-page of ed. 1605 it had then " bene divers and sundry times lately acted," and in a work called the Life and Death of Mr. Edmund Geninges, 1614, it is stated that " King Liere, a book so called," *hath applause.*

No. 218. Before King James.—It is certain that Shakespeare's tragedy was not produced before March, 1603, the date of the publication of Harsnet's Declaration, a book whence the names of some of the fiends mentioned by Edgar were, perhaps indirectly, taken, but the other notices in King Lear that have been thought to bear upon the question of its date are of a less decisive character. Such is the variation of the terms of British and English, but the former occurs more frequently than the latter in the older play ; while allusions to such matter as storms and eclipses are exceedingly treacherous criteria. Moreover, if the tragedy had been produced any length of time previously to the Christmas of 1606, it would be difficult to account for the evidences of its popularity accruing only in the following year. What are termed the æsthetic evidences are pureful fanciful. Thus we are told by one of the shrewdest of critics, that "in King Lear the Fool rises into heroic proportions, and shows not less than Lear himself the grand development of Shakespeare's mind at this period of maturity." But too extravagant is the hope of interpreting the development of a mind that had already produced the tragedy of Hamlet, and that development at all events is not likely to be faithfully traced in characteristics, which, in the hands of so unlimited a genius, may be fairly regarded as natural dramatic evolutions from an adherence to the outline of a popular story.

No. 219. Continued in the family.—The settled estates named in the poet's will consisted of his residence and grounds at New Place, the house in the Blackfriars, the land purchased from the Combes, and the Henley Street property. The entail of these was barred and a resettlement made in 1639, but the latter was abrogated by a new one, executed in 1647, by which Mrs. Nash became the owner of the estates subject to the life-interest of Susanna Hall and to a limitation in favour of her issue. Some years after the death of Mrs. Hall the Henley Street and Blackfriars estates came, under some unrecorded conditions, to be treated as fee-simples belonging to the testator's grand-daughter ; but the two other properties, New Place and the Combe land, were resettled in 1652 to the use of Mr. and Mrs. Barnard for their joint and survivorship lives, with a remainder to her children, and, in default of issue, to her appointment.

No. 220. The unities of character.—In venturing to suggest the preservation of these as one of the leading characteristics of Shakespeare's dramatic work, it is under the impression that in this respect he is essentially superior, certainly to Ben Jonson, and, I believe, to all contemporary writers. It is possible, indeed, that a skilful analyzer of every one of his numerous characters might occasionally meet with an apparent or even with a real discrepancy, but this would not materially endanger the integrity of the position here advanced. The few examples of this kind may be attributed either to Shakespeare's extreme rapidity of composition, or to circumstances that occasioned intermittent work, or even, on rare occasions, to the necessity of a compliance with the exigencies of the stage.

No 221. Continued to be one of mud.—" It is to be noticed that Dr. Davenport's old garden wall had not been erected more than thirty years, and was built where a mud wall, which had been standing there many years, was taken down, and the open ditch was filled up, and a culvert made to carry away the water," Defendant's Case in the Bree Suit at the Warwick Summer Assizes, 1807. The ditch here referred to was the one that was formerly on the south side of Chapel Lane.

No. 222. One of the valuable tithe-leases.—There is nothing to lead to the usual opinion that Quiney was referring to the lease the moiety of which was sold in 1605. When Sturley mentions " our tithes " and the " very great moment " Shakespeare's purchase of them would be " both to him and to us," he alludes, in all probability, to some in which they were likely to be interested as farmers in the event of an individual, who was practically a non-resident, becoming the owner. That Sturley and Adrian Quiney were likely to have officiated in such capacities is shown by a deposition, taken in 1590, respecting the tithe-hay of Clopton, " one Quiny and Abraham Sturley being farmers of the same," Worc. Episc. Reg. MS., a farmer being a person who collected and sold the tithe produce, paying over a stipulated amount to the lessee. The Corporation, who received, at that time, a fixed rent on each of the tithe divisions, would not have been affected by a change of ownership, neither could the latter have been of consequence to the inhabitants of the town.

No. 223. The same occupation.—There is this to be said in favour of Rowe's account, that it was formerly considered in many places that the eldest son had a kind of prescriptive right to be brought up to his father's occupation. Dr. Franklin mentions thisusage as one that was an invariable rule with his English ancestors ; Works, ed. 1793, i. 8.

No. 224. Allegorical characters.—The allegorical was the first deviation from the purely religious drama. The introduction of secular plays quickly followed, after which, from the close of the fifteenth century to the time of Shakespeare, there was a succession of interludes and other theatrical pieces in great variety, in many of which some of the characters were abstract personifications similar to those introduced into the moral-plays. The most ancient English secular drama which is known to exist was written about the year 1490 by the Rev. Henry

Medwall, chaplain to Morton, Archbishop of Canterbury, and afterwards printed by Rastell under the title of,—"a godely interlude of Fulgeus, Cenatoure of Rome, Lucres his doughter, Gayus Flaminius and Publius Cornelius, of the Disputacyon of Noblenes." Medwall was the author of at least two other lengthy pieces, in both of which, however, the characters were mainly allegorical, but he appears to have been the first writer who introduced a prose speech into an English play. His works, although rather dull even for his age, are superior both in construction and versification to those of his predecessors, and he may almost be said to be the founder of our famous national drama, that which lingered for generations after him in painful mediocrity until a little fervour, and more poetic beauty, were communicated to it by a small band of writers who were bestowing a literary character on the stage at the time of the poet's arrival in London. It was very shortly afterwards, and in the midst of this advance, that the English drama rose by a spirited bound to be first really worthy the name of art in the hands of Marlowe.

No. 225. The reckless gossip.—Aubrey was utterly wanting in either delicacy or charity when treating on matters that affected the reputations of others. Ben Jonson fared no better in his hands than Shakespeare. "Ben Johnson had one eie lower than tother and bigger, like Clun the player; perhaps he begott Clun," Aubrey's Lives, iii. 54, MS.

No. 226. Who had the free use of Aubreys papers.—In his memoir of Sir William Davenant he occasionally uses the exact words of Aubrey, and Warton's implied statement, that there is a notice of the scandal in one of Wood's own manuscripts, is erroneous.

No. 227. Unconscious of a secret.—This may be concluded from the kind and liberal arrangements made in his will, 1622, in favour of "my sonne William."

No. 228. All's one.—The half title, on the first page of the text, ed. 1608, runs as follows,—"All's One, or one of the foure plaies in one, called a York-shire Tragedy, as it was plaid by the kings Maiesties Plaiers." As this drama was entered at Stationers' Hall on May the 2nd, it may be assumed that it had been performed by Shakespeare's company before that day.

No. 229. Composed by other dramatists.—This appears from the following entry under the year 1599 in Henslowe's diary,—"this 16th of October, 99, received by me, Thomas Downton, of Phillipp Henchlow, to pay Mr. Munday, Mr. Drayton, and Mr. Wilson and Hathway, for the first parte of the Lyfe of Sir Jhon Ouldcasstell, and in earnest of the second parte, for the use of the companyny, ten pownd."

No. 230. Which of these editions is the first.—Pavier entered the First Part of Sir John Oldcastle, but without an author's name, on the Stationers' register of August, 1600, the drama having been produced by the Lord Admiral's company at the Rose in the previous November.

Henslowe, the manager of that theatre, was so well satisfied with the piece that, with unwonted liberality, he presented its authors with a gratuity on the occasion of its first performance. " Receved of Mr. Hincheloe, as a gefte for Mr. Mundaye and the reste of the poets, at the playnge of Sir John Oldcastell the ferste tyme, x.*s.*", Dulwich MS., 1599.

No. 231. No cancel of the poet's name.—Had the case been otherwise, it is all but impossible that copies with substituted title-pages should not have been discovered. If Pavier had withdrawn the name from the attributed drama after its publication, it is hardly likely that he would have been at the expense of printing an entirely new edition when the cancel of one leaf would have answered every purpose, that is to say, presuming that the withdrawal had been the result of any special remonstrance. Both editions of Sir John Oldcastle must have been issued in the latter part of the year, as Pavier did not enter into the publishing business until June, 1600.

No. 232. By inspiration not by design.—There is another theory which has met with considerable favour in recent times, the advocates of which would have us believe that Shakespeare's judgment throughout his dramatic writings was commensurate with his genius, and that, instead of troubling himself to weigh the chances of popularity, he was always working on an artistic and inner-life directed system to which the theatrical views of the day were altogether subordinate. Under the provisions of this theory has arisen, amongst other eccentric fancies, the arrangement of his works into definite Periods, each one being considered to represent a separate mental grade, and thus we are instructed by the inventor of this order how to discriminate between " the negative period of his perfection " and " the period of beauty " or " that of grandeur," while the last Period came, as we are informed in the explicit language of what is politely termed *the higher criticism*, " when the energies of intellect in the cycle of genius were, though in a rich and more potentiated form, becoming predominant over passion and creative self-manifestation," Coleridge's Notes and Lectures, ed. 1875, p. 81. It is difficult to understand the advantage of all this, but if classification of any kind is really thought to be of use, the most feasible, little as that most appears to be, is that which is deduced from variations in the style of composition and in range or character of knowledge and thought. It may certainly be possible to indicate a few of Shakespeare's dramas that undoubtedly belong to a period of comparative immaturity, but an enlarged division must necessarily be questionable in reference to the works of a dramatist who was endowed with a preternatural intelligence and an exhaustless versatility. Speculations on the exact periods of changes of personal taste in choice and treatment of subject are attended with even greater uncertainty, and involve the more than doubtful supposition that neither the managers of the theatre, nor the company of actors, nor the prevailing temper of the audiences, exercised an influence in the matter. It is also to be observed that much of the tone of a play would depend upon the nature of the story that the author was dramatizing. Can any one seriously imagine that if, for example, the composition epochs of Hamlet and Lear had been reversed, the treatment of either subject would on that account have materially varied from that which it received? Or that it is possible to gauge the writer's mental or perceptive expansion, if there were any, that accrued in the interval between the two compositions. Of all these matters it will be the wisest to believe, in the words of old Leonard Digges, that "some second Shakespeare must of Shakespeare write."

No. 233. The poet being then in London.—This is ascertained from the following passage in Sturley's letter of January the 24th,—"bi the instructions u can geve him (Shakespeare) theareof;" language which is not likely to have been used had the poet been at Stratford and accessible to the elder Quiney

No. 234. Was buried at Southwark.—"Burialles, December, 1607. —31. Edmund Shakspeare, a player, buried in the Church with a forenoone knell of the great bell, xx.*s.*," the Sexton's MS. note, St. Saviour's, Southwark. "1607, Decemb. 31, Edmond Shakespeare, a player, in the Church," parish bur. reg. The fee for burial "in any churchyard next the Church" was only two shillings, but we are told that "the churchwardens have for the ground for every man or woman that shall be buried in the Church, with an afternoones knell or without it, xx.*s.*," Duties belonging to the Church of St. Saviour, 1613. The fees for ringing the great bell amounted to eight shillings, whereas those for the use of the lesser one did not exceed twelve-pence, facts which indicate that no expense was spared in the conduct of Edmund's funeral.

No. 235. The road from Henley-in-Arden.—A tenement in Henley Street is described in a medieval deed as "unum mesuagium cum suis pertinenciis in villa de Stratford, illud, videlicet, quod jacet in illo vico qui se extendit versus Enley." In a similar manner there arose the names of Kent Street in Southwark, Dover Lane in Canterbury, Trumpington Street in Cambridge, &c.

No. 236. By the higher classes of Society.—So Chettle would appear to imply by using the expression, "divers of worship."

No. 237. The gradation of the author's mental changes.—If, indeed, we knew by positive testimony the exact order in which Shakespeare's dramas were composed, it might then be within the legitimate province of criticism to suggest biographical deductions from that order; but no one may reasonably assume that a special disposition must have pervaded him at a conjectural epoch, and then conclude that a drama which is fancied to be in harmony with the temperament so indicated belongs to that period of his life.

No. 238.   A single one of the actors.—Thomas Greene, the celebrated representative of Bubble in Tu Quoque, is said, on the doubtful authority of some lines quoted in the British Theatre, 1750, to have been one of Shakespeare's native acquaintances.   Those lines are, in all probability, spurious, but even if they express a truth, it is in the highest degree unlikely that the circumstance could have influenced the poet's attachment to the theatre.   This Thomas Greene, who was not the person of that name mentioned in the local records, is first heard of as an actor in the early part of the reign of James the First, when he was a member of Queen Anne's company, and there is no reason for believing that he was ever one of the colleagues of the great dramatist, while amongst the latter there was not one who is known to have been connected in any way with Stratford-on-Avon.   The oft-repeated statement, that Richard Burbage came from that locality, is unsupported by the faintest evidence, there being no pretence whatever for conjecturing that the Stratford family were in any way connected with that of the great actor.   The latter, moreover, were resident in London at least as early as 1576, and when Richard's brother Cuthbert exhibited his pedigree at the metropolitan visitation of 1634, he said nothing respecting a provincial descent.   The surname of Burbage was not an unusual one, and was to be met with, in Shakespeare's time, in various parts of England. There were Burbages in Warwickshire not merely at Stratford, but at Kineton, Fillongley, Coventry, Whitacre, Hartshill and Corley, a list which could no doubt be extended by further research.

No. 239.   Did not consider it necessary to deviate.—Preliminary to the formation of a modern impartial judgment on the authorship of Titus Andronicus, it will be only fair to dissociate Shakespeare entirely from the revolting details of the romance, and partially at least from their arrangement in the play itself.   A theory which denies the possibility of his having been unduly influenced by his intimate professional association with the elder drama, as well as with the managers and actors of the day, not only in this instance but in several of his compositions, is one that would lead to inadmissible speculations.   It must be recollected that, owing to the paucity of materials, we have very imperfect means of forming a judgment on the originality of his constructive art.

No. 240.   The traditional belief of his own day.—And also of that of a previous age.   Randolph, in his Hey for Honesty, 1651, speaking of the "vast power divine" of money, enquires affirmatively if for its sake "did not Shakespeare writ his comedy."   The metrical quotation in the text is from Pope's First Epistle of the Second Book of Horace Imitated, fol., 1737, p. 5, but the opinion given in those lines must be considered an expansion of a similar one which is found in the preface to his edition of the works of the great dramatist, 1725,—"Shakespeare, having at his first appearance no other aim in his writings than to procure a subsistance, directed his endeavours solely to hit the taste and humour that then prevailed."

No. 241. And popular.—This may be gathered from an allusion in Heywood's Apology for Actors, 1612, where it is classed with Henry the Fifth amongst the stirring dramatic histories of that period Capell, who was the first to print Edward the Third as the work of Shakespeare, mentions its attribution to him in a list of plays at the end of the Careless Shepherdess, 1656, and in an " Exact and Perfect Catalogue of all Playes that are Printed," perhaps the same list or another edition of it appended to some copies of Tom Tyler and his Wife, 1661, not only Edward the Third, but also Edward the Second and Edward the Fourth are ascribed to the great dramatist. It is scarcely necessary to observe that late catalogues of this kind are of no value whatever in questions of authorship.

No. 242. In or before the year 1595.—It was entered at Stationers' Hall by Cuthbert Burby on December the 1st, 1595, and printed in the following year, "as it hath bin sundrie times plaied about the Citie of London." Another edition, with merely a few trivial variations, appeared in the year 1599. Burby's widow in 1609 assigned the copyright to Welby, who parted with it to Snodham in 1618, but no seventeenth century edition of the play is known to exist.

No. 243. A fidelity to nature.—The verification of this fidelity is obviously in many cases beyond the reach of experience, but it is unconsciously acknowledged in all through an instinct that would resent the suggestion that a demonstration was necessary. It may, however, be as well to observe that, when we speak of the great dramatist as being true to nature, it is with the limitation that all but the spiritual fidelity was subject to the conventionalities of the ancient stage.

No. 244. The Vendor.—The estate came to Matthew Bacon, then or afterwards of Gray's Inn, in the year 1590, in pursuance of some friendly arrangements, and it was sold by him to Henry Walker in 1604 for the sum of £100. In the conveyance of the former date mention is made of a well in the plot of land at the back of the house.

No. 245. To redeem the mortgage.—In mortgages of this period it was usual to name a precise date for repayment, unaccompanied by provisions respecting the interest on, or the continuation of, the loan. It does not, therefore, follow that, in this case, Shakespeare complied with the strict terms of the arrangement, which were to the effect that the debt should be liquidated at the following Michaelmas. It is at all events clear, from the declaration of trust in 1618, that the legal estate was vested in the trustees when Shakespeare granted the lease to Robinson, and, in all probability, the mortgage was paid off by the Halls shortly before they executed the deed of release to the latter.

No. 246.   Of the same name.—For he did not appear in order to sign either of the deeds of 1613, and he was certainly in London about the time at which they were executed.   The trustees were probably nominated by the vendor, none being required for Shakespeare's own protection.   In the will of Hemmings, the actor, 1630, he describes himself as "citizen and grocer of London," but it is to be observed that Condell, in 1627, mentions him as "John Heminge, gentleman"   The latter surname was by no means an unusual one.

No. 247.   For enrollment.—"Indentura facta Willielmo Shakespeare, Willielmo Johnson, Johanni Jackson et Johanni Hemynge, per Henricum Walker," contemporary index to grantees, Rot. Claus., 11 Jac. I., pars 31, in v. Shakespeare.   At the end of the enrollment, which of course verbally follows the original deed, is this note,—"et memorandum quod undecimo die Marcii, anno suprascripto, prefatus Henricus Walker venit coram dicto domino rege in Cancellaria sua, et recognovit indenturam predictam, ac omnia et singula in eadem contenta et specificata, in forma supradicta.   Irrotulatur vicesimo-tercio die Aprilis, anno regni regis Jacobi Anglie undecimo."

No. 248.   Very near the locality.—This appears from the following descriptions of the parcels in the conveyance of the estate from Edward Bagley to Sir Heneage Fetherston in the year 1667, here given from an old abstract of title,—"all that piece or parcel of ground whereon, at the time of the late fire, two messuages or tenements which were formerly one messuage or tenement, and heretofore were in the tenure of Thomas Crane, and, at the time of the said fire, in the tenure of William Iles, lying in the parish of St. Ann, Blackfryers; and also all that piece or parcel of ground at the time of the said fire used for a yard, and adjoining to the said two messuages or tenements, or one of them, lying near Ireland Yard in the said parish, which said piece or parcel of ground does abbutt on the street leading to a dock called Puddle Dock, near the river Thames, on the east, and on other grounds of Sir Heneage Fetherston west, north, and south, and all vaults, cellars, &c."   The property is described in the settlements of 1639 and 1647 as then consisting of one messuage or tenement in the occupation of a shoemaker of the name of Dicks.

No. 249.   Ireland Yard.—Probably so named after the William Ireland, a haberdasher, who occupied the house at the time of Shakespeare's purchase of it in 1613.   His name is found, with a mark instead of a signature, as a witness to the conveyance-deed of 1604, but he did not enter on the tenancy until after the latter date.   He also rented other property in the immediate neighbourhood.

No. 250.   Followed the succession.—The Blackfriars house is included with the other entailed properties in the fine that was levied in Easter Term, 23 Car. I., in anticipation of the settlement of June, 1647.   It is curious, however, that, instead of one recovery only having been suffered in pursuance of the conditions of that settlement, there were two filed in Michaelmas Term, viz., one that referred to the Warwickshire estates and a separate one for " unum mesuagium cum pertinenciis in parochia sancte Anne, Blackfriars." This latter was preliminary no doubt to some contemplated arrangement, possibly for its sale, and it may be that such a transfer is alluded to in the following passage in Edward Nash's Bill of Complaint, Feb. 1647-8,—" and she, the said Elizabeth Nashe, by and with the consent and approbation of the said other partyes some or one of them, hath sould away part of the premisses devised unto your said orator and his heires, the certainty whereof nor the names nor vallue thereof your said orator cannot sett forth, but the same is very well knowne unto the said Elizabeth Nashe and the rest of the said partyes ; and she, the said Elizabeth Nashe, doth now give out and pretend that she had a good estate in the said premisses at the tyme she sould the same, and that she had full power and lawfull authoritie to make sale of the said premisses, albeit she and the rest of the said persons well know the contrary."

No. 251. Metrical tests.—These are the ignes fatui which, in recent years, have enticed many a deluded traveller out of the beaten path into strange quagmires. We may rest satisfied that no process which aims at establishing the periods of Shakespeare's diction with scientific accuracy, or, indeed, any system not grounded on the axioms of its spontaneous freedom and versatility,—of his complete indifference to rule or precedent in the adaptation of language to thought and stage elocution,—will ultimately be accepted. It is obvious that he adapted his metre generically to the theme, and specifically to character and sentiment ; so that, although he could not have adopted a definitively late metrical fashion at an early period of his literary career, we cannot assume with certainty that he would ever have abandoned the intermittent use of any known measures, if they chanced to harmonise with the treatment of the subject and the positions of the characters. The fallacies appear to consist in the endeavour to regulate, by a theoretical order, the sequence of desultory and subtle uses of various metrical structures, and in the curious presumption of attempting to determine the mental conditions of which the deviations of those uses are the supposed result.

No. 252. Most of those epochs.—The extravagant introduction of lines with the hypermetrical syllable did not come into vogue with our dramatists until in or about the year 1610. This is the only one of the metrical tests which has a positive chronological value, the others having, at the best, only a correlative importance, and being practically useless in the presence of other evidence. If more plays of the time had been preserved, we might have had an accurate idea of the extent to which

Shakespeare's metre followed or initiated that of his contemporaries. What few there are, however, encourage the suspicion that it often, if not always, reflected, in its general forms, the current usages of the day. This may have been the case with his later, as it is known to have been with his earlier, dramas ; and to a following of those usages may be fairly attributed not only some of his metrical adoptions, but much of what is now considered an artificial obscurity of diction.

No. 253. Or not very long afterwards.—The bill of complaint must have been drafted after the death of Thomas Combe in January, 1609, and before Lady Day, 1613. There is an obvious error in the notice of the unexpired term of Combe's lease.

No. 254. In favour of the complainants.—It would seem that, in 1626, all the tenants were liable to contribute, for in that year the Stratford Council "agreed that a bill in Chauncery shal be exhibited, and subpens taken forthe against and served on such as have not payde theire partes towardes Barkers Rente."

No. 255. A rent-charge of £34.—In a "Rent Rolle of all the Landes and Tenementes belonginge to the Bailiffe and Burgisses of the Boroughe of Stratforde-upon-Avon," 1598, is the following entry,— "thexecutours of Sir John Huband doe holde all maner of tythes of corne, grayne, and hey, in the townes, hamlettes, villages, and fieldes of Olde Stratford, Welcome and Bishopton, and all maner of tythes of woole, lambe, hempe, flaxe, and other small and privie tythes, for the yerely rent of xxxiiij.*li.* paiable at our Lady Day and Michaelmas." In the place of the executors of Huband there is inserted in Thomas Greene's later handwriting,—"Mr. Thomas Combes and Mr. William Shakespeare."

No. 256. A tendency towards increase.—It is at all events certain that about the time that the Corporation purchased their moiety from the poet's son-in-law in 1624, they obtained no less a sum than £90 for one year's product.

No. 257. Parted with the share in the tithes.—The Corporation arranged the purchase from John Hall in August, 1624, at the sum of £400, their tenancy to commence from the previous Lady Day ; but the conveyance was not executed till March the 1st, 1625, and the money was not paid until some months after the date of that indenture. According to the deed last named, there was excepted from the moiety that was sold, "the tythes of two closses late leased to William Combe, esquier, att the yearelie rente of twentie shillinges." The following paragraph in that indenture may be worth giving,—"and whereas the said William Shakespere, beinge possessed of the said moitie, or parcell of the said tythes, to him soe graunted and assigned by the said Raphe Huband, by his laste will and testamente, beareinge, date the fyve and twentythe day of Marche, in the yeares of the raigne of our Sovereigne Lord James, nowe Kinge over England the fower-teenthe, of Scotland the nyne and fortythe, did devise and will unto the said John Hall and Susanna his wiefe all the said moitye, or one halfe of the said tythes to him soe graunted or assigned by the said Raphe Huband, together with all his estate and terme of yeares therein then to come and unexpired ; by force and vertue whereof, or some other good assuraunce in lawe, the said John Hall and Susanna doe, or one of them doeth, nowe stand lawfullie estated and possessed of the said moitie of all and everie the said tythes for and dueringe the resydue of the said tyme of fourscore and twelve yeares yett to come and not expired."

No. 258. A free offspring of the ear.—Shakespeare probably wrote verse as easily as prose, and very few species of dramatic metre had then taken an absolute form by precedent. Even if it had been otherwise, the metrical ear, which, like that for music, is a natural gift, must, in his case, have revolted from a subjection to normal restrictions.

No. 259. A preliminary knowledge.—It should be recollected that the dramatic and theatrical arts are inseparable, that they bear no close analogy to any other, and that a real success in either is impossible without an efficient adaptation of the written matter to the conventionalities of the existing stage.

No. 260. On the stage.—The First Part of Henry the Fourth had been exhibited on the public stage before the name of Oldcastle had been altered to that of Falstaff. There is distinct evidence of this in the well-known allusion to the Honour speech in Field's Amends for Ladies, 1618, a piece which appears to be referred to in Stafford's Niobe Dissolv'd, 1611. Field must have written that comedy before he joined Shakespeare's company, and the only plausible explanation of the passage referring to Oldcastle is that the different names of the character long continued to be indiscriminately referred to by those who had witnessed the earliest representations of the play. At all events, it is certain that, after 1597, the name of the character was Falstaff on the public stage, as is clear from the title-pages of the early quarto editions of Shakespeare's play, and from there being allusions to him under that appellation in Every Man Out of his Humour, acted either in 1599 or early in 1600, and printed in the latter year ; the First Part of Sir John Oldcastle, written in 1599, printed in 1600 ; the Whipping of the Satyre, 1601 ; Sharpe's More Fooles Yet, 1610 ; New and Choise Characters of Severall Authors, 1615 ; and in numerous later works of the seventeenth century. It may be worth notice that the letter, in which Sir Toby Matthew curiously refers to Falstaff as the author of a speech he quotes, was certainly not written until after the death of Shakespeare. When the First Part of Henry the Fourth was acted at Court in 1613, it is mentioned under the titles of Sir John Falstaff and the Hotspur, and, in 1624, as the First Part of Sir John Falstaff.

No. 261.   The spring of the year.—Certainly not long before March the 5th, 1597, on which day Lord Cobham, who had been the Lord Chamberlain of the Household since the previous August, expired ; for if the name of Oldcastle had been thoughtlessly introduced into the comedy before that period, it is obvious that his lordship, under whom the poet then served, would not have required the Queen's authority for its suppression.   It was probably his son, Henry, Constable of Dover Castle, who brought the subject before Elizabeth.

No. 262.   By the composition of the Second Part.—The date is not known, but the name of Oldcastle was changed to that of Falstaff in or before February, 1598, as appears from the Stationers' Registers, and, in the printed edition of the Second Part, the prefix *Old* is accidentally left standing to one of Falstaff's speeches.   In the third act, Sir John is spoken of as Page to Thomas Mowbray, Duke of Norfolk, a fact which applies to Oldcastle, not to Falstaff.   These circumstances appear to show decisively that the name of Shakespeare's character was at first Oldcastle in the Second as well as in the First Part, and that the former play was *written* before the month above mentioned.   The time of its production is unknown, the earliest allusion to it as an acting play being in a reference to Justice Silence by Ben Jonson in 1599 or 1599-1600, but it is clear from the epilogue that it could not have been submitted to a public audience before the introduction of the name of Falstaff. The suggestion that this epilogue was not composed by Shakespeare is unsupported by any kind of evidence, and that it was written before the death of Elizabeth is proved by the concluding words.

No. 263.   Both these plays.—The Second Part never attained the height of popularity accorded to the First, but still it must have been very successful.   That the "humours of swaggering Pistol," as well as those of Falstaff, were specially appreciated, would appear from the title-page of the edition of 1600.   There are references to, or quotations from, the Second Part, in the Poetaster, 1601 ; Eastward Hoe, 1605 ; the Merry Devil of Edmonton, 1608 ; and in Ben Jonson's Silent Woman, ed. 1616, p. 550, first acted in 1609.   Justices Silence and Shallow rapidly became typical characters.   "No, ladie, this is a kinsman of Justice Silence," Every Man Out of his Humour, ed. 1600. "We must have false fiers to amaze these spangle babies, these true heires of Ma. Justice Shallow," Satiro-Mastix, 1602.   "When thou sittest to consult about any weighty matter, let either Justice Shallowe, or his cousen, Mr. Weathercocke, be foreman of the jurie," Woodhouse's Flea, 1605.   One of the most curious notices of these personages occurs in a letter from Sir Charles Percy to a Mr. Carlington, dated from "Dumbleton in Glocestshire this 27 of December," and endorsed 1600, —"Mr. Carlington,—I am heere so pestred with contrie businesse that I shall not bee able as yet to come to London ; if I stay heere long in this fashion, at my return I think you will find mee so dull that I shall bee taken for Justice Silence or Justice Shallow; wherefore I am to entreat you that you will take pittie of mee, and, as occurrences shall searve, to send mee such news from time to time as shall happen, the knowledge of the which, thoutgh perhaps thee will not exempt mee from the opinion of a Justice Shallow at London, yet, I will assure you, thee will make mee passe for a very sufficient gentleman in Glocestrshire." Allusions of this kind in a private letter assume the familiarity, both of the writer and his correspondent, with Shakespeare's play, and are interesting evidences of its popularity.

No. 264. Had been introduced as Sir John Oldcastle.—See the Prince's allusion to him under this name in the First Part of Henry the Fourth, i. 2,—"as the honey of Hybla, my old lad of the castle." Although the authors of the First Part of Sir John Oldcastle, 1600, mention Falstaff, they almost unconsciously identify the personality of their hero with Shakespeare's fat knight by making him refer to his exploits at Shrewsbury.

No. 265. Ordered Shakespeare to alter the name.—Stage-poets, says Fuller, in his Church History, ed. 1655, p. 168,—"have made themselves very bold with, and others very merry at, the memory of Sir John Oldcastle, whom they have fancied a boon companion, a jovial royster and yet a coward to boot; the best is, Sir John Falstaffe hath relieved the memory of Sir John Oldcastle, and of late is substituted buffoone in his place." According to Rowe, in his life of Shakespeare, 1709, the " part of Falstaff is said to have been originally written under the name of Oldcastle ; some of that family being then remaining, the Queen was pleas'd to command him to alter it ; upon which he made use of Falstaff." This account is partially confirmed by a much earlier one which occurs in a very curious dedicatory epistle addressed to Sir Henry Bourchier by Dr. Richard James, who died in 1638. It is annexed to an unpublished manuscript entitled, the Legend and Defence of the noble Knight and Martyr, Sir John Oldcastel, several copies of which, in the author's handwriting, varying slightly from each other, are still preserved. In the course of this epistle Dr. James relates that "in Shakespeare's first shew of Harrie the Fift the person with which he undertook to play a buffone was not Falstaffe, but Sir Jhon Oldcastle ; and that offence beinge worthily taken by personages descended from his title, as peradventure by manie others allso whoe ought to have him in honourable memorie, the poet was putt to make an ignorant shifte of abusing Sir Jhon Fastolphe, a man not inferior of vertue, though not so famous in pietie as the other." The writer no doubt intended to put "first shew of Harrie the Fourth," it being clear, from the epilogue to the Second Part of Henry the Fourth, that Shakespeare had altered the name of Oldcastle to that of Falstaff before he wrote Henry the Fifth.

The Doctor's suggestion,—"as peradventure by manie others allso whoe ought to have him in honourable memorie,"—may be said to be confirmed by Shakespeare's epilogue and by the authors of the drama of Sir John Oldcastle, published in 1600, who, in their Prologue, are careful to notice the apprehensions that might be raised in the minds of the audience by the "doubtful title," and to remove suspicion by the announcement that the delineation of the martyr's character was a "tribute of love" to his faith and loyalty.

No. 266. Sir John Oldcastle.—There was a play so called which was acted by Shakespeare's company at Somerset House on March the 6th, 1600, before Lord Hunsdon and his guests, the latter being the Ambassadors from the Spanish Low Countries. "All this weeke the lords have beene in London, and past away the tyme in feasting and plaies ; for Vereiken dined upon Wednesday with my Lord Treasurer, who made hym a roiall dinner ; upon Thursday my Lord Chamberlain feasted hym, and made hym very great, and a delicate dinner, and there in the afternoone his plaiers acted before Vereiken, *Sir John Old Castell,* to his great contentment,"—Rowland Whyte to Sir Robert Sydney, dated from Baynards Castell, Saturday, 8 March, 1599-1600, ap. Sydney Letters, ed. 1746, ii. 175. It is possible, certainly, but very unlikely that the play acted on this occasion was the one that was printed in 1600, and which belonged to another company ; and still more improbable that a drama so conspicuously announced as written in the Protestant cause should have been selected for representation before the ambassadors of a late Cardinal, the Archduke of Austria. There was, in all probability, another play on the subject of Sir John Oldcastle, now lost, that belonged to the Lord Chamberlain's company and included the real prototype of Falstaff, the latter being a distinction that certainly does not belong to the Famous Victories. Fuller, in his Worthies, 1662, speaks of Sir John Oldcastle as "being made the make-sport *in all plays* for a coward ;" and there are several other general allusions, some of an earlier date, which would indicate the former existence of more dramas on the subject than are now known to us. That there was, in the seventeenth century, a stage character of Oldcastle other than that in Henry the Fourth, in the printed drama of 1600, or the very meagre one exhibited in the Famous Victories, admits, indeed, of proof. This fourth Sir John was as fond of ale as Goodman Smug of Edmonton ; his nose was red and carbuncled ; and he was as fat as the hero of Eastcheap. "Ale is thought to be much adulterated, and nothing so good as Sir John Old-castle and Smugge the Smith was us'd to drink," Howell's Familiar Letters, ed. 1688. The appearance of the Knight's nose is thus alluded to in the play of Hey for Honesty, 1651,— "the sinke is paved with the rich rubies and incomparable carbuncles of Sir John Oldcastle's nose," reference to which is also made in

Gayton's Festivous Notes upon Don Quixote, 1654, p. 49. It appears from a passage in the Meeting of Gallants at an Ordinarie, or the Walkes in Powles, 1604, that Sir John Oldcastle was represented on the stage as a very fat man, which is certainly not the case in the drama which was printed under that title in 1600 ;—"now, signiors, how like you mine host? did I not tell you he was a madde round knave and a merrie one too? and if you chaunce to talke of *fatte* Sir John Oldcastle, he wil tell you he was his great grand-father, and not much unlike him *in paunch*, if you marke him well by all descriptions." The host, who is here described, returns to the gallants and entertains them with telling them stories. After his first tale, he says,—"nay, gallants, Ile fit you, and now I will serve in another as good as vineger and pepper to your roast beefe." Signor Kickshawe replies ;—"let's have it, let's taste on it, mine host, my noble *fat actor*." There is another passage to the same effect in a pamphlet entitled the Wandering Jew telling Fortunes to Englishmen, 4to. Lond., 1640, p. 38, in which a character named Glutton is made to say,—"a chaire, a chaire, sweet Master Jew, a chaire ; all that I say, is this ; I'me a fat man,—it has been a West-Indian voyage for me to come reeking hither ; a kitchen-stuffe wench might pick up a living by following me for the fat which I loose in stradling ; I doe not live by the sweat of my brows, but am almost dead with sweating ; I eate much, but can talke little ; Sir John Old-castle was my great grandfathers fathers uncle ; I come of a huge kindred." It may fairly be assumed that the preceding notices do not refer to the Oldcastle of the first manuscript of Henry the Fourth. In two of the instances they certainly do not, Shakespeare's Falstaff being also alluded to in Hey for Honesty, 1651, and in Gayton's Notes, 1654. There is more uncertainty in the attribution of a reference by Bagwell, who in his poem entitled the Merchant Distressed, 1644, speaking of idle cowardly captains, observes that, although they "have no skill in martiall discipline, yet they'le brag, as if they durst to fight,—with Sir John Oldcastle, that high-flowne knight."

No. 267. One of the few names invented by Shakespeare.—A general absence of sincerity, rather than insincerity, is one of the leading characteristics of Falstaff, but the selection of a name suggestive of duplicity was probably the result more of accident than of design. At all events, it is in the highest degree unlikely that Shakespeare meditated in the choice any reference whatever to the historic character of Fastolf, the warrior he had previously introduced into the First Part of Henry the Sixth, although the printer of the first folio edition of that drama inadvertently adopted the orthography of the then better known name. It is clear from Oldcastle having been the original appellation of Falstaff, that the cowardice of the latter was not suggested by that attributed to the Fastolf of the earlier play. Fastolf was, however, sometimes called Falstaff even in strictly historical works, as in Trussell's Continuation of the History of England, ed. 1685, p. 126. The confusion between the real and fictitious characters is lamented in Daniel's manuscript poem called Trinarchodia, 1649, and also by Fuller, in his Worthies, 1662. The error continued to be made by later writers, and may occasionally be detected in works of the present century. "Sir John Fastoff gave to the seven senior demies of Magdalen College a penny a week for augmentation of their vests, which being nowadays but a small pittance, those that have it are call'd, by such as have it not, Fastoff's buckram men," Hearne's Diary, 1721. In a Short View of English History by Bevil Higgons, 1748, the warrior of Henry the Sixth's time is stated to have "been ridiculed and misrepresented by the pen of a certain poet for an original of buffoonery and cowardice for no other reason but that some of his posterity had disobliged Mr. Shakespear." This tradition apparently belongs to the number of those which are either incorrectly recorded or are mere fabrications.

No. 268. Two editions.—Four leaves only of the first edition, discovered many years ago at Bristol concealed in the recesses of an old book-cover, are known to exist. This precious fragment, which I would not exchange for its surface in pearls, is one of the most cherished gems in the library at Hollingbury Copse. Although the arrangements of the forms in the first two editions materially differ, both impressions were no doubt published by Wise in 1598, and might be distinguished by the circumstance of the word *hystorie* in the head-line of the first being *historie* in that of the second. Such was the unsettled orthography of the period that its variation is no evidence in the question of priority, but that the fragment belongs to the first edition may be safely inferred from its containing a word found in no other impression, omission being the commonest error in early reprints. It is something, at this late day, to recover even a single lost word that was written by Shakespeare, Poins therein exclaiming,—"how the *fat* rogue roared!" When Wise entered the play on the registers of the Stationers' Company in February, 1598, the title there given varies considerably from that in the second edition of that year, so that the one belonging to the fragment, if ever discovered, might possibly agree with the wording of the copyright entry. There were thus no fewer than six editions published in the author's lifetime, a fact that testifies to the great popularity of this drama.

No. 269. Familiar household words.—Thus Meres is found quoting one of Falstaff's sayings, without considering it necessary to mention whence it was derived,—"as Aulus Persius Flaccus is reported among al writers to be of an honest life and upright conversation, so Michael Drayton among schollers, souldeers, poets, and all sorts of people, is helde for a man of vertuous disposition, honest conversation, and well governed cariage, which is almost meraculous among good wits in these declining and corrupt times, *when there is nothing but rogery in villanous man*, and when cheating and craftines is counted the cleanest wit and soundest wisdome," Palladis Tamia, 1598. This is from a literary work composed by one of Shakespeare's friends, but there is a similar testimony to the early popularity of the First Part of Henry the Fourth in a private familiar letter from Toby Matthew to Dudley Carleton, written in September, 1598, wherein he observes, speaking of some military officers, and with the evident notion that the quotation would be recognized,—"well, honour prickes them on, and the world thinckes that honour will quickly prick them of againe."

No. 270. The inimitable humour of Falstaff.—"In my time, before the wars, Lowin used to act, with mighty applause, Falstaffe, Morose, Vulpone, and Mammon," Historia Histrionica, 1699, p. 4. Lowin could not have been the original performer of Falstaff, as he did not join Shakespeare's company until long after the production of Henry the Fourth, but he may possibly have undertaken the part before the author's death, one for which his jovial expression of countenance must have been well adapted. "In some tract," observes Malone, "of which I forgot to preserve the title, Hemmings is said to have been the original performer of Falstaff," Historical Account of the English Stage, ed. 1790, p. 188.

No. 271. Opposite the lower grounds of New Place.—This is stated on the reasonable supposition, in fact, all but certainty, that the locality of the estate had not been changed between the time of Shakespeare and its ownership by the Cloptons early in the last century. Since that period the Chapel Lane Rowington copyhold has always been the one described in the text, its area corresponding to that given in the survey of 1604.

No. 272. At the annual rental of two shillings and sixpence.—In a survey of the manor taken in August, 1606, and preserved amongst the records of the Land Revenue Office, there is the following notice of this copyhold estate, the annual value of which and other particulars were evidently unknown to the compiler :—

Tenentes Custumarii.

Stratford-super-Avon. } Willielmus Shakespere tenet per copiam datam die . . . anno . . videlicet,
Domum mansionalem.
Reddendo per annum
Habendum.

} ij.s.
finis.
heriettum.
annualis valor.
dimittenda.

but in another survey taken October 24th, 1604, in a list of the "customary tenants in Stratforde parcell of the saide manor," is this entry,—"William Shakespere lykewise holdeth there one cottage and one garden, by estimation a quarter of one acre, and payeth rent yeerlye ij.*s*., vj.*d*." There is a discrepancy in the amounts of the rent which are given in the ancient records, the sum of two shillings being mentioned in a Longbridge manuscript survey of the *manerium de Rowington cum membris*, 1555, and in that of 1606 above quoted. In one of 1582, and in numerous other documents, two shillings and sixpence is named as the annual rental.

No. 273.   And then he surrendered it.—No record of this surrender has been discovered, but it is the most natural explanation of the terms in which the copyhold estate is mentioned in the poet's will. If this view be not accepted, it will be requisite to make the gratuitous assumption that the scrivener inserted a wholly unnecessary proviso through being unacquainted with the custom of the manor. "By the custome thereof the eldest sonne is to inherite, and for default of yssue male, the eldest daughter; the coppieholders for every messuage and for every tofft of a messuage paye a herriott, but a cottage and tofft of a cottage paye not herriotts," Rowington Survey, MS.

No. 274.   Was formally admitted.—There is evidence of the admission, but not of its date, in a letter written by a steward of the manor in the last century. "Stretford-super-Avon; Paule Barthlett, one mesuage, ij.*s*.; Mr. John Hall, for his coppiehold, ij.*s*. vj.*d*.," Rentall of the Mannor of Rowington, 1630, MS. The first of these individuals owned the little estate in Church Street. In October, 1633, *Johannes Hall gen.* was fined twelve-pence for not appearing to do service at the court; Rowington MSS. "Paid David Abby for mendinge the orchard wall att Mr. Nashes barne, 00.02.0," Stratford-on-Avon Corporation MSS., 1637. This last entry would seem to prove that the Shakespeare copyhold was then in the occupation of Thomas Nash, and that there was a barn to the south of the cottage.

No. 275.   Had previously taken place.—If the question be decided by a strictly legal standard, this inference, however reasonable on a balance of probabilities, is at least not one of absolute certainty. The provisions of the Scotch law mention six lunar months as the shortest period of gestation consistent with the viability of the child, and the French code regards as legitimate and viable all children born after one hundred and eighty days. See a full and able discussion of the subject in Dr. Montgomery's Exposition of the Signs and Symptoms of Pregnancy, ed. 1856, pp. 513-524. In the year 1710, the then leading physicians of Edinburgh made a legal declaration "that a child born in the beginning of the sixth lunar month may be alive and continue in life, which is consistent with our observation and experience;" and the words of the most eminent authority of all, Dr. Hunter, imply that healthy maturity can be attained by a child born in the middle of the seventh lunar month.

No. 276. No question of morals.—Assuming the existence of a pre-contract, Shakespeare and Anne Hathaway were, by virtue of that contract, to use the words of Bishop Watson, "perfectly married together;" although, as the Bishop continues to observe, "the marriage of them in the face of the Church afterward, by the ministration of the priest, is not superfluous, but much expedient for sundry causes," Doctrine of the Seven Sacraments, 1558. Even if there had been an informality in the pre-contract, the offence supposed to have been committed by Shakespeare would have been in itself a condition that would have rendered the arrangement legally valid. See Swinburne's Treatise of Spousals, 1686, p. 224.

No. 277. According to an early tradition.—See Hall's letter of 1694 in the Biographical Notices, No. 8, and the following manuscript note, written towards the end of the seventeenth century, which is preserved in a copy of the third folio,—"in the church of Strattford-uppon-Avon, uppon a stone in the chancell, these words were orderd to be cutt by Mr. Shackspeare, the town being the place of his birth and buriall."

No. 278. Another statement less probable.—The parish-clerk of Stratford-on-Avon informed Dowdall, in 1693, that the verses were "made by himselfe a little before his death," the word *himselfe* referring to Shakespeare. Roberts, in his answer to Pope's Preface, 1729, p. 47, mentions the epitaph in the following terms,—"if that were his writing, as the report goes it was." On the other hand, neither Dugdale in 1656, nor Rowe in 1709, take any notice of the presumed authorship.

No. 279. There has long been a tradition.—"At the side of the chancel is a charnel-house almost filled with human bones, skulls, &c.—the guide said that Shakespeare was so much affected by this charnel-house that he wrote the epitaph for himself to prevent his bones being thrown into it," notes of a visit made to Stratford-on-Avon in July 1777, first printed in the edition of Defoe's Tour issued in the next year, and transferred without acknowledgment into later works.

No. 280. A large degree of moisture.—In July, 1619, there was a resolution passed by the Town Council to "bestow some charge towardes the keeping dry the chauncell at the High Church."

No. 281. The owners.—When Heminges and Condell speak of Death having deprived Shakespeare of his *right* "to have set forth and overseen his own writings," they assuredly refer to a moral, not to a legal, privilege. There is no contemporary instance known of an author selling a play to a theatre and reserving to himself a copyright interest. There was of course nothing to prevent subsequent arrangements with proprietors, although it seems that, in those days, a vigilant protection of the copy was the only effectual mode of hindering the publication of a drama.

No. 282.   Successful and popular.—It is scarcely necessary to observe that these epithets are warranted by the appearance of four editions between the years 1597 and 1615, and the play seems to have been a favourite with Bodenham, who introduces a large number of quotations from it in his Belvedere, 1600.   It is also in the list of Shakespearean dramas given by Meres in 1598, but other early notices, where the authorship is not distinctly to be inferred, may relate to some of the plays on the same reign which were not the composition of the great dramatist.   The copyright entry of the first impression is here given in facsimile.

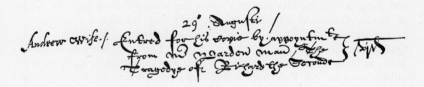

No. 283.   Was omitted.—The general context shows that the deposition scene belongs to the play as it was originally written, and that it could not have been a subsequent addition.   Its omission in the first and second impressions excludes the probability of Lord Bacon having referred to Shakespeare's drama when he wrote, in his charge against Oliver St. John,—"and for your comparison with Richard the Second, I see you follow the example of them that brought him upon the stage, and into print, in Queen Elizabeth's time"; the allusions here being almost certainly to the insurrection stage-performance and Hayward's Life of Henry IV.

No. 284.   Until some years after.—The deposition scene appeared for the first time in an edition published in 1608 by Law, who carelessly allowed the descriptive portion of the title-page to retain its Elizabethan form; but some time afterwards, and in the same year, he circulated another impression, the text being merely a reprint, from the same forms, of the previous copy, which he described as including "new additions of the Parliament Sceane and the deposing of King Richard." That the latter was the second issue may be safely inferred not merely from the fact of the company's title being therein rightly given, but from the circumstance of there having then been no one at all likely to have interfered with the public announcement of the deposition.

No. 285.   Objections having been made.—That this was the case may be inferred from the words of the title-pages of some copies (see the preceding note) of the edition of 1608, which imply that the deposition scene was a novelty on the stage, and that the play had then been recently introduced with that addition at the Globe Theatre.   Without placing too much reliance on the title-pages of the old quartos, the word *lately* is so rarely to be found in them, that special credit may be fairly claimed for its accuracy. The repetitions of the term in subsequent titles do not affect this position, for the reprinted ones all throughout the series of quarto editions are obviously valueless as authorities. In fact, in all cases in which statements respecting performances and authorship are verbally repeated in the title-pages of different editions of the same old play, those in the earliest are alone worth consideration.

No. 286. It was an exceedingly dangerous theme.—Hayward, who, in 1599, issued his account of the fall of Richard, and the elevation of her successor to the throne, under the title of the First Part of the Life and Raigne of King Henrie the Fourth, dedicating the work to the Earl of Essex, displeased Elizabeth so seriously that, through her influence, he was reprimanded by the Star Chamber and thrown into prison. The Queen continued to be so excitable on the subject that even in August, 1601, in an interview with Lambard, who was exhibiting a work on the public records, his Pandecta Rotulorum, on opening at the reign of Richard, she said, in allusion to the deposition of that Sovereign and to the recent insurrection, "I am Richard the Second, knowe yee not that?," to which he replied, "such a wicked immagination was determined and attempted by a most unkind gentleman ; the most adorned creature that ever your Majestie made." The latter part of the Queen's rejoinder is more significant than intelligible,—" he that will forget God will also forget his benefactors ; this tragedy was played fourtie times in open streets and houses."

No. 287. In its treatment of the deposition of Richard the Second.— It may be just worth notice that there was seen by Forman at the Globe in April, 1611, a play called Richard the Second, in which the author had dramatized incidents, some historical and others fanciful, dating from the period of Jack Straw's rebellion to the succession of Henry the Fourth. The deposition and murder of Richard may incidentally have been noticed, or the facts tacitly admitted, but if they had formed prominent features in the composition, Forman, in his somewhat elaborate account of the performance, could hardly have failed, as he has done, to have made special allusions to events of so telling a character. There is also an old play in MS. Eg. 1994, without either date or title, dealing with the history of the same reign, but it refers solely to events that occurred before the deposition.

No. 288. The conspirators had selected.—The Government fixed upon Sir Gelly Merrick as the chief agent in these proceedings, and in the official account of the conspiracy, which was published in the same year, 1601, it is stated,—"that the afternoone before the rebellion, Merricke, with a great company of others, that afterwards were all in the action, had procured to bee played before them the play of Deposing of

King Richard the Second ; neither was it casuall, but a play bespoken by Merrick ; and not so onely, but when it was told him by one of the players that the play was olde, and they should have losse in playing it, because fewe would come to it, there was fourty shillings extraordinarie given to play it, and so thereupon playd it was ; so earnest hee was to satisfie his eyes with the sight of that tragedie which hee thought soone after his lord should bring from the stage to the state ; but that God turned it upon their owne heads." This statement appears to be the authority upon which Camden relied when he notes that " Merick was accused that hee had with money procured an old out-worne play of the tragicall deposing of King Richard the Second to bee acted upon the publike stage before the conspirators, which the lawyers interpreted to bee done by him as if they should now behold that acted upon the stage which was the next day to bee acted in deposing the Queene," Annals or the Historie of Elizabeth, ed. 1635, p. 555, the term *exoleta* occupying, in the Latin original, the place of the words *old out-worne*. A third account is given in a contemporary narrative of the trial of Merrick, from which it appears that the Attorney-General, in arguing the case against him, observed,—" the story of Henry the Fourth being set forth in a play, and in that play there being set forth the killing of the king upon a stage, the Friday before, Sir Gilly and some others of the earl's train having an humour to see a play, they must needs have the play of Henry the Fourth ; the players told them that was stale, they should get nothing by playing of that, but no play else

would serve, and Sir Gilly gives fourty shillings to Philips the player to play this, besides whatsoever he could get," State Trials, ed. 1809, i. 1445, from a manuscript formerly belonging to Peter le Neve, sold at the auction of his library in 1731, Catalogue, p. 93, art. 378. In addition to these evidences, there are preserved amongst the national State Papers the original depositions of Phillipps and Merrick, both of which are exceedingly curious and interesting. The first, which is duly signed by the witness, the poet's colleague, is entitled, " the exam. of Augustyne Phillypps, Servant unto the L. Chamberleyne, and one of hys players, taken the xviij.th of Februarij, 1600, upon hys othe ;" and is as follows,—" he sayeth that on Fryday last was sennyght, or Thursday, Sir Charles Percye, Sir Jostlyne Percye, and the L. Montegle, with some thre more, spake to some of the players, in the presens of thys examinant, to have the playe of the deposyng and kyllyng of Kyng Rychard the Second to be played the Saterday next, promysyng to geve them xl.*s* more then their ordynary to play yt; when thys examinant and hys fellowes were determyned to have played some other play, holdyng that play of Kyng Rychard to be so old, and so long out of yous, that they should have small or no cumpany at yt; but, at theire request, this examinant and his fellowes were content to play yt the Saterday, and have theise xl.*s* more then theire ordynary for yt, and so played yt accordyngly." It will be observed that Phillipps, in this statement, does not even mention the name of Merrick, but the latter may, notwithstanding his own intimation to the contrary made in self-defence, have been one of the "some thre more." The affidavit of this person, which is entitled, "the examinacion of Sir Gelly Meryke, taken the xvij.th of February, 1600," that is, 1600–1, is recorded in the following terms,—"he sayeth that, upon Saterday last was sennyght, he dyned at Gunters in the company of the L. Montegle, Sir Christoffer Blont, Sir Charles Percye, Ellys Jones, and Edward Bushell, and who else he remembreth not; and after dynner that day, and at the motyon of Sir Charles Percy and the rest, they went all together to the Globe, over the water, wher the L. Chamberlen's men use to playe, and were ther sumwhat before the playe began, Sir Charles tellyng them that the playe wold be of Harry the iiij.th; whether Sir John Davyes wer ther, or not, this examinant can not tell, but he sayed he wold be ther, yf he cold;—he can not tell who procured that playe to be played at that tyme, except yt were Sir Charles Percy; but, as he thynketh, yt was Sir Charles Percye;—there he was at the same playe, and cam in sumwhat after yt was begone; and the playe was of Kyng Harry the iiij.th and of the kyllyng of Kyng Richard the Second, played by the L. Chamberlens players." Another notice of the visit of the conspirators to the theatre, from the examination of Sir William Constable, taken on the 16th inst., may also be worth giving,—" on Saterday, the seventh of this present month, this examinant, together with my L. Mounteagle, Sir Christofer Blunt, Sir Gilly Merick, Sir Charles Percy, Henry Cuffe, Edward Bushell, Ellis Jones,—and Sir John Davies, as hee thinketh,— at one Gunters house over against Temple Gate, and, for ought hee knoweth, they met by chaunce, and there they all dined; and after diner Thomas Lee came to the play, where they were all assembled saving Cuffe, at the Globe on the Bankside; and after the play this examinant and Edward Busshell came to Essex House, where hee supped and lay all night."

No. 289. With a portion of the reign of his successor.—It is specially worthy of notice that the Attorney-General, in his private memoranda of the evidences on the conspiracy, mentions the insurrection drama more than once as "the play of H. 4," in one significant instance using those words in connexion with the affidavit of Phillipps, his note being in the following terms,—"Phillipps for the play of H. 4, et confessione propria." It is also alluded to by Sir Charles Percy and in the report of the trial under the same title, one which is not at all likely to have been even casually given to Shakespeare's Richard the Second. The former was, in all probability, one of the numerous dramatic histories of the time the very names of most of which have long since disappeared ; and the practice of the old theatres certainly did not exclude from their repertories the admission of more than one composition on the same theme.

No. 290. Had so outgrown its popularity.—This circumstance increases the probability that Shakespeare was not the author of the insurrection drama. It is true that plays, in his day, frequently came to be considered old with extreme rapidity, but it may be doubted if his history of Richard the Second, which was certainly keeping its place on the stage in 1608, years after the events mentioned in the text, would have been denounced by his own intimate friend, or by any other member of the company, as one likely to prove, on the occasion of a single exceptional revival in 1601, entirely unattractive to the public. Phillipps, moreover, speaks of the deposition and murder of Richard as if they had constituted the main actions of the piece that was represented at the Globe on the seventh of February, while an eye-witness of the performance mentions it as "the playe of Kyng Harry the iiij.th and of the kyllyng of Kyng Richard the Second."

No. 291. A stepping-stone passage.—In the lane which is passed immediately before reaching that in which the Hathaway farm-house is situated. The stepping-stones continued in use until 1788, in which year a rustic bridge was erected over the streamlet.

No. 292. Richard Hathaway.—The son no doubt of the John who was the customary tenant of the Shottery estate from April, 1543, to October, 1556, and perhaps for some time afterwards. "John Hathewey, in goodes, x.*li.*," subsidy-roll, Old Stratford, 3 Edward VI. There was a Richard Hathaway who was a party in suits in the Court of Record, 1563 and 1566. "Richard Hatheway in bonis, iiij.*li.*," subsidy, 9 Eliz., for "Shotterey, Bishopton and Welcoume," MS. Longbridge. "April 12, Thomas, the sonne of Richard Hathaway," baptisms, 1569. "February 3, John, son to Richard Hathaway," ibid., 1575. "November 30, William, sonne to Richard Hathaway of Shottrey," ibid., 1578. "September 7, Richard Hathaway," burials, 1581.

No. 293. Richard Hathaway, the baker.—The identity of this individual with the second A. H. C. Richard is proved by the reference to Isabel in Bartholomew's will, for that same Isabel, born in 1608, is described in a settlement that was made in 1625, a few weeks after her marriage with Richard Walford, a draper of Stratford, as the daughter of Richard and Priscilla Hathaway. This Priscilla, who was married to him in 1607, is introduced in the baker's will, 1636, as "my deere beloved wife," and she continued the business after her husband's decease, residing in Bridge Street until her death in 1651.

No. 294. To six individuals.—See the terms of the legacies in the will itself, 1670, which is given at length in the collection of Domestic Records,—1. "Feb. 25, Judith, filia Thomæ Hathaway," baptisms, 1637–8; probably named after Shakespeare's daughter, Judith Quiney. —2. "August 29, Joanna, filia Thomæ Hatheway," baptisms, 1641.— 3. Edward Kent, son of the preceding.—4. "Novemb. 6, Rose, filia Thomas Hathaway," baptisms, 1642.—5. "January 10, Elizabeth, fillia Thomas Hathaway," baptisms, 1646–7.—6. "June 11, Sussanna, fillia Thomas Hathaway," baptisms, 1648; most likely a godchild of Susannah Hall, the Christian name having then been an unusual one in Hathaway families.

No. 295. My kinsman, Thomas Hathaway.—It is to be observed that Lady Barnard applies the same epithet, *kinsman*, to Thomas Hart, the grandson of the poet's sister. Thomas Nash, in a codicil to his will, 1647, "gave unto Elizabeth Hathwaye fiftie poundes, to Thomas Hathway fiftie poundes, to Judith Hathway tenn poundes," the Thomas here mentioned, it is reasonable to presume, being the joiner.

No. 296. The joiner here mentioned.—There were other Thomas Hathaways in the borough throughout the seventeenth century, and great care must be exercised in dealing with the various allusions to the name that are found in the local records. Amongst them was a baker who was occasionally honoured with the patronage of the Corporation, 1623–1632, and there was another who is returned as the occupier of one fire-hearth in Wood Street in 1663.

No. 297. Occasionally employed by the Town-Council.—"Att this halle it is agreed that Thomas Hathawaye shall have twentie shillings alowed him for his losse he hade in a table in the nue halle, and the remanynge timber of the same table," 14 December, 1643. Entries respecting his workmanship may also be seen in the chamberlains' books for 1642 and 1647.

No. 298. By his widow Jane.—"January 15, Thomas Hathaway," burials, 1654–5. "October 7, Jane Hathaway, widow," ibid., 1696. This Jane is returned as the occupier of two fire-hearths in 1670 and 1674, and she is frequently mentioned in the proceedings of the Court of Record, temp. Car. II. She is described in 1662 as "Jane Hathaway of Stratford-upon-Avon, in the county of Warwicke, late wife of Thomas Hathaway, late of Stratford-upon-Avon aforesaid, joyner, deceased," in a document in which there is also a notice of "Thomas Hathaway, cittizen and joyner of London, sone and heire of the said Thomas Hathaway, deceased." The last-mentioned Thomas, "whose daughter and heir" Susanna was living in 1697, resided in St. Giles's, Cripplegate, and administration of his goods, valued at £39. 4s. 6d., was granted to one of his creditors in June, 1684, his widow Alice refusing to act.

No. 299.   A place call'd Luddington.—When it is recollected that the locality of Shakespeare's marriage has been a subject of investigation from the early days of Malone (ed. 1790, i. 176) to the present time, it is incredible that a genuine tradition respecting it, current in the immediate neighbourhood of Stratford during the whole of that period should only have been publicly noticed in quite recent years.   It will take something more than aged persons' reminiscences of youthful hearsay to neutralize these considerations, and no small degree of credulity to enable us to place reliance upon the accuracy of the memory of an old lady who, according to Fullom's romantic History of Shakespeare, 1862, p. 202, "not only declared that she was told in her childhood that the marriage was solemnized at Luddington, but had seen the ancient tome in which it was registered."   It is also worth notice that Jordan, in a separate account of Luddington, makes no allusion to its marriage tradition ; nor had the late R. B. Wheler, up to the year 1821 or later, ever heard of such a belief.   This little hamlet, prettily situated on the rising banks of the Avon, was a chapelry in the time of Shakespeare, and Thomas Hunt, who had been one of the masters of the Stratford Grammar-school during the poet's boyhood is noticed as having been its curate in 1584, in which year he was suspended for open contumacy.   Both chapel and register have long disappeared, various conflicting accounts being given of the destruction of the latter.

No. 300.   Shotteriche.—One of the ancient names of Shottery, others being Schotrydy, Shotrech and Schotryth.

No. 301.   Till within these few years.—John Hathaway, who died in 1746, devised his A. H. C. estate to his mother Sarah for life, with remainder to his three sisters as tenants in common ; and when the words here quoted were penned, the house was in the occupation of William Taylor, the husband of one of those sisters.

No. 302.   Johanna Hatheway.—"Accio inter Johannam Hathway, querentem, et Willielmum Mountford, defendentem, finita est," register of the Court of Record, 23 December, 1584.   "Jone Hathewe is of houshold six," presentments made at the manor court for Shottery, 1595.

No. 303.   Bartholomew Hathaway.—"January 14, Annys, daughter to Bartholmew Hathaway," baptisms, 1584.   "February 8, John, sonne to Bartholmew Hathaway," ibid., 1586.   "June 1, an infante of Bartholmew Hathaways," burials, 1588.   "March 8, Edmund, sonne to Bartholmew Hathaway," baptisms, 1590.   October 20, Bartholomew Hathaway of Shottery," burials, 1624.   The inventory of his goods, taken a few days after his decease, is that of a plain English yeoman-farmer of the time, one not affected to luxury, new fashions or display.

No. 304. Into the hands of his son John.—Richard, the son of this individual and the grandson of Bartholomew, devised the estate in the following terms,—"I give and bequeath unto my sonne, John Hathaway, all that my messuage or tennement wherein I now dwell and inhabite in Shottery, and allso all those messuages or tennements, with th'appurtenances, in Shottery, now in the occupacion of Thomas Lambe and Edward Sands, togeather with all that my two yard land and a half of a yard land, with the appurtenances thereunto belonginge, lyeinge and beeinge in the common fields of Shottery aforesaid and Old Stratford, to have and to hold the said messuages or tennements, lands, closes and premisses, and every part and parcell thereof, with the appurtenances, unto my said son, John Hathaway, his heires and assignes for ever," will dated November the 26th, 1684. "Aperll 17, Richard Hathaway," burials, 1692.

No. 305. Issued by Rider.—In this view, which is more accurate than Ireland's, a large isolated barn is seen near the present entrance-side of the dwelling. It was removed many years ago, but, as I gathered from a person who witnessed the demolition, it was of unusual strength for an outhouse of that description, and parts of it may, therefore, have belonged to one that was on the spot in the days of the Richard Hathaway of 1581. In later sketches there will be observed a hovel which adjoined the building on the lower part of it near the road, but this was only a modern projection which has since been taken away.

No. 306. Compiled from his memoranda.—"The small village of Shottery, distant from Stratford one mile on the west, is supposed to be the place in which Shakspeare's wife, Anne Hathaway, resided before her marriage;—it is certain that the Hathaways, a numerous family, lived in this village about the period of Shakspeare's nuptials; and there is, consequently, reason for presuming that the popular tradition is correct;—a cottage is yet shewn as the identical tenement in which she dwelt when Shakspeare won her to his love; but of this circumstance no resemblance of proof has been adduced."—Brewer's Description of the County of Warwick, 1820, p. 259.

No. 307. Wild conjectures.—There are a large and apparently an ever increasing number of gratuitous theories respecting Shakespeare that are destitute of evidential or traditional foundation, and not a few of their advocates, treating a protest against the necessity of discussion as an acknowledgment that refutation is hopeless, assume a right to demand a controversy on their merits. These writers, however, are apt to forget that the burden of proof rests in such cases exclusively upon themselves, and that the impartial student, aware that a large number of specious arguments can be produced in favour of almost any conceivable hypothesis, may fairly be excused if he hesitates to misprize time by the examination of surmises that are based on parallels in thought or language, fanciful references, whimsical developments of prototypes, and such like; one conjecture not infrequently brought forward to support another, the combination then being presumed to be irresistible.   Many of these unsubstantial speculations are amusing and nearly all are harmless, but it may be doubted if any one, in the absence of a fragment of direct evidence, and on such grounds as those now indicated, can be justified, even in a paradoxical exercise, in maintaining that Shakespeare was not the real composer of the plays that have so long been attributed to him,—an assumption that involves the branding of a hallowed name as one belonging to a rank impostor, to a person, in short, who was so clever and artful a rogue that he was enabled to adopt the results of another man's genius as his own for upwards of twenty years without raising a whisper of contemporary suspicion; and all this in the midst of the innumerable questions that must have been submitted to the recognized author by his fellow-actors during the preliminary readings and elaborate rehearsals of nearly fourty dramas, to say nothing of his uniform adroitness in triumphantly deceiving so shrewd a critic as Ben Jonson and other literary friends.

No. 308.   That relates to the country and to rural life.—If, for example, there was a migratory bird that uniformly reached England on one particular day, and that day was April 23rd in the time of Shakespeare, it would now be first seen, according to our modern computation, on May 3rd, and so nearly accurate is the present Gregorian system of reckoning that more than three thousand years would have to elapse before there would be an error of a single day in the recognized period of the bird's arrival.

No. 309.   Tolerably successful in business.—It is extremely unlikely that the money for the purchase could have been derived from his father, who was still living and holding a farm under the Ardens.

No. 310.   Through an alliance.—He was married in all probability either at Aston-Cantlowe or Stratford, but the registers do not commence sufficiently early to enable us to ascertain the period of the ceremony. It must, however, have taken place at some time between November, 1556, and September, 1558, the dates respectively of Robert Arden's will and the baptism of Joan Shakespeare.

No. 311.   A wealthy farmer.—Robert Arden, or Ardern, the latter being the more usual form of the name in the earlier records, is described in an indenture of 1501 as the son "Thome Ardern de Wylmecote." He was most likely the grandson of a Robert Ardern who was the bailiff of Snitterfield about the middle of the fifteenth century, and who is also mentioned in a record of 1461 as *nuper firmarius terre dominice ibidem ;* but there is nothing in the evidences yet discovered to authorize a further conjecture respecting the primitive descent ; and it should be borne in mind that the surname is one that belonged, at these early periods, to numerous families in the midland counties.   The Robert who was the poet's maternal grandfather, owned considerable estates at Snitterfield, the larger portion of which, if not the whole, he purchased in 1519 and 1529, acquiring in the former year two messuages and land from Richard and Agnes Rushby, and in the latter one tenement and land from John Palmer, all of which are described as being "inter tenementum Ricardi Hardyng ex una parte, et terram domini ex altera parte." The place of his abode is not given in any of these conveyances, but his identity is shown in a release from the first-named vendors, 1521, in which he is described as "Robertus Ardern de Wylmcote, parochia de Aston Cantlowe." In the subsidy for that parish taken in 14–15 Henry VIII., he was assessed on goods of the value of £8, there being only four persons, including his father Thomas at £12, who paid on a higher estimate; and when, in the assessment collected in 1546, he was returned as holding lands of the annual value of £10, there was but one other individual who was rated at so large an amount.

No. 312. With about fifty acres at Wilmecote.—Nearly all the measures of land that are given in documents of the sixteenth century are conjectural, attempts at precise surveys being then of rare occurrence, and hence it is that serious variations are so often found in descriptions of parcels that refer to one and the same estate. It is thus impossible in many cases, and somewhat conspicuously in that of Asbies, to ascertain the exact dimensions. In the two most reliable evidences, the mortgage-deed of 1578, as quoted by Lambert, and the Bill of Complaint of 1589, the farm is said to have consisted of one yard and four acres of land, but in the fines of 1579 it is respectively mentioned as containing fifty-six and eighty-six acres, a "common of pasture" being added in each of the two latter instances; and the uncertainty attending these discrepancies is enhanced by the variable quantity of land that passed under the name of a yard. "Virgata terræ is a quantity of land various according to the place, as at Wimbleton in Surrey it is but fifteen acres, in other counties twenty, in some twenty-four, in some thirty, and in others forty acres," Cowel's Interpreter, ed. Manley, 1672. There is another estimate of a more recent period in a lease that was granted by Lord Abergavenny in 1708 of "one yard-land containing fourty-four acres" at Aston Cantlowe, the very parish in which Asbies was situated.

No. 313. During her girlhood.—Her age at the time of her marriage is unknown, but it may be fairly concluded that the youngest of so large a family, who survived till 1608 and outlived her sisters by many years, was in her teens when John Shakespeare had the good fortune to win her affections. It may be as well to add that this view is not inconsistent with her executorial appointment. "The testator hath power to appoint executors not onely persons of ful age, but also infants, and the act done by the infant as executor, as the releasing of the debt due to the testator, or the selling or distributing of the testators goods, is saide to be sufficient in law," Swinburn's Treatise of Testaments, ed. 1590, fol. 196.

No. 314. Towels.—Those that were employed for lavational purposes were called washing-towels, and are rarely noticed in inventories of the period alluded to in the text. Washing-basins are also seldom mentioned excepting in lists of articles that were used by barbers.

No. 315. As for the inmate and other labourers.—" Plaine people in the countrey, as carters, threshers, ditchers, colliers, and plowmen, use seldome times to washe their hands, as appereth by their filthines, and as very few times combe their heades, as it is seen by floxe, nyttes, grese, fethers, strawe, and suche lyke, whiche hangeth in their heares," Bullein's Government of Health, c. 1558.

No. 316. A substantial farmer of Bearley.—The will of this individual, the earliest recorded member of a family that was afterwards brought into intimate relations with the Shakespeares, seems to be worth giving at length.—" *Testamentum Johannis Hyll de Bereley.* In Dei nomine, amen,—in the yere of our Lorde God 1545, the xxvj. day off August, in the xxxvij. yere of the reigne of our sovereigne lorde Henry the viij.th, by the grace of God Kynge of England, France and Ireland, defendour of the fayth, and of the Churche of England and also of Ireland in erth supreme hed, I, John Hill of Berely, sycke in body, but hole and perfette of mynde, the Lorde be praysed, make my last will and testament in maner and forme folowinge. Fyrst, I bequeth my soule unto Almyghtie God and to his blessed Mother and virgyne Saynte Mary, and to all the blessed company of heven, and my body to be buryed in the churcheyarde of Wotton Wawene. Item, I bequeth unto John, my sonne, xl.*s.*, a heyfer of too yeres age and a quarter of barly, to be payd at xx. yeres of his age. Item, I gyve unto my doughtour Elenor xx.*s.*, a heyfer of ij. yeres age and a quarter of barly, to be payde at xx.ti yeres of hur age. Item, I bequeth unto Mary, my doughtur, xx.*s.*, a heyfer of too yeres of age, and a quarter of barly, to be payd at xx. yeres of hur age. Item, I gyve unto Thomas, my sonne, xl.*s.*, a heyfer of ij. yeres of age, and a quarter of barly, to be payd at xx.ti yeres of hys age. And if any of my said children do decease before the tyme of the receipte of ther legacyes or bequest, that then his or ther parte shall remayne unto the other, beynge alyve. Item, I gyve unto William Rawlyns, my servaunte, a calf of one yere of age. Item, I gyve unto every one of my godchildren iiij.*d*. Item, I gyve unto Agnes, my wyff, the lease of my farme in Bereley duringe hur lyff, and after hur decease John, my sone, to have yt. The residue of my goodes not afore bequethed, my dettes paid and my funerall expenses discharged, I gyve unto Agnes, my wyf, whom I make my hole executrice to dispose them as she shall thinke moost pleasinge to God and helth unto my soule. Also I make John Webbe and John Hewys to be oversears of this, my last wil, to se it performed. These witnesses,— Sir Thomas Peynton, John Cally, smyth, with other moo. Inv. exhib., xliij.*li.*, xij.*s.*, vj.*d.*" Proved on September the 7th, 1545.

No. 317. Could even write their own names.—There is no reasonable pretence for assuming that, in the time of John Shakespeare, whatever may have been the case at earlier periods, it was the practice for marks to be used by those who were capable of signing their names. No instance of the kind has been discovered amongst the numerous records of his era that are preserved at Stratford-on-Avon, while even a few rare examples in other districts, if such are to be found, would be insufficient to countenance a theory that he was able to write. All the known evidences point in the opposite direction, and it should be observed that, in common with many other of his illiterate contemporaries, he did not always adhere to the same kind of symbol, at one time contenting himself with a rudely-shaped cross and at another delineating a fairly good representation of a pair of dividers, an instrument that is used in several trades for making circles, or setting off equal lengths in leather and other materials. Joan Lambert, the poet's aunt, and Edmund, her husband, used respectively at least three and four differently-formed marks; and

the "sign-manual" that George Whateley, bailiff of Stratford, penned in September, 1564, is very different from one (here engraved) that he adopted in 1579.

No. 318. And fondly-loved.—It was clearly Robert Arden's wish to deal equitably with all the members of his family, but the terms of his will, especially in the selection of Mary and Alice for executors, may perhaps be thought to exhibit an inclination in favour of those two daughters.

No. 319. Who died in 1573.—"Alexander Webb was bureyd the seventeenth day of Aprill, 1573," Snitterfield Register. The earliest notice of this individual that has been discovered is found in one of the Arden conveyances of 1550, wherein he is introduced as Alexander Webbe de Berely, that is, Bearley, a hamlet in the parish of Snitterfield, and he is similarly described in a number of later documents. In his will, dated April the 15th, 1573, after recording a number of dispositions in favour of his wife, the poet's aunt, and their children, he adds,— "moreover I doe institute, appoynte and ordaine, to be my overseers to see this, my last will and testament performed, satisfied and fullfilled, according to my will, John Shackespere of Stretford-upon-Aven, John Hill of Bearley, and for theyre paynes taken I geve them xij.*d.* a-pece ; wittnes, John Wager, Henry Shaxspere, William Maydes, with others."

No. 320.   The mortgagee dying in April.—In the Bill that was filed in the Court of Queen's Bench, 1589, the death of Edmund Lambert is stated to have occurred on the 1st of March, 1587, but this is certainly an error. "Edmund Lambarte, senior, buried 23 April, 1587," parish register, Barton-on-the-Heath. His widow, one of Shakespeare's maternal aunts, died a few years afterwards. "1593. Joanna Lambarte, vidua, buried 30 November," reg. ibid.

No. 321.   In the following September. This arrangement, which appears to have been merely a verbal one, is not alluded to in the Chancery Bill that was filed ten years afterwards, and it is therein asserted by the Shakespeares that they tendered the £40 to John Lambert after the death of his father in 1587.

No. 322.   The best title.—It must be borne in mind that William was at this time the only one of the sons who had attained his majority, and that the concurrence of Gilbert was not yet available. The estate was left absolutely to the poet's mother, and that there was no marriage settlement bestowing vested interests in it upon her children is obvious from the fact of the loan of 1578 having been effected during their minority.

No. 323.   In the following autumn.—In the Bill of Complaint, 1597, the Shakespeares are represented as admitting that Edmund Lambert had occupied the estate for "three or four," instead of two, years before they tendered him the amount of the loan. But the terms of the Bill must either have been drawn up from oral information supplied by the aged plaintiffs, or from instructions given by the poet, and, in either case, this and other deviations from the precise facts may be reasonably explained as due to imperfect recollections. Even in the Replication, which was evidently prepared more carefully than the Bill, there is as inaccurate a reference to the period of Edmund's decease as there is in the allusion to the same event in the latter document.

No. 324.   All but the dwelling.—The land only is mentioned in the description of parcels which is given in the fine, and the words *cum pertinenciis* at the end of that description can hardly be thought to include the farm-house. It is possible that Lambert, in his Answer, 1597, may allude to its exclusion when he says "that the said messuage, yearde lande, and other the said premisses, *or the moste parte thereof,* have ever, sythence the purches therof by this defendantes father, byne in lease by the demise of the said complainante."

No. 325.   Afterwards exhibited.—It would seem from the Order of May, 1598, that John Shakespeare's Bill of Complaint was introduced after the delivery of the joint-bill to the defendant. The last-named Bill and the Answer were filed in Court on the same day, November the 24th, 1597, but it is obvious that Lambert must have been supplied with a copy of the former some time previously, for otherwise there would have been no time for the preparation of the reply.

No. 326. Was corresponding with the latter.—"I likewise beg to trouble you farther to make me a small drawing of the house at Wilncott, where Shakespeare's grandfather Arden lived;—you shew'd me a drawing of the house, you say, which I never remember to have seen, or I should certainly have gone over to have looked at it, and should have saved you the trouble of doing it by having made one myself," letter from Ireland to Jordan, 1794.

No. 327. Sheloyle.—It is just possible that this field may be the Shelfyll afterwards mentioned, and that it may be the one which is now called Shelshill, but it is not safe to infer that this is the case, the names of different plots of ground being often very nearly identical. Care must be taken to distinguish between either of these and the larger Shelfield, anciently Shelfhull, also situated in Aston Cantlowe.

No. 328. Aged and impotent.—This was the legal phrase that was generally used when a person was old and too infirm to undertake a long journey, and they are introduced into a formal declaration which was made by Agnes Arden on July the 5th, 1580, the purport of which was to disclose the extent of her interests in her late husband's Snitterfield estates, a bill respecting them having then been recently filed in Chancery against that lady and other defendants by one Thomas Mayowe. A commission for taking her depositions at her own residence was accordingly issued in the following November. The declaration abovementioned is here subjoined,—"To all and to whom thes presentes shall come, Agnes Arden of Wilmcote in the countie of Warr : widowe greting, knowe ye that I the sayd Agnes have receaved of Allexander Webb and still doe receave of his executors and assignes for twoe messuages one cottage and all landes and tenementes with thappurtenaunces belonginge to the same lying and being in Snitterfield in the countie aforesayd, one yearly rent of fortie shillinges, according to the demise thereof made by me the sayd Agnes to the sayd Allexander Webb bearing date the one and twenteth daie of Maij in the seconde yeare of the raigne of the Queenes Majesties that nowe is for the terme of fortie yeares, if I the sayd Agnes so long doe lyve ; Of which sayd messuage and premisses estate was made to me the sayd Agnes for terme of my lyffe by Roberte Arden my late husband in the fourth yeare of the raigne of the late King Edward the sixt, of which sayd estate for terme of my liffe I am yet seased. All which to be true I have thought good to testifie by this my wryting, and am and wil be readye to depose the same upon myne othe att all tymes and places if

I weare able to travell, being aged and impotent.   In wytnes wherof to thes presentes I have putt my seale the fifte daie of July, 1580.—*The marke + of Agnes Arden.*—Sealed and delyvered in the presence of Adam Palmer, and Anthony Osbaston, and Jhon Hill."

No. 329.   Absolved from bestowing larger gifts.—It has been generally believed that Agnes Arden was not on very friendly terms with the Shakespeares, and this merely because they are not liberally considered in her will, but few theories are more uncertain than those which are based upon indications of this description.   It is impossible for us to be acquainted with the whole of the circumstances by which a testator was surrounded or influenced, and, in this case, there might be broached, with equal reason, the highly improbable assumption that she had no great affection for the children of her brother, Alexander Webbe, each of whom received nothing beyond the pittance that was assigned in the same will to a godchild.   Her burial at Aston Cantlowe in 1580 is registered in the following terms,—"the xxix.th day of December was bureyd Agnis Arden, wydow."

No. 330.   The poet's widow had expired.—The notice of her burial is thus given in the parish-register of Stratford-on-Avon under the date of August, 1623,—

and this bracketed form of the entry has led to the suspicion that she re-married one Richard James,—Shakespeare Society's Papers, 1845, ii. 107.   This conjecture is altogether at variance with the terms of her monumental inscription, and brackets of a like description are to be seen in other parts of the register, no fewer than six occurring in the list of baptisms for the year in question, 1623.   The matter, however, is placed beyond all doubt by the record of the two funerals as it thus appears in a contemporary transcript of the original notes that were made on the occasion,—

> August 8.   Mrs. Ann Shakespeare.
> 8.   Ann, wyfe to Richard James.

and it may be just worth adding that in an enumeration of "persons remarkable," whose names were to be noticed in the Stratford register, and which was added to the volume towards the close of the seventeenth century, there is included the memorandum,—"1623, one Mrs. Shakespere was buried."

No. 331.   Or neighbouring registers.—There are notices of a Henry Shakespeare in the registers of Hampton Lucy and Clifford, but it has been clearly established that the poet's father was not the John Shakespeare of either of those parishes.   Ingon, the abode in the sixteenth century of one family of the name, is situated in the former locality.   "Lettyce, the daughter of Henrye Shakespere, was baptized the x.th of June," Hampton Lucy register, 1582.   "June 10, 1583, Henry, sonne unto Antony Shaxspere, buryd," Clifford register.   "Jeames, the sonne of Henrye Shakespere, was baptized the xvj.th of October," Hampton Lucy, 1585.

No. 332.   Were conducted exclusively.—It is difficult on any other hypothesis to account for the circumstance of both of the indentures of the fine having been discovered amongst the title-deeds that were delivered over to Sir Edward Walker, the purchaser of New Place in the year 1675.

No. 333.   In a paper of the time of Edward the Sixth.—The reference here is to an Answer filed in Chancery by William Clopton in reply to the complaint of Anne, the widow of Dr. Bentley, a lessee of New Place, who had died about the year 1549.   In the course of this document, which was no doubt written shortly after the last-named event, he states that "the said Thomas Bentlye ys deceassed out of this present lyf, and hath lefte the said manour place in great ruyne and decay and unrepayryd, and yt dothe styll remayne unrepayryd ever sythen the deathe of the same Thomas to the greate damage and los of the defendant."   In the original Bill the house is described as "one capytall messuage or mannour place in Stratforde-uppon-Haven, in the countye of Warwyck, called the Newe Place," and it is mentioned under the same title in an indenture of 1532.

No. 334.   It was renovated.—Theobald, who was acquainted with Sir Hugh Clopton, and furnished by that gentleman with traditional particulars respecting this house, writing in 1733, states that when Shakespeare purchased it, he, "having repair'd and modell'd it to his own mind, chang'd the name to New Place, which the mansion-house, since erected on the same spot, at this day retains."   Although this account of the origin of the name is erroneous, it does not follow that the whole statement is unfounded, the probability being that the worthy knight, having heard that the poet had made extensive repairs and alterations, rashly jumped to the conclusion that the otherwise some-what unintelligible title of the building had thence originated.   In connexion with this subject it is worth mentioning that, when the Corporation were repairing the Clopton Bridge in the year 1598, they made use of a load of stone which they had obtained from the great dramatist,—"paid to Mr. Shaxspere for on lod of ston, x.d,"—and this probably consisted of old material taken either from New Place or from its outbuildings, the strata under his newly-acquired estate yielding nothing of the kind. Old cut stone, moreover, would perhaps have

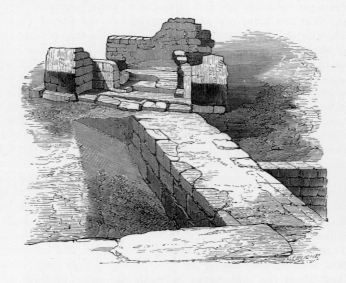

been more suitable for the work that was being conducted at the bridge than any that could have been readily obtained from the Wilmecote quarries; and that Shakespeare himself furnished the commodity may be reasonably assumed from its being next to impossible that his father could then have had it for sale, at the same time that there was no other Stratfordian of the name who would have been dubbed a Mr.

No. 335. Immediately preceding its demolition.—It has been frequently asserted that Sir John Clopton merely repaired and altered

Shakespeare's residence, but that he built an entirely new house is a fact that was placed beyond a doubt by the excavations that were made on the site in 1862. The only vestiges of the first structure that were permitted to remain, and those obviously by accident, were small portions of the ancient foundations, and that the later mansion was constructed on another ground-plan is seen, amongst other evidences, by the angle at which a modern fireplace has been erected across the old stone-work, the latter being two feet in thickness.

No. 336. By the Rev. Joseph Greene.—The notice given in the text is taken from the original manuscript now preserved at Hollingbury Copse. It may be observed, in confirmation of Grimmitt's account, that we know from other sources that Edward Clopton resided at New Place before its demolition, and that there was a brick wall in his time on the Chapel-lane side of the premises. "Clopton Edwardus, armiger, presented for not reparing the ground before his brick wall in the Chappell Lane," MS. dated 1694.

No. 337. There were two barns.—One of these barns, that nearest the house, is mentioned in 1590 as the property of William Underhill, who subsequently purchased the other one on the east, both of them being included in the fine that was levied on the occasion of the transfer of the estate to Shakespeare in 1597. "Willielmus Underhill, generosus tenet libere unum horreum per redditum per annum iij.*d*, secta curie ;—heres Willielmi Smyth tenet libere unum horreum per redditum per annum xij.*d*, secta curie ;—inhabitantes de Clyfford tenent libere unum horreum per redditum per annum vj.*d*, secta curie," manorial survey in 1590. The two barns are again mentioned in the fine of 1602, after which, with the exception of the notice of a stable that belonged to Sir John Barnard in 1670,—juratores presentant quod Johannes Barnard, miles, removeat nocumentum ante gardinum et stabula sua in le Chappell Lane,—we have no information respecting the outbuildings that were at New Place in the seventeenth century. The latter, or what may have been left of them, were no doubt removed when Sir John Clopton built the new house, for it is inconceivable that a person, who evidently meditated a liberal reconstruction that was to be in harmony with the contemporary notions of domestic splendor, should have permitted any of the older structures to remain, and that every adjunct of the mansion was then of a newly-fashioned character is virtually admitted in the settlement of 1702, in which he undertakes to complete, by the March of the following year, the "finishing both as to glaseing, wainscoateing, painteing, laying of flores, makeing the starecase, doors, walls and pertitions in and about the said house, brewhouse, stables, coachhouse and other buildings, and alsoe wallinge the garden, and layeing gravell walkes therein, and doeing all other things proper and reasonable in and about the said house to make the same inhabitable." It appears, moreover, from the earliest known plan of the locality, which was made shortly before the demolition of the second house in 1759, that the outbuildings that were by the side of the lane then extended without a break from the corner of the house, there being only seventy-five feet of open ground between their termination and the eastern boundary of the poet's land ; all this leading to the in-ference that the ancient character of the whole of the premises had been effaced.

No. 338.   On the Chapel-lane side of New Place.—It is most likely
that the two barns were not the only outbuildings that were here to be
found in the time of Shakespeare, but, if so, it is not at all probable that
the nature of the latter will ever be revealed.   There are, it is true, in
various places, under the surface that either adjoin or are near Chapel-
lane, fragments of stone-work of uncertain date that could not have
belonged to the house and that may be portions of other buildings, but
there is not one which is of sufficient importance to authorize the enunciation of a conjecture respecting its true character.   They all, however,
encourage the opinion that none of the adjuncts were left by Sir John
Clopton in their original form or position, and an illustration of this
probability will be observed in the annexed engraving of remains at the

side of the lane which were found at the distance of about a hundred
and eighty feet from the south-western end of the mansion, the rect-
angular concavity, the wall and the line of regular brick-work on the
left, being those portions that were unmistakably of modern date.   The
remaining part, which is presumably ancient, is constructed of lime-stone
one foot seven inches in depth, its top being about six inches below the
street level.

No. 339.   The eastern termination of the grounds.—In more recent
times there was a large barn at New Place, the frontage of which was in
Chapel-lane, its south-eastern corner being at a distance of seventy-five
feet from the termination mentioned in the text.   The earliest distinct
notice of this outbuilding that has yet been discovered bears the date of
1705, and it remained a barn for many years afterwards, but at some
time between March, 1775, and September, 1790, it was converted into

two cottages and a stable. The three latter were removed in 1862, the greatest care having been taken, before their demolition was ordered, to ascertain that there was not even a remote possibility of any of the constructional workmanship having belonged to the Shakespearean era. There were discovered, however, amongst the timbers, which were chiefly of elm, a number of pieces of oak that had been used in a former structure, a fact that was clearly elicited by some of them having mortises and grooves in useless and incongruous positions. It has hence been too hastily assumed that these oaken scantlings had been transferred from one of the poet's own barns, but such an inference is of course necessarily doubtful.

No. 340. An ancient well.—In the poet's time the well, which is now under one of the southern outer walls of Nash's House, was in a yard or passage at the back of New Place, and there can be little if any doubt that it was filled up by Sir John Clopton, and a new one formed at *y* for the supply of a pump for one of his kitchens, when the additions were made to the former residence in or about the year 1702. The first-named well, undoubtedly the one that furnished the water-supply to Shakespeare's household, widens very considerably as it increases in depth, the stone-work being laid in with clay; and thinking it very likely that relics of his dwelling might here be discovered, I attended a leisurely exhumation of its contents in 1863, examining with the minutest care each recurrent spade-full, so that I can confidently assert that there was not in the whole store a vestige of an object that could have belonged to a period as early as that of the great dramatist. It is advisable to mention this distinctly, one clever forgery at least, a stone with an inscription referring to Bott, a former owner of the estate, having been produced as an article that had been found amongst the *débris*. Even in cases where no deception has been practised, it is impossible to be too cautious in our reception of the assumed pristine history of those New Place relics that are of a movable description, it being obvious that nothing beyond the vague possibility of accuracy in a conjecture can be elicited from the mere fact of their discovery after so many generations had passed away, and in a locality that had been subjected to essential modifications throughout its entire area. This is of course said in reference to the very few examples that can be fairly considered to belong to the Shakespearean era, nearly all those of a later date, including one of Gastrell's candlesticks, being unworthy of either notice or preservation.

No. 341. Who was then residing.—The evidence of this singular fact is contained in a paper, in Greene's handwriting, respecting the premises of one George Browne, possession of which he was desirous of securing by Lady Day, 1610, with a view to have sufficient time to prepare them for his own occupation by the following Michaelmas. It appears that arrangements had been in progress, during the summer of

1609, to settle matters on this basis, but Browne having altered his mind on the subject, Greene drew up memoranda, entitled, "Some reasons to prove that G. Browne ment before this to have bene gone, besydes others that I will reserve to myself for use, yf need be." Amongst these reasons are the following,—"he doubted whether he might sowe his garden untill about my going to the terme;—seeing I could gett noe carryages to help me here with tymber, I was content to permytt yt without contradiction, *and the rather because I perceyved I might stay another yere at New Place,*" MS. dated September 9th, 1609, Greene being evidently more anxious to have facilities for putting the new premises in order than to turn Browne out of them. The house to which Greene removed was a large one adjoining the Churchyard, near to its present entrance at the bottom of Old Town, where he was certainly before June 21st, 1611, for on that day an order was made that the town was "to repare the churchyard wall at Mr. Green's dwelling-house, and to keepe yt sufficiently repar'd for the lenth of too hundred nintye and seaven foote of wallinge." The conditions under which he had been previously living at New Place are unknown, but it can scarcely be doubted that he had either been a lodger, or, following a custom very prevalent in those days, a temporary lessee of certain rooms in the building, it being contrary to all probability that he could have been a tenant of the whole to the exclusion of the poet's wife and daughter.

No. 342. Together with the Great Garden of New Place.—This garden was conveyed by a separate deed of March the 22nd, 1706.

No. 343. Joseph Hunt.—A lease was granted to this person by Sir Edward Walker in December, 1675, terminable at the end of four, eight or twelve years, from the preceding Michaelmas.

No. 344. Initiating.—The tenor of the dedication and address implies this, and the fact may be fairly said to be proved by the following words,—"we pray you do not envie his friends the office of their care and paine to have collected *and publish'd* them." That this was also the contemporary opinion is shown by the first lines of the poem by Digges in the same volume,—"Shake-speare, at length thy pious fellowes give the world thy Workes."

No. 345. Either by or under the directions.—It is difficult to say if the will, in its present state, was penned by the lawyer himself or by his clerk. Not having succeeded in discovering a single extraneous manuscript in the acknowledged handwriting of Collins, there is nothing but the attestation paragraph to rely upon. The latter, which seems to have been written by him, is not inconsistent with the belief that the composition and penmanship of the entire manuscript is to be assigned to that solicitor. The variation of style observable in his autograph is no positive criterion, a man's signature being often materially different in the forms of the letters from his other writings. There is a striking instance of this last assertion in the will of John Gibbs, of Stratford-on-Avon, transcribed by John Beddome in 1622, the latter signing his name in characters that do not in the least degree resemble those he used in his copy of the document itself.

No. 346. A solicitor residing at Warwick.—It may be worth mentioning that the Stratfordians of those days very rarely employed solicitors for testamentary purposes. In Shakespeare's case, however, the creation of an entail, so unusual with his townsmen, no doubt rendered legal assistance necessary, for the requisite form would hardly have been known to the clergyman or the non-professional inhabitants, the persons who at that time generally drew up local wills.

No. 347. A corrected draft.—In the record-room of Stratford-on-Avon there are preserved several documents which were evidently written by the same person who made or copied the poet's will, and one of them, the draft of the tithe-conveyance of 1605, is an exactly similar manuscript, the corrections being made by the transcriber himself. The erasures are mainly of the same character in both, that is to say, they are chiefly eliminations of unnecessary, informal, or erroneous words and sentences.

No. 348. The appointment for that day was postponed.—This new theory seems to be the only one which can reasonably account for the fact of the date appearing in the superscription before the whole document was engrossed. If it be assumed that the poet, on or about the eighteenth of January, gave written or oral instructions for his will, making arrangements at the same time for its execution at a meeting to take place between Collins and himself, either at Warwick or Stratford, on the following Thursday, and that, in the interval, circumstances induced him to postpone the appointment, all the apparently conflicting evidences will be reconciled.

No. 349. In perfect health.—This was not, as has been suggested, a mere legal formula. No conscientious solicitor would ever have used the words untruthfully, while the cognate description of a testator as " being sick in body, but of whole and perfect memory," is one that is continually met with in ancient wills.

No. 350. To secure the validity.—This was most likely the case, although there is no doubt that the adoption of such expedients was due more to individual caution than to an absolute legal necessity. In those days there was so much laxity in everything connected with testamentary formalities that inconvenience would seldom have arisen from any kind of carelessness. No one, excepting in subsequent litigation, would ever have dreamt of asking if erasures preceded signatures, how or when interlineations were added, if the witnesses were present at the execution, or, in fact, any questions at all. The officials thought nothing of even admitting to probate a mere copy of a will that was destitute of the signatures both of testator and witnesses, and, in one curious instance, a familiar letter addressed by a John Baker to his brother and sister was duly registered in London in 1601 as an efficient testamentary record. It is, however, to be observed that it would be difficult to find a will of the time so irregularly written as Shakespeare's. Amongst those proved in the local court, I have not met with one containing more than four interlineations.

No. 351. The alteration of the day of the month.—When March was substituted for January, it is most likely that the day of the month should also have been changed. There was otherwise, at least, a singular and improbable coincidence.

No. 352. Not from that of the testator's decease.—This is clearly the meaning intended, although the paragraph, *she living the said term after my decease,* appears to be inconsistent with the previous clause. Unless the lawyer has committed an oversight, these words may simply mean,—if she has lived the said term at the period of my decease. Most of this portion of the will is expressed in a clumsy style, but the paragraph above quoted appears to have been inserted merely to avoid the chance of the preceding sentences being interpreted in a sense adverse to the bequest of the reversions to Elizabeth Hall and Joan Hart.

No. 353. The undevisable property.—"And note that, in some places, chattels as heirloomes, as the *best bed,* table, pot, pan, cart, and other dead chattels moveable, may go to the heire, and the heire in that case may have an action for them at the common law," Coke's Commentarie upon Littleton, ed. 1629, fol. 18, b.

No. 354. Compensation for dower.—The following is part of the form of a codicil given in West's Simboleography, 1605,—"I give to E., my wife, in recompence of her thirds or reasonable portion of my goods, one hundreth poundes, and two of my best gueldinges, and two of my best beddes fully furnished." In a report of the proceedings in the Star Chamber for 1605 there is a notice of a bribe which consisted of "200 *li.,* a vellet gowne, spoones, and a fether-bedde."

No. 355. Free-bench.—"The first wief onlie shall have for her free-bench during her life all such landes and tenementes as her husband dyed seised of in possession of inheritance, yf so be her said husband have done noe act nor surrender to the contrary thereof, and shee shal be admitted to her said free-bench payeing onlie a penny for a fine as aforesaid," Customs of Rowington Manor, 1614.

No. 356. Subject to a careful revision.—Whether we regard the document as the work of either the lawyer or his clerk, it is exceedingly difficult to understand how the long provision commencing, *to be sett out,* afterwards erased, could have found its way into the manuscript, the introductory words, that alone would have rendered them intelligible, being wanting. This discarded portion of the will has been always presumed to refer to Judith, but it is perhaps more likely, to judge from the original state and subsequent alteration of the next paragraph, to be a portion of a cancelled bequest to the testator's grand-daughter, and its insertion may have arisen from some misapprehension of the original instructions.

No. 357. In the statement of the regnal years.—It would be easy to give too much weight to the error in the superscription which announces an unknown January, one which was in the fourteenth year of James of England and in the forty-ninth of his reign over Scotland. A similar chronological impossibility will be observed in the declaration issued by Shakespeare against Phillip Rogers in 1604, and cognate inaccuracies are occasionally met with in other documents of the time. Thus the will of Arthur Ange of Stratford-on-Avon is dated on March the 15th, 4 James I., the regnal year indicating 1606–7, whereas probate was granted in June, 1606. The date of 1616 in Shakespeare's will may apply to any of the early months, for it was not an invariable rule to adhere in numerals to the ancient calendar.

No. 359. The diminutive boards of the Curtain Theatre.—It has been generally believed that Shakespeare alludes to the Globe Theatre when he refers to "the wooden O" in Henry the Fifth, but, apart from the improbability of his making a disparaging allusion to the size of his company's new edifice, it is not at all likely that the building could have been completed before the return of Lord Essex from Ireland in September, 1599. The letter O was used in reference to any object of a circular formation, and there is every probability that it would have been applicable to the Curtain. Now Armin, who was one of Shakespeare's company playing at the Globe in 1600, speaks of himself in his Foole Upon Foole, published in that year, as the Clown at the Curtain Theatre. It may then be inferred that the former theatre was opened in 1600, and at some time before March the 25th, the latest date that can be assigned to the production of Every Man Out of his Humour.

No. 360. His apartment in Southwark.—The Southwark of Elizabeth and James is indissolubly connected with the biographical history of the great dramatist, and pity it is that all vestiges of its ancient theatres and their surroundings should have disappeared. An elaborate essay by Mr. William Rendle on the Bankside and its theatres appeared in 1877, but the most lucid and graphic account of the borough itself, and its former condition, will be found in the same writer's principal work, Old Southwark and its People, 4to. 1878.

No. 361. To an individual.—His name was John Lane, who "about five weekes past reported that the plaintiff had the runninge of the raynes, and had bin naught with Rafe Smith at John Palmer," July the 15th, 1613 ; contemporary notes in MS. Harl. 4064. The notice of the termination of the suit is gathered from the reports of it preserved in the episcopal registers at Worcester.

No. 362. This surreptitious edition.—The differences between the editions of 1603 and 1604 will be most conveniently studied by the aid of the parallel texts which were arranged and edited by Mr. Sam. Timmins, 8vo. 1860, one of the most really useful and valuable books in the embarrassing library of modern Shakespeareana.

No. 363. That I was not.—There is a singular obscurity which renders a correct interpretation of Greene's handwriting a matter of unusual difficulty. The pronoun in this entry is considered by Mr. Edward Scott of the British Museum, a very able judge, to be really the letter J, while Dr. Ingleby is of opinion that Greene, who was unquestionably a careless scribbler, intended to write *he.* But if Shakespeare had not favored the enclosure scheme, why should the majority of the Corporation have addressed one of their letters of remonstrance to him as well as to Manwaring, or why should Greene have troubled the former with "a note of the inconveniences" that would arise from the execution of the proposed design? The whole of Greene's diary has lately been published under the editorship of Dr. Ingleby, to whom I am indebted for the rectification of my *Thursday* disaster and for the correct reading, *tellyng,* in the last extract given in the text. It may here be mentioned that, in the Articles of Agreement, 1614, Estate Records, No. 13, *increasinge* is an obvious error for *decreasinge,* but the former word is that found in the original manuscript.

No. 364. A repugnance on his part.—See the extract, Biographical Notices, No. 8, from the very curious letter of 1694, which was recently discovered by the Rev. W. D. Macray in the Bodleian Library. The original is undated, but Mr. Macray has distinctly ascertained that it was written in December, 1694.

No. 365. The pleasant Willy of Spenser.—Dryden was the first to suggest that the "pleasant" individual here mentioned was no other than the great dramatist, but he had a very narrow acquaintance with the literature of the Elizabethan period, and the attribution to Shakespeare is at best purely conjectural. The only real evidence at present accessible is contained in an annotated copy of the 1611 edition of the Teares of the Muses, in which volume the manuscript note to the line commencing "Our pleasant Willy,"—*Tarlton died an. 1588,*—distinctly indicates that Spenser was referring to that celebrated actor and to his decease, the word *died* being expressed by a symbol, the interpretation of which is ascertained by other instances of its use. This memorandum was unquestionably penned within a few years after the publication of the work in which it appears, and as it is clearly seen, from other entries, that the annotator had a correct general knowledge of the objects of the Spenserian references, it is extremely unlikely that his mistakes should be restricted to this one special case. If his testimony be accepted, the words " dead of late " must be taken literally, and the allusion to "that same gentle spirit" will refer to another contemporary. The use of the sobriquet was common in Elizabeth's time, and Tarlton might have received the one in question from his extra-popular delivery of a song known under that name. The music to *Tarlton's Willy* is preserved in a seventeenth-century manuscript at Cambridge, MS. Univ. Lib. Dd. iv. 23. It is also worth notice that three days after a publisher named Wolfe had issued a contemporary ballad on Tarlton's decease, he entered another one,—" Peggies complaint for the death of her Willye,"—and it is by no means impossible that the simulated poetess was one of the great comedian's pet acquaintances. The burden of this latter production ran as follows,—" But now he is dead and gone,= Mine own sweet Willy is laid in his grave."

No. 366. The chronological order.—An essay on the Chronological Order of Shakespeare's Plays, by the Rev. H. P. Stokes, 8vo., 1878, is the ablest and most elaborate dissertation that has yet appeared upon the subject. It enters far more minutely into detail than would be within the scope of the present work.

No. 367. Municipal records.—There was not a single company of actors, in Shakespeare's time, which did not make professional visits through nearly all the English counties, and in the hope of discovering traces of his footsteps during his provincial tours I have personally examined the records of the following cities and towns,— Marlborough, Wells, Bath, Plymouth, Totnes, Andover, Basingstoke, Dartmouth, Godalming, Salisbury, Exeter, Arundel, Lymington, Romsey, Shaftesbury, Warwick, Bewdley, Dover, Lydd, Banbury, Shrewsbury, Oxford, Worcester, Hereford, Gloucester, Tewkesbury, Rochester, Guildford, Hastings, Saffron Walden, Abingdon, Carnarvon, Beaumaris, Oswestry, Liverpool, Chester, Reading, Conway, Gravesend, Bridgewater, Evesham, Droitwich, Kidderminster, Campden, Maidstone, Faversham, Southampton, Newport, Bridport, Yeovil, Weymouth, Lewes, Coventry, Bristol, Kingston-on-Thames, Lyme Regis, Dorchester, Canterbury, Sandwich, Queenborough, Ludlow, Stratford-on-Avon, Leominster, Folkestone, Winchelsea, New Romney, Barnstaple, Rye, York, Seaford, Newcastle-on-Tyne, Leicester, Hythe, St. Alban's, Henley-on-Thames, and Cambridge, the last being preserved in the library of Downing College. The time occupied in these researches has fluctuated immensely in various places, from an hour or even less in some few cases to several weeks in others. In no single instance have I at present found in any municipal record a notice of the poet himself, but curious material of an unsuspected nature respecting his company and theatrical surroundings has been discovered.

NOTES OF ACKNOWLEDGMENT.

1. A considerable number of the Latin documents, as well as a few of the English ones, have had the advantage of re-collations made by a very able paleographer, Mr. J. A. C. Vincent, to whom I am indebted for nearly the whole of the extensions, and who has also taken infinite pains, on several occasions, to establish the true readings in difficult cases in which I was at fault. For his assistance in these directions, especially at the Record Office, I wish to express my sincere thanks, and, in reference to the last-named institution, it is hardly necessary to record my gratitude,—for it is due from every visitor,—for the unvarying kindness and patience with which Mr. W. D. Selby is always ready to extend to others the advantages of his own wide knowledge and experience.

2. The Rev. T. P. Wadley, Rector of Naunton Beauchamp, kindly communicated the interesting notice of the poet's father that he had discovered in the will of Alexander Webbe, 1573; and when I was at Worcester some years ago he drew my attention to the following minute that appears in the episcopal register under the date of 27th November, 1582,—"item eodem die similis emanavit licencia inter Willielmum Shaxpere et Annam Whateley de Temple Grafton," the *licencia* being one *matrimonii*, as is shown by a previous entry. There is no note in the volume of a Shakespearean licence having been issued on the next day, and Mr. Wadley is of opinion that the one granted to the poet was applied for on the 27th. If this be so,—and he tells me that he has met with a similar variation of date in another instance,—the scribe must, through some exceptional accident, have mis-written the last four words, the bond itself being of course of infinitely higher authority than the entry, and Temple Grafton not being one of the hamlets of Stratford.

3. The note on the construction of Thomas Quiney's house is given on the excellent authority of Mr. Alderman Edward Gibbs, who has ever most liberally, in this and other questions of architectural detail, permitted me to have recourse to his unrivalled knowledge in all that relates to the ancient buildings of Stratford-on-Avon. It should also be mentioned that Mr. Gibbs was the first to indicate the unique conditions under which it has been possible to ascertain, even at this late day, the character and elevation of the original northern gable of the poet's residence.

4. It is to the sagacity of Mr. Joseph Hill of Perry Barr, Birmingham, who rescued them when they were positively on their way to the paper-mill, that students are indebted for the preservation of most of the interesting documents which relate to the history of the Eastern boundary of the Shakespeare Henley-street estate.

NOTES ON THE ENGRAVINGS.

The following notes are limited to observations on those engravings that appear to require some degree of explanation. There are a considerable number the natures and histories of which are fully exhibited either in or near the respective pages in which they occur.

Vol. i. p. 22. Copy of a sketch taken by R. B. Wheler, engraved by F. Eginton and published on 1 July, 1806.—Vol. i. p. 24. Reduced from a sketch taken by John Jordan, an inhabitant of Stratford-on-Avon. The details are clumsily and inaccurately given, as will be seen by comparing the view of the house on the extreme left with Mr. Robinson's truthful representation of the same building in vol. 2. p. 158.—Vol. i. p. 26. See vol. ii. p. 215.—Vol. i. p 32. From an original drawing by Richard Greene, the earliest one of the house known to exist.—Vol. i. p. 33. See vol. ii. p. 227.—Vol. i. p. 36. See vol. ii. pp. 224, 227.—Vol. i. p. 38. The marks and signatures of the members of the Corporation of Stratford-on-Avon, 1564.—Vol. i. p. 50. Facsimiles of a list of affeerors, including John Shakespeare, 1561, and of the conclusion of the Field inventory cited in vol. ii. p. 245.—Vol. i. p. 58. View of Stratford-on-Avon, engraved by J. T. Blight from a painting that was executed about the year 1740.—Vol. i. pp. 76, 77. A plan of some of the northern districts of the metropolis, copied from a more extensive one that was published by Braun in 1574.—Vol. i. p. 79. See vol. ii. pp. 242, 243.—Vol. i. pp. 94, 95. Plan of London by John Norden, 1593.—Vol. i. p. 121. Shakespeare's well, now hidden under one of the southern walls of Nash's House.—Vol. i. pp. 128, 129. Facsimile, from Aggas's plan of London, of the district in which the Theatre and Curtain were situated, carefully taken from the original by E. W. Ashbee.—Vol. i. p. 131. The ancient Clopton Bridge at Stratford-on-Avon, from a sketch taken by Richard Greene about the year 1750, the earliest one of the structure that is known to exist.—Vol. i. p. 166. From a view " graven by I. Hondius and are to be solde by I. Sudbury and George Humble in Popes Head Alley in London, 1610."—Vol. i. p. 188. One of the mud walls that used to be so prevalent at Stratford-on-Avon, sketched and engraved by J. T. Blight. They are probably now extinct, for I remember many years

ago having great difficulty in finding a genuine example of one.—Vol. i.
p. 236.   Facsimiles of Thomas Quiney's monogram, signatures and
French motto, from the first page of the account that he delivered to
the Corporation in the year 1623.   It should be mentioned that the
engraving of the signature in the right-hand corner is taken from a
separate example.—Vol. i. p. 254.   Autographs and seals of Susanna
Hall and Elizabeth Nash, from the deed of settlement of 1647.—Vol. i.
p. 289.   The second Globe Theatre, from an engraving published by
Visscher, c. 1620.—Vol. i. p. 353.   The dotted break in the facsimile
of the surname merely indicates the end of one line and the commencement of another.—Vol. ii. p. 42.   The market-cross and old houses in
Wood Street, Stratford-on-Avon, engraved by J. T. Blight from a sketch
taken about the year 1820.—Vol. ii. p. 95.   The back of Julius Shaw's
house, with parts of the adjoining buildings, from a sketch taken in the
the year 1862, exhibiting traces of Elizabethan work, a considerable
portion, however, unquestionably belonging to a much later period.—
Vol. ii. p. 109.   Autographs and seals of George Nash and Susanna
Hall, from the deed of settlement of 1639.—Vol. ii. pp. 112, 113.   The
first of these engravings is a plan of the cellar and foundation-walls, and
the second of the attic story, of Nash's House, from a measured survey
taken in the year 1874 by Mr. John Robinson of Whitehall, architect.
—Vol. ii. p. 132.   View of the second New Place, the Guild Chapel,
the Guild-hall, the Grammar-School, and the Falcon Tavern, from a
copy of an old drawing published by R. B. Wheler in the year 1806.—
Vol. ii. p. 214.   See vol. ii. p. 219, the three divisions of the facsimile
being side by side in the original, the top one being therein on the
extreme left and the next in the middle.—Vol. ii. p. 223.   See vol. ii.
pp. 224, 215.—Vol. ii. p. 226.   See vol. ii. pp. 242, 230.—Vol. ii.
p. 228.   See vol. ii. pp. 232, 224, 235, 227.—Vol. ii. p. 229.   See
vol. ii. pp. 230, 227.—Vol ii. p. 237.   See vol. ii. pp. 236, 241.—Vol. ii.
p. 240.   See vol. ii. pp. 238, 244, 216.—Vol. ii. pp. 254–255.   Part of
a map of Warwickshire, including Stratford-on-Avon, from a very rare
engraving that was published in the year 1603.—Vol. ii. p. 276.   Plan
of New Place and neighbourhood, the thick lines showing the boundaries
of the estate that was purchased by the great dramatist.   At V was the
frontage of the Clifford and Spurr estates, and R is the site of a barn
that was accidentally destroyed by fire about the year 1618.   The letters
L and M indicate the respective situations of the Rowington Copyhold
and the Falcon Tavern.

BIOGRAPHICAL INDEX.

Adam,—a tradition that Shakespeare undertook the performance of this character in a representation of As You Like It, i. 170, 171.

Addenbroke, John, — the poet's suit against him in the Court of Record for the recovery of a debt, i. 208. Copies of the orders and papers, ii. 78–80.

Æsthetic criticism,—of equivocal value in determining the chronological order of Shakespeare's works, or the nature of his temperament at the time of dramatic composition, i. 16, ii. 249.

All's Well that Ends Well,—note on its title and period of composition, ii. 272.

Antony and Cleopatra,—a few brief observations on its contemporary history, i. 206, ii 285, 286.

Arden, Agnes, second wife of the poet's maternal grandfather,—conditional bequest to her in her husband's will, ii. 53. Has a life-interest in his Snitterfield estates, ii. 173–176. Copy of a lease of them to Alexander Webbe, ii. 177. The opinion that she was not on friendly terms with the Shakespeares probably erroneous, i. 60, ii. 372. Her infirmities and decease, i. 60, ii. 371, 372. Copies of her will and inventory, ii. 54, 55. Table of her immediate descendants, ii. 247.

Arden, Mary, the poet's mother,—the agricultural and rural surroundings of her youth, i. 28. The style of living that prevailed in her father's house, i. 28, 29. Her illiteracy and mark-signatures, i. 28, 40. Owns the reversion to a portion of a valuable estate at Snitterfield, i. 29. Receives under the provisions of her father's will a handsome pecuniary legacy as well as an estate at Wilmecote called Asbies, i. 29, ii. 53. Is one of his executors and perhaps a favourite daughter, ii. 53, 369. Marries John Shakespeare, i. 27. Her probable age at the time, ii. 367. Disposal of her reversionary interests at Snitterfield, i. 59, 60. Copy of the fine that was levied on the occasion, ii. 176, 177. Her right to dower in the Henley Street estate probably merged in a liberal allowance from her son, i. 183. Burial, i. 207, ii. 52.

Arden, Robert, the poet's maternal grandfather,—a wealthy farmer, i. 27, ii. 366, 367. His probable descent, ii. 366. His property at Snitterfield, i. 27, ii. 173–176, 367. His estate called Asbies, q.v. The interior of his house, i. 27–29. Marries secondly Agnes, the widow of a substantial farmer of the name of Hill, i. 29. Copy of his will, ii. 53. The inventory of his goods, i. 27, ii. 53. Genealogical table of his descendants, ii. 174.

Armin, Robert, one of Shakespeare's fellow actors,—his account of a curious incident that occurred at Evesham and supposed to be alluded to in Troilus and Cressida, i. 295–297.

Asbies,—an estate at Wilmecote, near Stratford-on-Avon, belonging to Robert Arden, the poet's maternal grandfather, who devised it to his youngest daughter, i. 27, 29, ii. 53. Its probable extent, ii. 205, 367. Account of an estate erroneously supposed to have included it, ii. 199–201, 371. Copy of a fine relating to a lease of it that was granted by the Shakespeares, ii. 202, 203. Mortgaged by John and Mary Shakespeare, i. 59. Copy of the fine that was then levied, ii. 11. Their unsuccessful attempts to recover possession, i. 59. A Chancery suit ultimately instituted, most likely at the poet's expense, to effect that object, i. 137, 138, ii. 203, 370, 371. Copies of records and Orders in the suit, ii. 14–17, 204, 205. Its probable result, i. 140. Intermediate negociations for the surrender of the estate to John Lambert on terms that were recognized by the poet, i. 78, 80, ii. 370. Transcript of a Bill of Complaint that was filed in the Court of Queen's Bench to enforce a specific performance of those terms, ii. 11–13.

As you Like It,—observations on its contemporary history, i. 170, ii. 275.

Aubrey, John,—character of his biographical notices of Shakespeare, i. 10,

His association with Condell in the preparation of the First Folio, i. 262–270. Copies of their addresses to its patrons and readers, ii. 65, 66.

Henry the Eighth,—notes on its early history, i. 215, ii. 294, 295. Contemporary plays by other authors on the events of the same reign, i. 222, ii. 292–294.

Henry the Fifth,—observations on its contemporary history, i. 161, ii. 330, 381. Date of composition, i. 161.

Henry the Fourth,—notes on the two Parts and their early history, i. 141–143, ii. 257, 349–355. See also the verses written on Shakespeare by Leonard Digges, ii. 89. A play on the history of parts of the reigns of this sovereign and his predecessor acted by the Globe company on the day preceding the outbreak of the Essex Insurrection, i. 174–177, ii. 360–362.

Henry the Sixth,—notes on the three Parts of, their authenticity and early history, i. 85–88, 98, 266, ii. 267–272. See also the extract from Nash's Pierce Penilesse, ii. 81.

Henslowe, Phillip, a theatrical proprietor and manager, — Shakespeare's earliest dramas written for, i. 97, 110.

Heywood, Thomas,—the writer of poems that appeared under Shakespeare's name in the third edition of the Passionate Pilgrim, and his expostulation with the publisher on the subject, i. 218, 219, ii. 297.

Highways,—the poet's name in a list of subscribers towards the expense of attempting to carry a Bill through Parliament for the repair of the, i. 214.

Hill, John, a farmer of Bearley and the earliest recorded member of a family that was afterwards brought into intimate relations with the Shakespeares,—copy of his will, ii. 368–369. Table of his descendants, ii. 247.

Holinshed's Chronicles,—the edition of 1586 the one used by Shakespeare, i. 251.

Horneby, Thomas,—proceeded against by Shakespeare in the Court of Record owing to the non-appearance of John Addenbroke, for whom he had become bail, i. 208, ii. 79.

Horses,—Shakespeare obtaining a temporary living, soon after his arrival in London, by taking care of the horses of visitors to the theatre during the times of the performances, i. 69–75, ii. 286–288. The topography of the locality favourable to the reception of this traditional story, i. 328. Possibly engaged at James Burbage's livery-stables, i. 73.

Huband, Ralph,—a gentleman of Ipsley, co. Warwick, from whom Shakespeare purchased his moiety of the Tithes, q.v.

James the First,—grants a licence to Shakespeare and the other members of his company to perform in London at the Globe, and, in the provinces, at town-halls or other suitable buildings, i. 194, ii. 82. Copy of the licence, ii. 82, 83. Witnesses a theatrical performance by Shakespeare's company at Wilton, i. 194. The great dramatist in the procession that accompanied His Majesty in his triumphal excursion through London, i. 195.

John, King,—observations on its contemporary history, i. 156, 212, ii. 286.

Johnson, Gerard,—the sculptor of the poet's monumental effigy, i. 258.

Johnson, Robert, — one of the royal musicians and the original composer of the music to the Tempest, i. 214, ii. 309.

Jonson, Ben, — the acceptance of his comedy of Every Man in His Humour for representation due to the sagacity and good-nature of the great dramatist, i. 154, 155. The latter one of the original performers in that comedy, i. 154, and also in his Sejanus, i. 194. Allusion to his inferiority to Shakespeare in the Return from Parnassus, ii. 153. His wit-combats with him, ii. 70. Present at a convivial meeting with Shakespeare and Drayton in one of the Stratford taverns, i. 243, ii. 70. The loving interest taken by him in the publication of the first edition of Shakespeare's dramas, i. 270. His eulogistic poem on, i. 270, ii. 66, 67, and his biographical notices of, the great dramatist, ii. 69.

Julius Cæsar,—notes on its early history, ii. 257. See also the verses written on Shakespeare by Leonard Digges, ii. 89.

Kempe, William, a popular comic actor, —performed with Shakespeare and Burbage in two comedies that were represented before Queen Elizabeth at Greenwich Palace, i. 109. Is introduced into the Return from Parnassus in a dialogue in which he makes a speech alluding to Shakespeare, ii. 153.

Lambert, Edmund, husband of the poet's aunt,—notes of their burials, ii. 370. He lends money on Asbies, i. 59, ii. 202. Declines to reconvey the estate unless other debts, as well as the loan, are discharged, i. 59, ii. 16. Probability that he had verbally guaranteed the surrender on those conditions, ii. 203.

Lambert, John,—negociations for the surrender of the estate of Asbies to, i. 78, 80, ii. 11–13, 370. The subsequent Chancery proceedings against him, i. 137, 138, 140, ii. 14–17, 204, 205, 370.

Lane, John,—the defendant in an action for slander brought against him by the poet's eldest daughter, i. 224, 225, ii. 381.

Lawrence, Henry,—the scrivener who attended the completion of the Blackfriars

Nash, John,—remembered in Shakespeare's will by a gift of four nobles, ii. 170.

Nash, Thomas, son of the above-named Anthony and the first husband of Shakespeare's only grand-daughter,—baptism, ii. 51. The New Place library bequeathed to him by Hall, i. 251. Owner of the adjoining house, ii. 91–93. Notes on his career, i. 255, ii. 324, 325. Burial and grave, ii. 324.

Neighbours, Shakespeare's,—memoranda on those who were resident in Chapel Street, ii. 91–100.

New Place,—a mansion originally built for Sir Hugh Clopton in the fifteenth century, i. 119, ii. 101. Termed the Great House, i. 119, 120, ii. 101. Notices of it by Leland and Grimmitt, i. 120, ii. 102, 134. Its barns, i. 121, ii. 375. Its well, i. 121, ii. 377. Our knowledge of its structural formation exceedingly limited, i. 120. No authentic sketch of it known to exist, ii. 277, 278. Remnants of its foundations, i. 4, 123, ii. 123. Its purchase by Shakespeare, i. 119, ii. 105. Most likely in a dilapidated state at the time, i. 119, ii. 373. The corn accumulated in its barns, i. 122, 125, ii. 58. Arrangement of a fruit-orchard in its larger garden under the directions of the poet, i. 122. A flaw discovered in the validity of the title necessitating the levying of a second fine, i. 185, ii. 105. Entertainment of a preacher at, i. 225, 226. The original house demolished by Sir John Clopton, ii. 120, 121. A large new mansion, erected on the site, afterwards removed by the Rev. Francis Gastrell, ii. 121–125. Its history and topography, i. 119–122, ii. 101–135, 373–378.

Oldcastle,—the original name of the character afterwards termed Falstaff, q.v.

Oldcastle, Sir John,—a play so called and unblushingly announced as the work of Shakespeare, i. 164. Early editions, i. 164, ii. 341, 342. Its real authors, ii. 341. Another play with the same title performed by the Lord Chamberlain's servants, i. 169, ii. 352, 353.

Othello,—notes on its early history, i. 196, ii. 302, 303. See also the extract, with facsimile, from the journal of the Secretary to the German embassy, ii. 85, the commencement of the elegy on Burbage, ii. 88, and the verses on Shakespeare by Leonard Digges, ii. 89.

Oxford, — theatrical performances of Shakespeare's company before the Mayor and Corporation of, i. 197. The visits of the poet to the Crown Inn, the residence of John Davenant, an innkeeper of, i. 198, 199, ii. 44, 45, 49.

Passionate Pilgrim,—a little collection of minor poems fraudulently issued in 1599 under the name of Shakespeare, containing, however, very few that really emanated from his pen, i. 162, 163. Notes on the contents of the volume, i. 375–378. Two of the Sonnets first published in that work, i. 157, 162. No copy of the second edition known to exist, i. 378. The third, which appeared in 1612, also ascribed to Shakespeare, although it included poems of considerable length taken, without acknowledgement, from one of the published works of Thomas Heywood, i. 218. Displeasure of Shakespeare at the liberty that had been taken with his name, and consequent withdrawal of the title-page, i. 218, 219, 378, ii. 296, 297.

Percy, Sir Charles,—one of the Essex conspirators who was present at the interview that they held with Shakespeare's company two days before the outbreak of the insurrection, i. 177. Was greatly impressed by the humour of the Second Part of Henry the Fourth, ii. 350, 351.

Pericles,—observations on its contemporary history, i. 205, 212, ii. 336, 337.

Phillipps, Augustine, the poet's friend and colleague,—his proceedings in reference to a drama on the subject of Richard the Second that was acted at the Globe on the day before the outbreak of the Essex Insurrection, i. 174–176, ii. 360. His bequest of a gold piece to Shakespeare, i. 197.

Pleasant Willy,—an actor mentioned by Spenser and erroneously believed by Dryden and others to have been the great dramatist, ii. 382.

Plutarch's Lives, North's translation of,— the edition of 1595 the one probably read by Shakespeare, i. 251, ii. 285.

Pope, Alexander,—his notices of Shakespeare's appreciation of money and indifference to literary fame, i. 147, ii. 344.

Quiney, Adrian,—a mercer of Stratford, nominated, in conjunction with the poet's father, to undertake the management of some important legal business connected with the affairs of the borough, i. 152, ii. 232. Shakespeare communicates to him his intention of negociating for the purchase of land at Shottery, i. 153. Letter to his son Richard mentioning the poet, ii. 58, 59.

Quiney, Elizabeth, widow of Richard,— mistress of a tavern at Stratford-on-Avon, i. 153. Facsimile of her mark-signature, i. 153. Friendly with the poet's daughter, Judith Shakespeare, i. 153.

Quiney, Judith,—the marital name of the poet's younger daughter, Judith Shakespeare, q.v.

Quiney, Richard,—is urged to communicate with Shakespeare respecting the expediency of the latter acquiring property

of his literary education, i. 83, 85. Sketches of the known incidents in his literary career, *his plays and other works being indexed under their respective titles*, dispersedly in i. 85–225. Lampooned by Robert Greene, i. 86–89, 302. Chettle's apology for having been instrumental in its publication, i. 88, 303. The testimony of the latter to his respectable position as an actor and dramatist, i. 88, 89. His acquaintance with Richard Field, and personal superintendence of the typographical construction of Venus and Adonis, i. 89, 96. Its dedication to Lord Southampton, i. 91. The London of that day, Shakespeare's London, q.v. Dedication of his Lucrece to Lord Southampton, i. 107. His father's applications for a grant of coat-armour probably made at his suggestion and expense, i. 118, 162. Deaths of his son Hamnet and his uncle Henry, i. 117, ii. 52, 212. Purchase of New Place, q.v. Reported munificence of Lord Southampton, i. 133, 134. Most likely furnished the means for the prosecution of the Chancery suit for the recovery of Asbies, i. 137. Compelled to alter the name of Oldcastle, the original appellation of the hero of the Boar's Head tavern, i. 141, 142, ii. 350, 351. Contemplated purchase of land at Shottery or in the neighbourhood of Stratford, i. 145, 146, ii. 57. Recommends one of Ben Jonson's plays to the favourable notice of the Lord Chamberlain's company, i. 154, 155, ii. 75. Negociations with Richard Quiney on pecuniary matters, i. 148–152. Facsimile of the only letter to him that has yet been discovered, i. 148, 150. His rational appreciation of the value of money, i. 147, 170, 231, 242, ii. 77–80. Ordered by the Queen to write a play in which Falstaff was to appear in the character of a lover, i. 143, ii. 263, 264. His graceful compliment to the Earl of Essex, i. 161. Probable acquaintance with that nobleman, i. 176. The implication of his company in the transactions that were followed by the outbreak of the Essex Insurrection, i. 174–182, ii. 359–362. Loses his father, i. 182, ii. 52, 248. Succeeds as his heir-at-law to the Henley Street estate, i. 183. Purchase of arable land from the Combes, i. 184, ii. 17–19, 331, 333. Absent from Stratford at the period of the transfer, i. 184. Arranges with Hercules Underhill for the removal of a flaw that had been discovered in the title to New Place, i. 185, ii. 105. Purchase of the Rowington copyhold from Walter Getley, q.v. Marches in the royal procession from the Tower to Westminster, i. 195. Litigation respecting certain bushels of malt that he had sold to one Philip Rogers, i. 195, ii. 77, 78. In attendance at Somerset House on the occasion of the visit of the Spanish Ambassador, i. 195, 196. Death of his colleague, Augustine Phillipps, a few days after making a will in which he bequeaths a piece of gold to the great dramatist, i. 197. Purchases the unexpired term of the moiety of a lease of the Tithes, q.v. His frequent visits to his friend, John Davenant, q.v. One of the godfathers of Sir William Davenant, q.v. Gives his eldest daughter in marriage to John Hall, i. 202, ii. 52. Loses his brother Edmund, i. 204, ii. 343. His suit against John Addenbroke for the recovery of a debt, i. 208, ii. 78–80. Birth of his only grand-daughter, Elizabeth, i. 204, ii. 52. Loses his mother, i. 207, ii. 52. Was shortly afterwards godfather to William Walker, to whom he subsequently bequeathed a gold piece, i. 207. Involved in a litigation respecting the Tithes, q.v. Purchase of meadow land from the Combes, i. 211, ii. 25. Absent from London at the time of the conveyance, i. 211. His name found in a list of subscribers towards the expense of carrying a Highway Bill through Parliament, i. 214. His displeasure at the fraudulent use made of his name in the third edition of the Passionate Pilgrim, i. 218, 219. The sum of £5 bequeathed to him by John Combe, upon whom he is said, on doubtful evidences, to have written satirical verses, i. 226. Loses his brother Richard, i. 219, ii. 52. Purchase of a house in the parish of St. Anne, Blackfriars, q.v. His closing years passed in leisurely retirement at Stratford, i. 214, 231, ii. 70, 76. Traditional love of children, i. 205, ii. 43. His great affection for his grand-daughter, i. 204, 205. Familiarly known amongst his contemporaries as Will or Will Shakespeare, ii. 69, 154. His convivial proclivities and notices of the crab-tree tradition, i. 216–218, 243, ii. 325, 326, 328. Retained his literary intimacies to the end, i. 231, ii. 70. Is interested and takes a part in the proposed Enclosures, q.v. Instructions and arrangements respecting his will, i. 231–233, ii. 378–381. The nature of its provisions, i. 233–242. Marriage of his youngest daughter to Thomas Quiney, i. 234, ii. 52. Meets Drayton and Ben Jonson at a festive entertainment in one of the Stratford taverns, i. 243, ii. 70. Is attacked by a fever very shortly afterwards, i. 243, ii. 70. Death and burial, i. 243, 260, ii. 52. Dies in the Catholic faith, ii. 71. His will, a draft prepared for engrossment, proved in London by his son-in-law, John Hall, i. 246. A homely inscription on his

HARRISON AND SONS, PRINTERS IN ORDINARY TO HER MAJESTY, ST. MARTIN'S LANE.